GENERAL STATUTES OF C

MW00953492

TITLE 54 CRIMINAL PROCEDURE

WITH OFFICIAL NOTES

2018 EDITION

CONNECTICUT LEGISLATURE

TABLE OF CONTENTS

CHAPTER 959* COURT JURISDICTION AND POWER 4

    PART I 7

    ARREST AND ARRAIGNMENT 7

    PART II* SEARCHES 38

    PART III* 53

    SEIZED PROPERTY 53

CHAPTER 959A* WIRETAPPING AND ELECTRONIC SURVEILLANCE 69

CHAPTER 960* INFORMATION, PROCEDURE AND BAIL 84

CHAPTER 960A* YOUTHFUL OFFENDERS 190

CHAPTER 961* TRIAL AND PROCEEDINGS AFTER CONVICTION 206

    PART I DISCOVERY, TRIAL AND WITNESSES 213

    PART II SENTENCING AND APPEAL 258

    PART IIA HIV AND DNA TESTING OF OFFENDERS 280

    PART IIB TESTING FOR TUBERCULOSIS INFECTION 293

    PART IIC POST-CONVICTION REMEDIES 295

    PART III PROBATION, PAROLE AND PARDON 300

CHAPTER 962 COSTS, FEES AND EXPENSES IN CRIMINAL PROCEEDINGS OR PROSECUTIONS 362

CHAPTER 963* FRESH PURSUIT 369

CHAPTER 964* UNIFORM CRIMINAL EXTRADITION ACT 370

CHAPTER 965* DETAINERS 383

CHAPTER 966 LIMITATION OF PROSECUTIONS 392

CHAPTER 967 GENERAL PROVISIONS 396

CHAPTER 968 VICTIM SERVICES 399

CHAPTER 968A ADDRESS CONFIDENTIALITYPROGRAM 435

CHAPTER 969* REGISTRATION OF SEXUAL OFFENDERS 445

CHAPTER 969A REGISTRATION OF CERTAIN OFFENDERS 473

CHAPTER 970 CONNECTICUT SENTENCING COMMISSION 478

CHAPTER 959* COURT JURISDICTION AND POWER

*Cited. 228 C. 758.

Cited. 8 CA 673.

Rule that where several courts have concurrent jurisdiction of the same offense, the court which first acquires jurisdiction of the prosecution generally retains it to the exclusion of the other courts, held to have limited application in criminal cases. 21 CS 246.

Table of Contents

Secs. 54-1 and 54-1a. Criminal jurisdiction of trial justices; of Court of Common Pleas.

Sec. 54-1b. Arraignment of prisoner. Advice as to rights.

Sec. 54-1c. Admissibility of confession.

Sec. 54-1d. Place of arraignment. Multiple arrest warrants. Multiple credit card and automated teller machine offenses. Identity theft and related offenses.
    Violation of order of protection by electronic or telephonic means.

Sec. 54-1e. Election of place of trial when venue is in the geographical area of Derby, Ansonia, Shelton, and Seymour.

Sec. 54-1f. (Formerly Sec. 6-49). Arrest without warrant. Pursuit outside precincts.

Sec. 54-1g. Time of arraignment. Violation of protective order, standing criminal protective order or restraining order.

Sec. 54-1h. (Formerly Sec. 6-49a). Arrest by complaint and summons for commission of misdemeanor.

Sec. 54-1i. (Formerly Sec. 54-40a). Duty of law enforcement officer before charging with a crime a person found in unconscious condition.

Sec. 54-1j. Ascertainment that defendant understands possible immigration and naturalization consequences of guilty or nolo contendere plea.

Sec. 54-1k. Issuance of protective orders in cases of stalking, harassment, sexual assault, risk of injury to or impairing morals of a child.

Sec. 54-1*l*. Short title: Alvin W. Penn Racial Profiling Prohibition Act.

Sec. 54-1m. Adoption of policy prohibiting certain police actions. Traffic stop information. Standardized method. Data collection and reporting.

Sec. 54-1n. Complaint by victim of identity theft. Law enforcement agency's responsibilities.

Sec. 54-1o. Electronic recording of custodial interrogations.

Sec. 54-1p. Eyewitness identification procedures.

Sec. 54-1q. Court to advise defendant that guilty or nolo contendere plea may have consequence of suspension of driver's license.

Sec. 54-1r. Complaint by protected person re violation of order of protection by electronic or telephonic means. Law enforcement agency's responsibilities.

Sec. 54-1s. Racial Profiling Prohibition Project Advisory Board. Membership. Duties.

Sec. 54-1t. Adoption of policy re police use of electronic defense weapons. Data collection. Reports.

Sec. 54-2. Conviction and binding over by trial justice.

Sec. 54-2a. Issuance of bench warrants of arrest, subpoenas, capias and other criminal process. Release conditions. Service of court process. Entry of warrants and process into computer system.

Sec. 54-2b. Transferred

Sec. 54-2c. Traffic violator need not appear in court, when. Schedule of fines established.

Sec. 54-2d. Notation in computer network of actions taken by law enforcement agency to execute certain warrants.

Sec. 54-2e. Issuance of rearrest warrant or capias for failure to appear.

Secs. 54-3 and 54-4. Issue of warrant after arrest. Trial justice may issue criminal process to be served anywhere in the state.

Sec. 54-5. Transferred

Secs. 54-6 to 54-12. Criminal jurisdiction of municipal courts. Limit of jurisdiction of municipal courts. Jurisdiction over violations concerning overweight commercial vehicles. Bonds on adjournment of hearing. Copies of files and records for Superior Court and state's attorneys on bindover; notice when proceeding pending on seized property. Appointment of court interpreters in municipal and trial justice court. Appeal from municipal court or trial justice.

Secs. 54-13 and 54-14. Transferred

Secs. 54-15 and 54-16. Binding over on probable cause. Jurisdiction of Common Pleas Court on appeals.

Sec. 54-17. Transferred

Sec. 54-17a. Presentation in one judicial district for offenses charged in various districts where defendant to plead guilty.

Sec. 54-18. Transferred

Secs. 54-18a to 54-21. Transfer of criminal cases between Superior and Common Pleas Court. Certain cases to be tried at first term. Search when cruelty is suspected. Search warrants in cases of cruelty to animals.

Secs. 54-22 to 54-24. **Transferred**

Secs. 54-25 and 54-26. Release on recognizance. Witnesses in courts of other states.

Sec. 54-27. **Transferred**

Sec. 54-28. **Transferred**

Secs. 54-29 to 54-31. Seizure of obscene literature and gambling implements. Illegal articles and implements to be destroyed. Judges of city courts may act.

Sec. 54-32. **Transferred**

Sec. 54-33. Search warrants for gambling and lottery implements.

Sec. 54-33a. Issuance of search warrant, warrant for tracking device or warrant for foreign corporation records or data.

Sec. 54-33b. Search of person.

Sec. 54-33c. Warrant application, affidavits, execution and return. Copies. Orders.

Sec. 54-33d. Interference with search.

Sec. 54-33e. Destruction of property.

Sec. 54-33f. Motion for return of unlawfully seized property and suppression as evidence.

Sec. 54-33g. Forfeiture of moneys and property related to commission of criminal offense. In rem proceeding. Disposition. Secondary evidence of forfeited property.

Sec. 54-33h. (Formerly Sec. 53-279). Arrest of keeper of gambling equipment; seizure and disposition of property.

Sec. 54-33i. "Journalist", "news organization" and "news" defined.

Sec. 54-33j. Issuance of search warrant for property of journalist or news organization.

Sec. 54-33k. "Strip search" defined.

Sec. 54-33*l.* Strip searches. Procedure.

Sec. 54-33m. Failure to wear seat belt not probable cause for vehicle search.

Sec. 54-33n. Search of school lockers and property.

Secs. 54-34 and 54-35. Search of person. Condemnation of gambling implements, notice.

Sec. 54-36. Disposition of property held as evidence.

Sec. 54-36a. Definitions. Inventory. Return of stolen property. Disposition of other seized property. Return of compliance.

Sec. 54-36b. Examiner of seized property, appointment, duties.

Sec. 54-36c. Disposition of seized property on order of the examiner of seized property.

Sec. 54-36d. Proceedings under chapters 214, 220 and 490 concerning cigarettes, alcohol and fisheries and game, respectively, exempt from certain licensing and disposition requirements.

Sec. 54-36e. Firearms and ammunition to be turned over to state police. Sale at public auction.

Sec. 54-36f. Receipt for seized property to be given by law enforcement officials.

Sec. 54-36g. Destruction of controlled drugs, controlled substances and drug paraphernalia held as evidence in criminal proceedings. Petition, notice and hearing. Representative samples. Certificate of results. Destruction upon final disposition of criminal action. Records.

Sec. 54-36h. Forfeiture of moneys and property related to illegal sale or exchange of controlled substances or money laundering. In rem proceeding. Disposition.

Sec. 54-36i. Drug assets forfeiture revolving account. Allocation of moneys.

Secs. 54-36j to 54-36*l* Seizure and forfeiture of motor vehicle used in patronizing a prostitute. Innocent owner defense to forfeiture of motor vehicle used in patronizing a prostitute. Release of motor vehicle seized in connection with arrest for patronizing a prostitute; delivery or return of motor vehicle upon disposition of prosecution.

Sec. 54-36m. Impoundment of motor vehicle occupied by person arrested for patronizing a prostitute from a motor vehicle.

Sec. 54-36n. Identification and tracing of seized and recovered firearms and ammunition.

Sec. 54-36o. Property derived from identity theft subject to forfeiture to state. Exceptions. Proceeds.

Sec. 54-36p. Forfeiture of moneys and property related to sexual exploitation, prostitution and human trafficking. In rem proceeding. Disposition.

Secs. 54-37 to 54-39. Disposition of accused acquitted on ground of insanity. Release of persons confined under order prior to October 1, 1959. Petition for release. Disposition of insane person upon expiration of term.

Sec. 54-40. Transferred

Sec. 54-40a. Transferred

Sec. 54-41. Transferred

PART I

ARREST AND ARRAIGNMENT

Secs. 54-1 and 54-1a. Criminal jurisdiction of trial justices; of Court of Common Pleas. Sections 54-1 and 54-1a are repealed.

(1949 Rev., S. 8721; 1955, S. 3319d; 1957, P.A. 522, S. 1; 1959, P.A. 28, S. 25, 204; 1961, P.A. 78; 352; 1963, P.A. 177; February, 1965, P.A. 331, S. 35; 1967, P.A. 152, S. 43; 549, S. 8; 630, S. 12; 1971, P.A. 72, S. 15; 870, S. 1; P.A., 74-183, S. 7, 291; P.A. 76-436, S. 515, 681.)

Sec. 54-1b. Arraignment of prisoner. Advice as to rights.

Any accused, when he is arraigned before the Superior Court, shall be advised by a judge that he has a right to counsel, that he has a right to refuse to make any statement and that any statement he makes may be introduced in evidence against him. Each such person shall be allowed a reasonable opportunity to consult counsel.

(1963, P.A. 126, S. 1; February, 1965, P.A. 185, S. 1; 436, S. 1; 1967, P.A. 549, S. 9; 656, S. 58; 1972, P.A. 69, S. 2; P.A. 74-183, S. 125, 291; P.A. 76-436, S. 516, 681; P.A. 80-313, S. 27.)

History: 1965 acts provided bond would cover appearance in court to which accused was bound over, allowed judge to release accused on his own recognizance and added provision setting forth exceptions to requirement re presentment of accused to first session of court; 1967 acts substituted criminal "term" for criminal "session" and, effective October 1, 1968, provided accused be advised of his rights at his arraignment rather than when he is put to plea, provided alternatives to bail and added concept of incapacity in provision re exceptions to requirement for presentment of accused at first session; 1972 act added Subdiv. (4) in exception to requirement that accused be presented at first session re persons accused of misdemeanor or offenses with lesser penalties as specified; P.A. 74-183 replaced circuit court with court of common pleas, reflecting reorganization of judicial system and deleted provision first added in 1965 and amended in 1967 and 1972 re exceptions to requirement for presentment at first session of court, effective December 31, 1974; P.A. 76-436 replaced court of common pleas with superior court, reflecting transfer of all trial jurisdiction to superior court and specified that accused persons who are not released on bond or on their written promise to appear are to be committed to commissioner of correction until next criminal term of court or until discharged, effective July 1, 1978; P.A. 80-313 deleted provisions detailing conditions of release on bond or promise to appear.

See Sec. 51-296 re designation of public defender for indigent defendant or codefendant.

See Sec. 54-1j re court advice re possible immigration and naturalization ramifications of guilty or nolo contendere plea.

See Sec. 54-94a re conditional plea of nolo contendere.

Prior to act, held that neither failure to warn defendant of his constitutional rights nor his lack of counsel required conclusion that his confession was involuntary. 150 C. 169. Cited. 154 C. 314, 324. Presentation before circuit court session next held in circuit where offense is alleged to have been committed means the regular session of the circuit court next to be held, excluding any session on day of arrest. 155 C. 134. Right to counsel not denied where defendant made no request for same even though defendant's attorneys, during period from his arrest to his arraignment, made repeated unsuccessful efforts to communicate with him. Id., 155. Defendant was warned of his rights prior to his plea being offered but not prior to conversation with his daughter in police barracks wherein he admitted he was guilty of crimes charged. 157 C. 25. Cited. 164 C. 402. Admission into evidence of custodial statements not violation of section. 167 C. 408. Cited. 187 C. 6; 195 C. 505; 198 C. 517; 201 C. 489; 236 C. 388.

Cited. 34 CA 261; 43 CA 209.

Cited. 39 CS 347.

Cited. 2 Conn. Cir. Ct. 573. Compliance by the state with the requirements of section in no way adversely affected defendant's right to claim that his rights were violated because the court refused to appoint counsel to represent him. 3 Conn. Cir. Ct. 624, 630. Motion to dismiss on ground constitutional right to counsel had been violated should be made prior to not guilty plea. 4 Conn. Cir. Ct. 166. Court could conclude from statements and conduct of defendant that he had effectively waived his rights. Id., 168. On-the-scene questioning of person in investigation of crime without prior warning not precluded since such person is not under restraint. Id., 195. Purpose and necessity of arraignment or presentment of accused are to fix his identity, inform him of his constitutional rights and the charge against him and give him an opportunity to plead; before arraignment, there is no issue pending to which accused can plead and entry of nolle prosequi before arraignment is not a final judgment from which an appeal lies. Id., 466. Cited. 5 Conn. Cir. Ct. 35, 40. Collective statement of their rights to group of accused may be sufficient compliance with section but not as to defendants with linguistic difficulties or below average intelligence. Id., 178. Cited. Id., 243. Defendant waived his right to counsel where he had, for 6 months, obtained postponements on this ground. 6 Conn. Cir. Ct. 58.

Sec. 54-1c. Admissibility of confession.

Any admission, confession or statement, written or oral, obtained from an accused person who has not been presented to the first session of the court, or on the day specified for arraignment under the provisions of section 54-1g, or who has not been informed of such person's rights as provided by section 54-1b or 54-64b, shall be inadmissible.

(1963, P.A. 126, S. 3; February, 1965, P.A. 436, S. 2; P.A. 76-336, S. 2; P.A. 80-313, S. 28; P.A. 03-19, S. 127.)

History: 1965 act added "or on the day specified in ... section 54-1b"; P.A. 76-336 substituted day "for arraignment under the provisions of section 54-63c" for day specified "in subdivision (1), (2) or (3) of section 54-1b"; P.A. 80-313 added reference to Sec. 54-64b and substituted reference to Sec. 54-1g for reference to Sec. 54-63c; P.A. 03-19 made technical changes, effective May 12, 2003.

Proof of voluntariness of confession prerequisite to its admissibility if made during illegal detention. 151 C. 246, see 371 U.S. 471. Cited. 154 C. 314, 321; 155 C. 124, 133. Confession inadmissible as defendant was not advised he could have a lawyer's services prior to interrogation and that he had right to stop answering questions at any time. 157 C. 384. Cited. 164 C. 402. Admission into evidence of custodial statements not violation of section. 167 C. 408. Cited. 187 C. 6. Exclusionary effects of this statute do not apply to violations of Sec. 54-63c. 195 C. 505. Cited. 236 C. 388; 240 C. 205. Section not applicable to suppress a statement that was elicited from accused before expiration of the first court session when his presentment still would have been timely; legislature's use of past tense in the phrase "has not been presented" evinces an intent that the violation of not presenting the accused person to the court in a timely manner already must have occurred when the statement is obtained in order for section to apply; section was intended to embody federal rules in effect when section was enacted in 1963. 317 C. 1.

Cited. 11 CA 238; 37 CA 252; judgment reversed, see 236 C. 388; 43 CA 209; 44 CA 162. Section renders inadmissible any admission, confession or statement given by an accused person who remains in state custody after the time at which he should have been presented in court; section does not invalidate all statements made by defendant prior to that time due to later, unrelated wrongdoing by the police in prolonging the period of his pre-presentment detention. 145 CA 547; judgment affirmed, see 317 C. 1.

Cited. 2 Conn. Cir. Ct. 573; 3 Conn. Cir. Ct. 346; 5 Conn. Cir. Ct. 35, 40.

Sec. 54-1d. Place of arraignment. Multiple arrest warrants. Multiple credit card and automated teller machine offenses. Identity theft and related offenses. Violation of order of protection by electronic or telephonic means.

(a) For the purposes of this section, "geographical area" means the geographical area of the Superior Court established pursuant to section 51-348.

(b) Except as provided in subsections (d) and (e) of this section, defendants in criminal actions shall be presented for arraignment to:

(1) The court in the geographical area in which the crime was alleged to have been committed;

(2) If the arrest was by warrant, the court in the geographical area in which the crime was alleged to have been committed or in which the arrest was made; or

(3) If the arrest was by a warrant issued pursuant to section 53a-32 or for failure to appear as provided in section 53a-172 or 53a-173, the court in the geographical area in which the crime was alleged to have been committed or in which the arrest was made, or the superior court having jurisdiction over the underlying criminal prosecution.

(c) If the defendant was presented to the court in the geographical area in which the arrest was made for arraignment and was not released from custody after such arraignment, the defendant shall be presented to the court in the geographical area in which the crime was alleged to have been committed not later than the second court day following such arraignment. Except as provided in subsection (d) of this section, any defendant who has been presented to the court in accordance with this section and is the subject of one or more additional arrest warrants issued for crimes that were alleged to have been committed in one or more geographical areas, other than the geographical area in which the defendant is initially presented, shall subsequently be presented to the court in each geographical area in which such crimes were alleged to have been committed, in such order as the courts may determine, not later than the second court day following the prior arraignment. A criminal cause shall not fail on the ground that it has been submitted to a session of improper venue.

(d) Any defendant who is charged with multiple offenses under any provision of section 53a-127b or sections 53a-128a to 53a-128i, inclusive, where such offenses were alleged to have been committed in more than one geographical area, may be presented to the court in any one of such geographical areas. The court may consolidate all such offenses into a single criminal action and shall have jurisdiction over such action.

(e) Any defendant who is charged with a violation of section 53a-129a of the general statutes, revision of 1958, revised to January 1, 2003, section 53a-129b, 53a-129c, 53a-129d or 53a-129e, and any defendant who is charged with any other offense committed as a result of such violation may be presented to the court in the geographical area in which the person whose personal identifying information has been obtained and used by the defendant resides and may be prosecuted in such geographical area or judicial district.

(f) Any defendant who is charged with a violation of section 53a-223, 53a-223a or 53a-223b by means of electronic or telephonic communication may be presented to the court in the geographical area in which (1) the victim resides, (2) the victim received the communication, or (3) the communication was initiated. Such defendant may be prosecuted in any such geographical area or a corresponding judicial district.

(P.A. 74-183, S. 206, 291; P.A. 76-436, S. 517, 681; P.A. 80-313, S. 29; P.A. 95-105; P.A. 98-45; P.A. 03-156, S. 8; P.A. 05-152, S. 7; P.A. 06-152, S. 14; P.A. 09-239, S. 9; P.A. 12-114, S. 9.)

History: P.A. 76-436 replaced court of common pleas with superior court, reflecting transfer of all trial jurisdiction to superior court and substituted reference to Sec. 51-348 for reference to Sec. 51-156a, effective July 1, 1978; P.A. 80-313 deleted specific reference to superior court and rephrased protection for criminal causes submitted to session of improper venue; P.A. 95-105 authorized the defendant to be brought to the court in the geographical area in which the arrest was made for arraignment if the arrest was by warrant and added provision that if the defendant was brought to such court for arraignment and not released from custody, the defendant shall be presented to the court in the geographical area in which the crime was alleged to have been committed not later than the second court day following such arraignment; P.A. 98-45 designated existing provisions as Subsec. (a), added exception language and added new Subsec. (b) re consolidation of credit card and automated teller machine fraud offenses; P.A. 03-156 amended Subsec. (a) to add exception re Subsec. (c) and added new Subsec. (c) re place of presentment of defendant charged with identity theft or any other offense committed as a result of such violation; P.A. 05-152 amended Subsec. (a) by adding provision re arraignment at superior court having jurisdiction over underlying criminal prosecution if defendant is arrested on warrant issued pursuant to Sec. 53a-32 or for failure to appear as provided in Sec. 53a-172 or 53a-173 and by making technical changes; P.A. 06-152 added new Subsec. (a) defining "geographical area", divided existing Subsec. (a) into new Subsecs. (b)(1), (2) and (3) and (c) and made technical and conforming changes therein, inserted "in which the crime was alleged to have been committed or" in said Subsec. (b)(2), inserted "the court in the geographical area in which the crime was alleged to have been committed or in which the arrest was made, or" in said Subsec. (b)(3), added provision re presentment of defendant who is the subject of additional arrest warrants in said Subsec. (c), redesignated existing Subsec. (b) as Subsec. (d) and made a conforming change therein, and redesignated existing Subsec. (c) as Subsec. (e), effective June 6, 2006; P.A. 09-239 amended Subsec. (e) by adding reference to Sec. 53a-129e and provision re prosecution in geographical area or judicial district; P.A. 12-114 added Subsec. (f) re place of presentment of defendant charged with violation of Sec. 53a-223, 53a-223a or 53a-223b by means of electronic or telephonic communication.

Cited. 187 C. 264.

Cited. 39 CS 347.

Sec. 54-1e. Election of place of trial when venue is in the geographical area of Derby, Ansonia, Shelton, and Seymour. Section 54-1e is repealed.

(P.A. 75-578, S. 5; P.A. 76-436, S. 582, 681.)

Sec. 54-1f. (Formerly Sec. 6-49). Arrest without warrant. Pursuit outside precincts. (a) For purposes of this section, the respective precinct or jurisdiction of a state marshal or judicial marshal shall be wherever such marshal is required to perform duties. Peace officers, as defined in subdivision (9) of section 53a-3, in their respective precincts, shall arrest, without previous complaint and warrant, any person for any offense in their jurisdiction, when the person is taken or apprehended in the act or on the speedy information of others, provided that no constable elected pursuant to the provisions of section 9-200 shall be considered a peace officer for the purposes of this subsection, unless the town in which such constable holds office provides, by ordinance, that constables shall be considered peace officers for the purposes of this subsection.

(b) Members of the Division of State Police within the Department of Emergency Services and Public Protection or of any local police department or any chief inspector or inspector in the Division of Criminal Justice shall arrest, without previous complaint and warrant, any person who the officer has reasonable grounds to believe has committed or is committing a felony.

(c) Members of any local police department or the Office of State Capitol Police and constables and state marshals who are certified under the provisions of sections 7-294a to 7-294e, inclusive, and who perform criminal law enforcement duties, when in immediate pursuit of a person who may be arrested under the provisions of this section, except a person alleged to have violated only a municipal ordinance, are authorized to pursue such person outside of their respective precincts into any part of the state in order to effect the arrest. Such person may then be returned in the custody of such officer to the precinct in which the offense was committed.

(d) Any person arrested pursuant to this section shall be presented with reasonable promptness before proper authority.

what is reasonable? proper authority?

(1949 Rev., S. 465; 1953, S. 195d; 1961, P.A. 239; 1971, P.A. 754; P.A. 75-567, S. 69, 80; P.A. 76-111, S. 3; P.A. 77-614, S. 486, 610; P.A. 80-313, S. 1; 80-394, S. 7, 13; P.A. 81-472, S. 93, 159; P.A. 83-518, S. 2; P.A. 84-302, S. 2; P.A. 89-129, S. 1, 2; P.A. 96-219, S. 10; P.A. 00-99, S. 6, 154; P.A. 01-195, S. 70, 181; P.A. 11-51, S. 134; P.A. 15-83, S. 1.)

History: 1961 act added provision authorizing members of local police departments to pursue suspects beyond their precincts and return suspects, when caught to precinct where offense was committed; 1971 act deleted the word "organized" as qualifier of references to local police departments; P.A. 75-567 substituted detectives in the division of criminal justice for county detectives; P.A. 76-111 replaced detectives with chief inspectors and inspectors of criminal justice division; P.A. 77-614 made state police department a division within the department of public safety, effective January 1, 1979; Sec. 6-49 transferred to Sec. 54-1f in 1979; P.A. 80-313 divided section into Subsecs. and substituted references to peace officers for detailed listing of persons to which provisions apply, i.e. sheriffs, inspectors, constables, etc.; P.A. 80-394 specified applicability to sheriffs, deputy sheriffs and special deputy sheriffs, adding provision re precinct or jurisdiction of deputies and special deputies; P.A. 81-472 amended Subsec. (a) to delete reference to special deputy sheriffs since such sheriffs are included in definition of peace officers; P.A. 83-518 amended Subsec. (a) providing that constables shall not be considered peace officers for purposes of Subsec. (a) unless town ordinance so provides; P.A. 84-302 permitted certified constables who perform criminal law enforcement duties to pursue offenders outside of their precincts; P.A. 89-129 amended provision in Subsec. (c) authorizing pursuit outside of precinct to include members of the office of state capitol security; P.A. 96-219 amended Subsec. (c) by changing the name of the "Office of State Capitol Security" to the "Office of State Capitol Police"; P.A. 00-99 amended Subsec. (a) by changing reference to deputy or special deputy sheriff to state marshal or judicial marshal and amended Subsec. (c) by deleting reference to sheriffs, deputy sheriffs and special deputy sheriffs and adding reference to state marshals, effective December 1, 2000; P.A. 01-195 made technical changes for purposes of gender neutrality in Subsec. (a), effective July 11, 2001; pursuant to P.A. 11-51, "Department of Public Safety" was changed editorially by the Revisors to "Department of Emergency Services and Public Protection" in Subsec. (b), effective July 1, 2011; P.A. 15-83 amended Subsec. (c) by adding exception re person alleged to have violated only a municipal ordinance and making technical changes.

See Sec. 6-43 re special deputies.

Annotations to former section 6-49:

Facts held insufficient to authorize arrest without warrant. 37 C. 32. Arrest being lawful, officer is presumed to have performed all subsequent duties. 51 C. 432–434. Extends common law rule. 84 C. 167. Owner of goods stolen or any other person may retake them and tender thief to justice. 97 C. 137. Thief resisting capture is guilty of breach of the peace and may be arrested by anyone. Id., 138. Right of police to arrest for offenses in their presence and to seize implements used in law breaking. Id., 545. When officer must act on his own knowledge. Id., 701. Facts held sufficient to authorize arrest without warrant. 101 C. 229. Any arrest without a warrant, except as authorized by statute, is illegal. 115 C. 282. Police officers while off duty or out of uniform are included within the coverage of section. 120 C. 101. Speedy information which justifies arrest is information that person arrested was guilty of crime or at least implicated in it. 131 C. 224. Officer may act on speedy information if he has reasonable ground to accept it as accurate. Id., 231. Fact that defendant not taken before proper magistrate not sufficient to exclude confession. 137 C. 183. Cited. 147 C. 194. Intention of officer in pursuing person admissible as a fact to be weighed with other circumstances. 148 C. 27. An accused is lawfully taken or apprehended in the act if circumstances observed by officer preceding the arrest, viewed in light of common knowledge and his own training and experience, gave him probable cause to believe that a crime was being, or had just been, committed; evidence seized cannot be used to sustain validity of arrest. 149 C. 567. Illegal arrest and detention does not automatically render inadmissible confessions made after the arrest or during the period of detention. 150 C. 169. Officer entitled to exert force where grounds for "reasonable belief" are present. 151 C. 402. Person need not submit to unlawful arrest. 152 C. 296. In determining the validity of an arrest made without a warrant, "reasonable grounds" is to be equated with probable cause. 153 C. 41. Probable cause exists when the arresting officer has reasonably trustworthy information sufficient to believe a felony had been committed by the accused. Id., 42. Arrest made on strength of officer's own observation would be legal only if the circumstances he observed, when taken in connection with those before observed by him when weighed in the light of common knowledge, gave him probable reason or ground to believe that such a crime was being, or was about to be, committed. Id., 69, 70. Accused is lawfully taken or apprehended in the act if the circumstances observed by the arresting officer, viewed in light of common knowledge and his own training and experience, gave him probable cause to believe a crime was being, or had just been, committed; amount of evidence necessary to furnish probable cause for an arrest without a warrant is to be measured by facts of particular case and need not be evidence sufficient to convict; a reasonable search incident to a lawful arrest is not unlawful even though made without a warrant; a lawful entry is necessarily an essential element of a reasonable search of a dwelling. Id., 152. A police officer may make a reasonable search before or after an arrest without a warrant if the circumstances justified the arrest and the search was incidental to the arrest. Id., 154. Where larceny which constituted a misdemeanor was committed in New London and defendants were apprehended in Hartford by Hartford police, held that, since larceny is a continuing crime, defendants, if transportation of the merchandise was with a continuous felonious intent, were committing larceny in Hartford and defendants' claim that arrest or search without a warrant was illegal must fail. Id., 217, 218. Member of an organized local police department is authorized to arrest, without previous complaint and warrant, any person who officer has reasonable grounds to believe has committed or is committing a felony and may conduct a search incident thereto without a warrant. 155 C. 385. A legal arrest may be made without a warrant when defendant was apprehended just after his sale of drugs to an informer under police surveillance of the transaction and his person could be searched incidentally to such arrest. Id., 516. Police lieutenant's arrest of defendant on speedy information was clearly justifiable when defendant was sitting armed in his car at night with narcotics on his person. 157 C. 114. Arrest for misdemeanor of breach of the peace on speedy information of others by police was proper; search of car in which defendant was sitting made without warrant was lawful. Id., 222. Arrest of defendant for assault committed in officer's presence was lawful and search of trunk of defendant's car was lawful incident to the arrest. Id., 351. Officer's arresting defendant for disorderly conduct was proper and search incidental thereto of person was legal. Id., 485. Arrest of defendant operating stolen car could be made without warrant on grounds that he was apprehended in act and upon speedy information where arresting officer had been informed by police barracks car was a stolen car. 159 C. 201. Arrest permitted without warrant when person is "taken or apprehended in the act" if preceding arrest, circumstances in light of officers training and experience gave him probable cause for such arrest. 160 C. 140. An informant's tip as to description and location of criminal suspect and his truck having proved true was justifiable basis for arrest under statute. 161 C. 117. Cited. 163 C. 186. Felony provision cited. 171 C. 105. Cited. 174 C. 153; Id., 452; 178 C. 427; 183 C. 386; 220 C. 307.

Cited. 22 CS 6. An arrest by a police officer without a warrant is ground for an action for false imprisonment unless the arrest is authorized by section. Id., 311. Cited. 24 CS 32. Where offenses committed by defendant and with which he is charged occurred within the hour prior to his arrest, officer acted speedily on information he had obtained. 25 CS 108. If search is incident to arrest, no warrant is needed. Id., 216. Discussion of facts which constitute acting on speedy information or on reasonable belief that a felony has been committed or is being committed; no need for issuance of warrant for seizure of articles which are taken incidental to lawful arrest. 26 CS 297. Cited. 28 CS 313. "Speedy information" requirement was in derogation of common law re felonies; additional clause re felonies, added in 1945, is declaratory of common law. 34 CS 531. Modern trend prohibits warrantless entry to home to make an arrest unless there are exigent circumstances. Id., 539.

Arrest made hour after officer saw crime committed satisfied requirement of acting on "speedy information". 2 Conn. Cir. Ct. 247. Cited. Id., 467. Arrest without a warrant not unlawful merely because pursuit of defendant by Orange police officer was interrupted when defendant temporarily succeeded in eluding officer. 3 Conn. Cir. Ct. 42. Arrest made without warrant on "speedy information" of informer who purchased liquor sold by defendant illegally, made within half hour after sale, held lawful. 4 Conn. Cir. Ct. 125. Cited. Id., 533. Officers would have been justified in arresting defendants for bookmaking when telephone calls and other evidence of their illegal activity occurred in presence of officers who had entered house with search warrant, even if warrant had been illegal. Id., 603. Acting on speedy information defendant was committing crime of lascivious carriage, police officers rightfully entered her apartment building and observed her conduct from fire escape of apartment; police officers investigating a crime on speedy information who enter a building are licensees. 5 Conn. Cir. Ct. 35. Statute provides a less strict standard for arrests without a warrant for felonies provided they are made by members of an organized local police department. Id., 44, 50. Defendant's arrest by police officer who observed him in telephone booth, taking house bets on slips of paper officer could read, was properly made without warrant and reasonable search could be made on such arrest. Id., 51. Member of Derby police department was justified in arrest of defendant without warrant where New Haven police requested his arrest as one involved in felonious larceny in their jurisdiction. Id., 529. Defendant in resisting an unlawful arrest was not guilty of breach of the peace. 6 Conn. Cir. Ct. 42. Arrest by Trumbull officer of defendant as he drew up to his home in Bridgeport two hours after he had violated hit and run statute in Trumbull was valid as an arrest in immediate pursuit outside Trumbull precinct. Id., 55. Facts held sufficient to authorize arrest without warrant. Id., 228, 235, 236. Cited. Id., 613. Taken or apprehended defined. Id., 618.

Annotations to present section:

Cited. 179 C. 46; 180 C. 481; 181 C. 172. As a matter of constitutional law, where entry of dwelling is for purpose of conducting search under a valid search warrant, resident may be arrested under statute where police have probable cause to believe he committed a felony; arrest does not constitute violation of fourth amendment to U.S. Constitution. Id., 187. Cited. 188 C. 432, 442; 200 C. 82; 215 C. 667; 216 C. 172; 225 C. 921; 227 C. 363. Violation of Sec. 14-227a is an "offense" within meaning of this section. 228 C 758. Cited. 229 C. 125; 240 C. 489.

Cited. 15 CA 416; 20 CA 183; 23 CA 123; Id., 487; 27 CA 370; Id., 741; 29 CA 207; 30 CA 108; 31 CA 669; 33 CA 590; 34 CA 189; Id., 201; 46 CA 633. Where prior felony conviction formed basis of a charge under section, violation of section could not be established without presenting proof of such conviction. 64 CA 384. Does not prohibit "Terry" stops by extraterritorial police officers; rather, it prohibits full custodial arrests by extraterritorial police officers. 70 CA 297.

Cited. 38 CS 313.

Subsec. (a):

Cited. 191 C. 433; 210 C. 333; 224 C. 494; 227 C. 534; 228 C. 758. Section inapplicable to juveniles re commencement of delinquency proceedings by service of a summons alleging commission of criminal offenses. 297 C. 16.

Cited. 6 CA 124; 11 CA 11; 21 CA 326; 26 CA 481; judgment reversed, see 224 C. 494; Id., 805; 28 CA 708; 41 CA 779.

"Speedy information of others" does not preclude reliance on supplementary observations made by the officer. 37 CS 755. Officer's entry into apartment was lawful and in full compliance with statute; arrest was made on the speedy information of others; properly conducted search incidental to lawful arrest is not illegal even though made without a warrant. 38 CS 313. Cited. Id., 364; 39 CS 347; 40 CS 512.

Subsec. (b):

Cited. 183 C. 386; 189 C. 429; 195 C. 505; 220 C. 307; 236 C. 216; 248 C. 183.

Cited. 6 CA 124; 11 CA 11; 13 CA 69; Id., 214; 14 CA 388; 15 CA 569; 18 CA 184; 20 CA 168; judgment reversed, see 215 C. 667; Id., 521; 26 CA 481; judgment reversed, see 224 C. 494; 27 CA 128; 31 CA 548; 39 CA 579. Where probable cause for warrantless arrest was established using Aguilar-Spinelli factors, trial court improperly introduced second level of review under "totality of the circumstances" analysis. 47 CA 424. Phrase "reasonable grounds to believe" is synonymous with probable cause. 59 CA 272. Warrantless arrest based on probable cause was authorized under subsection. 74 CA 802. "Reasonable grounds" as used in statute is synonymous with probable cause. 78 CA 659.

Subsec. (c):

Appellate Court, in affirming defendant's conviction for operating motor vehicle while under the influence of intoxicating liquor, rejected defendant's argument that there can only be "immediate pursuit" for purposes of Subsec. when there are findings that arresting officer personally observed illegal conduct and then followed suspect across jurisdictional boundaries. 88 CA 110.

Cited. 37 CS 755.

Sec. 54-1g. Time of arraignment. Violation of protective order, standing criminal protective order or restraining order.

(a) Any arrested person who is not released sooner or who is charged with a family violence crime as defined in section 46b-38a or a violation of section 53a-181c, 53a-181d or 53a-181e shall be promptly presented before the superior court sitting next regularly for the geographical area where the offense is alleged to have been committed. If an arrested person is hospitalized, or has escaped or is otherwise incapacitated, the person shall be presented, if practicable, to the first regular sitting after return to police custody.

(b) Any arrested person who is charged with a violation of section 53a-223, 53a-223a or 53a-223b shall be promptly presented to the superior court next sitting for the geographical area where the offense is alleged to have been committed. If the alleged offense was committed in a geographical area of the Superior Court other than the geographical area where the protective order was issued, the prosecutorial official for the geographical area of the Superior Court where the alleged offense was committed shall notify the prosecutorial official for the geographical area where the protective order was issued of the

16

alleged violation of such protective order. On motion of any party or the court, the prosecution of such offense may be transferred to the superior court for the geographical area where the protective order was issued.

(P.A. 80-313, S. 26; P.A. 86-337, S. 10; P.A. 91-381, S. 5, 7; P.A. 93-75; P.A. 95-214, S. 2; P.A. 12-114, S. 21.)

History: P.A. 86-337 applied provisions to persons charged with a family violence crime as defined in Sec. 46b-38a; P.A. 91-381 added new Subsec. (b) re prompt presentment of arrested person charged with violation of Sec. 53a-110b to superior court where protective order was issued; P.A. 93-75 amended Subsec. (b) by adding procedure for determining geographic area of the superior court where person arrested for violation of protective order shall be prosecuted; P.A. 95-214 amended Subsec. (a) to include persons charged with "a violation of section 53a-181c, 53a-181d or 53a-181e"; P.A. 12-114 amended Subsec. (b) to add reference to violation of Sec. 53a-223a or 53a-223b.

Cited. 236 C. 388; 243 C. 205.

Cited. 11 CA 238; 43 CA 209; 44 CA 162.

Sec. 54-1h. (Formerly Sec. 6-49a). Arrest by complaint and summons for commission of misdemeanor.

Any person who has been arrested with or without a warrant for commission of a misdemeanor, or for an offense the penalty for which is imprisonment for not more than one year or a fine of not more than one thousand dollars, or both, may, in the discretion of the arresting officer, be issued a written complaint and summons and be released on his written promise to appear on a date and time specified. If any person so arrested and summoned fails to appear for trial at the place and time so specified, or on any court date thereafter, a warrant for his rearrest or a capias shall be issued and he shall also be subject to the provisions of section 53a-173.

(1972, P.A. 69, S. 1; P.A. 84-123, S. 1.)

History: Sec. 6-49a transferred to Sec. 54-1h in 1981; P.A. 84-123 added "or on any court date thereafter" and authorized issuance of a capias for person who fails to appear.

Sec. 54-1i. (Formerly Sec. 54-40a). Duty of law enforcement officer before charging with a crime a person found in unconscious condition.

(a) All law enforcement officers in this state shall make a diligent effort to determine if any person they find in a semiconscious or unconscious condition is wearing an identification bracelet or metal tag, or is carrying an identification card, bearing such person's name and any of the following information: A statement of an illness, such as epilepsy, diabetes or a cardiac condition, which might cause semiconsciousness or unconsciousness, a physician's name or identification of a medication, before such person may be charged with a crime. If any law enforcement officer shall determine that such a person is actually suffering from an affliction which would cause semiconsciousness or unconsciousness, he shall notify such person's physician immediately or have such person immediately transported to a physician or to some facility where the services of a physician are available.

(b) Any person who wilfully and knowingly falsifies such identification or deliberately misrepresents such an illness shall be guilty of a class A misdemeanor.

(P.A. 73-202, S. 1, 2.)

History: Sec. 54-40a transferred to Sec. 54-1i in 1981.

Sec. 54-1j. Ascertainment that defendant understands possible immigration and naturalization consequences of guilty or nolo contendere plea.

(a) The court shall not accept a plea of guilty or nolo contendere from any defendant in any criminal proceeding unless the court first addresses the defendant personally and determines that the defendant fully understands that if the defendant is not a citizen of the United States, conviction of the offense for which the defendant has been charged may have the consequences of deportation or removal from the United States, exclusion from readmission to the United States or denial of naturalization, pursuant to the laws of the United States. If the defendant has not discussed these possible consequences with the defendant's attorney, the court shall permit the defendant to do so prior to accepting the defendant's plea.

(b) The defendant shall not be required at the time of the plea to disclose the defendant's legal status in the United States to the court.

(c) If the court fails to address the defendant personally and determine that the defendant fully understands the possible consequences of the defendant's plea, as required in subsection (a) of this section, and the defendant not later than three years after the acceptance of the plea shows that the defendant's plea and conviction may have one of the enumerated consequences, the court, on the defendant's motion, shall vacate the judgment, and permit the defendant to withdraw the plea of guilty or nolo contendere, and enter a plea of not guilty.

(P.A. 82-177; P.A. 97-256, S. 6; P.A. 03-81, S. 1.)

History: P.A. 97-256 amended Subsec. (c) by imposing a three-year time period after the acceptance of the plea for the defendant to show that his plea and conviction may have one of the enumerated consequences, and deleting provision that, in the absence of a record that the court provided the required advice, the defendant is presumed not to have received such advice; P.A. 03-81 amended Subsec. (a) to replace former provision prohibiting the court accepting plea unless the court "advises" the defendant of the possible immigration or naturalization consequences of conviction if the defendant is not a citizen and setting forth specific language of such advisement with provision that prohibits the court accepting plea unless the court first addresses the defendant personally and determines that the defendant fully understands such possible consequences, add "removal" from the United States as a possible consequence and add provision requiring the court to permit the defendant to discuss these possible consequences with the defendant's attorney prior to accepting plea, amended Subsec. (b) to make a technical change for purposes of gender neutrality and amended Subsec. (c) to make provisions applicable

18

if court fails "to address the defendant personally and determine that the defendant fully understands the possible consequences of the defendant's plea, as required in subsection (a) of this section" rather than if court fails "to advise a defendant, as required in subsection (a) of this section" and make a technical change for purposes of gender neutrality.

Court found that the time limit for filing motion was procedural in nature and therefore could be applied retroactively. 251 C. 617. Warning of deportation and denial was substantial compliance with provisions of statute since defendant was warned guilty plea implicates immigration status. 257 C. 653.

Court need only inform defendant of potential deportation consequences rather than engaging defendant in a manner to ensure full understanding. 62 CA 805. Section is in place only to call defendant's attention to potential immigration consequences under federal law, not to inform defendant of every possible consequence of a plea. 68 CA 499. Court's inquiry of defense counsel as to whether there were any immigration issues and whether counsel talked to defendant about possible consequences of pleas cannot be construed as substantial compliance with requirements of Subsec. (a). 120 CA 489; judgment reversed, see 303 C. 527.

Subsec. (a):

Court properly relied upon representations by defense counsel that defendant understood immigration consequences of guilty plea and court was not required to address defendant personally; substantial compliance with section is sufficient. 303 C. 527.

Subsec. is plain and unambiguous, and requires that court address defendant personally and determine that defendant fully understands that immigration consequences may flow from entering a plea if a noncitizen, and court is only required to provide defendant an opportunity to discuss with defense counsel the possible immigration consequences of entering a plea if the court is made aware that defendant has not discussed those immigration consequences with defense counsel. 139 CA 308.

Subsec. (c):

Under 1999 revision, court does not have jurisdiction to hear motion filed outside of 3-year period. 306 C. 125.

Sec. 54-1k. Issuance of protective orders in cases of stalking, harassment, sexual assault, risk of injury to or impairing morals of a child.

(a) Upon the arrest of a person for a violation of subdivision (1) or (2) of subsection (a) of section 53-21, section 53a-70, 53a-70a, 53a-70c, 53a-71, 53a-72a, 53a-72b or 53a-73a, or any attempt thereof, or section 53a-181c, 53a-181d or 53a-181e, the court may issue a protective order pursuant to this section. Upon the arrest of a person for a violation of section 53a-182b or 53a-183, the court may issue a protective order pursuant to this section if it finds that such violation caused the victim to reasonably fear for his or her physical safety. Such order shall be an order of the court, and the clerk of the court shall cause (1) a copy of such order, or the information contained in such order, to be sent to the victim, and (2) a copy of such order, or the information contained in such order, to be sent by facsimile or other means not later than forty-eight hours after its issuance to the law enforcement agency or agencies for the town in which the victim resides, the town in which the victim is employed and the town in which the defendant resides. If the victim is enrolled in a public or private elementary or secondary school, including a technical high school, or an institution of higher education, as defined in section 10a-55, the clerk of the court shall, upon the request of the victim, send, by facsimile or other means, a copy of such order, or the information contained in such order, to such school or institution of higher education, the president of any institution of higher education at which the victim is enrolled and the special police force established pursuant to section 10a-156b, if any, at the institution of higher education at which the victim is enrolled.

(b) A protective order issued under this section may include provisions necessary to protect the victim from threats, harassment, injury or intimidation by the defendant, including but not limited to, an order enjoining the defendant from (1) imposing any restraint upon the person or liberty of the victim, (2) threatening, harassing, assaulting, molesting or sexually assaulting the victim, or (3) entering the dwelling of the victim. A protective order issued under this section may include provisions necessary to protect any animal owned or kept by the victim including, but not limited to, an order enjoining the defendant from injuring or threatening to injure such animal. Such order shall be made a condition of the bail or release of the defendant and shall contain the following language: "In accordance with section 53a-223 of the Connecticut general statutes, any violation of this order constitutes criminal violation of a protective order which is punishable by a term of imprisonment of not more than ten years, a fine of not more than ten thousand dollars, or both. Additionally, in accordance with section 53a-107 of the Connecticut general statutes, entering or remaining in a building or any other premises in violation of this order constitutes criminal trespass in the first degree which is punishable by a term of imprisonment of not more than one year, a fine of not more than two thousand dollars, or both. Violation of this order also violates a condition of your bail or release and may result in raising the amount of bail or revoking release.".

(c) The information contained in and concerning the issuance of any protective order issued under this section shall be entered in the registry of protective orders pursuant to section 51-5c.

(P.A. 95-214, S. 3; P.A. 02-132, S. 56; P.A. 05-147, S. 1; 05-288, S. 183; P.A. 07-78, S. 3; P.A. 08-84, S. 1; P.A. 10-144, S. 7; P.A. 12-114, S. 4; June 12 Sp. Sess. P.A. 12-2, S. 99; P.A. 14-217, S. 126.)

History: P.A. 02-132 replaced provisions re sending certified copy of order to law enforcement agency with provisions re sending copy of or information contained in order to law enforcement agency by facsimile or other means, replaced provisions re entry of protective orders in registry established under Sec. 46b-38c(e) with provisions re entry of information into registry of protective orders pursuant to Sec. 51-5c and made technical changes, effective January 1, 2003; P.A. 05-147 authorized the issuance of a protective order upon the arrest of a person for a violation of Sec. 53a-182b or 53a-183 if the violation caused the victim to reasonably fear for his or her physical safety and revised the language of the order to make technical changes and specify that a violation of Sec. 53a-223 is punishable by a term of imprisonment of not more than five years, a fine of not more than $5,000, or both, reflecting the increase in the penalty for said violation made by P.A. 02-127; P.A. 05-288 made technical changes and revised required language in order re penalty for criminal violation of a protective order, effective July 13, 2005; P.A. 07-78 added provision re authority of protective order to include provisions necessary to protect any animal owned or kept by the victim; P.A. 08-84 inserted Subsec. designators (a), (b) and (c), and amended Subsec. (a) to reference Secs. 53-21(a)(1) or (2), 53a-70, 53a-70a, 53a-70c, 53a-71, 53a-72a, 53a-72b or 53a-73a, or any attempt thereof; P.A. 10-144 amended Subsec. (a) to insert Subdiv. designators (1) and (2), to delete "certified" re copy of order and add "or the information contained in such order" in Subdiv. (1) and to substitute provision re law enforcement agency for town in which victim resides, town in which victim is employed and town in which defendant resides for provision re appropriate law enforcement agency in Subdiv. (2); P.A. 12-114 amended Subsec. (a) to add provision re clerk of court to send copy of order to school at which victim is enrolled, and made technical changes; June 12 Sp. Sess. P.A. 12-2 amended Subsec. (a) to substitute "technical high school" for "regional vocational technical school"; P.A. 14-217 amended Subsec. (b) to replace "five years" and "five thousand dollars" with "ten years" and "ten thousand dollars", respectively, in required order language re penalty for criminal violation of a protective order, effective January 1, 2015.

Nothing in section prohibits state from bringing charges for other criminal acts in addition to violation of protective order. 151 CA 590.

Sec. 54-1l. Short title: Alvin W. Penn Racial Profiling Prohibition Act.

(a) This section and section 54-1m shall be known as the "Alvin W. Penn Racial Profiling Prohibition Act".

(b) For the purposes of this section, "racial profiling" means the detention, interdiction or other disparate treatment of an individual solely on the basis of the racial or ethnic status of such individual.

(c) No member of the Division of State Police within the Department of Emergency Services and Public Protection, a municipal police department or any other law enforcement agency shall engage in racial profiling. The detention of an individual based on any noncriminal factor or combination of noncriminal factors is inconsistent with this policy.

(d) The race or ethnicity of an individual shall not be the sole factor in determining the existence of probable cause to place in custody or arrest an individual or in constituting a reasonable and articulable suspicion that an offense has been or is being committed so as to justify the detention of an individual or the investigatory stop of a motor vehicle.

(P.A. 99-198, S. 1; P.A. 03-160, S. 2; P.A. 11-51, S. 134.)

History: P.A. 03-160 inserted new Subsec. (a) providing that section and Sec. 54-1m shall be known as the "Alvin W. Penn Racial Profiling Prohibition Act" and redesignated existing Subsecs. (a) to (c) as new Subsecs. (b) to (d), effective June 26, 2003; pursuant to P.A. 11-51, "Department of Public Safety" was changed editorially by the Revisors to "Department of Emergency Services and Public Protection" in Subsec. (c), effective July 1, 2011.

Sec. 54-1m. Adoption of policy prohibiting certain police actions. Traffic stop information. Standardized method. Data collection and reporting.

(a) Each municipal police department, the Department of Emergency Services and Public Protection and any other department with authority to conduct a traffic stop shall adopt a written policy that prohibits the stopping, detention or search of any person when such action is solely motivated by considerations of race, color, ethnicity, age, gender or sexual orientation, and such action would constitute a violation of the civil rights of the person. For the purposes of this section: (1) "Department with authority to conduct a traffic stop" means any department that includes, or has oversight of, a police officer, and (2) "police officer" means a police officer within a municipal police department or the Department of Emergency Services and Public Protection or a person with the same authority pursuant to any provision of the general statutes to make arrests or issue citations for violation of any statute or regulation relating to motor vehicles and to enforce said statutes and regulations as policemen or state policemen have in their respective jurisdictions, including, but not limited to: (A) Special policemen or state policemen acting under the provisions of section 29-18, 17a-24 or 17a-465; (B) policemen acting under the provisions of section 29-19; (C) the Commissioner of Motor Vehicles, each deputy commissioner of the Department of Motor Vehicles and any salaried inspector of motor vehicles designated by the commissioner pursuant to section 14-8; (D) State Capitol Police officers acting under the provisions of section 2-1f; (E) special police forces acting under the provisions of section 10a-156b; (F) state policemen acting under the provisions of section 27-107; and (G) fire police officers acting under the provisions of section 7-313a.

(b) Not later than July 1, 2013, the Office of Policy and Management, in consultation with the Racial Profiling Prohibition Project Advisory Board established in section 54-1s, and the Criminal Justice Information System Governing Board shall, within available resources, develop and implement a standardized method:

(1) To be used by police officers of municipal police departments, the Department of Emergency Services and Public Protection and any other department with authority to conduct a traffic stop to record traffic stop information unless the police officer is required to leave the location of the stop prior to completing such form in order to respond to an emergency or due to some other exigent circumstance within the scope of such police officer's duties. The standardized method and any form developed and implemented pursuant to such standardized method shall allow the following information to be recorded: (A) The date and time of the stop; (B) the specific geographic location of the stop; (C) the unique identifying number of the police officer making the stop, or the name and title of the person making the stop if such person does not have a unique identifying number; (D) the race, color, ethnicity, age and gender of the operator of the motor vehicle that is stopped, provided the identification of such characteristics shall be based on the observation and perception of the police officer responsible for reporting the stop; (E) the nature of the alleged traffic violation or other violation that caused the stop to be made and the statutory citation for such violation; (F) the disposition of the stop including whether a warning, citation or summons was issued, whether a search was conducted, the authority for any search conducted, the result of any search conducted, the statute or regulation citation for any warning, citation or summons issued and whether a custodial arrest was made; and (G) any other information deemed appropriate. The method shall also provide for (i) notice to be given to the person stopped that if such person believes that such person has been stopped, detained or subjected to a search solely because of race, color, ethnicity, age, gender, sexual orientation, religion or membership in any other protected class, such person may file a complaint with the appropriate law enforcement agency unless the police officer was required to leave the location of the stop prior to providing such notice in order to respond to an emergency

or due to some other exigent circumstance within the scope of such police officer's duties, and (ii) instructions to be given to the person stopped on how to file such complaint unless the police officer was required to leave the location of the stop prior to providing such instructions in order to respond to an emergency or due to some other exigent circumstance within the scope of such police officer's duties;

(2) To be used to report complaints pursuant to this section by any person who believes such person has been subjected to a motor vehicle stop by a police officer solely on the basis of race, color, ethnicity, age, gender, sexual orientation or religion; and

(3) To be used by each municipal police department, the Department of Emergency Services and Public Protection and any other department with authority to conduct a traffic stop to report data to the Office of Policy and Management pursuant to subsection (h) of this section.

(c) Not later than July 1, 2013, the Office of Policy and Management, in consultation with the Racial Profiling Prohibition Project Advisory Board, shall develop and implement guidelines to be used by each municipal police department, the Department of Emergency Services and Public Protection and any other department with authority to conduct a traffic stop in (1) training police officers of such agency in the completion of the form developed and implemented pursuant to subdivision (1) of subsection (b) of this section, and (2) evaluating the information collected by police officers of such municipal police department, the Department of Emergency Services and Public Protection or other department with authority to conduct a traffic stop pursuant to subsection (e) of this section for use in the counseling and training of such police officers.

(d) (1) Prior to the date a standardized method and form have been developed and implemented pursuant to subdivision (1) of subsection (b) of this section, each municipal police department, the Department of Emergency Services and Public Protection and any other department with authority to conduct a traffic stop shall, using the form developed and promulgated pursuant to the provisions of subsection (h) in effect on January 1, 2012, record and retain the following information: (A) The number of persons stopped for traffic violations; (B) characteristics of race, color, ethnicity, gender and age of such persons, provided the identification of such characteristics shall be based on the observation and perception of the police officer responsible for reporting the stop and the information shall not be required to be provided by the person stopped; (C) the nature of the alleged traffic violation that resulted in the stop; (D) whether a warning or citation was issued, an arrest made or a search conducted as a result of the stop; and (E) any additional information that such municipal police department, the Department of Emergency Services and Public Protection or any other department with authority to conduct a traffic stop, as the case may be, deems appropriate, provided such information shall not include any other identifying information about any person stopped for a traffic violation such as the person's operator's license number, name or address.

(2) On and after the date a standardized method and form have been developed and implemented pursuant to subdivision (1) of subsection (h) of this section, each municipal police department, the Department of Emergency Services and Public Protection and any other department with authority to conduct a traffic stop shall record and retain the information required to be recorded pursuant to such standardized method and any additional information that such municipal police department or the Department of Emergency Services and Public Protection or other department with authority to conduct a traffic stop, as

the case may be, deems appropriate, provided such information shall not include any other identifying information about any person stopped for a traffic violation such as the person's operator's license number, name or address.

(e) Each municipal police department, the Department of Emergency Services and Public Protection and any other department with authority to conduct a traffic stop shall provide to the Chief State's Attorney and the Office of Policy and Management (1) a copy of each complaint received pursuant to this section, and (2) written notification of the review and disposition of such complaint. No copy of such complaint shall include any other identifying information about the complainant such as the complainant's operator's license number, name or address.

(f) Any police officer who in good faith records traffic stop information pursuant to the requirements of this section shall not be held civilly liable for the act of recording such information unless the officer's conduct was unreasonable or reckless.

(g) If a municipal police department, the Department of Emergency Services and Public Protection or any other department with authority to conduct a traffic stop fails to comply with the provisions of this section, the Office of Policy and Management shall recommend and the Secretary of the Office of Policy and Management may order an appropriate penalty in the form of the withholding of state funds from such municipal police department, the Department of Emergency Services and Public Protection or such other department with authority to conduct a traffic stop.

(h) Not later than October 1, 2012, each municipal police department and the Department of Emergency Services and Public Protection shall provide to the Office of Policy and Management a summary report of the information recorded pursuant to subsection (d) of this section. On and after October 1, 2013, each municipal police department, the Department of Emergency Services and Public Protection and any other department with authority to conduct a traffic stop shall provide to the Office of Policy and Management a monthly report of the information recorded pursuant to subsection (d) of this section for each traffic stop conducted, in a format prescribed by the Office of Policy and Management. On and after January 1, 2015, such information shall be submitted in electronic form, and shall be submitted in electronic form prior to said date to the extent practicable.

(i) The Office of Policy and Management shall, within available resources, review the prevalence and disposition of traffic stops and complaints reported pursuant to this section. Not later than July 1, 2014, and annually thereafter, the office shall report the results of any such review, including any recommendations, to the Governor, the General Assembly and any other entity deemed appropriate.

(P.A. 99-198, S. 2, 3; June Sp. Sess. P.A. 01-9, S. 128, 131; P.A. 03-160, S. 1; P.A. 04-27, S. 6; 04-257, S. 83; P.A. 11-51, S. 171; P.A. 12-74, S. 1; June 12 Sp. Sess. P.A. 12-1, S. 144; P.A. 13-75, S. 1; May Sp. Sess. P.A. 16-3, S. 168.)

History: (Revisor's note: A reference in Subsec. (f) to "the information recorded pursuant to subsection (d)" was changed editorially by the Revisors to "the information recorded pursuant to subsection (b)" for accuracy); June Sp. Sess. P.A. 01-9 amended Subsec. (h) to extend the effectiveness of Subsecs. (f) and (g) from January 1, 2002, to January 1, 2003, effective July 1, 2001; P.A. 03-160 amended Subsec. (b)(5) to provide that additional information does not include any other identifying information about any person stopped for a traffic violation such as his or her operator's license number, name or address, amended Subsec. (c) to require copy of the complaint and written notification of the review and disposition of such complaint to be provided to the African-American Affairs Commission and to provide that no such complaint shall contain any other identifying information about the complainant such as his or her operator's license number, name or address, amended Subsec. (f) to require that summary report be provided to the African-American Affairs Commission, amended Subsec. (g) to require the African-American Affairs Commission to review the prevalence and disposition of traffic stops and complaints and, not later than January 1, 2004, and annually thereafter, to report the results of such review to the Governor, the General Assembly and any other entity said commission deems appropriate and to delete references to the Chief State's Attorney, deleted former Subsec. (h) re limited period of effectiveness of Subsecs. (f) and (g), redesignated existing Subsec. (i) as Subsec. (h) and amended said Subsec. by substituting reference in Subdiv. (1) to personal identifying information with reference to race, color, ethnicity, gender and age, effective June 26, 2003; P.A. 04-27 made technical changes, effective April 28, 2004; P.A. 04-257 made a technical change in Subsec. (b), effective June 14, 2004; P.A. 11-51 replaced Commissioner and Department of Public Safety with Commissioner and Department of Emergency Services and Public Protection and amended Subsecs. (a), (b) and (h) to delete references to January 1, 2000, effective July 1, 2011; P.A. 12-74 added new Subsec. (b) re development and implementation of standardized method to record traffic stop information, added new Subsec. (c) re training and evaluation guidelines, redesignated existing Subsec. (b) as Subsec. (d) and amended same to provide that method be used on and after July 1, 2013, if developed and implemented, redesignated existing Subsecs. (c) to (g) as Subsecs. (e) to (i) and amended same to substitute references to Office of Policy and Management for references to African-American Affairs Commission re receipt of complaints, Chief State's Attorney re recommendation of penalty for failure to comply, Chief State's Attorney and commission re summary report, and commission re review, within available resources, and substitute "October 1, 2013" for "October 1, 2000" re summary report, added Subsec. (j) re report to judiciary committee, deleted former Subsec. (h) re development and promulgation of forms, and made technical changes, effective July 1, 2012; June 12 Sp. Sess. P.A. 12-1 amended Subsec. (d) to add Subdiv. (1) re use of form and recording of information, designate provisions re recording and retaining information under standardized method as Subdiv. (2) and add reference therein to municipal police department and Department of Emergency Services and Public Protection, amended Subsec. (h) to substitute "October 1, 2012" for "October 1, 2013" re summary report and delete provision re use of method and form, and made technical changes, effective July 1, 2012; P.A. 13-75 made section applicable to "any other department with authority to conduct a traffic stop", amended Subsec. (a) to add Subdiv. (1) defining "department with authority to conduct a traffic stop" and Subdiv. (2) defining "police officer", amended Subsec. (b)(1) to add provisions re exception to requirement to record traffic stop information and complaint information provided to person stopped when officer is required to leave in order to respond to emergency or due to other exigent circumstances within scope of duties, and to require that form include specific geographic location of stop, officer's unique identifying number or name, title of person making stop if such person has no unique identifying number, the authority for any search conducted, the result of any search conducted, and the citation for any warning, citation or summons issued, amended Subsec. (h) to require departments to provide Office of Policy and Management with monthly reports of information recorded under Subsec. (d), amended Subsec. (i) to substitute "July 1, 2014," for "January 1, 2014," re report, and amended Subsec. (j) to substitute "January 1, 2014," for "January 1, 2013," re report and add reference to public safety committee, the African-American Affairs Commission, the Latino and Puerto Rican Affairs Commission and the Black and Puerto Rican Caucus of the

General Assembly; May Sp. Sess. P.A. 16-3 deleted former Subsec. (j) re January 1, 2014, report on progress in developing standardized method and guidelines, effective July 1, 2016.

Sec. 54-1n. Complaint by victim of identity theft. Law enforcement agency's responsibilities.

Any person who believes that such person's personal identifying information has been obtained and used by another person in violation of section 53a-129a of the general statutes, revision of 1958, revised to January 1, 2003, or section 53a-129b, 53a-129c or 53a-129d may file a complaint reporting such alleged violation with the law enforcement agency for the town in which such person resides. Such law enforcement agency shall accept such complaint, prepare a police report on the matter, provide the complainant with a copy of such report and investigate such alleged violation and any other offenses allegedly committed as a result of such violation and shall, if necessary, coordinate such investigation with any other law enforcement agencies.

(P.A. 03-156, S. 7.)

Sec. 54-1o. Electronic recording of custodial interrogations.

(a) For the purposes of this section:

(1) "Custody" means the circumstance when (A) a person has been placed under formal arrest, or (B) there is a restraint on a person's freedom of movement of the degree associated with a formal arrest and a reasonable person, in view of all the circumstances, would have believed that he or she was not free to leave;

(2) "Interrogation" means questioning initiated by a law enforcement official or any words or actions on the part of a law enforcement official, other than those normally attendant to arrest and custody, that such official should know are reasonably likely to elicit an incriminating response from the person;

(3) "Custodial interrogation" means any interrogation of a person while such person is in custody;

(4) "Place of detention" means a police station or barracks, courthouse, correctional facility, community correctional center or detention facility; and

(5) "Electronic recording" means an audiovisual recording made by use of an electronic or digital audiovisual device.

(b) An oral, written or sign language statement of a person under investigation for or accused of a capital felony or a class A or B felony made as a result of a custodial interrogation at a place of detention shall be presumed to be inadmissible as evidence against the person in any criminal proceeding unless: (1) An electronic recording is made of the custodial interrogation, and (2) such recording is substantially accurate and not intentionally altered.

(c) Every electronic recording required under this section shall be preserved until such time as the person's conviction for any offense relating to the statement is final and all direct and habeas corpus appeals are exhausted or the prosecution is barred by law.

(d) If the court finds by a preponderance of the evidence that the person was subjected to a custodial interrogation in violation of this section, then any statements made by the person during or following that nonrecorded custodial interrogation, even if otherwise in compliance with this section, are presumed to be inadmissible in any criminal proceeding against the person except for the purposes of impeachment.

(e) Nothing in this section precludes the admission of:

(1) A statement made by the person in open court at his or her trial or at a preliminary hearing;

(2) A statement made during a custodial interrogation that was not recorded as required by this section because electronic recording was not feasible;

(3) A voluntary statement, whether or not the result of a custodial interrogation, that has a bearing on the credibility of the person as a witness;

(4) A spontaneous statement that is not made in response to a question;

(5) A statement made after questioning that is routinely asked during the processing of the arrest of the person;

(6) A statement made during a custodial interrogation by a person who requests, prior to making the statement, to respond to the interrogator's questions only if an electronic recording is not made of the statement, provided an electronic recording is made of the statement by the person agreeing to respond to the interrogator's question only if a recording is not made of the statement;

(7) A statement made during a custodial interrogation that is conducted out-of-state; and

(8) Any other statement that may be admissible under law.

(f) The state shall have the burden of proving, by a preponderance of the evidence, that one of the exceptions specified in subsection (e) of this section is applicable.

(g) Nothing in this section precludes the admission of a statement, otherwise inadmissible under this section, that is used only for impeachment and not as substantive evidence.

(h) The presumption of inadmissibility of a statement made by a person at a custodial interrogation at a place of detention may be overcome by a preponderance of the evidence that the statement was voluntarily given and is reliable, based on the totality of the circumstances.

(i) Any electronic recording of any statement made by a person at a custodial interrogation that is made by any law enforcement agency under this section shall be confidential and not subject to disclosure under the Freedom of Information Act, as defined in section 1-200, and the information shall not be transmitted to any person except as needed to comply with this section.

(P.A. 11-174, S. 1.)

History: P.A. 11-174 effective January 1, 2014.

Sec. 54-1p. Eyewitness identification procedures.

(a) For the purposes of this section:

(1) "Eyewitness" means a person who observes another person at or near the scene of an offense;

(2) "Photo lineup" means a procedure in which an array of photographs, including a photograph of the person suspected as the perpetrator of an offense and additional photographs of other persons not suspected of the offense, is presented to an eyewitness for the purpose of determining whether the eyewitness is able to identify the suspect as the perpetrator;

(3) "Live lineup" means a procedure in which a group of persons, including the person suspected as the perpetrator of an offense and other persons not suspected of the offense, is presented to an eyewitness for the purpose of determining whether the eyewitness is able to identify the suspect as the perpetrator;

(4) "Identification procedure" means either a photo lineup or a live lineup; and

(5) "Filler" means either a person or a photograph of a person who is not suspected of an offense and is included in an identification procedure.

(b) Not later than February 1, 2013, the Police Officer Standards and Training Council and the Division of State Police within the Department of Emergency Services and Public Protection shall jointly develop and promulgate uniform mandatory policies and appropriate guidelines for the conducting of eyewitness identification procedures that shall be based on best practices and be followed by all municipal and state law enforcement agencies. Said council and division shall also develop and promulgate a standardized form to be used by municipal and state law enforcement agencies when conducting an identification procedure and making a written record thereof.

(c) Not later than May 1, 2013, each municipal police department and the Department of Emergency Services and Public Protection shall adopt procedures for the conducting of photo lineups and live lineups that are in accordance with the policies and guidelines developed and promulgated by the Police Officer Standards and Training Council and the Division of State Police within the Department of Emergency Services and Public Protection pursuant to subsection (b) of this section and that comply with the following requirements:

(1) Whenever a specific person is suspected as the perpetrator of an offense, the photographs included in a photo lineup or the persons participating in a live lineup shall be presented sequentially so that the eyewitness views one photograph or one person at a time in accordance with the policies and

guidelines developed and promulgated by the Police Officer Standards and Training Council and the Division of State Police within the Department of Emergency Services and Public Protection pursuant to subsection (b) of this section;

(2) The identification procedure shall be conducted in such a manner that the person conducting the procedure does not know which person in the photo lineup or live lineup is suspected as the perpetrator of the offense, except that, if it is not practicable to conduct a photo lineup in such a manner, the photo lineup shall be conducted by the use of a folder shuffle method, computer program or other comparable method so that the person conducting the procedure does not know which photograph the eyewitness is viewing during the procedure;

(3) The eyewitness shall be instructed prior to the identification procedure:

(A) That the eyewitness will be asked to view an array of photographs or a group of persons, and that each photograph or person will be presented one at a time;

(B) That it is as important to exclude innocent persons as it is to identify the perpetrator;

(C) That the persons in a photo lineup or live lineup may not look exactly as they did on the date of the offense because features like facial or head hair can change;

(D) That the perpetrator may or may not be among the persons in the photo lineup or live lineup;

(E) That the eyewitness should not feel compelled to make an identification;

(F) That the eyewitness should take as much time as needed in making a decision; and

(G) That the police will continue to investigate the offense regardless of whether the eyewitness makes an identification;

(4) In addition to the instructions required by subdivision (3) of this subsection, the eyewitness shall be given such instructions as may be developed and promulgated by the Police Officer Standards and Training Council and the Division of State Police within the Department of Emergency Services and Public Protection pursuant to subsection (b) of this section;

(5) The photo lineup or live lineup shall be composed so that the fillers generally fit the description of the person suspected as the perpetrator and, in the case of a photo lineup, so that the photograph of the person suspected as the perpetrator resembles his or her appearance at the time of the offense and does not unduly stand out;

(6) If the eyewitness has previously viewed a photo lineup or live lineup in connection with the identification of another person suspected of involvement in the offense, the fillers in the lineup in which the person suspected as the perpetrator participates or in which the photograph of the person suspected as the perpetrator is included shall be different from the fillers used in any prior lineups;

(7) At least five fillers shall be included in the photo lineup and at least four fillers shall be included in the live lineup, in addition to the person suspected as the perpetrator;

(8) In a photo lineup, no writings or information concerning any previous arrest of the person suspected as the perpetrator shall be visible to the eyewitness;

(9) In a live lineup, any identification actions, such as speaking or making gestures or other movements, shall be performed by all lineup participants;

(10) In a live lineup, all lineup participants shall be out of the view of the eyewitness at the beginning of the identification procedure;

(11) The person suspected as the perpetrator shall be the only suspected perpetrator included in the identification procedure;

(12) Nothing shall be said to the eyewitness regarding the position in the photo lineup or the live lineup of the person suspected as the perpetrator;

(13) Nothing shall be said to the eyewitness that might influence the eyewitness's selection of the person suspected as the perpetrator;

(14) If the eyewitness identifies a person as the perpetrator, the eyewitness shall not be provided any information concerning such person prior to obtaining the eyewitness's statement regarding how certain he or she is of the selection; and

(15) A written record of the identification procedure shall be made that includes the following information:

(A) All identification and nonidentification results obtained during the identification procedure, signed by the eyewitness, including the eyewitness's own words regarding how certain he or she is of the selection;

(B) The names of all persons present at the identification procedure;

(C) The date and time of the identification procedure;

(D) In a photo lineup, the photographs presented to the eyewitness or copies thereof;

(E) In a photo lineup, identification information on all persons whose photograph was included in the lineup and the sources of all photographs used; and

(F) In a live lineup, identification information on all persons who participated in the lineup.

(P.A. 11-252, S. 1; P.A. 12-111, S. 1.)

History: (Revisor's note: In Subsec. (b), "Department of Public Safety" was changed editorially by the Revisors to "Department of Emergency Services and Public Protection" to conform with changes made by P.A. 11-51); P.A. 12-111 amended Subsec. (a) to replace "displayed" with "presented" in definitions of "photo lineup" and "live lineup", added new Subsec. (b) re development and promulgation by February 1, 2013, of uniform mandatory policies and appropriate guidelines for conducting of eyewitness identification procedures and development and promulgation of standardized form and redesignated existing Subsec. (b) as Subsec. (c) and amended same to replace "January 1, 2012" with "May 1, 2013" as deadline for adopting lineup procedures and require such procedures to be in accordance with policies and guidelines developed and promulgated pursuant to Subsec. (b), add new Subdiv. (1) re presentation of photographs or persons sequentially, replace former Subdiv. (1) re conducting of procedure, when practicable, by person not aware of which person in lineup is suspected as perpetrator with new Subdiv. (2) re conducting of procedure in such a manner that person conducting procedure does not know which person in lineup is suspected as perpetrator and, if it is not practicable to conduct photo lineup in such a manner, allowing photo lineup to be conducted using a method so that person conducting procedure does not know which photograph eyewitness is viewing, redesignate existing Subdiv. (2) as Subdiv. (3) and amend same to add new Subpara. (A) re viewing of array of photographs or group of persons and presentation of photographs or persons one at a time, add new Subpara. (B) re importance of excluding innocent persons, add new Subpara. (C) re difference in appearance because of change in features like facial or head hair, redesignate existing Subparas. (A) to (C) as Subparas. (D) to (F) and add new Subpara. (G) re continuation of police investigation, add new Subdiv. (4) re giving of additional instructions developed and promulgated pursuant to Subsec. (b), redesignate existing Subdivs. (3) to (11) as Subdivs. (5) to (13), redesignate existing Subdiv. (12) as Subdiv. (14) and amend same to replace "eyewitness's statement that he or she is certain of the selection" with "eyewitness's statement regarding how certain he or she is of the selection" and redesignate existing Subdiv. (13) as Subdiv. (15) and amend same by replacing in Subpara. (D) "the photographs themselves" with "the photographs presented to the eyewitness or copies thereof", effective July 1, 2012.

Sec. 54-1q. Court to advise defendant that guilty or nolo contendere plea may have consequence of suspension of driver's license.

The court shall not accept a plea of guilty or nolo contendere from a person in a proceeding with respect to a violation of section 14-110, subsection (b) or (c) of section 14-147, section 14-215, subsection (a) of section 14-222, subsection (a) or (b) of section 14-224 or section 53a-119b unless the court advises such person that conviction of the offense for which such person has been charged may have the consequence of the Commissioner of Motor Vehicles suspending such person's motor vehicle operator's license.

(P.A. 03-233, S. 3.)

Sec. 54-1r. Complaint by protected person re violation of order of protection by electronic or telephonic means. Law enforcement agency's responsibilities.

Any person listed as a protected person on a restraining order, protective order, standing criminal protective order or foreign order of protection who believes that an electronic or telephonic communication received by the person constitutes a violation of section 53a-223, 53a-223a or 53a-223b may file a complaint reporting such alleged violation with the law enforcement agency for the town in which (1) such person resides, (2) such person received the communication, or (3) such communication was initiated. Such law enforcement agency shall accept such complaint, prepare a police report on the matter, provide the complainant with a copy of such report and investigate such alleged violation and shall, if necessary, coordinate such investigation with any other law enforcement agencies and, upon request of the complainant, notify the law enforcement agency for the town in which the complainant resides.

(P.A. 12-114, S. 8.)

Sec. 54-1s. Racial Profiling Prohibition Project Advisory Board. Membership. Duties.

(a) There is established, within available resources, a Racial Profiling Prohibition Project Advisory Board for the purpose of advising the Office of Policy and Management with respect to the adoption of standardized methods and guidelines pursuant to section 54-1m. The board shall be within the Office of Policy and Management for administrative purposes only.

(b) The board shall include the following members:

(1) The Chief State's Attorney, or a designee;

(2) The Chief Public Defender, or a designee;

(3) The president of the Connecticut Police Chiefs Association, or a designee;

(4) The executive director of the Commission on Equity and Opportunity, or a designee;

(5) Two members of the Commission on Equity and Opportunity, designated by the executive director;

(6) The executive director of the Commission on Human Rights and Opportunities, or a designee;

(7) The Commissioner of Emergency Services and Public Protection, or a designee;

(8) The Commissioner of Transportation, or a designee;

(9) The director of the Institute for Municipal and Regional Policy at Central Connecticut State University, or a designee; and

(10) Such other members as the board may prescribe.

(c) The chairpersons of the joint standing committee of the General Assembly having cognizance of matters relating to the judiciary shall select two chairpersons of the board from among the members of the board.

(P.A. 12-74, S. 2; May Sp. Sess. P.A. 16-3, S. 169.)

History: P.A. 12-74 effective June 6, 2012; May Sp. Sess. P.A. 16-3 amended Subsec. (b) by replacing "African-American Affairs Commission" with "Commission on Equity and Opportunity" in Subdiv. (4), replacing reference to executive director of Latino and Puerto Rican Affairs Commission or designee with reference to two members of Commission on Equity and Opportunity designated by the executive director in Subdiv. (5), deleting former Subdiv. (6) re executive director of Asian Pacific American Affairs Commission or designee and redesignating existing Subdivs. (7) to (11) as Subdivs. (6) to (10), effective July 1, 2016.

See Sec. 4-38f for definition of "administrative purposes only".

Sec. 54-1t. Adoption of policy re police use of electronic defense weapons. Data collection. Reports.

(a) For purposes of this section, "law enforcement agency" means the Division of State Police within the Department of Emergency Services and Public Protection or any municipal police department, "police officer" means a state police officer or a sworn member of a municipal police department and "electronic defense weapon" has the same meaning as provided in section 53a-3.

(b) (1) Each law enforcement agency that authorizes a police officer employed by such agency to use an electronic defense weapon shall: (A) Not later than January 31, 2015, adopt and maintain a written policy that meets or exceeds the model policy developed by the Police Officer Standards and Training Council regarding the use of an electronic defense weapon; (B) require police officers to document any use of an electronic defense weapon in use-of-force reports; (C) not later than January fifteenth following each calendar year in which an electronic defense weapon is used, prepare an annual report using the form developed and promulgated by the Police Officer Standards and Training Council pursuant to section 7-294cc that details the use of electronic defense weapons by police officers employed by such agency and includes (i) data downloaded from the electronic defense weapons after their use, (ii) data compiled from the use-of-force reports, and (iii) statistics on each such use of an electronic defense weapon, including, but not limited to, (I) the race and gender of each person on whom the electronic defense weapon was used, provided the identification of such characteristics shall be based on the observation and perception of the police officer that used the electronic defense weapon, (II) the number of times the electronic defense weapon was activated and used on such person, (III) the injury, if any, suffered by such person against whom the electronic defense weapon was used, and (IV) if the electronic defense weapon that was used had different usage modes, the mode used; and (D) not later than January 15, 2016, and annually thereafter, submit the report to the Criminal Justice Policy and Planning Division within the Office of Policy and Management.

(2) Not later than January 15, 2016, and annually thereafter, a law enforcement agency that does not authorize police officers employed by such agency to use an electronic defense weapon shall submit a report to the Criminal Justice Policy and Planning Division within the Office of Policy and Management stating that such agency does not authorize its officers to use electronic defense weapons.

(c) The Office of Policy and Management shall post the annual reports submitted pursuant to subsection (b) of this section on its Internet web site.

(P.A. 14-149, S. 1.)

History: P.A. 14-149 effective January 1, 2015.

Sec. 54-2. Conviction and binding over by trial justice. Section 54-2 is repealed.

(1949 Rev., S. 8725; 1957, P.A. 522, S. 2; 1959, P.A. 28, S. 204.)

Sec. 54-2a. Issuance of bench warrants of arrest, subpoenas, capias and other criminal process. Release conditions. Service of court process. Entry of warrants and process into computer system.

(a) In all criminal cases the Superior Court, or any judge thereof, or any judge trial referee specifically designated by the Chief Justice to exercise the authority conferred by this section may issue (1) bench warrants of arrest upon application by a prosecutorial official if the court or judge determines that the affidavit accompanying the application shows that there is probable cause to believe that an offense has been committed and that the person complained against committed it, (2) subpoenas for witnesses, (3) capias for witnesses and for defendants who violate an order of the court regarding any court appearance, and (4) all other criminal process; and may administer justice in all criminal matters.

(b) The court, judge or judge trial referee issuing a bench warrant for the arrest of the person or persons complained against shall, in cases punishable by death, life imprisonment without the possibility of release or life imprisonment, set the conditions of release or indicate that the person or persons named in the warrant shall not be entitled to bail and may, in all other cases, set the conditions of release. The conditions of release, if included in the warrant, shall fix the first of the following conditions which the court, judge or judge trial referee finds necessary to assure such person's appearance in court: (1) Written promise to appear; (2) execution of a bond without surety in no greater amount than necessary; or (3) execution of a bond with surety in no greater amount than necessary.

(c) In lieu of a warrant for the rearrest of any defendant who fails to appear for trial at the place and time specified or on any court date thereafter the court, judge or judge trial referee may issue a capias.

(d) All process issued by said court or any judge thereof, or any judge trial referee shall be served by any proper officer, or an indifferent person when specially directed to do so, and shall be obeyed by any and all persons and officers to whom the same is directed or whom it may concern.

(e) Whenever a warrant or other criminal process is issued under this section or section 53a-32, the court, judge or judge trial referee may cause such warrant or process to be entered into a central computer system in accordance with policies and procedures established by the Chief Court Administrator. Existence of the warrant or other criminal process in the computer system shall constitute prima facie evidence of the issuance of the warrant or process. Any person named in the warrant or other criminal process may be arrested based on the existence of the warrant or process in the computer system and shall, upon any such arrest, be given a copy of the warrant or process.

(1959, P.A. 28, S. 27; February, 1965, P.A. 194, S. 1; 1967, P.A. 10, S. 1; 152, S. 44; 549, S. 10; P.A. 74-183, S. 126, 291; P.A. 76-436, S. 518, 681; P.A. 77-576, S. 38, 65; P.A. 79-216, S. 1; P.A. 80-313, S. 2; P.A. 84-123, S. 2; P.A. 00-209, S. 4; P.A. 01-72, S. 1; P.A. 04-127, S. 8; P.A. 10-43, S. 21; P.A. 12-5, S. 24.)

History: 1965 act added authority of judge to issue subpoenas and warrants; 1967 acts deleted language in last sentence qualifying power of judge as being "when the circuit court is not in session" and, effective October 1, 1968, added provisions for alternatives to bail; P.A. 74-183 replaced circuit court with court of common pleas, effective December 31, 1974; P.A. 76-436 replaced court of common pleas with superior court and deleted references to powers of other unspecified courts and judges, reflecting transfer of all trial jurisdiction to superior court, effective July 1, 1978; P.A. 77-576 added detailed provisions re procedure for issuance of bench warrants and clarified provisions with respect to crimes which are not bailable, effective July 1, 1978; P.A. 79-216 made minor wording changes; P.A. 80-313 divided section into Subsecs., restated power to issue bench warrants in Subsec. (a) and deleted detailed provisions re procedure re issuance of bench warrants and arrests made on bench warrant; P.A. 84-123 amended Subsec. (a) by authorizing the issuance of capias for defendants who violate a court order regarding any court appearance, added a new Subsec. (c) re the issuance of a capias in lieu of a rearrest warrant, and redesignated former Subsec. (c) as Subsec. (d); P.A. 00-209 made technical changes and added new Subsec. (e) authorizing the entry of a rearrest warrant into a central computer system, providing that the existence of the warrant in the computer system is prima facie evidence of its issuance and authorizing the arrest of a person based on the existence of the warrant in the computer system; P.A. 01-72 amended Subsec. (a) by adding "or any judge trial referee specifically designated by the Chief Justice to exercise the authority conferred by this section" and amended Subsecs. (b) to (e) by adding references to judge trial referee; P.A. 04-127 amended Subsec. (e) by deleting reference to "rearrest" warrant and adding reference to Sec. 53a-32; P.A. 10-43 amended Subsec. (e) to make provisions applicable to other criminal process and require that entry of warrant or process into central computer system be in accordance with policies and procedures established by Chief Court Administrator; P.A. 12-5 amended Subsec. (b) to add reference to cases punishable by life imprisonment without possibility of release, effective April 25, 2012.

See Sec. 52-56(d) re execution or service of capias in any precinct by state marshal of any precinct.

See Sec. 54-64b re release following arrest on court warrant.

Cited. 181 C. 562; 187 C. 292; 193 C. 612; 202 C. 443; 205 C. 298; 233 C. 403.

Cited. 27 CA 307.

Cited. 38 CS 377.

Subsec. (b):

Death penalty unconstitutional under Art. I, Secs. 8 and 9 of Connecticut Constitution. 318 C. 1.

Sec. 54-2b. Transferred to Chapter 960, Sec. 54-56a.

Sec. 54-2c. Traffic violator need not appear in court, when. Schedule of fines established. Section 54-2c is repealed.

(1967, P.A. 429; 1969, P.A. 455; 1971, P.A. 436; P.A. 74-183, S. 128, 291; P.A. 75-577, S. 123, 126.)

Sec. 54-2d. Notation in computer network of actions taken by law enforcement agency to execute certain warrants.

Not later than thirty days after the entry of the issuance of any rearrest warrant or arrest warrant for a violation of probation into the paperless rearrest warrant network, the law enforcement agency for the municipality in which the accused person resides shall, if such network is available and accessible to such agency, enter a notation in such network of the actions, if any, that have been taken by such agency to execute the warrant and apprehend the accused person.

(P.A. 06-99, S. 2.)

See Sec. 54-108c re availability on Internet of information on outstanding arrest warrants for probation violations.

Sec. 54-2e. Issuance of rearrest warrant or capias for failure to appear.

Unless good cause is shown, no court shall issue a rearrest warrant or a capias for failure to appear as provided in section 53a-173 prior to four o'clock p.m. of the day of the alleged failure to appear.

(P.A. 07-243, S. 3.)

Secs. 54-3 and 54-4. Issue of warrant after arrest. Trial justice may issue criminal process to be served anywhere in the state. Sections 54-3 and 54-4 are repealed.

(1949 Rev., S. 8722, 8723; 1959, P.A. 28, S. 204.)

Sec. 54-5. Transferred to Chapter 960, Sec. 54-56f.

Secs. 54-6 to 54-12. Criminal jurisdiction of municipal courts. Limit of jurisdiction of municipal courts. Jurisdiction over violations concerning overweight commercial vehicles. Bonds on adjournment of hearing. Copies of files and records for Superior Court and state's attorneys on bindover; notice when proceeding pending on seized property. Appointment of court interpreters in municipal and trial justice court. Appeal from municipal court or trial justice. Sections 54-6 to 54-12, inclusive, are repealed.

(1949 Rev., S. 7579, 8726, 8730, 8731, 8733, 8741; 1953, S. 3096d; 1955, S. 3097d; June, 1955, S. 3096d; November, 1955, S. N229; 1959, P.A. 28, S. 138, 204; 1961, P.A. 179; 1963, P.A. 49; 1971, P.A. 321; P.A. 73-116, S. 16; 73-667, S. 1, 2; P.A. 74-183, S. 130, 291; P.A. 76-336, S. 1; 76-436, S. 521, 681.)

Secs. 54-13 and 54-14. Transferred to Chapter 961, Secs. 54-96a and 54-96b, respectively.

Secs. 54-15 and 54-16. Binding over on probable cause. Jurisdiction of Common Pleas Court on appeals. Sections 54-15 and 54-16 are repealed.

(1949 Rev., S. 8727, 8742; 1949, S. 3320d; November, 1955, S. N230; 1959, P.A. 28, S. 141, 204; 1963, P.A. 642, S. 61.)

Sec. 54-17. Transferred to Chapter 961, Sec. 54-95a.

Sec. 54-17a. Presentation in one judicial district for offenses charged in various districts where defendant to plead guilty.

When any person is arrested in any judicial district upon a criminal charge within the jurisdiction of the Superior Court and any indictment or information is pending against him in the superior court for one or more other judicial districts, he may, with his consent and that of the state's attorney for each such judicial district, be presented in the judicial district where the first warrant served upon him originated for all of the offenses to which he intends to plead guilty.

(1961, P.A. 251; P.A. 73-116, S. 17; 73-667, S. 1, 2; P.A. 78-280, S. 2, 4, 127.)

History: P.A. 73-116 added references to judicial districts; P.A. 73-667 changed effective date of P.A. 73-116 from October 1, 1973, to April 25, 1973; P.A. 78-280 deleted references to counties.

Cited. 25 CS 202.

Sec. 54-18. Transferred to Chapter 890, Sec. 51-353a.

Secs. 54-18a to 54-21. Transfer of criminal cases between Superior and Common Pleas Court. Certain cases to be tried at first term. Search when cruelty is suspected. Search warrants in cases of cruelty to animals. Sections 54-18a to 54-21, inclusive, are repealed.

(1949 Rev., S. 8724, 8745, 8787; 1959, P.A. 28, S. 143; 1961, P.A. 517, S. 70; 1963, P.A. 642, S. 63; 652, S. 10; 1971, P.A. 590; P.A. 73-116, S. 19; 73-667, S. 1, 2; P.A. 74-183, S. 134, 291; P.A. 76-336, S. 10; 76-436, S. 525, 526, 681.)

Secs. 54-22 to 54-24. Transferred to Chapter 961, Secs. 54-82i to 54-82k, inclusive.

Secs. 54-25 and 54-26. Release on recognizance. Witnesses in courts of other states. Sections 54-25 and 54-26 are repealed.

(1949 Rev., S. 8746, 8762; 1959, P.A. 28, S. 147; P.A. 76-336, S. 10; P.A. 80-313, S. 61.)

Sec. 54-27. Transferred to Chapter 890, Sec. 51-348a.

Sec. 54-28. Transferred to Chapter 890, Sec. 51-352b.

Secs. 54-29 to 54-31. Seizure of obscene literature and gambling implements. Illegal articles and implements to be destroyed. Judges of city courts may act. Sections 54-29 to 54-31, inclusive, are repealed.

(1949 Rev., S. 8752–8754; 1959, P.A. 28, S. 148, 204; 1963, P.A. 652, S. 10.)

Sec. 54-32. Transferred to Chapter 945, Sec. 53-243a.

PART II* SEARCHES

*Cited. 14 CA 356.

Sec. 54-33. Search warrants for gambling and lottery implements. Section 54-33 is repealed.

(1949 Rev., S. 8756; 1959, P.A. 28, S. 149; 1963, P.A. 652, S. 10.)

Sec. 54-33a. Issuance of search warrant, warrant for tracking device or warrant for foreign corporation records or data. (a) As used in sections 54-33a to 54-33g, inclusive, "property" includes, but is not limited to, documents, books, papers, films, recordings, records, data and any other tangible thing; and "tracking device" means an electronic or mechanical device that permits the tracking of the movement of a person or object.

(b) Upon complaint on oath by any state's attorney or assistant state's attorney or by any two credible persons, to any judge of the Superior Court or judge trial referee, that such state's attorney or assistant state's attorney or such persons have probable cause to believe that any property (1) possessed, controlled, designed or intended for use or which is or has been used or which may be used as the means of committing any criminal offense; or (2) which was stolen or embezzled; or (3) which constitutes evidence of an offense, or which constitutes evidence that a particular person participated in the commission of an offense, is within or upon any place, thing or person, such judge or judge trial referee, except as provided in section 54-33j, may issue a warrant commanding a proper officer to enter into or upon such place or thing, search such place, thing or person and take into such officer's custody all such property named in the warrant.

(c) Upon complaint on oath by any state's attorney or assistant state's attorney or by any two credible persons, to any judge of the Superior Court or judge trial referee, that such state's attorney or assistant state's attorney or such persons have probable cause to believe that a criminal offense has been, is being, or will be committed and that the use of a tracking device will yield evidence of the commission of that offense, such judge or judge trial referee may issue a warrant authorizing the installation and use of a tracking device. The complaint shall identify the person on which or the property to, in or on which the tracking device is to be installed, and, if known, the owner of such property.

(d) A warrant may issue only on affidavit sworn to by the complainant or complainants before the judge or judge trial referee and establishing the grounds for issuing the warrant, which affidavit shall be part of the arrest file. If the judge or judge trial referee is satisfied that grounds for the application exist or that there is probable cause to believe that grounds for the application exist, the judge or judge trial referee shall issue a warrant identifying the property and naming or describing the person, place or thing to be searched or authorizing the installation and use of a tracking device and identifying the person on which or the property to, in or on which the tracking device is to be installed. The warrant shall be directed to any police officer of a regularly organized police department or any state police officer, to an inspector in the Division of Criminal Justice, to a conservation officer, special conservation officer or patrolman acting pursuant to section 26-6 or to a sworn motor vehicle inspector acting under the authority of section 14-8. Except for a warrant for the installation and use of a tracking device, the warrant shall state the date and time of its issuance and the grounds or probable cause for its issuance and shall command the officer to search within a reasonable time the person, place or thing named, for the property specified. A warrant for the installation and use of a tracking device shall state the date and time of its issuance and the grounds or probable cause for its issuance and shall command the officer to complete the installation of the device within a specified period not later than ten days after the date of its issuance and authorize the installation and use of the tracking device, including the collection of data through such tracking device, for a reasonable period of time not to exceed thirty days from the date the tracking device is installed. Upon request and a showing of good cause, a judge or judge trial referee may authorize the use of the tracking device for an additional period of thirty days.

(e) A judge or judge trial referee may issue a warrant pursuant to this section for records or data that are in the actual or constructive possession of a foreign corporation or business entity that transacts business in this state, including, but not limited to, a foreign corporation or business entity that provides electronic communication services or remote computing services to the public. Such a warrant may be served on an authorized representative of the foreign corporation or business entity by hand, mail, commercial delivery, facsimile or electronic transmission, provided proof of delivery can be established. When properly served with a warrant issued pursuant to this section, the foreign corporation or business entity shall provide to the applicant all records or data sought by the warrant within fourteen business days of being served with the warrant, unless the judge or judge trial referee determines that a shorter or longer period of time is necessary or appropriate.

(f) The inadvertent failure of the issuing judge or judge trial referee to state on the warrant the time of its issuance shall not in and of itself invalidate the warrant.

(1963, P.A. 652, S. 1, 3; February, 1965, P.A. 439; 574, S. 46; P.A. 74-183, S. 138, 291; P.A. 76-436, S. 530, 681; P.A. 77-504; P.A. 79-14, S. 3; P.A. 80-313, S. 8; P.A. 81-227, S. 3; June Sp. Sess. P.A. 98-1, S. 39, 121; P.A. 00-31; P.A. 01-72, S. 2; P.A. 04-147, S. 2; P.A. 13-271, S. 42; P.A. 14-233, S. 9.)

History: 1965 acts authorized search of person and made grammatical correction; P.A. 74-183 replaced circuit court with court of common pleas in Subsec. (b), reflecting reorganization of judicial system, effective December 31, 1974; P.A. 76-436 added reference to assistant state's attorneys and deleted reference to prosecuting attorneys and to court of common pleas in Subsec. (b), reflecting transfer of all trial jurisdiction to superior court, effective July 1, 1978; P.A. 77-504 added Subsec. (b)(3) authorizing issuance of search warrant to discover property constituting evidence of offense or evidence that a person participated in the commission of an offense; P.A. 79-14 added exception re Sec. 54-33j in Subsec. (b)(3); P.A. 80-313 substituted "may" for "shall" in Subsec. (c) provision re issuance of warrant on sworn affidavit; P.A. 81-227 amended Subsec. (c) by authorizing judges to direct search warrants to conservation officers and patrolmen acting pursuant to Sec. 26-6; June Sp. Sess. P.A. 98-1 made a technical change in Subsec. (c), effective June 24, 1998; P.A. 00-31 amended Subsec. (c) to require the warrant to state the date and time of its issuance and to add provision that the inadvertent failure of the issuing judge to state on the warrant the time of its issuance shall not in and of itself invalidate the warrant, and made technical changes in Subsecs. (b) and (c) for purposes of gender neutrality; P.A. 01-72 added references to judge trial referee in Subsecs. (b) and (c); P.A. 04-147 amended Subsec. (c) to authorize a warrant to be directed to an inspector in the Division of Criminal Justice and make a technical change for purposes of gender neutrality; P.A. 13-271 amended Subsec. (c) to authorize warrant to be directed to a sworn motor vehicle inspector acting under authority of Sec. 14-8, effective July 1, 2013; P.A. 14-233 amended Subsec. (a) to add provision defining "tracking device", added new Subsec. (c) re warrant for tracking device, redesignated existing Subsec. (c) as Subsec. (d) and amended same to add provisions re warrant for tracking device and person or property subject to tracking device, added Subsec. (e) re warrant for records or data in actual or constructive possession of foreign corporation or business entity, designated existing provision re failure to state on warrant time of issuance as Subsec. (f), and made technical changes.

See Sec. 54-154 re taxing of expenses in search and seizure cases.

Former statute did not authorize seizure of contraceptive material. 126 C. 428. Under former statute, obscene materials could be seized regardless of who possessed them or of knowledge or intent in such possession. 146 C. 78. This section and sections 54-33b to 54-33g passed subsequent to *Mapp v. Ohio*, 367 U.S. 643, which held that evidence obtained by unlawful search and seizure is inadmissible in state courts; prior to such passage if search and seizure were incidental to lawful arrest, they were not unreasonable. 149 C. 567. Cited. 153 C. 8. Judge issuing search warrant not required to recite in warrant the grounds on which he found probable cause. Id., 708, 709. Warrant calling for search and seizure of passenger automobile includes whatever was an integral part or component of that automobile, e.g., dust on floor, stains on interior, seats and cushions. 155 C. 145. Neither the recital that affiant had information from reliable informant nor statement that apartment sought to be searched had been under surveillance were sufficient grounds for issuance of warrant; warrant issued was illegal. Id., 385. Cited. 165 C. 239; 169 C. 322; 170 C. 618; 181 C. 562; 196 C. 471; 206 C. 90; 219 C. 529; 224 C. 29; 226 C. 514.

Cited. 10 CA 561; 30 CA 249.

Search and seizure which, though without warrant, is consented to is not within exclusionary rule; but mere acquiescence in and peaceful submission to demands of searching officers is not to be construed as consent; defendant's application for order to return articles illegally seized was denied. 23 CS 41. Where search warrant is issued and executed, presumption is that proper legal procedure was observed and burden is on defendant to overcome presumption. Id., 405. Even though evidence was obtained as result of illegal search and seizure, defendant was not entitled to motion to suppress evidence in advance of trial. 24 CS 36. Arrest for minor traffic violation did not justify search of car without a warrant; if stolen goods were in plain sight, search might have been justified. 25 CS 229. Reference in warrant, after specifying drugs and named instruments for using them, concluded "and any other paraphernalia" which could be used in taking drugs and was too broad; items not specifically mentioned in warrant could not be used in evidence. 28 CS 19. Cited. 41 CS 1.

Where judge had before him no information which permitted him to make an independent judicial determination of the existence of probable cause for the issuance of a search and seizure warrant, the issuance of such warrant was in violation of the constitution and the evidence seized as a result of its execution is not admissible in defendants' trial. 3 Conn. Cir. Ct. 97, 98. An unsigned and undated search warrant is fatally defective, invalid and void and confers no authority to act thereunder. Id., 641, 644. Supporting affidavit sufficient when it recited several instances of information by others of defendant operating his home for pool selling and police surveillance of activity of defendant in community; name of informant need not be disclosed. 4 Conn. Cir. Ct. 603. Cited. 5 Conn. Cir. Ct. 44, 46. Motion to suppress evidence obtained by search and seizure under warrant issued fourteen days before actual seizure granted on grounds execution of warrant was not made within reasonable time. Id., 468. Affidavit in support of search warrant for violation of pool selling statute, that set forth underlying circumstances, reasons informants were reliable, actual betting transactions and personal observation of defendant by affiants was sufficient. Id., 669.

Subsec. (b):

Cited. 179 C. 23; 192 C. 98; 229 C. 125.

Cited. 1 CA 315. Possession or control of property is relevant, not ownership. 57 CA 396.

Subsec. (d) (former Subsec. (c)):

Sec. 54-33b. Search of person.

The officer serving a search warrant may, if such officer has reason to believe that any of the property described in the warrant is concealed in the garments of any person in or upon the place or thing to be searched, search the person for the purpose of seizing the same. When the person to be searched is a woman, the search shall be made by a policewoman or other woman assisting in the service of the warrant, or by a woman designated by the judge or judge trial referee issuing the warrant.

(1963, P.A. 652, S. 2; P.A. 80-313, S. 9; P.A. 01-72, S. 4.)

History: P.A. 80-313 rephrased provisions but made no substantive changes; P.A. 01-72 made a technical change for purposes of gender neutrality and added reference to judge trial referee.

Sec. 54-33c. Warrant application, affidavits, execution and return. Copies. Orders.

(a) The applicant for a search warrant shall file the application for the warrant and all affidavits upon which the warrant is based with the clerk of the court for the geographical area within which any person who may be arrested in connection with or subsequent to the execution of the search warrant would be presented with the return of the warrant. Upon the arrest of any person in connection with or subsequent to the execution of the search warrant, the law enforcement agency that arrested the person shall notify the clerk of such court of the return of the warrant by completing a form prescribed by the Chief Court Administrator and filing such form with the clerk together with any applicable uniform arrest report or misdemeanor summons.

(b) Except for a warrant for the installation and use of a tracking device: (1) The warrant shall be executed within ten days and returned with reasonable promptness consistent with due process of law and shall be accompanied by a written inventory of all property seized; (2) a copy of such warrant shall be given to the owner or occupant of the dwelling, structure, motor vehicle or place designated in the warrant, or the person named in the warrant; and (3) within forty-eight hours of such search, a copy of the application for the warrant and a copy of all affidavits upon which the warrant is based shall be given to such owner, occupant or person. The judge or judge trial referee may, by order, dispense with the requirement of giving a copy of the affidavits to such owner, occupant or person at such time if the applicant for the warrant files a detailed affidavit with the judge or judge trial referee which demonstrates to the judge or judge trial referee that (A) the personal safety of a confidential informant would be jeopardized by the giving of a copy of the affidavits at such time, or (B) the search is part of a continuing investigation which would be adversely affected by the giving of a copy of the affidavits at such time, or (C) the giving of a copy of the affidavits at such time would require disclosure of information or material prohibited from being disclosed by chapter 959a.

(c) A warrant for the installation and use of a tracking device shall be returned with reasonable promptness consistent with due process of law and after the period authorized for tracking, including any extension period authorized under subsection (d) of section 54-33a, has expired. Within ten days after the use of the tracking device has ended, a copy of the application for the warrant and a copy of all affidavits upon which the warrant is based shall be given to the person who was tracked or the owner of the property to, in or on which the tracking device was installed. The judge or judge trial referee may, by order, dispense with the requirement of giving a copy of the affidavits to the person who was tracked or the owner of the property to, in or on which the tracking device was installed if the applicant for the warrant files a detailed affidavit with the judge or judge trial referee which demonstrates to the judge or judge trial referee that (1) the personal safety of a confidential informant would be jeopardized by the giving of a copy of the affidavits at such time, or (2) the search is part of a continuing investigation which would be adversely affected by the giving of a copy of the affidavits at such time, or (3) the giving of a copy of the affidavits at such time would require disclosure of information or material prohibited from being disclosed by chapter 959a.

(d) If the judge or judge trial referee dispenses with the requirement of giving a copy of the affidavits at such time pursuant to subsection (b) or (c) of this section, such order shall not affect the right of such owner, occupant or person to obtain such copy at any subsequent time. No such order shall limit the disclosure of such affidavits to the attorney for a person arrested in connection with or subsequent to the execution of a search warrant unless, upon motion of the prosecuting authority within two weeks of such person's arraignment, the court finds that the state's interest in continuing nondisclosure substantially outweighs the defendant's right to disclosure.

(e) Any order entered pursuant to subsection (b) or (c) of this section dispensing with the requirement of giving a copy of the affidavits to such owner, occupant or person shall be for a specific period of time, not to exceed (1) two weeks beyond the date the warrant is executed, or (2) with respect to a warrant for the installation and use of a tracking device, two weeks after any extension period authorized under subsection (d) of section 54-33a has expired. Within the applicable time period set forth in subdivision (1) or (2) of this subsection, the prosecuting authority may seek an extension of such period of time. Upon the execution and return of the warrant, affidavits which have been the subject of such an order shall remain in the custody of the clerk's office in a secure location apart from the remainder of the court file.

(1963, P.A. 652, S. 4; 1971, P.A. 291; P.A. 76-155; P.A. 85-306; P.A. 89-247; P.A. 97-40, S. 8; P.A. 99-215, S. 9; P.A. 01-72, S. 5; P.A. 14-233, S. 10.)

History: 1971 act set ten-day deadline for execution of warrant and required that copy of warrant be given to owner or occupant of dwelling, structure etc. to be searched or to the person named in the warrant; P.A. 76-155 set 48-hour deadline for giving copy of warrant and added provisions re requirement that copy of warrant application, affidavits be given to owner, occupant or person named in warrant; P.A. 85-306 required the applicant to file a detailed affidavit with the judge before the judge may dispense with the requirement of giving a copy of the affidavits; P.A. 89-247 added provisions re filing of copy of search warrant application with clerk of court, re prohibition of clerks' disclosing information pertinent to the application, re protection of rights of an arrested person's attorney to disclosure of affidavits and re time limits on orders which dispense with requirement that copy of warrant application and affidavits be given to interested parties within 48 hours and divided section into Subsecs.; P.A. 97-40 changed "issuance" to "execution" of warrant in Subsec. (a); P.A. 99-215 amended Subsec. (a) by deleting provision requiring filing of copy of warrant and that search be conducted within one business day of execution and prohibiting clerk from disclosure of information re application or affidavits of search warrant and substituting provision that any person arrested in connection with or subsequent to execution of search warrant would be presented with return of warrant; P.A. 01-72 amended Subsec. (a) by adding references to judge trial referee; P.A. 14-233 amended Subsec. (a) to add provision requiring law enforcement agency that arrests person in execution of search warrant to notify clerk of court, designated existing provisions re execution of warrant as new Subsec. (b) and amended same to add provision re exception for warrant for tracking device, insert Subdiv. (1) to (3) designators and redesignate existing Subdivs. (1) to (3) as Subparas. (A) to (C), added Subsec. (c) re return of warrant for tracking device, 10-day deadline for giving copy of application for warrant and affidavits after tracking device use has ended, and exception to requirement to give copy of affidavits, designated existing provisions re dispensing of requirement to give copy of affidavits as Subsec. (d), redesignated existing Subsec. (b) as Subsec. (e) and amended same to designate existing provision re 2 weeks beyond date warrant is executed as Subdiv. (1) and add Subdiv. (2) re warrant for installation and use of tracking device, and made technical and conforming changes.

Return on search warrant, not defective. 163 C. 107. Cited. 165 C. 239; 239 C. 793.

Cited. 7 CA 265; 10 CA 347; 14 CA 356; 15 CA 251; 18 CA 477.

Cited. 28 CS 23. Omission of signature from copies of warrant and affidavits served on defendant held harmless error; exclusionary rule discussed. 35 CS 225. Cited. 36 CS 570; 40 CS 20.

Cited. 5 Conn. Cir. Ct. 44, 46. Execution of search and seizure warrant 14 days after its issuance held unreasonable lapse of time although officers' daily surveillance made this the opportune date for search; motion to suppress evidence seized granted. Id., 468.

Sec. 54-33d. Interference with search.

Any person who forcibly assaults, resists, opposes, impedes, intimidates or interferes with any person authorized to serve or execute search warrants or to make searches and seizures while engaged in the performance of his duties with regard thereto or on account of the performance of such duties, shall be fined not more than one thousand dollars or imprisoned not more than one year or both; and any person who in committing any violation of this section uses any deadly or dangerous weapon shall be fined not more than ten thousand dollars or imprisoned not more than ten years or both.

(1963, P.A. 652, S. 5.)

Cited. 165 C. 239.

Cited. 11 CA 47; 24 CA 330. Act of clenching mouth shut to avert DNA swab constitutes use of physical force to evade search warrant in violation of section. 144 CA 353.

Cited. 30 CS 211.

Cited. 6 Conn. Cir. Ct. 176.

Sec. 54-33e. Destruction of property.

Any person who, before, during or after seizure of any property by any police officer authorized to make searches and seizures, in order to prevent the seizure or securing of any property named in the warrant by such police officer, breaks, destroys or removes or causes the breaking, destruction or removal of the same, shall be fined not more than one thousand dollars or imprisoned not more than one year or both.

(1963, P.A. 652, S. 6.)

Cited. 165 C. 239; 173 C. 450.

Cited. 26 CA 667.

Cited. 30 CS 211.

Cited. 5 Conn. Cir. Ct. 44, 46; 6 Conn. Cir. Ct. 176.

Sec. 54-33f. Motion for return of unlawfully seized property and suppression as evidence.

(a) A person aggrieved by search and seizure may move the court which has jurisdiction of such person's case or, if such jurisdiction has not yet been invoked, then the court which issued the warrant, or the court in which such person's case is pending, for the return of the property and to suppress for use as evidence anything so obtained on the ground that: (1) The property was seized without a warrant, or (2) the warrant is insufficient on its face, or (3) the property seized is not that described in the warrant, or (4) there was not probable cause for believing the existence of the grounds on which the warrant was issued, or (5) the warrant was illegally executed. In no case may the judge or judge trial referee who signed the warrant preside at the hearing on the motion.

(b) The motion shall be made before trial or hearing unless opportunity therefor did not exist or the defendant was not aware of the grounds for the motion, but the court in its discretion may entertain the motion at the trial or hearing.

(c) The court shall receive evidence on any issue of fact necessary to the decision of the motion. If the motion is granted, the property shall be restored unless otherwise subject to lawful detention and it shall not be admissible in evidence at any hearing or trial.

(1963, P.A. 652, S. 7; 1967, P.A. 4; 1969, P.A. 292, S. 1; P.A. 80-313, S. 10; P.A. 01-72, S. 6.)

History: 1967 act added proviso prohibiting judge who signed warrant from presiding at hearing on motion; 1969 act authorized aggrieved person to make motion "in the court in which his case is pending" for return of property and to suppress its use as evidence; P.A. 80-313 reorganized provisions and divided section into Subsecs.; P.A. 01-72 amended Subsec. (a) by making technical changes for purposes of gender neutrality and adding reference to judge trial referee.

History discussed. 152 C. 90. Cited. 154 C. 314, 321. Neither statement that affiant had information from reliable informant nor that apartment sought to be searched had been under police surveillance was sufficient grounds for issuance of warrant, hence search warrant was illegal. 155 C. 385. Motion to suppress evidence consisting of several marked bills found on defendant immediately after he was observed selling narcotics to an informer, obtained by search incident to his lawful arrest for commission of felony of illegal sale of narcotics, properly denied. Id., 516. Ruling denying defendant's motion to suppress evidence of narcotics seized by arresting officer from stolen car in defendant's possession without obtaining search warrant was superseded by ruling during trial admitting narcotics as evidence; where defendant driver of stolen car had been arrested and drugs were found in car on custodial search by arresting officer, motion to suppress use of drugs in evidence properly denied. 159 C. 201. Cited. 169 C. 322. Person aggrieved by search and seizure may move to suppress for use as evidence anything obtained upon warrant when there is not probable cause for believing the existence of grounds for warrant. 170 C. 618. Cited. 195 C. 668; 216 C. 150, see also 26 CA 423, 27 CA 291, 223 C. 902 and 225 C. 10, reversing judgment of Appellate Court in *State v. Marsala,* 223 C. 903; 226 C. 514; 239 C. 793.

Cited. 10 CA 561; 14 CA 605; 15 CA 251; 27 CA 370; 31 CA 548.

Use of motion to suppress. 29 CS 423. Motion to dismiss, motion to suppress, difference. 30 CS 211. Section implements fourth amendment of U.S. Constitution and Art. I, Sec. 7 of the Connecticut Constitution and is analogous to rule 41 of Federal Rules of Criminal Procedure; purposes of rule. 33 CS 129.

Evidence obtained by an immediate search of defendant's apartment after her arrest for liquor violation was admissible; search without warrant was an incident to a lawful arrest. 4 Conn. Cir. Ct. 125. Where officers went beyond directives of warrant for search of defendant and certain premises and searched automobiles, evidence obtained was suppressed, but articles taken were not returned in absence of demand or request. Id., 422, 423. Property sought to be suppressed was voluntarily handed over to police officers by defendant's wife who was not party to defendant's appeal; he has no standing to claim violation of wife's constitutional rights as these are personal to her. Id., 605. Testimony or information, although not tangible, come within purview of statute. 5 Conn. Cir. Ct. 44. Although not expressly required, it is better practice for motion to suppress to be in writing. Id., 51. Motion by defendant to suppress evidence seized in search of his car dismissed by Circuit Court where prosecuting attorney had instituted bindover proceedings in Superior Court. Id., 119. While it is better practice to test legality of seizure in preliminary hearing, court may entertain motion to suppress at trial; officers did not search for papers where they had defendant under surveillance in his store and saw him putting papers under rafters of hatchway and picked them up upon arrest. Id., 613. Where there was probable cause to believe that defendant was in business of pool selling from allegations of affidavit, search warrant was properly issued. Id, 669. Burden of proof relative to the illegality of search and seizure is on accused; newspaper, policy sheet and pen discarded by accused were abandoned property and apprehension of them by police is not seizure of defendant's property. 6 Conn. Cir. Ct. 17. Doctrine of retroactivity not applied to procedural problem of this kind. Id., 192, 194. Motion to suppress must specify item to be suppressed. Id., 454. Cited. Id., 574, 584.

Sec. 54-33g. Forfeiture of moneys and property related to commission of criminal offense. In rem proceeding. Disposition. Secondary evidence of forfeited property.

(a) When any property believed to be possessed, controlled, designed or intended for use or which is or has been used or which may be used as a means of committing any criminal offense, or which constitutes the proceeds of the commission of any criminal offense, except a violation of section 21a-267, 21a-277, 21a-278 or 21a-279, has been seized as a result of a lawful arrest or lawful search, which the state claims to be a nuisance and desires to have destroyed or disposed of in accordance with the provisions of this section, the Chief State's Attorney or a deputy chief state's attorney, state's attorney or assistant or deputy assistant state's attorney may petition the court not later than ninety days after the seizure, in the nature of a proceeding in rem, to order forfeiture of such property. Such proceeding shall be deemed a civil suit in equity, in which the state shall have the burden of proving all material facts by clear and convincing evidence. The court shall identify the owner of such property and any other person as appears to have an interest in such property, and order the state to give notice to such owner and any interested person by certified or registered mail. The court shall promptly, but not less than two weeks after such notice, hold a hearing on the petition.

(b) If the court finds the allegations made in such petition to be true and that the property has been possessed, controlled or designed for use, or is or has been or is intended to be used, with intent to violate or in violation of any of the criminal laws of this state, or constitutes the proceeds of a violation of any of the criminal laws of this state, except a violation of section 21a-267, 21a-277, 21a-278 or 21a-279, the court shall render judgment that such property is a nuisance and order the property to be destroyed or disposed of to a charitable or educational institution or to a governmental agency or institution, except that if any such property is subject to a bona fide mortgage, assignment of lease or rent, lien or security interest, such property shall not be so destroyed or disposed of in violation of the rights of the holder of such mortgage, assignment of lease or rent, lien or security interest.

(c) (1) When the condemned property is money (A) on and after October 1, 2014, and prior to July 1, 2016, the court shall order that such money be distributed as follows: (i) Seventy per cent shall be allocated to the law enforcement agency, including the Department of Emergency Services and Public Protection and local police departments, responsible for investigating the criminal violation and seizing the money, and such local police departments shall use such money for the detection, investigation, apprehension and prosecution of persons for the violation of criminal laws, and any money allocated to the Department of Emergency Services and Public Protection shall be deposited in the General Fund; (ii) twenty per cent shall be deposited in the Criminal Injuries Compensation Fund established in section 54-215; and (iii) ten per cent shall be allocated to the Division of Criminal Justice and deposited in the General Fund; and (B) on and after July 1, 2016, such money shall be deposited in the General Fund.

(2) When the condemned property is a valuable prize, which is subject to a bona fide mortgage, assignment of lease or rent, lien or security interest, such property shall remain subject to such mortgage, assignment of lease or rent, lien or security interest.

(d) When any property or valuable prize has been declared a nuisance and condemned under this section, the court may also order that such property be sold in accordance with procedures approved by the Commissioner of Administrative Services. Proceeds of such sale shall first be allocated toward the balance of any mortgage, assignment of lease or rent, lien or security interest, and the remaining proceeds of such sale, if any, shall be allocated in accordance with subparagraphs (A) to (C), inclusive, of subdivision (1) of subsection (c) of this section. In any criminal prosecution, secondary evidence of property condemned and destroyed pursuant to this section shall be admissible against the defendant to the same extent as such evidence would have been admissible had the property not been condemned and destroyed.

(e) If the court finds the allegations not to be true, or that the property has not been kept with intent to violate or in violation of the criminal laws of this state, or that the property does not constitute the proceeds of a violation of the criminal laws of this state, or that the property is the property of a person who is not a defendant, the court shall order the property returned to the owner forthwith and the party in possession of such property pending such determination shall be responsible and personally liable for such property from the time of seizure and shall immediately comply with such order.

(f) Failure of the state to proceed against such property in accordance with the provisions of this section shall not prevent the use of such property as evidence in any criminal trial.

(1963, P.A. 652, S. 8; February, 1965, P.A. 215; 574, S. 47; 1972, P.A. 49; P.A. 75-54, S. 1, 3; P.A. 76-77, S. 4; 76-436, S. 531, 681; P.A. 80-313, S. 11; P.A. 84-540, S. 4, 7; P.A. 87-294, S. 1; P.A. 89-269, S. 3; P.A. 14-233, S. 1.)

History: 1965 acts specified applicability of provisions to seized property "which the state claims to be a nuisance and desires to have destroyed or disposed of in accordance with the provisions of this section" and added provision allowing use of property which state has failed to proceed against as evidence in criminal trial; 1972 act referred to property "possessed, controlled or designed for use ... or intended to be used" in violation of criminal laws rather than to property "kept" in connection with violation of law and added proviso re superior court's assumption of trial jurisdiction; P.A. 75-54 changed deadline for issuing summons from 48 hours after seizure to 10 days after seizure and clarified applicability re property which is subject to liens; P.A. 76-77 added provision re sale of property at public auction; P.A. 76-436 replaced prosecuting attorneys with assistant state's attorneys and deleted proviso re superior court's assumption of trial jurisdiction rendered obsolete because of transfer of all trial jurisdiction to that court, effective July 1, 1978; P.A. 80-313 divided section into Subsecs. and moved provision re final destruction or disposal of property but made no substantive changes; P.A. 84-540 deleted reference in Subsec. (a) to property seized "pursuant to subdivision (1) of subsection (b) of section 54-33a" and substituted reference to property "believed to be possessed, controlled, designed or intended for use or which is or has been used as a means of committing any criminal offense" seized "as a result of a search incident to an arrest, a warrantless arrest or a search warrant"; expanded provision in Subsec. (a) requiring judge or court "issuing the warrant" to issue a summons to include judge or court "before whom the arrested person is to be arraigned"; P.A. 87-294 amended Subsec. (c) to specify that property which is money shall be deposited in the general fund; P.A. 89-269 amended Subsec. (a) to add exception for "a violation of section 21a-267, 21a-277, 21a-278 or 21a-279", to require that the property has been seized as a result of a "lawful arrest or lawful search" rather than a "search incident to an arrest, a warrantless arrest or a search warrant", and to delete provision that the summons notify the owner to appear "then and there to show cause why such property should not be adjudged a nuisance and ordered to be destroyed or otherwise disposed of as herein provided", amended Subsec. (b) to place on the state's attorney or assistant state's attorney "the burden of proving all material facts by clear and convincing evidence" and amended Subsec. (c) to add exception for "a violation of section 21a-267, 21a-277, 21a-278 or 21a-279"; P.A. 14-233 substantially revised section by amending Subsec. (a) to add provision making section applicable to proceeds of commission of a criminal offense and replacing provisions re judge or court issuing warrant and summons with provisions authorizing state's attorney to petition court, after seizure of property, for forfeiture order in a civil proceeding in rem after notice to owner or interested party by certified or registered mail, deleting former Subsec. (b) re owner of property claiming interest, redesignating existing Subsec. (c) as Subsec. (b), inserting new Subsec. (c)(1) and (2) designators, replacing provision re money or prize seized with provisions re distribution of money, adding provisions re when property is a valuable prize, designating existing provisions re nuisance as new Subsec. (d) and amending same to replace provisions re sale at public auction and use of property as evidence with provisions re sale in accordance with procedures approved by Commissioner of Administrative Services, allocation of balance of proceeds and admissibility of secondary evidence of condemned property, redesignating existing Subsecs. (d) and (e) as Subsecs. (e) and (f), and making technical and conforming changes.

Origin of former statute. 126 C. 433. Under former statute, obscene materials could be destroyed regardless of who possessed them or of knowledge or intent in such possession. 146 C. 78. Intervening federal tax lien has precedence over state's inchoate claim which is not perfected until a final adjudication of forfeiture. 176 C. 339. Cited. 192 C. 98; 194 C. 589; 196 C. 471; 204 C. 259; 207 C. 743.

Statute requires that the issuance of the warrant, pursuant to which the property sought to be confiscated is seized, precede the seizure and that the seizure take place pursuant to that warrant. 1 CA 315. Statute, being a forfeiture statute, must be read and applied strictly. 5 CA 540. Cited. 15 CA 589; 19 CA 195; Id., 588; 39 CA 40.

Cited. 36 CS 551.

Seizure warrant is prerequisite to condemnation of gambling device; action to condemn is civil and state has right to appeal. 2 Conn. Cir. Ct. 399. Cited. 3 Conn. Cir. Ct. 96. Defendant's lack of knowledge his car was being used by person to whom he entrusted it for policy playing is no defense to forfeiture proceeding. 5 Conn. Cir. Ct. 1. Cited. Id., 44, 46; 6 Conn. Cir. Ct. 283. Not a criminal statute, but provides for forfeiture of car used in violation of law by in rem civil action. Id., 284.

Subsec. (a):

Time limit is directory, not mandatory. 19 CA 195. Cited. 23 CA 724.

Sec. 54-33h. (Formerly Sec. 53-279). Arrest of keeper of gambling equipment; seizure and disposition of property. Section 54-33h is repealed.

(1949 Rev., S. 8656; 1959, P.A. 28, S. 191; 1963, P.A. 652, S. 9; 1969, P.A. 169; P.A. 73-455, S. 9.)

Sec. 54-33i. "Journalist", "news organization" and "news" defined.

For the purposes of this section and sections 54-33a and 54-33j:

(1) "Journalist" means a person engaged in the business of investigating, collecting or writing news, or of supervising such activity, with the intent of publication or presentation or for publication or presentation to the public through a news organization.

(2) "News organization" means (A) an individual, partnership, corporation or other association engaged in the business, whether or not for profit, of (i) publishing a newspaper or other periodical that reports news events and that is issued at regular intervals or has a general circulation; or (ii) providing newsreels or other motion picture news for public showing; or (iii) broadcasting news to the public by wire, radio, television or facsimile; and (B) a press association or other association of individuals, partnerships, corporations or other associations described in subparagraph (A) of this subdivision or in subdivision (1) of this section engaged in gathering news and disseminating it to its members for publication.

(3) "News" means any compilation of facts, theories, rumors or opinions concerning any subject for the purpose of informing the public.

(P.A. 79-14, S. 1; P.A. 80-313, S. 12.)

History: P.A. 80-313 replaced alphabetic Subdiv. indicators with numeric indicators and made corresponding format changes in Subpara. indicators but made no substantive changes.

Sec. 54-33j. Issuance of search warrant for property of journalist or news organization.

(a) No search warrant, as provided in section 54-33a, may be issued to search any place or seize anything in the possession, custody or control of any journalist or news organization unless such warrant is issued upon probable cause that such person or organization has committed or is committing the offense related to the property named in the warrant or such property constitutes contraband or an instrumentality of a crime.

(b) Nothing in this section shall be construed as limiting the right to subpoena any such evidence if such subpoena is otherwise permitted by law.

(P.A. 79-14, S. 2.)

Sec. 54-33k. "Strip search" defined.

For the purposes of this section and section 54-33l, "strip search" means having an arrested person remove or arrange some or all of his or her clothing or, if an arrested person refuses to remove or arrange his or her clothing, having a peace officer or employee of the police department remove or arrange the clothing of the arrested person so as to permit a visual inspection of the genitals, buttocks, anus, female breasts or undergarments used to clothe said anatomical parts of the body.

(P.A. 80-93, S. 1; P.A. 81-234, S. 1.)

History: P.A. 81-234 amended the definition of strip search to include the removing or arranging of the clothing of an arrested person by a peace officer or an employee of the police department when the arrested person refuses to remove or arrange the clothing.

Section does not address those strip searches that are conducted incident to lawful arrest on a felony charge. 82 CA 111.

Sec. 54-33l. Strip searches. Procedure.

(a) No person arrested for a motor vehicle violation or a misdemeanor shall be strip searched unless there is reasonable belief that the individual is concealing a weapon, a controlled substance or contraband.

(b) No search of any body cavity other than the mouth shall be conducted without a search warrant. Any warrant authorizing a body cavity search shall specify that the search is required to be performed under sanitary conditions and conducted either by or under the supervision of a person licensed to practice medicine in accordance with chapter 370.

(c) All strip searches shall be performed by a person of the same sex as the arrested person and on premises where the search cannot be observed by persons not physically conducting the search or not absolutely necessary to conduct the search.

(d) Any peace officer or employee of a police department conducting a strip search shall (1) obtain the written permission of the police chief or an agent thereof designated for the purposes of authorizing a strip search in accordance with this section and section 54-33k and (2) prepare a report of the strip search. The report shall include the written authorization required by subdivision (1) of this subsection, the name of the person subjected to the search, the name of any person conducting the search and the time, date and place of the search. A copy of the report shall be provided to the person subjected to the search.

(e) Nothing in this section shall preclude prosecution of a peace officer or employee under any other provision of the general statutes.

(f) Nothing in this section shall be construed as limiting any statutory or common law rights of any person for purposes of any civil action or injunctive relief.

(g) The provisions of this section and section 54-33k shall not apply when the person is remanded to a correctional institution pursuant to a court order.

(P.A. 80-93, S. 2; P.A. 81-234, S. 2.)

History: P.A. 81-234 amended Subsec. (a) to clarify the exception to the prohibition on strip searches and to provide that a person may be strip searched if there is reasonable belief he is concealing contraband, amended Subsec. (b) by replacing "licensed practitioner, as defined in section 20-184a" with "person licensed to practice medicine in accordance with chapter 370", and amended Subsec. (c) by providing that a strip search shall be performed where it cannot be observed by persons not absolutely necessary to conduct it.

Section does not address those strip searches that are conducted incident to lawful arrest on a felony charge. 82 CA 111. Language of section suggests that a strip search and a body cavity search are two discrete searches and, therefore, when a search constitutes a strip search, it does not necessarily amount to a body cavity search under statute; although the two types of searches appear within same statutory provision, the two terms are used independently of each other. 105 CA 179.

Sec. 54-33m. Failure to wear seat belt not probable cause for vehicle search.

The failure of an operator of, or front seat passenger in, a private passenger motor vehicle or vanpool vehicle to wear a seat safety belt as required by section 14-100a shall not constitute probable cause for a law enforcement official to conduct a search of such vehicle and its contents.

(P.A. 85-429, S. 7, 8.)

Sec. 54-33n. Search of school lockers and property.

All local and regional boards of education and all private elementary and secondary schools may authorize the search by school or law enforcement officials of lockers and other school property available for use by students for the presence of weapons, contraband or the fruits of a crime if (1) the search is justified at its inception and (2) the search as actually conducted is reasonably related in scope to the circumstances which justified the interference in the first place. A search is justified at its inception when there are reasonable grounds for suspecting that the search will turn up evidence that the student has violated or is violating either the law or the rules of the school. A search is reasonably related in scope when the measures adopted are reasonably related to the objectives of the search and not excessively intrusive in light of the age and sex of the student and the nature of the infraction.

(P.A. 94-115.)

Secs. 54-34 and 54-35. Search of person. Condemnation of gambling implements, notice. Sections 54-34 and 54-35 are repealed.

(1949 Rev., S. 8757, 8758; 1961, P.A. 214; 255, S. 1; 1963, P.A. 652, S. 10.)

PART III*

SEIZED PROPERTY

*Cited. 26 CA 910.

Sec. 54-36. Disposition of property held as evidence. Section 54-36 is repealed.

(1949 Rev., S. 8759; 1969, P.A. 699, S. 31; P.A. 73-116, S. 22; 73-667, S. 1, 2; P.A. 74-221, S. 9.)

Sec. 54-36a. Definitions. Inventory. Return of stolen property. Disposition of other seized property. Return of compliance.

(a) As used in this section, sections 53-278c and 54-36c: (1) "Contraband" means any property, the possession of which is prohibited by any provision of the general statutes; (2) "stolen property" shall include, but not be limited to, cash or the proceeds from the sale of such property obtained by theft or other illegal means; (3) "owner" means a person or persons entitled to seized property as a matter of law or fact.

(b) (1) Whenever property is seized in connection with a criminal arrest or seized pursuant to a search warrant without an arrest, the law enforcement agency seizing such property shall file, on forms provided for this purpose by the Office of the Chief Court Administrator, an inventory of the property seized. The inventory, together with the uniform arrest report, in the case of an arrest, shall be filed with the clerk of the court for the geographical area in which the criminal offense is alleged to have been committed; except, when the property is stolen property and, in the opinion of the law enforcement officer, does not exceed one thousand dollars in value, or when an attempt was made to steal the property but the property at all times remained on the premises in a sealed container, the filing of an inventory shall not be required and such property may be returned to the owner. In the case of property seized in connection with a search warrant without an arrest, the inventory shall be attached to the warrant and shall be filed with the clerk of the court for the geographical area in which the search warrant was issued. If any criminal proceeding is transferred to another court location, then the clerk with whom the inventory is filed shall transfer such inventory to the clerk of the court location to which such action is transferred.

(2) If the seized property is stolen property, within ten days of the seizure, the law enforcement agency seizing the property shall notify the owner of the property if known, or, if the owner of the property is unknown at the time of seizure, such agency shall within ten days of any subsequent ascertainment of the owner notify such owner, and, on a form prescribed by the Office of the Chief Court Administrator, advise the owner of such owner's rights concerning the property and the location of the property. Such written notice shall include a request form for the return of the property. The owner may request the return of the property by filing such request form with such law enforcement agency, and upon receipt of such request, the law enforcement agency shall forward it to the clerk of the court for the geographical area in which the criminal offense is alleged to have been committed. The clerk of the court shall notify the defendant or defendants of the request to return the property. The court shall order the return of the property within thirty days of the date of filing such return request by the owner, except that for good cause shown, the court may order retention of the property for a period to be determined by the court. Any secondary evidence of the identity, description or value of such property shall be admissible in evidence against such defendant in the trial of such case. The fact that the evidence is secondary in nature may be shown to affect the weight of such evidence, but not to affect its admissibility. If the stolen property is a motor vehicle, a photograph of the motor vehicle and a sworn affidavit attesting to the vehicle identification number of such motor vehicle shall be sufficient evidence of the identity of the motor vehicle. For the purposes of this subdivision, "motor vehicle" means a passenger or commercial motor vehicle or a motorcycle, as defined in section 14-1, and includes construction equipment, agricultural tractors and farm implements.

(3) (A) If the seized property is currency and is stolen property, the law enforcement agency seizing the currency shall follow the procedures set forth in subdivision (2) of this subsection.

(B) If the seized property is currency and is not stolen property, the law enforcement agency seizing the currency shall, within ten days of such seizure, notify the defendant or defendants, if such currency was seized in connection with a criminal arrest, or the person or persons having a possessory interest in the premises from which such currency was seized, if such currency was seized pursuant to a search warrant without an arrest, that such defendant or person has the right to a hearing before the Superior Court on the disposition of the currency. Such defendant or person may, not later than thirty days after receiving such notice, request a hearing before the Superior Court. The court may, after any such hearing, order that the law enforcement agency, after taking reasonable measures to preserve the evidentiary value of the currency, deposit the currency in a deposit account in the name of the law enforcement agency as custodian for evidentiary funds at a financial institution in this state or order, for good cause shown, that the currency be retained for a period to be determined by the court. If such defendant or person does not request a hearing, the law enforcement agency may, after taking reasonable measures to preserve the evidentiary value of the currency, deposit the currency in a deposit account in the name of the law enforcement agency as custodian for evidentiary funds at a financial institution in this state.

(C) If the currency is deposited in a deposit account at a financial institution in this state pursuant to subparagraph (B) of this subdivision, the financial institution at which such deposit account is established shall not be required to segregate the currency deposited in such deposit account. No funds may be withdrawn from such deposit account except pursuant to a court order directed to the financial institution. Any withdrawal of funds from such deposit account shall be in the form of a check issued by the financial institution to the law enforcement agency or to such other payee as the court may order. Nothing in this subdivision shall prohibit a financial institution from charging a fee for the maintenance and administration of such deposit account and for the review of the court order.

(D) If the currency is deposited in a deposit account at a financial institution in this state pursuant to subparagraph (B) of this subdivision, any secondary evidence of the identity, description or value of such currency shall be admissible in evidence against a defendant in the trial of a criminal offense. The fact that the evidence is secondary in nature may be shown to affect the weight of such evidence, but not to affect its admissibility.

(c) Unless such seized property is stolen property and is ordered returned pursuant to subsection (b) of this section or unless such seized property is adjudicated a nuisance in accordance with section 54-33g, or unless the court finds that such property shall be forfeited or is contraband, or finds that such property is a controlled drug, a controlled substance or drug paraphernalia as defined in subdivision (8), (9) or (20) of section 21a-240, it shall, at the final disposition of the criminal action or as soon thereafter as is practical, or, if there is no criminal action, at any time upon motion of the prosecuting official of such court, order the return of such property to its owner within six months upon proper claim therefor.

(d) When the court orders the return of the seized property to the owner, the order shall provide that if the seized property is not claimed by the owner within six months, the property shall be destroyed or be given to a charitable or educational institution or to a governmental agency or institution, except that (1) if such property is money it shall be remitted to the state and shall be deposited in the General Fund or (2) if such property is a valuable prize it shall be disposed of by public auction or private sale in which case the proceeds shall become the property of the state and shall be deposited in the General Fund; provided any person who has a bona fide mortgage, assignment of lease or rent, lien or security interest in such property shall have the same right to the proceeds as he had in the property prior to the sale.

(e) If such seized property is adjudicated a nuisance or if the court finds that such property shall be forfeited or is contraband other than a controlled drug, a controlled substance or drug paraphernalia as defined in subdivision (8), (9) or (20) of section 21a-240, the court shall order that such property be destroyed or be given to a charitable or educational institution or to a governmental agency or institution, except that (1) if such property is money, the court shall order that it be remitted to the state and be deposited in the General Fund or (2) if such property is a valuable prize, the court shall order that it be disposed of by public auction or private sale in which case the proceeds shall become the property of the state and shall be deposited in the General Fund; provided any person who has a bona fide mortgage, assignment of lease or rent, lien or security interest in such property shall have the same right to the proceeds as he had in the property prior to sale.

(f) If the court finds that such seized property is fireworks as defined in section 29-356, the court shall order the forfeiture and destruction of such property. Any secondary evidence of the identity, description or value of such property shall be admissible in evidence against the defendant in the trial of the case. A photograph of the fireworks and a sworn affidavit describing such fireworks shall be sufficient evidence of the identity of the fireworks. The fact that the evidence is secondary in nature may be shown to affect the weight of such evidence, but not to affect its admissibility.

(g) If the court finds that such seized property is a controlled drug, a controlled substance or drug paraphernalia as defined in subdivision (8), (9) or (20) of section 21a-240, the court shall order the forfeiture and destruction of such property or order it delivered to the Commissioner of Consumer Protection pursuant to section 54-36g.

(h) Any order made under the provisions of subsections (b), (c), (d), (e), (f) and (g) of this section or section 54-33f or 54-33g, shall upon notification from the clerk, be complied with by the person or department having custody or possession of such property.

(i) A return of compliance with the court order, on a form prescribed by the Office of the Chief Court Administrator, shall be filed with the clerk of the court by the person or department to whom notice is sent in accordance with the provisions of subsection (h) of this section. If the court ordered the seized property returned to the owner within six months upon proper claim therefor, the return of the compliance shall be filed within seventy-two hours of the return of the property to the owner. If the owner does not claim the property within six months, then the return of compliance shall be filed within seventy-two hours of compliance with the order of the court pursuant to subsection (d) of this section. Failure to comply with the court order within ninety days following expiration of the period within which the owner of the property may claim the property shall constitute criminal contempt. If the court renders an order concerning the disposition of the property other than an order to return the property to the owner, the return of compliance shall be filed with the clerk within seventy-two hours of compliance with the court order. Failure to comply with the court order within ninety days of receipt of such order shall constitute criminal contempt. Failure to file a return of compliance as set forth in this subsection shall constitute criminal contempt. Anyone convicted of criminal contempt may be punished by a fine of not more than one hundred dollars. Each failure to comply with a court order and each failure to file a return of compliance within the required period shall constitute a separate criminal contempt.

(P.A. 74-221, S. 1-6; P.A. 75-530, S. 16, 17, 35; P.A. 76-77, S. 1; P.A. 78-280, S. 1, 127; P.A. 79-392; P.A. 81-240, S. 1, 3; P.A. 82-235; P.A. 85-263, S. 1; P.A. 87-243; 87-294, S. 2; P.A. 99-247, S. 5; P.A. 01-104; 01-186, S. 8; June 30 Sp. Sess. P.A. 03-6, S. 146(c); P.A. 04-189, S. 1; P.A. 07-246, S. 5; P.A. 12-72, S. 1.)

History: P.A. 75-530 amended Subsec. (b) to make clear distinctions between filing procedure for inventories of property seized in arrest or under a search warrant, and to add provisions specifically applicable to stolen property and restated Subsec. (c); P.A. 76-77 required that uniform arrest report or search warrant, as the case may be, be filed with inventory, added exception to inventory requirement in connection with arrest re stolen property not exceeding $50 in value and added provision re return of stolen property upon its owner's application to court in Subsec. (b) and changed applicable time periods re claims for property and return of property in Subsecs. (c) to (f) from one year to six months; P.A. 78-280 deleted references to filing of inventories in counties; P.A. 79-392 added definitions of "stolen property" and "owner" in Subsec. (a) and substituted reference to Sec. 54-36c for reference to Sec. 54-36b; P.A. 81-240 replaced previous provisions re return of stolen property with new provisions re notification of the owner of stolen property, procedure for return of stolen property within 30 days of request therefor, except for good cause shown and specified that secondary nature of evidence may affect weight of evidence but not admissibility in Subsec. (b) and deleted provision in Subsec. (e) whereby return of compliance was filed after return of property to owner or at the end of six months in cases where court orders return within that time period; P.A. 82-235 required office of chief court administrator to provide forms for return of stolen property, required notice of stolen property within 10 days instead of 48 hours, provided procedure for return of seized property, other than stolen property or contraband, within six months, eliminated sentence of imprisonment for criminal contempt for failure to file the return of compliance and required that any sale of unclaimed seized property ordered by the court shall be public; P.A. 85-263 amended Subsec. (b) by adding exceptions of stolen property which does not exceed $250 in value or when an attempt was made to steal property but property remained on premises in sealed container, amended Subsec. (c) by adding "finds that such property is a controlled drug" and "drug paraphernalia", and added provisions re order of return of property by court, property adjudicated a nuisance, disposition of controlled drugs, controlled substances and drug paraphernalia and immediate filing of return of compliance if owner fails to claim property within six months; P.A. 87-243 added new Subsec. (f) re the forfeiture and destruction of fireworks and the admissibility of secondary evidence of such fireworks, and relettered the remaining subsections and internal references accordingly; P.A. 87-294 specified that property which is money and sale or auction proceeds be deposited in the general fund; P.A. 99-247 amended Subsec. (b) to insert Subdiv. indicators, reposition provision re transfer of inventory and add new Subdiv. (3) re the deposit of seized currency in a safe deposit box in a financial institution, the removal of such currency and the responsibility of such financial institution with respect to such safe deposit box and its contents; P.A. 01-104 amended Subsec. (b) by making a technical change for purposes of gender neutrality and adding provisions re motor vehicles in Subdiv. (2), deleting former Subdiv. (3) and adding new Subdiv. (3) re currency; P.A. 01-186 amended Subsec. (i) by requiring return of compliance to be filed within 72 hours of return of property or court order, providing that failure to comply with court order within 90 days shall constitute criminal contempt, adding provision re each failure to file return of compliance within required period shall constitute a separate criminal contempt and making conforming changes; June 30 Sp. Sess. P.A. 03-6 replaced Commissioner of Consumer Protection with Commissioner of Agriculture and Consumer Protection, effective July 1, 2004; P.A. 04-189 repealed Sec. 146 of June 30 Sp. Sess. P.A. 03-6, thereby reversing the merger of the Departments of Agriculture and Consumer Protection, effective June 1, 2004; P.A. 07-246 amended Subsec. (f) to provide that a photograph and affidavit shall be sufficient evidence of the identity of fireworks; P.A. 12-72 amended Subsec. (b)(1) to increase from $250 to $1,000 the maximum value of stolen property re when police may return the property to the owner without filing an inventory.

Cited. 181 C. 388; 192 C. 98; 204 C. 259; 242 C. 666.

Cited. 5 CA 540; 10 CA 130; 23 CA 215; 30 CA 249; 33 CA 409. Denial of request for return of seized property pursuant to statute was appealable and plaintiff improperly brought a writ of error. 107 CA 760. Statute does not apply to money found near drugs and seized at the same time as an arrest for violations of drug laws. 108 CA 533.

Cited. 35 CS 659; 36 CS 352; 39 CS 392.

Subsec. (a):

The mere possibility of civil judgment concluding that defendant holds legal lien or security interest in property at issue was insufficient to establish defendant as the owner of such property for purposes of Subsec. 154 CA 405.

Subsec. (b):

Where stolen jewelry was inadvertently returned to owner without notifying defendant, admission of secondary evidence not improper where defendant had opportunity to cross-examine and challenge value of stolen property claimed by state. 133 CA 681.

Subsec. (c):

Statute authorizes the forfeiture in this case, prior to enactment of the 1984 amendment to Sec. 54-33g, which incorporated seizure as a result of a warrantless arrest. 196 C. 471.

Use of radar detection device not "crime" so as to warrant forfeiture of device. 36 CS 551.

Sec. 54-36b. Examiner of seized property, appointment, duties.

There shall be an examiner of seized property who shall be appointed and be subject to supervision by the Chief Court Administrator of the Judicial Department. The examiner of seized property may prescribe forms and procedures to be used in identifying and labeling seized property, shall recommend to the judges any procedures which may be necessary to implement the provisions of this section, sections 53-278c and 54-36a, may inspect records maintained by clerks of court in connection with accounting for seized property, and may inspect offices where seized property is kept to insure the filing of inventories and compliance with other provisions of said sections. The examiner of seized property shall conduct or contract for any public auction required pursuant to the provisions of section 54-36a, section 54-33g and section 53-278c and, at his discretion, such property may be sold by him to the highest bidder in whatever locality of the state he determines affords the most favorable market. The examiner of seized property may decline the highest bid at any such sale and reoffer the property at a later sale if he considers the bid insufficient. He may dispose of any such property by private sale if, in his opinion, the probable cost of public sale will exceed the value of the property. He may also, at his discretion, dispose of such property to a charitable or educational institution or to a governmental agency or institution.

(P.A. 74-221, S. 7; P.A. 75-530, S. 18, 35; P.A. 76-77, S. 2; P.A. 85-140, S. 6; 85-263, S. 3.)

History: P.A. 75-530 authorized examiner to contract for public auction, allowed sale to highest bidder in locality affording the most favorable market and added provisions authorizing examiner to decline highest bid and hold another sale, to dispose of property by private sale and to dispose of property to charitable, educational or government institution; P.A. 76-77 added reference to Sec. 54-33q; P.A. 85-140 provided that the examiner be appointed and subject to supervision by the chief court administrator rather than the executive secretary of the judicial department; P.A. 85-263 deleted references to Secs. 54-36a(f) and 53-278(c).

Sec. 54-36c. Disposition of seized property on order of the examiner of seized property.

If there is no criminal action, property seized prior to October 1, 1974, held by law enforcement agencies in connection with a crime, which has not been claimed by the owner, except property held for disposition pursuant to section 54-33g, shall, upon notification by the police authority, be disposed of on the order of the examiner of seized property if he obtains the consent of the prosecuting official of such court. Property, seized after October 1, 1974, in connection with a crime for which an inventory need not be filed and held by law enforcement agencies for six months and which has not been claimed by the owner, shall be disposed of by an order of the examiner of seized property if he obtains the consent of the prosecuting official of such court. In disposing of property pursuant to this section, the examiner of seized property may order that such property be destroyed or be given to a charitable or educational institution or to a governmental agency or institution; provided, (1) if such property is money, he shall order that it be remitted to the state and be deposited in the General Fund or (2), if such property is a valuable prize, he shall order that it be disposed of by public auction or private sale, in which case the proceeds shall become the property of the state and shall be deposited in the General Fund; provided any person who has a bona fide mortgage, assignment of lease or rent, lien or security interest in such property shall have the same right to the proceeds as he had in the property prior to sale.

(P.A. 75-530, S. 19, 35; P.A. 76-77, S. 3; P.A. 87-294, S. 3.)

History: P.A. 76-77 amended provisions to recognize hearing of Sec. 54-36a created in 1974 and to require that examiner obtain consent of prosecuting officials before disposing of property; P.A. 87-294 amended section to specify that property which is money and sale or auction proceeds be deposited in the general fund.

Sec. 54-36d. Proceedings under chapters 214, 220 and 490 concerning cigarettes, alcohol and fisheries and game, respectively, exempt from certain licensing and disposition requirements.

Sections 21-1, 54-36a, 54-36b and 54-36c, shall not be applicable to the proceedings taken pursuant to chapters 214, 220 and 490.

(P.A. 75-530, S. 23, 35.)

Sec. 54-36e. Firearms and ammunition to be turned over to state police. Sale at public auction.

(a) Except as provided in sections 26-85 and 26-90, firearms and ammunition, adjudged by the court to be contraband pursuant to subsection (c) of section 54-36a, or adjudicated a nuisance pursuant to section 54-33g, shall be turned over to the Bureau of Identification of the Connecticut Division of State Police within the Department of Emergency Services and Public Protection for destruction or appropriate use or disposal by sale at public auction.

(b) Firearms and ammunition turned over to the state police pursuant to subsection (a) of this section which are not destroyed or retained for appropriate use shall be sold at public auctions, conducted by the Commissioner of Administrative Services or said commissioner's designee. Pistols and revolvers, as defined in section 53a-3, which are antiques, as defined in section 29-33, or curios or relics, as defined in the Code of Federal Regulations, Title 27, Chapter 1, Part 178, or modern pistols and revolvers which have a current retail value of one hundred dollars or more may be sold at such public auctions, provided such pistols and revolvers shall be sold only to persons who have a valid permit to sell a pistol or revolver, or a valid permit to carry a pistol or revolver, issued pursuant to section 29-28. Rifles and shotguns, as defined in section 53a-3, shall be sold only to persons qualified under federal law to purchase such rifles and shotguns and who have a valid long gun eligibility certificate issued pursuant to section 29-37p. The proceeds of any such sale shall be paid to the State Treasurer and deposited by the State Treasurer in the forfeit firearms account within the General Fund.

(P.A. 76-77, S. 5; P.A. 77-614, S. 486, 610; P.A. 85-263, S. 4; P.A. 87-257; P.A. 00-192, S. 42, 102; P.A. 11-51, S. 134; P.A. 13-3, S. 9, 39.)

History: P.A. 77-614 made state police department a division within the department of public safety, effective January 1, 1979; P.A. 85-263 added provisions re disposal of firearms at public auction; P.A. 87-257 amended Subsec. (b) to permit more than one annual auction of firearms by deleting restriction that firearms be sold at a public "auction held annually on or before the thirtieth of June"; P.A. 00-192 amended Subsec. (b) to require sale proceeds to be deposited in forfeit firearms account and made technical changes for purposes of gender neutrality, effective July 1, 2000; pursuant to P.A. 11-51, "Department of Public Safety" was changed editorially by the Revisors to "Department of Emergency Services and Public Protection" in Subsec. (a), effective July 1, 2011; P.A. 13-3 amended Subsec. (b) to add requirement that rifles and shotguns only be sold to persons who have a valid long gun eligibility certificate issued pursuant to Sec. 29-37p and make a technical change, effective July 1, 2013, and made section applicable to ammunition adjudged to be contraband or adjudicated a nuisance, effective October 1, 2013.

Sec. 54-36f. Receipt for seized property to be given by law enforcement officials.

Whenever property is seized in connection with a criminal arrest or seized pursuant to a search warrant without an arrest, the law enforcement agency seizing such property shall give a receipt therefor to the person or persons from whom such property was seized or to the person or persons having a possessory interest in the premises from which such property was seized. The receipt, on a form provided for this purpose by the Office of the Chief Court

Administrator, shall list with specificity the property seized, be signed by the law enforcement official or officials who seized the property and be given to the person or persons from whose person or premises the property was seized at the time of such seizure or, if the property was seized from premises in the absence of the person or persons having a possessory interest therein, be mailed to such person or persons by registered or certified mail within five days of such seizure.

(P.A. 84-222.)

Sec. 54-36g. Destruction of controlled drugs, controlled substances and drug paraphernalia held as evidence in criminal proceedings. Petition, notice and hearing. Representative samples. Certificate of results. Destruction upon final disposition of criminal action. Records.

(a) At any time after the seizure of a controlled drug or a controlled substance, as defined in subdivision (8) or (9) of section 21a-240, or drug paraphernalia, as defined in subdivision (20) of section 21a-240, in connection with a criminal arrest or pursuant to a search warrant without an arrest, the prosecuting official of the court for the geographical area in which the criminal offense is alleged to have been committed may petition the court for destruction of such controlled drug, controlled substance or drug paraphernalia. After notice, by certified or registered mail to the defendant and his attorney, and hearing on the petition, the court may order the forfeiture and destruction of such controlled drug, controlled substance or drug paraphernalia, under procedures and to the extent determined by the court, or order it delivered to the Commissioner of Consumer Protection as soon as possible. Such order shall be in writing and shall provide for the analysis of representative samples of such controlled drug, controlled substance or drug paraphernalia. The results of such analysis shall be recorded on a certificate signed by the person making the analysis, witnessed and acknowledged pursuant to section 1-29. Such certificate shall be prima facie evidence of the composition and quality of such controlled drug, controlled substance or drug paraphernalia.

(b) Upon final disposition of the criminal action or, if there is no criminal action, at any time upon motion of the prosecuting official, the court shall order the destruction of any controlled drug, controlled substance or drug paraphernalia not previously destroyed pursuant to an order under subsection (a) of this section, or order it delivered to the Commissioner of Consumer Protection as soon as possible.

(c) The law enforcement agency seizing the controlled drug, controlled substance or drug paraphernalia shall keep a full and complete record of the time and place where such controlled drug, controlled substance or drug paraphernalia was seized, the kinds, quantities and weight of drugs received, by whom the controlled drug, controlled substance or drug paraphernalia were delivered and received and the date and manner of destruction or disposition of such controlled drug, controlled substance or drug paraphernalia. Such record and the certificate of the results of the analysis shall be disclosed only to attorneys of record in the case, the defendant and to federal and state officers charged with enforcement of federal and state narcotic laws.

(P.A. 84-44, S. 1; P.A. 85-263, S. 2; June 30 Sp. Sess. P.A. 03-6, S. 146(c); P.A. 04-189, S. 1.)

Sec. 54-36h. Forfeiture of moneys and property related to illegal sale or exchange of controlled substances or money laundering. In rem proceeding. Disposition.

(a) The following property shall be subject to forfeiture to the state pursuant to subsection (b) of this section:

(1) All moneys used, or intended for use, in the procurement, manufacture, compounding, processing, delivery or distribution of any controlled substance, as defined in subdivision (9) of section 21a-240;

(2) All property constituting the proceeds obtained, directly or indirectly, from any sale or exchange of any such controlled substance in violation of section 21a-277 or 21a-278;

(3) All property derived from the proceeds obtained, directly or indirectly, from any sale or exchange for pecuniary gain of any such controlled substance in violation of section 21a-277 or 21a-278;

(4) All property used or intended for use, in any manner or part, to commit or facilitate the commission of a violation for pecuniary gain of section 21a-277 or 21a-278;

(5) All property constituting, or derived from, the proceeds obtained, directly or indirectly, by a corporation as a result of a violation of section 53a-276, 53a-277 or 53a-278.

(b) Not later than ninety days after the seizure of moneys or property subject to forfeiture pursuant to subsection (a) of this section, in connection with a lawful criminal arrest or a lawful search, the Chief State's Attorney or a deputy chief state's attorney, state's attorney or assistant or deputy assistant state's attorney may petition the court in the nature of a proceeding in rem to order forfeiture of said moneys or property. Such proceeding shall be deemed a civil suit in equity, in which the state shall have the burden of proving all material facts by clear and convincing evidence. The court shall identify the owner of said moneys or property and any other person as appears to have an interest therein, and order the state to give notice to such owner and any interested person by certified or registered mail, and shall promptly, but not less than two weeks after notice, hold a hearing on the petition. No testimony offered or evidence produced by such owner or interested person at such hearing and no evidence discovered as a result of or otherwise derived from such testimony or evidence, may be used against such owner or interested person in any proceeding, except that no such owner or interested person shall be immune from prosecution for perjury or contempt committed while giving such testimony or producing such evidence. At such hearing the court shall hear evidence and make findings of fact and enter conclusions of law and shall issue a final order, from which the parties shall have such right of appeal as from a decree in equity.

(c) No property shall be forfeited under this section to the extent of the interest of an owner or lienholder by reason of any act or omission committed by another person if such owner or lienholder did not know and could not have reasonably known that such property was being used or was intended to be used in, or was derived from, criminal activity.

(d) Notwithstanding the provisions of subsection (a) of this section, no moneys or property used or intended to be used by the owner thereof to pay legitimate attorney's fees in connection with his defense in a criminal prosecution shall be subject to forfeiture under this section.

(e) Any property ordered forfeited pursuant to subsection (b) of this section shall be sold at public auction conducted by the Commissioner of Administrative Services or his designee.

(f) The proceeds from any sale of property under subsection (e) of this section and any moneys forfeited under this section shall be applied: (1) To payment of the balance due on any lien preserved by the court in the forfeiture proceedings; (2) to payment of any costs incurred for the storage, maintenance, security and forfeiture of such property; and (3) to payment of court costs. The balance, if any, shall be deposited in the drug assets forfeiture revolving account established under section 54-36i.

(P.A. 86-404, S. 3, 4; P.A. 88-364, S. 71, 123; P.A. 89-269, S. 1.)

History: P.A. 88-364 amended Subsec. (b) by substituting "moneys" for "property"; P.A. 89-269 amended Subsec. (a) to restructure provisions, to insert Subdiv. indicators, to replace in Subdiv. (2) "the proceeds of any sale of any such controlled substance in violation of any provision of the general statutes" with "All property constituting the proceeds obtained, directly or indirectly, from any sale or exchange of any controlled substance in violation of section 21a-277 or 21a-278", and to add Subdivs. (3), (4) and (5) re other property subject to forfeiture, amended Subsec. (b) to authorize the "chief state's attorney or a deputy chief state's attorney, state's attorney or assistant or deputy assistant state's attorney" rather than "the prosecuting official of the court for the geographical area in which the criminal offense is alleged to have been committed" to petition the court "Not later than ninety days" after the seizure rather than "At any time" after the seizure, to make provisions applicable to moneys "or property" seized, to require the seizure to be "in connection with a lawful criminal arrest or a lawful search" rather than "in connection with a criminal arrest or pursuant to a search warrant without an arrest", to change the state's burden of proof from a preponderance of the evidence to clear and convincing evidence, to require the court to identify the owner of the moneys or property and any person with an interest therein, and to add provision prohibiting the use of certain testimony or evidence against the owner or interested person, added Subsec. (c) re the forfeiture of property when the owner or lienholder has no knowledge of the criminal activity, added Subsec. (d) re the forfeiture of moneys or property used or intended to be used to pay attorney's fees, added Subsec. (e) re the sale at public auction of forfeited property, and added Subsec. (f) re the allocation of the proceeds from the sale of forfeited property or any forfeited moneys; (Revisor's note: In 1995 the word "fund" in the phrase "drug assets forfeiture revolving fund" was replaced editorially by the Revisors with the word "account" to conform section with Sec. 54-36i as amended by P.A. 94-95).

Money found near drugs and seized at same time as arrest for violations of drug laws is not property subject to forfeiture proceedings. 108 CA 533.

Subsec. (b):

Time limit in section is substantive and a jurisdictional prerequisite. 43 CS 203.

Sec. 54-36i. Drug assets forfeiture revolving account. Allocation of moneys.

(a) There is established and created an account of the General Fund to be known as the "drug assets forfeiture revolving account" for the purpose of providing funds for substance abuse treatment and education programs and for use in the detection, investigation, apprehension and prosecution of persons for the violation of the laws pertaining to the illegal manufacture, sale, distribution or possession of controlled substances.

(b) The account shall consist of the proceeds from the sale of property and moneys received and deposited pursuant to section 54-36h.

(c) Moneys in such account shall be distributed as follows: (1) Seventy per cent shall be allocated to the Department of Emergency Services and Public Protection and local police departments pursuant to subsection (d) of this section, fifteen per cent of which shall be used for purposes of drug education and eighty-five per cent of which shall be used for the detection, investigation, apprehension and prosecution of persons for the violation of laws pertaining to the illegal manufacture, sale, distribution or possession of controlled substances and for the purposes of police training on gang-related violence as required by section 7-294*l,* (2) twenty per cent shall be allocated to the Department of Mental Health and Addiction Services for substance abuse treatment and education programs and tobacco prevention and enforcement positions engaged in compliance activities as required by the federal government as a condition of receipt of substance abuse prevention and treatment block grant funds, and (3) ten per cent shall be allocated to the Division of Criminal Justice for use in the prosecution of persons for the violation of laws pertaining to the illegal manufacture, sale, distribution or possession of controlled substances.

(d) Expenditures from the account allocated to the Department of Emergency Services and Public Protection and local police departments shall be authorized by a panel composed of: (1) The Commissioner of Emergency Services and Public Protection or his designee, (2) the commander of the state-wide narcotics task force or his designee, and (3) the president of the Connecticut Police Chiefs Association or his designee. The panel shall adopt procedures for the orderly authorization of expenditures, subject to the approval of the Comptroller. Such expenditures may be authorized only to the Department of

Emergency Services and Public Protection and to organized local police departments within this state. Such expenditures shall be held by the Department of Emergency Services and Public Protection and the various organized local police departments in accounts or funds established for that purpose. In no event shall the expenditures be placed in a state or town general fund and in no event shall the expenditures be used for purposes other than those provided in subdivision (1) of subsection (c) of this section. The panel shall ensure the equitable allocation of expenditures to the Department of Emergency Services and Public Protection or any local police department which participated directly in any of the acts which led to the seizure or forfeiture of the property so as to reflect generally the contribution of said department or such local police department in such acts. The panel shall authorize expenditures from the account for the reimbursement of any organized local police department which has used its own funds in the detection, investigation, apprehension and prosecution of persons for the violation of laws pertaining to the illegal manufacture, sale, distribution or possession of controlled substances and which makes application to the panel for reimbursement.

(e) Moneys remaining in the drug assets forfeiture revolving account at the end of a fiscal year shall not revert to the General Fund but shall remain in the revolving account to be used for the purposes set forth in this section.

(P.A. 89-269, S. 2; P.A. 90-230, S. 95, 101; P.A. 91-406, S. 20, 29; P.A. 93-381, S. 9, 39; 93-416, S. 9, 10; P.A. 94-95, S. 15; P.A. 95-257, S. 5, 58; P.A. 96-180, S. 162, 166; P.A. 09-2, S. 6; P.A. 11-51, S. 134.)

History: P.A. 90-230 corrected an internal reference in Subsec. (d); P.A. 91-406 confirmed the numbering of this section as Sec. 54-36i, thereby correcting a typographical error; P.A. 93-381 replaced Connecticut alcohol and drug abuse commission with department of public health and addiction services, effective July 1, 1993; P.A. 93-416 amended Subsec. (c)(1) to include police training on gang-related violence as another purpose for which fund moneys shall be used, effective June 29, 1993; P.A. 94-95 changed name of fund from "drug assets forfeiture revolving fund" to "drug assets forfeiture revolving account"; P.A. 95-257 replaced Commissioner and Department of Public Health and Addiction Services with Commissioner and Department of Mental Health and Addiction Services, effective July 1, 1995; P.A. 96-180 amended Subsec. (d)(3) to substitute "Connecticut Police Chiefs Association" for "Connecticut Chiefs of Police Association"; P.A. 09-2 amended Subsec. (c)(2) to extend use of funds to specified tobacco prevention and enforcement positions, effective April 1, 2009; pursuant to P.A. 11-51, "Commissioner of Public Safety" and "Department of Public Safety" were changed editorially by the Revisors to "Commissioner of Emergency Services and Public Protection" and "Department of Emergency Services and Public Protection", respectively, effective July 1, 2011.

Secs. 54-36j to 54-36l. Seizure and forfeiture of motor vehicle used in patronizing a prostitute. Innocent owner defense to forfeiture of motor vehicle used in patronizing a prostitute. Release of motor vehicle seized in connection with arrest for patronizing a prostitute; delivery or return of motor vehicle upon disposition of prosecution. Sections 54-36j to 54-36l, inclusive, are repealed, effective October 1, 1997.

(P.A. 93-265, S. 3-5; 93-398, S. 1, 2; P.A. 96-180, S. 163, 166; P.A. 97-279, S. 3.)

Sec. 54-36m. Impoundment of motor vehicle occupied by person arrested for patronizing a prostitute from a motor vehicle.

(a) Any police officer who arrests a person for a violation of section 53a-83a shall cause the motor vehicle such person was occupying at the time of the alleged offense to be impounded for a period of forty-eight hours after such arrest, until such person is arraigned or until such motor vehicle is released by order of the court, whichever occurs first.

(b) The owner of such motor vehicle may reclaim such motor vehicle after the expiration of such forty-eight-hour period, the arraignment of the arrested person or the issuance of a court order releasing such motor vehicle, as the case may be, upon payment of all towing and storage costs, except that if the owner of such motor vehicle is a person, firm or corporation licensed under the provisions of section 14-15, such owner may reclaim such motor vehicle at any time upon payment of all towing and storage costs.

(P.A. 97-279, S. 1.)

Sec. 54-36n. Identification and tracing of seized and recovered firearms and ammunition.

(a) Whenever a law enforcement agency seizes a firearm in connection with a criminal arrest or pursuant to a search warrant without an arrest or otherwise recovers a firearm, such agency shall forthwith take all appropriate steps to identify and trace the history of such firearm.

(b) In complying with the provisions of subsection (a) of this section, a law enforcement agency shall use the National Tracing Center of the Federal Bureau of Alcohol, Tobacco and Firearms. Such law enforcement agency shall immediately transmit to the National Tracing Center, by facsimile or by entering such information on the Connecticut On-Line Law Enforcement Communications Teleprocessing (COLLECT) System when said system becomes available for transmitting such information directly to the National Tracing Center, all information necessary to comply with the provisions of subsection (a) of this section.

(c) The Department of Emergency Services and Public Protection shall take appropriate action to allow the COLLECT System to be used by law enforcement agencies in complying with the provisions of this section.

(d) Whenever a firearm is identified and is determined to have been stolen, the law enforcement agency shall return such firearm, and any ammunition seized or recovered with such firearm that is determined to be stolen, to the rightful owner thereof, provided such owner is not prohibited from possessing such firearm or ammunition and such agency does not need to retain such firearm or ammunition as evidence in a criminal prosecution.

(P.A. 98-129, S. 3; P.A. 11-51, S. 134; P.A. 13-3, S. 41.)

History: Pursuant to P.A. 11-51, "Department of Public Safety" was changed editorially by the Revisors to "Department of Emergency Services and Public Protection" in Subsec. (c), effective July 1, 2011; P.A. 13-3 amended Subsec. (d) to add provision re return of ammunition that is seized or recovered with a firearm that is determined to be stolen and made conforming changes.

Sec. 54-36o. Property derived from identity theft subject to forfeiture to state. Exceptions. Proceeds.

(a) All property constituting, or derived from, the proceeds obtained, directly or indirectly, by a person as a result of a violation of section 53a-129a of the general statutes, revision of 1958, revised to January 1, 2003, or section 53a-127g, 53a-129b, 53a-129c, 53a-129d, 53a-129e, 53a-130, 21-120 or 21-121 shall be subject to forfeiture to the state pursuant to subsection (b) of this section.

(b) Not later than ninety days after the seizure of property subject to forfeiture pursuant to subsection (a) of this section, the Chief State's Attorney or a deputy chief state's attorney, state's attorney or assistant or deputy assistant state's attorney may petition the court in the nature of a proceeding in rem to order forfeiture of said moneys or property. Such proceeding shall be deemed a civil suit in equity, in which the state shall have the burden of proving all material facts by clear and convincing evidence. The court shall identify the owner of such property and any other person as appears to have an interest therein, and order the state to give notice to such owner and any interested person by certified or registered mail, and shall promptly, but not less than two weeks after notice, hold a hearing on the petition. No testimony offered or evidence produced by such owner or interested person at such hearing and no evidence discovered as a result of or otherwise derived from such testimony or evidence, may be used against such owner or interested person in any proceeding, except that no such owner or interested person shall be immune from prosecution for perjury or contempt committed while giving such testimony or producing such evidence. At such hearing the court shall hear evidence and make findings of fact and enter conclusions of law and shall issue a final order, from which the parties shall have such right of appeal as from a decree in equity.

(c) No property shall be forfeited under this section to the extent of the interest of an owner or lienholder by reason of any act or omission committed by another person if such owner or lienholder did not know and could not have reasonably known that such property was being used or was intended to be used in, or was derived from, criminal activity.

(d) Notwithstanding the provisions of subsection (a) of this section, no property used or intended to be used by the owner thereof to pay legitimate attorney's fees in connection with his defense in a criminal prosecution shall be subject to forfeiture under this section.

(e) Any property ordered forfeited pursuant to subsection (b) of this section shall be sold at public auction conducted by the Commissioner of Administrative Services.

(f) The proceeds from any sale of property under subsection (e) of this section shall be applied: (1) To payment of the balance due on any lien preserved by the court in the forfeiture proceedings; (2) to payment of any costs incurred for the storage, maintenance, security and forfeiture of such property; and (3) to payment of court costs. The balance, if any, shall be deposited in the privacy protection guaranty and enforcement account established under section 42-472a.

(P.A. 09-239, S. 12; June 12 Sp. Sess. P.A. 12-2, S. 90.)

History: June 12 Sp. Sess. P.A. 12-2 made a technical change in Subsec. (f).

Sec. 54-36p. Forfeiture of moneys and property related to sexual exploitation, prostitution and human trafficking. In rem proceeding. Disposition.

(a) The following property shall be subject to forfeiture to the state pursuant to subsection (b) of this section:

(1) All moneys used, or intended for use, in a violation of subdivision (3) of subsection (a) of section 53-21 or section 53a-86, 53a-87, 53a-88, 53a-90a, 53a-189a, 53a-189b, 53a-192a, 53a-196a, 53a-196b, 53a-196c or 53a-196i;

(2) All property constituting the proceeds obtained, directly or indirectly, from a violation of subdivision (3) of subsection (a) of section 53-21 or section 53a-86, 53a-87, 53a-88, 53a-90a, 53a-189a, 53a-189b, 53a-192a, 53a-196a, 53a-196b, 53a-196c or 53a-196i;

(3) All property derived from the proceeds obtained, directly or indirectly, from a violation of subdivision (3) of subsection (a) of section 53-21 or section 53a-86, 53a-87, 53a-88, 53a-90a, 53a-189a, 53a-189b, 53a-192a, 53a-196a, 53a-196b, 53a-196c or 53a-196i;

(4) All property used or intended for use, in any manner or part, to commit or facilitate the commission of a violation of subdivision (3) of subsection (a) of section 53-21 or section 53a-83, 53a-83a, 53a-86, 53a-87, 53a-88, 53a-90a, 53a-189a, 53a-189b, 53a-192a, 53a-196a, 53a-196b, 53a-196c or 53a-196i.

(b) Not later than ninety days after the seizure of moneys or property subject to forfeiture pursuant to subsection (a) of this section, in connection with a lawful criminal arrest or a lawful search, the Chief State's Attorney or a deputy chief state's attorney, state's attorney or assistant or deputy assistant state's attorney may petition the court in the nature of a proceeding in rem to order forfeiture of such moneys or property. Such proceeding shall be deemed a civil suit in equity in which the state shall have the burden of proving all material facts by clear and convincing evidence. The court shall identify the owner of such moneys or property and any other person as appears to have an interest therein, and order the state to give notice to such owner and any interested person, including any victim of the crime with respect to which such moneys or property were seized, by certified or registered mail. The court shall promptly, but not less than two weeks after such notice, hold a hearing on the petition. No testimony offered or evidence produced by such owner or interested person at such hearing and no evidence discovered as a result of or otherwise derived from such testimony or evidence may be used against such owner or interested person in any proceeding, except that no such owner or interested person shall be immune from prosecution for perjury or contempt committed while giving such testimony or producing such evidence. At such hearing, the court shall hear evidence and make findings of fact and enter conclusions of law and shall issue a final order from which the parties shall have such right of appeal as from a decree in equity.

(c) No moneys or property shall be forfeited under this section to the extent of the interest of an owner or lienholder by reason of any act or omission committed by another person if such owner or lienholder did not know and could not have reasonably known that such moneys or property was being used or was intended to be used in, or was derived from, criminal activity.

(d) Notwithstanding the provisions of subsection (a) of this section, no moneys or property used or intended to be used by the owner thereof to pay legitimate attorney's fees in connection with his or her defense in a criminal prosecution shall be subject to forfeiture under this section.

(e) Any property ordered forfeited pursuant to subsection (b) of this section shall be sold at public auction conducted by the Commissioner of Administrative Services or the commissioner's designee.

(f) The proceeds from any sale of property under subsection (e) of this section and any moneys forfeited under this section shall be applied: (1) To payment of the balance due on any lien preserved by the court in the forfeiture proceedings; (2) to payment of any costs incurred for the storage, maintenance, security and forfeiture of any such property; and (3) to payment of court costs. The balance, if any, shall be deposited in the Criminal Injuries Compensation Fund established in section 54-215.

(P.A. 10-112, S. 1; P.A. 13-166, S. 1; P.A. 14-233, S. 2; P.A. 16-71, S. 11.)

History: P.A. 13-166 amended Subsec. (a) to add references to violations of Secs. 53a-82, 53a-88 and 53a-196i and amended Subsec. (f) to provide that balance of proceeds be deposited in Criminal Injuries Compensation Fund, rather than General Fund; P.A. 14-233 amended Subsec. (a) to delete references to pecuniary gain in Subdivs. (3) and (4); P.A. 16-71 amended Subsec. (a) by deleting references to Sec. 53a-82 and, in Subdiv. (4), adding references to Secs. 53a-83 and 53a-83a.

Secs. 54-37 to 54-39. Disposition of accused acquitted on ground of insanity. Release of persons confined under order prior to October 1, 1959. Petition for release. Disposition of insane person upon expiration of term. Sections 54-37 to 54-39, inclusive, are repealed.

(1949 Rev., S. 8749-8751; 1953, S. 3321d, 3322d; 1955, S. 3322d; 1959, P.A. 28, S. 150; 523, S. 1; 1963, P.A. 642, S. 65, 84; February, 1965, P.A. 435, S. 2; 557; 1967, P.A. 261, S. 2; 1971, P.A. 871, S. 129; P.A. 80-146.)

Sec. 54-40. Transferred to Chapter 960, Sec. 54-56d.

Sec. 54-40a. Transferred to Chapter 959, Sec. 54-1i.

Sec. 54-41. Transferred to Chapter 890, Sec. 51-352c.

CHAPTER 959a* WIRETAPPING AND ELECTRONIC SURVEILLANCE

*See chapter 952, part XVII re tampering with private communications, eavesdropping and voyeurism.

Cited. 171 C. 524. Federal, Connecticut and New York wiretap statutes discussed. 176 C. 17. Cited. 189 C. 42; 191 C. 360; 194 C. 447; 212 C. 195. Monitoring and tape recording of cordless telephone conversations without a judicial wiretap order was unlawful interception under wiretap act. 224 C. 593. Cited. 238 C. 253; Id., 692.

Cited. 3 CA 477; 5 CA 634; 14 CA 605; 16 CA 245; 44 CA 247.

Table of Contents

Sec. 54-41a. Definitions.

Sec. 54-41b. Application for order authorizing interception.

Sec. 54-41c. Information in application.

Sec. 54-41d. Issuance of order.

Sec. 54-41e. Statement by panel on issuance of order. Contents of order.

Sec. 54-41f. Execution of order; progress reports.

Sec. 54-41g. Extensions of order.

Sec. 54-41h. Privileged wire communications; issuance of order and interception prohibited.

Sec. 54-41i. Recording of interception; sealing, custody and destruction.

Sec. 54-41j. Sealing, custody, storage and destruction of applications and orders.

Sec. 54-41k. Service of notice of interception; inspection of intercepted communications, applications and orders; postponement of service.

Sec. 54-41l. Intercepted communication admissible as evidence, when.

Sec. 54-41m. Motion to suppress.

Sec. 54-41n. Report by panel to Chief Court Administrator.

Sec. 54-41o. Reports by state's attorneys.

Sec. 54-41p. Disclosure of contents of wire communication. Unauthorized disclosure: Class D felony.

Sec. 54-41q. Authority of communication common carrier to intercept, disclose or use wire communication.

Sec. 54-41r. Remedies of party intercepted; defense.

Sec. 54-41s. Illegal possession, sale, distribution of equipment: Class D felony.

Sec. 54-41t. Unauthorized or illegal interception: Class C felony.

Sec. 54-41u. Admissibility of intercepted wire communication obtained pursuant to federal law.

Sec. 54-41a. Definitions.

The following words and phrases, as used in this chapter, shall have the following meanings, unless the context otherwise requires:

(1) "Wire communication" means any communication made in whole or in part through the use of facilities for the transmission of communications by the aid of telephone or telegraph between the point of origin and the point of reception furnished or operated by any person engaged as a common carrier in providing or operating such facilities for the transmission of intrastate, interstate or foreign communications;

(2) "Intercept" means the intentional overhearing or recording of a wire communication through the use of any electronic, mechanical or other device;

(3) "Electronic, mechanical or other device" means any device or apparatus which can be used to intercept a wire communication other than (A) any telephone or telegraph instrument, equipment or facility, or any component thereof (i) furnished to the subscriber or used by a communications common carrier in the ordinary course of its business and being used by the subscriber or user in the ordinary course of its business, or (ii) being used by a communications common carrier in the ordinary course of its business, (B) a hearing aid or similar device being used to correct subnormal hearing to not better than normal;

(4) "Person" means any officer, agent or employee of the state of Connecticut or any political subdivision thereof, and any individual, partnership, association, joint stock company, trust, limited liability company or corporation;

(5) "Investigative officer" means (A) any officer of the Connecticut state police, (B) the chief inspector or any inspector in the Division of Criminal Justice who is empowered by law to conduct investigations of or to make arrests for offenses enumerated in this chapter, (C) any municipal police officer who has been duly sworn as a special state police officer under the provisions of section 29-177 and who is currently assigned to the state-wide narcotics task force or the state-wide organized crime investigative task force and is acting under the direct authority of the Connecticut state police, and (D) any attorney authorized by law to prosecute or participate in the prosecution of offenses enumerated in this chapter;

(6) "Law enforcement officer" means any officer of any organized police department of this state or of the state police of any other state, an official of the Federal Bureau of Investigation, Drug Enforcement Administration or United States Customs Service, or the United States attorney for the district of Connecticut or a person designated by him in writing to receive the contents of any wire communication or evidence derived therefrom;

(7) "Contents", when used with respect to any wire communication, means and includes any information concerning the identity of the parties to such communication or the existence, substance, purport or meaning of that communication;

(8) "Panel of judges" or "panel" means any panel or panels of three Superior Court judges specifically designated by the Chief Justice of the Supreme Court from time to time to receive applications for, and to enter orders authorizing, interceptions of wire communications in accordance with the provisions of this chapter;

(9) "Communication common carrier" means any person engaged as a common carrier for hire in the transmission of communications by wire or radio;

(10) "Aggrieved person" means a person who was a party to any intercepted wire communication, a person against whom the interception was directed, a person named in any order authorizing an interception, or a person having a property interest in any premises involved in any interception.

(1971, P.A. 68, S. 1; P.A. 79-179, S. 1; P.A. 82-368, S. 1; P.A. 83-543, S. 1; P.A. 87-229; P.A. 95-79, S. 184, 189.)

History: P.A. 79-179 replaced single definition for "investigative or law enforcement officer" with a separate definition for each, applying existing definition to investigative officers and adding chief inspectors and inspectors of criminal justice division; P.A. 82-368 expanded the definitions of "investigative office" to include municipal police officers as specified and "law enforcement officer" to include state police of other states and FBI or Drug Enforcement Administration officials; P.A. 83-543 expanded the definition of "law enforcement officer" to include the U.S. attorney for Connecticut or his designee; P.A. 87-229 expanded the definition of "law enforcement officer" to include an official of the United States Customs Service; P.A. 95-79 redefined "person" to include a limited liability company, effective May 31, 1995.

Cited. 171 C. 524; 191 C. 360; 194 C. 447. "Wire communication" as defined in section includes the radio wave portion of a cordless telephone conversation. 224 C. 593. Cited. 238 C. 253; Id., 692.

Cited. 8 CA 673; 10 CA 347.

Sec. 54-41b. Application for order authorizing interception.

The Chief State's Attorney or the state's attorney for the judicial district in which the interception is to be conducted may make application to a panel of judges for an order authorizing the interception of any wire communication by investigative officers having responsibility for the investigation of offenses as to which the application is made when such interception may provide evidence of the commission of offenses involving gambling, bribery, violations of section 53-395, violations of section 53a-70c, violations of subsection (a) of section 53a-90a, violations of section 53a-192a, violations of section 53a-196, violations of section 21a-277, felonious crimes of violence or felonies involving the unlawful use or threatened use of physical force or violence committed with the intent to intimidate or coerce the civilian population or a unit of government.

(1971, P.A. 68, S. 2; P.A. 78-280, S. 1, 127; P.A. 79-179, S. 2; P.A. 82-368, S. 2; P.A. 83-543, S. 2; P.A. 02-97, S. 13; P.A. 15-195, S. 5.)

History: P.A. 78-280 substituted "judicial district" for "county"; P.A. 79-179 deleted reference to law enforcement officers; P.A. 82-368 added bribery and violations of Sec. 53-395 ("CORA") as crimes for which an application can be made for an interception; P.A. 83-543 authorized the chief state's attorney to make application for interception order; P.A. 02-97 added felonies involving the unlawful use or threatened use of physical force or violence committed with the intent to intimidate or coerce the civilian population or a unit of government as crimes for which an application may be made for an interception; P.A. 15-195 added provision re violations of Secs. 53a-70c, 53a-90a(a), 53a-192a and 53a-196.

Cited. 171 C. 524; 176 C. 17. Application defective for failure of state's attorney to make formal oath or affirmation. 180 C. 345. Cited. 191 C. 360; 194 C. 447; 199 C. 591; 212 C. 485; 223 C. 906; 224 C. 322; 234 C. 539; 238 C. 692.

Cited. 7 CA 660; 8 CA 673; 27 CA 596; 44 CA 249.

Sec. 54-41c. Information in application.

Each application for an order authorizing the interception of a wire communication shall be made in writing upon oath or affirmation to a panel of judges. Each application shall include the following information: (1) The identity of the applicant and his authority to make such application; (2) the identity and qualifications of the investigative officers or agency for whom the authority to intercept a wire communication is sought; (3) the identity and qualifications of the investigative or law enforcement officers to whom disclosure of the contents of any intercepted wire communication or evidence derived therefrom might be made; (4) a statement of the use to which the contents of any intercepted wire communication or any evidence derived therefrom will be put; (5) a full and complete statement of the facts and circumstances relied upon by the applicant, to justify his reasonable belief that the wire communication of a particularly described person will constitute evidence of a crime enumerated in section 54-41b that has been or is being committed or that such communication will materially aid in the apprehension of the perpetrator of such crime and that an order should be issued, including (A) details as to the particular offense that has been or is being committed, (B) a particular description of the nature and location of the facilities from which or the place where the communication is to be intercepted, (C) a particular description of the type of communications sought to be intercepted, (D) the identity of the person, if known, who has committed or is committing the offense and whose communications are to be intercepted, (E) the time and date when the facts and circumstances relied upon by the applicant were first received by him or by the investigative or law enforcement officer conducting the investigation, whichever is earlier, (F) the way in which the intercepted wire communication will constitute material evidence of the particularly described offense or will materially aid in the apprehension of the perpetrator of such offense, (G) the hours of the day or night during which wire communication may be reasonably expected to occur; (6) a full and complete statement of facts showing that other normal investigative procedures with respect to the offense have been tried and have failed or reasonably appear to be unlikely to succeed if tried or to be too dangerous to employ, (7) a statement of the period of time for which the interception is required to be maintained. No order authorizing or approving the interception of a wire communication shall be issued if the facts and circumstances relied upon by the applicant were discovered more than twenty days next preceding the date of the application. If the nature of the investigation is such that the authorization for interception should not automatically terminate when the described type of communication has been first obtained, a particular description of facts establishing probable cause to believe that additional communications of the same type will occur thereafter; (8) a full and complete statement of the facts concerning all previous applications known to the individual making the application, made to any panel of judges, for authorization to intercept, or for approval of interceptions of, wire communications involving any of the same persons, facilities or places specified in the application, and the action taken by the panel on each such application; (9) a statement that the wire communications sought are material to a particularly described investigation or prosecution and that such communications are not legally privileged; (10) if it is reasonably necessary to make a secret entry upon a private place or premises in order to install an intercepting device to effectuate the interception, a statement to that effect and to the effect that no practicable alternative method of executing the order which will preserve the secrecy of its execution exists; (11) where the application is for the extension of an order, a statement setting forth the results thus far obtained from the interception, or a reasonable explanation of the failure to obtain such results; (12) where the application is for an order authorizing interception in excess of thirty-five orders previously issued by all panels in a calendar year, a statement setting forth the nature of the emergency situation which may result in imminent peril to the public health, safety or welfare, and the nature of that imminent peril, which requires the issuance of an additional interception order. The state's attorney shall inform the Governor and the joint standing committee of the General Assembly having cognizance of matters relating to criminal law and procedure of the nature of the emergency situation which may result in imminent peril to the public health, safety or welfare, and the nature of that imminent peril; (13) such additional testimony or documentary evidence in support of fact in the application as the panel of judges may require. Allegations of fact in the application may be based either upon the personal knowledge of the applicant or upon information and belief. If the applicant personally knows the facts alleged, it must be so stated. If the facts establishing such probable cause are derived in whole or part from the statements of persons other than the applicant, the sources of such information and belief shall be either disclosed or described, and the application shall contain facts establishing the existence and reliability of the informant, or the reliability of the information supplied by him. The application shall also state the basis of the informant's knowledge or belief. If the applicant's information and belief are derived from tangible evidence or recorded oral evidence, a copy or detailed description thereof shall be annexed to or included in the application. Affidavits of persons other than the applicant may be submitted in conjunction with the application if they tend to support any fact or conclusion alleged therein. Such accompanying affidavits may be based either on personal knowledge of the affiant, or information and belief with the source thereof and reason therefor specified.

(1971, P.A. 68, S. 3; P.A. 79-179, S. 3; P.A. 82-368, S. 3.)

History: P.A. 79-179 removed reference to law enforcement officers in Subdiv. (2); P.A. 82-368 changed the time limit on reliable information from 15 to 20 days and included the provision dealing with application for the thirty-sixth and subsequent emergency orders as new Subdiv. (12), renumbering accordingly.

Read with Sec. 54-41b, oath or affirmation required can only be that of the state's attorney applicant; acknowledgment is insufficient. 176 C. 17. Application defective for failure of state's attorney to make formal oath or affirmation; statute requires disclosure of prior applications to intercept the conversations of a particular person, not prior interceptions of conversations to which that person was a party. 180 C. 345. Cited. 191 C. 360; 194 C. 447; 199 C. 591; 224 C. 593; 238 C. 692.

Sec. 54-41d. Issuance of order.

Upon such application the panel of judges, by unanimous vote, may enter an ex parte order authorizing the interception of wire communications within the state of Connecticut, if the panel determines on the basis of the facts submitted by the applicant that there is probable cause to believe that: (1) An individual has committed or is committing an offense enumerated in section 54-41b; (2) particular communications will constitute material evidence that an offense enumerated in section 54-41b has been committed or is being committed or will materially aid in the apprehension of the perpetrator of such offense; (3) such communications are not otherwise privileged; (4) other normal investigative procedures with respect to the offense have been tried and have failed or reasonably appear to be unlikely to succeed if tried or to be too dangerous to employ; (5) the facilities from which, or the place where, the wire communications are to be intercepted are being used, or are about to be used, in connection with the commission of such offense, or are leased to, listed in the name of, or commonly used by such individual; (6) such facilities or places are not those described in section 54-41h; (7) if the facilities from which a wire communication is to be intercepted are public, a special need exists to intercept wire communications over such facilities; (8) the investigative officers to be authorized to intercept the wire communication are qualified by training and experience to execute the interception sought; (9) not more than thirty-four orders authorizing interception have been previously issued by all panels in the calendar year in which the application is made, except that upon a showing of an emergency situation in which the commission of an offense enumerated in section 54-41b may result in imminent peril to public health, safety or welfare, such panel may issue additional orders authorizing interception.

(1971, P.A. 68, S. 4; P.A. 79-179, S. 4; P.A. 82-368, S. 4; P.A. 83-295, S. 11.)

History: P.A. 79-179 removed reference to law enforcement officers in Subdiv. (8); P.A. 82-368 included a provision dealing with the issuance of emergency orders involving danger to public health, safety or welfare; P.A. 83-295 amended Subdiv. (9) by replacing "a violation of" with "the commission of an offense enumerated in".

Sec. 54-41e. Statement by panel on issuance of order. Contents of order.

Each order authorizing the interception of any wire communication shall be accompanied by a written statement of the panel setting forth in detail its determination made in accordance with the provisions of section 54-41d and the grounds therefor and shall specify: (1) The identity of the person, if known, whose communications are to be intercepted; (2) the nature and location of the communication facilities as to which or the place where authority to intercept is granted; (3) a particular description of the type of communication sought to be intercepted, and a statement of the particular offense to which it relates; (4) the identity of the investigative officers authorized to intercept such wire communications; (5) the identity of the investigative or law enforcement officers to whom disclosure of the contents of any intercepted wire communication or any evidence derived therefrom may be made; (6) the use to which the contents of any intercepted wire communication or any evidence derived therefrom may be put; (7) the identity of the person making the application and his authority; (8) the identity of the panel and its authority to issue an order; (9) the period of time during which such interception is authorized, including a statement that the interception shall automatically terminate when the desired communication has been first obtained; (10) express authorization to make secret entry onto private premises to install any device, provided no such secret entry shall be authorized if there exists a practicable alternative method of executing the order which will preserve the secrecy of its execution; (11) the date of issuance of the order and its effective date. Every order and extension thereof shall contain a provision that the authorization to intercept shall be executed as soon as practicable, shall be conducted in such a way as to minimize the interception of communications not otherwise subject to interception in accordance with the provisions of this chapter, and shall terminate upon attainment of the authorized objective, or in any event within fifteen days next succeeding the date of issuance of such order. An order authorizing the interception of a wire communication shall, upon request of the applicant, direct that a communication common carrier, landlord, custodian or other person shall furnish the applicant forthwith all information, facilities and technical assistance necessary to accomplish the interception unobtrusively and with a minimum of interference with the services that such carrier, landlord, custodian or person is according the person whose communications are to be intercepted. Any communication common carrier, landlord, custodian or other person furnishing such facilities or technical assistance shall be compensated therefor by the applicant at the prevailing rates.

(1971, P.A. 68, S. 5; P.A. 79-179, S. 5; P.A. 82-368, S. 5; P.A. 99-215, S. 10.)

History: P.A. 79-179 removed reference to law enforcement officers in Subdiv. (4); P.A. 82-368 increased from 10 to 15 days the maximum duration of an order authorizing the interception of a wire communication; P.A. 99-215 deleted "issuing" before "panel".

Cited. 176 C. 17. The remedy of total suppression considered entirely appropriate when execution of wiretap in complete disregard of minimization occurred; minimization requirement discussed. 191 C. 360. Cited. 210 C. 804; Id., 805; 212 C. 485; 224 C. 593; 238 C. 692.

Cited. 5 CA 207; Id., 634; 8 CA 673; 9 CA 182; 16 CA 245.

Sec. 54-41f. Execution of order; progress reports.

Any order entered in accordance with the provisions of this chapter may be executed pursuant to its terms only by the investigative officers expressly authorized therein. The order may be executed according to its terms only during the hours specified therein, and for the period authorized or part thereof. No order may authorize the interception of any wire communication for any period longer than is necessary to achieve the objective of the authorization, nor in any event longer than fifteen days. Whenever an order authorizing an interception is entered in accordance with the provisions of this chapter, the order may require reports to be made to the panel showing what progress has been made toward achievement of the authorized objective and the need for continued interception. Such reports shall be made at such intervals as such panel may require.

(1971, P.A. 68, S. 6; P.A. 79-179, S. 6; P.A. 82-368, S. 6; P.A. 99-215, S. 11.)

History: P.A. 79-179 removed reference to power of law enforcement officers to execute orders; P.A. 82-368 increased from 10 to 15 days the maximum duration of an interception; P.A. 99-215 deleted "which issued the order" after "panel".

Cited. 191 C. 360; 212 C. 485; 238 C. 692.

Sec. 54-41g. Extensions of order.

No more than three extensions of an order may be granted by the panel and only upon application for an extension made in accordance with the provisions of section 54-41c, which shall, in addition, contain the results of the interceptions conducted thus far, and findings by the panel as required by the provisions of section 54-41d. The period of any extension shall be no longer than the panel deems necessary to achieve the purposes for which it was granted and in no event longer than fifteen days.

(1971, P.A. 68, S. 7; P.A. 82-368, S. 7; P.A. 99-215, S. 12.)

History: P.A. 82-368 increased from 10 to 15 days the maximum period of an extension; P.A. 99-215 deleted "issuing" before "panel".

Cited. 191 C. 360; 212 C. 485; 238 C. 692.

Sec. 54-41h. Privileged wire communications; issuance of order and interception prohibited. If the facilities from which, or the place where, the wire communications are to be intercepted are being used, or are about to be used, or are leased to, listed in the name of, or commonly used by, a licensed physician, an attorney-at-law or a practicing clergyman, no order shall be issued and no wire communications shall be intercepted over such facilities or in such places. No otherwise privileged wire communications intercepted in accordance with, or in violation of, the provisions of this chapter shall lose their privileged character, nor shall any evidence derived therefrom be used for any purpose.

(1971, P.A. 68, S. 8.)

Cited. 191 C. 360; 212 C. 485; 238 C. 692.

Sec. 54-41i. Recording of interception; sealing, custody and destruction. The contents of any wire communication intercepted by any means authorized by this chapter shall, if possible, be recorded on tape or wire or other comparable device. The recording of the contents of any wire communication in accordance with the provisions of this section shall be done in such manner as will protect the recording from editing or other alterations. Immediately upon the expiration of the period of the order, or extensions thereof, such recordings shall be made available to the panel and sealed under its directions and custody of such recordings shall be wherever the panel so directs. They shall not be destroyed except upon an order of the panel and, if not so destroyed, they shall be kept for ten years. Duplicate recordings may be made by the applicant for his use or for disclosure pursuant to the provisions of section 54-41p for investigations. The presence of the seal provided for by this section, or a satisfactory explanation for the absence thereof, shall be a prerequisite for the use or disclosure of the contents of any wire communication or evidence derived therefrom under the provisions of section 54-41p.

(1971, P.A. 68, S. 9; P.A. 99-215, S. 13.)

History: P.A. 99-215 deleted "issuing such order" after "panel" and "issuing or denying" before "panel".

Cited. 191 C. 360; 212 C. 485; 238 C. 692.

Cited. 8 CA 673; 16 CA 245.

Sec. 54-41j. Sealing, custody, storage and destruction of applications and orders.

Applications made and orders granted in accordance with the provisions of this chapter shall be sealed by the panel and transferred to the custody of the Chief Court Administrator. Except as otherwise provided, such applications and orders shall be disclosed only upon a showing of good cause to the Chief Court Administrator. Applications and orders shall be stored in a secure place which shall be designated by the Chief Court Administrator to which access shall be denied to all persons except the Chief Court Administrator or such court officers or administrative personnel as he shall designate. Applications and orders shall not be destroyed except upon order of the Chief Court Administrator and if not so destroyed they shall be kept for ten years. Any person who violates any of the provisions of this section may be punished in accordance with the provisions of section 51-33.

(1971, P.A. 68, S. 10; P.A. 76-436, S. 10a, 533, 681; P.A. 99-215, S. 14.)

History: P.A. 76-436 made no changes, Sec. 10a of the act cancelling amendments called for in Sec. 533; P.A. 99-215 deleted "issuing or denying" before "panel".

Cited. 191 C. 360; 212 C. 485; 238 C. 692.

Sec. 54-41k. Service of notice of interception; inspection of intercepted communications, applications and orders; postponement of service.

Within a reasonable time but not later than ninety days next succeeding the termination of the period of an order or extensions thereof, the panel may cause to be served on the persons named in the order or the application, and shall cause to be served on persons not named in the order or application whose communications were intercepted, an inventory which shall include notice of the fact of the entry of the order or the application; the date of the entry and the period of authorized interception, or the denial of the application; and the fact that during the period wire communications were or were not intercepted. The panel shall make available to such person or his counsel for inspection the intercepted communications, applications and orders immediately upon the filing of a motion requesting such information. On an ex parte showing of good cause approved unanimously by the panel the serving of the inventory required by this section may be postponed for a period not to exceed sixty days. Not more than one such postponement shall be authorized and under no circumstances shall the serving of the inventory required by this section be made later than one hundred fifty days after the termination of the period of an order or extensions thereof.

(1971, P.A. 68, S. 11; P.A. 82-368, S. 8; P.A. 99-215, S. 15.)

History: P.A. 82-368 gave the panel discretion in ordering the service of an inventory, included persons not named in the order whose communications were intercepted as entitled to any such inventory and extended from 90 to 150 days the maximum period of postponement of such inventory; P.A. 99-215 deleted "issuing or denying" before "panel".

Cited. 191 C. 360; 212 C. 485; 224 C. 593; 238 C. 692.

Strict compliance with provisions of statute is mandatory. 3 CA 477. Cited. 10 CA 347. Service of inventory requirement discussed. 14 CA 605. Cited. 16 CA 245.

When delivery of document to defendant's attorney deemed adequate service. 30 CS 302.

Sec. 54-41*l*. Intercepted communication admissible as evidence, when.

The contents of any intercepted wire communication or evidence derived therefrom shall not be received in evidence or otherwise disclosed in any trial, hearing or other proceeding in a court of this state unless each aggrieved person, not less than thirty days before such trial, hearing or proceeding, has been served with a copy of the court order, and accompanying application, under which the interception was authorized.

(1971, P.A. 68, S. 12.)

Cited. 191 C. 360; 212 C. 485; 238 C. 253; Id., 692.

Notice not required prior to issuance of bench warrant. 30 CS 302.

Sec. 54-41m. Motion to suppress.

Any aggrieved person in any trial, hearing or proceeding in or before any court, department, officer, agency, regulatory body or other authority of the state of Connecticut, or of a political subdivision thereof, may move to suppress the contents of any intercepted wire communication, or evidence derived therefrom, on the grounds that the communication was unlawfully intercepted under the provisions of this chapter; the order of authorization or approval under which it was intercepted is insufficient on its face; or the interception was not made in conformity with the order of authorization or approval. Such motion shall be made before the trial, hearing or proceeding unless there was no opportunity to make such motion or the person was not aware of the grounds of the motion, in which case such motion may be made at any time during the course of such trial, hearing or proceeding. If the motion is granted, the contents of the intercepted wire communication, or evidence derived therefrom, shall be treated as having been obtained in violation of this chapter and shall not be received in evidence in any such trial, hearing or proceeding. The panel, upon the filing of such motion by the aggrieved person, shall make available to the aggrieved person or his counsel for inspection the intercepted communication and evidence derived therefrom.

(1971, P.A. 68, S. 13.)

Cited. 176 C. 17. Motion to suppress upheld since state's attorney failed to make formal oath or affirmation in connection with application. 180 C. 345. Cited. 191 C. 360; 194 C. 447; 199 C. 591; 212 C. 485; 224 C. 593; 238 C. 692.

Cited. 3 CA 477; 5 CA 634; 7 CA 660; 10 CA 347; 14 CA 605; 27 CA 596; 44 CA 249.

Cited. 30 CS 302.

Sec. 54-41n. Report by panel to Chief Court Administrator.

In addition to any reports required by federal law, within thirty days next succeeding the expiration of an order or an extension thereof, or the denial of an application, the panel shall report to the Chief Court Administrator the fact that an order or extension was applied for; the fact that the order or extension was granted as applied for, was modified or was denied; the period of interceptions authorized by the order, and the number and duration of any extensions of the order; the offense or offenses specified in the order or application, or extension of an order; the identity of the person making the application and the nature of the facilities from which or the place where communications were to be intercepted.

(1971, P.A. 68, S. 14; P.A. 76-436, S. 10a, 534, 681; P.A. 99-215, S. 16.)

History: P.A. 76-436 made no change, Sec. 10a of the act cancelling amendment called for in Sec. 534; P.A. 99-215 deleted "issuing or denying" before "panel".

Cited. 191 C. 360; 212 C. 485; 238 C. 692.

Sec. 54-41o. **Reports by state's attorneys.** (a) In January of each year each state's attorney shall report to the administrative office of the United States courts and to the Chief Court Administrator, who shall in turn report to the Governor and the General Assembly, the information required by this section with respect to each application for an order or extension made during the preceding calendar year; a general description of the interception made under such order or extension, including (1) the approximate nature and frequency of incriminating communications intercepted, (2) the approximate nature and frequency of other communications intercepted, (3) the approximate number of persons whose communications were intercepted, and (4) the approximate nature, amount and cost of the manpower and other resources used in the interceptions; the number of arrests resulting from interceptions made under such order or extension, and the offenses for which arrests were made; the number of trials resulting from such interceptions; the number of motions to suppress made with respect to such interceptions, and the number granted or denied; the number of convictions resulting from such interceptions and the offenses for which the convictions were obtained and a general assessment of the importance of the interceptions; and the information required by this section with respect to orders or extensions obtained in the calendar year next preceding.

(b) In January of each year, the Chief State's Attorney shall make a report to the joint standing committee of the General Assembly having cognizance of matters relating to criminal law and procedure, based upon reports filed with him by each state's attorney covering the prior calendar year. The Chief State's Attorney's report shall include the following information: (1) The number of orders authorizing an interception, and the number of extensions thereof; (2) the number of additional orders granted based upon an emergency situation, and the nature of the emergency; (3) the nature of the particular offense to which each order was directed; (4) a general description of the interception made under each order or extension, including (A) the nature and frequency of incriminating communications intercepted, (B) the nature and frequency of other communications intercepted, (C) the number of persons whose communications were intercepted, and (D) the nature, amount and cost of the manpower and other resources used in the interceptions; (5) the number of arrests resulting from interceptions made under each order or extension, and the offenses for which such arrests were made; (6) the number of trials resulting from such interceptions; (7) the number of motions to suppress made with respect to such interceptions, and the number granted or denied; (8) the number of convictions resulting from such interceptions and the offenses for which the convictions were obtained and (9) the number of persons who were not named in an order or application for the interception of wire communications and whose communications were intercepted.

(1971, P.A. 68, S. 15; P.A. 76-436, S. 10a, 535, 681; P.A. 79-631, S. 34, 111; P.A. 82-368, S. 9; P.A. 83-587, S. 66, 96.)

History: P.A. 76-436 made no changes. Sec. 10a of the act cancelling amendment called for in Sec. 535; P.A. 79-631 deleted requirement that chief court administrator report to the judicial council; P.A. 82-368 added Subsec. (b) dealing with the report by the chief state's attorney to the joint standing committee of the general assembly having cognizance of matters relating to criminal law and procedure; P.A. 83-587 made a technical amendment to Subsec. (b).

Cited. 191 C. 360; 212 C. 485; 238 C. 692.

Sec. 54-41p. **Disclosure of contents of wire communication. Unauthorized disclosure: Class D felony.**

(a) Any investigative officer who, by any means authorized by this chapter, has obtained knowledge of the contents of any wire communication, or evidence derived therefrom, may, if specially authorized by the order authorizing the interception of such communication, disclose such contents to any investigative or law enforcement officer designated in such order to the extent that such disclosure is appropriate to the conduct of the investigation specified in the application for such order.

(b) Any person who has received, by any means authorized by this chapter, any information concerning a wire communication, or evidence derived therefrom, intercepted in accordance with the provisions of this chapter may disclose the contents of that communication or such derivative evidence insofar as it relates to the crimes set forth in section 54-41b while giving testimony under oath or affirmation in any criminal proceeding before any court or grand jury.

(c) If an investigative officer, while engaged in the interception of wire communications in accordance with the provisions of this chapter, intercepts wire communications relating to any crime not specified in the order authorizing such interception, the contents of such intercepted communications and evidence derived therefrom may be disclosed as otherwise provided in subsection (a) of this section.

(d) Any investigative officer who discloses the contents of any intercepted wire communication or evidence derived therefrom (1) to any person not authorized to receive such information or (2) in a manner otherwise than authorized by the provisions of this chapter shall be guilty of a class D felony.

(1971, P.A. 68, S. 16; P.A. 79-179, S. 7; P.A. 82-368, S. 10; P.A. 05-288, S. 184.)

History: P.A. 79-179 removed law enforcement officers' power to disclose contents of wire communication to an investigative officer or to another law enforcement officer; P.A. 82-368 designated previous provisions as Subsecs. (a) and (b) and added Subsecs. (c) and (d) re interception of communications unrelated to crimes specified in the order and re consideration of unauthorized disclosure as a class D felony; P.A. 05-288 made a technical change in Subsec. (c), effective July 13, 2005.

Cited. 191 C. 360; 212 C. 485; 223 C. 906; 224 C. 322; Id., 593; 238 C. 692.

Cited. 27 CA 596.

Sec. 54-41q. Authority of communication common carrier to intercept, disclose or use wire communication.

(a) It shall not be unlawful under this chapter for an operator of a switchboard, or an officer, employee or agent of any communication common carrier whose facilities are used in the transmission of a wire communication, to intercept, disclose or use that communication in the normal course of his employment while engaged in any activity which is a necessary incident to the rendition of his service or to the protection of the rights or property of the carrier of such communication, provided such communication common carriers shall not utilize service observing or random monitoring except for mechanical or service quality control checks.

(b) It shall not be unlawful under this chapter for an officer, employee or agent of any communications common carrier to provide information or facilities to an investigative officer who, pursuant to this chapter, is authorized to intercept a wire communication.

(1971, P.A. 68, S. 17; P.A. 79-179, S. 8.)

History: P.A. 79-179 authorized officer, employee or agent of communications common carrier to provide information or facilities to investigative officers rather than to law enforcement officers in Subsec. (b).

Cited. 191 C. 360; 212 C. 485.

Sec. 54-41r. Remedies of party intercepted; defense.

Any person whose wire communication is intercepted, disclosed or used in violation of this chapter or of sections 53a-187 to 53a-189, inclusive, shall (1) have a civil cause of action against any person who intercepts, discloses or uses, or procures any other person to intercept, disclose or use, such communication, and (2) be entitled to recover from any such person actual damages but not less than liquidated damages computed at the rate of one hundred dollars per day for each day of violation or one thousand dollars, whichever is higher; punitive damages; and a reasonable attorney's fee and other litigation costs reasonably incurred. A good faith reliance on a court order shall constitute a complete defense to any civil or criminal action brought in accordance with the provisions of this chapter or any other law.

(1971, P.A. 68, S. 18.)

Cited. 191 C. 360; 212 C. 485; 224 C. 593.

Cited. 3 CA 477; 14 CA 605.

Cited. 30 CS 302.

Sec. 54-41s. Illegal possession, sale, distribution of equipment: Class D felony

. A person is guilty of the illegal possession, sale or distribution of electronic surveillance equipment when he possesses, sells or distributes an electronic, mechanical or other device, as defined in section 54-41a for use in violation of section 53a-188 or 53a-189. The illegal possession, sale or distribution of electronic surveillance equipment is a class D felony.

(P.A. 73-639, S. 22.)

Cited. 191 C. 360; 212 C. 485; 224 C. 593.

Sec. 54-41t. Unauthorized or illegal interception: Class C felony. Any investigative officer who intercepts the wire communications of any person in violation of the provisions of this chapter shall be guilty of a class C felony.

(P.A. 82-368, S. 11.)

Cited. 191 C. 360; 212 C. 485; 224 C. 593; 238 C. 692.

Cited. 16 CA 245.

Sec. 54-41u. Admissibility of intercepted wire communication obtained pursuant to federal law.

Nothing in this chapter shall preclude the receipt in evidence in a court of this state of any intercepted wire communication obtained in conformity with 18 USC 2510 et seq.

(P.A. 02-97, S. 14.)

CHAPTER 960* INFORMATION, PROCEDURE AND BAIL

*Until a statement, or an act, or a writing is determined to come within the definition of a confession, there is no requirement that the corpus delicti be established before the admission of the evidence. 22 CS 507.

Table of Contents

Secs. 54-42 to 54-44. Original information in Superior Court. Bench warrant; procedure on arrest; previous bond in Court of Common Pleas. Admissibility of confession. Informations in cases appealed to Superior Court.

Sec. 54-45. When grand jury is required. Selecting grand jury. Alternate grand jurors.

Sec. 54-45a. Record of grand jury proceedings. Transcripts.

Sec. 54-46. Prosecution on complaint or information.

Sec. 54-46a. Probable cause hearing for persons charged with crimes punishable by death, life imprisonment without possibility of release or life imprisonment.

Sec. 54-47. Investigations into commission of crime.

Sec. 54-47a. Compelling testimony of witness. Immunity from prosecution.

Sec. 54-47b. Investigatory grand jury. Definitions.

Sec. 54-47c. Application for investigation into commission of crime.

Sec. 54-47d. Appointment of investigatory grand jury. Duration and scope of investigation.

Sec. 54-47e. Sealing of order and application. Summary of scope of investigation. Disclosure.

Sec. 54-47f. Conduct of investigation. Testimony of witnesses.

Sec. 54-47g. Finding and record of investigation. Disclosure. Hearing. Access to testimony.

Sec. 54-47h. Report.

Sec. 54-47i. Authority of investigation ordered prior to October 1, 1985.

Secs. 54-47j to 54-47z. **Reserved**

Sec. 54-47aa. Ex parte order to compel disclosure of or direct application to carrier or provider for certain telephone and Internet records.

Sec. 54-48. Reward for arrest of capital offender or felon.

Sec. 54-49. Reward for information as to high crime or crime resulting in death of police officer or firefighter.

Sec. 54-50. Reward for information as to unlawful disinterment of corpse.

Sec. 54-51. Reward for information as to theft of motor vehicle, livestock or poultry.

Sec. 54-52. Determination of claims to reward.

Sec. 54-53. Release by correctional officials.

Sec. 54-53a. Detention of persons who have not made bail.

Secs. 54-54 and 54-55. Original information in Court of Common Pleas. Information in cases appealed to Court of Common Pleas.

Sec. 54-56. Dismissal of information by court.

Sec. 54-56a. (Formerly Sec. 54-2b). Pleading by mail in certain motor vehicle cases.

Sec. 54-56b. Right to dismissal or trial on nolle.

Sec. 54-56c. Request for privileged trial status.

Sec. 54-56d. (Formerly Sec. 54-40). Competency to stand trial.

Sec. 54-56e. (Formerly Sec. 54-76p). Accelerated pretrial rehabilitation.

Sec. 54-56f. (Formerly Sec. 54-5). Requirements of sureties of the peace.

Sec. 54-56g. Pretrial alcohol education program.

Sec. 54-56h. Consideration of defendant's contribution to Criminal Injuries Compensation Fund or of community service work hours. Payment of monetary contribution to fund.

Sec. 54-56i. Pretrial drug education and community service program.

Sec. 54-56j. Pretrial school violence prevention program.

Sec. 54-56k. Pretrial account.

Sec. 54-56l. Pretrial supervised diversionary program for persons with psychiatric disabilities and veterans.

Sec. 54-56m. Mediation programs.

Sec. 54-56n. Pretrial and diversionary program data collection and reporting.

Sec. 54-56o. Nolle prosequi in certain family violence cases.

Sec. 54-56p. Program for young persons charged with a motor vehicle violation or alcohol-related offense.

Sec. 54-57. Joinder of offenses of the same character.

Sec. 54-58. Description of money in complaint or information.

Sec. 54-59. Statement of ownership, partnership or joint tenancy in indictment, information or complaint.

Sec. 54-60. Allegations in criminal cases.

Sec. 54-61. Complaints for offenses specified in special acts, ordinances and bylaws.

Sec. 54-62. Allegation of previous conviction.

Sec. 54-63. Mode of informing against larceny by embezzlement.

Sec. 54-63a. Definitions.

Sec. 54-63b. Pretrial release of arrested persons. Duties of Court Support Services Division. Uniform weighted release criteria.

Sec. 54-63c. Duties of law enforcement officer or probation officer serving warrant re arrested person. Interview and release of arrested person.

Sec. 54-63d. Release by bail commissioner or intake, assessment and referral specialist. Information, files and reports held by Court Support Services Division.

Sec. 54-63e. Bond or promise conditioned on appearance.

Sec. 54-63f. Release after conviction and pending sentence or appeal.

Sec. 54-63g. Appeal from court order re release.

Sec. 54-64. Police officials and clerks of court to take promise to appear or bond.

Sec. 54-64a. Release by judicial authority.

Sec. 54-64b. Release following arrest on court warrant.

Sec. 54-64c. Notice of appearance after release.

Sec. 54-64d. Release of person taken into custody on a capias.

Sec. 54-64e. Noncriminal behavior as condition of release. Notice of conditions of release and sanctions for violation.

Sec. 54-64f. Violation of conditions of release. Imposition of different or additional conditions. Revocation of release.

Sec. 54-64g. Surveillance of serious felony offenders released on bond.

Sec. 54-65. Procedure when surety believes principal intends to abscond. Application for release of surety from bond if principal absconds.

Sec. 54-65a. Forfeiture of bond for failure to appear. Issuance of rearrest warrant or capias. Termination or reinstatement of bond. Rebate to surety.

Sec. 54-65b. Verification of rearrest warrant or capias upon request.

Sec. 54-65c. Vacating forfeiture of bond.

Sec. 54-66. Acceptance and disposition of bail. Pledge of real property as lien. Forfeiture of bond for failure to appear. Issuance of rearrest warrant or capias.
Termination or reinstatement of bond.

Sec. 54-66a. Automatic termination of bail bonds.

Sec. 54-67. When attorneys not allowed to give bonds.

Sec. 54-68. Persons charged with gaming to give bonds.

Sec. 54-69. Motion of parties to modify conditions of release.

Sec. 54-69a. Motion of bail commissioner or intake, assessment and referral specialist to modify conditions of release.

Sec. 54-69b. Authority of court to modify conditions of release.

Sec. 54-70. Compromise of forfeited bonds.

Sec. 54-71. Mistake in form of recognizance.

Sec. 54-71a. No civil liability for release.

Sec. 54-72. Fines and forfeitures; prosecutions; liability of corporation.

Sec. 54-73. Collection and disposition of forfeitures.

Sec. 54-74. Remission of fine.

Sec. 54-75. Employment of detectives.

Sec. 54-76. **Transferred**

Sec. 54-76a. Procedure at hearing in probable cause.

Secs. 54-42 to 54-44. Original information in Superior Court. Bench warrant; procedure on arrest; previous bond in Court of Common Pleas. Admissibility of confession. Informations in cases appealed to Superior Court. Sections 54-42 to 54-44, inclusive, are repealed.

(1949 Rev., S. 8764-8766; 1963, P.A. 126, S. 2, 3; 1967, P.A. 656, S. 60; 1969, P.A. 803, S. 1; P.A. 73-116, S. 23; 73-667, S. 1, 2; P.A. 76-106, S. 1; 76-436, S. 536, 681; P.A. 77-452, S. 38, 72; 77-576, S. 39, 65; P.A. 80-313, S. 61; 80-483, S. 136, 186.)

Sec. 54-45. When grand jury is required. Selecting grand jury. Alternate grand jurors.

(a) The Superior Court may, when necessary, order a grand jury of eighteen electors of the judicial district where said court is sitting to be summoned, impaneled and sworn to inquire after and present such offenses as are cognizable by said court. Said court may, in its discretion, order one or two additional electors to be added to the grand jury as alternate grand jurors. Such alternate jurors shall be sworn separately from those constituting the regular panel and shall not counsel or confer with members of the regular panel as to any matters before the grand jury unless they become a part of the regular panel as hereinafter provided. They shall attend the sessions of the grand jury and shall be seated with or near the members of the regular panel, with equal opportunity to see and hear all matters adduced in the proceedings. If for any reason a grand juror is unable to further perform his duty, the court may excuse him and, if any grand juror is so excused or dies, the court may order that the alternate juror or, if more than one, that one who is designated by lot drawn by the clerk of the Superior Court, shall become a part of the regular panel and the inquiry shall then proceed as though such grand juror had been a member of the regular panel from the beginning of the inquiry.

(b) No person shall be put to plea or held to trial for any crime the punishment of which may be death or imprisonment for life, charged by the state before May 26, 1983, unless an indictment has been found against him for such crime by a grand jury legally impaneled and sworn, and no bill shall be presented by any grand jury unless at least twelve of the jurors agree to it.

(1949 Rev., S. 8747; February, 1965, P.A. 173; P.A. 73-116, S. 1; 73-667, S. 1, 2; P.A. 78-280, S. 2, 127; P.A. 80-313, S. 3; P.A. 83-210, S. 3, 5.)

History: 1965 act added provisions for alternate grand jurors; P.A. 73-116 added reference to judicial districts; P.A. 73-667 changed effective date of P.A. 73-116 from October 1, 1973, to April 25, 1973; P.A. 78-280 deleted reference to counties; P.A. 80-313 divided section into Subsecs; P.A. 83-210 amended Subsec. (b) to require a grand jury indictment for crimes punishable by death or imprisonment for life "charged by the state before May 26, 1983" to reflect the establishment of a probable cause hearing pursuant to Sec. 54-46a in place of a grand jury proceeding for persons accused of such crimes.

See Sec. 1-25 re forms of oaths for jurors.

Powers and duties of grand jury. 1 C. 428. Where death or imprisonment for life is not penalty, no grand jury necessary. 3 C. 112. Inquiry before grand jury must be secret. 16 C. 467. Not necessary that accused be present. 21 C. 279. Quaere, whether member of grand jury may be challenged for favor; if absolute disqualification is discovered after indictment found, it may be pleaded in avoidance. 47 C. 106. The endorsement of a "true bill" on an indictment cannot be contradicted by parol evidence on habeas corpus proceedings; 67 C. 553; and, in habeas corpus proceedings in U.S. courts, failure to so endorse is not regarded. 160 U.S. 231. When required, an interpreter may be present in the grand jury room. 106 C. 721. When an accused person is confined for a crime punishable by death or life imprisonment, it is the duty of the court to order a grand jury; and this may be done before opening of term to which accused was bound over. Id., 719. When court may select members of grand jury. 126 C. 64. In a general investigation by grand jury, state's attorney may be present to aid in examination of witnesses. Id., 66. Jury may have stenographer present; what evidence jury may elicit. Id., 71. Constitution does not protect a person from being questioned by grand jury but only gives immunity from answering particular questions; history and nature of grand jury. Id., 72. Cited. 135 C. 269. Requires an indictment by a grand jury in all cases in which the penalty to be imposed may be life imprisonment. 144 C. 295. Grand jury in which 7 out of 18 are attorneys not in itself illegal where there is no evidence of an intentional and systematic exclusion of any group. 146 C. 137. Cited. Id., 227; 153 C. 325. There is no federal constitutional impediment to dispensing entirely with grand jury in state prosecutions. 155 C. 367. In absence of contrary evidence, presumption arises that selection of grand jury was made without discrimination and fairly by officer in charge of selection. 158 C. 341. Cited. 159 C. 264; 164 C. 402; 176 C. 270; 181 C. 268; 183 C. 299; 184 C. 597. Presence of counsel before grand jury discussed; grand jury transcript available to defendant under Subsec. (a) is made available under the inherent supervisory powers of the Superior Court and evidentiary uses of it by defendant are restricted to impeaching a witness, attacking the credibility of a witness or proving inconsistent statements of a witness. 187 C. 281. Trial court's denial of motion to quash the ordering of second grand jury is not one of those few presentence orders deemed final for purposes of appeal. 191 C. 27. During period between November 24, 1982, and May 26, 1983, statute provided authorization for use of grand juries in cases punishable by death or life imprisonment. 192 C. 671. Cited. Id., 700; 194 C. 416; Id., 692; 197 C. 247; Id., 280; Id., 507; 199 C. 163; 202 C. 18; 203 C. 641; 204 C. 259; 207 C. 276; 226 C. 601.

Cited. 4 CA 544; 10 CA 103; 27 CA 643; Id., 675.

Cited. 6 CS 221; 22 CS 6, 7. Person not given right to counsel before grand jury decision; this is not "critical stage" in proceedings against him. 25 CS 61. Grand jury is not prohibited from receiving hearsay evidence; that such evidence may have been considered by the grand jury would not entitle one who had been indicted to have the indictment quashed. Id., 388. Counsel for the accused may not accompany him before the grand jury. Id., 389. Section was fully complied with by the court and its officers in summoning grand jury in absence of a showing that any of the members were disqualified for any reason. 26 CS 211. Nature of grand jury discussed; not the state's burden to prove that the method of selection of grand jury was fair and nondiscriminatory. Id., 213. Charge to grand jury that presumption of sanity was adequate basis on which to find, so far as element of soundness of mind was concerned, probable cause to hold accused for trial, was accurate; constitutional right of accused to counsel does not include representation by counsel before a grand jury. Id., 214. Indictment insufficient in law may be attacked by demurrer; provision that grand jurors come from county where court sits is broad enough to comply with federal constitutional requirement that there must be no intentional or systematic exclusion of group or class from grand jury. 29 CS 119. Exclusion of aliens from grand jury service does not make statute unconstitutional since citizenship requirement bears rational relationship to demands of jury service. 35 CS 98. Cited. 36 CS 141; 45 CS 1.

Sec. 54-45a. Record of grand jury proceedings. Transcripts.

(a) In any grand jury proceeding ordered pursuant to the provisions of section 54-45, the official stenographer of the Superior Court or his assistant shall make a record of the proceedings excluding the deliberations, which shall be confidential and filed with the court. Access to the transcript shall be available only to the prosecutorial official or any person accused of crime as a result of the grand jury investigation or the accused person's attorney. The prosecutorial official or the person accused of a crime as a result of such grand jury investigation or the accused person's attorney may obtain a copy of the transcript by paying for it.

(b) The transcript of such proceedings may not be used as evidence in any proceeding against the accused except for the purpose of impeaching a witness, attacking the credibility of a witness or proving inconsistent statements of a witness. The transcript may also be used as evidence in a prosecution for perjury committed by a witness while giving such testimony.

(P.A. 78-289, S. 1; P.A. 80-313, S. 4.)

History: P.A. 80-313 divided section into Subsecs. and reworded provisions.

Cited. 177 C. 677; 181 C. 268; 186 C. 476. Availability and use of grand jury transcripts discussed. 187 C. 281. Cited. 193 C. 350; 194 C. 469; Id., 530; 197 C. 698; 198 C. 644; 200 C. 323; 201 C. 534. Statute governs indicting grand juries and expressly prohibits subsequent use of grand jury testimony. 250 C. 188.

Cited. 10 CA 103.

Transcript may not be used to impeach a grand jury finding of a true bill. 36 CS 141. Cited. 42 CS 10; 45 CS 1.

Sec. 54-46. Prosecution on complaint or information.

For all crimes charged by the state on or after May 26, 1983, the prosecution may be by complaint or information. For all crimes punishable by death or imprisonment for life charged by the state before May 26, 1983, the prosecution shall be by indictment.

(1949 Rev., S. 8775; P.A. 75-376; P.A. 76-336, S. 15; 76-436, S. 537, 681; P.A. 79-157; P.A. 80-313, S. 7; P.A. 83-210, S. 4, 5.)

History: P.A. 75-376 added provisions re trial on nolle prosequi; P.A. 76-336 clarified nolle provisions, substituting "At any stage in such prosecution" for "In any such prosecution"; P.A. 76-436 removed from exception cases involving nolle entered in common pleas court on matter bound over to superior court or upon recommendation of prosecutor that bench warrant is being requested or issued by superior court for arrest for same transaction, reflecting transfer of all trial jurisdiction to superior court, effective July 1, 1978; P.A. 79-157 designated previous provisions as Subsecs. (a) and (b) and added Subsec. (c) re effect of not guilty plea on privilege with respect to assignment for trial; P.A. 80-313 specified prosecution by indictment required for all crimes punishable by death or life imprisonment and deleted former Subsecs. (b) and (c) re nolle prosequi and assignment for trial; P.A. 83-210 amended the section to reflect the establishment of a probable cause hearing to replace a grand jury proceeding by providing that prosecution by complaint or information would apply to all crimes "charged by the state on or after May 26, 1983" and prosecution by indictment would only apply to persons accused of crimes punishable by death or life imprisonment "charged by the state before May 26, 1983".

See Sec. 54-56b re right to dismissal or trial on nolle.

See Sec. 54-56c re request for privileged trial status.

Section is constitutional. 60 C. 94; 135 C. 262. Information may be amended after evidence has been offered. 35 C. 319. As to particularity required. 39 C. 230; 93 C. 646. Must charge all essential elements of crime; 72 C. 606; 73 C. 407; thus, specific intent must be charged. 66 C. 250; 80 C. 614; 81 C. 699. Charging offense in words of statute. 66 C. 9; Id., 657; 72 C. 606; 73 C. 18; 80 C. 321; 81 C. 696; 83 C. 304; 97 C. 730, 735; 99 C. 117; or of city ordinance. 60 C. 106; 88 C. 715; 91 C. 68. If effect is to include acts not in purview of statute, it is not sufficient; 82 C. 321; 93 C. 646; a more particular description may limit proof. 80 C. 321. Necessity of negativing exception. 69 C. 198; 88 C. 353. Old rules as to strictness relaxed; 81 C. 696; general rule as to certainty. 85 C. 322. Aider by verdict; 68 C. 512; 81 C. 696; amendable defect not ground for new trial. 80 C. 614. Necessity of identifying person with reference to whom crime is committed; 66 C. 558; of correctly alleging date of crime. 81 C. 98. Alleging matters by legal effect; act of principal as act of agent. 69 C. 86. Allegation of former conviction. 68 C. 512; 94 C. 701; 96 C. 172. Against one as accessory. 82 C. 213. Conspiracy and acts done in pursuance of it may be alleged in one count; 75 C. 206; so keeping disorderly house and one where lewd persons resort, 66 C. 8; so keeping place for registering bets and selling pools. 66 C. 250. Merger defined; is a doctrine of very limited application. 99 C. 114; 108 C. 215. Identity of offenses. Id., 214. Cited. 151 C. 524; 153 C. 325; Id., 451. There is no federal constitutional impediment to dispensing entirely with grand jury in state prosecutions. 155 C. 367. Prosecution by information for infamous crime was not violation of defendant's rights under U.S. Constitution. 156 C. 391. Cited. 159 C. 264; 184 C. 597; 192 C. 671; 202 C. 443; 229 C. 691.

Cited. 22 CS 7. Not a denial of equal protection clause of fourteenth amendment of federal constitution to indict person by an information in larceny case. 25 CS 509.

Sec. 54-46a. Probable cause hearing for persons charged with crimes punishable by death, life imprisonment without possibility of release or life imprisonment.

(a) No person charged by the state, who has not been indicted by a grand jury prior to May 26, 1983, shall be put to plea or held to trial for any crime punishable by death, life imprisonment without the possibility of release or life imprisonment unless the court at a preliminary hearing determines there is probable cause to believe that the offense charged has been committed and that the accused person has committed it. The accused person may knowingly and voluntarily waive such preliminary hearing to determine probable cause.

(b) Unless waived by the accused person or extended by the court for good cause shown, such preliminary hearing shall be conducted within sixty days of the filing of the complaint or information in Superior Court. The court shall be confined to the rules of evidence, except that written reports of expert witnesses shall be admissible in evidence and matters involving chain of custody shall be exempt from such rules. No motion to suppress or for discovery shall be allowed in connection with such hearing. The accused person shall have the right to counsel and may attend and, either individually or by counsel, participate in such hearing, present argument to the court, cross-examine witnesses against him and obtain a transcript of the proceedings at his own expense. At the close of the prosecution's case, if the court finds that, based on the evidence presented by the prosecution, probable cause exists, the accused person may make a specific offer of proof, including the names of witnesses who would testify or produce the evidence offered. The court shall not allow the accused person to present such evidence unless the court determines that such evidence would be sufficient to rebut the finding of probable cause.

(c) If, from the evidence presented pursuant to subsection (b) of this section, it appears to the court that there is probable cause to believe that the accused person has committed the offense charged, the court shall so find and approve the continuance of the accused person's prosecution for that offense. A determination by the court that there is not probable cause to require the accused person to be put to trial for the offense charged shall not operate to prevent a subsequent prosecution of such accused person for the same offense.

(P.A. 83-210, S. 1, 5; P.A. 87-260, S. 5; P.A. 12-5, S. 25.)

History: P.A. 87-260 amended Subsec. (a) to change the applicability of the requirement of a preliminary hearing from a person charged by the state "on or after May 26, 1983" to a person charged by the state "who has not been indicted by a grand jury prior to May 26, 1983"; P.A. 12-5 amended Subsec. (a) to add reference to crime punishable by life imprisonment without possibility of release, effective April 25, 2012.

Constitutional right to a probable cause hearing vested immediately for all defendants not yet indicted on May 26, 1983; portion of statute conferring right to probable cause hearing only on those charged on and after May 26, 1983, is unconstitutional and therefore invalid. 192 C. 671. Cited. 201 C. 598. Validity is not subject to constitutional attack as a violation of separation of powers. 203 C. 641. Cited. 206 C. 323; 210 C. 631; Id., 652; 211 C. 289; 213 C. 161; Id., 708; 214 C. 132; Id., 454; Id., 476; Id., 616; 218 C. 714; 220 C. 270; 221 C. 109; 222 C. 506; 223 C. 127; 224 C. 29; 228 C. 62. Probable cause hearing required by section applies only to criminal prosecutions, not to an action for adjudication of delinquency. 229 C. 691. Cited. 233 C. 106; 234 C. 97; 237 C. 58; 240 C. 727; Id., 743; 242 C. 409. Deprivation of counsel at a probable cause hearing constitutes procedural error for which harmless error review is proper. 279 C. 493.

Cited. 7 CA 457; 26 CA 165; 28 CA 34; 29 CA 499; 30 CA 381; 34 CA 58; judgment reversed, see 232 C. 537; 35 CA 762; 36 CA 250; Id., 364; 37 CA 404; 46 CA 545. Second probable cause hearing which was held after the 60-day time limit was valid because the first hearing was held within the statutory time limit and the second hearing was scheduled based on defendant's request so that defendant could be represented by counsel. 75 CA 223. Right to be heard by an impartial tribunal is guaranteed by the state and federal constitutions and need not be recited in each section delineating criminal procedure, therefore section is constitutional. 151 CA 574.

Cited. 40 CS 38; 42 CS 426; 43 CS 38; Id., 367.

Subsec. (a):

Cited. 204 C. 120; 209 C. 133. Death penalty unconstitutional under Art. I, Secs. 8 and 9 of Connecticut Constitution. 318 C. 1.

Cited. 19 CA 571; 41 CA 809; 44 CA 790. By unconditionally accepting a plea deal and pleading guilty, petitioner waived any challenge to court's jurisdiction over his person; statute on its face contains terms "any crime", "the offense" and "it" when mandating that defendant exposed to punishment of life imprisonment or death be given preliminary hearing in probable cause; there is nothing in the statute that refers to crimes, offenses or an aggregation of crimes or offenses, and petitioner has referred to no case law or other statute that has interpreted the statute to require probable cause hearing when the aggregate of the charges exposes defendant to 60 years imprisonment, but the crimes, when considered individually, expose defendant to less than 60 years on each charge; when the state amends an information and defendant no longer faces possibility of a life sentence, it is not improper for trial court to proceed without affording defendant a hearing in probable cause. 105 CA 124.

Subsec. (b):

Court concluded statute constitutional when read in conjunction with prosecution's ongoing constitutional duty to disclose exculpatory material to a criminal defendant independent of a defense motion or request. 200 C. 323. Cited. 216 C. 492. No constitutional duty requires a court to entertain motions to suppress at a probable cause hearing. 218 C. 151. Cited. 229 C. 716; 238 C. 588. Waiver of time period in which to hold hearing may be asserted by attorney for defendant and does not require defendant personally to appear and be canvassed. 245 C. 301.

Legislature, in enacting Subsec., required that probable cause hearing must be conducted within 60 days of filing of the complaint or information unless waived by defendant or extended by the court for good cause shown. 79 CA 535.

Sec. 54-47. Investigations into commission of crime. Section 54-47 is repealed.

(1949 Rev., S. 8777; 1953, S. 3324d; 1969, P.A. 631, S. 2; 1971, P.A. 860; P.A. 73-116, S. 2; 73-667, S. 1, 2; P.A. 74-183, S. 139, 291; 74-186, S. 2, 12; P.A. 76-436, S. 10a, 538, 681; P.A. 78-280, S. 1, 127; P.A. 80-313, S. 5; P.A. 85-611, S. 9.)

Sec. 54-47a. Compelling testimony of witness. Immunity from prosecution.

(a) Whenever in the judgment of the Chief State's Attorney, a state's attorney or the deputy chief state's attorney, the testimony of any witness or the production of books, papers or other evidence of any witness (1) in any criminal proceeding involving narcotics, arson, bribery, gambling, election law violations, felonious crimes of violence, any violation which is an offense under the provisions of title 22a, corruption in the executive, legislative or judicial branch of state government or in the government of any political subdivision of the state, fraud by a vendor of goods or services in the medical assistance program under Title XIX of the Social Security Act amendments of 1965, as amended, any violation of chapter 949c, or any other class A, B or C felony or unclassified felony punishable by a term of imprisonment in excess of five years for which the Chief State's Attorney or state's attorney demonstrates that he has no other means of obtaining sufficient information as to whether a crime has been committed or the identity of the person or persons who may have committed a crime, before a court or grand jury of this state or (2) in any investigation conducted by an investigatory grand jury as provided in sections 54-47b to 54-47g, inclusive, is necessary to the public interest, the Chief State's Attorney, the state's attorney, or the deputy chief state's attorney, may, with notice to the witness, after the witness has claimed his privilege against self-incrimination, make application to the court for an order directing the witness to testify or produce evidence subject to the provisions of this section.

(b) Upon the issuance of the order such witness shall not be excused from testifying or from producing books, papers or other evidence in such case or proceeding on the ground that the testimony or evidence required of him may tend to incriminate him or subject him to a penalty or forfeiture. No such witness may be prosecuted or subjected to any penalty or forfeiture for or on account of any transaction, matter or thing concerning which he is compelled to testify or produce evidence, and no testimony or evidence so compelled, and no evidence discovered as a result of or otherwise derived from testimony or evidence so compelled, may be used as evidence against him in any proceeding, except that no witness shall be immune from prosecution for perjury or contempt committed while giving such testimony or producing such evidence. Whenever evidence is objected to as inadmissible because it was discovered as a result of or otherwise derived from compelled testimony or evidence, the burden shall be upon the person offering the challenged evidence to establish a source independent of the compelled testimony or evidence.

(1969, P.A. 631, S. 1; P.A. 74-183, S. 140, 291; 74-227, S. 1, 2; P.A. 76-436, S. 539, 681; P.A. 78-96, S. 3-5; P.A. 80-313, S. 6; P.A. 81-104; P.A. 85-611, S. 8; P.A. 87-350, S. 4, 6.)

History: P.A. 74-183 replaced circuit court with court of common pleas in accordance with reorganization of the judicial system, effective December 31, 1974; P.A. 74-227 deleted reference to prosecuting attorneys, added references to chief state's attorney, deputy chief state's attorneys, state referees, superior court judges and three-judge panels and extended applicability of provisions to cases involving violation of election laws; P.A. 76-436 deleted references to court of common pleas, reflecting transfer of all trial jurisdiction to superior court, effective July 1, 1978; P.A. 78-96 applied provisions to violations which are offenses under Title 25 provisions; P.A. 80-313 divided section into Subsecs. and made minor wording changes in Subsec. (b); P.A. 81-104 provided that immunity from prosecution may be granted to any witness in a criminal proceeding involving arson or bribery; P.A. 85-611 amended Subsec. (a) to replace reference to repealed Sec. 54-47 with provision that testimony or evidence may be compelled "in any investigation conducted by an investigatory grand jury as provided in sections 54-47b to 54-47g, inclusive"; P.A. 87-350 added provisions re criminal proceeding involving violation of title 22a, corruption in executive, legislative or judicial branch of state government or in government of political subdivision of state, fraud by a vendor of goods or services in the medical assistance program under Title XIX of the Social Security Act amendments of 1965, any violation of chapter 949c or any other class A, B or C felony or unclassified felony punishable by a term of imprisonment in excess of five years for which chief state's attorney or state's attorney demonstrates that he has no other means of obtaining sufficient information as to whether crime has been committed or identity of person who may have committed a crime.

Section to be used to secure testimony for prosecution; as there is no other statutory authority granting immunity, there is no basis for granting immunity to witness for the defense. 170 C. 206. Cited. 172 C. 542, 561. Assistant state's attorney has authority pursuant to this section, in conjunction with Sec. 51-278, to make applications for immunity grants. 174 C. 16. One who has been granted immunity is not incompetent witness, although fact of immunity may bear upon weight given testimony of witness granted immunity. Id., 287. Cited. 191 C. 670; 201 C. 559; 202 C. 541; 204 C. 259. Defendant lacks standing to challenge procedure by which a witness has been immunized. 206 C. 203. Cited. 207 C. 98; 213 C. 66; 221 C. 625. A grant of immunity pursuant to section includes both use immunity and transactional immunity. 298 C. 404.

Cited. 16 CA 679; 17 CA 395; 20 CA 447; 33 CA 521.

Cited. 45 CS 1.

Sec. 54-47b. Investigatory grand jury. Definitions.

For the purposes of sections 54-47a to 54-47h, inclusive:

(1) "Applicant" means any judge of the Superior Court, Appellate Court or Supreme Court, the Chief State's Attorney or a state's attorney who makes an application to a panel of judges for an investigation into the commission of a crime or crimes.

(2) "Crime or crimes" means (A) any crime or crimes involving corruption in the executive, legislative or judicial branch of state government or in the government of any political subdivision of the state, (B) fraud by a vendor of goods or services in the medical assistance program under Title XIX of the Social Security Act Amendments of 1965, as amended, (C) any violation of chapter 949c, (D) any violation of the election laws of the state, (E) any felony involving the unlawful use or threatened use of physical force or violence committed with the intent to intimidate or coerce the civilian population or a unit of government, and (F) any other class A, B or C felony or any unclassified felony punishable by a term of imprisonment in excess of five years for which the Chief State's Attorney or state's attorney demonstrates that he or she has no other means of obtaining sufficient information as to whether a crime has been committed or the identity of the person or persons who may have committed a crime.

(3) "Investigatory grand jury" means a judge, constitutional state referee or any three judges of the Superior Court, other than a judge designated by the Chief Justice to serve on the panel, appointed by the Chief Court Administrator to conduct an investigation into the commission of a crime or crimes.

(4) "Panel of judges" or "panel" means a panel of three Superior Court judges designated by the Chief Justice of the Supreme Court from time to time to receive applications for investigations into the commission of crimes in accordance with the provisions of sections 54-47a to 54-47h, inclusive, one of whom may be the Chief Court Administrator.

(P.A. 85-611, S. 1; P.A. 87-350, S. 1, 6; P.A. 02-97, S. 11.)

History: P.A. 87-350 added any violation of the election laws of the state or any unclassified felony punishable by a term of imprisonment in excess of five years to definition of "crime or crimes", added "or state's attorney" after "chief states attorney" and added "or the identity of the person or persons who may have committed a crime"; P.A. 02-97 amended definition of "crime or crimes" in Subdiv. (2) by adding new Subpara. (E) re any felony involving the unlawful use or threatened use of physical force or violence committed with the intent to intimidate or coerce the civilian population or a unit of government, redesignating former Subpara. (E) as Subpara. (F) and making a technical change for purposes of gender neutrality.

Cited. 202 C. 541; 204 C. 259; 207 C. 98; 213 C. 66; 221 C. 625.

Cited. 16 CA 679; 17 CA 395; 20 CA 447.

Cited. 45 CS 1.

Sec. 54-47c. Application for investigation into commission of crime. (a) Any judge of the Superior Court, Appellate Court or Supreme Court, the Chief State's Attorney or a state's attorney may make application to a panel of judges for an investigation into the commission of a crime or crimes whenever such applicant has reasonable belief that the administration of justice requires an investigation to determine whether or not there is probable cause to believe that a crime or crimes have been committed.

(b) Each application for an investigation into the commission of a crime or crimes shall be made in writing upon oath or affirmation to a panel of judges. Each application shall include the following information: (1) The identity of the applicant and his authority to make such application; (2) a full and complete statement of the facts and circumstances relied upon by the applicant to justify his reasonable belief that the investigation will lead to a finding of probable cause that a crime or crimes have been committed; and (3) a full and complete statement of the facts concerning all previous applications known to the applicant, made to any panel of judges, for investigation of any one or more of the same criminal offenses involving any of the same persons specified in the application, including the action taken by the panel on each such application. The panel of judges may require such additional testimony or documentary evidence in support of facts in the application as it deems necessary. Such additional testimony shall be transcribed.

(c) If the application is made by the Chief State's Attorney or a state's attorney, it shall also include (1) a full and complete statement of the status of the investigation and of the evidence collected as of the date of such application, (2) if other normal investigative procedures have been tried with respect to the alleged crime, a full and complete statement specifying the other normal investigative procedures that have been tried and the reasons such procedures have failed or the specific nature of the alleged crime or the nature of the investigation that leads the applicant to reasonably conclude that the use of normal investigative procedures would not result in the obtaining of information that would advance the investigation or would fail to secure and preserve evidence or testimony that might otherwise be compromised, (3) if other normal investigative procedures have not been tried, a full and complete statement of the reasons such procedures reasonably appear to be unlikely to succeed if tried or be too dangerous to employ, and (4) a full and complete statement of the reasons for the applicant's belief that the appointment of an investigatory grand jury and the investigative procedures employed by such investigatory grand jury will lead to a finding of probable cause that a crime or crimes have been committed.

(d) The panel may approve the application and order an investigation into the commission of a crime or crimes if it finds that (1) the administration of justice requires an investigation to determine whether or not there is probable cause to believe that a crime or crimes have been committed, (2) if the application was made by the Chief State's Attorney or a state's attorney, other normal investigative procedures with respect to the alleged crime have been tried and have failed or reasonably appear to be unlikely to succeed if tried or be too dangerous to employ or, due to the specific nature of the alleged crime or the nature of the investigation, it is reasonable to conclude that the use of normal investigative procedures would not result in the obtaining of information that would advance the investigation or would fail to secure and preserve evidence or testimony that might otherwise be compromised, and (3) the investigative procedures employed by an investigatory grand jury appear likely to succeed in determining whether or not there is probable cause to believe that a crime or crimes have been committed.

(P.A. 85-611, S. 2; P.A. 87-350, S. 2, 6; P.A. 98-48, S. 2; P.A. 03-273, S. 1.)

History: P.A. 87-350 added provision re transcription of additional testimony; P.A. 98-48 designated provisions of Subsec. (b) re requirements of an application made by the Chief State's Attorney or a state's attorney as new Subsec. (c), amended said Subsec. (c) to designate provisions re the use of other normal investigative procedures as Subdivs. (2) and (3) and rephrase said provisions, add Subdiv. (1) requiring a statement of the status of the investigation and of the evidence collected as of the date of the application and add Subdiv. (4) requiring a statement of the reasons for the applicant's belief that the appointment of an investigatory grand jury and the investigative procedures employed by such grand jury will lead to a finding of probable cause that a crime or crimes have been committed, and added new Subsec. (d) authorizing the panel to approve the application and order an investigation if it makes certain findings and specifying said findings; P.A. 03-273 amended Subsec. (c)(2) to add provision re statement that specifies the specific nature of the alleged crime or the nature of the investigation that leads the applicant to reasonably conclude that the use of normal investigative procedures would not result in the obtaining of information that would advance the investigation or would fail to secure and preserve evidence or testimony that might otherwise be compromised and amended Subsec. (d)(2) to add provision re finding that, due to the specific nature of the alleged crime or the nature of the investigation, it is reasonable to conclude that the use of normal investigative procedures would not result in the obtaining of information that would advance the investigation or would fail to secure and preserve evidence or testimony that might otherwise be compromised.

Cited. 202 C. 541; 204 C. 259; 206 C. 203; 207 C. 98; 213 C. 66; 221 C. 625; 224 C. 29.

Sec. 54-47d. Appointment of investigatory grand jury. Duration and scope of investigation. (a) If the panel approves the application and orders an investigation into the commission of a crime or crimes, the Chief Court Administrator shall (1) appoint an investigatory grand jury to conduct the investigation, and (2) designate the court location in the judicial district where any motions to quash and any contempt proceedings shall be heard and any findings and records of the investigation shall be filed.

(b) Each order authorizing the investigation into the commission of a crime or crimes by the panel shall specify: (1) The date of issuance of the order, (2) the period of time within which the investigation is to be conducted, provided in no event shall the investigation be longer than six months from the date the Chief Court Administrator appoints the investigatory grand jury to conduct the investigation, unless an application for an extension of time is filed and granted pursuant to subsection (c) of this section, (3) the scope of the investigation, and (4) the panel's reasons for finding that (A) the administration of justice requires an investigation to determine whether or not there is probable cause to believe that a crime or crimes have been committed, (B) if the application was made by the Chief State's Attorney or a state's attorney, other normal investigative procedures with respect to the alleged crime have been tried and have failed or reasonably appear to be unlikely to succeed if tried or be too dangerous to employ, or, due to the specific nature of the alleged crime or the nature of the investigation, it is reasonable to conclude that the use of normal investigative procedures would not result in the obtaining of information that would advance the investigation or would fail to secure and preserve evidence or testimony that might otherwise be compromised, and (C) the investigative procedures employed by the investigatory grand jury appear likely to succeed in determining whether or not there is probable cause to believe that a crime or crimes have been committed. The panel shall retain a copy of the order and the original application and shall transmit to the investigatory grand jury, appointed pursuant to subsection (a) of this section, the original order and a copy of the application filed with the panel.

(c) The investigatory grand jury may make an application to the panel of judges for an extension of time within which to conduct its investigation or for an amendment to the scope of its investigation. The application for extension or amendment shall set forth the reasons for the necessity of such extension or amendment. No more than two extensions or amendments of an order may be granted by the issuing panel. The period of any extension shall be no longer than the panel deems necessary to achieve the purposes for which it was granted and in no event shall any extension be for a period longer than six months.

(P.A. 85-611, S. 3; P.A. 87-350, S. 3, 6; P.A. 98-48, S. 3; P.A. 03-273, S. 2.)

History: P.A. 87-350 made technical changes in Subsec. (a) and deleted provision in Subsec. (c) requiring extension or amendment to contain the findings thus far made; P.A. 98-48 amended Subsec. (b)(4) to insert Subpara. indicators and add Subpara. (B) re the panel's reasons for finding that other normal investigative procedures have failed or are unlikely to succeed if tried or be too dangerous to employ and Subpara. (C) re the panel's reasons for finding that the investigative procedures employed by the investigatory grand jury appear likely to succeed in determining whether or not there is probable cause to believe that a crime or crimes have been committed; P.A. 03-273 made a technical change in Subsec. (a) and amended Subsec. (b)(4)(B) to add provision re finding that due to the specific nature of the alleged crime or the nature of the investigation, it is reasonable to conclude that the use of normal investigative procedures would not result in the obtaining of information that would advance the investigation or would fail to secure and preserve evidence or testimony that might otherwise be compromised.

Cited. 202 C. 541; 204 C. 259; 206 C. 203; 207 C. 98; 213 C. 66; 221 C. 625.

Cited. 16 CA 679; 17 CA 395; 20 CA 447. An application and order transmitted by an investigatory grand jury panel pursuant to Subsec. (b) are part of the record of the investigatory grand jury. 104 CA 398; judgment reversed, see 293 C. 247.

Cited. 45 CS 1.

P['

Sec. 54-47e. Sealing of order and application. Summary of scope of investigation. Disclosure.

Any order authorizing the investigation into the commission of a crime or crimes and any application filed with the panel pursuant to section 54-47c or subsection (c) of section 54-47d shall be sealed. The panel shall submit to the Chief Court Administrator a summary of the scope of the investigation, any recommendation as to the court location at which any motions to quash and any contempt proceedings are to be heard and the finding and record of the investigation are to be filed. Such summary shall be public unless the panel determines, by majority vote, that such summary be sealed for purposes of (1) ensuring the public safety of any individual, (2) ensuring that the investigation would not be adversely affected or (3) complying with other provisions of the general statutes or rules of court which prohibit disclosure of such information. Any investigation by the investigatory grand jury shall be conducted in private, provided the panel, by a majority vote, may order the investigation or any portion thereof to be public when such disclosure or order is deemed by the panel to be in the public interest.

(P.A. 85-611, S. 4; P.A. 88-345, S. 2, 3.)

History: P.A. 88-345 deleted former provisions re discretionary disclosure of fact that matter has been referred to the grand jury and added provisions re submission by panel of summary of scope of investigation, recommendation as to court location and disclosure of such summary, effective June 7, 1988, and applicable to findings filed on or after June 7, 1988.

Cited. 202 C. 541; 204 C. 259. Does not apply to disclosure of material accumulated by grand jury investigation convened under authority of repealed Sec. 54-47. 207 C. 98. Cited. 213 C. 66; 221 C. 625. Legislature has vested the grand jury and the panel with discretion to disclose evidence gathered as

Sec. 54-47f. Conduct of investigation. Testimony of witnesses.

(a) The investigatory grand jury, in conducting the investigation, may (1) seek the assistance of the Chief State's Attorney or state's attorney who filed the application, or his designee, (2) appoint an attorney to provide assistance if a judge of the Superior Court, Appellate Court or Supreme Court filed the application or (3) appoint any other attorney to provide assistance when necessary in the interest of justice.

(b) The attendance of witnesses and the production of documents at such investigation may be compelled by subpoena, signed by any official authorized to issue such process.

(c) If any witness properly summoned fails to appear or to produce any documents included in the subpoena, or if he fails to answer any proper question, the investigatory grand jury conducting the investigation may report the matter to the state's attorney for the judicial district which has been designated in subsection (a) of section 54-47d unless such state's attorney is the applicant or has been appointed to assist in such investigation, in which case the investigatory grand jury shall report the matter to the Chief State's Attorney, and such state's attorney or Chief State's Attorney, as the case may be, may file a complaint setting forth the facts at any criminal session of the superior court in such judicial district. The court shall thereupon issue a citation to the witness to appear before the court and show cause why he should not be punished as for a contempt, and if, after hearing, the court finds that he failed to appear without due cause or failed to produce any document properly to be presented to the investigatory grand jury or failed to answer any proper question in the course of the investigation, it may punish him as it might a witness failing to appear, to produce a document properly to be considered or to answer a proper question before the court.

(d) Witnesses may be examined by the investigatory grand jury conducting the investigation or by any attorney or attorneys appointed by such investigatory grand jury for such purpose. At the hearing, the official conducting the investigation shall inform the witness that he has the right to have counsel present and to consult with such counsel.

(e) The official conducting the investigation shall inform any witness who is a target of the investigation that he is a target and shall advise him that he has the right under the Constitution of the United States and the Constitution of Connecticut not to be compelled to be a witness, or to give evidence, against himself.

(f) Any attorney appointed to assist in conducting the investigation shall disclose to the investigatory grand jury any exculpatory information or material in his possession, custody or control concerning any person who is a target of the investigation.

(g) An official stenographer of the Superior Court or his assistant shall record any testimony taken at the investigation.

(P.A. 85-611, S. 5; P.A. 01-84, S. 24, 26.)

History: P.A. 01-84 made a technical change in Subsec. (b), effective July 1, 2001.

Cited. 202 C. 541; 204 C. 259; 207 C. 98; 213 C. 66; 221 C. 625.

Cited. 16 CA 679; 17 CA 395; 20 CA 447.

Cited. 45 CS 1.

Sec. 54-47g. Finding and record of investigation. Disclosure. Hearing. Access to testimony.

(a) Within sixty days of the conclusion of the investigation, the investigatory grand jury conducting such investigation shall file its finding with the court of the judicial district designated by the Chief Court Administrator pursuant to subsection (a) of section 54-47d, and shall file a copy of its finding with the panel and with the Chief State's Attorney or a state's attorney if such Chief State's Attorney or state's attorney made application for the investigation. The stenographer shall file any record of the investigation with the court of the judicial district designated by the Chief Court Administrator pursuant to subsection (a) of section 54-47d and the panel and the Chief State's Attorney or a state's attorney, if such Chief State's Attorney or state's attorney made application for the investigation, shall have access to such record upon request made to the clerk of the court without a hearing. Such finding shall state whether or not there is probable cause to believe that a crime or crimes have been committed. Except as otherwise provided in this section, any part of the record of the investigation not disclosed with the finding pursuant to subsection (b) of this section shall be sealed, provided any person may file an application with the panel for disclosure of any such part of the record. Upon receipt of such application, the panel shall, after notice, hold a hearing and the panel, by a majority vote, may disclose any such part of the record when such disclosure is deemed by the panel to be in the public interest, except that no part of the record shall be disclosed which contains allegations of the commission of a crime by an individual if the investigatory grand jury failed to find probable cause that such individual committed such crime unless such individual requests the release of such part of the record. Any person aggrieved by an order of the panel shall have the right to appeal such order by filing a petition for review with the Appellate Court within seventy-two hours from the issuance of such order.

(b) The finding of the investigation shall be open to public inspection and copying at the court where it has been filed seven calendar days after it has been filed, unless within that period the Chief State's Attorney or a state's attorney with whom the finding was filed files a motion with the investigatory grand jury requesting that a part or all of such finding not be so disclosed. The finding may include all or such part of the record as the investigatory grand jury may determine, except that no part of the record shall be disclosed which contains allegations of the commission of a crime by an individual if the investigatory grand jury failed to find probable cause that such individual committed such crime unless such individual requests the release of such part of the record. In such event as much of the finding as has not been sought to be withheld from disclosure shall be disclosed promptly upon the expiration of said seven-calendar-day period.

(c) Within fifteen calendar days of the filing of such motion, the investigatory grand jury shall conduct a hearing. The investigatory grand jury shall give written notice of such hearing to the person filing such motion and any other person the investigatory grand jury deems to be an interested party to the proceedings, which may include, but not be limited to, persons who testified or were the subject of testimony before the investigatory grand jury. Within five calendar days of the conclusion of the hearing, the investigatory grand jury shall render its decision, and shall send copies thereof to all those to whom it gave notice of the hearing. It shall deny any such motion unless it makes specific findings of fact on the record that there is a substantial probability that one of the following interests will be prejudiced by publicity that nondisclosure would prevent, and that reasonable alternatives to nondisclosure cannot adequately protect that interest: (1) The right of a person to a fair trial; (2) the prevention of potential defendants from fleeing; (3) the prevention of subornation of perjury or tampering with witnesses; or (4) the protection of the lives and reputations of innocent persons which would be significantly damaged by the release of uncorroborated information. Any order of nondisclosure shall be drawn to protect the interest so found.

(d) Any person aggrieved by an order of the investigatory grand jury shall have the right to appeal such order by filing a petition for review with the Appellate Court within seventy-two hours from issuance of such order.

(e) The Appellate Court shall provide an expedited hearing on such petition in accordance with such rules as the judges of the Appellate Court may adopt, consistent with the rights of the petitioner and the parties.

(f) Notwithstanding the existence of an order of nondisclosure under this section, any witness may apply in writing to the presiding judge of the criminal session of the court of the judicial district wherein the record of the investigation has been filed, or his designee, for access to and a copy of the record of his own testimony. Any witness shall be allowed access, at all reasonable times, to the record of his own testimony and be allowed to obtain a copy of such record unless said judge or his designee finds after a hearing and for good cause shown that it is not in the best interest of justice to allow the witness to have access to and a copy of the record of his testimony.

(g) Notwithstanding the existence of an order of nondisclosure under this section, the presiding judge of the criminal session of the court of the judicial district wherein the record of the investigation has been filed, or his designee, shall grant any written request of a person accused of a crime as a result of the investigation to have access, at all reasonable times, to the record of his own testimony and to obtain a copy of such record.

(P.A. 85-611, S. 6; P.A. 87-350, S. 5, 6; P.A. 88-148; 88-345, S. 1, 3; P.A. 05-288, S. 185.)

History: P.A. 87-350 added provisions re duty of stenographer to file copies of finding and record of investigation, application of witness to presiding judge for access to record of investigation, right of witness to access at all reasonable times to access of record of own testimony and granting written request by person accused of crime as result of investigation to access of record of own testimony; P.A. 88-148 amended Subsec. (b) to authorize any witness to apply for and, unless the presiding judge or his designee disallows it, to obtain a copy of the record of his own testimony, and amended Subsec. (c) to require the presiding judge or his designee to grant the written request of a person accused of a crime as a result of the investigation to obtain a copy of the record of his own testimony; P.A. 88-345 amended Subsec. (a) to permit person to make application to panel for disclosure of record and panel to disclose any part of the record, except such part which contains allegations re individual if grand jury failed to find probable cause and re right of appeal within 72 hours of order, and added new provisions as Subsecs. (b) to (e), inclusive, re disclosure of finding, hearing on motion for nondisclosure, specific findings of fact necessary for granting such motion, right of appeal of order of grand jury and expedited hearing on petition by appellate court, relettering prior provisions accordingly, effective June 7, 1988, and applicable to findings filed on or after June 7, 1988; P.A. 05-288 made a technical change in Subsec. (a), effective July 13, 2005.

Cited. 202 C. 541; 204 C. 259; 207 C. 98; 213 C. 66; 219 C. 905; 221 C. 625. State's right of access to testimony of grand jury witness includes right to use that testimony in its case-in-chief in subsequent criminal prosecution of that witness; to the extent that trial court's ruling is predicated on grand juror's order of secrecy, it lacks support in record because defendant never established that he relied to his detriment on grand juror's order of secrecy. 250 C. 188. Order and application are not part of the record of the grand jury investigation and must be sealed pursuant to Sec. 54-47e since the legislature did not vest the grand jury or panel with discretion to make public disclosure of order and application. 293 C. 247.

Cited. 16 CA 679; 17 CA 395; 19 CA 230.

Cited. 45 CS 1.

Subsec. (a):

Cited. 222 C. 331; 229 C. 178.

Initial determination of "public interest" left to grand jury panel. 20 CA 447. Cited. 43 CA 851.

Because prosecution has right of access under statute to record of testimony from investigatory grand jury proceedings, it could provide to defendants, without request for hearing, those categories of materials normally subject to disclosure in criminal cases, as such disclosure is very much part of prosecutorial function, although disclosure must be only for purpose of pending criminal case and any discovery ordered by trial court pursuant to defense request should be accompanied by protective order. 50 CS 23.

Subsec. (c):

Legislature intended for grand jury to have discretion as to whether to grant a motion to seal its report if there was a substantial probability that information in the report would prejudice a person's right to a fair trial to a degree that is more than de minimis and that the prejudice could be prevented by nondisclosure; "reasonable alternatives" portion requires grand jury to consider alternatives to nondisclosure when the alternatives would protect the enumerated interests in the first instance, but does not require grand jury to injure an enumerated interest through disclosure and then craft remedies to cure that injury; "innocent persons" does not include persons who have been arrested as the result of grand jury's finding of probable cause. 293 C. 464.

Sec. 54-47h. Report.

In January of each year, the panel of judges appointed pursuant to section 54-47b shall report to the Chief Court Administrator, who shall in turn report to the Chief Justice, Governor and General Assembly, the following information with respect to applications made during the preceding calendar year: (1) The number of applications for an investigation into the commission of a crime or crimes filed with the panel; (2) the number of applications approved by the panel; and (3) the number of applications approved for extensions of time or amendments to the order.

(P.A. 85-611, S. 7.)

Cited. 202 C. 541; 204 C. 259; 207 C. 98; 213 C. 66. Appellate review under section must be forwarded on an action brought to the trial court; there was no basis for appeal from determinations of grand jury panel before effective date of P.A. 88-345, i.e. June 7, 1988. 221 C. 625.

Cited. 16 CA 679; 17 CA 395; 20 CA 447.

Cited. 45 CS 1.

Sec. 54-47i. Authority of investigation ordered prior to October 1, 1985.

(a) The authority of any judge, state referee or three judges of the Superior Court to conduct an inquiry to determine whether or not there is probable cause to believe that a crime or crimes have been committed, where such inquiry was ordered prior to October 1, 1985, in accordance with section 54-47 of the general statutes, revision of 1958, revised to January 1, 1985, shall continue until the conclusion of such inquiry and a final report has been filed with the court pursuant to said section, and any action taken or caused to be taken by such judge, state referee or three judges of the Superior Court pursuant to such inquiry, otherwise valid, shall be valid notwithstanding that such action was or is taken or caused to be taken on or after October 1, 1985, and any evidence obtained pursuant to such inquiry, otherwise admissible, shall be admissible in any criminal prosecution of a person accused as a result of such inquiry notwithstanding that such evidence was or is obtained on or after October 1, 1985.

(b) The appointment of any judge or referee after October 1, 1985, to replace a judge or referee ordered to conduct an inquiry to determine whether or not probable cause to believe that a crime or crimes have been committed, where such inquiry was ordered prior to October 1, 1985, in accordance with section 54-47 of the general statutes, revised to January 1, 1985, shall not be deemed to create a new inquiry and the authority of such judge so appointed shall continue as provided in subsection (a) of this section.

(P.A. 86-317, S. 1, 2.)

P.A. 85-611 as clarified by P.A. 86-317 did not revoke the authority of or alter the procedures governing investigatory grand juries that had been properly authorized before October 1, 1985. 202 C. 189. Section validates any action taken or evidence obtained on or after October 1, 1985, pursuant to authority contained in former Sec. 54-47; considered to be clarifying. Id., 541. Cited. 207 C. 98; 213 C. 66.

Cited. 45 CS 1.

Secs. 54-47j to 54-47z. Reserved for future use.

Sec. 54-47aa. Ex parte order to compel disclosure of or direct application to carrier or provider for certain telephone and Internet records.

(a) For the purposes of this section:

(1) "Basic subscriber information" means: (A) Name, (B) address, (C) local and long distance telephone connection records or records of session times and durations, (D) length of service, including start date, and types of services utilized, (E) telephone or instrument number or other subscriber number or identity, including any assigned Internet protocol address, and (F) means and source of payment for such service, including any credit card or bank account number;

(2) "Call-identifying information" means dialing or signaling information that identifies the origin, direction, destination or termination of each communication generated or received by a subscriber or customer, excluding geo-location data, by means of any equipment, facility or service of a telecommunications carrier;

(3) "Electronic communication service" means "electronic communication service" as defined in 18 USC 2510, as amended from time to time;

(4) "Exigent circumstance" means an emergency involving danger of serious physical injury to or death of a person;

(5) "Geo-location data" means information concerning the location of an electronic device, including the real-time and historical location of the device, that, in whole or in part, is generated by, derived from or obtained by the operation of an electronic device, including, but not limited to, a cellular telephone surveillance device;

(6) "Law enforcement official" means the Chief State's Attorney, a state's attorney, an inspector with the Division of Criminal Justice, a sworn member of the Division of State Police within the Department of Emergency Services and Public Protection or a sworn member of an organized local police department;

(7) "Remote computing service" means "remote computing service" as defined in section 18 USC 2711, as amended from time to time; and

(8) "Telecommunications carrier" means "telecommunications carrier" as defined in 47 USC 1001, as amended from time to time.

(b) A law enforcement official may apply for an ex parte order from a judge of the Superior Court to compel (1) a telecommunications carrier to disclose call-identifying information pertaining to a subscriber or customer, (2) a provider of electronic communication service or remote computing service to disclose basic subscriber information pertaining to a subscriber or customer, or (3) a telecommunications carrier or a provider of electronic communication service or remote computing service to disclose the content of a subscriber's or customer's communications or geo-location data associated with a subscriber's or customer's call-identifying information. The judge shall grant such order if the law enforcement official swears under oath to a statement of (A) a reasonable and articulable suspicion that a crime has been or is being committed and such call-identifying or basic subscriber information is relevant and material to an ongoing criminal investigation, in which case such order shall not authorize disclosure of the content of any communication or geo-location data, or (B) probable cause to believe that a crime has been or is being committed and the content of such subscriber's or customer's communications or the geo-location data associated with such subscriber's or customer's call-identifying information is relevant and material to an ongoing criminal investigation, in which case such order shall authorize the disclosure of such information, content or geo-location data. Any such order entered pursuant to this subsection shall state upon its face the case number assigned to such investigation, the date and time of issuance and the name of the judge authorizing the order. The law enforcement official shall have any ex parte order issued pursuant to this subsection signed by the authorizing judge within forty-eight hours or not later than the next business day, whichever is earlier. No order pursuant to this subsection shall authorize the disclosure of any such information, content or data for a period in excess of fourteen days.

(c) A law enforcement official may apply directly to a telecommunications carrier or provider of electronic communication service or remote computing service for production of geo-location data for a period not in excess of forty-eight hours, including real-time or historical geo-location data, or any combination of such data, pertaining to an identified subscriber or customer. The telecommunications carrier or provider of electronic telecommunication service or remote computing service may provide the requested geo-location data upon the applicant stating under oath: (1) That facts exist upon which to base a belief that the data sought is relevant and material to an ongoing criminal investigation; (2) a belief that exigent circumstances exist; and (3) the facts supporting the belief that exigent circumstances exist. Any subsequent application for information from the same telecommunication carrier or provider of electronic communication service or remote computing service for production of geo-location data in connection with the same investigation shall be made pursuant to subsection (b) of this section.

(d) A telecommunications carrier shall disclose call-identifying information and a provider of electronic communication service or remote computing service shall disclose basic subscriber information to a law enforcement official when an order is issued pursuant to subsection (b) of this section.

106

(e) Not later than forty-eight hours after the issuance of an order pursuant to subsection (b) of this section, the law enforcement official shall mail notice of the issuance of such order to the subscriber or customer whose call-identifying information or basic subscriber information is the subject of such order, except that such notification may be delayed for a period of up to ninety days upon the execution of a written certification of such official to the judge who authorized the order that there is reason to believe that notification of the existence of the order may result in (1) endangering the life or physical safety of an individual, (2) flight from prosecution, (3) destruction of or tampering with evidence, (4) intimidation of potential witnesses, or (5) otherwise seriously jeopardizing the investigation. The law enforcement official shall maintain a true copy of such certification. During such ninety-day period, the law enforcement official may request the court to extend such period of delayed notification. Such period may be extended beyond ninety days only upon approval of the court. The applicant shall file a copy of the notice with the clerk of the court that issued such order. If information is provided in response to the order, the applicant shall, not later than ten days after receiving such information, file with the clerk a return containing an inventory of the information received. If a judge finds there is a significant likelihood that such notification would seriously jeopardize the investigation and issues an order authorizing delayed notification under this subsection, the telecommunications carrier or provider of electronic communication service or remote computing service from whom the call-identifying information or basic subscriber information is sought shall not notify any person, other than legal counsel for the telecommunications carrier or provider of electronic communication service or remote computing service and the law enforcement official that requested the ex parte order, of the existence of the ex parte order. Any information provided in response to the court order shall be disclosed to the defense counsel.

(f) A telecommunications carrier or provider of electronic communication service or remote computing service that provides information pursuant to an order issued pursuant to subsection (b) of this section or pursuant to an application made pursuant to subsection (c) of this section shall be compensated for the reasonable expenses incurred in providing such information.

(g) Any telecommunications carrier or provider of electronic communication service or remote computing service that provides information pursuant to an order issued pursuant to subsection (b) of this section or an application made pursuant to subsection (c) of this section shall be afforded the legal protections provided under 18 USC 3124, as amended from time to time, with regard to such actions.

(h) No information obtained pursuant to subsection (b) or (c) of this section shall be retained for a period in excess of fourteen days, unless such information relates to an ongoing criminal investigation. Any information provided pursuant to said subsection (b) or (c) shall be disclosed to the defense counsel.

(i) Not later than January fifteenth of each year, each law enforcement official shall report to the Chief State's Attorney the information required by this subsection with respect to each order issued pursuant to subsection (b) of this section and each application made pursuant to subsection (c) of this section in the preceding calendar year. The Chief State's Attorney shall, based upon the reports filed by each law enforcement official and not later than January thirty-first of each year, submit a report, in accordance with the provisions of section 11-4a, to the joint standing committee of the General Assembly having cognizance of matters relating to criminal law and procedure concerning orders issued pursuant to subsection (b) of this section and applications made pursuant to subsection (c) of this section in the preceding calendar year. The report shall include the following information: (1) The number of orders issued pursuant to subsection (b) of this subsection and the number of applications submitted to telecommunications carriers or providers of electronic communication service or remote computing service pursuant to subsection (c) of this section, (2) whether the order was directed to a telecommunications carrier, provider of electronic communication service or provider of remote computing service, (3) whether the information sought was call-identifying information or basic subscriber information, (4) the statutory offense or offenses that were the subject of the investigation, (5) the number of notifications that were delayed pursuant to subsection (e) of this section, and the reason for such delayed notification, (6) the number of motions to vacate an order that were filed, and the number of motions granted or denied, (7) the number of investigations concluded and the final result of such investigations, and (8) the status of any criminal prosecution resulting from the investigation.

(P.A. 05-182, S. 1, 2; P.A. 11-51, S. 134; P.A. 16-148, S. 1.)

History: Pursuant to P.A. 11-51, "Department of Public Safety" was changed editorially by the Revisors to "Department of Emergency Services and Public Protection" in Subsec. (a)(4), effective July 1, 2011; P.A. 16-148 amended Subsec. (a) by redefining "call-identifying information" in Subdiv. (2), adding new Subdiv. (4) defining "exigent circumstance", adding new Subdiv. (5) defining "geo-location data" and redesignating existing Subdivs. (4) to (6) as Subdivs. (6) to (8), amended Subsec. (b) by replacing "may request an ex parte order" with "may apply for an ex parte order", adding Subdiv. (3) re disclosure of content of subscriber's or customer's communications or geo-location data, replacing "law enforcement official states a reasonable and articulable suspicion" with "law enforcement official swears under oath to a statement of (A) a reasonable and articulable suspicion", deleting reference to exigent circumstances, adding provisions re disclosure of content of communication or geo-location data not authorized, adding Subpara. (B) re probable cause to believe that crime has been or is being committed and content of subscriber's or customer's communications or geo-location data is relevant and material to ongoing criminal investigation, and adding provision re no order to authorize disclosure of information, content or data for a period in excess of 14 days, added new Subsec. (c) re law enforcement official may apply directly to telecommunications carrier or provider of electronic communication service or remote computing service for production of geo-location data, redesignated existing Subsecs. (c) to (f) as Subsecs. (d) to (g), amended redesignated Subsec. (e) by adding provisions re applicant to file copy of notice with clerk of court that issued order and re disclosure of information to defense counsel, amended redesignated Subsecs. (f) and (g) by adding references to application made pursuant to Subsec. (c), added Subsec. (h) re retention of information and disclosure of information to defense counsel, redesignated existing Subsec. (g) as Subsec. (i) and amended same by adding references to application made pursuant to Subsec. (c) and, in Subdiv. (1), adding provision re number of applications submitted, and made technical and conforming changes.

There is nothing in section to suggest that defendant is to receive notice re a third party's phone records; the fact that victim's phone records show that she received calls from defendant does not, in itself, make notice provisions of Subsec. (d) applicable. 161 CA 10.

Sec. 54-48. Reward for arrest of capital offender or felon.

When any crime punishable by death or imprisonment for more than one year has been committed, the Governor, upon application of the state's attorney for the judicial district in which it has been committed, may offer, publicly, a reward not exceeding fifty thousand dollars, to the person who gives information leading to the arrest and conviction of the guilty person, or, if such guilty person has fled after conviction of a felony in a court of this state, to the person who gives information leading to the arrest and detention of the convicted felon, whether found within the state or elsewhere, which reward shall be paid to the informer by the state, by order of the court before which such conviction is had.

(1949 Rev., S. 8269; P.A. 73-116, S. 3; 73-667, S. 1, 2; P.A. 77-604, S. 55, 84; P.A. 78-276; 78-280, S. 2, 127; P.A. 97-52.)

History: P.A. 73-116 substituted "Connecticut Correctional Institution, Somers" for "State Prison" and added reference to judicial districts; P.A. 73-667 changed effective date of P.A. 73-116 from October 1, 1973, to April 25, 1973; P.A. 77-604 deleted specific reference to imprisonment at Somers referring instead to imprisonment "for more than one year"; P.A. 78-276 deleted reference to counties (as did P.A. 78-280) and increased maximum amount of reward from $3,000 to $20,000; P.A. 97-52 increased the maximum amount of the reward to $50,000.

Does not recompense one who had wholly performed before the offer was made. 143 C. 462.

Sec. 54-49. Reward for information as to high crime or crime resulting in death of police officer or firefighter.

(a) When any high crime has been committed in any municipality, the chief executive officer of such municipality, as described in section 7-193, may offer, publicly, a reward not exceeding two thousand five hundred dollars, to the person who gives information leading to the arrest and conviction of the guilty person; which reward shall be paid to the informer by the municipality, by order of the court before which such conviction is had.

(b) When any crime has been committed in any municipality which results in the death of any police officer or firefighter, the chief executive officer of such municipality, upon the affirmative vote of two-thirds of the legislative body of such municipality, or when the legislative body is the town meeting, at least two-thirds of those present and voting, may offer publicly, a reward not exceeding twenty thousand dollars, to the person who gives information leading to the arrest and conviction of the guilty person, which reward shall be paid to the informer by the municipality, by order of the court before which such conviction is had.

(1949 Rev., S. 8270; P.A. 84-540, S. 5, 7; P.A. 93-425, S. 1.)

History: P.A. 84-540 added Subsec. (b) authorizing the chief executive officer of a municipality in which a crime has been committed which results in the death of a police officer or firefighter, to offer a reward for information leading to arrest and conviction of guilty person; P.A. 93-425 amended Subsec. (a) by deleting "town, its selectmen" and adding "municipality, the chief executive officer of such municipality, as described in section 7-193", increasing reward from amount not exceeding $200 to $2,500, and deleting "town" and substituting "municipality".

Sec. 54-50. Reward for information as to unlawful disinterment of corpse.

For any violation of the provisions of section 53-334, the Governor, upon application of the selectmen of the town where the offense has been committed, shall, publicly, offer a reward, not exceeding two hundred dollars, for the apprehension of the guilty person; and, if the offender is convicted, such reward shall be paid to the informer by the state, upon order of the court before which the conviction is had.

(1949 Rev., S. 8271.)

Sec. 54-51. Reward for information as to theft of motor vehicle, livestock or poultry. Section 54-51 is repealed, effective October 1, 2003.

(1949 Rev., S. 8272; P.A. 74-338, S. 55, 94; P.A. 03-9, S. 1.)

Sec. 54-52. Determination of claims to reward.

When any reward is offered for the recovery of stolen property, or for information which may lead to the conviction of any criminal, or for both, the court before which conviction is had or the superior court for the judicial district where the offense was committed, at a criminal term, may decide upon the claims of the parties interested in such reward. If there is more than one claimant for the reward, the court in which the conviction was secured or the court for the judicial district wherein the offense was committed, or the presiding judge of such court, shall determine who are justly entitled to the reward, and may apportion it equitably among them.

(1949 Rev., S. 8268, 8273; P.A. 73-116, S. 24; 73-667, S. 1, 2; P.A. 76-436, S. 540, 681; P.A. 78-280, S. 1, 127.)

History: P.A. 73-116 added reference to judicial districts; P.A. 73-667 changed effective date of P.A. 73-116 from October 1, 1973, to April 25, 1973; P.A. 76-436 deleted provision whereby presiding judge of court to which accused was bound over determines amount of reward when accused forfeits his recognizance and authorized court for county or judicial district where offense was committed to determine reward, reflecting transfer of all trial jurisdiction to superior court, effective July 1, 1978; P.A. 78-280 deleted references to counties.

Sec. 54-53. Release by correctional officials.

Each person detained in a community correctional center pursuant to the issuance of a bench warrant of arrest or for arraignment, sentencing or trial for an offense not punishable by death shall be entitled to bail and shall be released from such institution upon entering into a recognizance, with sufficient surety, or upon posting cash bail as provided in section 54-66, for the detained person's appearance before the court having cognizance of the offense, to be taken by any person designated by the Commissioner of Correction at the institution where the person is detained. The person so designated shall deliver the recognizance or cash bail to the clerk of the appropriate court before the opening of the court on the first court day thereafter. When cash bail in excess of ten thousand dollars is received for a detained person accused of a felony, where the underlying facts and circumstances of the felony involve the use, attempted use or threatened use of physical force against another person, the person so designated shall prepare a report that contains (1) the name, address and taxpayer identification number of the detained person, (2) the name, address and taxpayer identification number of each person offering the cash bail, other than a person licensed as a professional bondsman under chapter 533 or a surety bail bond agent under chapter 700f, (3) the amount of cash received, and (4) the date the cash was received. Not later than fifteen days after receipt of such cash bail, the person so designated shall file the report with the Department of Revenue Services and mail a copy of the report to the state's attorney for the judicial district in which the alleged offense was committed and to each person offering the cash bail.

(1949 Rev., S. 8778; 1961, P.A. 517, S. 50; February, 1965, P.A. 606; 1969, P.A. 803, S. 2; P.A. 80-313, S. 17; P.A. 99-240, S. 15.)

History: 1961 act deleted obsolete reference to county commissioners; 1965 act made section applicable to person awaiting arraignment or sentencing as well as trial, offered the alternative of posting cash bail and substituted present provisions for taking bail for prior provision of taking by the court, a judge or clerk; 1969 act replaced jail administrator with commissioner of correction, substituted references to community correctional centers for references to jails and specified applicability to persons detained "pursuant to the issuance of a bench warrant"; P.A. 80-313 made minor changes in wording; P.A. 99-240 added provisions requiring the person designated by the commissioner to prepare a report when cash bail in excess of $10,000 is received for a detained person accused of a felony involving the use, attempted use or threatened use of physical force against another person, specifying the contents of such report and requiring such designated person not later than 15 days after receipt of such cash bail to file such report with the Department of Revenue Services and mail a copy of such report to the appropriate state's attorney and each person offering the cash bail.

Not permitted to one under sentence for prior offense. K. 260. Sheriff may take bail and release prisoner. 2 D. 11. Not the practice to issue a special order to clerk for commitment of prisoner to jail; there is a continuing order to that effect. 36 C. 251. Bail where state appeals; 65 C. 282; where accused appeals to Supreme Court and sentence is stayed. 71 C. 457. Liabilities on bail bond. 83 C. 688. Nature of act of taking bail; law authorizing clerk to take bail will not permit him to fix amount. 89 C. 301. Application to Supreme Court to admit accused to bail denied; procedure there must be to have finding of facts made by referee unless they are admitted by state's attorney. 109 C. 738. Cited. 140 C. 326. In capital cases, refusal of bail must be restricted to cases where proof is evident or presumption great in accord with Art. I, Sec. 8 of state constitution; burden of proof that proof is evident or presumption great in capital offenses as grounds for refusing bail is on state and not met by fact of grand jury indictment. 159 C. 264.

Only an act of God or an act of law or an act of the obligee excuses a surety whose principal does not appear before court; sleepiness constitutes no reason for relaxation of the law. 23 CS 3

Sec. 54-53a. Detention of persons who have not made bail.

(a) No person who has not made bail may be detained in a community correctional center pursuant to the issuance of a bench warrant of arrest or for arraignment, sentencing or trial for an offense not punishable by death, for longer than forty-five days, unless at the expiration of the forty-five days he is presented to the court having cognizance of the offense. On each such presentment, the court may reduce, modify or discharge the bail, or may for cause shown remand the person to the custody of the Commissioner of Correction. On the expiration of each successive forty-five-day period, the person may again by motion be presented to the court for such purpose.

(b) Notwithstanding the provisions of subsection (a) of this section, any person who has not made bail and is detained in a community correctional center pursuant to the issuance of a bench warrant of arrest or for arraignment, sentencing or trial for an offense classified as a class D or E felony or as a misdemeanor, except a person charged with a crime in another state and detained pursuant to chapter 964 or a person detained for violation of his parole pending a parole revocation hearing, shall be presented to the court having cognizance of the offense within thirty days of the date of his detention. On such presentment, the court may reduce, modify or discharge the bail or may for cause shown remand the person to the custody of the Commissioner of Correction. On the expiration of each successive thirty-day period, the person shall again be presented to the court for such purpose.

(c) Notwithstanding the provisions of subsections (a) and (b) of this section, any person who has not made bail may be heard by the court upon a motion for modification of the bail at any time.

(1971, P.A. 513; P.A. 74-186, S. 1, 12; P.A. 80-313, S. 25; P.A. 82-244; P.A. 89-166; P.A. 13-258, S. 8.)

History: P.A. 74-186 made minor changes in wording and specified that presentment is to occur at the expiration of each successive 45-day period; P.A. 80-313 made minor changes in wording, substituting "the" for "such" etc; P.A. 82-244 added Subsec. (b) requiring a bail review hearing every 30 days for persons charged with a class D felony or a misdemeanor; P.A. 89-166 added Subsec. (c) providing that any person who has not made bail may be heard by the court upon a motion for modification of the bail at any time; P.A. 13-258 amended Subsec. (b) to add reference to a class E felony.

See Sec. 51-180 re criminal terms and sessions of court.

See Sec. 51-180a re special session held when accused is confined for want of bail.

Cited. 169 C. 438. Section, which requires review of bail every 45 days for persons held in custody while mandating procedure for implementing right to be released on bail, provides no sanction for a violation of that procedure; denial of any right created by section is not a violation of fundamental constitutional right. 171 C. 395.

Cited. 29 CS 434. Provides no sanction in event of a violation; defendant not entitled to dismissal of information without showing of prejudice. 43 CS 211.

Secs. 54-54 and 54-55. Original information in Court of Common Pleas. Information in cases appealed to Court of Common Pleas. Sections 54-54 and 54-55 are repealed.

(1949 Rev., S. 8767, 8768; 1961, P.A. 517, S. 71.)

Sec. 54-56. Dismissal of information by court.

All courts having jurisdiction of criminal cases shall at all times have jurisdiction and control over informations and criminal cases pending therein and may, at any time, upon motion by the defendant, dismiss any information and order such defendant discharged if, in the opinion of the court, there is not sufficient evidence or cause to justify the bringing or continuing of such information or the placing of the person accused therein on trial.

(1949 Rev., S. 8769.)

Cited. 170 C. 337. In absence of statutory authority, court may not of its own motion dismiss a criminal prosecution unless there is fundamental legal defect in information or indictment or constitutional defect such as denial of speedy trial or illegality of arrest. 172 C. 608. Cited. 189 C. 42; 193 C. 474; Id., 602; 198 C. 435; 200 C. 440. Trial court did not abuse its discretion having properly found "cause" to dismiss with prejudice. Id., 453. Cited. 204 C. 187; 207 C. 374; 209 C. 225; 213 C. 708; 214 C. 657; 229 C. 716; 242 C. 409. Absent compliance with section, trial court did not have authority to dismiss pending misdemeanor charge because, in trial court's view, case was not sufficiently important to warrant time and expense of jury trial. 243 C. 690. Dismissal of an information may be predicated upon either insufficient evidence or insufficient cause, but only in the most compelling of circumstances. 305 C. 330.

Cited. 4 CA 520; 5 CA 347; 7 CA 46; 8 CA 607; 11 CA 224. Insufficient cause "prong" of statute is inappropriate basis for dismissal of information preceded by arrest warrant where no trial has yet been held. 19 CA 495. Cited. 20 CA 321; 21 CA 210; 24 CA 195; 29 CA 689; 40 CA 789; 45 CA 722.

Purpose and history of law. 13 CS 112. Cited. 21 CS 246. Resort to section is not proper method to raise issue of jurisdiction of court over person of defendant. 28 CS 512. Purpose of motion to dismiss is to prevent unchecked powers by prosecuting attorney. 29 CS 118. Insufficient evidence and insufficient cause grounds of section may not be raised through pretrial dismissal motion in case where defendant was arrested on warrant signed by a judge. 49 CS 248.

Motion to dismiss count having been previously granted, motion for directed verdict on that count was properly denied. 5 Conn. Cir. Ct. 78.

Sec. 54-56a. (Formerly Sec. 54-2b). Pleading by mail in certain motor vehicle cases.

In any criminal action arising out of an alleged violation of the law relating to motor vehicles, except a violation of section 14-219 specified in subsection (e) of said section 14-219, appearances, pleas of not guilty and requests for trial by jury or court may be made by or on behalf of the defendant by mailing such pleas and requests by first-class mail, postage prepaid, to the clerk of the court in which such case is to be tried, which pleas and requests shall be received by said clerk not later than the court day next preceding the court day on which the defendant is to appear. Said pleas and claims shall be filed on forms approved by the Office of the Chief Court Administrator.

(1963, P.A. 475; P.A. 74-183, S. 127, 291; P.A. 76-381, S. 3; 76-436, S. 519, 681; P.A. 77-452, S. 34, 72; P.A. 79-196; P.A. 85-446, S. 4, 6; P.A. 90-213, S. 12.)

History: P.A. 74-183 replaced circuit court with court of common pleas, reflecting reorganization of judicial system, effective December 31, 1974; P.A. 76-381 amended section to specify applicability re actions arising out of alleged commission of an infraction; P.A. 76-436 and P.A. 77-452 replaced court of common pleas with superior court, reflecting transfer of all trial jurisdiction to superior court, effective July 1, 1978; P.A. 79-196 required that forms for filing pleas and claims be approved by chief court administrator's office rather than by superior court judges; Sec. 54-2b transferred to Sec. 54-56a in 1981; P.A. 85-446 deleted references to procedures for an alleged commission of an infraction, effective October 1, 1986; P.A. 90-213 added exception for a violation of Sec. 14-219 specified in Subsec. (e) of said Sec. 14-219.

Annotation to former section 54-2b:

Cited. 29 CS 155.

Sec. 54-56b. Right to dismissal or trial on nolle.

A nolle prosequi may not be entered as to any count in a complaint or information if the accused objects to the nolle prosequi and demands either a trial or dismissal, except with respect to prosecutions in which a nolle prosequi is entered upon a representation to the court by the prosecuting official that a material witness has died, disappeared or become disabled or that material evidence has disappeared or has been destroyed and that a further investigation is therefore necessary.

(P.A. 80-313, S. 30.)

Cited. 180 C. 153. The court must accept the entry of nolle prosequi for the record unless it is persuaded that prosecutor's exercise of discretion is clearly contrary to manifest public interest. 185 C. 199. Cited. 191 C. 27; 198 C. 435. Entry of nolles over defendant's objection fits within exception to rule of finality allowing appeal of interlocutory trial court rulings that, if erroneous, cannot later be remedied. 209 C. 52. Gives defendant the right to have criminal charge disposed of with finality by dismissal with prejudice. Id., 133. Cited. 214 C. 616; 233 C. 44; 240 C. 590. Trial court properly allowed the entry of nolle prosequi based on the state's representations that a key witness against defendant was unavailable due to the witness' intent to assert his fifth amendment privilege against self-incrimination, and the court was not required to conduct an evidentiary hearing re the state's representations; nolle prosequi functionally converted into a dismissal without prejudice pursuant to Sec. 54-142a(c) after 13 months had elapsed, therefore the state was not barred from bringing charges against defendant 4 years later and defendant's right to a speedy trial was not violated. 289 C. 598.

Cited. 5 CA 347; 10 CA 217; 11 CA 224; 40 CA 705; judgment reversed, see 240 C. 590; 44 CA 162. Defendant's objection to entry of nolle made 7 weeks after it had been entered was not timely and fell outside limited jurisdiction retained by the court following the entry of nolle. 111 CA 397. Defendant's infraction ticket was a complaint and, therefore, he was entitled to object to the entry of nolle and demand a trial or a dismissal. 143 CA 194.

Sec. 54-56c. Request for privileged trial status.

If the accused enters a plea of not guilty, the state's attorney, assistant state's attorney or deputy assistant state's attorney may, in accordance with rules adopted by the judges of the Superior Court, request that the case be privileged with respect to assignment for trial.

(P.A. 80-313, S. 31.)

Sec. 54-56d. (Formerly Sec. 54-40). Competency to stand trial.

(a) **Competency requirement. Definition.** A defendant shall not be tried, convicted or sentenced while the defendant is not competent. For the purposes of this section, a defendant is not competent if the defendant is unable to understand the proceedings against him or her or to assist in his or her own defense.

(b) **Presumption of competency.** A defendant is presumed to be competent. The burden of proving that the defendant is not competent by a preponderance of the evidence and the burden of going forward with the evidence are on the party raising the issue. The burden of going forward with the evidence shall be on the state if the court raises the issue. The court may call its own witnesses and conduct its own inquiry.

(c) **Request for examination.** If, at any time during a criminal proceeding, it appears that the defendant is not competent, counsel for the defendant or for the state, or the court, on its own motion, may request an examination to determine the defendant's competency.

(d) **Examination of defendant. Report.** If the court finds that the request for an examination is justified and that, in accordance with procedures established by the judges of the Superior Court, there is probable cause to believe that the defendant has committed the crime for which the defendant is charged, the court shall order an examination of the defendant as to his or her competency. The court may (1) appoint one or more physicians specializing in psychiatry to examine the defendant, or (2) order the Commissioner of Mental Health and Addiction Services to conduct the examination either (A) by a clinical team consisting of a physician specializing in psychiatry, a clinical psychologist and one of the following: A clinical social worker licensed pursuant to chapter 383b or a psychiatric nurse clinical specialist holding a master's degree in nursing, or (B) by one or more physicians specializing in psychiatry, except that no employee of the Department of Mental Health and Addiction Services who has served as a member of a clinical team in the course of such employment for at least five years prior to October 1, 1995, shall be precluded from being appointed as a member of a clinical team. If the Commissioner of Mental Health and Addiction Services is ordered to conduct the examination, the commissioner shall select the members of the clinical team or the physician or physicians. When performing an examination under this section, the examiners shall have access to information on treatment dates and locations in the defendant's treatment history contained in the Department of Mental Health and Addiction Services' database of treatment episodes for the purpose of requesting a release of treatment information from the defendant. If the examiners determine that the defendant is not competent, the examiners shall then determine whether there is a substantial probability that the defendant, if provided with a course of treatment, will regain competency within the maximum period of any placement order under this section. If the examiners determine that there is a substantial probability that the defendant, if provided with a course of treatment, will regain competency within the maximum period of any placement order under this section, the examiners shall then determine whether the defendant appears to be eligible for civil commitment, with monitoring by the Court Support Services Division, pursuant to subdivision (2) of subsection (h) of this section. If the examiners determine that there is not a substantial probability that the defendant, if provided with a course of treatment, will regain competency within the maximum period of any placement order under this section, the examiners shall then determine whether the defendant appears to be eligible for civil commitment to a hospital for psychiatric disabilities pursuant to subsection (m) of this section and make a recommendation to the court regarding the appropriateness of such civil commitment. The court may authorize a physician specializing in psychiatry, a clinical psychologist, a clinical social worker licensed pursuant to chapter 383b or a psychiatric nurse clinical specialist holding a master's degree in nursing selected by the defendant to observe the examination. Counsel for the defendant may observe the examination. The examination shall be completed within fifteen business days from the date it was ordered and the examiners shall prepare and sign, without notarization, a written report and file such report with the court within twenty-one business days of the date of the order. On receipt of the written report, the clerk of the court shall cause copies to be delivered immediately to the state's attorney and to counsel for the defendant.

(e) **Hearing. Evidence.** The court shall hold a hearing as to the competency of the defendant not later than ten days after the court receives the written report. Any evidence regarding the defendant's competency, including the written report, may be introduced at the hearing by either the defendant or the state, except that no treatment information contained in the Department of Mental Health and Addiction Services' database of treatment episodes may be included in the written report or introduced at the hearing unless the defendant released the treatment information pursuant to subsection (d) of this section. If the written report is introduced, at least one of the examiners shall be present to testify as to the determinations in the report, unless the examiner's presence is waived by the defendant and the state. Any member of the clinical team shall be considered competent to testify as to the team's determinations. A defendant and the defendant's counsel may waive the court hearing only if the examiners, in the written report, determine without qualification that the defendant is competent. Nothing in this subsection shall limit any other release or use of information from said database permitted by law.

(f) **Court finding of competency or incompetency.** If the court, after the hearing, finds that the defendant is competent, the court shall continue with the criminal proceedings. If the court finds that the defendant is not competent, the court shall also find whether there is a substantial probability that the defendant, if provided with a course of treatment, will regain competency within the maximum period of any placement order permitted under this section.

(g) **Court procedure if finding that defendant will not regain competency.** If, at the hearing, the court finds that there is not a substantial probability that the defendant, if provided with a course of treatment, will regain competency within the period of any placement order under this section, the court shall follow the procedure set forth in subsection (m) of this section.

(h) **Court procedure if finding that defendant will regain competency. Placement of defendant for treatment or pending civil commitment proceedings. Progress report.** (1) If, at the hearing, the court finds that there is a substantial probability that the defendant, if provided with a course of treatment, will regain competency within the period of any placement order under this section, the court shall either (A) order placement of the defendant for treatment for the purpose of rendering the defendant competent, or (B) order placement of the defendant at a treatment facility pending civil commitment proceedings pursuant to subdivision (2) of this subsection.

(2) (A) Except as provided in subparagraph (B) of this subdivision, if the court makes a finding pursuant to subdivision (1) of this subsection and does not order placement pursuant to subparagraph (A) of said subdivision, the court shall, on its own motion or on motion of the state or the defendant, order placement of the defendant in the custody of the Commissioner of Mental Health and Addiction Services at a treatment facility pending civil commitment proceedings. The treatment facility shall be determined by the Commissioner of Mental Health and Addiction Services. Such order shall: (i) Include an authorization for the Commissioner of Mental Health and Addiction Services to apply for civil commitment of such defendant pursuant to sections 17a-495 to 17a-528, inclusive; (ii) permit the defendant to agree to request voluntarily to be admitted under section 17a-506 and participate voluntarily in a treatment plan prepared by the Commissioner of Mental Health and Addiction Services, and require that the defendant comply with such treatment plan; and (iii) provide that if the application for civil commitment is denied or not pursued by the Commissioner of Mental Health and Addiction Services, or if the defendant is unwilling or unable to comply with a treatment plan despite reasonable efforts of the treatment facility to encourage the defendant's compliance, the person in charge of the treatment facility, or such person's designee, shall submit a written progress report to the court and the defendant shall be returned to the court for a hearing pursuant to subsection (k) of this section. Such written progress report shall include the status of any civil commitment proceedings concerning the defendant, the defendant's compliance with the treatment plan, an opinion regarding the defendant's current competency to stand trial, the clinical findings of the person submitting the report and the facts upon which the findings are based, and any other information concerning the defendant requested by the court, including, but not limited to, the method of treatment or the type, dosage and effect of any medication the defendant is receiving. The Court Support Services Division shall monitor the defendant's compliance with any applicable provisions of such order. The period of placement and monitoring under such order shall not exceed the period of the maximum sentence which the defendant could receive on conviction of the charges against such defendant, or eighteen months, whichever is less. If the defendant has complied with such treatment plan and any applicable provisions of such order,

at the end of the period of placement and monitoring, the court shall approve the entry of a nolle prosequi to the charges against the defendant or shall dismiss such charges.

(B) This subdivision shall not apply: (i) To any person charged with a class A felony, a class B felony, except a violation of section 53a-122 that does not involve the use, attempted use or threatened use of physical force against another person, or a violation of section 14-227a or 14-227m, subdivision (1) or (2) of subsection (a) of section 14-227n, subdivision (2) of subsection (a) of section 53-21 or section 53a-56b, 53a-60d, 53a-70, 53a-70a, 53a-70b, 53a-71, 53a-72a or 53a-72b; (ii) to any person charged with a crime or motor vehicle violation who, as a result of the commission of such crime or motor vehicle violation, causes the death of another person; or (iii) unless good cause is shown, to any person charged with a class C felony.

(i) **Placement for treatment. Conditions.** The placement of the defendant for treatment for the purpose of rendering the defendant competent shall comply with the following conditions: (1) The period of placement under the order or combination of orders shall not exceed the period of the maximum sentence which the defendant could receive on conviction of the charges against the defendant or eighteen months, whichever is less; (2) the placement shall be either (A) in the custody of the Commissioner of Mental Health and Addiction Services, the Commissioner of Children and Families or the Commissioner of Developmental Services, except that any defendant placed for treatment with the Commissioner of Mental Health and Addiction Services may remain in the custody of the Department of Correction pursuant to subsection (p) of this section; or, (B) if the defendant or the appropriate commissioner agrees to provide payment, in the custody of any appropriate mental health facility or treatment program which agrees to provide treatment to the defendant and to adhere to the requirements of this section; and (3) the court shall order the placement, on either an inpatient or an outpatient basis, which the court finds is the least restrictive placement appropriate and available to restore competency. If outpatient treatment is the least restrictive placement for a defendant who has not yet been released from a correctional facility, the court shall consider whether the availability of such treatment is a sufficient basis on which to release the defendant on a promise to appear, conditions of release, cash bail or bond. If the court determines that the defendant may not be so released, the court shall order treatment of the defendant on an inpatient basis at a mental health facility or facility for persons with intellectual disability. Not later than twenty-four hours after the court orders placement of the defendant for treatment for the purpose of rendering the defendant competent, the examiners shall transmit information obtained about the defendant during the course of an examination pursuant to subsection (d) of this section to the health care provider named in the court's order.

(j) **Progress reports re treatment.** The person in charge of the treatment facility, or such person's designee, or the Commissioner of Mental Health and Addiction Services with respect to any defendant who is in the custody of the Commissioner of Correction pursuant to subsection (p) of this section, shall submit a written progress report to the court (1) at least seven days prior to the date of any hearing on the issue of the defendant's competency; (2) whenever he or she believes that the defendant has attained competency; (3) whenever he or she believes that there is not a substantial probability that the defendant will attain competency within the period covered by the placement order; (4) whenever, within the first one hundred twenty days of the period covered by the placement order, he or she believes that the defendant would be eligible for civil commitment pursuant to subdivision (2) of subsection (h) of this section; or (5) whenever he or she believes that the defendant is still not competent but has improved sufficiently such that continued inpatient commitment is no longer the least restrictive placement appropriate and available to restore competency. The progress report shall contain: (A) The clinical findings of the person submitting the report and the facts on which the findings are based; (B) the opinion of the person submitting the report as to whether the defendant has attained competency or as to whether the defendant is making progress, under treatment, toward attaining competency within the period covered by the placement order; (C) the opinion of the person submitting the report as to whether the defendant appears to be eligible for civil commitment to a hospital for psychiatric disabilities pursuant to subsection (m) of this section and the appropriateness of such civil commitment, if there is not a substantial probability that the defendant will attain competency within the period covered by the placement order; and (D) any other information concerning the defendant requested by the court, including, but not limited to, the method of treatment or the type, dosage and effect of any medication the defendant is receiving. Not later than five business days after the court finds either that the defendant will not attain competency within the period of any placement order under this section or that the defendant has regained competency, the person in charge of the treatment facility, or such person's designee, or the Commissioner of Mental Health and Addiction Services with respect to any defendant who is in the custody of the Commissioner of Correction pursuant to subsection (p) of this section, shall provide a copy of the written progress report to the examiners who examined the defendant pursuant to subsection (d) of this section.

(k) **Reconsideration of competency. Hearing. Involuntary medication. Appointment and duties of health care guardian.** (1) Whenever any placement order for treatment is rendered or continued, the court shall set a date for a hearing, to be held within ninety days, for reconsideration of the issue of the defendant's competency. Whenever the court (A) receives a report pursuant to subsection (j) of this section which indicates that (i) the defendant has attained competency, (ii) the defendant will not attain competency within the remainder of the period covered by the placement order, (iii) the defendant will not attain competency within the remainder of the period covered by the placement order absent administration of psychiatric medication for which the defendant is unwilling or unable to provide consent, (iv) the defendant would be eligible for civil commitment pursuant to subdivision (2) of subsection (h) of this section, or (v) the defendant is still not competent but has improved sufficiently such that continued inpatient commitment is no longer the least restrictive placement appropriate and available to restore competency, or (B) receives a report pursuant to subparagraph (A)(iii) of subdivision (2) of subsection (h) of this section which indicates that (i) the application for civil commitment of the defendant has been denied or has not been pursued by the Commissioner of Mental Health and Addiction Services, or (ii) the defendant is unwilling or unable to comply with a treatment plan despite reasonable efforts of the treatment facility to encourage the defendant's compliance, the court shall set the matter for a hearing not later than ten days after the report is received. The hearing may be waived by the defendant only if the report indicates that the defendant is competent. With respect to a defendant who is in the custody of the Commissioner of Correction pursuant to subsection (p) of this section, the Commissioner of Mental Health and Addiction Services shall retain responsibility for providing testimony at any hearing under this subsection. The court shall determine whether the defendant is competent or is making progress toward attaining competency within the period covered by the placement order. If the court finds that the defendant is competent, the defendant shall be returned to the custody of the Commissioner of Correction or released, if the defendant has met the conditions for release, and the court shall continue with the criminal proceedings. If the court finds that the defendant is still not competent but that the defendant is making progress toward attaining competency, the court may continue or modify the placement order. If the court finds that the defendant is still not competent but that the defendant is making progress toward attaining competency and inpatient placement is no longer the least restrictive placement appropriate and available to restore competency, the court shall consider whether the availability of such less restrictive placement is a sufficient basis on which to release the defendant on a promise to appear, conditions of release, cash bail or bond and may order continued treatment to restore competency on an outpatient basis. If the court finds that the defendant is still not competent and will not attain competency within the remainder of the period covered by the placement order absent administration of psychiatric medication for which the defendant is unwilling or unable to provide consent, the court shall proceed as provided in subdivisions (2), (3) and (4) of this subsection. If the court finds that the defendant is eligible for civil commitment, the court may order placement of the defendant at a treatment facility pending civil commitment proceedings pursuant to subdivision (2) of subsection (h) of this section.

(2) If the court finds that the defendant will not attain competency within the remainder of the period covered by the placement order absent administration of psychiatric medication for which the defendant is unwilling or unable to provide consent, and after any hearing held pursuant to subdivision (3) of this subsection, the court may order the involuntary medication of the defendant if the court finds by clear and convincing evidence that: (A) To a reasonable degree of medical certainty, involuntary medication of the defendant will render the defendant competent to stand trial, (B) an adjudication of guilt or innocence cannot be had using less intrusive means, (C) the proposed treatment plan is narrowly tailored to minimize intrusion on the defendant's liberty and privacy interests, (D) the proposed drug regimen will not cause an unnecessary risk to the defendant's health, and (E) the seriousness of the alleged crime is such that the criminal law enforcement interest of the state in fairly and accurately determining the defendant's guilt or innocence overrides the defendant's interest in self-determination.

(3) (A) If the court finds that the defendant is unwilling or unable to provide consent for the administration of psychiatric medication, and prior to deciding whether to order the involuntary medication of the defendant under subdivision (2) of this subsection, the court shall appoint a health care guardian who shall be a licensed health care provider with specialized training in the treatment of persons with psychiatric disabilities to represent the health care interests of the defendant before the court. Notwithstanding the provisions of section 52-146e, such health care guardian shall have access to the psychiatric records of the defendant. Such health care guardian shall file a report with the court not later than thirty days after his or her appointment. The report shall set forth such health care guardian's findings and recommendations concerning the administration of psychiatric medication to the defendant, including the risks and benefits of such medication, the likelihood and seriousness of any adverse side effects and the prognosis with and without such medication. The court shall hold a hearing on the matter not later than ten days after receipt of such health care guardian's report and shall, in deciding whether to order the involuntary medication of the defendant, take into account such health care guardian's opinion concerning the health care interests of the defendant.

(B) The court, in anticipation of considering continued involuntary medication of the defendant under subdivision (4) of this subsection, shall order the health care guardian to file a supplemental report updating the findings and recommendations contained in the health care guardian's report filed under subparagraph (A) of this subdivision.

(4) If, after the defendant has been found to have attained competency by means of involuntary medication ordered under subdivision (2) of this subsection, the court determines by clear and convincing evidence that the defendant will not remain competent absent the continued administration of psychiatric medication for which the defendant is unable to provide consent, and after any hearing held pursuant to subdivision (3) of this subsection and consideration of the supplemental report of the health care guardian, the court may order continued involuntary medication of the defendant if the court finds by clear and convincing evidence that: (A) To a reasonable degree of medical certainty, continued involuntary medication of the defendant will maintain the defendant's competency to stand trial, (B) an adjudication of guilt or innocence cannot be had using less intrusive means, (C) the proposed treatment plan is narrowly tailored to minimize intrusion on the defendant's liberty and privacy interests, (D) the proposed drug regimen will not cause an unnecessary risk to the defendant's health, and (E) the seriousness of the alleged crime is such that the criminal law enforcement interest of the state in fairly and accurately determining the defendant's guilt or innocence overrides the defendant's interest in self-determination. Continued involuntary medication ordered under this subdivision may be administered to the defendant while the criminal charges against the defendant are pending and the defendant is in the custody of the Commissioner of Correction or the Commissioner of Mental Health and Addiction Services. An order for continued involuntary medication of the defendant under this subdivision shall be reviewed by the court every one hundred eighty days while such order remains in effect. The court shall order the health care guardian to file a supplemental report for each such review. After any hearing held pursuant to subdivision (3) of this subsection and consideration of the supplemental report of the health care guardian, the court may continue such order if the court finds, by clear and convincing evidence, that the criteria enumerated in subparagraphs (A) to (E), inclusive, of this subdivision are met.

(5) The state shall hold harmless and indemnify any health care guardian appointed by the court pursuant to subdivision (3) of this subsection from financial loss and expense arising out of any claim, demand, suit or judgment by reason of such health care guardian's alleged negligence or alleged deprivation of any person's civil rights or other act or omission resulting in damage or injury, provided the health care guardian is found to have been acting in the discharge of his or her duties pursuant to said subdivision and such act or omission is found not to have been wanton, reckless or malicious. The provisions of subsections (b), (c) and (d) of section 5-141d shall apply to such health care guardian. The provisions of chapter 53 shall not apply to a claim against such health care guardian.

(l) **Failure of defendant to return to treatment facility in accordance with terms and conditions of release.** If a defendant who has been ordered placed for treatment on an inpatient basis at a mental health facility or a facility for persons with intellectual disability is released from such facility on a furlough or for work, therapy or any other reason and fails to return to the facility in accordance with the terms and conditions of the defendant's release, the person in charge of the facility, or such person's designee, shall, within twenty-four hours of the defendant's failure to return, report such failure to the prosecuting authority for the court location which ordered the placement of the defendant. Upon receipt of such a report, the prosecuting authority shall, within available resources, make reasonable efforts to notify any victim or victims of the crime for which the defendant is charged of such defendant's failure to return to the facility. No civil liability shall be incurred by the state or the prosecuting authority for failure to notify any victim or victims in accordance with this subsection.

The failure of a defendant to return to the facility in which the defendant has been placed may constitute sufficient cause for the defendant's rearrest upon order by the court.

(m) **Release or placement of defendant who will not attain competency. Report to court prior to release from placement.** (1) If at any time the court determines that there is not a substantial probability that the defendant will attain competency within the period of treatment allowed by this section, or if at the end of such period the court finds that the defendant is still not competent, the court shall consider any recommendation made by the examiners pursuant to subsection (d) of this section and any opinion submitted by the treatment facility pursuant to subparagraph (C) of subsection (j) of this section regarding eligibility for, and the appropriateness of, civil commitment to a hospital for psychiatric disabilities and shall either release the defendant from custody or order the defendant placed in the custody of the Commissioner of Mental Health and Addiction Services, the Commissioner of Children and Families or the Commissioner of Developmental Services. If the court orders the defendant placed in the custody of the Commissioner of Children and Families or the Commissioner of Developmental Services, the commissioner given custody, or the commissioner's designee, shall then apply for civil commitment in accordance with sections 17a-75 to 17a-83, inclusive, or 17a-270 to 17a-282, inclusive. If the court orders the defendant placed in the custody of the Commissioner of Mental Health and Addiction Services, the court may order the commissioner, or the commissioner's designee, to apply for civil commitment in accordance with sections 17a-495 to 17a-528, inclusive, or order the commissioner, or the commissioner's designee, to provide services to the defendant in a less restrictive setting, provided the examiners have determined in the written report filed pursuant to subsection (d) of this section or have testified pursuant to subsection (e) of this section that such services are available and appropriate. If the court orders the defendant placed in the custody of the Commissioner of Mental Health and Addiction Services and orders the commissioner to apply for civil commitment pursuant to this subsection, the court may order the commissioner to give the court notice when the defendant is released from the commissioner's custody if such release is prior to the expiration of the time within which the defendant may be prosecuted for the crime with which the defendant is charged, provided such order indicates when such time expires. If the court orders the defendant placed in the custody of the Commissioner of Developmental Services for purposes of commitment under any provision of sections 17a-270 to 17a-282, inclusive, the court may order the Commissioner of Developmental Services to give the court notice when the defendant's commitment is terminated if such termination is prior to the expiration of the time within which the defendant may be prosecuted for the crime with which the defendant is charged, provided such order indicates when such time expires.

(2) The court shall hear arguments as to whether the defendant should be released or should be placed in the custody of the Commissioner of Mental Health and Addiction Services, the Commissioner of Children and Families or the Commissioner of Developmental Services.

(3) If the court orders the release of a defendant charged with the commission of a crime that resulted in the death or serious physical injury, as defined in section 53a-3, of another person, or with a violation of subdivision (2) of subsection (a) of section 53-21, subdivision (2) of subsection (a) of section 53a-60 or section 53a-60a, 53a-70, 53a-70a, 53a-70b, 53a-71, 53a-72a or 53a-72b, or orders the placement of such defendant in the custody of the Commissioner of Mental Health and Addiction Services or the Commissioner of Developmental Services, the court may, on its own motion or on motion of the prosecuting authority, order, as a condition of such release or placement, periodic examinations of the defendant as to the defendant's competency at

intervals of not less than six months. Such an examination shall be conducted in accordance with subsection (d) of this section. Periodic examinations ordered by the court under this subsection shall continue until the court finds that the defendant has attained competency or until the time within which the defendant may be prosecuted for the crime with which the defendant is charged, as provided in section 54-193 or 54-193a, has expired, whichever occurs first.

(4) Upon receipt of the written report as provided in subsection (d) of this section, the court shall, upon the request of either party filed not later than thirty days after the court receives such report, conduct a hearing as provided in subsection (e) of this section. Such hearing shall be held not later than ninety days after the court receives such report. If the court finds that the defendant has attained competency, the defendant shall be returned to the custody of the Commissioner of Correction or released, if the defendant has met the conditions for release, and the court shall continue with the criminal proceedings.

(5) The court shall dismiss, with or without prejudice, any charges for which a nolle prosequi is not entered when the time within which the defendant may be prosecuted for the crime with which the defendant is charged, as provided in section 54-193 or 54-193a, has expired. Notwithstanding the record erasure provisions of section 54-142a, police and court records and records of any state's attorney pertaining to a charge which is nolled or dismissed without prejudice while the defendant is not competent shall not be erased until the time for the prosecution of the defendant expires under section 54-193 or 54-193a. A defendant who is not civilly committed as a result of an application made by the Commissioner of Mental Health and Addiction Services, the Commissioner of Children and Families or the Commissioner of Developmental Services pursuant to this section shall be released. A defendant who is civilly committed pursuant to such an application shall be treated in the same manner as any other civilly committed person.

(n) **Payment of costs.** The cost of the examination effected by the Commissioner of Mental Health and Addiction Services and of testimony of persons conducting the examination effected by the commissioner shall be paid by the Department of Mental Health and Addiction Services. The cost of the examination and testimony by physicians appointed by the court shall be paid by the Judicial Department. If the defendant is indigent, the fee of the person selected by the defendant to observe the examination and to testify on the defendant's behalf shall be paid by the Public Defender Services Commission. The expense of treating a defendant placed in the custody of the Commissioner of Mental Health and Addiction Services, the Commissioner of Children and Families or the Commissioner of Developmental Services pursuant to subdivision (2) of subsection (h) of this section or subsection (i) of this section shall be computed and paid for in the same manner as is provided for persons committed by a probate court under the provisions of sections 17b-122, 17b-124 to 17b-132, inclusive, 17b-136 to 17b-138, inclusive, 17b-194 to 17b-197, inclusive, 17b-222 to 17b-250, inclusive, 17b-256, 17b-263, 17b-340 to 17b-350, inclusive, 17b-689b and 17b-743 to 17b-747, inclusive.

(o) **Custody of defendant prior to hearing.** Until the hearing is held, the defendant, if not released on a promise to appear, conditions of release, cash bail or bond, shall remain in the custody of the Commissioner of Correction unless hospitalized as provided in sections 17a-512 to 17a-517, inclusive.

(p) **Placement of defendant who presents significant security, safety or medical risk. Defendant remaining in custody of Commissioner of Correction.** (1) This section shall not be construed to require the Commissioner of Mental Health and Addiction Services to place any defendant who presents a significant security, safety or medical risk in a hospital for psychiatric disabilities which does not have the trained staff, facilities or security to accommodate such a person, as determined by the Commissioner of Mental Health and Addiction Services in consultation with the Commissioner of Correction.

(2) If a defendant is placed for treatment with the Commissioner of Mental Health and Addiction Services pursuant to subsection (i) of this section and such defendant is not placed in a hospital for psychiatric disabilities pursuant to a determination made by the Commissioner of Mental Health and Addiction Services under subdivision (1) of this subsection, the defendant shall remain in the custody of the Commissioner of Correction. The Commissioner of Correction shall be responsible for the medical and psychiatric care of the defendant, and the Commissioner of Mental Health and Addiction Services shall remain responsible to provide other appropriate services to restore competency.

(3) If a defendant remains in the custody of the Commissioner of Correction pursuant to subdivision (2) of this subsection and the court finds that the defendant is still not competent and will not attain competency within the remainder of the period covered by the placement order absent administration of psychiatric medication for which the defendant is unwilling or unable to provide consent, the court shall proceed as provided in subdivisions (2), (3) and (4) of subsection (k) of this section. Nothing in this subdivision shall prevent the court from making any other finding or order set forth in subsection (k) of this section.

(q) **Defense of defendant prior to trial.** This section shall not prevent counsel for the defendant from raising, prior to trial and while the defendant is not competent, any issue susceptible of fair determination.

(r) **Credit for time in confinement on inpatient basis.** Actual time spent in confinement on an inpatient basis pursuant to this section shall be credited against any sentence imposed on the defendant in the pending criminal case or in any other case arising out of the same conduct in the same manner as time is credited for time spent in a correctional facility awaiting trial.

(1949 Rev., S. 8748; 1959, P.A. 523, S. 2; 1967, P.A. 670; 1969, P.A. 828, S. 213; P.A. 74-306, S. 1–4; P.A. 75-476, S. 1–3, 6; P.A. 76-353; 76-436, S. 532, 681; P.A. 77-415, S. 1, 2; P.A. 78-280, S. 117, 127; P.A. 80-313, S. 32; P.A. 81-365; P.A. 83-183, S. 1–5; P.A. 84-506; P.A. 85-288; 85-613, S. 79, 154; P.A. 93-91, S. 1, 2; P.A. 94-27, S. 16, 17; P.A. 95-146; 95-257, S. 11, 58; P.A. 96-90; 96-180, S. 128, 166; 96-215, S. 3, 4; P.A. 98-88, S. 1, 2; P.A. 01-41; June 30 Sp. Sess. P.A. 03-3, S. 13–17, 97; P.A. 04-28, S. 1; 04-76, S. 57; P.A. 05-19, S. 2, 3; P.A. 06-36, S. 1; P.A. 07-71, S. 1; 07-73, S. 2(b); 07-153, S. 1; P.A. 09-79, S. 1; P.A. 10-28, S. 1; P.A. 11-15, S. 1, 2; 11-129, S. 19; June 12 Sp. Sess. P.A. 12-1, S. 142; P.A. 16-126, S. 31.)

History: 1959 act added provision re computation and payment of hospital expense during confinement; 1967 act divided section into Subsecs., added qualification of inability to assist in his own defense to Subsecs. (a) and (c) and authority of judge to act on his own motion in Subsec. (a), amended Subsec. (b) to make mandatory the appointment of at least two psychiatrists rather than discretionary appointment of two or three physicians to examine accused and added provisions re commitment to state hospital for mental illness for examination, re physician's witnessing of examination and re filing of examination report; 1969 act added Subsec. (d) re maximum periods of commitment; P.A. 74-306 amended Subsec. (b) to make judge's appointment of examiners optional rather than mandatory, to change number appointed from "at least two" to "one or more", to replace provision re commitment to state hospital with provisions re commitment to commissioner of mental health and examination by clinical team, to impose 15-day deadline for filing written report, to require hearing and to specify when hearing may be waived, amended Subsecs. (c) and (d) to reflect changes in Subsec. (b), imposing 15-day deadline for hearing in Subsec. (c) and provision re application of Sec. 17-197 in Subsec. (d), and added Subsecs. (e) and (f) re commitment of violent person and re cost of examinations; P.A. 75-476 restated and clarified Subsec. (b) adding procedural details and limiting examinations to a determination of accused's ability to understand proceeding and assist in his own defense where previously determination was of accused's "mental condition", made similar changes in Subsec. (c), eliminating references to insanity and mental defectiveness and deleting provision stating that expenses are to be paid in same manner as expenses in superior court criminal prosecutions, and amended Subsec. (d) to replace previous provisions re maximum commitment for period equaling maximum sentence for the particular crime or for 25 years if case involves class A felony with maximum commitment period of 18 months, to make changes conforming provisions to changes in Subsecs. (b) and (c) and to add provisions re hearing procedure and options to proceed with trial, reconfine accused, etc.; P.A. 76-353 amended Subsec. (b) to set 10-day deadline for hearing where previously "prompt" hearing was required, amended Subsec. (c) to add references to commissioner of mental retardation, to require hearing within ten rather than 15 days and to add reference to possibility that accused will not be able to understand proceeding and assist in his own defense within remainder of commitment period, amended Subsec. (d) to conform with changes in Subsec. (c) and to restore optional maximum commitment for maximum period of sentence which may be imposed for the crime he is accused of and repealed Subsecs. (e) and (f) by omission; P.A. 76-436 amended section to reflect substitution of assistant state's attorneys for prosecuting attorneys, effective July 1, 1978; P.A. 77-415 restated provisions, reorganized Subsecs. and added Subsecs. (f) and (g) restoring provisions omitted by P.A. 76-353; P.A. 78-280 made technical grammatical change in Subsec. (b); P.A. 80-313 restated and reordered provisions, and revised subsection divisions but made no substantive changes; Sec. 54-40 transferred to Sec. 54-56d in 1981; P.A. 81-365 replaced previous section which was declared unconstitutional; P.A. 83-183 authorized placement of defendant in custody of children and youth services commissioner in Subsecs. (g), (i), (l) and (m) and specified that court may order treatment at mental retardation facilities in Subsec. (i); P.A. 84-506 amended Subsec. (d) to require the examiner to "prepare and sign, without notarization" a written report and file it with the court within 10 days of the examination, amended Subsec. (g) to replace provision requiring court to either release the defendant or place him in the custody of the commissioner of mental health, children and youth services or mental retardation with provision that the court shall "follow the procedure set forth in Subsec. (m)", added a new Subsec. (l) re the responsibilities of the person in charge of a treatment facility and the prosecuting authority when a defendant fails to return to such facility, and relettered remaining Subsecs. accordingly; P.A. 85-288 amended Subsec. (m) to provide that the court shall dismiss, with or without prejudice, any charges for which a nolle prosequi is not entered when the time within which the defendant may be prosecuted for the crime with which he is charged has expired; P.A. 85-613 made technical change in Subsec. (m), substituting reference to chapter 368t for reference to chapter 365a; P.A. 93-91 substituted commissioner and department of children and families for commissioner and department of children and youth services, effective July 1, 1993; P.A. 94-27 amended Subsec. (m) to delete reference to Secs. 17a-580 to 17a-603, inclusive, effective July 1, 1994; P.A. 95-146 amended Subsec. (d) to revise the composition of the clinical team by replacing "a psychiatric social worker" with "one of the following:

A clinical independent social worker certified pursuant to chapter 383b or a psychiatric nurse clinical specialist holding a master's degree in nursing", to add exception re appointment of an employee of the Department of Mental Health as a member of a clinical team, to revise the list of professionals authorized to observe the examination by deleting "a psychiatric social worker" and adding "a clinical independent social worker certified pursuant to chapter 383b or a psychiatric nurse clinical specialist holding a master's degree in nursing" and to require the report to be filed within 21 business days of the "date of the order" rather than within 10 days of the "completion of the examination"; P.A. 95-257 replaced Commissioner and Department of Mental Health with Commissioner and Department of Mental Health and Addiction Services, effective July 1, 1995; P.A. 96-90 amended Subsec. (m) to delete references to Secs. 17a-450 to 17a-484, inclusive, 17a-540 to 17a-550, inclusive, 17a-560 to 17a-576, inclusive, 17a-615 to 17a-618, inclusive, and 46a-11a to 46a-11g, inclusive; P.A. 96-180 made technical changes in Subsec. (d) by replacing references to "clinical independent social worker certified pursuant to chapter 383b" with "clinical social worker licensed pursuant to chapter 383b", effective June 3, 1996; P.A. 96-215 amended Subsec. (b) by deleting "clear and convincing" evidence and inserting "preponderance of the" evidence in lieu thereof, effective June 4, 1996; (Revisor's note: In 1997 the references to "17b-115 to 17b-138" and "17b-689 to 17b-693, inclusive," in Subsec. (n) were changed editorially by the Revisors to "17b-116 to 17b-138" and "17b-689, 17b-689b", respectively, to reflect the repeal of certain sections by Sec. 164 of June 18 Sp. Sess. P.A. 97-2); P.A. 98-88 amended Subsec. (k) to designate existing provisions as Subdiv. (1), redesignating former Subdivs. (1) and (2) as Subparas. (A) and (B), respectively, adding Subpara. (C) re a report that the defendant will not attain competency absent administration of psychiatric medication for which the defendant is unwilling or unable to provide consent and adding provision requiring the court to proceed as provided in Subdivs. (2) and (3) if it finds that the defendant will not attain competency absent administration of psychiatric medication for which the defendant is unwilling or unable to provide consent, to add new Subdiv. (2) authorizing the court to order the involuntary medication of the defendant if it makes certain findings by clear and convincing evidence, and to add new Subdiv. (3) requiring the appointment of a licensed health care provider to represent the health care interests of the defendant if the defendant is unable to provide consent for the administration of psychiatric medication, requiring such person to file a report with the court setting forth his findings and recommendations re the administration of psychiatric medication to the defendant and requiring the court to hold a hearing on the matter and consider such person's opinion in deciding whether to order the involuntary medication of the defendant, and amended Subsec. (m) to authorize a court when it releases a defendant charged with a crime that resulted in the death or serious physical injury of another person to order periodic examinations of the defendant, set forth the procedure for conducting such an examination and a subsequent hearing by the court, require the continuation of criminal proceedings if the defendant is found to have attained competency, specify the duration of such periodic examinations and add references to Sec. 54-193a; P.A. 01-41 amended Subsec. (k) to designate as "a health care guardian" the person appointed in Subdiv. (3) to represent the health care interests of the defendant, add Subdiv. (4) re indemnification of health care guardians and make technical changes in Subdivs. (1) and (2); June 30 Sp. Sess. P.A. 03-3 amended Subsec. (d) by adding provision re whether defendant appears eligible for civil commitment with monitoring by Court Support Services Division pursuant to Subsec. (h)(2), adding Subdiv. and Subpara. designators and making technical changes, amended Subsec. (h) by designating existing provisions as Subdiv. (1) and amending said Subdiv. by designating provisions re ordering placement for treatment as Subpara. (A) and adding Subpara. (B) re ordering placement at treatment facility pending civil commitment proceedings, and by adding Subdiv. (2) re placement of defendant in custody of Commissioner of Mental Health and Addiction Services at treatment facility pending civil commitment proceedings, amended Subsec. (j) by adding Subdiv. (4) re report whenever defendant has been placed for treatment pending civil commitment proceedings and application for civil commitment is denied or not pursued and by making technical changes, amended Subsec. (m) by adding provision re if court orders placement of defendant in custody of Commissioner of Mental Health and Addiction Services and by making technical changes, and amended Subsec. (n) by adding reference to Subsec. (h)(2), effective August 20, 2003, and, in repealing Secs. 17b-19, 17b-62 to 17b-65, inclusive, 17b-116, 17b-116a, 17b-116b, 17b-117, 17b-120, 17b-121, 17b-123, 17b-134, 17b-135, 17b-220, 17b-259 and 17b-287, also authorized deletion of internal references to said sections in this section, effective March 1, 2004; P.A. 04-28 amended Subsec. (d) by changing "or" to "and" re determinations of probability that defendant will regain competency and whether defendant appears eligible for civil commitment, effective April 28, 2004; P.A. 04-76 amended Subsec. (n) by deleting references to Secs. 17b-118b and 17b-221 that were repealed by the same act; (Revisor's note: In 2005, a reference in Subsec. (m) to Sec. 17a-283 was changed editorially by the Revisors to Sec. 17a-282 to reflect the repeal of Sec. 17a-283 by P.A. 04-54); P.A. 05-19 amended Subsec. (k)(1) by adding Subpara. (D) re denial of application for civil commitment of defendant and amended Subsec. (p) by deleting provision re state policeman to guard violent defendant after necessary placement in facility; P.A. 06-36 amended Subsec. (d) by adding provision re action of examiners upon determination of substantial probability that defendant will regain competency within maximum period of placement order, amended Subsec. (h)(2) by adding provision re request for voluntary admission under Sec. 17a-506, replacing provision re defendant ceasing voluntary participation in treatment plan with provision re defendant unwilling or unable to comply with treatment plan despite reasonable efforts of treatment facility to encourage compliance, deleting reference to Subsec. (j) and adding provision re contents of written progress report, amended Subsec. (j)(4) by adding provision re first 120 days of period covered by placement order, replacing "has been placed for treatment pending civil commitment proceedings" with "would be eligible for civil commitment" and deleting provision re application for civil commitment is denied or not pursued, amended Subsec. (k)(1) by replacing "has been placed for treatment pending civil commitment proceedings" with "would be eligible for civil commitment", deleting provision re application for civil commitment is denied or not pursued, adding provision re receipt of report pursuant to Subsec. (h)(2)(A)(iii) and adding provision re placement order upon finding that defendant is eligible for civil commitment, amended Subsec. (k)(3) by inserting "unwilling or" and made technical changes throughout section; P.A. 07-71 amended Subsec. (k) by making a conforming change in Subdiv. (1), making a technical change in Subdiv. (2), designating existing provisions of Subdiv. (3) as Subdiv. (3)(A) and making a technical change therein, adding Subdiv. (3)(B) re supplemental report of health care guardian, adding new Subdiv. (4) re continued involuntary medication of defendant and redesignating existing Subdiv. (4) as Subdiv. (5); pursuant to P.A. 07-73 "Commissioner of Mental Retardation" was changed editorially by the Revisors to "Commissioner of Developmental Services", effective October 1, 2007; P.A. 07-153 amended Subsec. (d) by adding provision re examiners' determination and recommendation re civil commitment of incompetent defendant to hospital for psychiatric disabilities, amended Subsec. (j) by adding new Subpara. (C) requiring progress report to contain opinion re eligibility for and appropriateness of such commitment and redesignating existing Subpara. (C) as Subpara. (D), made technical changes in Subsec. (k) and amended Subsec. (m) by adding provision re consideration of examiners' recommendation and treatment facility opinion re such commitment, distinguishing between commitment procedures applicable to placement of defendant in custody of Commissioner of Children and Families or Commissioner of Developmental Services and commitment procedures applicable to placement of defendant in custody of Commissioner of Mental Health and Addiction Services and authorizing the court to order the latter commissioner to provide services in a less restrictive setting; P.A. 09-79 amended Subsec. (d) to add provision re examiners' access to information on treatment dates and locations in department's database of treatment episodes for purpose of obtaining release of information from defendant and to provide that examination be completed within 15 business days, rather than 15 days, amended Subsec. (e) to add provision re exclusion of treatment information in database of treatment episodes unless defendant released the information and to provide that nothing in subsection shall limit other release or use of information from said database permitted by law, amended Subsec. (i) to require evaluators to transmit information obtained about defendant not later than 24 hours after court orders placement, amended Subsec. (j) to require person in charge of treatment facility or designee to provide written progress report to examiners not later than 5 business days after court finds defendant will not attain competency within period of placement order or defendant has regained competency, and made technical changes, effective June 2, 2009; P.A. 10-28 amended Subsec. (i) to substitute "examiners" for "evaluators" and "examination" for "evaluation", and amended Subsec. (m) to divide existing provisions into Subdivs. (1) to (5), to add provision allowing court to order commissioner to give court notice prior to committed defendant's release if release is prior to expiration of time within which defendant may be prosecuted in Subdiv. (1), to add provision re violation of Sec. 53-21(a)(2), 53a-60(a)(2), 53a-60a, 53a-70, 53a-70a, 53a-70b, 53a-71, 53a-72a or 53a-72b, provide that periodic examinations occur at intervals of not less than 6 months and reposition provision re continuation of periodic examinations in Subdiv. (3), and to add "record" re erasure in Subdiv. (5); P.A. 11-15 added Subsecs. (j)(5) and (k)(1)(A)(v) re defendant who is not competent but has improved sufficiently that inpatient commitment is no longer the least restrictive placement appropriate and available to restore competency, amended Subsec. (k)(1) to add provision re court consideration of whether availability of such less restrictive placement is a sufficient basis on which to release such defendant on a promise to appear, conditions of release, cash bail or bond, and made technical changes; P.A. 11-129 amended Subsec. (i) to substitute "facility for persons with intellectual disability" for "mental retardation facility"; June 12 Sp. Sess. P.A. 12-1 amended Subsec. (i)(2) to insert Subpara. designators (A) and (B) and add exception in Subpara. (A) that defendant placed with Commissioner of Mental Health and Addiction Services may remain in custody of Department of Correction, amended Subsec. (j) to make provisions applicable to Commissioner of Mental Health and Addiction Services re defendant in custody of Commissioner of Correction, amended Subsec. (k)(1) to provide that Commissioner of Mental Health and Addiction Services retain responsibility for providing testimony at hearing re defendant in custody of Commissioner of Correction, amended Subsec. (l) to substitute "a facility for persons with intellectual disability" for "mental retardation facility", amended Subsec. (m) to add provision in Subdiv. (1) allowing court to order Commissioner of Developmental Services to give court notice prior to committed defendant's release if release is prior to expiration of time within which defendant may be prosecuted, and add provision in Subdiv. (3) allowing court to order periodic examinations of defendant placed with Commissioner of Developmental Services, amended Subsec. (p) to designate existing provisions as Subdiv. (1) and amend same to replace provisions re placement of violent defendant with provisions re defendant who presents a significant security, safety or medical risk, add Subdiv. (2) re defendant remaining in custody of Commissioner of Correction and, add Subdiv. (3) re defendant in custody of Commissioner of Correction who the court finds is still not competent and will not attain competency absent administration of psychiatric medication; P.A. 16-126 amended Subsec. (h)(2)(B) by adding references to Secs. 14-227m and 14-227n(a)(1) and (2).

See Sec. 17a-543a re appointment of special limited conservator for and administration of medication to defendant placed in custody of Commissioner of Mental Health and Addiction Services.

See Sec. 17a-566 re required examination for signs of mental illness of persons convicted of certain crimes.

Annotations to former section 54-40:

Cited. 134 C. 45; 161 C. 20. A person who is "insane" within the meaning of the rule exempting mentally disabled persons from execution is not necessarily "insane" within the meaning of the rules precluding incompetent persons from trial, conviction and sentencing. 169 C. 13. Cited. 171 C. 454; 193 C. 526; 198 C. 273.

Cited. 14 CS 33.

Commitment under section operates in all particulars as civil commitment by Probate Court and committed person's assets must be used for his support; section applies to those already committed at time of enactment and is not ex post facto as it is not a criminal statute. 5 Conn. Cir. Ct. 542.

Annotations to present section:

Cited. 186 C. 476; 189 C. 61; 192 C. 383; Id., 520; 198 C. 598; 199 C. 359; 200 C. 224; 205 C. 673; 210 C. 304; 214 C. 476; 222 C. 312; 223 C. 557; 224 C. 29; Id., 907; 225 C. 524; 227 C. 930; 229 C. 228; 230 C. 109; Id., 572; 233 C. 44; Id., 813; 235 C. 671; 237 C. 633. Trial court improperly failed to canvass defendant personally and relied on old competency report despite defense counsel's representations that competency issues had newly surfaced; even when defendant is competent at commencement of trial, trial court must be alert to circumstances suggesting a change that would render defendant unable to meet the standards of competence to stand trial. 315 C. 151.

Cited. 5 CA 79; 6 CA 476; 8 CA 491; 9 CA 587; 14 CA 140; Id., 586; 17 CA 602; 20 CA 212; 22 CA 477; 25 CA 741; 28 CA 360; judgment reversed, see 229 C. 529; Id., 548; 30 CA 428; 32 CA 553; 34 CA 236; 36 CA 135; Id., 641; 54 CA 361. Defendant is presumed competent and burden to show otherwise is on party alleging incompetence. 62 CA 367. Trial court did not improperly fail to order competency hearing in light of court's observations of defendant at trial and various evaluation reports from mental health facility in which he had been treated, all of which concluded that he was competent to stand trial and that he was engaging in a deliberate pattern of behavior to delay his trial; trial court did not abuse its discretion in determining defendant was malingering in order to delay trial and that competency hearing under section was not required. 81 CA 294. Although defense counsel expressed concerns about defendant's competency, court had opportunity to observe defendant on numerous occasions and did not abuse its discretion by denying defendant's motion for a competency evaluation. 113 CA 651. To demonstrate that trial counsel was ineffective for purposes of this section, petitioner must show that trial counsel had substantial evidence to raise a reasonable doubt regarding petitioner's lack of competence, but failed to act on it by moving for a competency hearing, and such evidence required trial counsel to investigate petitioner's competence further, but failed to do so. 166 CA 707.

Cited. 44 CS 101. Juvenile, age 11, failed to meet burden of proving that he is not competent to stand trial because expert's opinion that juvenile is not competent lacks sufficient foundation and is based upon expert's age-bias for juvenile competency. 52 CS 267.

Subsec. (a):

No abuse of discretion in finding defendant competent to stand trial. 68 CA 470. Despite egregious and repeated outbursts during trial, defendant legally competent to stand trial since his demeanor and condition remained unchanged from the final pretrial evaluation and his conduct resulted not from mental incapacity but from his deliberate choice to obstruct the proceedings. 158 CA 119.

Subsec. (b):

Defendant who refuses to cooperate with evaluation process is presumed to be competent under Subsec. 124 CA 249.

Subsec. (i):

Placements for treatment must be treated cumulatively for purposes of applying the 18-month time limitation. 288 C. 610.

Subsec. (k):

Subdiv. (2): State's interest in trying defendant for intent to sell and manufacture of marijuana overrides defendant's right to self-determination because the offenses were serious and carried a mandatory minimum sentence of 7 years imprisonment. 299 C. 141.

Discussion of whether trial court correctly used standards set forth in statute in determining whether to order forced medication of defendant to render him competent to stand trial; confirmation that statute makes it mandatory to appoint a licensed health care provider to represent health care interests of defendant if court finds that defendant is unable to provide consent for involuntary medication. 70 CA 488.

State did not establish by clear and convincing evidence that forced administration of antipsychotic drugs either is substantially likely to render defendant competent to stand trial or, to a reasonable degree of medical certainty, will render defendant competent to stand trial, or that administration of antipsychotic drugs is narrowly tailored and substantially unlikely to have side effects that will interfere significantly with defendant's ability to assist counsel in preparing for trial and at trial. 53 CS 290.

Subsec. (m):

The term "defendant" includes a respondent in a juvenile matter. 291 C. 556. Subdiv. (5): Provision applies to all charges pending against defendant who has been found incompetent and not restorable to competency; the applicable statute of limitations runs continuously from the date that defendant committed the offense and not from the date that defendant had been found incompetent and not restorable to competency. 301 C. 630.

Unconditional release under statute is a reasonable legislative determination. 22 CA 199. Section, as amended by P.A. 98-88, applies retroactively to authorize court to order periodic competency evaluations of incompetent defendant charged with the commission of a crime that resulted in death or serious

Sec. 54-56e. (Formerly Sec. 54-76p). Accelerated pretrial rehabilitation.

(a) There shall be a pretrial program for accelerated rehabilitation of persons accused of a crime or crimes or a motor vehicle violation or violations for which a sentence to a term of imprisonment may be imposed, which crimes or violations are not of a serious nature. Upon application by any such person for participation in the program, the court shall, but only as to the public, order the court file sealed.

(b) The court may, in its discretion, invoke such program on motion of the defendant or on motion of a state's attorney or prosecuting attorney with respect to a defendant (1) who, the court believes, will probably not offend in the future, (2) who has no previous record of conviction of a crime or of a violation of section 14-196, subsection (c) of section 14-215, section 14-222a, subsection (a) or subdivision (1) of subsection (b) of section 14-224, section 14-227a or 14-227m or subdivision (1) or (2) of subsection (a) of section 14-227n, and (3) who states under oath, in open court or before any person designated by the clerk and duly authorized to administer oaths, under the penalties of perjury, (A) that the defendant has never had such program invoked on the defendant's behalf or that the defendant was charged with a misdemeanor or a motor vehicle violation for which a term of imprisonment of one year or less may be imposed and ten or more years have passed since the date that any charge or charges for which the program was invoked on the defendant's behalf were dismissed by the court, or (B) with respect to a defendant who is a veteran, that the defendant has not had such program invoked in the defendant's behalf more than once previously, provided the defendant shall agree thereto and provided notice has been given by the defendant, on a form prescribed by the Office of the Chief Court Administrator, to the victim or victims of such crime or motor vehicle violation, if any, by registered or certified mail and such victim or victims have an opportunity to be heard thereon. Any defendant who makes application for participation in such program shall pay to the court an application fee of thirty-five dollars. No defendant shall be allowed to participate in the pretrial program for accelerated rehabilitation more than two times. For the purposes of this section, "veteran" means any person who was discharged or released under conditions other than dishonorable from active service in the armed forces as defined in section 27-103.

(c) This section shall not be applicable: (1) To any person charged with (A) a class A felony, (B) a class B felony, except a violation of subdivision (1), (2) or (3) of subsection (a) of section 53a-122 that does not involve the use, attempted use or threatened use of physical force against another person, or a violation of subdivision (4) of subsection (a) of section 53a-122 that does not involve the use, attempted use or threatened use of physical force against another person and does not involve a violation by a person who is a public official, as defined in section 1-110, or a state or municipal employee, as defined in section 1-110, or (C) a violation of section 14-227a or 14-227m, subdivision (1) or (2) of subsection (a) of section 14-227n, subdivision (2) of subsection (a) of section 53-21 or section 53a-56b, 53a-60d, 53a-70, 53a-70a, 53a-70b, 53a-71, except as provided in subdivision (5) of this subsection, 53a-72a,

131

53a-72b, 53a-90a, 53a-196e or 53a-196f, (2) to any person charged with a crime or motor vehicle violation who, as a result of the commission of such crime or motor vehicle violation, causes the death of another person, (3) to any person accused of a family violence crime as defined in section 46b-38a who (A) is eligible for the pretrial family violence education program established under section 46b-38c, or (B) has previously had the pretrial family violence education program invoked in such person's behalf, (4) to any person charged with a violation of section 21a-267 or 21a-279 who (A) is eligible for the pretrial drug education and community service program established under section 54-56i, or (B) has previously had the pretrial drug education program or the pretrial drug education and community service program invoked on such person's behalf, (5) unless good cause is shown, to (A) any person charged with a class C felony, or (B) any person charged with committing a violation of subdivision (1) of subsection (a) of section 53a-71 while such person was less than four years older than the other person, (6) to any person charged with a violation of section 9-359 or 9-359a, (7) to any person charged with a motor vehicle violation (A) while operating a commercial motor vehicle, as defined in section 14-1, or (B) who holds a commercial driver's license or commercial driver's instruction permit at the time of the violation, (8) to any person charged with a violation of subdivision (6) of subsection (a) of section 53a-60, or (9) to a health care provider or vendor participating in the state's Medicaid program charged with a violation of section 53a-122 or subdivision (4) of subsection (a) of section 53a-123.

(d) Except as provided in subsection (e) of this section, any defendant who enters such program shall pay to the court a participation fee of one hundred dollars. Any defendant who enters such program shall agree to the tolling of any statute of limitations with respect to such crime and to a waiver of the right to a speedy trial. Any such defendant shall appear in court and shall, under such conditions as the court shall order, be released to the custody of the Court Support Services Division, except that, if a criminal docket for drug-dependent persons has been established pursuant to section 51-181b in the judicial district, such defendant may be transferred, under such conditions as the court shall order, to the court handling such docket for supervision by such court. If the defendant refuses to accept, or, having accepted, violates such conditions, the defendant's case shall be brought to trial. The period of such probation or supervision, or both, shall not exceed two years. If the defendant has reached the age of sixteen years but has not reached the age of eighteen years, the court may order that as a condition of such probation the defendant be referred for services to a youth service bureau established pursuant to section 10-19m, provided the court finds, through an assessment by a youth service bureau or its designee, that the defendant is in need of and likely to benefit from such services. When determining any conditions of probation to order for a person entering such program who was charged with a misdemeanor that did not involve the use, attempted use or threatened use of physical force against another person or a motor vehicle violation, the court shall consider ordering the person to perform community service in the community in which the offense or violation occurred. If the court determines that community service is appropriate, such community service may be implemented by a community court established in accordance with section 51-181c if the offense or violation occurred within the jurisdiction of a community court established by said section. If the defendant is charged with a violation of section 46a-58, 53-37a, 53a-181j, 53a-181k or 53a-181ℓ the court may order that as a condition of such probation the defendant participate in a hate crimes diversion program as provided in subsection (e) of this section. If a defendant is charged with a violation of section 53-247, the court may order that as a condition of such probation the defendant undergo psychiatric or psychological counseling or participate in an animal cruelty prevention and education program provided such a program exists and is available to the defendant.

(e) If the court orders the defendant to participate in a hate crimes diversion program as a condition of probation, the defendant shall pay to the court a participation fee of four hundred twenty-five dollars. No person may be excluded from such program for inability to pay such fee, provided (1) such person files with the court an affidavit of indigency or inability to pay, (2) such indigency or inability to pay is confirmed by the Court Support Services Division, and (3) the court enters a finding thereof. The Judicial Department shall contract with service providers, develop standards and oversee appropriate hate crimes diversion programs to meet the requirements of this section. Any defendant whose employment or residence makes it unreasonable to attend a hate crimes diversion program in this state may attend a program in another state which has standards substantially similar to, or higher than, those of this state, subject to the approval of the court and payment of the application and program fees as provided in this section. The hate crimes diversion program shall consist of an educational program and supervised community service.

(f) If a defendant released to the custody of the Court Support Services Division satisfactorily completes such defendant's period of probation, such defendant may apply for dismissal of the charges against such defendant and the court, on finding such satisfactory completion, shall dismiss such charges. If the defendant does not apply for dismissal of the charges against such defendant after satisfactorily completing such defendant's period of probation, the court, upon receipt of a report submitted by the Court Support Services Division that the defendant satisfactorily completed such defendant's period of probation, may on its own motion make a finding of such satisfactory completion and dismiss such charges. If a defendant transferred to the court handling the criminal docket for drug-dependent persons satisfactorily completes such defendant's period of supervision, the court shall release the defendant to the custody of the Court Support Services Division under such conditions as the court shall order or shall dismiss such charges. Upon dismissal, all records of such charges shall be erased pursuant to section 54-142a. An order of the court denying a motion to dismiss the charges against a defendant who has completed such defendant's period of probation or supervision or terminating the participation of a defendant in such program shall be a final judgment for purposes of appeal.

(P.A. 73-641, S. 1, 2; P.A. 74-38; P.A. 76-53; 76-179; P.A. 79-581, S. 11; 79-585, S. 10, 15; P.A. 81-446, S. 4; P.A. 82-9; P.A. 83-534, S. 7; P.A. 85-350, S. 2; 85-374; P.A. 87-343, S. 3, 4; P.A. 87-567, S. 5, 7; P.A. 88-145; P.A. 89-219, S. 7, 10; P.A. 91-24, S. 6; May Sp. Sess. P.A. 92-6, S. 116, 117; P.A. 93-138; P.A. 95-142, S. 4; 95-154; 95-225, S. 31; P.A. 97-248, S. 10, 12; P.A. 98-81, S. 16, 20; 98-208, S. 1, 2; P.A. 99-148, S. 3, 4; 99-187, S. 5; P.A. 00-72, S. 4, 12; 00-196, S. 39; 00-209, S. 5; P.A. 01-16; 01-84, S. 19, 26; P.A. 02-132, S. 34; P.A. 03-208, S. 2; P.A. 04-139, S. 9; P.A. 05-235, S. 5; P.A. 07-217, S. 192; P.A. 10-43, S. 22; P.A. 11-158, S. 1; P.A. 12-42, S. 2; P.A. 13-159, S. 3; 13-271, S. 43; P.A. 14-56, S. 3; 14-130, S. 34; 14-220, S. 2; 14-233, S. 7; P.A. 15-85, S. 19; 15-211, S. 10; P.A. 16-126, S. 32; 16-193, S. 29.)

History: P.A. 74-38 transferred power to invoke accelerated rehabilitation program from state's attorney or prosecuting attorney to the court and replaced provision which made section inapplicable to persons accused of class A, B or C felony with provision specifying that section is inapplicable in such cases "unless good cause is shown"; P.A. 76-53 clarified provision requiring that crime victims be given opportunity to express their views by specifying notice procedure; P.A. 76-179 required that candidate for rehabilitation state under oath that he has not previously had the program invoked on his behalf; P.A. 79-581 rendered provisions inapplicable to youths previously adjudged youthful offenders; P.A. 79-585 substituted office of adult probation for commission on adult probation; Sec. 54-76p transferred to Sec. 54-56e in 1981; P.A. 81-446 excluded persons charged with a violation of Sec. 14-227a from the provisions of this section; P.A. 82-9 substituted "in the future" for "again" and added provision re erasure of records pursuant to Sec. 54-142a upon dismissal; P.A. 83-534 excluded persons charged with a violation of Sec. 53a-56b or 53a-60d from the provisions of this section; P.A. 85-350 added provision that if the defendant does not apply for dismissal of the charges against him after satisfactory completion of the program the court may on its own motion make a finding of satisfactory completion and dismiss the charges; P.A. 85-374 added provision that certain court orders are final judgments for purposes of appeal; P.A. 87-343 made persons accused of a motor vehicle violation for which a sentence to a term of imprisonment may be imposed eligible for the program; P.A. 87-567 specified that section will not apply to persons accused of a family violence crime who are eligible for pretrial family education program established under Sec. 46b-38c or who have previously had pretrial family violence education program invoked in their behalf; P.A. 88-145 precluded from the program an accused who has a previous record of conviction of "a violation of section 14-196, subsection (c) of section 14-215, section 14-222a, subsection (a) of section 14-224 or section 14-227a", and made a technical change to conform with the changes made by P.A. 87-343 by requiring the accused to give notice to the victim or victims of such crime "or motor vehicle violation"; P.A. 89-219 established an application fee of $25 and a participation fee of $100; P.A. 91-24 added provision permitting the defendant to make a sworn statement "before any person designated by the clerk and duly authorized to administer oaths"; May Sp. Sess. P.A. 92-6 increased application fee from $25 to $35; P.A. 93-138 made persons accused of more than one crime or motor vehicle violation eligible for the program; P.A. 95-142 made ineligible for the program any person charged with a violation of Sec. 53-21(2), 53a-70, 53a-70a, 53a-70b, 53a-71, 53a-72a or 53a-72b; P.A. 95-154 made ineligible for the program any person charged with a class A or B felony and any person who has previously been adjudged a youthful offender for the commission of a class B felony, however provision re youthful offenders failed to take effect because of irreconcilable conflict with P.A. 95-225, the provisions of that act having taken precedence; P.A. 95-225 made ineligible for the program any person who has previously been adjudged a youthful offender where formerly a "youth" who has previously been adjudged a youthful offender was ineligible unless good cause was shown, and added provision authorizing the court to order certain defendants be referred for services to a youth service bureau as a condition of probation if the court finds that they are in need of and likely to benefit from such services; P.A. 97-248 authorized the transfer of a defendant to the court handling the criminal docket for drug-dependent persons if such a docket has been established in the judicial district, specified that the period of probation or supervision or both not exceed two years and provided that if a defendant transferred to the court handling the criminal docket for drug-dependent persons satisfactorily completes his period of supervision the court shall release the defendant to the Office of Adult Probation or dismiss the charges, effective July 1, 1997; P.A. 98-81 after "who has not been adjudged a youthful offender" added "on or after October 1, 1995", effective May 22, 1998; P.A. 98-208 inserted Subsec., Subdiv. and Subpara. indicators and added Subsec. (c)(2) making provisions inapplicable to any person charged with a crime or motor vehicle violation who, as a result of the commission of such crime or motor vehicle violation, causes the death of another person, effective July 1, 1998; P.A. 99-148 added Subsec. (c)(4) making provisions inapplicable to any person charged with a violation of Sec. 21a-267 or 21a-279 who is eligible for the pretrial drug education program under Sec. 54-56i or has previously had such program invoked in such person's behalf and made provisions of section gender neutral, effective July 1, 1999; P.A. 99-187 amended Subsec. (d) to add provision authorizing the court to order as a condition of probation that the defendant participate in the zero-tolerance drug supervision program established pursuant to Sec. 53a-39d and to make technical changes for purposes of gender neutrality; P.A. 00-72 amended Subsec. (d) to add exception re amount of the participation fee and add provision authorizing the court to order participation in a hate crimes diversion program as a condition of probation for defendants charged with a violation of Sec. 46a-58, 53-37a, 53a-181j, 53a-181k or 53a-181*l,* added new Subsec. (e) re hate crimes diversion program and redesignated former Subsec. (e) as Subsec. (f), effective July 1, 2001; P.A. 00-196 amended Subsec. (d) to add provisions requiring the court to consider ordering a person charged with a misdemeanor that did not involve the use, attempted use or threatened use of physical force against another person or a motor vehicle violation to perform community service as a condition of probation and authorizing such community service to be implemented by a community court if the offense or violation occurred within the jurisdiction of a community court, which provisions were formerly incorporated in Sec. 53a-28(e) and were deleted therefrom by same public act; P.A. 00-209 amended Subsec. (b)(3) to replace condition that defendant "has not previously been adjudged a youthful offender on or after October 1, 1995," with condition that defendant "has not been adjudged a youthful offender within the preceding five years", and to add provision that in determining whether to grant an application for a person who has been adjudged a youthful offender more than five years prior to the date of the application, the court shall have access to the youthful offender records of such person and may consider the crime such person was charged with as a youth; P.A. 01-16 amended Subsec. (c)(1) to add exception re eligibility of any person charged with a violation of Sec. 53a-122 that does not involve the use, attempted use or threatened use of physical force against another person and to make a technical change; P.A. 01-84 amended Subsec. (c)(1) to replace reference to "subdivision (2) of section 53-21" with "subdivision (2) of subsection (a) of section 53-21", effective July 1, 2001; P.A. 02-132 replaced "Office of Adult Probation" with "Court Support Services Division" in Subsecs. (d), (e) and (f) and replaced "Office of Adult Probation" with "Judicial Department" re authority for contracting with service providers in Subsec. (e); P.A. 03-208 amended Subsec. (d) to add provision authorizing the court to order counseling or participation in an animal cruelty prevention and education program for a defendant charged with a violation of Sec. 53-247; P.A. 04-139 amended Subsec. (c)(1) to make section inapplicable to a person charged with a violation of Sec. 53a-90a, 53a-196e or 53a-196f; P.A. 05-235 added Subsec. (c)(6) making section inapplicable to any person charged with a violation of Sec. 9-359 or 9-359a, effective July 1, 2005, and applicable to elections, primaries and referenda held on or after September 1, 2005; P.A. 07-217 made a technical change in Subsec. (d), effective July 12, 2007; P.A. 10-43 amended Subsec. (d) to delete provision authorizing court to order as condition of probation that defendant participate in zero-tolerance drug supervision program; P.A. 11-158 amended Subsec. (b) to delete Subdiv. (3) re condition that person not have been adjudged youthful offender within preceding 5 years, redesignate existing Subdiv. (4) as Subdiv. (3) and delete provision re court access to youthful offender records of person adjudged youthful offender more than 5 years prior to the application and consideration of crime such person was charged with as a youth; P.A. 12-42 amended Subsec. (b) to add provisions re defendant who is a veteran and re definition of "veteran"; P.A. 13-159 amended Subsec. (c) to add "except as provided in subdivision (5) of this subsection" in Subdiv. (1), substitute "pretrial drug education and community service program" for "pretrial drug education program" and make a conforming change in Subdiv. (4), and add Subpara. (A) designator re person charged with a class C felony and add Subpara. (B) re person charged under Sec. 53a-71(a)(1) for violation committed while less than 4 years older than the other person in Subdiv. (5); P.A. 13-271 amended Subsec. (c) to add Subdiv. (7) re person charged with motor vehicle violation while operating a commercial motor vehicle or who holds commercial driver's license or commercial driver's instruction permit at time of violation, effective January 1, 2014; P.A. 14-56 amended Subsec. (b) to redefine "veteran", effective May 23, 2014; P.A. 14-130 amended Subsec. (b)(2) to add reference to Sec. 14-224(b)(1); P.A. 14-220 amended Subsec. (c) to add Subdiv. (8) re person charged with violation of Sec. 53a-60(a)(6); P.A. 14-233 amended Subsec. (a) to add provision re court to order file sealed as to public upon application for participation in program, amended Subsec. (b) to add Subpara. (A) and (B) designators and provision re defendant charged with misdemeanor or motor vehicle violation when 10 years have passed since program was previously invoked and related charges were dismissed in Subdiv. (3), and to add provision re no defendant may participate in program more than 2 times, amended Subsec. (c) to add reference to violation of Sec. 53a-122(a)(1), (2) or (3) and add provision re public official or state or municipal employee charged with violation of Sec. 53a-122(a)(4), and made technical changes; P.A. 15-85 amended Subsec. (b) by substituting "form prescribed by the Office of the Chief Court Administrator" for "form approved by rule of court"; P.A. 15-211 amended Subsec. (c) by adding Subpara. designators (A) to (C) in Subdiv. (1) and adding Subdiv. (9) re health care provider or vendor participating in the Medicaid program charged with a violation of Sec. 53a-122 or 53a-123(a)(4); P.A. 16-126 amended Subsecs. (b)(2) and (c)(1) by adding references to Secs. 14-227m and 14-227n(a)(1) and (2); P.A. 16-193 made technical changes in Subsec. (c)(8) and (9).

Annotations to former section 54-76p:

Cited. 36 CS 527. Found error in denial of application for accelerated rehabilitation; detailed discussion in dissent. 37 CS 767.

Annotations to present section:

Claim to a dismissal of charges based on successful completion of conditions imposed under statute is interlocutory and review of claim not deemed proper as an exception to the ground rule requiring final judgment; exceptions discussed. 194 C. 650. Cited. 206 C. 512; 219 C. 752; 222 C. 331. Arbitrator improperly relied on employee's admission into accelerated rehabilitation program as evidence of cause for employee's discharge from employment despite clear and significant public policy that acceptance of accelerated rehabilitation is not evidence of guilt, that it cannot be used as evidence of guilt, and that it has no probative value on the issues of guilt or innocence of the charged offenses. 298 C. 824. Under 2014 Supplement, because the purpose of accelerated rehabilitation is to grant onetime offenders an opportunity to maintain a clean criminal record, a conviction obtained while participating in the program violates the purpose of section and requires a finding of unsatisfactory completion. 313 C. 590.

Denial of application for accelerated rehabilitation is not appealable following plea of nolo contendere. 2 CA 219. "Crime" means a single criminal act or transaction out of which one or more criminal charges might arise; determinative criterion governing statute is whether charges arise out of same act or transaction. 6 CA 505. Cited. 8 CA 273; 9 CA 631; judgment reversed, see 205 C. 352; Id., 686; 23 CA 559. Defendant charged with more than one single criminal act or transaction is ineligible for accelerated rehabilitation. 25 CA 235. Cited. 27 CA 635. Section is mandatory in nature; failure to complete satisfactorily the period of pretrial probation requires that case be returned to docket for trial. 45 CA 722. Court's appraisal of sufficiency of required apology to victim upheld, where defendant initiated other litigation that may have been impacted by wording of apology. 108 CA 605. Mere arrest of defendant, without more, was not sufficient ground to terminate defendant's accelerated rehabilitation. 110 CA 814.

Mere arrest of defendant, without more, is an insufficient ground for revoking his eligibility for dismissal of charges pursuant to accelerated rehabilitation program. 37 CS 853. Cited. Id., 864. Denial of application for accelerated rehabilitation not a final judgment from which right of appeal lies. 38 CS 552. Cited. Id., 689; 41 CS 454.

Subsec. (a):

After defendant's completion of program, court must act affirmatively by making a finding of satisfactory completion in order to dismiss charges against defendant and state's failure to terminate his status in the program during period of probation does not require court to dismiss the underlying charge. 98 CA 111. Legislature's use of both the singular "crime" and the plural "crimes" reflects the legislature's intent that statute may be invoked with respect to defendant accused of either one crime or multiple crimes, regardless of whether those crimes are temporally or otherwise related. 110 CA 442.

Sec. 54-56f. (Formerly Sec. 54-5). Requirements of sureties of the peace.

Any judge of the Superior Court may, from his personal knowledge or upon complaint of another, require sureties of the peace and good behavior from any person who threatens to beat or kill another or resists or abuses any officer in the execution of his office or contends with angry words or, by any unlawful act, terrifies or disturbs any person. When any person complains on oath to a judge of the Superior Court that he has just cause to fear that another will imprison, beat or kill the complainant, or procure others to do so, and that he is under fear of bodily harm, such judge may, if he believes such person has just cause for such fear, require sureties of the peace and good behavior from the person so complained of. Upon refusal of the person so required to find sureties of the peace in any of such cases, such judge may commit him to a community correctional center to remain until he is discharged by due course of law or until the next term of the superior court having criminal jurisdiction in such judicial district, which may make further order relating to the subject matter of any such offense; but, in all cases in which any person so complains on oath, such judge shall require of him a sufficient bond to prosecute his complaint to effect; and, if the person complained of is discharged by such judge for want of probable cause, the complainant shall pay all the expenses of such prosecution and such judge shall tax the same against the complainant and issue execution against him therefor, and the same when collected shall be paid into the hands of such judge, to be by him paid to those to whom the same may be due.

(1949 Rev., S. 8729; 1959, P.A. 28, S. 205; 1963, P.A. 642, S. 59; 1967, P.A. 656, S. 59; P.A. 73-116, S. 15; 73-667, S. 1, 2; P.A. 74-183, S. 129, 291; P.A. 76-436, S. 520, 681; P.A. 78-280, S. 1, 127.)

History: 1959 act substituted circuit court judge for trial justice and deleted provision for person who abuses justice of the peace; 1963 act deleted specification commitment be to jail "in county"; 1967 act changed court "session" to court "term"; P.A. 73-116 replaced "jail" with "community correctional center" and added reference to judicial districts; P.A. 73-667 changed effective date of P.A. 73-116 from October 1, 1973, to April 25, 1973; P.A. 74-183 replaced circuit court with court of common pleas, reflecting reorganization of judicial system, effective December 31, 1974; P.A. 76-436 replaced court of

Sec. 54-56g. Pretrial alcohol education program.

(a)(1) There shall be a pretrial alcohol education program for persons charged with a violation of section 14-227a, 14-227g or 14-227m, subdivision (1) or (2) of subsection (a) of section 14-227n or section 15-133 or 15-140n. Upon application by any such person for participation in such program and payment to the court of an application fee of one hundred dollars and a nonrefundable evaluation fee of one hundred dollars, the court shall, but only as to the public, order the court file sealed, provided such person states under oath, in open court or before any person designated by the clerk and duly authorized to administer oaths, under penalties of perjury that: (A) If such person is charged with a violation of section 14-227a, 14-227g or 14-227m, subdivision (1) or (2) of subsection (a) of section 14-227n, subsection (d) of section 15-133 or section 15-140n, such person has not had such program invoked in such person's behalf within the preceding ten years for a violation of section 14-227a, 14-227g or 14-227m, subdivision (1) or (2) of subsection (a) of section 14-227n, subsection (d) of section 15-133 or section 15-140n, (B) such person has not been convicted of a violation of section 53a-56b or 53a-60d, a violation of subsection (a) of section 14-227a before, on or after October 1, 1981, a violation of subdivision (1) or (2) of subsection (a) of section 14-227a on or after October 1, 1985, a violation of section 14-227g, a violation of section 14-227m or a violation of subdivision (1) or (2) of subsection (a) of section 14-227n, (C) such person has not been convicted of a violation of section 15-132a, subsection (d) of section 15-133, section 15-140/or section 15-140n, (D) such person has not been convicted in any other state at any time of an offense the essential elements of which are substantially the same as section 53a-56b, 53a-60d, 15-132a, 15-140/or 15-140n, subdivision (1) or (2) of subsection (a) of section 14-227a, section 14-227m, subdivision (1) or (2) of subsection (a) of section 14-227n or subsection (d) of section 15-133, and (E) notice has been given by such person, by registered or certified mail on a form prescribed by the Office of the Chief Court Administrator, to each victim who sustained a serious physical injury, as defined in section 53a-3, which was caused by such person's alleged violation, that such person has applied to participate in the pretrial alcohol education program and that such victim has an opportunity to be heard by the court on the application.

(2) The court shall provide each such victim who sustained a serious physical injury an opportunity to be heard prior to granting an application under this section. Unless good cause is shown, a person shall be ineligible for participation in such pretrial alcohol education program if such person's alleged violation of section 14-227a, 14-227g or 14-227m, subdivision (1) or (2) of subsection (a) of section 14-227n or subsection (d) of section 15-133 caused the serious physical injury, as defined in section 53a-3, of another person.

(3) The application fee imposed under this subsection shall be credited to the Criminal Injuries Compensation Fund established under section 54-215. The evaluation fee imposed under this subsection shall be credited to the pretrial account established under section 54-56k.

(b) The court, after consideration of the recommendation of the state's attorney, assistant state's attorney or deputy assistant state's attorney in charge of the case, may, in its discretion, grant such application. If the court grants such application, the court shall refer such person to the Court Support Services Division for assessment and confirmation of the eligibility of the applicant and to the Department of Mental Health and Addiction Services for evaluation. The Court Support Services Division, in making its assessment and confirmation, may rely on the representations made by the applicant under oath in open court with respect to convictions in other states of offenses specified in subsection (a) of this section. Upon confirmation of eligibility and receipt of the evaluation report, the defendant shall be referred to the Department of Mental Health and Addiction Services by the Court Support Services Division for placement in an appropriate alcohol intervention program for one year, or be placed in a state-licensed substance abuse treatment program. The alcohol intervention program shall include a ten-session intervention program and a fifteen-session intervention program. Any person who enters the pretrial alcohol education program shall agree: (1) To the tolling of the statute of limitations with respect to such crime, (2) to a waiver of such person's right to a speedy trial, (3) to complete ten or fifteen counseling sessions in an alcohol intervention program or successfully complete a substance abuse treatment program of not less than twelve sessions pursuant to this section dependent upon the evaluation report and the court order, (4) to commence participation in an alcohol intervention program or substance abuse treatment program not later than ninety days after the date of entry of the court order unless granted a delayed entry into a program by the court, (5) upon completion of participation in the alcohol intervention program, to accept placement in a substance abuse treatment program upon the recommendation of a provider under contract with the Department of Mental Health and Addiction Services pursuant to subsection (f) of this section or placement in a state-licensed substance abuse treatment program which meets standards established by the Department of Mental Health and Addiction Services, if the Court Support Services Division deems it appropriate, and (6) if ordered by the court, to participate in at least one victim impact panel. The suspension of the motor vehicle operator's license of any such person pursuant to section 14-227b shall be effective during the period such person is participating in the pretrial alcohol education program, provided such person shall have the option of not commencing the participation in such program until the period of such suspension is completed. If the Court Support Services Division informs the court that the defendant is ineligible for such program and the court makes a determination of ineligibility or if the program provider certifies to the court that the defendant did not successfully complete the assigned program or is no longer amenable to treatment and such person does not request, or the court denies, program reinstatement under subsection (e) of this section, the court shall order the court file to be unsealed, enter a plea of not guilty for such defendant and immediately place the case on the trial list. If such defendant satisfactorily completes the assigned program, such defendant may apply for dismissal of the charges against such defendant and the court, on reviewing the record of the defendant's participation in such program submitted by the Court Support Services Division and on finding such satisfactory completion, shall dismiss the charges. If the defendant does not apply for dismissal of the charges against such defendant after satisfactorily completing the assigned program the court, upon receipt of the record of the defendant's participation in such program submitted by the Court Support Services Division, may on its own motion make a finding of such satisfactory completion and dismiss the charges. Upon motion of the defendant and a showing of good cause, the court may extend the one-year placement period for a reasonable period for the defendant to complete the assigned program. A record of participation in such program shall be retained by the Court Support Services Division for a period of ten years from the date the court grants the application for participation in such program. The Court Support Services Division shall transmit to the Department of Motor Vehicles a record of participation in such program for each person who satisfactorily completes such program. The Department of Motor Vehicles shall maintain for a period of ten years the record of a person's participation in such program as part of such person's driving record. The Court Support Services Division shall transmit to the Department of Energy and Environmental Protection the record of participation of any person who satisfactorily completes such program who has been charged with a violation of the provisions of subsection (d) of section 15-133 or section 15-140n. The Department of Energy and Environmental Protection shall maintain for a period of ten years the record of a person's participation in such program as a part of such person's boater certification record.

(c) At the time the court grants the application for participation in the pretrial alcohol education program, such person shall also pay to the court a nonrefundable program fee of three hundred fifty dollars if such person is ordered to participate in the ten-session intervention program and a nonrefundable program fee of five hundred dollars if such person is ordered to participate in the fifteen-session intervention program. If the court grants the application for participation in the pretrial alcohol education program and such person is ordered to participate in a substance abuse treatment program, such person shall be responsible for the costs associated with participation in such program. No person may be excluded from either program for inability to pay such fee or cost, provided (1) such person files with the court an affidavit of indigency or inability to pay, (2) such indigency or inability to pay is confirmed by the Court Support Services Division, and (3) the court enters a finding thereof. If the court finds that a person is indigent or unable to pay for a treatment program, the costs of such program shall be paid from the pretrial account established under section 54-56k. If the court finds that a person is indigent or unable to pay for an intervention program, the court may waive all or any portion of the fee for such intervention program. If the court denies the application, such person shall not be required to pay the program fee. If the court grants the application and such person is later determined to be ineligible for participation in such pretrial alcohol education program or fails to complete the assigned program, the program fee shall not be refunded. All program fees shall be credited to the pretrial account established under section 54-56k.

(d) If a person returns to court with certification from a program provider that such person did not successfully complete the assigned program or is no longer amenable to treatment, the provider, to the extent practicable, shall include a recommendation to the court as to whether a ten-session intervention program, a fifteen-session intervention program or placement in a state-licensed substance abuse treatment program would best serve such person's needs. The provider shall also indicate whether the current program referral was an initial referral or a reinstatement to the program.

(e) When a person subsequently requests reinstatement into an alcohol intervention program or a substance abuse treatment program and the Court Support Services Division verifies that such person is eligible for reinstatement into such program and thereafter the court favorably acts on such request, such person shall pay a nonrefundable program fee of one hundred seventy-five dollars if ordered to complete a ten-session intervention program or two hundred fifty dollars if ordered to complete a fifteen-session intervention program, as the case may be. Unless good cause is shown, such fees shall not be waived. If the court grants a person's request to be reinstated into a treatment program, such person shall be responsible for the costs, if any, associated with being reinstated into the treatment program. All program fees collected in connection with a reinstatement to an intervention program shall be credited to the pretrial account established under section 54-56k. No person shall be permitted more than two program reinstatements pursuant to this subsection.

(f) The Department of Mental Health and Addiction Services shall contract with service providers, develop standards and oversee appropriate alcohol programs to meet the requirements of this section. Said department shall adopt regulations, in accordance with chapter 54, to establish standards for such alcohol programs. Any person ordered to participate in a treatment program shall do so at a state-licensed treatment program which meets the standards established by said department. Any defendant whose employment or residence makes it unreasonable to attend an alcohol intervention program or a substance abuse treatment program in this state may attend a program in another state which has standards substantially similar to, or higher than, those of this state, subject to the approval of the court and payment of the application, evaluation and program fees and treatment costs, as appropriate, as provided in this section.

(g) The court may, as a condition of granting such application, require that such person participate in a victim impact panel program approved by the Court Support Services Division of the Judicial Department. Such victim impact panel program shall provide a nonconfrontational forum for the victims of alcohol-related or drug-related offenses and offenders to share experiences on the impact of alcohol-related or drug-related incidents in their lives. Such victim impact panel program shall be conducted by a nonprofit organization that advocates on behalf of victims of accidents caused by persons who operated a motor vehicle while under the influence of intoxicating liquor or any drug, or both. Such organization may assess a participation fee of not more than seventy-five dollars on any person required by the court to participate in such program, provided such organization shall offer a hardship waiver when it has determined that the imposition of a fee would pose an economic hardship for such person.

(h) The provisions of this section shall not be applicable in the case of any person charged with a violation of section 14-227a or 14-227m or subdivision (1) or (2) of subsection (a) of section 14-227n (1) while operating a commercial motor vehicle, as defined in section 14-1, or (2) who holds a commercial driver's license or commercial driver's instruction permit at the time of the violation.

(P.A. 81-446, S. 1; P.A. 82-408, S. 1; 82-472, S. 166, 183; P.A. 83-508, S. 1, 5; 83-571, S. 1; P.A. 85-350, S. 3; 85-417; 85-529, S. 1, 4; 85-596, S. 3; P.A. 86-403, S. 91, 132; P.A. 89-110, S. 1–3; 89-219, S. 8, 10; 89-314, S. 4, 5; P.A. 91-24, S. 7; 91-243; May Sp. Sess. P.A. 92-6, S. 81, 117; P.A. 93-381, S. 9, 39; P.A. 94-135, S. 8; P.A. 95-257, S. 5, 58; P.A. 96-180, S. 129, 166; P.A. 97-309, S. 14, 23; 97-322, S. 7, 9; June 18 Sp. Sess. P.A. 97-8, S. 32, 88; P.A. 98-81, S. 11; P.A. 99-255, S. 3; P.A. 01-201, S. 2, 3; June Sp. Sess. P.A. 01-8, S. 9, 13; P.A. 02-132, S. 35; May 9 Sp. Sess. P.A. 02-1, S. 117; P.A. 03-244, S. 11, 13; June 30 Sp. Sess. P.A. 03-6, S. 177; P.A. 04-217, S. 19; 04-250, S. 2; P.A. 06-130, S. 21; P.A. 07-167, S. 42; June Sp. Sess. P.A. 07-4, S. 20; P.A. 09-110, S. 11; Sept. Sp. Sess. P.A. 09-3, S. 51; P.A. 10-18, S. 24; 10-30, S. 1; P.A. 11-80, S. 1; P.A. 13-271, S. 44; P.A. 14-110, S. 1; P.A. 15-85, S. 20; 15-211, S. 11; P.A. 16-126, S. 4, 5.)

History: P.A. 82-408 added "before or after October 1, 1982" after "14-227a" in Subsec. (a), in Subsec. (b) changed "grants" to "may, in its discretion, grant" and eliminated provision that license suspension shall be ineffective during period of participation in program and reversed upon satisfactory completion of program, in Subsec. (d) changed "office of adult probation" to "Connecticut alcohol and drug abuse commission" and "Connecticut alcohol and drug abuse commission" to "service providers" and in Subsec. (e) after "fund" added "from which all moneys except administrative costs, shall be transferred to the Connecticut alcohol and drug abuse commission"; P.A. 82-472 changed date applicable to violations of Sec. 14-227a from October 1, 1982, to October 1, 1981; P.A. 83-508 repealed provision establishing alcohol education and treatment revolving fund from which moneys shall be transferred to Connecticut alcohol and drug abuse commission for education and treatment programs and provided that $200 fee shall be credited to the general fund instead of being deposited in revolving fund and that any balance in the revolving fund on July 1, 1983, shall be transferred to the general fund; P.A. 83-571 amended Subsec. (b) to provide that a person who enters the system agrees to accept more intensive treatment or other forms of education or treatment or to participate in additional meetings or counseling sessions if the office of adult probation deems it appropriate, to provide that the case of a defendant "no longer amenable to treatment under such program" shall be placed on the trial list, and to replace the provision that a defendant's "case shall be brought to trial" with provision that the court shall "enter a plea of not guilty for such defendant and immediately place the case on the trial list", to require the office of adult probation to transmit to the department of motor vehicles a record of participation for each person who satisfactorily completes such program and to require the department of motor vehicles to maintain for 7 years a record of a person's participation in the program, and amended Subsec. (c) to increase the fee for participation from $200 to $250; P.A. 85-350 amended Subsec. (a) to provide that unless good cause is shown a person is ineligible for the program if his violation caused the serious physical injury of another person, and amended Subsec. (b) to provide that if the defendant does not apply for dismissal of the charges against him after satisfactory completion of the program the court may on its own motion make a finding of satisfactory completion and dismiss the charges; P.A. 85-417 replaced references to office of adult probation with references to bail commission; P.A. 85-529 amended Subsec. (a) to establish an application fee of $15 and provide that said fee be credited to the criminal injuries compensation fund; P.A. 85-596 amended Subsec. (a) to exclude persons convicted of a violation of "subsection (a)" of section 14-227a before or after October 1, 1981, or "a violation of subdivision (1) or (2) of subsection (a) of section 14-227a on or after October 1, 1985"; P.A. 86-403 made technical change in Subsec. (b); P.A. 89-110 amended Subsec. (a) to exclude persons convicted of a violation of Sec. 53a-56b or 53a-60d or convicted in any other state at any time of an offense the essential elements of which are substantially the same as Sec. 53a-56b, 53a-60d or 14-227a(a)(1) or (2), amended Subsec. (b) to authorize the bail commission to rely on the representations made by the applicant re convictions in other states, and amended Subsec. (d) to authorize a defendant to attend an alcohol education and treatment program in another state under certain conditions; P.A. 89-219 amended Subsec. (a) to raise the application fee from $15 to $50; P.A. 89-314 amended Subsec. (b) to add proviso that a person whose license has been suspended pursuant to Sec. 14-227b shall have the option of not commencing participation in the program until the period of such suspension is completed; P.A. 91-24 amended Subsec. (a) to add provision permitting the person to make a sworn statement "before any person designated by the clerk and duly authorized to administer oaths"; P.A. 91-243 amended Subsec. (b) to make technical language changes to clarify the role of the Connecticut alcohol and drug abuse commission in the pretrial alcohol education system and repealed obsolete Subsec. (e) re transfer of moneys in alcohol education and treatment fund to general fund; May Sp. Sess. P.A. 92-6 amended Subsec. (c) to raise fee from $250 to $350; P.A. 93-381 replaced Connecticut alcohol and drug abuse commission and executive director with department and commissioner of public health and addiction services, respectively, effective July 1, 1993; P.A. 94-135 amended Subsec. (b) to provide referral to bail commissioner for assessment and confirmation of eligibility for program, and amended Subsec. (c) to require payment of nonrefundable program fee at time court grants application and to specify that payment of such fee is not required if court denies application, but that fee is not refundable if ineligibility is determined at a later time or applicant does not complete the program; P.A. 95-257 replaced Commissioner and Department of Public Health and Addiction Services with Commissioner and Department of Mental Health and Addiction Services, effective July 1, 1995; P.A. 96-180 made technical change in Subsec. (d), substituting "department" for "commission", effective June 3, 1996; P.A. 97-309 and June 18 Sp. Sess. P.A. 97-8 both changed eight meetings or counseling sessions to ten counseling sessions in Subsec. (b) and in Subsec. (c) increased the program fee from $350 to $425, effective July 1, 1997; P.A. 97-322 revised effective date of P.A. 97-309 but without affecting this section; P.A. 98-81 amended Subsecs. (a) and (b) by changing "information or complaint" to "court file"; P.A. 99-255 amended Subsec. (b) to require a person who enters the system to agree to participate in at least fifteen counseling sessions if such person was charged with a violation of Sec. 14-227a(a)(2) and had a blood alcohol ratio of 0.16% or more of alcohol, by weight, amended Subsec. (c) to establish a program fee of $600 if the person was charged with a violation of Sec. 14-227a(a)(2) and had a blood alcohol ratio of 0.16% or more of alcohol, by weight, and made technical changes for purposes of gender neutrality (Revisor's note: In Subsec. (b) a reference to "sixteen-hundredths of one per cent of more of alcohol" was changed editorially by the Revisors to "sixteen-hundredths of one per cent or more of alcohol" for consistency with language in Subsec. (c)); P.A. 01-201 added Subsec. (b)(5) requiring a person who enters the system to agree to participate in at least one victim impact panel if ordered by the court and added Subsec. (e) to authorize the court to require participation in a victim impact panel program as a condition of granting the application, specify the nature of the program and the organization that will conduct the program and authorize the organization to assess a participation fee; June Sp. Sess. P.A. 01-8 amended Subsec. (c) by changing "General Fund" to "pretrial account", effective July 1, 2001; P.A. 02-132 replaced "Bail Commission" with "Court Support Services Division" in Subsecs. (b) and (c); May 9 Sp. Sess. P.A. 02-1 amended Subsec. (a) to require a pretrial alcohol education system for persons charged with a violation of Sec. 14-227g and a nonrefundable evaluation fee of $100, to require the court to order the court file sealed provided there is a statement under oath that, if such person is charged with a violation of Sec. 14-227a, such person has not had such system invoked in his or her behalf within the preceding 10 years for a violation of said section, and, if such person is charged with a violation of Sec. 14-227g, such person has never had such system invoked in his or her behalf for a violation of Sec. 14-227a or 14-227g, and to make technical changes, amended Subsec. (b) to require the court to refer applicants to the Department of Mental Health and Addiction Services for evaluation, to require any person who enters the system to agree to complete ten or fifteen counseling sessions in an alcohol intervention program dependent upon the evaluation report and the court order and to make technical changes, amended Subsec. (c) to require payment to the court of a nonrefundable program fee of $325 if such person is ordered to participate in the ten-session program and a nonrefundable program fee of $500 if such person is ordered to participate in the fifteen-session program and to make technical changes, and amended Subsec. (d) to add provision re payment of the evaluation fee, effective July 1, 2002; P.A. 03-244 amended Subsec. (a) to include reference to Secs. 15-133, 15-140l and 15-140n and amended Subsec. (b) to provide for transmittal of the record of participation to the Department of Environmental Protection for persons who violated Sec. 15-133, 15-140l or 15-140n; June 30 Sp. Sess. P.A. 03-6 amended Subsec. (a) to restore existing statutory language inadvertently omitted in the drafting of public act 03-244; P.A. 04-217 added Subsec. (f) providing section not applicable where person charged with violation of Sec. 14-227a while operating commercial motor vehicle, effective January 1, 2005; P.A. 04-250 amended Subsec.

(a) to make technical changes, amended Subsec. (b) to authorize the placement of the defendant in a state-licensed substance abuse treatment program, add as an alternative in Subdiv. (3) successful completion of a substance abuse treatment program of not less than twelve sessions, add in Subdiv. (4) that the person agrees to accept placement in a treatment program "upon completion of participation in the alcohol intervention program" and replace in Subdiv. (4) "placement in a treatment program which has standards substantially similar to, or higher than, a program of a provider under contract with the Department of Mental Health and Addiction Services" with "placement in a state-licensed treatment program which meets standards established by" said department, amended Subsec. (c) to replace "application for participation in the pretrial alcohol education system" with "application for participation in the alcohol intervention program", add provision that if the court grants participation in a treatment program the person is responsible for the costs associated with participation in such program, add provision that if the court finds a person is indigent or unable to pay for a treatment program the costs of such program shall be paid from the pretrial account established under Sec. 54-56k and make technical changes and amended Subsec. (d) to require any person ordered to participate in a treatment program to do so at a state-licensed treatment program which meets the standards established by said department and replace "an alcohol program" with "an alcohol intervention program or a treatment program"; P.A. 06-130 amended Subsec. (f) by making section inapplicable to holders of commercial driver's licenses, effective July 1, 2006; P.A. 07-167 amended Subsec. (f) by deleting provision re holder of a commercial driver's license, effective July 1, 2007; June Sp. Sess. P.A. 07-4 amended Subsec. (e) to increase fee from $25 to $75 and to permit a waiver where fee would pose economic hardship; P.A. 09-140 amended Subsecs. (a) and (b) by adding references to Sec. 15-132a and making a technical change, effective July 1, 2009; Sept. Sp. Sess. P.A. 09-3 amended Subsec. (a) by replacing pretrial alcohol education system with pretrial alcohol education program, increasing application fee from $50 to $100 and specifying that evaluation fee shall be credited to pretrial account established under Sec. 54-56k, amended Subsec. (b) by providing that alcohol intervention program shall include 10-session and 15-session intervention programs, adding new Subdiv. (4) re commencing participation in program not later than 90 days after date of entry of court order, redesignating existing Subdivs. (4) and (5) as Subdivs. (5) and (6), adding provision re entry of not guilty plea for any person who does not pursue or who is denied program reinstatement by the court under Subsec. (e), extending from 7 to 10 years the record retention requirements re program participation for Departments of Motor Vehicles and Environmental Protection and making a technical change, amended Subsec. (c) by increasing alcohol intervention program fee from $325 to $350 and deleting "such evaluation and" re fees credited to pretrial account, added new Subsec. (d) re recommendations from program providers re persons who do not successfully complete assigned program, added new Subsec. (e) re reinstatement into intervention or treatment program and redesignated existing Subsecs. (d) to (f) as Subsecs. (f) to (h), effective January 1, 2010; P.A. 10-18 amended Subsecs. (a) to (c) by replacing references to "system" with references to "program"; P.A. 10-30 made technical changes and substituted references to "program" for references to "system", amended Subsec. (b) to substitute "ten years from the date the court grants the application for participation in such program" for "seven years from the date of application", amended Subsec. (c) to allow waiver of fees if court finds person indigent or unable to pay for intervention program, and amended Subsec. (f) to reference treatment costs, effective July 1, 2010; pursuant to P.A. 11-80, "Department of Environmental Protection" was changed editorially by the Revisors to "Department of Energy and Environmental Protection" in Subsec. (b), effective July 1, 2011; P.A. 13-271 amended Subsec. (h) to add Subdiv. (1) designator re operating a commercial motor vehicle and add Subdiv. (2) re person who holds commercial driver's license or commercial driver's instruction permit at time of violation, effective January 1, 2014; P.A. 14-110 amended Subsec. (a) to add new Subdiv. (1) to (3) designators, redesignate existing Subdivs. (1) to (4) as Subparas. (A) to (D) and add Subpara. (E) re notice to victim who sustained serious physical injury caused by alleged violation in Subdiv. (1), add provision re victim's opportunity to be heard prior to granting of application in Subdiv. (2), and make technical changes; P.A. 15-85 amended Subsec. (a)(1)(E) by substituting "form prescribed by the Office of the Chief Court Administrator" for "form approved by rule of court"; P.A. 15-211 amended Subsec. (a)(1) by deleting references to Secs. 15-132a and 15-140*l*, adding references to Secs. 14-227g, 15-133(d) and 15-140n, deleting former Subpara. (B) re person charged with violation of Sec. 14-227g, redesignating existing Subpara. (C) as Subpara. (B) and adding reference to violation of Sec. 14-227g therein, adding new Subpara. (C) re person not convicted of violation of Sec. 15-132a, 15-133(d), 15-140*l* or 15-140n, and adding references to Secs. 15-132a, 15-133(d), 15-140*l* and 15-140n in Subpara. (D), amended Subsec. (a)(2) by adding reference to Sec. 15-133(d), and amended Subsec. (b) by replacing references to Secs. 15-132a, 15-133 and 15-140*l* with reference to Sec. 15-133(d); P.A. 16-126 amended Subsecs. (a) and (h) by adding references to Secs. 14-227m and 14-227n(a)(1) and (2).

Trial court might reasonably have determined that defendant lost her eligibility to continue in the system of alcohol education when, shortly after she had been admitted, she again operated her vehicle while intoxicated. 200 C. 102. Pretrial alcohol education program cited. Id., 615.

Cited. 39 CA 11; 45 CA 722. Program is a pretrial diversionary program designed to avoid trial and therefore court did not abuse its discretion in denying application for participation in program after jury selection had commenced. 86 CA 751.

Cited. 37 CS 767; 38 CS 675; Id., 689.

Subsec. (a):

Subdiv. (1)(D) plain and unambiguous; trial court properly denied application and related motion to dismiss because of defendant's 1997 New York conviction since statute expressly states that persons with out of state convictions, at any time, are not eligible for program. 162 CA 145.

Subsec. (f):

Defendant was ineligible for pretrial alcohol education program because she was the holder of a commercial driver's license at the time she was charged with violating Sec. 14-227a concerning operation of a motor vehicle while under the influence of intoxicating liquor or drugs. 110 CA 836.

Sec. 54-56h. Consideration of defendant's contribution to Criminal Injuries Compensation Fund or of community service work hours. Payment of monetary contribution to fund.

(a) The court may, in the disposition of any criminal or motor vehicle case, including a dismissal or the imposition of a sentence, consider the fact that the defendant has made a monetary contribution to the Criminal Injuries Compensation Fund established under section 54-215 or a contribution of community service work hours to a private nonprofit charity or other nonprofit organization.

(b) In entering a nolle prosequi, the state's attorney, assistant state's attorney or deputy assistant state's attorney in charge of the case may consider the fact that the defendant has made a monetary contribution to the Criminal Injuries Compensation Fund or a contribution of community service work hours to a private nonprofit charity or other nonprofit organization.

(c) A monetary contribution made by a defendant to the Criminal Injuries Compensation Fund as provided in this section may be paid to either the clerk of the court or the Office of Victim Services.

(P.A. 91-85; P.A. 97-257, S. 7, 13; P.A. 06-152, S. 9.)

History: P.A. 97-257 added references to contributions to "Criminal Injuries Compensation Fund established under section 54-215", effective July 1, 1997; P.A. 06-152 made a technical change in Subsec. (b) and added Subsec. (c) re payment of monetary contribution to Criminal Injuries Compensation Fund, effective July 1, 2006.

Sec. 54-56i. Pretrial drug education and community service program.

(a) There is established a pretrial drug education and community service program for persons charged with a violation of section 21a-267, 21a-279 or 21a-279a. The pretrial drug education and community service program shall include a fifteen-session drug education program and a substance abuse treatment program of not less than fifteen sessions, and the performance of community service.

(b) Upon application by any such person for participation in such program and payment to the court of an application fee of one hundred dollars and a nonrefundable evaluation fee of one hundred fifty dollars, the court shall, but only as to the public, order the court file sealed. A person shall be ineligible for participation in such pretrial drug education and community service program if such person has twice previously participated in (1) the pretrial drug education program established under the provisions of this section in effect prior to October 1, 2013, (2) the community service labor program established under section 53a-39c, (3) the pretrial drug education and community service program established under this section, or (4) any of such programs, except that the court may allow a person who has twice previously participated in such programs to participate in the pretrial drug education and community service program one additional time, for good cause shown. The evaluation and application fee imposed under this subsection shall be credited to the pretrial account established under section 54-56k.

(c) The court, after consideration of the recommendation of the state's attorney, assistant state's attorney or deputy assistant state's attorney in charge of the case, may, in its discretion, grant such application. If the court grants such application, the court shall refer such person (1) to the Court Support

146

Services Division for confirmation of the eligibility of the applicant, (2) to the Department of Mental Health and Addiction Services for evaluation and determination of an appropriate drug education or substance abuse treatment program for the first or second time such application is granted, and (3) to a state-licensed substance abuse treatment program for evaluation and determination of an appropriate substance abuse treatment program for the third time such application is granted, except that, if such person is a veteran, the court may refer such person to the Department of Veterans Affairs or the United States Department of Veterans Affairs, as applicable, for any such evaluation and determination. For the purposes of this subsection and subsection (d) of this section, "veteran" means any person who was discharged or released under conditions other than dishonorable from active service in the armed forces as defined in section 27-103.

(d) (1) (A) Upon confirmation of eligibility and receipt of the evaluation and determination required under subsection (c) of this section, such person shall be placed in the pretrial drug education and community service program and referred by the Court Support Services Division for the purpose of receiving appropriate drug education services or substance abuse treatment program services, as recommended by the evaluation conducted pursuant to subsection (c) of this section and ordered by the court, to the Department of Mental Health and Addiction Services or to a state-licensed substance abuse treatment program for placement in the appropriate drug education or substance abuse treatment program, except that, if such person is a veteran, the division may refer such person to the Department of Veterans Affairs or the United States Department of Veterans Affairs, subject to the provisions of subdivision (2) of this subsection.

(B) Persons who have been granted entry into the pretrial drug education and community service program for the first time shall participate in either a fifteen-session drug education program or a substance abuse treatment program of not less than fifteen sessions, as ordered by the court on the basis of the evaluation and determination required under subsection (c) of this section. Persons who have been granted entry into the pretrial drug education and community service program for the second time shall participate in either a fifteen-session drug education program or a substance abuse treatment program of not less than fifteen sessions, as ordered by the court based on the evaluation and determination required under subsection (c) of this section. Persons who have been granted entry into the pretrial drug education and community service program for a third time shall be referred to a state-licensed substance abuse program for evaluation and participation in a course of treatment as ordered by the court based on the evaluation and determination required under subsection (c) of this section.

(C) Persons who have been granted entry into the pretrial drug education and community service program shall also participate in a community service program administered by the Court Support Services Division pursuant to section 53a-39c. Persons who have been granted entry into the pretrial drug education and community service program for the first time shall participate in the community service program for a period of five days. Persons who have been granted entry into the pretrial drug education and community service program for the second time shall participate in the community service program for a period of fifteen days. Persons who have been granted entry into the pretrial drug education and community service program for a third or additional time shall participate in the community service program for a period of thirty days.

(D) Placement in the pretrial drug education and community service program pursuant to this section shall not exceed one year. Persons receiving substance abuse treatment program services in accordance with the provisions of this section shall only receive such services at state-licensed substance abuse treatment program facilities that are in compliance with all state standards governing the operation of such facilities, except that, if such person is a veteran, such person may receive services from facilities under the supervision of the Department of Veterans Affairs or the United States Department of Veterans Affairs, subject to the provisions of subdivision (2) of this subsection.

(E) Any person who enters the pretrial drug education and community service program shall agree: (i) To the tolling of the statute of limitations with respect to such crime; (ii) to a waiver of such person's right to a speedy trial; (iii) to complete participation in the pretrial drug education and community service program, as ordered by the court; (iv) to commence participation in the pretrial drug education and community service program not later than ninety days after the date of entry of the court order unless granted a delayed entry into the program by the court; and (v) upon completion of participation in the pretrial drug education and community service program, to accept (I) placement in a treatment program upon the recommendation of a provider under contract with the Department of Mental Health and Addiction Services or a provider under the supervision of the Department of Veterans Affairs or the United States Department of Veterans Affairs, or (II) placement in a treatment program that has standards substantially similar to, or higher than, a program of a provider under contract with the Department of Mental Health and Addiction Services, if the Court Support Services Division deems it appropriate.

(2) The Court Support Services Division may only refer a veteran to the Department of Veterans Affairs or the United States Department of Veterans Affairs for the receipt of services under the program if (A) the division determines that such services will be provided in a timely manner under standards substantially similar to, or higher than, standards for services provided by the Department of Mental Health and Addiction Services under the program, and (B) the applicable department agrees to submit timely program participation and completion reports to the division in the manner required by the division.

(e) If the Court Support Services Division informs the court that such person is ineligible for the program and the court makes a determination of ineligibility or if the program provider certifies to the court that such person did not successfully complete the assigned program and such person did not request, or the court denied, reinstatement in the program under subsection (i) of this section, the court shall order the court file to be unsealed, enter a plea of not guilty for such person and immediately place the case on the trial list.

(f) If such person satisfactorily completes the assigned program, such person may apply for dismissal of the charges against such person and the court, on reviewing the record of such person's participation in such program submitted by the Court Support Services Division and on finding such satisfactory completion, shall dismiss the charges. If such person does not apply for dismissal of the charges against such person after satisfactorily completing the assigned program, the court, upon receipt of the record of such person's participation in such program submitted by the Court Support Services Division, may on its own motion make a finding of such satisfactory completion and dismiss the charges. Upon motion of such person and a showing of good cause, the court may extend the placement period for a reasonable period of time to allow such person to complete the assigned program. A record of participation in such program shall be retained by the Court Support Services Division for a period of ten years from the date the court grants the application for participation in the program.

(g) At the time the court grants the application for participation in the pretrial drug education and community service program, any person ordered to participate in such drug education program shall pay to the court a nonrefundable program fee of six hundred dollars. If the court orders participation in a substance abuse treatment program, such person shall pay to the court a nonrefundable program fee of one hundred dollars and shall be responsible for the costs associated with such program. No person may be excluded from any such program for inability to pay such fee or cost, provided (1) such person files with the court an affidavit of indigency or inability to pay, (2) such indigency or inability to pay is confirmed by the Court Support Services Division, and (3) the court enters a finding thereof. The court may waive all or any portion of such fee depending on such person's ability to pay. If the court finds that a person is indigent or unable to pay for a substance abuse treatment program, the costs of such program shall be paid from the pretrial account established under section 54-56k. If the court denies the application, such person shall not be required to pay the program fee. If the court grants the application, and such person is later determined to be ineligible for participation in such pretrial drug education and community service program or fails to complete the assigned program, the program fee shall not be refunded. All program fees shall be credited to the pretrial account established under section 54-56k.

(h) If a person returns to court with certification from a program provider that such person did not successfully complete the assigned program or is no longer amenable to treatment, the provider, to the extent practicable, shall include a recommendation to the court as to whether placement in a drug education program or placement in a substance abuse treatment program would best serve such person's needs. The provider shall also indicate whether the current program referral was an initial referral or a reinstatement to the program.

(i) When a person subsequently requests reinstatement into a drug education program or a substance abuse treatment program and the Court Support Services Division verifies that such person is eligible for reinstatement into such program and thereafter the court favorably acts on such request, any person reinstated into such drug education program shall pay a nonrefundable program fee of two hundred fifty dollars, and any person reinstated into a substance abuse treatment program shall be responsible for the costs, if any, associated with being reinstated into the treatment program. Unless good cause is shown, such program fee shall not be waived. All program fees collected in connection with a reinstatement to a drug education program shall be credited to the pretrial account established under section 54-56k. No person shall be permitted more than two program reinstatements pursuant to this subsection.

(j) The Department of Mental Health and Addiction Services shall develop standards and oversee appropriate drug education programs that it administers to meet the requirements of this section and may contract with service providers to provide such programs. The department shall adopt regulations, in accordance with chapter 54, to establish standards for such drug education programs.

(k) Any person whose employment or residence or schooling makes it unreasonable to attend a drug education program or substance abuse treatment program in this state may attend a program in another state that has standards similar to, or higher than, those of this state, subject to the approval of the court and payment of the program fee or costs as provided in this section.

(P.A. 97-248, S. 7, 12; June 18 Sp. Sess. P.A. 97-8, S. 76, 88; P.A. 99-148, S. 1, 4; 99-215, S. 21, 29; June Sp. Sess. P.A. 01-8, S. 10, 13; P.A. 02-132, S. 36; P.A. 07-148, S. 17; Sept. Sp. Sess. P.A. 09-3, S. 55; P.A. 10-18, S. 25, 26; 10-30, S. 2; P.A. 12-42, S. 3; P.A. 13-159, S. 1; P.A. 14-56, S. 4; 14-173, S. 6–8; P.A. 15-211, S. 12; P.A. 16-167, S. 45.)

History: P.A. 97-248 effective July 1, 1997; June 18 Sp. Sess. P.A. 97-8 amended Subsec. (a) to change the deadline for establishing the program from October 1, 1997 to January 1, 1998, effective July 1, 1997; P.A. 99-148 amended Subsec. (a) to make program available to any person charged with a violation of Sec. 21a-279 rather than a violation of only "subsection (c)" of said section, added Subsec. (d)(4) requiring the person to accept placement in a treatment program, amended Subsec. (g) to reduce the program fee from $600 to $350, added new Subsec. (i) to authorize a person to attend a drug program in another state under certain circumstances, and made technical changes for purposes of gender neutrality, effective July 1, 1999; P.A. 99-215 amended Subsec. (b) by deleting "such information or complaint to be filed as a sealed information or complaint" and substituting "the court file sealed" and amended Subsec. (e) by deleting "information or complaint" and substituting "court file", effective June 29, 1999; June Sp. Sess. P.A. 01-8 amended Subsec. (g) by changing "General Fund" to "pretrial account", effective July 1, 2001; P.A. 02-132 replaced "Bail Commission" with "Court Support Services Division" in Subsecs. (c) to (g) and made technical changes in Subsec. (h); P.A. 07-148 amended Subsec. (a) by deleting reference to pilot research drug education program under Sec. 17a-715; Sept. Sp. Sess. P.A. 09-3 amended Subsec. (a) by specifying that drug education program includes a 10-session and 15-session drug intervention program and a drug treatment program and removing provision re date for establishment of program, amended Subsec. (b) by adding provision re $100 application and evaluation fees, specifying that previous participation in 8, 10 or 15-session drug program or substance abuse treatment under section are grounds for ineligibility in pretrial drug education program and specifying that evaluation and application fees shall be credited to pretrial account, amended Subsec. (c) by adding provision re referral to Department of Mental Health and Addiction Services for evaluation, amended Subsec. (d) by adding provision re receipt of appropriate services at state licensed facilities for duration not to exceed 1 year, deleting former Subdiv. (3), adding new Subdivs. (3) and (4) re participants agreeing to complete participation in program as recommended by evaluation and to commence participation in program not later than 90 days after date of entry of court order, redesignating existing Subdiv. (4) as Subdiv. (5) and adding therein "upon completion of participation in the pretrial drug education program", and revising provision re participation in community service labor program, amended Subsec. (e) by adding "and such person did not pursue or the court denied reinstatement in the program under subsection (i) of this section", amended Subsec. (f) by extending record retention requirements at Court Support Services Division from 7 to 10 years, amended Subsec. (g) to specify $350 fee for 10-session drug intervention program, $500 fee for 15-session drug intervention program, that when court orders participation in a drug treatment program, participant shall be responsible for costs associated with such program and that all program fees shall not be refunded and shall be credited to pretrial account, added new Subsec. (h) re recommendations from program providers when participants do not complete assigned program, added new Subsec. (i) re reinstatement into drug intervention program or substance abuse treatment program, redesignated existing Subsecs. (h) and (i) as Subsecs. (j) and (k) and amended the latter to change "drug program" to "drug intervention program" and add "or substance abuse treatment program", effective January 1, 2010; P.A. 10-18 made technical changes in Subsecs. (d) and (g); P.A. 10-30 made technical changes, amended Subsec. (d) to substitute "Court Support Services Division" for "department", amended Subsec. (f) to substitute "date the court grants the application for participation in the program" for "date of application", amended Subsec. (g) to provide that costs of program be paid from pretrial account if court finds that person is indigent or unable to pay for treatment program, and amended Subsecs. (g) and (k) to reference costs, effective July 1, 2010; P.A. 12-42 amended Subsecs. (c) and (d) by adding provisions re referral of and services for persons who are veterans, and made technical changes; P.A. 13-159 amended Subsec. (a) to change name of program from "pretrial drug education program" to "pretrial drug education and community service program", make persons charged with violation of Sec. 21a-279a eligible for program, change 10-session drug intervention program to 15-week drug education program, provide that substance abuse treatment program be not less than 15 sessions, and require performance of community service, amended Subsec. (b) to change nonrefundable evaluation fee from $100 to $150 and eliminate requirement that person state under oath that such person has never had program invoked on person's behalf, allow person to be eligible who has previously participated in same program or community service labor program, and allow person to participate one additional time for good cause shown, amended Subsecs. (c) and (d) to add provisions re referral to Department of Mental Health and Addiction Services for evaluation and determination of appropriate program for first or second application granted, and to a state-licensed substance abuse treatment program for third application granted, amended Subsec. (d)(1) to designate existing provisions as Subparas. (A), (D) and (E), add Subpara. (B) re participation requirements upon entry to the program for a first, second or third time, add Subpara. (C) re participation in community service program and, in Subpara. (E), delete condition of participation in drug education program that person also participate in community service labor program under Sec. 53a-39c, amended Subsec. (g) to replace $350 fee for 10-session program or $500 fee for 15-session program with $600 fee and nonrefundable program fee of $100, amended Subsec. (i) to substitute "drug education program" for "drug intervention program" and add provision re any person reinstated into a substance abuse treatment program to be responsible for costs associated with being reinstated, and made technical and conforming changes; P.A. 14-56 amended Subsec. (c) to redefine "veteran", effective May 23, 2014; P.A. 14-173 amended Subsec. (a) to delete reference to 15-session drug intervention program, amended Subsec. (c) to add "and determination" re referral of veteran, and amended Subsec. (d)(1) to substitute "drug education" for "drug intervention" re services in Subpara. (A) and add provision re substance abuse treatment program of not less than 15 sessions in Subpara. (B); P.A. 15-211 amended Subsecs. (a), (b) and (d) by replacing references to drug education and community service program with references to pretrial drug education and community service program, amended Subsecs. (a) and (d) by substituting "fifteen-session" for "fifteen-week", and made technical changes in Subsecs. (g) and (i); P.A. 16-167 amended Subsecs. (c) and (d) to replace "Department of Veterans' Affairs" with "Department of Veterans Affairs", effective July 1, 2016.

Sec. 54-56j. Pretrial school violence prevention program.

(a) There shall be a school violence prevention program for students of a public or private secondary school charged with an offense involving the use or threatened use of physical violence in or on the real property comprising a public or private elementary or secondary school or at a school-sponsored activity as defined in subsection (h) of section 10-233a. Upon application by any such person for participation in such program, the court shall, but only as to the public, order the court file sealed, provided such person states under oath, in open court or before any person designated by the clerk and duly authorized to administer oaths, under penalties of perjury that such person has never had such system invoked in such person's behalf and that such person has not been convicted of an offense involving the threatened use of physical violence in or on the real property comprising a public or private elementary or secondary school or at a school-sponsored activity as defined in subsection (h) of section 10-233a, and that such person has not been convicted in any other state at any time of an offense the essential elements of which are substantially the same as such an offense.

(b) The court, after consideration of the recommendation of the state's attorney, assistant state's attorney or deputy assistant state's attorney in charge of the case, may, in its discretion, grant such application. If the court grants such application, it shall refer such person to the Court Support Services Division for assessment and confirmation of the eligibility of the applicant. The Court Support Services Division, in making its assessment and confirmation, may rely on the representations made by the applicant under oath in open court with respect to convictions in other states of offenses specified in subsection (a) of this section. As a condition of eligibility for participation in such program, the student and the parents or guardian of such student shall certify under penalty of false statement that, to the best of such person's knowledge and belief, such person does not possess any firearms, dangerous weapons, controlled substances or other property or materials the possession of which is prohibited by law or in violation of the law. Upon confirmation of eligibility, the defendant shall be referred to the Court Support Services Division for evaluation and placement in an appropriate school violence prevention program for one year.

(c) Any person who enters the program shall agree: (1) To the tolling of the statute of limitations with respect to such crime, (2) to a waiver of the right to a speedy trial, (3) to participate in a school violence prevention program offered by a provider under contract with the Court Support Services Division pursuant to subsection (g) of this section, and (4) to successfully complete the assigned program. If the Court Support Services Division informs the court that the defendant is ineligible for the program and the court makes a determination of ineligibility or if the program provider certifies to the court that the defendant did not successfully complete the assigned program, the court shall order the court file to be unsealed, enter a plea of not guilty for such defendant and immediately place the case on the trial list.

(d) The Court Support Services Division shall monitor the defendant's participation in the assigned program and the defendant's compliance with the orders of the court including, but not limited to, maintaining contact with the student and officials of the student's school.

(e) If such defendant satisfactorily completes the assigned program and one year has elapsed since the defendant was placed in the program, such defendant may apply for dismissal of the charges against such defendant and the court, on reviewing the record of such defendant's participation in such program submitted by the Court Support Services Division and on finding such satisfactory completion, shall dismiss the charges. If the defendant does not apply for dismissal of the charges against the defendant after satisfactorily completing the assigned program and one year has elapsed since the defendant was placed in the program, the court, upon receipt of the record of the defendant's participation in such program submitted by the Court Support Services Division, may on its own motion make a finding of such satisfactory completion and dismiss the charges.

(f) The cost of participation in such program shall be paid by the parent or guardian of such student, except that no student shall be excluded from such program for inability to pay such cost provided (1) the parent or guardian of such student files with the court an affidavit of indigency or inability to pay, and (2) the court enters a finding thereof.

(g) The Court Support Services Division shall contract with service providers, develop standards and oversee appropriate school violence prevention programs to meet the requirements of this section.

(h) The school violence prevention program shall consist of at least eight group counseling sessions in anger management and nonviolent conflict resolution.

(P.A. 99-259, S. 2, 3; P.A. 10-43, S. 23.)

History: P.A. 99-259 effective January 1, 2000; P.A. 10-43 replaced "Bail Commission" and "Office of Alternative Sanctions" with "Court Support Services Division", effective May 18, 2010.

See Sec. 46b-133e re suspension of delinquency proceedings for participation in school violence prevention program.

Sec. 54-56k. Pretrial account. (a) There is established an account to be known as the pretrial account. The account shall contain any moneys required by law to be deposited in the account and shall be a separate, nonlapsing account of the General Fund. Investment earnings credited to the account shall become part of the assets of the account. Any balance remaining in said account at the end of any fiscal year shall be carried forward in the account for the next fiscal year.

(b) There shall be deposited in the pretrial account all evaluation fees collected pursuant to subsection (a) of section 54-56g and subsection (b) of section 54-56i and all program fees collected pursuant to subsections (c) and (e) of section 54-56g and subsections (g) and (i) of section 54-56i and funds appropriated in subsection (a) of section 47 of special act 01-1 of the June special session.

(c) Amounts in the pretrial account shall be available to fund the cost of operating the pretrial alcohol and drug education programs established under sections 54-56g and 54-56i.

(June Sp. Sess. P.A. 01-8, S. 8, 13; P.A. 10-30, S. 6.)

History: June Sp. Sess. P.A. 01-8 effective July 1, 2001; P.A. 10-30 amended Subsec. (b) to reference evaluation fees collected pursuant to Secs. 54-56g(a) and 54-56i(b) and program fees collected pursuant to Secs. 54-56g(e) and 54-56i(i), effective July 1, 2010.

Sec. 54-56l. Pretrial supervised diversionary program for persons with psychiatric disabilities and veterans.

(a) There shall be a supervised diversionary program for persons with psychiatric disabilities, or persons who are veterans, who are accused of a crime or crimes or a motor vehicle violation or violations for which a sentence to a term of imprisonment may be imposed, which crimes or violations are not of a serious nature. For the purposes of this section, (1) "psychiatric disability" means a mental or emotional condition, other than solely substance abuse, that

(A) has substantial adverse effects on the defendant's ability to function, and (B) requires care and treatment, and (2) "veteran" means a person who is found, pursuant to subsection (d) of this section, to have a mental health condition that is amenable to treatment, and who was discharged or released under conditions other than dishonorable from active service in the armed forces as defined in section 27-103.

(b) A person shall be ineligible to participate in such supervised diversionary program if such person (1) is ineligible to participate in the pretrial program for accelerated rehabilitation under subsection (c) of section 54-56e, except if a person's ineligibility is based on the person's being eligible for the pretrial family violence education program established under section 46b-38c, the court may permit such person to participate in the supervised diversionary program if it finds that the supervised diversionary program is the more appropriate program under the circumstances of the case, or (2) has twice previously participated in such supervised diversionary program.

(c) Upon application by any such person for participation in such program, the court shall, but only as to the public, order the court file sealed, provided such person states under oath, in open court or before any person designated by the clerk and duly authorized to administer oaths, under penalties of perjury, that such person has not had such program invoked in such person's behalf more than once. Court personnel shall provide notice, on a form prescribed by the Office of the Chief Court Administrator, to any victim of such crime or motor vehicle violation, by registered or certified mail, that such person has applied to participate in the program and that such victim has an opportunity to be heard by the court on the matter.

(d) The court shall refer such person to the Court Support Services Division for confirmation of eligibility and assessment of the person's mental health condition. The prosecuting attorney shall provide the division with a copy of the police report in the case to assist the division in its assessment. The division shall determine if the person is amenable to treatment and if appropriate community supervision, treatment and services are available. If the division determines that the person is amenable to treatment and that appropriate community supervision, treatment and services are available, the division shall develop a treatment plan tailored to the person and shall present the treatment plan to the court.

(e) Upon confirmation of eligibility and consideration of the treatment plan presented by the Court Support Services Division, the court may grant the application for participation in the program. If the court grants the application, such person shall be referred to the division. The division may collaborate with the Department of Mental Health and Addiction Services, the Department of Veterans Affairs or the United States Department of Veterans Affairs, as applicable, to place such person in a program that provides appropriate community supervision, treatment and services. The person shall be subject to the supervision of a probation officer who has a reduced caseload and specialized training in working with persons with psychiatric disabilities.

(f) The Court Support Services Division shall establish policies and procedures to require division employees to notify any victim of the person admitted to the program of any conditions ordered by the court that directly affect the victim and of such person's scheduled court appearances with respect to the case.

(g) Any person who enters the program shall agree: (1) To the tolling of the statute of limitations with respect to such crime or violation; (2) to a waiver of such person's right to a speedy trial; and (3) to any conditions that may be established by the division concerning participation in the supervised diversionary program including conditions concerning participation in meetings or sessions of the program.

(h) If the Court Support Services Division informs the court that such person is ineligible for the program and the court makes a determination of ineligibility or if the division certifies to the court that such person did not successfully complete the assigned program, the court shall order the court file to be unsealed, enter a plea of not guilty for such person and immediately place the case on the trial list.

(i) If such person satisfactorily completes the assigned program, such person may apply for dismissal of the charges against such person and the court, on reviewing the record of such person's participation in such program submitted by the Court Support Services Division and on finding such satisfactory completion, shall dismiss the charges. If such person does not apply for dismissal of the charges against such person after satisfactorily completing the assigned program, the court, upon receipt of the record of such person's participation in such program submitted by the Court Support Services Division, may on its own motion make a finding of such satisfactory completion and dismiss the charges. Except as provided in subsection (j) of this section, upon dismissal, all records of such charges shall be erased pursuant to section 54-142a. An order of the court denying a motion to dismiss the charges against a person who has completed such person's period of probation or supervision or terminating the participation of a person in such program shall be a final judgment for purposes of appeal.

(j) The Court Support Services Division shall develop and maintain a database of information concerning persons admitted to the supervised diversionary program that shall be available to the state police and organized local police departments for use by sworn police officers when responding to incidents involving such persons. Such information shall include the person's name, date of birth, Social Security number, the violation or violations with which the person was charged, the dates of program participation and whether a deadly weapon or dangerous instrument was involved in the violation or violations for which the program was granted. The division shall enter such information in the database upon such person's entry into the program, update such information as necessary and retain such information for a period of five years after the date of such person's entry into the program.

(k) The Court Support Services Division, in consultation with the Department of Mental Health and Addiction Services, shall develop standards and oversee appropriate treatment programs to meet the requirements of this section and may contract with service providers to provide such programs.

(l) The Court Support Services Division shall retain the police report provided to it by the prosecuting attorney and the record of supervision including the dates of supervision and shall provide such information to the court, prosecuting attorney and defense counsel whenever a court is considering whether to grant an application by such person for participation in the supervised diversionary program for a second time.

(Jan. Sp. Sess. P.A. 08-1, S. 41; P.A. 12-42, S. 1; P.A. 14-56, S. 5; P.A. 15-85, S. 21; 15-211, S. 13; P.A. 16-167, S. 46.)

History: P.A. 12-42 amended Subsec. (a) by adding provisions re program for persons who are veterans, amended Subsec. (d) by adding references to community supervision and treatment, amended Subsec. (e) by replacing "shall" with "may" re division collaborating with departments and adding "the Department of Veterans' Affairs or the United States Department of Veterans Affairs, as applicable", amended Subsec. (k) by replacing "collaboration" with "consultation", and made technical changes; P.A. 14-56 amended Subsec. (a)(2) to redefine "veteran", effective May 23, 2014; P.A. 15-85 amended Subsec. (c) by substituting "form prescribed by the Office of the Chief Court Administrator" for "form approved by rule of court"; P.A. 15-211 amended Subsec. (b)(1) by adding provision re court may permit participation in supervised diversionary program when person's ineligibility is based on being eligible for pretrial family violence education program; P.A. 16-167 amended Subsec. (e) to replace "Department of Veterans' Affairs" with "Department of Veterans Affairs", effective July 1, 2016.

(Return to Chapter Table of Contents)

(Return to List of Chapters)

(Return to List of Titles)

Sec. 54-56m. Mediation programs.

(a) There shall be established, in the geographical area of the Superior Court for the towns of Berlin, New Britain, Newington, Rocky Hill and Wethersfield, the geographical area of the Superior Court for the towns of Bethlehem, Middlebury, Naugatuck, Prospect, Southbury, Watertown, Wolcott, Woodbury and Waterbury, and such other geographical areas of the Superior Court as the Chief Court Administrator may designate, programs of mediation wherein the court may refer a criminal prosecution to mediation for resolution. For the purposes of this section, "mediation" means the process where two or more persons to a dispute agree to meet with an impartial third party to work toward a resolution of the dispute which is satisfactory to all parties in accordance with principles of mediation commonly used in labor management disputes.

(b) If mediation is successful, the prosecuting authority, upon recommendation of the family relations counselor or mediation officer, shall enter a nolle prosequi and the prosecution shall be terminated and the defendant released from custody.

(c) If mediation is unsuccessful or the defendant fails to comply with the terms of any mediation agreement, the family relations counselor or mediation officer shall notify the prosecuting authority and prosecution of the defendant may be initiated.

(d) There shall be established, in the two geographical areas of the Superior Court enumerated in subsection (a) of this section and in such other geographical areas of the Superior Court as the Chief Court Administrator may designate, units to provide mediation services in cases referred by the court to mediation. In addition, mediation services in cases referred by the court to mediation may also be provided by private agencies under contract with the Judicial Department.

(P.A. 82-383, S. 1; P.A. 85-344; P.A. 95-225, S. 48, 52; P.A. 02-132, S. 37.)

History: P.A. 85-344 made mediation programs permanent rather than "pilot" programs and authorized instituting programs in geographical areas beyond those initially involved in pilot programs; P.A. 95-225 amended Subsec. (d) to add provision authorizing mediation services to also be provided by private agencies under contract with the Judicial Department, effective June 28, 1995; P.A. 02-132 made technical changes in Subsec. (a), changed family relations officer to family relations counselor in Subsecs. (b) and (c) and deleted reference to the Family Division of the Superior Court, added provision re other geographical areas designated by the Chief Court Administrator and made technical changes in Subsec. (d).

(Return to Chapter Table of Contents)

(Return to List of Chapters)

(Return to List of Titles)

Sec. 54-56n. Pretrial and diversionary program data collection and reporting.

(a) The Judicial Branch shall collect data on the number of members of the armed forces, veterans and nonveterans who, on and after January 1, 2016, apply for and are granted admission or are denied entry into (1) the pretrial program for accelerated rehabilitation established pursuant to section 54-56e, (2) the supervised diversionary program established pursuant to section 54-56*l*, or (3) the pretrial drug education and community service program established pursuant to section 54-56i. Data compiled pursuant to this section shall be based on information provided by applicants at the time of application to any such program. For the purposes of this section, "veteran" means any person who was discharged or released under conditions other than dishonorable from active service in the armed forces and "armed forces" has the same meaning as provided in section 27-103.

(b) Not later than January 15, 2017, and annually thereafter, the Judicial Branch shall submit a report detailing the data compiled for the previous calendar year pursuant to subsection (a) of this section to the joint standing committees of the General Assembly having cognizance of matters relating to veterans' and military affairs and the judiciary, in accordance with the provisions of section 11-4a.

(P.A. 15-246, S. 3.)

History: P.A. 15-246 effective January 1, 2016.

Sec. 54-56o. Nolle prosequi in certain family violence cases.

For any family violence case initiated on or after July 1, 2016, that is not referred to the local family violence intervention unit as provided in subsection (g) of section 46b-38c, the prosecuting authority shall not enter a nolle prosequi as to any charge of a family violence crime, as defined in section 46b-38a, unless the prosecuting authority states in open court his or her reasons for the nolle prosequi and, if the reasons include consideration of the defendant's participation in a counseling or treatment program, a representation that such counseling or treatment program complies with the program standards promulgated under section 46b-38*l*.

(P.A. 15-211, S. 22.)

History: P.A. 15-211 effective January 1, 2016.

Sec. 54-56p. Program for young persons charged with a motor vehicle violation or alcohol-related offense.

(a) The court may, in its discretion, invoke a program on motion of a defendant or on motion of a state's attorney or prosecuting attorney with respect to a defendant who (1) is under twenty-one years of age, (2) is charged with a motor vehicle violation, or a violation of section 30-88a, subsection (a) or (b) of section 30-89 or section 30-89a, and (3) has not previously had such program invoked in such person's behalf.

(b) This section shall not be applicable to any person charged with a motor vehicle violation causing serious injury or death, a motor vehicle violation classified as a felony unless good cause is shown, or a violation of section 14-227a or 14-227g.

(c) The court shall refer such person to the Court Support Services Division of the Judicial Branch for confirmation of eligibility of such person. Such program shall provide a nonconfrontational forum for such defendants to hear from victims who have been affected by underage drinking, drunk driving, distracted driving or other motor vehicle violations. Such program shall be approved by the Court Support Services Division conducted by a nonprofit organization that advocates on behalf of victims of accidents caused by persons who operated a motor vehicle while under the influence of intoxicating liquor or drugs or both. Such organization may assess a participation fee of not more than fifty dollars on any defendant required by the court to participate in such program.

(d) Such organization shall report whether the defendant satisfactorily completed the program to the Court Support Services Division. If the defendant satisfactorily completed the program, not later than nine months after the date on which the program was invoked pursuant to subsection (a) of this section, the charges against the defendant shall be dismissed. If the defendant does not satisfactorily complete the program not later than nine months after the invocation of such program, the charges against the defendant shall be reinstated.

(P.A. 16-182, S. 1.)

Sec. 54-57. Joinder of offenses of the same character.

Whenever two or more cases are pending at the same time against the same party in the same court for offenses of the same character, counts for such offenses may be joined in one information unless the court orders otherwise.

(1949 Rev., S. 8770.)

Court may compel state to elect between counts; 75 C. 201; 81 C. 1; or direct jury to find separately on each count. 34 C. 299. Effect of general verdict. 34 C. 299; 70 C. 73. Where same offense is charged in different counts. 74 C. 525. Where one count only is good. 66 C. 255. Right of accused to call for separate verdicts. 83 C. 298. Relation of counts to each other. 96 C. 427. One count charging two accused as principals may properly be joined with a second count charging one as principal and the other as accessory. 98 C. 460. Refusal to compel state to elect between counts held proper. Id., 461. Cited. 126 C. 84. Whether there shall be separate trials on different counts joined in indictment or information lies within trial court's discretion. 134 C. 109. Whenever two or more cases are pending at the same time against the same party in the same court for offenses of the same character, counts for such offenses may be joined in one information. 169 C. 566. Whether joinder of indictments and informations is controlled by statute or Sec. 829 of the 1978 Practice Book discussed; since rule regulates court procedure and does not infringe on any substantive right, rule controlled and court did not abuse its discretion by ordering joinder of two informations not of the same character. 187 C. 292; judgment reversed, see 303 C. 538. Cited. 204 C. 714; 205 C. 61; 209 C. 458; 210 C. 78; 215 C. 538; 216 C. 647; 234 C. 324; 235 C. 748; 236 C. 112. Joinder of manslaughter count and risk of injury to minor count permissible when factors weighed. 243 C. 523. Defendant did not suffer substantial prejudice by consolidation of charges against him because the evidence in both cases would have been cross admissible at separate trials to show a common scheme or plan on the part of the defendant. 287 C. 608. Under section, there is no blanket presumption in favor of joinder; section is directed at prosecutors and governs whether they may join multiple charges in a single information, while Practice Book is directed at trial courts; trial court abused its discretion in finding defendant's alleged conduct in felony murder case not so brutal or shocking to require separate trials, but error was harmless. 303 C. 538.

Cited. 10 CA 503; Id., 624; Id., 709; 14 CA 526; Id., 710; 15 CA 161; 18 CA 406; Id., 482; 19 CA 48; 24 CA 502; 25 CA 181; Id., 503; 28 CA 645; 33 CA 133; 35 CA 781; 36 CA 805; 37 CA 437; 41 CA 584; 42 CA 382; 43 CA 527; Id., 680; 45 CA 207. Joinder permitted where defendant holding knife injured victim while attacking her because physical harm not brutal or shocking; consolidation of three informations for trial ameliorated by court's explicit instruction to jury that offenses should be considered separately. 59 CA 529. Trial court is authorized by statute and rule to order a joint trial of charges against the same defendant. 70 CA 462. Joinder was proper because evidence relating to each crime would have been admissible in each separate trial to prove a common plan or scheme. 87 CA 150. Defendant was not subject to substantial injustice or deprived of due process when trial court granted state's motion for joinder because the matters were not so complex as to confuse a jury. 112 CA 711. Court did not abuse its discretion by joining charges of violating a protective order and threatening in the second degree because evidence from incidents on the relevant date for which defendant was charged for both crimes was admissible in both cases. 132 CA 414.

Where defendants were put to plea on a single information charging similar offenses concerning different complainants, court did not abuse its discretion in making such joinder. 2 Conn. Cir. Ct. 514. Cited. Id., 585.

Sec. 54-58. Description of money in complaint or information.

When it is necessary to describe any bill issued by the United States or by any national banking association or to describe any United States coin issued as money, it shall be a sufficient description to set forth in the complaint or information that the same is lawful money of the United States, and the value thereof, which value need not be proved as alleged.

(1949 Rev., S. 8771.)

Sec. 54-59. Statement of ownership, partnership or joint tenancy in indictment, information or complaint.

When in any indictment, information or complaint it is necessary to state the ownership of any property owned or possessed by more persons than one, it shall be sufficient to name one of them, and to state such property to belong to him and another or others, as the case may be; or, if it is necessary to mention for any purpose any partners, joint tenants, coparceners, tenants in common or trustees of joint stock companies, not incorporated by the laws of this state, it shall be sufficient to describe them in like manner.

(1949 Rev., S. 8772.)

(Return to Chapter Table of Contents)

(Return to List of Chapters)

(Return to List of Titles)

Sec. 54-60. Allegations in criminal cases.

Whenever any indictment, information or complaint is pending before any court, a conviction may be had for any offense sufficiently alleged therein or for an attempt to commit such offense, and the accused may be convicted or such court may accept a plea of guilty for any of such offenses.

(1949 Rev., S. 8774.)

Cited. 94 C. 706. State may designate an accused by an alias; motion to expunge "The Cowboy" as such an alias from indictment held properly denied. 98 C. 460. A plea of guilty to a specific criminal charge, which is relevant to the circumstances in a civil action, may be admissible as a verbal admission in such civil action. 147 C. 625. Cited. Id., 704.

Section is constitutionally sufficient to put a criminal defendant on notice he can be convicted of attempt to commit crime charged as well as any included lesser offenses. 39 CA 267.

Court will not allow party to enter a plea of guilty until satisfied that it is freely made and that the party making it understands its import and effect; if accused did not understand the charge against him, judgment should be opened and defendant allowed to withdraw plea of guilty. 23 CS 176.

Sec. 54-61. Complaints for offenses specified in special acts, ordinances and bylaws.

In any complaint or other process for an offense against the provisions of a special act or of an ordinance or bylaw of any town, city or borough, it shall be sufficient to set forth the offense in the same manner as in the case of an offense against the provisions of a public act.

(1949 Rev., S. 8786.)

If an offense is created by statute, it is sufficient to set it forth in the words of the statute. 60 C. 106; 88 C. 715.

Sec. 54-62. Allegation of previous conviction.

When, in any criminal complaint or information, it is necessary to set out a previous conviction for a similar offense, such previous conviction shall be held to be sufficiently alleged by naming the date when, the town or city where, the crime for which and the court wherein such conviction was had.

(1949 Rev., S. 8785.)

Defects may be cured by verdict. 68 C. 512. Former convictions should be set up in information or complaint. Id.; 94 C. 703; 96 C. 172. Information should be in two parts, each signed by the prosecutor, and the offense charged set out in one part and the prior conviction in another; the plea of accused to entire information should be taken in absence of the jury, and the trial should proceed on the first part only of the information; if a verdict of guilty is rendered, the trial should then proceed on the second part of the information. Id., 171. Cited. 147 C. 296. To prove prior conviction it is necessary to show it by record of valid subsisting final judgment of rendering court. 151 C. 213.

Cited. 45 CA 369.

Cited. 24 CS 362.

Sec. 54-63. Mode of informing against larceny by embezzlement. I

n any complaint or information for the crime of larceny by embezzlement, when it is unknown to the informing officer whether the total sum taken and appropriated was taken and appropriated at one or different times, it shall be sufficient to charge the total sum taken by the accused as having been taken at one and the same time.

(1949 Rev., S. 8788; P.A. 80-313, S. 57.)

History: P.A. 80-313 applied provisions to complaints or informations for crime of "larceny by" embezzlement, reflecting change in official term for the offense.

(Return to Chapter
Table of Contents)

(Return to
List of Chapters)

(Return to
List of Titles)

Sec. 54-63a. Definitions. As used in sections 54-63a to 54-63g, inclusive, and section 54-64a, "arrested person" means a person taken into custody for violation of any law, ordinance, regulation or bylaw of the state or of any town, city, borough, district or municipal corporation or authority, and "Court Support Services Division" means the division of the Judicial Department established pursuant to section 51-1d.

(1967, P.A. 549, S. 1; P.A. 02-132, S. 38.)

History: P.A. 02-132 replaced definition of "Bail Commission" with definition of "Court Support Services Division" and made technical changes.

Sec. 54-63b. Pretrial release of arrested persons. Duties of Court Support Services Division. Uniform weighted release criteria.

(a) The duties of the Court Support Services Division shall include: (1) To promptly interview, prior to arraignment, any person referred by the police pursuant to section 54-63c or by a judge. Such interview shall include, but not be limited to, information concerning the accused person, his or her family, community ties, prior criminal record and physical and mental condition. Any interview of a person held at a police station may be conducted by video conference; (2) to seek independent verification of information obtained during the interview, if practicable; (3) to determine, as provided in section 54-63d, or to make recommendations on request of any judge, concerning the terms and conditions of the release of arrested persons from custody pending final disposition of their cases; (4) to prepare a written report on all persons interviewed and, upon request and pursuant to the procedures established under subsection (f) of section 54-63d, provide copies of the report to the court, defense counsel and state's attorney. Such report shall contain the information obtained during the interview and verification process, the person's prior criminal record, where possible, and the determination or recommendation of the commissioner pursuant to section 54-63d concerning the terms and conditions of the release of the persons so interviewed; (5) to give prior notice of each required court appearance to each person released following an interview by a bail commissioner or an intake, assessment and referral specialist employed by the Judicial Branch; (6) to supervise pursuant to the direction of the court those persons released on nonfinancial conditions; (7) to inform the court and the state's attorney of any failure to comply with terms and conditions of release, including the arrest of persons released under its supervision; (8) to monitor, evaluate and provide information concerning terms and conditions of release and the release criteria established under subsection (b) of this section, to prepare periodic reports on its activities, and to provide such other information as is needed to assist in the improvement of the pretrial release process; (9) to perform such other functions as the Chief Court Administrator may, from time to time, assign.

(b) The Court Support Services Division shall establish written uniform weighted release criteria based upon the premise that the least restrictive condition or conditions of release necessary to ensure the appearance in court of the defendant and sufficient to reasonably ensure the safety of any other person will not be endangered is the pretrial release alternative of choice. Such criteria shall be based on, but not be limited to, the following considerations: (1) The nature and circumstances of the offense insofar as they are relevant to the risk of nonappearance; (2) the defendant's record of previous convictions; (3) the defendant's past record of appearance in court after being admitted to bail; (4) the defendant's family ties; (5) the defendant's employment record; (6) the defendant's financial resources, character and mental condition; and (7) the defendant's community ties.

(1967, P.A. 549, S. 2; 1969, P.A. 826, S. 1; P.A. 74-183, S. 141, 291; P.A. 76-436, S. 541, 681; P.A. 78-280, S. 118, 127; P.A. 80-313, S. 58; P.A. 81-437, S. 3, 12; P.A. 99-186, S. 11; P.A. 02-132, S. 39; P.A. 12-114, S. 5; 12-133, S. 35.)

History: 1969 act amended Subsec. (b) to authorize appointment of assistant chief bail commissioners and assistant bail commissioners and added provision empowering chief judge of circuit court to appoint additional bail commissioners; P.A. 74-183 revised provisions to reflect transfer of circuit court functions to court of common pleas, adding Subsec. (d) continuing bail commissioners for the balance of their terms, effective December 31, 1974; P.A. 76-436 amended section to reflect transfer of all trial jurisdiction to superior court, replacing references to former circuits with references to geographical areas, replacing chief judge of common pleas court with chief court administrator or his designee, etc., effective July 1, 1978; P.A. 78-280 added provision in Subsec. (b) authorizing judges to fill vacancies in bail commissioners' offices; P.A. 80-313 substituted reference to Sec. 54-63d for reference to Sec. 54-63c in Subsec. (a); P.A. 81-437 replaced previous provisions concerning the bail commission and chief bail commissioner, expanding duties and placing office of the bail commission within the judicial department; P.A. 99-186 amended Subsec. (a) to make a technical change in a statutory reference; P.A. 02-132 amended Subsec. (a) by deleting provision re Office of the Bail Commission within the Judicial Department, adding provision re duties of the Court Support Services Division and, in Subdiv. (5), replacing "the Bail Commission" with "a bail commissioner", deleted former Subsecs. (b), (c) and (d) re Chief Bail Commissioner, Assistant Chief Bail Commissioner and appointment of bail commissioners and other personnel and added new Subsec. (b) re uniform weighted release criteria; P.A. 12-114 amended Subsec. (b) to add provision re release criteria sufficient to reasonably ensure the safety of any other person will not be endangered, and made technical changes; P.A. 12-133 amended Subsec. (a) by adding provision re interview of person held at police station conducted by videoconference in Subdiv. (1) and adding "or an intake, assessment and referral specialist employed by the Judicial Branch" in Subdiv. (5).

Sec. 54-63c. Duties of law enforcement officer or probation officer serving warrant re arrested person. Interview and release of arrested person.

(a) Except in cases of arrest pursuant to a bench warrant of arrest in which the court or a judge thereof has indicated that bail should be denied or ordered that the officer or indifferent person making such arrest shall, without undue delay, bring such person before the clerk or assistant clerk of the superior court for the geographical area under section 54-2a, when any person is arrested for a bailable offense, the chief of police, or the chief's authorized designee, of the police department having custody of the arrested person or any probation officer serving a violation of probation warrant shall promptly advise such person of the person's rights under section 54-1b, and of the person's right to be interviewed concerning the terms and conditions of release. Unless the arrested person waives or refuses such interview, the police officer or probation officer shall promptly interview the arrested person to obtain information relevant to the terms and conditions of the person's release from custody, and shall seek independent verification of such information where necessary. At the request of the arrested person, the person's counsel may be present during the interview. No statement made by the arrested person in response to any question during the interview related to the terms and conditions of release shall be admissible as evidence against the arrested person in any proceeding arising from the incident for which the conditions of release were set. After such a waiver, refusal or interview, the police officer or probation officer shall promptly order release of the arrested person upon the execution of a written promise to appear or the posting of such bond as may be set by the police officer or probation officer, except that no condition of release set by the court or a judge thereof may be modified by such officers and no person shall be released upon the execution of a written promise to appear or the posting of a bond without surety if the person is charged with the commission of a family violence crime, as defined in section 46b-38a, and in the commission of such crime the person used or threatened the use of a firearm.

(b) If the person is charged with the commission of a family violence crime, as defined in section 46b-38a, and the police officer does not intend to impose nonfinancial conditions of release pursuant to this subsection, the police officer shall, pursuant to the procedure set forth in subsection (a) of this section, promptly order the release of such person upon the execution of a written promise to appear or the posting of such bond as may be set by the police officer. If such person is not so released, the police officer shall make reasonable efforts to immediately contact a bail commissioner or an intake, assessment and referral specialist employed by the Judicial Branch to set the conditions of such person's release pursuant to section 54-63d. If, after making such reasonable efforts, the police officer is unable to contact a bail commissioner or an intake, assessment and referral specialist or contacts a bail commissioner or an intake, assessment and referral specialist but such bail commissioner or intake, assessment and referral specialist is unavailable to promptly perform such bail commissioner's or intake, assessment and referral specialist's duties pursuant to section 54-63d, the police officer shall, pursuant to the procedure set forth in subsection (a) of this section, order the release of such person upon the execution of a written promise to appear or the posting of such bond as may be set by the police officer and may impose nonfinancial conditions of release which may require that the arrested person do one or more of the following: (1) Avoid all contact with the alleged victim of the crime, (2) comply with specified restrictions on the person's travel, association or place of abode that are directly related to the protection of the alleged victim of the crime, or (3) not use or possess a dangerous weapon, intoxicant or controlled substance. Any such nonfinancial conditions of release shall be indicated on a form prescribed by the Judicial Branch and sworn to by the police officer. Such form shall articulate (A) the efforts that were made to contact a bail commissioner or an intake, assessment and referral specialist, (B) the specific factual basis relied upon by the police officer to impose the nonfinancial conditions of release, and (C) if the arrested person was non-English-speaking, that the services of a translation service or interpreter were used. A copy of that portion of the form that indicates the nonfinancial conditions of release shall immediately be provided to the arrested person. A copy of the entire form shall be provided to counsel for the arrested person at arraignment. Any nonfinancial conditions of release imposed pursuant to this subsection shall remain in effect until the arrested person is presented before the Superior Court pursuant to subsection (a) of section 54-1g. On such date, the court shall conduct a hearing pursuant to section 46b-38c at which the defendant is entitled to be heard with respect to the issuance of a protective order.

(c) When cash bail in excess of ten thousand dollars is received for a detained person accused of a felony, where the underlying facts and circumstances of the felony involve the use, attempted use or threatened use of physical force against another person, the police officer shall prepare a report that contains

(1) the name, address and taxpayer identification number of the accused person, (2) the name, address and taxpayer identification number of each person offering the cash bail, other than a person licensed as a professional bondsman under chapter 533 or a surety bail bond agent under chapter 700f, (3) the amount of cash received, and (4) the date the cash was received. Not later than fifteen days after receipt of such cash bail, the police officer shall file the report with the Department of Revenue Services and mail a copy of the report to the state's attorney for the judicial district in which the alleged offense was committed and to each person offering the cash bail.

(d) No police officer or probation officer serving a violation of probation warrant shall set the terms and conditions of a person's release, set a bond for a person or release a person from custody under this section unless the police officer or probation officer has first checked the National Crime Information Center (NCIC) computerized index of criminal justice information to determine if such person is listed in such index.

(e) If the arrested person has not posted bail, the police officer or probation officer serving a violation of probation warrant shall immediately notify a bail commissioner or an intake, assessment and referral specialist.

(f) The chief, acting chief, superintendent of police, the Commissioner of Emergency Services and Public Protection, any captain or lieutenant of any local police department or the Division of State Police within the Department of Emergency Services and Public Protection or any person lawfully exercising the powers of any such officer may take a written promise to appear or a bond with or without surety from an arrested person as provided in subsection (a) of this section, or as fixed by the court or any judge thereof, may administer such oaths as are necessary in the taking of promises or bonds and shall file any report required under subsection (c) of this section.

(1967, P.A. 549, S. 3; 1969, P.A. 826, S. 2; P.A. 74-183, S. 142, 291; P.A. 76-336, S. 3; 76-436, S. 542, 681; P.A. 79-216, S. 2; P.A. 80-313, S. 14; P.A. 99-186, S. 8; 99-240, S. 16; P.A. 00-196, S. 41; P.A. 03-173, S. 1; P.A. 07-123, S. 1; P.A. 11-51, S. 134; P.A. 12-133, S. 36; P.A. 14-233, S. 3.)

History: 1969 act transferred duty to notify arrested person of his rights, etc. from bail commissioner to chief of police or his designee and added provisions re bail commissioner's investigation and decision re release on bail in Subsec. (a); P.A. 74-183 amended section to reflect transfer of circuit court functions to court of common pleas, effective December 1, 1974; P.A. 76-336 deleted provisions which implied officer's or bail commissioner's right to deny release on bail if he "finds custody to be necessary to provide reasonable assurance of such person's appearance in court"; P.A. 76-436 reworded exception in Subsec. (a) to clearly distinguish between bench warrants and arrest warrants in which court or judge has set conditions of release, replaced references to prosecuting attorneys with references to various categories of state's attorneys and deleted references to court of common pleas, reflecting transfer of all trial jurisdiction to superior court, effective July 1, 1978; P.A. 79-216 rephrased exception in Subsec. (a) to replace reference to condition of release with specific orders of judge or court re denial of bail, etc. and further amended subsection to specify that officer or bail commissioner may not modify condition of release set by court or judge; P.A. 80-313 deleted detailed provisions re bail procedure formerly comprising latter part of Subsec. (a) and Subsecs. (b) to (f), restated remaining provisions of Subsec. (a) and added new Subsec. (b) containing general statement of police officers' powers; P.A. 99-186 amended Subsec. (a) to prohibit the release of a person on the execution of a written promise to appear or the posting of a bond without surety if such person is charged with the commission of a family violence crime in which such person used or threatened the use of a firearm and to make technical changes for purposes of gender neutrality; P.A. 99-240 amended Subsec. (a) to add provisions requiring the police officer to prepare a report when cash bail in excess of $10,000 is received for a person accused of a felony involving the use, attempted use or threatened use of physical force against another person, specifying the contents of such report and requiring such police officer not later than 15 days after receipt of such cash bail to file such report with the Department of Revenue Services and mail a copy of such report to the state's attorney and each person offering the cash bail and amended Subsec. (b) to require any of the specified officials authorized to take action under said Subsec. to file any report required under Subsec. (a); P.A. 00-196 made technical changes in Subsec. (a); P.A. 03-173 amended Subsec. (a) to add provision prohibiting a police officer setting the terms and conditions of a person's release, setting a bond for a person or releasing a person from custody unless the officer first checks the National Crime Information Center computerized index of criminal justice information to determine if such person is listed in such index; P.A. 07-123 amended Subsec. (a) to provide that no statement made by arrested person in response to any question during the interview related to terms and conditions of release shall be admissible as evidence against arrested person in any proceeding arising from the incident for which conditions of release were set, added new Subsec. (b) specifying procedure for release of a person charged with a family violence crime, authorizing police officer to impose nonfinancial conditions of release for such person and specifying types of nonfinancial conditions that may be imposed, procedure for their imposition and their duration, designated existing provisions re procedure when cash bail in excess of $10,000 is received as Subsec. (c), designated existing provision requiring police officer to first check National Crime Information Center computerized index of criminal justice information as Subsec. (d) and amended same to make a technical change, designated existing provision requiring police officer to immediately notify a bail commissioner if arrested person has not posted bail as Subsec. (e), and redesignated existing Subsec. (b) re authority and duties of police personnel as Subsec. (f) and amended same to make a technical change; pursuant to P.A. 11-51, "Commissioner of Public Safety" and "Department of Public Safety" were changed editorially by the Revisors to "Commissioner of Emergency Services and Public Protection" and "Department of Emergency Services and Public Protection", respectively, in Subsec. (f), effective July 1, 2011; P.A. 12-133 amended Subsecs. (b) and (e) by adding references to intake, assessment and referral specialist; P.A. 14-233 amended Subsecs. (a), (d) and (e) to add provisions re probation officer serving a violation of probation warrant.

See Sec. 54-1g re time for arraignment.

See Sec. 54-64c re notice of required appearance after release on bond or promise to appear.

See Sec. 54-69b re court's authority to modify conditions of release.

See Sec. 54-71a re lack of liability of bail commissioners, police department employees and others in action for damages on account of a person's release.

Exclusionary effects of Sec. 54-1c do not apply to violations of this section. 195 C. 505. Trial court may issue a criminal protective order at defendant's arraignment after consideration of oral argument and family violence intervention unit's report; trial court is required to hold, at defendant's request at arraignment, a subsequent hearing within a reasonable period of time at which the state will be required to prove the continued necessity of the order by a fair preponderance of the evidence, which may include reliable hearsay testimony, and defendant will have an opportunity to proffer relevant evidence; legislature did not intend for Subsec. (b) and Sec. 46b-38c to entitle defendant to an evidentiary hearing beyond consideration of parties' arguments and unit's report prior to the initial issuance of a criminal protective order at arraignment, which may occur within hours of the alleged incident of family violence. 294 C. 1.

Cited. 28 CS 313.

(Return to Chapter Table of Contents)

(Return to List of Chapters)

(Return to List of Titles)

Sec. 54-63d. Release by bail commissioner or intake, assessment and referral specialist. Information, files and reports held by Court Support Services Division. (a) Upon notification by a police officer pursuant to section 54-63c that an arrested person has not posted bail, a bail commissioner or an intake, assessment and referral specialist employed by the Judicial Branch shall promptly conduct an interview and investigation as specified in subdivisions (1) and (2) of subsection (a) of section 54-63b and, based upon the criteria established pursuant to subsection (b) of section 54-63b and except as provided in subsection (b) of this section, the bail commissioner or intake, assessment and referral specialist shall promptly order release of such person on the first of the following conditions of release found sufficient to provide reasonable assurance of the person's appearance in court: (1) Upon the execution of a written promise to appear without special conditions; (2) upon the execution of a written promise to appear with any of the nonfinancial conditions as specified in subsection (c) of this section; (3) upon the execution of a bond without surety in no greater amount than necessary; or (4) upon the execution of a bond with surety in no greater amount than necessary. If the person is unable to meet the conditions of release ordered by the bail commissioner or intake, assessment and referral specialist, the bail commissioner or intake, assessment and referral specialist shall so inform the court in a report prepared pursuant to subdivision (4) of subsection (a) of section 54-63b.

(b) No person shall be released upon the execution of a written promise to appear or the execution of a bond without surety if the person is charged with the commission of a family violence crime, as defined in section 46b-38a, and in the commission of such crime the person used or threatened the use of a firearm.

(c) In addition to or in conjunction with any of the conditions enumerated in subdivisions (1) to (4), inclusive, of subsection (a) of this section, the bail commissioner or intake, assessment and referral specialist may impose nonfinancial conditions of release, which may require that the arrested person do any of the following: (1) Remain under the supervision of a designated person or organization; (2) comply with specified restrictions on the person's travel, association or place of abode; (3) not engage in specified activities, including the use or possession of a dangerous weapon, an intoxicant or controlled substance; (4) avoid all contact with an alleged victim of the crime and with a potential witness who may testify concerning the offense; or (5) satisfy any other condition that is reasonably necessary to ensure the appearance of the person in court. Any of the conditions imposed under subsection (a) of this section and this subsection by the bail commissioner or intake, assessment and referral specialist shall be effective until the appearance of such person in court.

(d) The police department shall promptly comply with the order of release of the bail commissioner or intake, assessment and referral specialist, except that if the department objects to the order or any of its conditions, the department shall promptly so advise a state's attorney or assistant state's attorney, the bail commissioner or intake, assessment and referral specialist and the arrested person. The state's attorney or assistant state's attorney may authorize the police department to delay release, until a hearing can be had before the court then sitting for the geographical area which includes the municipality in which the arrested person is being detained or, if the court is not then sitting, until the next sitting of said court. When cash bail in excess of ten thousand dollars is received for a detained person accused of a felony, where the underlying facts and circumstances of the felony involve the use, attempted use or threatened use of physical force against another person, the police department shall prepare a report that contains (1) the name, address and taxpayer identification number of the accused person, (2) the name, address and taxpayer identification number of each person offering the cash bail, other than a person licensed as a professional bondsman under chapter 533 or a surety bail bond agent under chapter 700f, (3) the amount of cash received, and (4) the date the cash was received. Not later than fifteen days after receipt of such cash bail, the police department shall file the report with the Department of Revenue Services and mail a copy of the report to the state's attorney for the judicial district in which the alleged offense was committed and to each person offering the cash bail.

(e) Except as provided in subsections (f) and (g) of this section, all information provided to the Court Support Services Division shall be for the sole purpose of determining and recommending the conditions of release, and shall otherwise be confidential and retained in the files of the Court Support Services Division, and not be subject to subpoena or other court process for use in any other proceeding or for any other purpose.

(f) The Court Support Services Division shall establish written procedures for the release of information contained in reports and files of the Court Support Services Division, such procedures to be approved by the executive committee of the judges of the Superior Court. Such procedures shall allow access to (1) nonidentifying information by qualified persons for purposes of research related to the administration of criminal justice; (2) all information provided to the Court Support Services Division by probation officers for the purposes of compiling presentence reports; and (3) all information provided to the Court Support Services Division concerning any person convicted of a crime and held in custody by the Department of Correction.

(g) Any files and reports held by the Court Support Services Division may be accessed and disclosed by employees of the division in accordance with policies and procedures adopted by the Chief Court Administrator.

(1967, P.A. 549, S. 4; P.A. 80-313, S. 15; P.A. 81-437, S. 4, 12; P.A. 82-383, S. 3; P.A. 95-225, S. 32; 95-261, S. 2; P.A. 97-53; P.A. 98-90, S. 3; P.A. 99-186, S. 9; 99-187, S. 1; 99-240, S. 17; P.A. 00-196, S. 42; P.A. 02-132, S. 40; P.A. 10-43, S. 24; P.A. 12-133, S. 37; P.A. 14-122, S. 59.)

History: P.A. 80-313 designated previous provisions as Subsec. (c), inserting new Subsecs. (a) and (b) containing provisions formerly found in Subsecs. (a) and (b) of Sec. 54-63b; P.A. 81-437 amended provisions concerning investigation by bail commissioner and criteria for release and added provisions re financial conditions of release and added new Subsec. (d) re written procedures for release of information in reports and files of office of the bail commission; P.A. 82-383 amended Subsec. (a) to provide that a term or condition of release recommended by a bail commissioner may include a term of supervision; P.A. 95-225 and 95-261 both amended Subsec. (c) to add exception for Subsec. (e) and added nearly identical provisions as new Subsec. (e) authorizing the Office of the Bail Commission to disclose reports and files to the Office of Adult Probation for the purposes of conducting investigations and supervising persons placed on probation; P.A. 97-53 amended Subsec. (a)(1) by adding "without special conditions" after "appear", added Subsec. (a)(2) re nonfinancial conditions as specified in Subsec. (b), renumbering existing Subdivs. (2) and (3) as Subdivs. (3) and (4), changing "financial" conditions of release to "the" conditions of release, and deleting provisions re bail commissioner's recommendation to the court, added Subsec. (b) re nonfinancial conditions and redesignated existing Subsecs. (b) to (e), inclusive, as Subsecs. (c) to (f), inclusive; P.A. 98-90 added Subsec. (f)(2) and (3) authorizing the Office of the Bail Commission to disclose files and reports to the Family Division of the Superior Court for the purpose of preparing written or oral reports and to agencies and organizations under contract with the Office of Alternative Sanctions for the purpose of monitoring arrested persons, respectively; P.A. 99-186 amended Subsec. (a) to add provision that the release of a person by the bail commissioner is subject to the exception in Subsec. (b), added new Subsec. (b) to prohibit the release of a person on the execution of a written promise to appear or the execution of a bond without surety if such person is charged with the commission of a family violence crime in which such person used or threatened the use of a firearm, relettering former Subdivs. (b) to (f) as Subdivs. (c) to (g), respectively, and made technical changes to revise statutory references and make provisions gender neutral; P.A. 99-187 amended former Subsec. (b) to add new Subdiv. (4) providing that the arrested person may be required as a condition of release to participate in the zero-tolerance drug supervision program established under Sec. 53a-39d, renumbering existing Subdivs. (4) and (5) as Subdivs. (5) and (6), respectively, and to make a technical change for purposes of gender neutrality; P.A. 99-240 amended former Subsec. (c) to add provisions requiring the police department to prepare a report when cash bail in excess of $10,000 is received for a detained person accused of a felony involving the use, attempted use or threatened use of physical force against another person, specifying the contents of such report and requiring such police department not later than 15 days after receipt of such cash bail to file such report with the Department of Revenue Services and mail a copy of such report to the state's attorney and each person offering the cash bail; P.A. 00-196 made technical changes in Subsec. (b); P.A. 02-132 amended Subsec. (a) by making technical and conforming changes, amended Subsecs. (e) and (f) by replacing "Office of the Bail Commission" and "Chief Bail Commissioner" with "Court Support Services Division" and deleted former Subsec. (g)(1), (2) and (3) re disclosure of files and reports held by Office of the Bail Commission, replacing "Office of the Bail Commission" with "Court Support Services Division" and adding provision re access and disclosure in accordance with policies and procedures adopted by the Chief Court Administrator; P.A. 10-43 amended Subsec. (c) to delete former Subdiv. (4) re participation in zero-tolerance drug supervision program and redesignate existing Subdivs. (5) and (6) as Subdivs. (4) and (5); P.A. 12-133 amended Subsecs. (a), (c) and (d) by adding references to intake, assessment and referral specialist; P.A. 14-122 made a technical change in Subsec. (c)(5).

See Secs. 53a-222, 53a-222a re criminal penalties for violation of certain conditions of release.

Sec. 54-63e. Bond or promise conditioned on appearance

. Whenever any arrested person is released upon his written promise to appear or upon bond without or with surety, such promise or bond shall be conditioned that he shall appear before the Superior Court. Any promise or bond without or with surety, and any fee paid for a bond with surety, shall also cover any appearance of such person, unless modified, and if modified any such fee which has been paid shall be credited toward the fee of any increased or new bond with surety.

(1967, P.A. 549, S. 5; P.A. 74-183, S. 143, 291; P.A. 76-106, S. 2; 76-436, S. 543, 681; P.A. 77-452, S. 37, 72.)

History: P.A. 74-183 replaced circuit court with court of common pleas, reflecting reorganization of judicial system, effective December 31, 1974; P.A. 76-106 added provisions re acceptance or modification of release conditions by superior court where accused previously entered into bond set by common pleas court in connection with same offense or offenses; P.A. 76-436 amended section to reflect transfer of all trial jurisdiction to superior court, omitting provisions added by P.A. 76-106 rendered obsolete by the change, effective July 1, 1978; P.A. 77-452 confirmed omission of P.A. 76-106 provisions.

Sec. 54-63f. Release after conviction and pending sentence or appeal.

A person who has been convicted of any offense, except a violation of section 53a-54a, 53a-54b, 53a-54c or 53a-54d or any offense involving the use, attempted use or threatened use of physical force against another person, and is either awaiting sentence or has given oral or written notice of such person's intention to appeal or file a petition for certification or a writ of certiorari may be released pending final disposition of the case, unless the court finds custody to be necessary to provide reasonable assurance of such person's appearance in court, upon the first of the following conditions of release found sufficient by the court to provide such assurance: (1) Upon such person's execution of a written promise to appear, (2) upon such person's execution of a bond without surety in no greater amount than necessary, (3) upon such person's execution of a bond with surety in no greater amount than necessary, (4) upon such person's deposit, with the clerk of the court having jurisdiction of the offense with which such person stands convicted or any assistant clerk of such court who is bonded in the same manner as the clerk or any person or officer authorized to accept bail, a sum of money equal to the amount called for by the bond required by the court, or (5) upon such person's pledge of real property, the equity of which is equal to the amount called for by the bond required by the court, provided the person pledging such property is the owner of such property. When cash bail is offered, such bond shall be executed and the money shall be received in lieu of a surety or sureties upon such bond. Such cash bail shall be retained by the clerk of such court until a final order of the court disposing of the same is passed, provided, if such bond is forfeited, the clerk of such court shall pay the money to the payee named therein, according to the terms and conditions of the bond.

(1967, P.A. 549, S. 14; P.A. 89-47; P.A. 98-51; P.A. 00-200, S. 5.)

History: P.A. 89-47 added Subdivs. (4) and (5) authorizing release upon the deposit of a sum of money or upon the pledge of real property, respectively, and added provisions re the execution of the bond when cash bail is offered and the retention and disposition of such cash bail; P.A. 98-51 prohibited the release of a person convicted of violating Sec. 53a-54a, 53a-54b, 53a-54c or 53a-54d; P.A. 00-200 prohibited the release of a person convicted of "any offense involving the use, attempted use or threatened use of physical force against another person" and made technical changes.

Bail under section is entirely disconnected from preconviction bail and presumption of innocence and should be granted with great caution. 159 C. 264. Section violates separation of powers provision contained in Art. II of the Connecticut Constitution, as amended by Art. XVIII of the amendments, insofar as it prohibits trial court from releasing on bail any person who has been convicted of an offense "involving the use, attempted use or threatened use of physical force against another person" because it presents significant interference with the orderly functioning of Superior Court's judicial role. 261 C. 492.

Supreme Court's determination of unconstitutionality in 261 C. 492 should be applied retroactively, as it could have impact on defendant's sentence. 89 CA 729.

Cited. 29 CS 339.

Sec. 54-63g. Appeal from court order re release.

Any accused person or the state, aggrieved by an order of the Superior Court concerning release, may petition the Appellate Court for review of such order. Any such petition shall have precedence over any other matter before said Appellate Court and any hearing shall be heard expeditiously with reasonable notice.

(1967, P.A. 549, S. 17; 1972, P.A. 108, S. 13; P.A. 74-183, S. 144, 291; P.A. 76-436, S. 544, 681; June Sp. Sess. P.A. 83-29, S. 17, 82.)

History: 1972 act replaced circuit court with court of common pleas, effective September 1, 1972, except that courts with cases pending retain jurisdiction; P.A. 74-183 replaced circuit court with court of common pleas, replaced appellate division of common pleas court with superior court and required hearing be "heard expeditiously with reasonable notice" rather than "held on one-day notice to the parties concerned", effective December 31, 1974; P.A. 76-436 replaced court of common pleas with superior court and deleted provisions re superior court's power to review common pleas court orders, leaving supreme court with sole power of review, reflecting transfer of all trial jurisdiction to superior court, effective July 1, 1978; June Sp. Sess. P.A. 83-29 deleted reference to supreme court and substituted appellate court in lieu thereof.

Appeal from refusal of bail in capital case allowed and new hearing ordered to determine whether case falls in constitutional exception to bail in capital case where proof is evident or presumption great. 159 C. 264. Cited. 222 C. 331; 230 C. 441; 233 C. 44; 237 C. 339; 240 C. 623.

Sec. 54-64. Police officials and clerks of court to take promise to appear or bond. Section 54-64 is repealed.

(1949 Rev., S. 8779; 1959, P.A. 28, S. 151; 1961, P.A. 203, S. 1; 1967, P.A. 549, S. 11; P.A. 74-183, S. 145, 291; P.A. 76-436, S. 545, 681; P.A. 77-614, S. 486, 610; P.A. 79-216, S. 3; P.A. 80-313, S. 61.)

Sec. 54-64a. Release by judicial authority. (a)(1) Except as provided in subsection (b) of this section, when any arrested person is presented before the Superior Court, said court shall, in bailable offenses, promptly order the release of such person upon the first of the following conditions of release found sufficient to reasonably ensure the appearance of the arrested person in court: (A) Upon his execution of a written promise to appear without special conditions, (B) upon his execution of a written promise to appear with nonfinancial conditions, (C) upon his execution of a bond without surety in no greater amount than necessary, (D) upon his execution of a bond with surety in no greater amount than necessary. In addition to or in conjunction with any of the conditions enumerated in subparagraphs (A) to (D), inclusive, of this subdivision the court may, when it has reason to believe that the person is drug-dependent and where necessary, reasonable and appropriate, order the person to submit to a urinalysis drug test and to participate in a program of periodic drug testing and treatment. The results of any such drug test shall not be admissible in any criminal proceeding concerning such person.

(2) The court may, in determining what conditions of release will reasonably ensure the appearance of the arrested person in court, consider the following factors: (A) The nature and circumstances of the offense, (B) such person's record of previous convictions, (C) such person's past record of appearance in court after being admitted to bail, (D) such person's family ties, (E) such person's employment record, (F) such person's financial resources, character and mental condition, and (G) such person's community ties.

(b) (1) When any arrested person charged with the commission of a class A felony, a class B felony, except a violation of section 53a-86 or 53a-122, a class C felony, except a violation of section 53a-87, 53a-152 or 53a-153, or a class D felony under sections 53a-60 to 53a-60c, inclusive, section 53a-72a, 53a-95, 53a-103, 53a-103a, 53a-114, 53a-136 or 53a-216, or a family violence crime, as defined in section 46b-38a, is presented before the Superior Court, said court shall, in bailable offenses, promptly order the release of such person upon the first of the following conditions of release found sufficient to reasonably ensure the appearance of the arrested person in court and that the safety of any other person will not be endangered: (A) Upon such person's execution of a written promise to appear without special conditions, (B) upon such person's execution of a written promise to appear with nonfinancial conditions, (C) upon such person's execution of a bond without surety in no greater amount than necessary, (D) upon such person's execution of a bond with surety in no greater amount than necessary. In addition to or in conjunction with any of the conditions enumerated in subparagraphs (A) to (D), inclusive, of this subdivision, the court may, when it has reason to believe that the person is drug-dependent and where necessary, reasonable and appropriate, order the person to submit to a urinalysis drug test and to participate in a program of periodic drug testing and treatment. The results of any such drug test shall not be admissible in any criminal proceeding concerning such person.

(2) The court may, in determining what conditions of release will reasonably ensure the appearance of the arrested person in court and that the safety of any other person will not be endangered, consider the following factors: (A) The nature and circumstances of the offense, (B) such person's record of previous convictions, (C) such person's past record of appearance in court after being admitted to bail, (D) such person's family ties, (E) such person's employment record, (F) such person's financial resources, character and mental condition, (G) such person's community ties, (H) the number and seriousness of charges pending against the arrested person, (I) the weight of the evidence against the arrested person, (J) the arrested person's history of violence, (K) whether the arrested person has previously been convicted of similar offenses while released on bond, and (L) the likelihood based upon the expressed intention of the arrested person that such person will commit another crime while released.

(3) When imposing conditions of release under this subsection, the court shall state for the record any factors under subdivision (2) of this subsection that it considered and the findings that it made as to the danger, if any, that the arrested person might pose to the safety of any other person upon the arrested person's release that caused the court to impose the specific conditions of release that it imposed.

(c) If the court determines that a nonfinancial condition of release should be imposed pursuant to subparagraph (B) of subdivision (1) of subsection (a) or (b) of this section, the court shall order the pretrial release of the person subject to the least restrictive condition or combination of conditions that the court determines will reasonably ensure the appearance of the arrested person in court and, with respect to the release of the person pursuant to subsection (b) of this section, that the safety of any other person will not be endangered, which conditions may include an order that the arrested person do one or more of the following: (1) Remain under the supervision of a designated person or organization; (2) comply with specified restrictions on such person's travel, association or place of abode; (3) not engage in specified activities, including the use or possession of a dangerous weapon, an intoxicant or a controlled substance; (4) provide sureties of the peace pursuant to section 54-56f under supervision of a designated bail commissioner or intake, assessment and referral specialist employed by the Judicial Branch; (5) avoid all contact with an alleged victim of the crime and with a potential witness who may testify concerning the offense; (6) maintain employment or, if unemployed, actively seek employment; (7) maintain or commence an educational program; (8) be subject to electronic monitoring; or (9) satisfy any other condition that is reasonably necessary to ensure the appearance of the person in court and that the safety of any other person will not be endangered. The court shall state on the record its reasons for imposing any such nonfinancial condition.

(d) If the arrested person is not released, the court shall order him committed to the custody of the Commissioner of Correction until he is released or discharged in due course of law.

(e) The court may require that the person subject to electronic monitoring pursuant to subsection (c) of this section pay directly to the electronic monitoring service provider a fee for the cost of such electronic monitoring services. If the court finds that the person subject to electronic monitoring is indigent and unable to pay the costs of electronic monitoring services, the court shall waive such costs. Any contract entered into by the Judicial Branch and the electronic monitoring service provider shall include a provision stating that the total cost for electronic monitoring services shall not exceed five dollars per day. Such amount shall be indexed annually to reflect the rate of inflation.

(1961, P.A. 38; 1963, P.A. 11; 1967, P.A. 549, S. 12; P.A. 74-183, S. 146, 291; P.A. 76-436, S. 546, 681; P.A. 77-452, S. 39, 72; P.A. 80-313, S. 16; P.A. 81-437, S. 9, 12; P.A. 89-390, S. 13, 37; P.A. 90-213, S. 51; 90-261, S. 9; P.A. 91-406, S. 13, 29; P.A. 99-186, S. 5; 99-187, S. 2; P.A. 00-141, S. 2, 3; P.A. 01-84, S. 25, 26; P.A. 03-278, S. 107; Jan. Sp. Sess. P.A. 08-1, S. 25; P.A. 10-43, S. 25; P.A. 12-133, S. 38; June 12 Sp. Sess. P.A. 12-2, S. 94; P.A. 14-122, S. 60.)

History: 1963 act added authority for taking a bond when court was not in criminal session by any one authorized under Sec. 54-64; 1967 act, effective October 1, 1968, provided for alternatives to bond with surety and provided for making release arrangements when accused is presented before court; P.A. 74-183 replaced circuit court with court of common pleas, effective December 31, 1974; P.A. 76-436 replaced court of common pleas with superior court, effective July 1, 1978; P.A. 77-452 deleted wording which implies power to refuse accused bail if "custody is found to be necessary to provide reasonable assurance of his appearance", effective July 1, 1978; P.A. 80-313 restated existing provisions and required that arrested person who is not released be committed to custody of commissioner of correction until released or discharged in due course of law; P.A. 81-437 added provision distinguishing between two types of release upon execution of written promise to appear without special conditions and with nonfinancial conditions; P.A. 89-390 added provisions authorizing the court to order a drug-dependent person to submit to a urinalysis drug test and participate in a program of periodic drug testing and treatment and specifying that the results of any such drug test shall be inadmissible in a criminal proceeding concerning such person; P.A. 90-213 designated former provisions re conditions of release and drug testing as Subsec. (a) and amended said Subsec. to provide that the court find the condition of release sufficient to reasonably assure "that the safety of any other person will not be endangered", added Subsec. (b) authorizing the court to consider certain enumerated factors in determining the conditions of release that will reasonably assure the appearance of the arrested person in court and that the safety of any other person will not be endangered, added Subsec. (c) specifying conditions the court is authorized to order the arrested person to satisfy when a nonfinancial condition of release is imposed, and designated former provisions re the commitment to the custody of the commissioner of correction of an arrested person who is not released as Subsec. (d); P.A. 90-261 designated former provisions of Subsec. (a) Subsec. (a)(1) and amended said Subdiv. to delete provision requiring court to find the condition of release sufficient to reasonably assure that the safety of any other person will not be endangered and to redesignate Subdivs. (1) to (4) as Subparas. (A) to (D), respectively, redesignated former Subsec. (b) as Subsec. (a)(2) and amended said Subdiv. to redesignate Subdivs. (1) to (7) as Subparas. (A) to (G), respectively, and to delete former Subdiv. (8) re number and seriousness of pending charges, Subdiv. (9) re weight of the evidence, Subdiv. (10) re history of violence, Subdiv. (11) re previous convictions of similar offenses committed while released on bond and Subdiv. (12) re likelihood of commission of another crime while released, added new Subsec. (b) consisting of Subdivs. (1) and (2) being identical to former Subsecs. (a) and (b), respectively, as enacted by P.A. 90-213, but made provisions applicable to persons charged with certain serious specified felonies, and amended Subsec. (c) to revise internal references and provide that the requirement that the condition of release reasonably assure that the safety of any other person will not be endangered is applicable "with respect to the release of the person pursuant to subsection (b) of this section"; P.A. 91-406 substituted "Except as provided in subsection (b) of this section, when" for "when" at the beginning of Subsec. (a)(1); P.A. 99-186 amended Subsec. (b) to make provisions applicable to a person charged with the commission of a family violence crime as defined in Sec. 46b-38a; P.A. 99-187 added new Subsec. (c)(4) providing that the arrested person may be ordered as a condition of release to participate in the zero-tolerance drug supervision program established under Sec. 53a-39d, renumbering Subdivs. (4) to (8) as Subdivs. (5) to (9), respectively, and making technical changes for purposes of gender neutrality; P.A. 00-141 added new Subsec. (c)(9) re electronic monitoring, redesignating former Subdiv. (9) as Subdiv. (10), and added Subsec. (e) re electronic monitoring services; P.A. 01-84 amended Subsec. (b)(1) to delete reference to Sec. 53a-72b as a class D felony since violation of said section was reclassified as a class C felony by June Sp. Sess. P.A. 99-2, and to make technical changes for purposes of gender neutrality, effective July 1, 2001; P.A. 03-278 made technical changes in Subsec. (e), effective July 9, 2003; Jan. Sp. Sess. P.A. 08-1 amended Subsec. (b) to add Subdiv. (3) requiring court to state for the record any factors under Subdiv. (2) that it considered and the findings that it made re danger, if any, that arrested person might pose to safety of any other person upon release that caused the court to impose the specific conditions of release that it imposed, effective January 25, 2008; P.A. 10-43 amended Subsec. (c) to delete former Subdiv. (4) re participation in zero-tolerance drug supervision program and redesignate existing Subdivs. (5) to (10) as Subdivs. (4) to (9); P.A. 12-133 amended Subsec. (c)(4) by adding "or intake, assessment and referral specialist employed by the Judicial Branch"; June 12 Sp. Sess. P.A. 12-2 made a technical change in Subsec. (b)(1); P.A. 14-122 made technical changes.

See Sec. 18-100f re release by Commissioner of Correction.

See Secs. 53a-222, 53a-222a re criminal penalties for violation of certain conditions of release.

Cited. 201 C. 115; 222 C. 331. Section affords Superior Court judge broad discretion in fixing nonfinancial conditions of defendant's release for purpose of ensuring, inter alia, the safety of others, including restrictions on entering a specific place of abode and on having contact with alleged victim of the crime with which defendant has been charged. 273 C. 418.

Cited. 22 CA 199.

Sec. 54-64b. Release following arrest on court warrant.

(a) When any person is arrested on a bench warrant of arrest issued by order of the Superior Court or, when said court is not in session, by a judge thereof, in which the court or judge issuing the warrant indicated that bail should be denied or ordered that the person to be arrested should be brought before a clerk or assistant clerk of the Superior Court, the officer or indifferent person making the arrest shall without undue delay bring the arrested person before the clerk or assistant clerk of the superior court for the geographical area where the offense is alleged to have been committed during the office hours of the clerk and if the clerk's office is not open, the officer or indifferent person shall, without undue delay, bring the arrested person to a community correctional center within the geographical area where the offense is alleged to have been committed or, if there is no such correctional center within such geographical area, to the nearest community correctional center, or the York Correctional Institution, as the case may be. The clerk or assistant clerk or a person designated by the Commissioner of Correction shall thereupon advise the arrested person of his rights under section 54-1b, and, when the court or judge has not indicated that bail should be denied, shall order the arrested person to enter into the condition of release pursuant to the condition fixed by the judge or court conditioned that the arrested person shall appear before the superior court having criminal jurisdiction in and for the geographical area to answer to the bench warrant of arrest and information filed in the case. Upon the failure of the arrested person to enter into the condition of release fixed by the court or judge or if the person has been arrested for an offense which is not bailable, the clerk or assistant clerk or the person designated by the Commissioner of Correction shall issue a mittimus committing the arrested person to a community correctional center, or the York Correctional Institution, as the case may be, until he is discharged by due course of law.

(b) When any person is arrested on a bench warrant of arrest issued by order of the Superior Court or by a judge thereof, in which the court or judge has not indicated that bail should be denied or has not ordered that the officer or indifferent person making such arrest shall without undue delay bring such person before the clerk or assistant clerk of the superior court for the geographical area, the officer or indifferent person making the arrest shall without undue delay, comply with the provisions of sections 54-63c and 54-63d in setting the conditions of release for the person or persons arrested under the warrant.

(c) The clerk or assistant clerk and the person designated by the Commissioner of Correction may take a written promise to appear on a bond without or with surety from an arrested person in accordance with the conditions of release fixed by the court or judge and may administer such oaths as are necessary in the taking of promises or bonds.

(P.A. 80-313, S. 13; P.A. 85-309; P.A. 15-14, S. 36.)

History: P.A. 85-309 amended Subsec. (a) to authorize commitment of person under arrest to Connecticut Correctional Institution, Niantic; P.A. 15-14 made technical changes in Subsec. (a).

Cited. 187 C. 6; 195 C. 505; 201 C. 115; 236 C. 388.

Sec. 54-64c. Notice of appearance after release.

The person taking any promise or bond shall give the person released a copy of the promise or bond, which shall notify the person of the time when and the place where he is next to appear and of the penalty for failure so to appear.

(P.A. 80-313, S. 18.)

Sec. 54-64d. Release of person taken into custody on a capias. (a) When any person is taken into custody on a capias issued by order of the Superior Court, the proper officer or state police officer taking the person into custody shall, without undue delay, bring such person before the court that issued the capias.

(b) If a courthouse lockup operated by the Judicial Branch is available at the court that issued the capias and is operational at the time the proper officer or state police officer brings the person taken into custody to the court, the proper officer or state police officer shall transfer the custody of such person to a judicial marshal at the court unless such person requires medical attention or there is insufficient space for such person at such lockup.

(1) If the court is in session, the judicial marshal shall present such person before the court. If the court is not in session but the clerk's office is open, the judicial marshal shall present such person before the clerk or assistant clerk or a person designated by the Chief Court Administrator.

(2) If the court is not in session and the clerk's office is closed, and such person indicates to the judicial marshal that he or she can meet the conditions of release fixed by the court, the judicial marshal shall, without undue delay, either (A) transport such person to a community correctional center within the judicial district or, if there is no community correctional center within the judicial district, to the nearest community correctional center, for the purpose of entering into the condition of release fixed by the court, or (B) if more expedient, hold the person in custody until the clerk's office is open or the next session of the court, for the purpose of entering into the condition of release fixed by the court. If such person does not indicate to the judicial marshal that he or she can meet the conditions of release fixed by the court, the judicial marshal shall hold the person in custody until the clerk's office is open or the next session of the court, for the purpose of entering into the condition of release fixed by the court.

(c) If a courthouse lockup operated by the Judicial Branch is not available at the court that issued the capias, or is available but is not operational or has insufficient space, the proper officer or state police officer taking the person into custody shall, without undue delay, transport such person to a community correctional center within the judicial district or, if there is no community correctional center within the judicial district, to the nearest community correctional center for the purpose of entering into the condition of release fixed by the court.

(d) The clerk or assistant clerk or a person designated by the Commissioner of Correction or by the Chief Court Administrator shall order the person taken into custody on the capias to enter into the condition of release fixed by the court on the condition that such person shall appear before the next session of the superior court that issued the capias. Upon the failure of such person to enter into the condition of release fixed by the court, the person shall be held in the correctional center pursuant to the capias until the next session of the court.

(P.A. 87-102; P.A. 03-224, S. 15; P.A. 05-152, S. 8.)

History: P.A. 03-224 added provisions re transfer of custody to judicial marshal if courthouse lockup is available and operational and added provision re designation by Chief Court Administrator, effective July 2, 2003; P.A. 05-152 divided section into Subsecs. (a), (b) and (d), amended Subsec. (a) by adding provision re person taken into custody by a state police officer and making a technical change, amended Subsec. (b) by adding provisions re transfer of custody by state police officer, making technical changes and replacing provisions re duties of proper officer with Subdivs. (1) and (2) re duties of judicial marshal, added Subsec. (c) re duties of proper officer or state police officer if courthouse lockup is not available, is not operational or has insufficient space, and made technical changes in Subsec. (d).

Sec. 54-64e. Noncriminal behavior as condition of release. Notice of conditions of release and sanctions for violation.

(a) When any person is released pursuant to the provisions of sections 54-63a to 54-63g, inclusive, or sections 54-64a to 54-64c, inclusive, it shall be a condition of such release that the person released not commit a federal, state or local crime during the period of release.

(b) When any person is released pursuant to the provisions of sections 54-63a to 54-63g, inclusive, or sections 54-64a to 54-64c, inclusive, such person shall be notified in writing at the time of release: (1) Of the condition specified in subsection (a) of this section and any additional conditions of release; (2) that violation of any condition of release may result in the imposition of different or additional conditions of release; (3) that if he is released with respect to an offense for which a term of imprisonment of ten or more years may be imposed and the court finds that he has violated any condition of release and the safety of any other person is endangered while he is on release, his release may be revoked; and (4) that any crime committed while on release may subject him to enhanced penalties pursuant to section 53a-40b.

(P.A. 90-213, S. 52, 56.)

Cited. 222 C. 331.

Sec. 54-64f. Violation of conditions of release. Imposition of different or additional conditions. Revocation of release.

(a) Upon application by the prosecuting authority alleging that a defendant has violated the conditions of the defendant's release, the court may, if probable cause is found, order that the defendant appear in court for an evidentiary hearing upon such allegations. An order to appear shall be served upon the defendant by any law enforcement officer delivering a copy to the defendant personally, or by leaving it at the defendant's usual place of abode with a person of suitable age and discretion then residing therein, or mailing it by registered or certified mail to the last-known address of the defendant.

(b) If the court, after an evidentiary hearing at which hearsay or secondary evidence shall be admissible, finds by clear and convincing evidence that the defendant has violated reasonable conditions imposed on the defendant's release it may impose different or additional conditions upon the defendant's release. If the defendant is on release with respect to an offense for which a term of imprisonment of ten or more years may be imposed and the court, after an evidentiary hearing at which hearsay or secondary evidence shall be admissible, finds by clear and convincing evidence that the defendant has violated reasonable conditions of the defendant's release and that the safety of any other person is endangered while the defendant is on release, it may revoke such release.

(c) If the defendant is on release with respect to an offense for which a term of imprisonment of ten or more years may be imposed and the court, after an evidentiary hearing at which hearsay or secondary evidence shall be admissible, finds by clear and convincing evidence that the safety of any other person is endangered while the defendant is on release and that there is probable cause to believe that the defendant has committed a federal, state or local crime while on release, there shall be a rebuttable presumption that the defendant's release should be revoked.

(d) The revocation of a defendant's release pursuant to this section shall cause any bond posted in the criminal proceeding to be automatically terminated and the surety to be released.

(P.A. 90-213, S. 53; P.A. 99-240, S. 11.)

History: P.A. 99-240 made hearsay or secondary evidence admissible at an evidentiary hearing and made technical changes for purposes of gender neutrality.

See Secs. 53a-222, 53a-222a re criminal penalties for violation of certain conditions of release.

Cited. 220 C. 922; 224 C. 29.

Subsec. (c):

As applied to defendant, statute did not violate right of bail provision of Art. I, Sec. 8 of the Connecticut Constitution, as amended by Art. XVII of the amendments. 222 C. 331.

Sec. 54-64g. Surveillance of serious felony offenders released on bond.

The office of the Chief State's Attorney shall, in consultation with the Commissioner of Emergency Services and Public Protection and the Connecticut Police Chiefs Association, develop protocols for the surveillance by state police officers or municipal police officers, or both, of persons charged with the commission of a serious felony offense, as defined in section 54-82t, who are released on bond.

(P.A. 99-240, S. 10; P.A. 11-51, S. 172.)

History: P.A. 11-51 replaced "Commissioner of Public Safety" with "Commissioner of Emergency Services and Public Protection" and deleted reference to January 1, 2000, effective July 1, 2011.

Sec. 54-65. Procedure when surety believes principal intends to abscond. Application for release of surety from bond if principal absconds.

(a) Any surety in a recognizance in criminal proceedings, who believes that such surety's principal intends to abscond, shall apply to a judge of the Superior Court, produce such surety's bail bond or evidence of being a surety, and verify the reason of such surety's application by oath or otherwise. Thereupon, the judge shall immediately grant a mittimus, directed to a proper officer or indifferent person, commanding such officer or indifferent person immediately to arrest the principal and commit the principal to a community correctional center. The Community Correctional Center Administrator shall receive the principal and retain the principal in a community correctional center until discharged by due order of law. The surrender of the principal shall be a full discharge of the surety upon such surety's bond or recognizance.

(b) If the principal of a surety in a recognizance in criminal proceedings absconds, such surety may apply, prior to six months after the date the bond is ordered forfeited, to a judge of the Superior Court to be released from such bond. The judge may release such surety from such bond for good cause shown.

(1949 Rev., S. 8780; P.A. 81-410, S. 12; P.A. 90-288, S. 1; P.A. 14-184, S. 1.)

History: P.A. 81-410 replaced previous provision re rights of surety with the language of former Sec. 52-319; P.A. 90-288 made provision re application to a judge by a surety who believes his principal intends to abscond mandatory rather than discretionary; P.A. 14-184 designated existing provisions as Subsec. (a) and amended same to make technical changes, and added Subsec. (b) re application for release of surety from bond for good cause shown when principal of surety absconds.

Right of person giving bail to retake prisoner; arrest of prisoner in another state no defense to action on hand. 16 Wall. 371; 160 U.S. 246. Cited. 140 C. 326; 175 C. 149. Has no application to facts of case. 199 C. 537.

Sec. 54-65a. Forfeiture of bond for failure to appear. Issuance of rearrest warrant or capias. Termination or reinstatement of bond. Rebate to surety.

(a)(1) Whenever an arrested person is released upon the execution of a bond with surety in an amount of five hundred dollars or more and such bond is ordered forfeited because the principal failed to appear in court as conditioned in such bond, the court shall, at the time of ordering the bond forfeited: (A) Issue a rearrest warrant or a capias directing a proper officer to take the defendant into custody, (B) provide written notice to the surety on the bond that the principal has failed to appear in court as conditioned in such bond, except that if the surety on the bond is an insurer, as defined in section 38a-660, the court shall provide such notice to such insurer and not to the surety bail bond agent, as defined in section 38a-660, and (C) order a stay of execution upon the forfeiture for six months. The court may, in its discretion and for good cause shown, extend such stay of execution. A stay of execution shall not prevent the issuance of a rearrest warrant or a capias.

(2) When the principal whose bond has been forfeited is returned to custody pursuant to the rearrest warrant or a capias within six months after the date such bond was ordered forfeited or, if a stay of execution was extended, within the time period inclusive of such extension of the date such bond was ordered

forfeited, the bond shall be automatically terminated and the surety released and the court shall order new conditions of release for the defendant in accordance with section 54-64a.

(3) When the principal whose bond has been forfeited returns to court voluntarily within five business days after the date such bond was ordered forfeited, the court may, in its discretion, and after finding that the defendant's failure to appear was not wilful, vacate the forfeiture order and reinstate the bond.

(b) Whenever an arrested person, whose bond has been forfeited, is returned to the jurisdiction of the court within one year after the date such bond was ordered forfeited, the surety on such bond shall be entitled to a rebate of that portion of the forfeited amount as may be fixed by the court or as may be established by a schedule adopted by rule of the judges of the court.

(P.A. 77-455; P.A. 79-461; P.A. 84-123, S. 3; P.A. 87-343, S. 1; P.A. 96-96; 96-164, S. 2; P.A. 99-62; P.A. 03-202, S. 21; P.A. 14-184, S. 2.)

History: P.A. 79-461 amended Subsec. (a) to specify applicability where bond is $500 or more and to add provisions re stay of execution on forfeiture; P.A. 84-123 amended Subsec. (a) to authorize a court to issue a capias for a defendant who fails to appear in court and to delete reference to issuance of a mittimus; P.A. 87-343 amended Subsec. (a) to provide automatic reinstatement of the bond and release of the surety when the arrested person is returned to custody within six months of the bond forfeiture; P.A. 96-96 amended Subsec. (a) to provide that when the "principal", rather than the "arrested person", is returned to custody "pursuant to the rearrest warrant or a capias" within six months of the forfeiture the bond shall be automatically "terminated", rather than "reinstated", and "the court shall order new conditions of release for the defendant in accordance with section 54-64a" and to add provision that when the principal returns to court voluntarily within two business days of the forfeiture, the court may vacate the forfeiture order and reinstate the bond if it finds the failure to appear was not wilful; P.A. 96-164 amended Subsec. (a) to extend from two to five business days the period after the date of forfeiture within which if the principal returns to court voluntarily the court may vacate the forfeiture order and reinstate the bond; P.A. 99-62 added new Subsec. (a)(2) requiring the court to provide written notice to the surety on the bond that the principal has failed to appear in court as conditioned in such bond, renumbering former Subdiv. (2) as Subdiv. (3); P.A. 03-202 amended Subsec. (a)(2) by adding provision re notice to insurer that is the surety on the bond, effective April 1, 2004; P.A. 14-184 amended Subsec. (a) to insert new Subdiv. (1), (2) and (3) designators, add provision allowing court to extend stay of execution for good cause shown and make conforming changes in Subdiv. (1), and add provision re time period inclusive of extension of date bond was ordered forfeited in Subdiv. (2), and made technical changes.

Statute can coexist with common law right of bail bondsman to apprehend and surrender his principal; nothing in wording of statute abrogates that right. 199 C. 537. The proper legal standard for determining whether a surety may be relieved of its obligation on a bail bond continues to be the common law rule set forth in *Taylor v. Taintor*, 83 U.S. 366, i.e. that a surety will be released only when the appearance of the principal at trial is made impossible by an act of God, an act of the state or pursuant to law. 301 C. 617.

Sec. 54-65b. Verification of rearrest warrant or capias upon request.

Upon the request during regular business hours of a person licensed as (1) a professional bondsman under chapter 533, (2) a surety bail bond agent under section 38a-660, or (3) a bail enforcement agent under sections 29-152f to 29-152i, inclusive, the Judicial Branch shall verify in the central computer system set forth in subsection (e) of section 54-2a whether a rearrest warrant or capias issued pursuant to section 54-65a is still outstanding.

(P.A. 11-45, S. 23.)

Sec. 54-65c. Vacating forfeiture of bond.

A court shall vacate an order forfeiting a bail bond and release the professional bondsman, as defined in section 29-144, or the surety bail bond agent and the insurer, as both terms are defined in section 38a-660, if (1) the principal on the bail bond (A) is detained or incarcerated (i) in another state, territory or country, or (ii) by a federal agency, or (B) has been removed by United States Immigration and Customs Enforcement, and (2) the professional bondsman, the surety bail bond agent or the insurer provides satisfactory proof of such detention, incarceration or removal to the court and the state's attorney prosecuting the case, and (3) the state's attorney prosecuting the case declines to seek extradition of the principal.

(P.A. 11-45, S. 24; P.A. 14-184, S. 4.)

History: P.A. 14-184 amended Subdiv. (1) by designating existing provision re principal detained or incarcerated as Subpara. (A), adding "or (ii) by a federal agency" therein, and adding Subpara. (B) re removal by United States Immigration and Customs Enforcement, amended Subdiv. (2) to add "satisfactory" re proof and add reference to removal, and made technical changes.

Sec. 54-66. Acceptance and disposition of bail. Pledge of real property as lien. Forfeiture of bond for failure to appear. Issuance of rearrest warrant or capias. Termination or reinstatement of bond.

(a)(1) In any criminal case in which a bond is allowable or required and the amount of such bond has been determined, the accused person, or any person on the accused person's behalf, (A) may deposit, with the clerk of the court having jurisdiction of the offense with which the accused person stands charged or any assistant clerk of such court who is bonded in the same manner as the clerk or any person or officer authorized to accept bail, a sum of money equal to the amount called for by such bond, or (B) may pledge real property, the equity of which is equal to the amount called for by such bond, provided the person pledging such property is the owner of such real property, and such accused person shall thereupon be admitted to bail.

182

(2) When cash bail is offered, such bond shall be executed and the money shall be received in lieu of a surety or sureties upon such bond. Such cash bail shall be retained by the clerk of such court until a final order of the court disposing of the same is passed, except that if such bond is forfeited, the clerk of such court shall pay the money to the payee named therein, according to the terms and conditions of the bond. When cash bail in excess of ten thousand dollars is received for a person accused of a felony, where the underlying facts and circumstances of the felony involve the use, attempted use or threatened use of physical force against another person, the clerk of such court shall prepare a report that contains (A) the name, address and taxpayer identification number of the accused person, (B) the name, address and taxpayer identification number of each person offering the cash bail, other than a person licensed as a professional bondsman under chapter 533 or a surety bail bond agent under chapter 700f, (C) the amount of cash received, and (D) the date the cash was received. Not later than fifteen days after receipt of such cash bail, the clerk of such court shall file the report with the Department of Revenue Services and mail a copy of the report to the state's attorney for the judicial district in which the court is located and to each person offering the cash bail.

(3) When real property is pledged, the pledge shall constitute a lien on the real property upon the filing of a notice of lien in the office of the town clerk of the town in which the real property is located. The lien shall be in an amount equal to the bond set by the court. The notice of lien shall be on a form prescribed by the Office of the Chief Court Administrator. Upon order of forfeiture of the underlying bond, the state's attorney for the judicial district in which the forfeiture is ordered shall refer the matter to the Attorney General and the Attorney General may, on behalf of the state, foreclose such lien in the same manner as a mortgage. The lien created by this subsection shall expire six years after the forfeiture is ordered unless the Attorney General commences an action to foreclose it within that period of time and records a notice of lis pendens in evidence thereof on the land records of the town in which the real property is located. If the bond has not been ordered forfeited, the clerk of the court shall authorize the recording of a release of such lien upon final disposition of the criminal matter or upon order of the court. The release shall be on a form prescribed by the Office of the Chief Court Administrator.

(b) (1) Whenever an accused person is released upon the deposit by a person on behalf of the accused person of a sum of money equal to the amount called for by such bond or upon the pledge by a person on behalf of the accused person of real property, the equity of which is equal to the amount called for by such bond, and such bond is ordered forfeited because the accused person failed to appear in court as conditioned in such bond, the court shall, at the time of ordering the bond forfeited: (A) Issue a rearrest warrant or a capias directing a proper officer to take the accused person into custody, (B) provide written notice to the person who offered cash bail or pledged real property on behalf of the accused person that the accused person has failed to appear in court as conditioned in such bond, and (C) order a stay of execution upon the forfeiture for six months. The court may, in its discretion and for good cause shown, extend such stay of execution. A stay of execution shall not prevent the issuance of a rearrest warrant or a capias.

(2) When the accused person whose bond has been forfeited is returned to custody pursuant to the rearrest warrant or a capias within six months of the date such bond was ordered forfeited or, if a stay of execution was extended, within the time period inclusive of such extension of the date such bond was ordered forfeited, the bond shall be automatically terminated and the person who offered cash bail or pledged real property on behalf of the accused person shall be released from such obligation and the court shall order new conditions of release for the accused person in accordance with section 54-64a.

(3) When the accused person whose bond has been forfeited returns to court voluntarily within five business days of the date such bond was ordered forfeited, the court may, in its discretion, and after finding that the accused person's failure to appear was not wilful, vacate the forfeiture order and reinstate the bond.

(1949 Rev., S. 8781; 1959, P.A. 28, S. 152; P.A. 81-246; P.A. 93-265, S. 1; P.A. 99-240, S. 14; P.A. 01-186, S. 18; P.A. 14-184, S. 3.)

History: 1959 act deleted references to trial justices and included assistant court clerk; P.A. 81-246 permitted the accused person to pledge real property in order to be admitted to bail; P.A. 93-265 added Subsec. (b) to provide that the pledge of real property constitutes a lien on the property when a notice of lien is filed and to specify the procedure for the foreclosure or release of such lien; P.A. 99-240 amended Subsec. (a) to add provisions requiring the clerk of the court to prepare a report when cash bail in excess of $10,000 is received for a person accused of a felony involving the use, attempted use or threatened use of physical force against another person, specifying the contents of such report and requiring said clerk not later than 15 days after receipt of such cash bail to file such report with the Department of Revenue Services and mail a copy of such report to the state's attorney and each person offering the cash bail; P.A. 01-186 added Subsec. (c) re forfeiture of bond for failure to appear, issuance of rearrest warrant or capias, stay of execution upon forfeiture of bond for six months from date bond ordered forfeited, automatic termination of bond if accused is returned to custody as result of rearrest warrant or capias and reinstatement of bond if accused returns to court voluntarily within 5 business days of order of forfeiture; P.A. 14-184 amended Subsec. (a) to designate existing provisions as Subdivs. (1) and (2) and redesignate existing Subdivs. (1) and (2) as Subparas. (A) and (B), redesignated existing Subsec. (b) as Subsec. (a)(3), redesignated existing Subsec. (c) as Subsec. (b)(1), (2) and (3), amended redesignated Subsec. (b)(1) to add provision allowing court, for good cause shown, to extend stay of execution, amended redesignated Subsec. (b)(2) to add provision re extension of stay of execution within time period inclusive of extension of date bond was ordered forfeited, amended redesignated Subsec. (b)(3) to delete provision re prevention of issuance of rearrest warrant or capias, and made technical changes.

Cash bail remains in custody of court until order for return is made, even though accused has appeared and been discharged; garnishment of such a fund. 96 C. 358. Cited. 119 C. 25.

Cited. 25 CA 643. This section and Sec. 54-65a do not expressly provide for, or preclude, granting of rebate to a depositor of cash bail when defendant has been returned to the jurisdiction more than 6 months after the bond is called, but it is within the power of Connecticut courts to ensure defendant's appearance and thus trial court's award of such a rebate was proper. 68 CA 849.

Sec. 54-66a. Automatic termination of bail bonds.

Any bail bond posted in any criminal proceeding in this state shall be automatically terminated and released whenever the defendant: (1) Is granted accelerated rehabilitation pursuant to section 54-56e; (2) is granted admission to the pretrial alcohol education program pursuant to section 54-56g; (3) is granted admission to the pretrial family violence education program pursuant to section 46b-38c; (4) is granted admission to the pretrial drug education and community service program pursuant to section 54-56i; (5) has the complaint or information filed against such defendant dismissed; (6) has the prosecution of the complaint or information filed against such defendant terminated by entry of a nolle prosequi; (7) is acquitted; (8) is sentenced by the court and a stay of such sentence, if any, is lifted; (9) is granted admission to the pretrial school violence prevention program pursuant to section 54-56j; (10) is charged with a violation of section 29-33, 53-202*l* or 53-202w, and prosecution has been suspended pursuant to subsection (h) of section 29-33; (11) is charged with a violation of section 29-37a and prosecution has been suspended pursuant to subsection (i) of section 29-37a; or (12) is granted admission to the supervised diversionary program for persons with psychiatric disabilities, or persons who are veterans, pursuant to section 54-56*l*.

(P.A. 79-469; P.A. 86-118; P.A. 90-288, S. 2; P.A. 91-218; P.A. 92-139; 92-256, S. 5; May Sp. Sess. P.A. 92-11, S. 50, 70; P.A. 97-287, S. 14; P.A. 98-21, S. 1; 98-59, S. 2, 3; P.A. 01-186, S. 9; P.A. 10-18, S. 27; 10-30, S. 5; P.A. 12-133, S. 22; P.A. 13-159, S. 4; P.A. 14-184, S. 5; 14-207, S. 8.)

History: P.A. 86-118 added provision re the termination and release of a bail bond upon defendant's admission to the pretrial alcohol education system; P.A. 90-288 added provision re the termination and release of a bail bond upon defendant's admission to the pretrial family violence education program; P.A. 91-218 replaced provisions requiring the automatic termination and release of a bail bond whenever a defendant has a fine imposed by the court, whether or not a stay is had or the fine is vacated by the court, or is sentenced by the court but a stay of execution or other delay of imposition of sentence is granted with provisions requiring such automatic termination and release whenever a defendant has the complaint or information filed against him dismissed, is acquitted or is convicted; P.A. 92-139 amended Subdiv. (6) by deleting "is convicted" and inserting "is sentenced by the court"; P.A. 92-256 and May Sp. Sess. P.A. 92-11 changed effective date of P.A. 92-139 from October 1, 1992, to May 27, 1992; P.A. 97-287 added new Subdiv. (4) re automatic termination and release of a bail bond when the defendant is granted admission to the community service labor program pursuant to Sec. 53a-39c, renumbering the remaining Subdivs. accordingly; P.A. 98-21 added new Subdiv. (5) re automatic termination and release of a bail bond when the defendant is granted admission to the pretrial drug education program pursuant to Sec. 54-56i, renumbering the remaining Subdivs. accordingly; P.A. 98-59 revised effective date of P.A. 98-21, but without affecting this section; P.A. 01-186 made a technical change for purposes of gender neutrality in Subsec. (6) and added Subdivs. (9) and (10) re automatic termination of bail bond when defendant is granted admission into pretrial school violence prevention program or is charged with violation of Sec. 29-33 and prosecution is suspended; P.A. 10-18 amended Subdiv. (2) by replacing "system" with "program"; P.A. 10-30 made identical change as P.A. 10-18, effective July 1, 2010; P.A. 12-133 added Subdiv. (11) re automatic termination of bail bond when defendant is granted admission to supervised diversionary program for persons with psychiatric disabilities; P.A. 13-159 substituted "pretrial drug education and community service program" for "pretrial drug education program" in Subdiv. (5); P.A. 14-184 amended Subdiv. (11) to add reference to persons who are veterans; P.A. 14-207 deleted former Subdiv. (4) re admission to the community service labor program pursuant to Sec. 53a-39c, redesignated existing Subdivs. (5) and (6) as Subdivs. (4) and (5), added new Subdiv. (6) re prosecution of complaint or information terminated by entry of nolle prosequi, amended Subdiv. (8) by adding "and a stay of such sentence, if any, is lifted", amended Subdiv. (10) by adding references to Secs. 53-202*l* and 53-202w, added new Subdiv. (11) re defendant charged with violation of Sec. 29-37a and prosecution suspended pursuant to Sec. 29-37a(i), and redesignated existing Subdiv. (11) as Subdiv. (12).

Sec. 54-67. When attorneys not allowed to give bonds.

No attorney-at-law may give any bond or recognizance in any criminal action or proceeding in which he is interested as attorney.

(1949 Rev., S. 8782; P.A. 80-313, S. 19.)

History: P.A. 80-313 substituted "may" for "shall".

Bond for costs on an appeal, given by appellant's attorney, not within prohibition of statute. 61 C. 500.

Sec. 54-68. Persons charged with gaming to give bonds. Section 54-68 is repealed.

(1949 Rev., S. 8789.; P.A. 76-336, S. 10.)

Sec. 54-69. Motion of parties to modify conditions of release.

(a) Whenever in any criminal prosecution the state's attorney for any judicial district or the assistant state's attorney is of the opinion that the bond without or with surety given by any accused person is excessive or insufficient in amount or security, or that the written promise of such person to appear is inadequate, or whenever any accused person alleges that the amount or security of the bond given by such accused person is excessive, such state's attorney or assistant state's attorney or the accused person may bring an application to the court in which the prosecution is pending or to any judge thereof, alleging such excess, insufficiency, or inadequacy, and, after notice as hereinafter provided and hearing, such judge shall in bailable offenses continue, modify or set conditions of release upon the first of the following conditions of release found sufficient to provide reasonable assurance of the appearance of the accused in court: (1) Upon such person's execution of a written promise to appear, (2) upon such person's execution of a bond without surety in no greater amount than necessary, (3) upon such person's execution of a bond with surety in no greater amount than necessary.

(b) No hearing upon any such application shall be had until a copy of such application, together with a notice of the time and place of hearing thereon, has been served upon the surety or sureties upon such bond, if any, and upon the appropriate bail commissioner or intake, assessment and referral specialist employed by the Judicial Branch and, in the case of an application by an accused person, upon any such state's attorney, or, in the case of the application by any such state's attorney, upon the accused person.

(c) Notwithstanding the provisions of subsection (b) of this section, a hearing may be had on an application by any such state's attorney without a copy of such application and notice of the hearing being served upon the surety or sureties upon such bond, if any, the appropriate bail commissioner or intake, assessment and referral specialist and the accused person if the accused person is charged with the commission of a family violence crime, as defined in section 46b-38a, or a violation of section 53a-181c, 53a-181d, 53a-181e, 53a-223, 53a-223a or 53a-223b and is being presented at the next sitting of the Superior Court as required by section 54-1g.

(1949 Rev., S. 8790; 1961, P.A. 517, S. 72; 1967, P.A. 549, S. 13; 656, S. 61; P.A. 74-183, S. 147, 291; P.A. 76-436, S. 548, 681; P.A. 78-280, S. 1, 127; P.A. 80-313, S. 23; P.A. 99-186, S. 6; P.A. 02-127, S. 5; P.A. 12-114, S. 22; 12-133, S. 39.)

History: 1961 act substituted circuit court for court of common pleas; 1967 acts included bond without surety or written promise as alternative to bond with surety, effective October 1, 1968, and allowed presentation of application to judge at any time rather than only when court is not in session; P.A. 74-183 replaced circuit court with court of common pleas and added reference to judicial districts, effective December 31, 1974; P.A. 76-436 deleted specific mention of common pleas court and replaced references to prosecuting attorneys with references to state's attorneys and assistant state's attorneys, reflecting transfer of all trial jurisdiction to superior court, effective July 1, 1978; P.A. 78-280 deleted reference to counties; P.A. 80-313 restated provision to delete implication that judge has power to deny bail for bailable offenses if "he finds custody to be necessary to provide reasonable assurance of the appearance of the accused in court"; P.A. 99-186 inserted Subsec. indicators, added new Subsec. (c) to permit a hearing to be held on an application by a state's attorney without serving a copy of the application and notice of the hearing on the surety or sureties on the bond, the bail commissioner and the accused person, as required by Subsec. (b), if the accused person is charged with the commission of a family violence crime, as defined in Sec. 46b-38a, or a violation of Sec. 53a-110b, 53a-181c, 53a-181d or 53a-181e and is being presented at the next court date as required by Sec. 54-1g, and made technical changes for purposes of gender neutrality; P.A. 02-127 amended Subsec. (c) to include a violation of Sec. 53a-223b; P.A. 12-114 amended Subsec. (c) to add reference to violation of Sec. 53a-223a; P.A. 12-133 amended Subsecs. (b) and (c) by adding references to intake, assessment and referral specialist.

Bond includes recognizance. 110 C. 173. Cited. 140 C. 326; 222 C. 331; 241 C. 413.

Cited. 4 Conn. Cir. Ct. 116.

Sec. 54-69a. Motion of bail commissioner or intake, assessment and referral specialist to modify conditions of release.

A bail commissioner or an intake, assessment and referral specialist employed by the Judicial Branch who has reason to believe that a person released under any of the provisions of sections 54-63a to 54-63g, inclusive, 54-64a, 54-64b and 54-69 intends not to appear in court as required by the conditions of release may apply to a judge of the court before which the person is required to appear, and verify by oath or otherwise the reason for his or her belief, and request that the person be brought before the court in order that the conditions of such person's release be reviewed. Upon finding reasonable grounds that the released person intends not to appear, the judge shall forthwith issue a capias directed to a proper officer or indifferent person, commanding such proper officer or indifferent person forthwith to arrest and bring the person to the court for a hearing to review the conditions of release. Such hearing shall be upon due notice as provided in section 54-69.

(1967, P.A. 549, S. 16; P.A. 80-313, S. 24; P.A. 12-133, S. 40.)

History: P.A. 80-313 updated list of applicable sections and made minor changes in wording; P.A. 12-133 added reference to intake, assessment and referral specialist employed by Judicial Branch and made technical changes.

Cited. 222 C. 331.

Sec. 54-69b. Authority of court to modify conditions of release.

The provisions of any promise or bond taken under section 54-63c or section 54-63d may at any time be modified by the court or any judge thereof as provided in section 54-69.

(P.A. 80-313, S. 22.)

Cited. 222 C. 331.

Sec. 54-70. Compromise of forfeited bonds. Section 54-70 is repealed.

(1949 Rev., S. 8791; 1959, P.A. 28, S. 193; 1963, P.A. 642, S. 66; P.A. 73-116, S. 32; 73-667, S. 1, 2; P.A. 78-280, S. 4, 119, 127; P.A. 83-279, S. 3, 4.)

Sec. 54-71. Mistake in form of recognizance.

No recognizance given by the accused in a criminal prosecution for his appearance before any court may be discharged for any mistake in form, if its terms are in substantial compliance with the requirements of law.

(1949 Rev., S. 8792; P.A. 80-313, S. 20.)

History: P.A. 80-313 substituted "may" for "shall".

Cited. 45 C. 352. Bond should receive liberal construction. 48 C. 59. Cited. 222 C. 331.

Sec. 54-71a. No civil liability for release.

No bail commissioner or intake, assessment and referral specialist employed by the Judicial Branch, no employee of any police department, no state's attorney or assistant state's attorney and no municipality may be held liable in a civil action for damages on account of the release of any person under any of the provisions of sections 54-63a to 54-63g, inclusive, 54-64a, 54-64b and 54-69.

(P.A. 80-313, S. 21; P.A. 12-133, S. 41.)

History: P.A. 12-133 added reference to intake, assessment and referral specialist employed by Judicial Branch.

Sec. 54-72. Fines and forfeitures; prosecutions; liability of corporation.

All fines, forfeitures and penalties, unless otherwise expressly disposed of by law, if imposed on any person by the Superior Court, shall belong to the state. When a fine, penalty or forfeiture is imposed by any statute as a punishment for any offense, and any part thereof is given to the person aggrieved or to him who sues therefor and the other part to the state, all proper informing officers shall make presentment of such offense to the court having cognizance thereof; and the whole of such fine, penalty or forfeiture shall in such case belong to the state. Whenever any corporation has incurred a penalty or forfeiture or is liable to a fine, the state's attorney in the judicial district wherein such corporation is located or has its principal place of business in this state may bring a civil action under the provisions of this section, in the name of the state, to recover such penalty, forfeiture or fine. The court shall render judgment, under the limitations of law, for the recovery of such penalty, forfeiture or fine, and issue execution therefor.

(1949 Rev., S. 8776; 1959, P.A. 28, S. 153; 152, S. 80; 1963, P.A. 642, S. 67; P.A. 73-116, S. 4; 73-667, S. 1, 2; P.A. 74-183, S. 148, 291; P.A. 76-436, S. 549, 681; P.A. 78-280, S. 1, 127.)

History: 1959 acts deleted references to fines imposed by trial justices, included circuit court and deleted provision for fines belonging to county, county government having been abolished; 1963 act deleted obsolete provision for fines imposed by common pleas court; P.A. 73-116 added reference to judicial districts; P.A. 73-667 changed effective date of P.A. 73-116 from October 1, 1973, to April 25, 1973; P.A. 74-183 replaced circuit court with court of common pleas, effective December 31, 1974; P.A. 76-436 deleted reference to power of court of common pleas to impose fines, forfeitures and penalties and deleted provision whereby jurisdiction was to be determined according to maximum penalty, forfeiture or fine which may be imposed, reflecting transfer of all trial jurisdiction to superior court, effective July 1, 1978; P.A. 78-280 deleted reference to counties.

See Sec. 51-56a re accounting for receipts by court clerks or executors.

Defendants in qui tam actions, if acquitted, entitled to costs. 2 R. 137. When may be brought in name of informer and town treasurer; form of judgment in such case. 5 C. 291. When state may prosecute for whole penalty. 7 C. 185. Court has no control over disposition of fines; statute controls. 18 C. 442. Cited. 222 C. 331.

Sec. 54-73. Collection and disposition of forfeitures.

The state's attorney in the judicial district in which any forfeiture to the state accrues shall collect and pay it to the State Treasurer; and, if in the opinion of the court the plaintiff is an improper person to collect it, a separate execution may be issued in favor of the state.

(1949 Rev., S. 8773; 1959, P.A. 152, S. 81; P.A. 73-116, S. 5; 73-667, S. 1, 2; P.A. 78-280, S. 2, 127.)

History: 1959 act deleted provision for forfeiture to county, county government having been abolished; P.A. 73-116 added reference to judicial districts; P.A. 73-667 changed effective date of P.A. 73-116 from October 1, 1973, to April 25, 1973; P.A. 78-280 deleted reference to counties.

Cited. 222 C. 331.

Sec. 54-74. Remission of fine.

Any judge of the Superior Court may remit any fine, if in his judgment such course will tend to the reformation of offenders or the furtherance of the ends of justice.

(1949 Rev., S. 8740; 1959, P.A. 28, S. 154; 1963, P.A. 642, S. 68; P.A. 74-183, S. 149, 291; P.A. 76-436, S. 550, 681.)

History: 1959 act substituted circuit court for trial justice or municipal court; 1963 act removed common pleas court from purview of section; P.A. 74-183 replaced circuit court with court of common pleas, effective December 31, 1974; P.A. 76-436 removed court of common pleas from purview of section, reflecting transfer of all trial jurisdiction to superior court, effective July 1, 1978.

Cited. 222 C. 331; 231 C. 514.

Sec. 54-75. Employment of detectives. Section 54-75 is repealed.

(1949 Rev., S. 8783; 1953, S. 3325d; 1961, P.A. 517, S. 73; 1967, P.A. 260; P.A. 73-122, S. 26, 27.)

Sec. 54-76. Transferred to Chapter 886, Sec. 51-286c.

Sec. 54-76a. Procedure at hearing in probable cause. Section 54-76a is repealed.

(1959, P.A. 548; February, 1965, P.A. 321; P.A. 76-336, S. 5, P.A. 78-280, S. 126, 127; 78-331, S. 54, 58.)

CHAPTER 960a* YOUTHFUL OFFENDERS

*Denial of defendant's application to be treated as a youthful offender is a final appealable judgment. 179 C. 98. Cited. 188 C. 565; 195 C. 303; 196 C. 122.

Table of Contents

Sec. 54-76b. Youthful offenders: Definitions; applicability of interstate compact.

Sec. 54-76c. Eligibility to be adjudged a youthful offender. Transfer of cases.

Sec. 54-76d. Investigations. Determinations by court. Waiver of proceedings.

Sec. 54-76e. Trial to determine youthful offender status.

Sec. 54-76f. Statements of defendant inadmissible.

Sec. 54-76g. Judgment of youthful offender status.

Sec. 54-76h. Proceedings private. Segregation of defendant in place of detention. Presence of victim at proceeding.

Sec. 54-76i. Court powers over person of defendant.

Sec. 54-76j. Disposition upon adjudication as youthful offender.

Sec. 54-76k. Determination of youthful offender status not to disqualify for office, license, etc.

Sec. 54-76l. Records or other information of youth to be confidential. Exceptions.

Sec. 54-76m. Age of defendant at time of crime controlling.

Sec. 54-76n. Application of criminal law.

Sec. 54-76o. Erasure of police and court records of youthful offender.

Sec. 54-76p. **Transferred**

Sec. 54-76q. Statement of victim regarding plea agreement or sentence.

Sec. 54-76b. Youthful offenders: Definitions; applicability of interstate compact.

(a) For the purposes of sections 54-76b to 54-76n, inclusive:

(1) "Youth" means (A) a minor who has reached the age of sixteen years but has not reached the age of eighteen years at the time of the alleged offense, or (B) a child who has been transferred to the regular criminal docket of the Superior Court pursuant to section 46b-127; and

191

(2) "Youthful offender" means a youth who (A) is charged with the commission of a crime which is not a class A felony or a violation of section 14-222a, subsection (a) or subdivision (1) of subsection (b) of section 14-224, section 14-227a, 14-227g or 14-227m, subdivision (1) or (2) of subsection (a) of section 14-227n, subdivision (2) of subsection (a) of section 53-21 or section 53a-70, 53a-70a, 53a-70b, 53a-71, 53a-72a or 53a-72b, except a violation involving consensual sexual intercourse or sexual contact between the youth and another person who is thirteen years of age or older but under sixteen years of age, and (B) has not previously been convicted of a felony in the regular criminal docket of the Superior Court or been previously adjudged a serious juvenile offender or serious juvenile repeat offender, as defined in section 46b-120.

(b) The Interstate Compact for Adult Offender Supervision under section 54-133 shall apply to youthful offenders.

(1971, P.A. 72, S. 1; P.A. 79-581, S. 9; P.A. 81-472, S. 94, 159; P.A. 89-383, S. 15, 16; July Sp. Sess. P.A. 94-2, S. 7; P.A. 95-142, S. 5; 95-225, S. 33; P.A. 01-84, S. 20, 26; 01-211, S. 18; P.A. 03-243, S. 4; P.A. 05-232, S. 1; P.A. 08-32, S. 10; P.A. 14-130, S. 35; P.A. 16-126, S. 33.)

History: P.A. 79-581 specified that those who have "been afforded a pretrial program for accelerated rehabilitation under section 54-76p" are not to be considered as youthful offenders; P.A. 81-472 made technical changes; P.A. 89-383 revised in part definition of "youthful offender" by replacing "a youth who has committed a crime or crimes which are not class A felonies" with "a youth who is charged with the commission of a crime which is not a violation of section 53a-70a or a class A felony"; July Sp. Sess. P.A. 94-2 included in the definition of "youth" a child who has been transferred to the regular criminal docket pursuant to Sec. 46b-127(a)(2); P.A. 95-142 redefined "youthful offender" to exclude a youth who is charged with the commission of a violation of Sec. 53-21(2) or of Sec. 53a-70, 53a-70b, 53a-71, 53a-72a or 53a-72b; P.A. 95-225 redefined "youthful offender" to exclude a youth who has previously been adjudged a serious juvenile offender or a serious juvenile repeat offender and made a technical change; P.A. 01-84 replaced reference to "subdivision (2) of section 53-21" with "subdivision (2) of subsection (a) of section 53-21", effective July 1, 2001; P.A. 01-211 inserted Subdiv. indicators and amended Subdiv. (1) to replace reference to "subdivision (2) of section 53-21" with "subdivision (2) of subsection (a) of section 53-21" and to add exception re violation involving consensual sexual intercourse or sexual contact between the youth and another person who is 13 years of age or older but under 16 years of age; P.A. 03-243 replaced provision re Interstate Compact on Juveniles with provision re Interstate Compact for Adult Offender Supervision under Sec. 54-133 and deleted "to the same extent as to minors below sixteen years of age"; P.A. 05-232 designated definitions as Subsec. (a) and made technical changes therein, redefined "youth" in Subsec. (a)(1) by adding provisions re age at time of the alleged offense and re docket of the Superior Court, redefined "youthful offender" in Subsec. (a)(2) by adding provision re felony conviction in regular docket of the Superior Court and deleting provisions re adjudication as a youthful offender and prior accelerated rehabilitation, and designated provision re applicability of interstate compact as Subsec. (b), effective January 1, 2006; P.A. 08-32 amended Subsec. (a)(2) to redefine "youthful offender" by excluding a youth who is charged with a violation of Sec. 14-222a, 14-224(a), 14-227a or 14-227g, effective August 1, 2008; P.A. 14-130 amended Subdiv. (2)(A) by adding reference to Sec. 14-224(b)(1); P.A. 16-126 amended Subsec. (a)(2) by adding references to Secs. 14-227m and 14-227n(a)(1) and (2).

Sec. 54-76c. Eligibility to be adjudged a youthful offender. Transfer of cases.

(a) In any case where an information or complaint has been laid charging a defendant with the commission of a crime, and where it appears that the defendant is a youth, such defendant shall be presumed to be eligible to be adjudged a youthful offender and the court having jurisdiction shall, but only as to the public, order the court file sealed, unless such defendant (1) is charged with the commission of a crime which is a class A felony or a violation of section 14-222a, subsection (a) or subdivision (1) of subsection (b) of section 14-224, section 14-227a, 14-227g or 14-227m, subdivision (1) or (2) of subsection (a) of section 14-227n, subdivision (2) of subsection (a) of section 53-21 or section 53a-70, 53a-70a, 53a-70b, 53a-71, 53a-72a or 53a-72b, except a violation involving consensual sexual intercourse or sexual contact between the youth and another person who is thirteen years of age or older but under sixteen years of age, or (2) has been previously convicted of a felony in the regular criminal docket of the Superior Court or been previously adjudged a serious juvenile offender or serious juvenile repeat offender, as defined in section 46b-120. Except as provided in subsection (b) of this section, upon motion of the prosecuting official, the court may order that an investigation be made of such defendant under section 54-76d, for the purpose of determining whether such defendant is ineligible to be adjudged a youthful offender, provided the court file shall remain sealed, but only as to the public, during such investigation.

(b) (1) Upon motion of the prosecuting official and order of the court, the case of any defendant who is a youth and is charged with the commission of a felony, other than a felony set forth in subsection (a) of this section, shall be transferred from the youthful offender docket to the regular criminal docket of the Superior Court, provided the court finds that there is probable cause to believe the defendant has committed the act for which he or she is charged. The defendant shall be arraigned in the regular criminal docket of the Superior Court by the next court business day following such transfer, provided any proceedings held prior to the finalization of such transfer shall be private and shall be conducted in such parts of the courthouse or the building wherein court is located as shall be separate and apart from the other parts of the court which are then being held for proceedings pertaining to adults charged with crimes. The file of any case so transferred shall remain sealed until the end of the tenth working day following such arraignment, unless the prosecuting official has filed a motion pursuant to subdivision (2) of this subsection, in which case such file shall remain sealed until the court makes a decision on the motion.

(2) A prosecuting official may, not later than ten working days after such arraignment, file a motion to transfer the case of any defendant who is a youth and is charged with the commission of a felony, other than a felony set forth in subsection (a) of this section, from the regular criminal docket of the Superior Court to the youthful offender docket for proceedings in accordance with the provisions of sections 54-76b to 54-76n, inclusive. The court sitting for the regular criminal docket of the Superior Court shall, after hearing and not later than ten working days after the filing of such motion, decide such motion.

(1971, P.A. 72, S. 2; P.A. 98-81, S. 9; P.A. 05-232, S. 2; P.A. 08-32, S. 11; P.A. 14-130, S. 36; P.A. 16-126, S. 34.)

History: P.A. 98-81 changed "information or complaint" to "court file"; P.A. 05-232 designated existing provisions as Subsec. (a) and amended same by replacing provisions re investigation of defendant for purpose of determining eligibility to be adjudged a youthful offender with provisions re presumption of eligibility, exceptions to eligibility and investigation to determine ineligibility to be adjudged a youthful offender, and added Subsec. (b) re transfer of cases, effective January 1, 2006; P.A. 08-32 amended Subsec. (a)(1) to add violations of Sec. 14-222a, 14-224(a), 14-227a and 14-227g to list of violations to which presumption of eligibility and sealing of the court file does not apply, effective August 1, 2008; P.A. 14-130 amended Subsec. (a)(1) by adding reference to Sec. 14-224(b)(1); P.A. 16-126 amended Subsec. (a) by adding references to Secs. 14-227m and 14-227n(a)(1) and (2).

Cited. 173 C. 414; 179 C. 98; 188 C. 565; 192 C. 85. Trial court order transferring defendant's case from youthful offender docket to regular criminal docket is not an appealable interlocutory order under 191 C. 27 because it does not conclude the rights of defendant regarding his status as a youthful offender. 300 C. 764.

Cited. 8 CA 607.

Cited. 30 CS 71. Because statutory benefits afforded to defendant under section constitute a liberty interest in youthful offender status and the discretionary transfer of a youthful offender docket to regular criminal docket vests such liberty interest in eligible defendants, due process requires notice and hearing for court to determine independently whether such transfer is appropriate. 51 CS 342.

Subsec. (b):

Subdiv. (1) does not require notice and a hearing before a case may be transferred from youthful offender docket to regular criminal docket, but Subsec. implicitly requires notice and a hearing by the court on regular criminal docket prior to finalization of a transfer of a case from youthful offender docket. 300 C. 748.

Sec. 54-76d. Investigations. Determinations by court. Waiver of proceedings.

(a) If the court grants a motion under subsection (a) of section 54-76c or if the court on its own motion determines that the defendant should be investigated under this section, and the defendant consents to physical and mental examinations, if deemed necessary, and to investigation and questioning, and to a trial without a jury, should a trial be had, the information or complaint shall be held in abeyance and no further action shall be taken in connection with such information or complaint until such examinations, investigation and questioning are had of the defendant. Investigations under this section shall be made by an adult probation officer. When the information or complaint charges commission of a felony, the adult probation officer shall include in the investigation a summary of any unerased juvenile record of adjudications of the defendant.

(b) Upon the termination of such examinations, investigation and questioning, the court, in its discretion based on the severity of the crime, which shall also take into consideration whether or not the defendant took advantage of the victim because of the victim's advanced age or physical incapacity, and the results of the examinations, investigation and questioning, shall determine whether such defendant is eligible or ineligible to be adjudged a youthful offender. If the court determines that the defendant is eligible to be so adjudged, no further action shall be taken on the information or complaint and the defendant shall be required to enter a plea of "guilty" or "not guilty" to the charge of being a youthful offender. If the court determines that the defendant is ineligible to be so adjudged, it shall order the information or complaint to be unsealed and the defendant shall be prosecuted as though the proceedings under sections 54-76b to 54-76n, inclusive, had not been had.

(c) If no motion is made by the prosecuting official under subsection (a) or (b) of section 54-76c or by the court under subsection (a) of this section, and the defendant consents to a trial without a jury, should a trial be had, no further action shall be taken on the information or complaint and the defendant shall be required to enter a plea of "guilty" or "not guilty" to the charge of being a youthful offender.

(d) At any time prior to trial as provided in section 54-76e or at any time prior to entering a plea of "guilty" to the charge of being a youthful offender, the defendant, on motion and with the concurrence of the defendant's parent or guardian and the defendant's attorney, if any, may waive further proceedings under the provisions of sections 54-76b to 54-76n, inclusive, and request a trial by jury in the regular criminal docket of the Superior Court. If the court, after making a thorough inquiry, is satisfied that such waiver is knowingly and voluntarily made, the court may grant such motion and order the information or complaint to be unsealed and the defendant shall be prosecuted as though the proceedings under sections 54-76b to 54-76n, inclusive, had not been had.

(e) At any point, if the court determines that a defendant is ineligible to be a youthful offender, the court shall order the information or complaint to be unsealed and the defendant shall be prosecuted as though the proceedings under sections 54-76b to 54-76n, inclusive, had not been had.

(1971, P.A. 72, S. 3; P.A. 77-362; P.A. 79-581, S. 10; P.A. 05-232, S. 3.)

History. P.A. 77-362 required consideration of whether or not defendant took advantage of victim because of victim's advanced age or physical incapacity in determining eligibility for youthful offender status in Subsec. (b); P.A. 79-581 amended Subsec. (a) to require inclusion of summary of unreleased juvenile record of adjudications in investigation where information or complaint charges commission of a felony; P.A. 05-232 amended Subsec. (a) by adding reference to motion under Sec. 54-76c(a) and making technical changes, amended Subsec. (b) by adding provision re determination whether defendant is ineligible to be adjudged a youthful offender and making technical changes, and added Subsecs. (c) re procedure if no motion is made, (d) re waiver of further proceedings and (e) re determination of ineligibility at any point, effective January 1, 2006.

Cited. 173 C. 414; 179 C. 98; 188 C. 565; 192 C. 85.

Cited. 8 CA 607.

Cited. 30 CS 71; 37 CS 755.

Sec. 54-76e. Trial to determine youthful offender status.

If the defendant enters a plea of "not guilty" or if the court on its own motion so directs, the defendant shall be tried for the purpose of determining whether he shall be adjudged a youthful offender. The trial shall be held by the court without a jury.

(1971, P.A. 72, S. 4.)

Cited. 173 C. 414; 179 C. 98; 192 C. 85.

Cited. 8 CA 607.

Cited. 30 CS 71; 37 CS 755.

Sec. 54-76f. Statements of defendant inadmissible.

No statement, admission or confession made by the defendant to the court or to any person designated by the court to conduct the examinations, investigation and questioning referred to in section 54-76d shall ever be admissible as evidence against him or his interest, except that the court may take such statement, admission or confession into consideration at the time of sentencing such defendant, if the defendant has been adjudged a youthful offender, or has been found guilty of the crime charged in the information or complaint upon which the proceedings hereunder were based, or any subsequent crime.

(1971, P.A. 72, S. 5.)

Cited. 173 C. 414.

Cited. 30 CS 71.

Sec. 54-76g. Judgment of youthful offender status.

If the defendant enters a plea of guilty to the charge of being a youthful offender or if, after trial, the court finds that he committed the acts charged against him in the information or complaint, the court shall adjudge the defendant to be a youthful offender and the information or complaint shall be considered a nullity and of no force or effect.

(1971, P.A. 72, S. 6.)

Cited. 173 C. 414; 179 C. 98; 190 C. 715.

Cited. 8 CA 607; 21 CA 645.

Cited. 30 CS 71.

Sec. 54-76h. Proceedings private. Segregation of defendant in place of detention. Presence of victim at proceeding.

(a) All of the proceedings had under the provisions of sections 54-76b to 54-76n, inclusive, shall be private and shall be conducted in such parts of the courthouse or the building wherein court is located as shall be separate and apart from the other parts of the court which are then being held for proceedings pertaining to adults charged with crimes. If the defendant is committed while any examination and investigation under section 54-76d is pending, before trial, during trial or after judgment and before sentence, those persons in charge of the place of detention shall segregate the defendant, to the extent of their facilities, from defendants over the age of eighteen years charged with crime.

(b) In a proceeding under sections 54-76b to 54-76n, inclusive, the court shall not exclude any victim from such proceeding or any portion thereof unless, after hearing from the parties and the victim and for good cause shown, which shall be clearly and specifically stated on the record, the court orders otherwise. For the purposes of this subsection, "victim" means a person who is the victim of a crime for which a youth is charged, a parent or guardian of such person, the legal representative of such person or a victim advocate for such person under section 54-220.

(1971, P.A. 72, S. 7; P.A. 05-169, S. 2; 05-232, S. 4; P.A. 10-43, S. 33.)

History: P.A. 05-169 designated existing provisions as Subsec. (a), made technical changes therein and added Subsec. (b) re presence of victim at proceeding; P.A. 05-232 deleted exception for proceedings on motion under Sec. 54-76c, added reference to investigation under Sec. 54-76d and made technical changes, effective January 1, 2006; P.A. 10-43 amended Subsec. (b) to replace "an advocate appointed for such person pursuant to section 54-221" with "a victim advocate for such person under section 54-220".

Cited. 173 C. 414; 179 C. 98; 192 C. 85; 195 C. 303; 240 C. 743.

Sec. 54-76i. Court powers over person of defendant.

Pending and during the investigation, trial, adjudication or acquittal of the defendant, or any other proceedings under sections 54-76b to 54-76n, inclusive, the court having jurisdiction shall have the same powers over the person of the defendant as it would have in the case of an adult charged with crime.

(1971, P.A. 72, S. 8; P.A. 05-232, S. 5.)

History: P.A. 05-232 replaced provision re court to which recommendation for investigation has been made with provision re court having jurisdiction, effective January 1, 2006.

Sec. 54-76j. Disposition upon adjudication as youthful offender.

(a) The court, upon the adjudication of any person as a youthful offender, may: (1) Commit the defendant; (2) impose a fine not exceeding one thousand dollars; (3) impose a sentence of conditional discharge or a sentence of unconditional discharge; (4) impose a sentence of community service; (5) impose a sentence to a term of imprisonment not greater than that authorized for the crime committed by the defendant, but in no event shall any such term exceed four years; (6) impose sentence and suspend the execution of the sentence, entirely or after a period set by the court; (7) order treatment pursuant to section 17a-699; or (8) if a criminal docket for drug-dependent persons has been established pursuant to section 51-181b in the judicial district in which the defendant was adjudicated a youthful offender, transfer the supervision of the defendant to the court handling such docket.

(b) If execution of the sentence is suspended under subdivision (6) of subsection (a) of this section, the defendant may be placed on probation or conditional discharge for a period not to exceed three years, provided, at any time during the period of probation, after hearing and for good cause shown, the court may extend the period as deemed appropriate by the court. If the court places the person adjudicated to be a youthful offender on probation, the court may order that, as a condition of such probation, the person be referred for services to a youth service bureau established pursuant to section 10-19m, provided the court finds, through an assessment by a youth service bureau or its designee, that the person is in need of and likely to benefit from such services. If the court places a youthful offender on probation, school and class attendance on a regular basis and satisfactory compliance with school policies

198

on student conduct and discipline may be a condition of such probation and, in such a case, failure to so attend or comply shall be a violation of probation. If the court has reason to believe that the person adjudicated to be a youthful offender is or has been an unlawful user of narcotic drugs, as defined in section 21a-240, and the court places such youthful offender on probation, the conditions of probation, among other things, shall include a requirement that such person shall submit to periodic tests to determine, by the use of "synthetic opiate antinarcotic in action", nalline test or other detection tests, at a hospital or other facility, equipped to make such tests, whether such person is using narcotic drugs. A failure to report for such tests or a determination that such person is unlawfully using narcotic drugs shall constitute a violation of probation. If the court places a person adjudicated as a youthful offender for a violation of section 53-247 on probation, the court may order that, as a condition of such probation, the person undergo psychiatric or psychological counseling or participate in an animal cruelty prevention and education program, provided such a program exists and is available to the person.

(c) Commitment under this section shall be for a period not to exceed the term of imprisonment authorized for the crime committed by the defendant, but in no event shall any such period exceed four years, and shall be to any religious, charitable or other correctional institution authorized by law to receive persons over the age of sixteen years. Whenever a youthful offender is committed by the court to any duly authorized religious, charitable or other institution, other than an institution supported or controlled by the state or a subdivision thereof, such commitment shall be made, when practicable, to a religious, charitable or other institution under the control of persons of the same religious faith or persuasion as that of the youthful offender. If a youthful offender is committed by the court to any institution other than an institution supported or controlled by the state or a subdivision thereof, which is under the control of persons of a religion or persuasion different from that of the youthful offender, the court shall state or recite the facts which impel it to make such disposition, and such statement shall be made a part of the record of the proceedings.

(1971, P.A. 72, S. 9; P.A. 78-17; P.A. 79-269; P.A. 94-136, S. 1; 94-221, S. 12; P.A. 95-225, S. 43; P.A. 97-248, S. 9, 12; P.A. 99-187, S. 6; P.A. 03-208, S. 4; P.A. 05-232, S. 6; 05-288, S. 226; P.A. 10-43, S. 26.)

History: P.A. 78-17 replaced suspended sentence with imposition of conditional or unconditional discharge and authorized placement of defendant on probation for cases where sentence imposed but execution of judgment suspended where previously probation was authorized for suspended sentence as well; P.A. 79-269 authorized imposition of sentence of community service; P.A. 94-136 inserted Subsec. indicators, amended Subsec. (a) to add a new Subdiv. (5) authorizing the court to impose a sentence to a term of imprisonment not greater than that authorized for the crime committed by the defendant, renumber former Subdiv. (5) as Subdiv. (6) and authorize the court to suspend execution of the sentence "entirely or after a period set by the court" and add Subdiv. (7) authorizing the court to order treatment pursuant to Sec. 17a-656, amended Subsec. (b) to authorize the court to place the defendant on conditional discharge and amended Subsec. (c) to change the maximum period of commitment from three years to "the term of imprisonment authorized for the crime committed by the defendant"; P.A. 94-221 authorized requiring school and class attendance and compliance with school policies on student conduct and discipline to be a condition of probation and, in such a case, made failure to so attend and comply a violation of probation; P.A. 95-225 amended Subsec. (b) to add provision authorizing the court to order that as a condition of probation the person be referred for services to a youth service bureau if the court finds that the person is in need of and likely to benefit from such services; P.A. 97-248 amended Subsec. (a) to correct a statutory reference in

Subdiv. (7) and add Subdiv. (8) to authorize the court to transfer the supervision of the defendant to the court handling the criminal docket for drug-dependent persons if such a docket has been established in the judicial district, effective July 1, 1997; P.A. 99-187 amended Subsec. (b) to add provision authorizing the court to order as a condition of probation that the person participate in the zero-tolerance drug supervision program established pursuant to Sec. 53a-39d; P.A. 03-208 amended Subsec. (b) to make a technical change and add provision authorizing the court to order counseling or participation in an animal cruelty prevention and education program as a condition of probation for a person adjudicated as a youthful offender for a violation of Sec. 53-247; P.A. 05-232 amended Subsec. (a)(5) by adding provision re maximum term of four years, amended Subsec. (b) by replacing provision re extension of probation for period not to exceed five years, including original probationary period, with provision re extension of period of probation or conditional discharge as deemed appropriate by the court after hearing and for good cause shown, amended Subsec. (c) by adding provisions re maximum period of four years and made technical changes, effective January 1, 2006; P.A. 05-288 made technical changes in Subsec. (b); P.A. 10-43 amended Subsec. (b) to delete provision authorizing court to order as condition of probation that person participate in zero-tolerance drug supervision program.

Cited. 173 C. 414; 190 C. 715; 240 C. 743.

Only one penalty allowed upon adjudication as a youthful offender in one or more matters. 8 CA 607.

Conflict with Sec. 18-75. 30 CS 71.

Sec. 54-76k. Determination of youthful offender status not to disqualify for office, license, etc.

No determination made under the provisions of sections 54-76b to 54-76n, inclusive, shall operate as a disqualification of any youth subsequently to hold public office or public employment, or as a forfeiture of any right or privilege to receive any license granted by public authority and no youth shall be denominated a criminal by reason of such determination, nor shall such determination be deemed a conviction.

(1971, P.A. 72, S. 10.)

Cited. 173 C. 414; 196 C. 122; 240 C. 743.

Cited. 32 CA 687.

Cited. 30 CS 71.

Sec. 54-76*l*. Records or other information of youth to be confidential. Exceptions.

(a) The records or other information of a youth, other than a youth arrested for or charged with the commission of a crime which is a class A felony or a violation of section 14-222a, subsection (a) or subdivision (1) of subsection (b) of section 14-224, section 14-227a, 14-227g or 14-227m, subdivision (1) or (2) of subsection (a) of section 14-227n, subdivision (2) of subsection (a) of section 53-21 or section 53a-70, 53a-70a, 53a-70b, 53a-71, 53a-72a or 53a-72b, except a violation involving consensual sexual intercourse or sexual contact between the youth and another person who is thirteen years of age or older but under sixteen years of age, including fingerprints, photographs and physical descriptions, shall be confidential and shall not be open to public inspection or be disclosed except as provided in this section, but such fingerprints, photographs and physical descriptions submitted to the State Police Bureau of Identification of the Division of State Police within the Department of Emergency Services and Public Protection at the time of the arrest of a person subsequently adjudged, or subsequently presumed or determined to be eligible to be adjudged, a youthful offender shall be retained as confidential matter in the files of the bureau and be opened to inspection only as provided in this section. Other data ordinarily received by the bureau, with regard to persons arrested for a crime, shall be forwarded to the bureau to be filed, in addition to such fingerprints, photographs and physical descriptions, and be retained in the division as confidential information, open to inspection only as provided in this section.

(b) The records of any such youth, or any part thereof, may be disclosed to and between individuals and agencies, and employees of such agencies, providing services directly to the youth, including law enforcement officials, state and federal prosecutorial officials, school officials in accordance with section 10-233h, court officials, the Division of Criminal Justice, the Court Support Services Division and a victim advocate under section 54-220 for a victim of a crime committed by the youth. Such records shall also be available to the attorney representing the youth, in any proceedings in which such records are relevant, to the parents or guardian of such youth, until such time as the youth reaches the age of majority or is emancipated, and to the youth upon his or her emancipation or attainment of the age of majority, provided proof of the identity of such youth is submitted in accordance with guidelines prescribed by the Chief Court Administrator. Such records shall also be available to members and employees of the Board of Pardons and Paroles and employees of the Department of Correction who, in the performance of their duties, require access to such records, provided the subject of the record has been adjudged a youthful offender and sentenced to a term of imprisonment or been convicted of a crime in the regular criminal docket of the Superior Court, and such records are relevant to the performance of a risk and needs assessment of such person while such person is incarcerated, the determination of such person's suitability for release from incarceration or for a pardon, or the determination of the supervision and treatment needs of such person while on parole or other supervised release. Such records shall also be available to law enforcement officials and prosecutorial officials conducting legitimate criminal investigations. Such records disclosed pursuant to this subsection shall not be further disclosed.

(c) The records of any such youth, or any part thereof, may be disclosed upon order of the court to any person who has a legitimate interest in the information and is identified in such order. Records or information disclosed pursuant to this subsection shall not be further disclosed.

(d) The records of any such youth, or any part thereof, shall be available to the victim of the crime committed by such youth to the same extent as the record of the case of a defendant in a criminal proceeding in the regular criminal docket of the Superior Court is available to a victim of the crime committed by such defendant. The court shall designate an official from whom such victim may request such information. Information disclosed pursuant to this subsection shall not be further disclosed.

(e) Any reports and files held by the Court Support Services Division regarding any such youth who served a period of probation may be accessed and disclosed by employees of the division for the purpose of performing the duties contained in section 54-63b.

(f) Information concerning any such youth who has escaped from an institution to which such youth has been committed or for whom an arrest warrant has been issued may be disclosed by law enforcement officials.

(g) Information concerning any such youth in the custody of the Department of Correction may be disclosed by the department to the parents or guardian of such youth.

(h) The information contained in and concerning the issuance of any protective order issued in a case in which a person is presumed or determined to be eligible to be adjudged a youthful offender shall be entered in the registry of protective orders pursuant to section 51-5c and may be further disclosed as specified in said section.

(i) The records of any youth adjudged a youthful offender for a violation of section 14-215 or 14-222, subsection (b) of section 14-223 or subdivision (2) or (3) of subsection (b) or subsection (c) of section 14-224 shall be disclosed to the Department of Motor Vehicles for administrative use in determining whether suspension of such person's motor vehicle operator's license is warranted. Such records disclosed pursuant to this subsection shall not be further disclosed.

(j) The provisions of this section, as amended by public act 05-232*, apply to offenses committed after January 1, 2006, and do not affect any cases pending on said date or any investigations involving offenses committed prior to said date.

(1971, P.A. 72, S. 11; P.A. 76-333, S. 6; P.A. 77-486, S. 4, 5; 77-614, S. 486, 610; P.A. 80-165, S. 2; P.A. 81-472, S. 95, 159; P.A. 82-140, S. 2; P.A. 94-221, S. 16; July Sp. Sess. P.A. 94-2, S. 11; P.A. 95-225, S. 34; 95-261, S. 3; P.A. 98-81, S. 10; 98-256, S. 12; P.A. 99-215, S. 17; P.A. 00-209, S. 3; P.A. 02-132, S. 57; P.A. 04-234, S. 2; P.A. 05-232, S. 7; P.A. 06-196, S. 186; Jan. Sp. Sess. P.A. 08-1, S. 24; P.A. 08-32, S. 12; P.A. 10-43, S. 34; 10-180, S. 5; P.A. 11-39, S. 1; 11-51, S. 134; P.A. 12-81, S. 27; P.A. 14-130, S. 37, 38; P.A. 16-126, S. 35.)

*Note: Public act 05-232 is entitled "An Act Concerning Youthful Offender Proceedings". (See Reference Table captioned "Public Acts of 2005" in Volume 16 which lists the sections amended, created or repealed by the act.)

History: P.A. 76-333 added the word "police" in agency designated as "state police bureau of identification"; P.A. 77-486 required that records be made available to judges and adult probation officers in connection with sentencing procedures; P.A. 77-614 made state police department a division within the department of public safety, effective January 1, 1979; P.A. 80-165 added provision re availability of records to crime victims; P.A. 81-472 made technical corrections; P.A. 82-140 permitted disclosure of identity of person charged to the victim if victim intends to bring a civil action for damages or person is adjudged a youthful offender; P.A. 94-221 replaced alphabetic with numeric Subdiv. indicators and added Subdiv. (3) re the disclosure of the identity of a person who is adjudged a youthful offender to the superintendent of schools for the school district in which such person resides and limited the use of such information by the superintendent; July Sp. Sess. P.A. 94-2 added a new Subdiv. (3) re the availability to a state's attorney of records concerning a youth adjudged a youthful offender for the violation of certain firearm-related offenses, renumbering former Subdiv. (3) as Subdiv. (4); P.A. 95-225 substantially revised section by designating existing provisions as Subsec. (a) and amending said Subsec. to specify that the records shall be confidential and not be disclosed except as provided in this section, delete former Subdivs. (1) to (4), inclusive, re exceptions to the prohibition on disclosure and delete provision that granted any institution to which a youth is committed the right to inspect any of the records of any person committed to it as a youthful offender without a court order, adding Subsec. (b) re disclosure of the records to certain individuals and agencies, adding Subsec. (c) re disclosure of the records to any person who has a legitimate interest therein upon order of the court and adding Subsec. (d) re availability of the records to the victim of the crime; P.A. 95-261 added Subsec. (b), designated by the Revisors as Subsec. (e), re disclosure of reports and files of Office of Adult Probation re youth adjudged youthful offender to Office of the Bail Commission; P.A. 98-81 amended Subsec. (b) by adding provision that records be available to attorney representing youth, parent or guardian, until youth reaches age of majority or is emancipated, and to youth upon attainment of age of majority, provided proof of identity of such youth is submitted to court in accordance with guidelines prescribed by Chief Court Administrator; P.A. 98-256 amended Subsec. (b) to make provisions applicable to records of a youth adjudged a youthful offender "on or after October 1, 1995"; P.A. 99-215 amended Subsec. (b) by adding "emancipation or" and making a technical change; P.A. 00-209 added new Subsec. (f) authorizing the disclosure by law enforcement officials of information concerning a youth who has escaped from an institution or for whom an arrest warrant has been issued; P.A. 02-132 amended Subsec. (a) by making technical changes, amended Subsec. (b) by replacing "Office of Adult Probation, the Office of the Bail Commission" with "Court Support Services Division", amended Subsec. (e) by replacing "Office of Adult Probation" with "Court Support Services Division", replacing "disclosed to the Office of the Bail Commission" with "accessed and disclosed by employees of the division" and adding provision re youthful offender who served a period of probation and added Subsec. (g) re entry of information into registry of protective orders pursuant to Sec. 51-5c, effective January 1, 2003; P.A. 04-234 replaced Board of Parole with Board of Pardons and Paroles, effective July 1, 2004; P.A. 05-232 amended Subsec. (a) by adding "or other information", replacing "any youth adjudged a youthful offender" with "a youth", adding exception for youth arrested for or charged with certain crimes and adding "or subsequently presumed or determined to be eligible to be adjudged", amended Subsec. (b) by replacing "any youth adjudged a youthful offender on or after October 1, 1995," with "any such youth" and making a technical change, amended Subsecs. (c), (d), (e) and (f) by replacing "any youth adjudged a youthful offender" with "any such youth", amended Subsec. (g) by replacing "found eligible" with "presumed or determined to be eligible" and added Subsec. (h) re applicability of amended section, effective January 1, 2006; P.A. 06-196 made a technical change in Subsec. (d), effective June 7, 2006; Jan. Sp. Sess. P.A. 08-1 amended Subsec. (b) to delete Board of Pardons and Paroles from existing list of service providing individuals and agencies to which records may be disclosed and add provision re availability of records to members and employees of Board of Pardons and Paroles and employees of Department of Correction, effective January 25, 2008; P.A. 08-32 amended Subsec. (a) to provide that confidentiality provisions do not apply to records or other information of a youth arrested for or charged with the commission of a violation of Sec. 14-222a, 14-224(a), 14-227a or 14-227g, added new Subsec. (h) re disclosure to Department of Motor Vehicles of records of youth adjudged youthful offender for violation of Sec. 14-215, 14-222, 14-223(b) or 14-224(b) or (c), suspension of the operator's license of any such youth and prohibition on further disclosure, and redesignated existing Subsec. (h) as Subsec. (i), effective August 1, 2008; P.A. 10-43 amended Subsec. (b) to replace "an advocate appointed pursuant to section 54-221" with "a victim advocate under section 54-220"; P.A. 10-180 amended Subsec. (b) to add provision re availability of records to law enforcement officials and prosecutorial officials conducting legitimate criminal investigations; P.A. 11-39 added new Subsec. (g) re disclosure of information to parents or guardian of youth in custody of Department of Correction and redesignated existing Subsecs. (g), (h) and (i) as Subsecs. (h), (i) and (j), effective June 3, 2011; pursuant to P.A. 11-51, "Department of Public Safety" was changed editorially by the Revisors to "Department of Emergency Services and Public Protection" in Subsec. (a), effective July 1, 2011; P.A. 12-81 amended Subsec. (i) to delete provision requiring Commissioner of Motor Vehicles to suspend operator's license of youth adjudged a youthful offender for 6 months for first offense and 1 year for second or subsequent offense; P.A. 14-130 amended Subsec. (a) by adding reference to Sec. 14-224(b)(1) and amended Subsec. (i) by adding reference to Sec. 14-224(b)(2) or (3) and making a technical change; P.A. 16-126 amended Subsec. (a) by adding references to Secs. 14-227m and 14-227n(a)(1) and (2).

Cited. 173 C. 414; 179 C. 98; 192 C. 85; 240 C. 743.

Cited. 34 CA 535. Confidentiality restrictions do not extend to records held by FBI because no language in section provides for such extension. 152 CA 300.

Cited. 30 CS 71; 33 CS 599; 38 CS 675.

Sec. 54-76m. Age of defendant at time of crime controlling.

The age of the youthful offender at the time of the commission of the crime set forth in the information or complaint shall determine whether he is entitled to the benefits provided by sections 54-76b to 54-76n, inclusive, and the provisions thereof shall apply to crimes committed prior, as well as subsequent, to October 1, 1971.

(1971, P.A. 72, S. 12.)

Cited. 173 C. 414.

Cited. 30 CS 71.

Sec. 54-76n. Application of criminal law.

The provisions of titles 53, 53a and 54, including the right of appeal, shall apply to sections 54-76b to 54-76m, inclusive, insofar as they are applicable and not inconsistent herewith.

(1971, P.A. 72, S. 13.)

Sec. 54-76o. Erasure of police and court records of youthful offender.

Whenever any person has been adjudicated a youthful offender and has subsequently been discharged from the supervision of the court or from the care of any institution or agency to whom he has been committed by the court, all police and court records pertaining to such youthful offender shall be automatically erased when such person attains twenty-one years of age, provided such person has not subsequent to being adjudged a youthful offender been convicted of a felony, as defined in section 53a-25, prior to attaining such age. Youthful offender status shall not be deemed conviction of a crime for the purposes of this section. Upon the entry of such an erasure order, all references including arrest, complaint, referrals, petitions, reports and orders, shall be removed from all agency, official and institutional files. The persons in charge of such records shall not disclose to any person, except the subject of the record, upon submission of satisfactory proof of the subject's identity in accordance with guidelines prescribed by the Chief Court Administrator, information pertaining to the record so erased. No youth who has been the subject of such an erasure order shall be deemed to have been arrested ab initio, within the meaning of the general statutes, with respect to proceedings so erased. Copies of the erasure order shall be sent to all persons, agencies, officials or institutions known to have information pertaining to the proceedings affecting such youth.

(1972, P.A. 20, S. 1; P.A. 77-486, S. 3, 5; P.A. 92-115, S. 1, 2.)

History: P.A. 77-486 replaced provision which had required erasure of records pertaining to youthful offenders upon receipt of petition filed by youths, their parents or guardians if two years have elapsed from date of discharge with new provisions requiring automatic erasure when offenders reach 21 if they have not subsequently been convicted of a felony and specifying that youthful offender status is not deemed to be conviction of a crime; P.A. 92-115 added provision that records may be disclosed to subject of the record, upon submission of proof of identity in accordance with guidelines prescribed by chief court administrator.

Sec. 54-76p. Transferred to Chapter 960, Sec. 54-56e.

Sec. 54-76q. Statement of victim regarding plea agreement or sentence.

In a proceeding under sections 54-76b to 54-76n, inclusive, concerning the acceptance of a plea pursuant to a plea agreement entered into by a youth or the imposition of sentence upon such youth, the court shall permit any victim of the crime for which such youth is charged to submit a written statement for the record, or to appear before the court and make a statement for the record, regarding such plea agreement or sentence.

(P.A. 05-169, S. 3.)

CHAPTER 961* TRIAL AND PROCEEDINGS AFTER CONVICTION

*In a criminal matter, unless the state makes out a prima facie case of guilt, no unfavorable inference may be drawn from the failure of the accused to testify. 147 C. 502. The fact that one or more persons jointly charged with the commission of a crime pleaded guilty is not admissible, on the trial of another person so charged, to establish that the crime was committed; a plea of guilty is, in effect, a confession of guilt which, having been made by one of those charged with the crime, can be no more than hearsay as to another who is so charged; the state must prove the whole case against any accused; sequestration of witnesses is in discretion of trial court; request must be seasonably made, must be specific and supported by sound reasons, and it must appear probable that, if witnesses were to hear one another's testimony, they would attempt falsely to give corroborating testimony; if these conditions are met, a denial of the motion could constitute an abuse of discretion; it is within the discretion of the court to grant or deny defendant the right to inspect statements of the state's witnesses in the possession of the state's attorney. 150 C. 195.

The corpus delicti, that is, that the crime charged has been committed by someone, cannot be established by the extrajudicial confession of defendant unsupported by corroborative evidence. 22 CS 385; 23 CS 420. In a criminal case, the accused cannot compel the prosecution to produce documents which he himself has made; facts sought to be disclosed must be shown to be exclusively within the knowledge of the state. Id., 41. Proof of guilt must exclude not every possible, but every reasonable, supposition of the innocence of the accused. Id., 299. In a criminal case, the state may rest its case upon evidence sufficient to make out prima facie case; prima facie case is made out when the evidence indicates to a reasonable person such a strong probability of guilt that a denial or explanation by defendant is reasonably called for; when the state has made out a prima facie case of guilt, an adverse inference may be drawn from the failure of defendant to testify in his own behalf. Id., 412. Information disclosed to a prosecuting attorney to enable him to perform the duties of his office is privileged on grounds of public policy, and the adverse party has no right to demand its production. Id., 459. If accused has reason to believe witness under examination had made prior statement which was contradictory to his testimony, accused may request statement to be produced for examination by court; further use of such statement rests in discretion of court. 24 CS 377.

Table of Contents

Sec. 54-77. **Transferred**

Sec. 54-77a. Establishing venue and selecting jurors for the town of Plymouth.

Sec. 54-77b. **Transferred**

Sec. 54-78. **Transferred**

Sec. 54-79. **Transferred**

Secs. 54-80 to 54-81b. Public defenders. Assistant public defenders; office; assistance. Expenses. Appointment of special defender. Public defenders for

Common Pleas Court. Representation of accused on bindover.

Sec. 54-82. Accused's election of trial by court or by jury. Number of jurors.

Sec. 54-82a. Test of insanity as defense.

Sec. 54-82b. Right to trial by jury.

Sec. 54-82c. (Formerly Sec. 54-139). Prisoner's right to speedy trial on pending charges.

Sec. 54-82d. (Formerly Sec. 54-140). Dismissal of charges on failure to grant prisoner speedy trial.

Sec. 54-82e. (Formerly Sec. 54-141). Mentally ill person not covered.

Sec. 54-82f. Voir dire examination.

Sec. 54-82g. (Formerly Sec. 51-242). Peremptory challenges in criminal prosecution.

Sec. 54-82h. Alternate jurors in criminal cases. Peremptory challenges.

Sec. 54-82i. (Formerly Sec. 54-22). Attendance of witnesses in criminal proceedings.

Sec. 54-82j. (Formerly Sec. 54-23). Detention of witnesses. Warrant.

Sec. 54-82k. (Formerly Sec. 54-24). Recognizance; commitment; release; fees.

Sec. 54-82l. Rules re speedy trial to be adopted by judges of Superior Court effective July 1, 1983.

Sec. 54-82m. Rules re speedy trial to be adopted by judges of Superior Court effective July 1, 1985.

Secs. 54-82n to 54-82p. **Reserved**

Sec. 54-82q. Temporary restraining order prohibiting harassment of witness.

Sec. 54-82r. Protective order prohibiting harassment of witness.

Sec. 54-82s. The Leroy Brown, Jr. and Karen Clarke Witness Protection Program.

Sec. 54-82t. Protective services for witness at risk of harm.

Sec. 54-82u. Witness protection agreement.

Sec. 54-83. Testimony in case where crime is punishable by death or life imprisonment without possibility of release.

Sec. 54-84. Testimony or silence of accused.

Sec. 54-84a. Testimony against spouse.

Sec. 54-84b. Testimony of spouse re confidential communications.

Sec. 54-85. Witness to testify with regard to bribery at elections.

Sec. 54-85a. Sequestering of witnesses in criminal prosecution.

Sec. 54-85b. Employment protection for witnesses and victims of crime. Penalty. Action for damages and reinstatement.

Sec. 54-85c. Representative of homicide victim entitled to be present at trial of defendant. Exclusion. Hearing.

Sec. 54-85d. Employer not to discharge employee who attends court as family member of or person designated by homicide victim.

Sec. 54-85e. Photograph of deceased victim shown to jury during opening and closing arguments.

Sec. 54-85f. Victim of violent crime or representative of deceased victim permitted to attend court proceedings.

Sec. 54-85g. Advisement to crime victims re constitutional rights by judge at arraignment.

Sec. 54-86. Depositions.

Sec. 54-86a. Certain evidence to be made available to defendant.

Sec. 54-86b. Right of accused to examine statements.

Sec. 54-86c. Disclosure of exculpatory information or material.

Sec. 54-86d. Nondisclosure of address and telephone number by victims of certain crimes.

Sec. 54-86e. Confidentiality of identifying information pertaining to victims of certain crimes. Availability of information to accused. Protective order information to be entered in registry.

Sec. 54-86f. Admissibility of evidence of sexual conduct.

Sec. 54-86g. Testimony of victim of child abuse. Court may order testimony taken outside courtroom. Procedure.

Sec. 54-86h. Competency of child as witness.

Sec. 54-86i. Testimony of expert witness re mental state or condition of defendant.

Sec. 54-86j. Polygraph examination of victims of sexual assault restricted.

Sec. 54-86k. Admissibility of results of DNA analysis.

Sec. 54-86l. Admissibility in criminal or juvenile proceeding of statement by child twelve years of age or younger at time of statement relating to sexual offense or offense involving physical abuse against the child.

Sec. 54-86m. Reproduction of property or material that constitutes child pornography prohibited.

Sec. 54-86n. Appointment of advocate in proceeding re the welfare or custody of a cat or dog. Advocate's duties. Department of Agriculture to maintain list of eligible advocates.

Sec. 54-87. Demurrer.

Sec. 54-88. State to open and close arguments.

Sec. 54-89. Direction of court to jury.

Sec. 54-89a. Court to inform jury on consequences of a finding of not guilty by reason of mental disease or defect.

Secs. 54-90 and 54-90a. **Transferred**

Sec. 54-91. When sentence to be passed.

Sec. 54-91a. (Formerly Sec. 54-109). Presentence investigation of defendant.

Sec. 54-91b. (Formerly Sec. 54-109a). Defendant may request copy of prior record and presentence investigation report.

Sec. 54-91c. Testimony of victim or representative of deceased victim prior to acceptance of plea agreement and at sentencing hearing. Terms of proposed

    plea agreement. Notification by state's attorney.

Sec. 54-91d. Referral of persons to youth service bureaus.

Sec. 54-91e. Notification of victim through automated system prior to acceptance of plea agreement.

Sec. 54-91f. Apology to victim by person convicted of motor vehicle offense that resulted in death or serious physical injury to another. Inadmissibility in civil

    or criminal proceeding.

Sec. 54-91g. Sentencing of a child for class A or B felony.

Sec. 54-92. Pronouncement of sentence.

Sec. 54-92a. (Formerly Sec. 54-120). Commitment to custody of Commissioner of Correction.

Sec. 54-92b. (Formerly Sec. 54-122). Discharge from community correctional center when held for nonpayment of fine.

Sec. 54-92c. (Formerly Sec. 17-381). Women attendants.

Sec. 54-93. Clerks to notify warden of Connecticut Correctional Institution, Somers, of sentences.

Sec. 54-93a. Court order to correct public record containing false information as a result of identity theft.

Sec. 54-94. Sentence of persons between sixteen and seventeen.

Sec. 54-94a. Conditional nolo contendere plea. Appeal of denial of motion to suppress or dismiss.

Sec. 54-95. Appeal by defendant in criminal prosecution; stay of execution.

Sec. 54-95a. (Formerly Sec. 54-17). Jurisdiction of Superior Court.

Sec. 54-95b. Reopening judgment in certain motor vehicle and criminal cases.

Sec. 54-95c. Application to vacate prostitution conviction on basis of being a victim of trafficking in persons. Prosecutor's response. Court order.

Sec. 54-96. Appeals by the state from Superior Court in criminal cases.

Sec. 54-96a. (Formerly Sec. 54-13). Appeal vacated by payment of fine.

Sec. 54-96b. (Formerly Sec. 54-14). Withdrawal of appeal of person committed to community correctional center.

Sec. 54-97. Mittimus required for commitment to correctional facility.

Sec. 54-98. Execution of mittimus for commitment to Connecticut Correctional Institution, Somers.

Sec. 54-99. Period within which death penalty inflicted.

Sec. 54-100. Method of inflicting death penalty. Attendance at execution.

Sec. 54-100a. Committee on news media access to executions. Selection of news media witnesses.

Sec. 54-101. Disposition of person becoming insane after death sentence.

Sec. 54-102. Burial or disposal of body of executed criminal.

Sec. 54-102a. (Formerly Sec. 53a-90). Venereal examination and HIV testing of persons charged with certain sexual offenses.

Sec. 54-102b. HIV testing of persons convicted of certain sexual offenses.

Sec. 54-102c. HIV information and test results provided to victim.

Secs. 54-102d to 54-102f. **Reserved**

Sec. 54-102g. Blood or other biological sample required from certain arrested or convicted persons for DNA analysis.

Sec. 54-102h. Procedure for collection of blood or other biological sample for DNA analysis.

Sec. 54-102i. Procedure for conducting DNA analysis of blood or other biological sample.

Sec. 54-102j. Dissemination of information in DNA data bank.

Sec. 54-102k. Unauthorized dissemination or use of DNA data bank information. Obtaining blood sample without authority. Penalties.

Sec. 54-102*l.* Expungement of DNA data bank records and destruction of samples.

Sec. 54-102m. DNA Data Bank Oversight Panel.

Secs. 54-102n to 54-102q. **Reserved**

Sec. 54-102r. Registration of persons convicted of sexual assault upon release from correctional facility or completion or termination of probation.

Sec. 54-102s. **Transferred**

Secs. 54-102t to 54-102z. **Reserved**

Sec. 54-102aa. Tuberculosis testing: Definitions. Requirements.

Sec. 54-102bb. Procedures for evaluation of tuberculosis infection.

Sec. 54-102cc. Tuberculosis infection control committee.

Sec. 54-102dd. Inmates with infectious tuberculosis required to be isolated. Persons exposed encouraged to be tested.

Sec. 54-102ee. Department contract option for testing of tuberculosis.

Secs. 54-102ff to 54-102ii. **Reserved**

Sec. 54-102jj. Preservation of biological evidence.

Sec. 54-102kk. DNA testing of biological evidence.

Secs. 54-102// to 54-102oo. **Reserved**

Sec. 54-102pp. Review of wrongful convictions.

Secs. 54-102qq to 54-102tt. **Reserved**

Sec. 54-102uu. Compensation for wrongful incarceration.

Sec. 54-103. Commission on Adult Probation.

Sec. 54-103a. Office of Adult Probation.

Sec. 54-103b. Services for probation referrals. Duties of Court Support Services Division. Contractual services and alternative incarceration program.

Sec. 54-104. Appointment of Director of Probation and probation officers. Qualifying examinations.

Sec. 54-105. Duties of executive director of Court Support Services Division re probation. Intensive probation program. Community service program. Caseload limitation.

Sec. 54-105a. Funds for the probation transition program and technical violation units.

Secs. 54-106 and 54-107. General Assembly to provide for expenses; central office; quarters. Appointment of probation officers.

Sec. 54-108. Duties of probation officers.

Sec. 54-108a. Supervision of probationers.

Sec. 54-108b. Risk assessment and monitoring standards developed by Chief Court Administrator.

Sec. 54-108c. Availability of information on outstanding arrest warrants for probation violations.

Sec. 54-108d. Authority of probation officers to detain certain persons, seize contraband and act as member of fugitive task force.

Sec. 54-108e. Duties of probation officers. Availability of information contained in alternative sentencing plan or community release plan.

Sec. 54-108f. Issuance of certificate of rehabilitation by Court Support Services Division. Modification or revocation.

Sec. 54-108g. Prohibition against disclosure of personal information of probation officers to certain individuals under the Freedom of Information Act.

Secs. 54-109 and 54-109a. **Transferred**

Secs. 54-110 to 54-119. Report on person with prior conviction. Restitution investigation and report. Information to be included in report. Appointment of restitution specialists and other personnel. Optional treatment of person found guilty of crime. Probation or suspension of sentence, generally. Penalty for common law high crimes and misdemeanors. Punishment upon second and third conviction. Second and subsequent convictions of crimes while armed with firearm. Additional penalties for conviction of crimes while armed with firearm. Court may impose additional sentence.

Sec. 54-120. **Transferred**

Sec. 54-121. Indeterminate sentence.

Sec. 54-122. **Transferred**

Sec. 54-123. Transportation of prisoner discharged from jail.

211

Sec. 54-123a. Judicial Department duties re alternative sanctions and incarceration programs.

Secs. 54-123b and 54-123c. Advisory committee concerning adult offenders. Advisory committee concerning juvenile offenders.

Sec. 54-123d. Establishment of alternative incarceration center providing mental health services.

Sec. 54-124. Board of Parole. Appointment and duties of executive secretary.

Sec. 54-124a. Board of Pardons and Paroles.

Sec. 54-124b. Caseload of parole officers.

Sec. 54-124c. Responsibility of the Department of Correction for supervision of persons released from confinement.

Sec. 54-124d. Criminal history records check of Board of Parole personnel.

Sec. 54-124e. Board of Pardons and Paroles as successor department to Board of Pardons and Board of Parole.

Sec. 54-125. Parole of prisoner serving indeterminate sentence.

Sec. 54-125a. Parole of inmate serving sentence of more than two years. Eligibility. Hearing to determine suitability for parole release of certain inmates.

Sec. 54-125b. Parole of prisoner after administrative review without a hearing.

Sec. 54-125c. Sexual offender treatment as precondition for parole hearing.

Sec. 54-125d. Deportation parole of aliens.

Sec. 54-125e. Special parole. Conditions. Duration. Violation. Hearing. Disposition.

Sec. 54-125f. Pilot zero-tolerance drug supervision program.

Sec. 54-125g. Parole of prisoner nearing end of maximum sentence.

Sec. 54-125h. Transfer of prisoner granted parole and nearing parole release date.

Sec. 54-125i. Parole of prisoner without a hearing.

Sec. 54-126. Rules and regulations concerning parole. Enforcement.

Sec. 54-126a. Testimony of crime victim at parole hearing. Notification to victim.

Sec. 54-127. Rearrest.

Sec. 54-127a. Parole revocation and rescission hearings.

Sec. 54-128. Period of confinement in correctional institution after parole violation.

Sec. 54-129. Discharge of paroled prisoner.

Sec. 54-130. State Prison for Women not covered.

Sec. 54-130a. (Formerly Sec. 18-26). Jurisdiction and authority of board to grant commutations of punishment, releases, pardons and certificates of rehabilitation.

Sec. 54-130b. (Formerly Sec. 18-26a). Commutation of punishment and deportation of inmates who are aliens.

212

Sec. 54-130c. (Formerly Sec. 18-30). Information about prisoner.

Sec. 54-130d. (Formerly Sec. 18-27a). Testimony of crime victim at session of board. Notification of Office of Victim Services of board's action.

Sec. 54-130e. Provisional pardons. Certificates of rehabilitation.

Sec. 54-130f. Pardon eligibility notice.

Sec. 54-130g. Pardon for violation of certain provisions of section 53a-61aa or 53a-62. Criteria.

Sec. 54-131. Employment of paroled or discharged prisoners. Interviews.

Sec. 54-131a. Release of inmate on medical parole.

Sec. 54-131b. Eligibility for medical parole.

Sec. 54-131c. Medical diagnosis.

Sec. 54-131d. Conditions of release on medical parole.

Sec. 54-131e. Requests for medical diagnosis.

Sec. 54-131f. Special panel. Emergency review.

Sec. 54-131g. Effect on parole or other release.

Secs. 54-131h to 54-131j. Reserved

Sec. 54-131k. Compassionate parole release.

Sec. 54-132. Definitions.

Sec. 54-133. Interstate Compact for Adult Offender Supervision.

Sec. 54-133a. Motor vehicle violation deemed a criminal offense for purposes of Interstate Compact for Adult Offender Supervision.

Secs. 54-134 to 54-138b. Designation of "Compact Institutions". Transfers to other correctional institutions. Incarceration in receiving state not to affect rights in sending state. Reimbursement for expenses. Ratification; regulations. Retaking of parolee. Unauthorized residency by parolee from another state; penalty.

Secs. 54-139 to 54-141. Transferred

Sec. 54-142. Destruction of notes received for unpaid fines.

PART I DISCOVERY, TRIAL AND WITNESSES

Sec. 54-77. Transferred to Chapter 890, Sec. 51-352.

Sec. 54-77a. Establishing venue and selecting jurors for the town of Plymouth. Section 54-77a is repealed.

(P.A. 75-26, S. 1, 8; P.A. 76-436, S. 664, 681; P.A. 77-576, S. 11, 65.)

Sec. 54-77b. Transferred to Chapter 890, Sec. 51-352a.

Sec. 54-78. Transferred to Chapter 890, Sec. 51-353.

Sec. 54-79. Transferred to Chapter 890, Sec. 51-353b.

Secs. 54-80 to 54-81b. Public defenders. Assistant public defenders; office; assistance. Expenses. Appointment of special defender. Public defenders for Common Pleas Court. Representation of accused on bindover. Sections 54-80 to 54-81b, inclusive, are repealed.

(1949 Rev., S. 3615, 8796; 1959, P.A. 28, S. 13; 1961, P.A. 564, S. 1–3; 1963, P.A. 642, S. 69, 70; February, 1965, P.A. 178, S. 1, 2; 218; 1967, P.A. 34, S. 1; 189; 622, S. 8; 1969, P.A. 655, S. 2; 1971, P.A. 871, S. 121; 1972, P.A. 281, S. 22, 23; P.A. 73-116, S. 25, 26; 73-667, S. 1, 2; P.A. 74-183, S. 150, 151, 291; 74-317, S. 12, 14.)

Sec. 54-82. Accused's election of trial by court or by jury. Number of jurors.

(a) In any criminal case, prosecution or proceeding, the accused may, if the accused so elects when called upon to plead, be tried by the court instead of by the jury; and, in such case, the court shall have jurisdiction to hear and try such case and render judgment and sentence thereon.

(b) If the accused is charged with a crime punishable by death, life imprisonment without the possibility of release or life imprisonment and elects to be tried by the court, the court shall be composed of three judges to be designated by the Chief Court Administrator, or the Chief Court Administrator's designee, who shall name one such judge to preside over the trial. Such judges, or a majority of them, shall have power to decide all questions of law and fact arising upon the trial and render judgment accordingly.

(c) If the accused does not elect to be tried by the court, the accused shall be tried by a jury of six except that no person charged with an offense which is punishable by death, life imprisonment without the possibility of release or life imprisonment, shall be tried by a jury of less than twelve without such person's consent.

(1949 Rev., S. 8797; 1953, S. 3326d; 1967, P.A. 656, S. 62; P.A. 73-576, S. 3, 4; 73-616, S. 41, 67; P.A. 76-336, S. 4; P.A. 77-474, S. 1, 2; P.A. 80-313, S. 36; P.A. 81-47; P.A. 12-5, S. 26.)

History: 1967 act provided for designation of judges by chief court administrator instead of chief justice; P.A. 73-576 substituted "Connecticut Correctional Institution, Somers" for "State Prison" and replaced provision calling for trial by jury of six unless defendant claims twelve-person jury or case is punishable by death or life imprisonment with provision calling for jury of six except in cases involving capital offense which require trial by twelve-person jury unless defendant consents to jury of six; P.A. 73-616 transferred duty to select panel judges from chief court administrator to chief justice; P.A. 76-336 deleted specific references to imprisonment at Somers Correctional Institution; P.A. 77-474 required jury of twelve in cases involving offenses punishable by death or life imprisonment rather than in cases involving capital offenses; P.A. 80-313 divided section into Subsecs.; P.A. 81-47 amended Subsec. (b) by replacing provision re appointment of judges by chief justice with provision that three judges shall be designated by chief court administrator or his designee, who shall name one such judge to preside over the trial; P.A. 12-5 added provisions re crimes punishable by life imprisonment without possibility of release and made technical changes, effective April 25, 2012.

Application by accused for leave to withdraw election made under statute is addressed to court's discretion; refusal to permit withdrawal held no error. 102 C. 51. The court's determination of guilt or innocence upon the evidence should be raised on appeal by an assignment of error; not necessary to make a motion to set aside verdict. 105 C. 332; 109 C. 126; 110 C. 552. Court fulfills function of jury; its additional power under statute does not authorize convicting of robbery a defendant charged with murder. 132 C. 43. Cited. 142 C. 114. It is not violative of the constitutional guarantee of the right to a jury trial for the legislature to enact a statute which changes the form of jury procedure if it still maintains the substance of the institution. 144 C. 228. Insofar as it provides that an accused shall be tried to a jury of 6 unless at the time he is put to plea he demands a jury of 12, it does not deprive any defendant of his right of trial by jury. Id., 230. Cited. 146 C. 78; 147 C. 95; 153 C. 328; 161 C. 413. Since determination of jury size is not a matter presently or historically lying exclusively within control of the judiciary, section, which regulates size of criminal juries, does not violate separation of powers clause of Connecticut Constitution. 171 C. 395. Cited. 173 C. 450; 174 C. 22; 176 C. 224; 182 C. 353; 190 C. 639; 191 C. 506; 197 C. 247; 198 C. 77; 223 C. 384; 227 C. 448; 231 C. 235. Death penalty unconstitutional under Art. I, Secs. 8 and 9 of Connecticut Constitution. 318 C. 1.

Cited. 34 CA 58; judgment reversed, see 232 C. 537; 41 CA 361; Id., 831. 3-judge court not required to deliberate with respect to all charges when only one charge carried maximum penalty of death or life in prison. 69 CA 267.

Cited. 33 CS 739; 34 CS 674; 39 CS 347.

Accused cannot postpone trial of his case indefinitely by repeatedly changing his election concerning trial by jury. 6 Conn. Cir. Ct. 218, 222, 223.

Subsec. (b):

Cited. 184 C. 455; 201 C. 534; 203 C. 4. Defendant's decision to forgo a jury determination in capital felony sentencing proceeding and opt for sentencing by a 3-judge panel was knowing, voluntary and intelligent; formulaic canvass of defendant is not required and validity of jury waiver is determined by examination of totality of the circumstances. 303 C. 71.

Cited. 13 CA 667; 22 CA 265. Court's instruction to defendant that he could not change his decision to waive his right to a jury trial simply because he had rethought his position was not legally inaccurate or in contradiction of the provisions of section. 120 CA 768.

Sec. 54-82a. Test of insanity as defense. Section 54-82a is repealed.

(1967, P.A. 336, S. 1, 2; 1969, P.A. 828, S. 214.)

Sec. 54-82b. Right to trial by jury.

(a) The party accused in a criminal action in the Superior Court may demand a trial by jury of issues which are triable of right by a jury. There is no right to trial by jury in criminal actions where the maximum penalty is a fine of one hundred ninety-nine dollars or in any matter involving violations payable through the Centralized Infractions Bureau where the maximum penalty is a fine of five hundred dollars or less.

(b) In criminal proceedings the judge shall advise the accused of his right to trial by jury at the time he is put to plea and, if the accused does not then claim a jury, his right thereto shall be deemed waived, but if a judge acting on motion made by the accused within ten days after judgment finds that such waiver was made when the accused was not fully cognizant of his rights or when, in the opinion of the judge, the proper administration of justice requires it, the judge shall vacate the judgment and cause the proceeding to be set for jury trial.

(c) In any criminal trial by a jury, except as otherwise provided by law, such trial shall be by a jury of six.

(P.A. 80-313, S. 35; P.A. 86-227; P.A. 87-241; May Sp. Sess. P.A. 92-6, S. 82, 117.)

History: P.A. 86-227 provided that "The party accused", rather than "Any party", may demand a jury trial and increased from $99 to $199 the maximum fine threshold for a jury trial; P.A. 87-241 amended Subsec. (a) by deleting reference to maximum penalty of sentence of 30 days or penalty consisting of both fine and imprisonment; May Sp. Sess. P.A. 92-6 amended Subsec. (a) to provide that there is no right to trial by jury in any matter involving violations payable through the centralized infractions bureau where the maximum penalty is a fine of $500 or less.

See Sec. 51-180 re criminal terms and sessions of court.

See Sec. 51-180a re special session held when an accused is confined for want of bail.

Right to jury trial discussed. 188 C. 697. Cited. 190 C. 639; 191 C. 506; 197 C. 247; 198 C. 77; 201 C. 489; 205 C. 456; 222 C. 591; 223 C. 384; 225 C. 355; 226 C. 618.

Cited. 9 CA 255; 10 CA 692; 39 CA 702; 41 CA 454; 46 CA 486. When defendant knowingly, voluntarily and intelligently waives right to a jury trial and is subsequently charged with additional crimes, if defendant again elects to waive right to a jury trial, defendant cannot complain on appeal that election for a court trial to the additional charges was compromised. 145 CA 767.

Subsec. (a):

Sec. 54-82c. (Formerly Sec. 54-139). Prisoner's right to speedy trial on pending charges.

(a) Whenever a person has entered upon a term of imprisonment in a correctional institution of this state and, during the continuance of the term of imprisonment, there is pending in this state any untried indictment or information against such prisoner, he shall be brought to trial within one hundred twenty days after he has caused to be delivered, to the state's attorney or assistant state's attorney of the judicial district or geographical area, in which the indictment or information is pending, and to the appropriate court, written notice of the place of his imprisonment and his request for final disposition to be made of the indictment or information. For good cause shown in open court, the prisoner or his counsel being present, the court may grant any necessary or reasonable continuance. The request of the prisoner shall be accompanied by a certificate of the warden, Community Correctional Center Administrator or other official having custody of the prisoner, stating the term of commitment under which the prisoner is being held, the time already served, the time remaining to be served on the sentence, the amount of good time earned, the time of parole eligibility of the prisoner and any decisions of the Board of Pardons and Paroles relating to the prisoner.

(b) The written notice and request for final disposition referred to in subsection (a) hereof shall be given or sent by the prisoner to the warden, Community Correctional Center Administrator or other official having custody of him, who shall promptly forward it together with the certificate to the appropriate prosecuting official and court by registered or certified mail, return receipt requested.

(c) The warden, Community Correctional Center Administrator or other official having custody of the prisoner shall promptly inform him in writing of the source and contents of any untried indictment or information against him concerning which the warden, administrator or other official has knowledge and of his right to make a request for final disposition thereof.

(d) Escape from custody by the prisoner subsequent to his execution of the request for final disposition referred to in subsection (a) hereof shall void the request.

(1957, P.A. 551, S. 1; 1961, P.A. 465; 1963, P.A. 642, S. 79; P.A. 73-116, S. 14; 73-667, S. 1, 2; P.A. 74-183, S. 156, 291; P.A. 76-436, S. 558, 681; P.A. 80-313, S. 37; June Sp. Sess. P.A. 98-1, S. 74, 121; P.A. 04-234, S. 2.)

History: 1961 act specified, in Subsec. (a), request and notice be to state's attorney or prosecuting attorney and added circuit court; 1963 act stipulated state's attorney be of the county, deleted reference to prosecuting attorney of county and substituted jail administrator for sheriff; P.A. 73-116 added reference to judicial districts and replaced jail administrator with community correctional center administrator; P.A. 73-667 changed effective date of P.A. 73-116 from October 1, 1973, to April 25, 1973; P.A. 74-183 replaced circuit court with court of common pleas, reflecting reorganization of judicial system, effective December 31, 1974; P.A. 76-436 replaced prosecuting attorneys of common pleas court with assistant state's attorneys and deleted reference to various courts' jurisdiction, reflecting transfer of all trial jurisdiction to superior court, effective July 1, 1978; P.A. 80-313 deleted reference to counties and made slight change in wording; Sec. 54-139 transferred to Sec. 54-82c in 1981; June Sp. Sess. P.A. 98-1 made a technical change in Subsec. (a), effective June 24, 1998; P.A. 04-234 replaced Board of Parole with Board of Pardons and Paroles, effective July 1, 2004.

Annotations to former section 54-139:

Phrase "has caused to be delivered" is equivalent of "has delivered" and 120-day period runs from completion of delivery of both request and supplemental information. 149 C. 250. Cited. 153 C. 28. Statute permits court to grant continuance for good cause shown even where facts which lead court to grant continuance are beyond defendant's control. 171 C. 487. Cited. 185 C. 118; 194 C. 297; 198 C. 573.

Cited. 40 CA 757.

Does not apply to prisoner in federal institution in Connecticut; does not purport to place a limit on time within which information should be made. 24 CS 308. Cited. 36 CS 327, 330.

Annotations to present section:

Cited. 193 C. 270; 194 C. 297; 197 C. 166; 198 C. 573; 202 C. 93; 221 C. 921; 224 C. 163; 242 C. 409.

Cited. 12 CA 1; 14 CA 244; Id., 493; 20 CA 205; 26 CA 698; 28 CA 195; 29 CA 694; 32 CA 38; 33 CA 184; judgment reversed, see 232 C. 707; 40 CA 757. In absence of any evidence to the contrary, it is presumed that officials acted properly under statute and therefore, because written notice was not delivered to state's attorney, the statutory 120-day period did not commence. 107 CA 517. For purposes of speedy trial calculations, delays attributable to initiations of the defense are excludable. 110 CA 245. Time limits under section excluded entire period of time during which defendant's competency claim was considered and resolved. 132 CA 24.

Sec. 54-82d. (Formerly Sec. 54-140). Dismissal of charges on failure to grant prisoner speedy trial.

If an action is not assigned for trial within the period of time as provided in section 54-82c, no court of this state shall any longer have jurisdiction thereof, nor shall the untried indictment or information be of any further force or effect, and the court shall enter an order dismissing the same.

(1957, P.A. 551, S. 2; P.A. 80-313, S. 38.)

History: P.A. 80-313 added specific reference to Sec. 54-139 and made slight change in wording; Sec. 54-140 transferred to Sec. 54-82d in 1981 and reference to Sec. 54-139 revised to reflect its transfer as well.

Annotations to former section 54-140:

Period of time construed to run from completion of delivery of both request and supplemental information. 149 C. 250. Cited. 171 C. 487; 185 C. 118.

Annotations to present section:

Cited. 194 C. 297; Id., 510; 197 C. 166; 198 C. 573. Failure to bring to trial within time limit prescribed by Sec. 54-82c may be waived; statute affects personal jurisdiction not subject matter jurisdiction. 202 C. 93. Cited. 221 C. 921; 224 C. 163.

Cited. 12 CA 1; 14 CA 244; 20 CA 205; 26 CA 698; 28 CA 195; 29 CA 694; 40 CA 757.

Sec. 54-82e. (Formerly Sec. 54-141). Mentally ill person not covered.

The provisions of sections 54-82c and 54-82d shall not apply to any person adjudged to be mentally ill.

(1957, P.A. 551, S. 3.)

History: Sec. 54-141 transferred to Sec. 54-82e in 1981 and revised references to other sections within provisions as necessary to reflect their transfer.

Cited. 194 C. 297.

Sec. 54-82f. Voir dire examination.

In any criminal action tried before a jury, either party shall have the right to examine, personally or by his counsel, each juror outside the presence of other prospective jurors as to his qualifications to sit as a juror in the action, or as to his interest, if any, in the subject matter of the action, or as to his relations with the parties thereto. If the judge before whom the examination is held is of the opinion from the examination that any juror would be unable to render a fair and impartial verdict, the juror shall be excused by the judge from any further service upon the panel, or in the action, as the judge determines. The right of such examination shall not be abridged by requiring questions to be put to any juror in writing and submitted in advance of the commencement of said action.

(P.A. 80-313, S. 39.)

Cited. 196 C. 667; 197 C. 314; 200 C. 586; 201 C. 125; 203 C. 506; 204 C. 156; Id., 377; 205 C. 61; 218 C. 309; 222 C. 1; 223 C. 299; 226 C. 237; Id., 618; 230 C. 385, see also 37 CA 801; 233 C. 215; Id., 813; 237 C. 238; Id., 454. Nothing in section requires trial court to permit a party to ascertain prospective jurors' views on specific evidence during voir dire. 269 C. 213. Trial court did not abuse its discretion by precluding defense counsel from asking venirepersons specifically about self-defense. 292 C. 656.

Sec. 54-82g. (Formerly Sec. 51-242). Peremptory challenges in criminal prosecution.

The accused may challenge peremptorily, in any criminal trial before the Superior Court for any offense punishable by death or life imprisonment without the possibility of release, twenty-five jurors; for any offense punishable by life imprisonment, fifteen jurors; for any offense the punishment for which may be imprisonment for more than one year and for less than life, six jurors; and for any other offense, three jurors. In any criminal trial in which the accused is charged with more than one count on the information or where there is more than one information, the number of challenges is determined by the count carrying the highest maximum punishment. The state, on the trial of any criminal prosecution, may challenge peremptorily the same number of jurors as the accused.

(1949 Rev., S. 8798; 1953, S. 3327d; 1959, P.A. 28, S. 210; February, 1965, P.A. 574, S. 39; P.A. 73-576, S. 1, 4; P.A. 74-183, S. 55, 291; P.A. 76-336, S. 16; P.A. 76-436, S. 105, 681; P.A. 77-452, S. 19, 72; P.A. 80-152; 80-313, S. 40, 62; P.A. 12-5, S. 27.)

History: 1959 act added circuit court; 1965 act deleted obsolete reference to common pleas court, its criminal jurisdiction having been abolished in 1959; P.A. 73-576 replaced "State Prison" with "Connecticut Correctional Institution, Somers" and deleted provisions which pertained to twelve-person juries and allowed for eight challenges in trials where offense is punishable by sentence of less than life and four challenges for other offenses, retaining six challenges and four challenges, respectively, previously applicable to six-person juries and now made generally applicable, effective June 12, 1973, and applicable to all prosecutions claimed for jury trial on and after that date; P.A. 74-183 replaced circuit court with court of common pleas, reflecting reorganization of judicial system, effective December 31, 1974; P.A. 76-336 specified that six challenges are allowed where imprisonment may be for "more than one year" and deleted specific mention of Somers institution as place of imprisonment; P.A. 76-436 reiterated changes of P.A. 76-336 and deleted reference to arraignment before court of common pleas, reflecting transfer of all trial jurisdiction to superior court, effective July 1, 1978; P.A. 77-452 made technical grammatical change; P.A. 80-152 deleted specific reference to superior court arraignments, referring instead to arraignment "in any criminal trial" and added provision re determination of challenges allowed in cases involving more than one court or more than one information; P.A. 80-313 reiterated deletion of reference to arraignment in superior court; Sec. 51-242 transferred to Sec. 54-82g in 1981; P.A. 12-5 added provision re offense punishable by life imprisonment without possibility of release and made a technical change, effective April 25, 2012.

Annotations to former section 51-242:

Sec. 54-82h. Alternate jurors in criminal cases. Peremptory challenges. (a) In any criminal prosecution to be tried to the jury in the Superior Court if it appears to the court that the trial is likely to be protracted, the court may, in its discretion, direct that, after a jury has been selected, two or more additional jurors shall be added to the jury panel, to be known as "alternate jurors". Such alternate jurors shall have the same qualifications and be selected and subject to examination and challenge in the same manner and to the same extent as the jurors constituting the regular panel, provided, in any case when the court directs the selection of alternate jurors, the number of peremptory challenges allowed shall be as follows: In any criminal prosecution the state and the accused may each peremptorily challenge thirty jurors if the offense for which the accused is arraigned is punishable by death or life imprisonment without the possibility of release, eighteen jurors if the offense is punishable by life imprisonment, eight jurors if the offense is punishable by imprisonment for more than one year and for less than life, and four jurors in any other case.

(b) Alternate jurors shall be sworn separately from those constituting the regular panel, and the oaths to be administered shall be as provided in section 1-25.

(c) Alternate jurors shall attend at all times upon trial of the cause. They shall be seated when the case is on trial with or near the jurors constituting the regular panel, with equal opportunity to see and hear all matters adduced in the trial of the case. If, at any time, any juror shall, for any reason, become unable to further perform the duty of a juror, the court may excuse such juror and, if any juror is so excused or dies, the court may order that an alternate juror who is designated by lot to be drawn by the clerk shall become a part of the regular panel and the trial or deliberation shall then proceed with appropriate instructions from the court as though such juror had been a member of the regular panel from the time when the trial or deliberation began. If the alternate juror becomes a member of the regular panel after deliberations began, the jury shall be instructed by the court that deliberations by the jury shall begin anew. A juror who has been selected to serve as an alternate shall not be segregated from the regular panel except when the case is given to the regular panel for deliberation at which time such alternate juror may be dismissed from further service on said case or may remain in service under the direction of the court.

(P.A. 80-313, S. 41; P.A. 82-307, S. 5, 8; P.A. 00-116, S. 6; P.A. 12-5, S. 28.)

History: P.A. 82-307 amended Subsec. (a) by changing the number of alternate jurors from "one or two" to two "or more" and amended Subsec. (c) to reflect this change; P.A. 00-116 amended Subsec. (c) by making technical changes, by permitting alternate juror to become part of the deliberation and proceed with appropriate instructions from the court as though alternate juror was part of the regular panel when the trial or deliberation began, by providing if alternate juror becomes member of panel after deliberations began, the jury shall be instructed by the court that deliberations by the jury shall begin anew, and by adding provision allowing alternate juror to remain in service under the direction of the court during deliberation of regular panel; P.A. 12-5 amended Subsec. (a) to add provision re offense punishable by life imprisonment without possibility of release, effective April 25, 2012.

See Sec. 51-243 re alternate jurors in civil cases.

Cited. 190 C. 219; 195 C. 421; 200 C. 615; 209 C. 564; 223 C. 299; 226 C. 618; 233 C. 813.

Cited. 7 CA 503; 8 CA 158; 34 CA 58; judgment reversed, see 232 C. 537; 35 CA 541; 36 CA 631; 38 CA 231; 41 CA 831.

Subsec. (a):

Death penalty unconstitutional under Art. I, Secs. 8 and 9 of Connecticut Constitution. 318 C. 1.

Subsec. (c):

Cited. 199 C. 163; 216 C. 367; 231 C. 235. Statute requires alternate jurors to be dismissed after commencement of jury deliberations and substitution of alternate juror after commencement of deliberations is prohibited; substitution of alternate juror after commencement of deliberations in violation of statute is not harmless error. 254 C. 472. Statute now explicitly permits substitution of a juror after deliberations have begun. 257 C. 192. Process for selecting and dismissing alternate jurors, including under Subsec., does not implicate constitutional rights. 272 C. 432. Trial court could not reconsider its decision to dismiss juror once it had communicated its decision to her since such communication caused her to lose her status as a juror and she was no longer qualified to participate in the remainder of the proceedings. 303 C. 378.

Judgments of conviction reversed due to substitution of two nonjurors, formerly alternate jurors who were dismissed by trial court after deliberations had begun, for regular jurors in the jury by the trial court. 67 CA 734. Defendant's constitutional right to fair trial before jury drawn from a fair cross-section of

Sec. 54-82i. (Formerly Sec. 54-22). Attendance of witnesses in criminal proceedings. (a) **Definitions.** The following words, when used in this section, have the meaning specified, unless the context otherwise indicates: "Witness" means a person whose testimony is desired in any proceeding or investigation by a grand jury or in a criminal action, prosecution or proceeding; "state" includes any territory of the United States and the District of Columbia, and "summons" means a subpoena, order or other notice requiring the appearance of a witness.

(b) **Summoning witness in this state to testify in another state.** If a judge of a court of record in any state which by its laws has made provision for commanding persons within that state to attend and testify in this state certifies, under the seal of such court, that there is a criminal prosecution pending in such court, or that a grand jury investigation has commenced or is about to commence, that a person being within this state is a material witness in such prosecution or grand jury investigation and that the presence of such witness will be required for a specified number of days, upon presentation of such certificate to any judge of a court of record in the judicial district in which such person is, such judge shall fix a time and place for a hearing and shall make an order directing the witness to appear at such time and place for such hearing. If, at such hearing, the judge determines that the witness is material and necessary, that it will not cause undue hardship to the witness to be compelled to attend and testify in the prosecution or a grand jury investigation in the other state and that the laws of such other state and the laws of any other state through which the witness may be required to pass by ordinary course of travel will give to such witness protection from arrest and from the service of civil or criminal process, the judge shall issue a summons, with a copy of the certificate attached, directing the witness to attend and testify in the court where the prosecution is pending, or where a grand jury investigation has commenced or is about to commence at a time and place specified in the summons. At any such hearing, the certificate shall be prima facie evidence of all the facts stated therein. If such certificate recommends that the witness be taken into immediate custody and delivered to an officer of the requesting state to assure the attendance of the witness in such state, such judge may, in lieu of notification of the hearing, direct that such witness be forthwith brought before such judge for such hearing, and, being satisfied, at such hearing, of the desirability of such custody and delivery, of which desirability such certificate shall be prima facie proof, may, in lieu of issuing a subpoena or summons, order that such witness be forthwith taken into custody and delivered to an officer of the requesting state. If such witness, after being paid or tendered by an authorized person the same amount per mile as provided for state employees pursuant to section 5-141c for each mile by the ordinary traveled route to and from the court where the prosecution is pending and five dollars each day that such witness is required to travel and attend as a witness, fails, without good cause, to attend and testify as directed in the summons, the witness shall be punished in the manner provided for the punishment of any witness who disobeys a summons issued from a court of record in this state.

(c) **Witness from another state summoned to testify in this state.** If a person in any state, which by its laws has made provision for commanding persons within its borders to attend and testify in criminal prosecutions or in grand jury investigations commenced or about to commence in this state, is a material witness in a prosecution pending in a court of record in this state, or in a grand jury investigation which has commenced or is about to commence, a judge of such court may issue a certificate under the seal of the court, stating such facts and specifying the number of days the witness will be required. Such certificate may include a recommendation that the witness be taken into immediate custody and delivered to an officer of this state to assure the attendance of the witness in this state. Such certificate shall be presented to a judge of a court of record in the judicial district in which the witness is found. If the witness is summoned to attend and testify in this state, the witness shall be tendered the same amount per mile as provided for state employees pursuant to section 5-141c for each mile by the ordinary traveled route to and from the court where the prosecution is pending, and five dollars for each day that such witness is required to travel and attend as a witness. A witness who has appeared in accordance with the provisions of the summons shall not be required to remain within this state a longer period of time than the period mentioned in the certificate, unless otherwise ordered by the court. If such witness, after coming into this state, fails, without good cause, to attend and testify as directed in the summons, the witness shall be punished in the manner provided for the punishment of any witness who disobeys a summons issued from a court of record in this state.

(d) **Exemption from arrest and service of process.** If a person comes into this state in obedience to a summons directing him to attend and testify in this state, he shall not, while in this state pursuant to such summons, be subject to arrest or the service of process, civil or criminal, in connection with matters which arose before his entrance into this state under such summons. If a person passes through this state while going to another state in obedience to a summons to attend and testify in that state or while returning therefrom, he shall not, while so passing through this state, be subject to arrest or the service of process, civil or criminal, in connection with matters which arose before his entrance into this state under such summons.

(e) **Interpretation.** This section shall be so interpreted and construed as to effectuate its general purpose to make uniform the laws of the states which enact it.

(1949 Rev., S. 8732; P.A. 78-280, S. 2, 127; P.A. 01-186, S. 10, 11.)

History: P.A. 78-280 substituted "judicial district" for "county"; Sec. 54-22 transferred to Sec. 54-82i in 1981; P.A. 01-186 amended Subsec. (b) by replacing "sum of ten cents a mile" with provision re payment of same amount per mile as provided for state employees pursuant to Sec. 5-141c and making technical changes for purposes of gender neutrality and amended Subsec. (c) by replacing "sum of ten cents for each mile" with provision allowing witness the same amount per mile as provided for state employees pursuant to Sec. 5-141c and making technical changes for purposes of gender neutrality.

Annotations to former section 54-22:

Cited. 171 C. 47; 179 C. 102.

Sec. 54-82j. (Formerly Sec. 54-23). Detention of witnesses. Warrant. Upon the written complaint of any state's attorney addressed to the clerk of the superior court for the judicial district wherein such state's attorney resides, alleging (1) that a person named therein is or will be a material witness in a criminal proceeding then pending before or returnable to the superior court for such judicial district, and in which proceeding any person is or may be charged with an offense punishable by death or imprisonment for more than one year, and (2) that the state's attorney believes that such witness is likely to disappear from the state, secrete himself or otherwise avoid the service of subpoena upon him, or refuse or fail to appear and attend in and before such superior court as a witness, when desired, the clerk or any assistant clerk of the court shall issue a warrant addressed to any proper officer or indifferent person, for the arrest of the person named as a witness, and directing that such person be forthwith brought before any judge of the superior court for such judicial district, for examination. The person serving the warrant shall bring the person so arrested before the judge for examination as soon as is reasonably possible and hold him subject to the further orders of the judge. The person serving the warrant shall also notify the state's attorney of such arrest and of the time and place of such examination.

(1949 Rev., S. 8760; 1959, P.A. 28, S. 144; February, 1965, P.A. 574, S. 44; P.A. 73-116, S. 20; 73-667, S. 1, 2; P.A. 74-183, S. 135, 291; P.A. 76-436, S. 527, 681; P.A. 78-280, S. 1, 127; P.A. 80-313, S. 42.)

History; 1959 act substituted circuit court for trial justice or municipal court; 1965 act deleted obsolete provision for bringing arrested witness before common pleas court judge; P.A. 73-116 added references to judicial districts and substituted "Connecticut Correctional Institution, Somers" for "State Prison"; P.A. 73-667 changed effective date of P.A. 73-116 from October 1, 1973, to April 25, 1973; P.A. 74-183 replaced circuit court with court of common pleas, reflecting reorganization of judicial system, effective December 31, 1974; P.A. 76-436 deleted reference to proceedings pending before common pleas court, reflecting transfer of all trial jurisdiction to superior court, and applied provisions to cases involving imprisonment for more than one year, deleting specific reference to imprisonment in Somers facility, effective July 1, 1978; P.A. 78-280 deleted references to counties; P.A. 80-313 made minor changes in wording but made no substantive changes; Sec. 54-23 transferred to Sec. 54-82j in 1981.

Cited. 5 CA 347.

Sec. 54-82k. (Formerly Sec. 54-24). Recognizance; commitment; release; fees. (a) If, upon the examination provided for in section 54-82j, the judge is of the opinion that the interests of justice so require, he may order that a recognizance to the state be entered into by one or more persons of sufficient responsibility, conditioned that the person named as a witness shall appear before the superior court before which the proceeding is pending or to which it is returnable and abide the order of said superior court in the case.

(b) If such recognizance is not entered into, the judge shall order the person to be committed to a community correctional center until the next criminal term of the Superior Court to be held in the judicial district, or until he is legally discharged, and the judge shall issue a proper mittimus for his commitment in the case. Any person so committed to a community correctional center shall not, upon such commitment, be confined or associated in the center with persons confined therein upon conviction of or charged with any criminal offense, and the state's attorney for the judicial district wherein the person is so detained may release the bond and order the discharge of the person if, in his judgment, the requirements of justice so demand. When any person is confined in a community correctional center under the provisions of this section and section 54-82j, he shall receive, in addition to his legal fees as a witness, two dollars for each day that he is so confined, and the fees and expenses incurred under the provisions of this section and section 54-82j, shall be taxed by the court and paid as other expenses in criminal proceedings.

(c) Any person committed under the provisions of this section shall be released from confinement upon the giving of the required recognizance, which shall be taken as provided in case of imprisonment in a community correctional center upon criminal process.

(d) "State's attorney", as used in section 54-82j, and in this section, includes assistant state's attorneys.

(1949 Rev., S. 8761; 1959, P.A. 28, S. 145; 1963, P.A. 642, S. 64; P.A. 73-116, S. 21; 73-667, S. 1, 2; P.A. 74-183, S. 136, 291; P.A. 76-436, S. 528, 681; P.A. 78-280, S. 1, 127; P.A. 80-313, S. 43.)

History: 1959 act substituted circuit court for municipal court or trial justice, which were abolished; 1963 act deleted stipulation commitment be to jail in county where court has jurisdiction; P.A. 73-116 added references to judicial districts and substituted "community correctional center" for "jail" where appearing; P.A. 73-667 changed effective date of P.A. 73-116 from October 1, 1973, to April 25, 1973; P.A. 74-183 replaced circuit court with court of common pleas, reflecting reorganization of judicial system, effective December 31, 1974; P.A. 76-436 amended section to delete references to proceedings before court of common pleas, reflecting transfer of all trial jurisdiction to superior court, effective July 1, 1978; P.A. 78-280 deleted references to counties;

Sec. 54-82l. Rules re speedy trial to be adopted by judges of Superior Court effective July 1, 1983. In accordance with the provisions of section 51-14, the judges of the Superior Court shall make such rules as they deem necessary to provide a procedure to assure a speedy trial for any person charged with a criminal offense on or after July 1, 1983. Such rules shall provide that (1) in any case in which a plea of not guilty is entered, the trial of a defendant charged in an information or indictment with the commission of a criminal offense shall commence within eighteen months from the filing date of the information or indictment or from the date of the arrest, whichever is later, except that when such defendant is incarcerated in a correctional institution of this state pending such trial and is not subject to the provisions of section 54-82c, the trial of such defendant shall commence within twelve months from the filing date of the information or indictment or from the date of the arrest, whichever is later; and (2) if a defendant is not brought to trial within the time limit set forth in subdivision (1) of this section and a trial is not commenced within thirty days of a motion for a speedy trial made by the defendant at any time after such time limit has passed, the information or indictment shall be dismissed. Such rules shall include provisions to identify periods of delay caused by the action of the defendant, or the defendant's inability to stand trial, to be excluded in computing the time limits set forth in subdivision (1) of this section.

(P.A. 82-349, S. 1, 4; P.A. 83-1, S. 1, 3; P.A. 07-217, S. 193.)

History: P.A. 82-349, S. 1, effective July 1, 1983; P.A. 83-1 made provisions applicable to person charged with criminal offense on or after July 1, 1983, effective March 24, 1983; P.A. 07-217 made technical changes, effective July 12, 2007.

Cited. 198 C. 542.

Cited. 3 CA 349; 5 CA 347; 12 CA 364.

Sec. 54-82m. Rules re speedy trial to be adopted by judges of Superior Court effective July 1, 1985. In accordance with the provisions of section 51-14, the judges of the Superior Court shall make such rules as they deem necessary to provide a procedure to assure a speedy trial for any person charged with a criminal offense on or after July 1, 1985. Such rules shall provide that (1) in any case in which a plea of not guilty is entered, the trial of a defendant charged in an information or indictment with the commission of a criminal offense shall commence within twelve months from the filing date of the information or indictment or from the date of the arrest, whichever is later, except that when such defendant is incarcerated in a correctional institution of this state pending such trial and is not subject to the provisions of section 54-82c, the trial of such defendant shall commence within eight months from the filing date of the information or indictment or from the date of arrest, whichever is later; and (2) if a defendant is not brought to trial within the time limit set forth in subdivision (1) of this section and a trial is not commenced within thirty days of a motion for a speedy trial made by the defendant at any time after such time limit has passed, the information or indictment shall be dismissed. Such rules shall include provisions to identify periods of delay caused by the action of the defendant, or the defendant's inability to stand trial, to be excluded in computing the time limits set forth in subdivision (1) of this section.

(P.A. 82-349, S. 2, 4; P.A. 83-1, S. 2, 3; P.A. 07-217, S. 194.)

History: P.A. 82-349, S. 2, effective July 1, 1985; P.A. 83-1 made provisions applicable to person charged with criminal offense on or after July 1, 1985, effective March 24, 1983; P.A. 07-217 made technical changes, effective July 12, 2007.

Cited. 202 C. 443; 218 C. 85; 233 C. 813. Exception to 60-day limitation period for acts of God and misconduct on part of defendant is a necessary implication. 242 C. 389. Cited. 243 C. 115. Trial court properly determined that the time that co-defendant's attorney was unavailable was excludable time for computing the commencement of defendant's trial. 252 C. 714. Administrative incompetence, whether founded in negligence, recklessness or a serious dereliction of duty, does not constitute "exceptional circumstances", and therefore "good cause", for the failure to bring defendant to trial before the 30-day period has expired. 265 C. 437.

Cited. 14 CA 244; 33 CA 184; judgment reversed, see 232 C. 707; 37 CA 384; 38 CA 868. Statutory right to speedy trial cited. 40 CA 483. Cited. Id., 643; Id., 757; 42 CA 144; 43 CA 488. Right to protection of statute waived by withdrawing motion and not filing for dismissal. 47 CA 91. Cited. 54 CA 361. Section codifies defendant's constitutional right to speedy trial and confers on Superior Court judges authority to make such rules as they deem necessary to establish procedure for implementing that right. 66 CA 357. Defendant not deprived of right to speedy trial when trial delay was occasioned by continuances requested by defendant's counsel, rather than by defendant, and defendant did not object. 78 CA 659.

Secs. 54-82n to 54-82p. Reserved for future use.

Sec. 54-82q. Temporary restraining order prohibiting harassment of witness. (a) Upon application of a prosecutorial official, a court may issue a temporary restraining order prohibiting the harassment of a witness in a criminal case if the court finds, from specific facts shown by affidavit or verified complaint, that there are reasonable grounds to believe that harassment of an identified witness in a criminal case exists or that such order is necessary to prevent and restrain the commission of an offense under section 53a-151 or 53a-151a.

(b) A temporary restraining order may be issued under this section without written or oral notice to the adverse party or such party's attorney if the court finds, upon written certification of facts by the prosecutorial official, that such notice should not be required and that there is a reasonable probability that the state will prevail on the merits. A temporary restraining order shall set forth the reasons for the issuance of such order, be specific in its terms and describe in reasonable detail, and not by reference to the complaint or other document, the act or acts being restrained.

(c) A temporary restraining order issued without notice under this section shall be endorsed with the date and hour of issuance and be filed forthwith in the office of the clerk of the court that issued the order.

(d) A temporary restraining order issued under this section shall expire at such time as the court directs, not to exceed ten days from issuance. The court, for good cause shown before expiration of the order, may extend the expiration date of the order for not more than ten days or for a longer period if agreed to by the adverse party. If the prosecutorial official files an application for a protective order pursuant to section 54-82r prior to the expiration date of the temporary restraining order, the temporary restraining order shall remain in effect until the court makes a decision on the issuance of such protective order.

(e) If, on two days' notice to the prosecutorial official or on such shorter notice as the court may prescribe, the adverse party appears and moves to dissolve or modify the temporary restraining order, the court shall proceed to hear and determine such motion expeditiously.

(f) When a temporary restraining order is issued without notice, an application for a protective order filed pursuant to section 54-82r shall be privileged in assignment for hearing and shall take precedence over all other matters except matters of the same character, and, if the prosecutorial official does not proceed with such application at such hearing, the temporary restraining order shall be dissolved.

(P.A. 99-240, S. 2.)

See Sec. 51-5c re automated registry of protective orders.

Sec. 54-82r. Protective order prohibiting harassment of witness. (a) Upon application of a prosecutorial official, a court may issue a protective order prohibiting the harassment of a witness in a criminal case if the court, after a hearing at which hearsay evidence shall be admissible, finds by a preponderance of the evidence that harassment of an identified witness in a criminal case exists or that such order is necessary to prevent and restrain the commission of a violation of section 53a-151 or 53a-151a. Any adverse party named in the complaint has the right to present evidence and cross-examine witnesses at such hearing. Such order shall be an order of the court, and the clerk of the court shall cause a certified copy of such order to be sent to the witness, and a copy of such order, or the information contained in such order, to be sent by facsimile or other means within forty-eight hours of its issuance to the appropriate law enforcement agency.

(b) A protective order shall set forth the reasons for the issuance of such order, be specific in terms and describe in reasonable detail, and not by reference to the complaint or other document, the act or acts being restrained. A protective order issued under this section may include provisions necessary to protect the witness from threats, harassment, injury or intimidation by the adverse party including, but not limited to, enjoining the adverse party from (1) imposing any restraint upon the person or liberty of the witness, (2) threatening, harassing, assaulting, molesting or sexually assaulting the witness, or (3) entering the dwelling of the witness. Such order shall contain the following language: "In accordance with section 53a-223 of the Connecticut general statutes, any violation of this order constitutes criminal violation of a protective order which is punishable by a term of imprisonment of not more than ten years, a fine of not more than ten thousand dollars, or both. Additionally, in accordance with section 53a-107 of the Connecticut general statutes, entering or remaining in a building or any other premises in violation of this order constitutes criminal trespass in the first degree which is punishable by a term of imprisonment of not more than one year, a fine of not more than two thousand dollars, or both.". If the adverse party is the defendant in the criminal case, such order shall be made a condition of the bail or release of the defendant and shall also contain the following language: "Violation of this order also violates a condition of your bail or release and may result in raising the amount of bail or revoking release.".

(c) The protective order shall remain in effect for the duration of the criminal case except as otherwise ordered by the court.

(P.A. 99-240, S. 3; P.A. 02-132, S. 58; P.A. 05-288, S. 186; P.A. 14-217, S. 127.)

History: P.A. 02-132 amended Subsec. (a) by replacing provisions re sending certified copy of order to law enforcement agency with provisions re sending copy of or information contained in order to law enforcement agency by facsimile or other means, effective January 1, 2003; P.A. 05-288 amended Subsec. (b) by making technical changes and revising required language in order re penalty for criminal violation of a protective order, effective July 13, 2005; P.A. 14-217 amended Subsec. (b) to replace "five years" and "five thousand" with "ten years" and "ten thousand", respectively, in required order language re penalty for criminal violation of a protective order and make technical changes, effective January 1, 2015.

See Sec. 51-5c re automated registry of protective orders.

Sec. 54-82s. The Leroy Brown, Jr. and Karen Clarke Witness Protection Program.

The program of providing protective services to witnesses under sections 54-82t and 54-82u shall be known as the "The Leroy Brown, Jr. and Karen Clarke Witness Protection Program".

(P.A. 99-247, S. 6.)

Sec. 54-82t. Protective services for witness at risk of harm.

(a) For the purposes of this section and section 54-82u:

(1) "Witness" means any person who is summoned, or who may be summoned, to give testimony in a criminal proceeding, and includes a member of the immediate family of such person.

(2) "Witness at risk of harm" means a witness who, as a result of cooperating in an investigation or prosecution of a serious felony offense, has been, or is reasonably likely to be, intimidated, harassed, threatened, retaliated against or subjected to physical violence.

(3) "Serious felony offense" means any felony that involves the use, attempted use or threatened use of physical force against another person or results in the serious physical injury or death of another person.

(b) In any investigation or prosecution of a serious felony offense, the prosecutorial official shall review all witnesses to the offense and may identify any witness as a witness at risk of harm. Upon such identification, the prosecutorial official shall then determine whether a witness at risk of harm is critical to a criminal investigation or prosecution. If the witness at risk of harm is determined to be critical to such investigation or prosecution, the prosecutorial official may (1) certify that the witness receive protective services, or (2) if the prosecutorial official finds a compelling need to temporarily relocate the witness, certify that the witness receive protective services including temporary relocation services. In determining whether a witness should receive protective services, the prosecutorial official shall give special consideration to a witness who is a child, elderly or handicapped or otherwise more at risk of being intimidated, harassed, threatened, retaliated against or subjected to physical violence or who is a witness in a case involving organized crime, gang activities or drug trafficking or involving a high degree of risk to the witness.

(c) When a witness is certified as provided in subsection (b) of this section, the Chief State's Attorney shall provide appropriate protective services to such witness. The Chief State's Attorney shall coordinate the efforts of state and local agencies to provide protective services to a witness.

(d) Protective services provided to such witness may include, but are not limited to:

(1) Armed protection, escort, marked or unmarked surveillance or periodic visits or contact by law enforcement officials prior, during or subsequent to the official proceeding;

(2) Temporary physical relocation to an alternate residence;

(3) Housing expenses;

(4) Transportation or storage of personal possessions;

(5) Basic living expenses including, but not limited to, food, transportation, utility costs and health care; or

(6) Other services as needed and approved by the Chief State's Attorney.

(e) Protective services may be provided for the duration of the criminal case or until the risk giving rise to certification has diminished, whichever occurs first.

(f) In addition to the protective services provided pursuant to subsection (d) of this section, the Chief State's Attorney shall provide such witness with (1) information on the responsibilities and risks of being a witness, and (2) the names and telephone numbers of persons to contact if such witness has questions or concerns for such witness's safety, including at least one telephone number that may be called twenty-four hours a day.

(g) If a witness declines to receive protective services under this section, the Chief State's Attorney shall request the witness to make such declination in writing. Such declination shall set forth (1) the type of protective services offered, (2) that the offer of protective services has been explained in detail to the witness, and (3) a telephone number that the witness may call twenty-four hours a day if the witness has concerns for the witness's safety or reconsiders the witness's decision to decline protective services.

(h) If the parent or parents or guardian of a child who is certified as a witness at risk of harm critical to a criminal investigation or prosecution as provided in subsection (b) of this section, declines the provision of protective services under this section, the Office of the Chief State's Attorney shall be notified within twenty-four hours after such declination. Upon receipt of such notice, the Chief State's Attorney shall make reasonable efforts to confer with a victim advocate providing services for the Office of Victim Services and shall, not later than three days after such declination, determine if the matter should be referred to the Department of Children and Families for investigation as to whether such child is neglected, as defined in section 46b-120, and whether the department should provide protective services or take other action pursuant to chapter 319a or 815t with respect to such child.

(i) The costs of providing protective services to witnesses under this section shall be shared by the state and local agencies providing such services pursuant to the witness protection policy established by the Office of the Chief State's Attorney.

(j) Any record of the Division of Criminal Justice or other governmental agency that, in the reasonable judgment of the Chief State's Attorney or a state's attorney, would disclose or would reasonably result in the disclosure of the identity or location of any person receiving or considered for the receipt of protective services under this section or of law enforcement techniques not otherwise known to the general public that are used in protecting witnesses, shall be confidential and not subject to disclosure under the Freedom of Information Act, as defined in section 1-200.

(k) The Division of Criminal Justice may utilize the resources of other state agencies in order to provide protective services to witnesses under this section. All offices of the state's attorneys and other agencies requesting assistance under this section shall comply with the provisions of the witness protection policy established by the Office of the Chief State's Attorney.

(l) The Chief State's Attorney, pursuant to his authority under section 51-279, shall implement the provisions of this section and section 54-82u. The Chief State's Attorney may adopt regulations in accordance with chapter 54 to implement the provisions of this section and section 54-82u.

(m) Not later than November 15, 2001, and annually thereafter, the Chief State's Attorney shall submit a report to the General Assembly on the fiscal and operational status of the program to provide protective services to witnesses under this section.

(P.A. 99-240, S. 6.)

(Return to Chapter

Table of Contents)

(Return to

List of Chapters)

(Return to

List of Titles)

Sec. 54-82u. Witness protection agreement. (a) In order to receive protective services under section 54-82t, the witness shall enter into a written agreement with the Chief State's Attorney. The witness protection agreement shall be in writing and shall specify the responsibilities of the witness that establish the conditions for the Chief State's Attorney to provide protective services. The witness shall agree to all of the following:

(1) To testify in and provide information to all appropriate law enforcement officials concerning all appropriate proceedings;

(2) To refrain from committing any crime;

(3) To take all necessary steps to avoid detection by other persons of the facts concerning the protective services provided to the witness under section 54-82t;

(4) To comply with legal obligations and civil judgments against the witness;

(5) To cooperate with all reasonable requests of officers and employees of the state or any municipality who are providing protective services under section 54-82t;

(6) To designate another person to act as agent for service of process;

(7) To make a sworn statement of all outstanding legal obligations, including obligations concerning child custody and visitation;

(8) To disclose if the witness is on probation or parole and, if so, any conditions of probation or parole;

(9) To inform regularly the appropriate official of the witness's activities and current address; and

(10) To comply with any other lawful and appropriate conditions as determined by the Office of the Chief State's Attorney.

(b) The Chief State's Attorney shall not be liable for any condition in the witness protection agreement that cannot reasonably be met due to a witness committing a crime during participation in the program.

(P.A. 99-240, S. 7.)

(Return to Chapter

Table of Contents)

(Return to

List of Chapters)

(Return to

List of Titles)

Sec. 54-83. Testimony in case where crime is punishable by death or life imprisonment without possibility of release. No person may be convicted of any crime punishable by death or life imprisonment without the possibility of release without the testimony of at least two witnesses, or that which is equivalent thereto.

(1949 Rev., S. 8799; P.A. 80-313, S. 47; P.A. 12-5, S. 29.)

History: P.A. 80-313 substituted "may" for "shall"; P.A. 12-5 added provision re crime punishable by life imprisonment without possibility of release, effective April 25, 2012.

Not necessary that there should be two witnesses to every material fact; true rule stated. 49 C. 385; 77 C. 274; 78 C. 18; 93 C. 246; 97 C. 465; 103 C. 467; 106 C. 705; 122 C. 533; 126 C. 57. Whether requirement is met is for the jury to say. 81 C. 27; 90 C. 126; 93 C. 246; 97 C. 465; 103 C. 467. Charge embodying rule approved. 97 C. 465. Cited. 123 C. 673. If testimony of one or more witnesses tends to prove that a murder has been committed, testimony of only one other witness implicating defendant is sufficient to satisfy statute. 139 C. 475. The proof of all the essential elements of a capital crime charged shall not depend upon the testimony of one witness. 142 C. 113. Cited. 147 C. 95. One witness may testify to some of the essential facts and another to the rest of the essential facts and the statute may be satisfied. Id., 194. Adoption of Wigmore definition of "corpus delicti"; previous cases defining "corpus delicti" overruled. 152 C. 15. Cited. 182 C. 511; 229 C. 125; 230 C. 183; 233 C. 813; 235 C. 206. Confession and independent circumstantial evidence satisfied the two witness rule. 251 C. 285. Death penalty unconstitutional under Art. I, Secs. 8 and 9 of Connecticut Constitution. 318 C. 1.

Evidentiary burden imposed by section is not constitutionally compelled. 121 CA 699.

(Return to Chapter

Table of Contents)

(Return to

List of Chapters)

(Return to

List of Titles)

Sec. 54-84. Testimony or silence of accused. (a) Any person on trial for crime shall be a competent witness, and at his or her option may testify or refuse to testify upon such trial. The neglect or refusal of an accused party to testify shall not be commented upon by the court or prosecuting official, except as provided in subsection (b) of this section.

(b) Unless the accused requests otherwise, the court shall instruct the jury that they may draw no unfavorable inferences from the accused's failure to testify. In cases tried to the court, no unfavorable inferences shall be drawn by the court from the accused's silence.

(1949 Rev., S. 8800; 1971, P.A. 237; 871, S. 122; P.A. 77-360; P.A. 80-313, S. 44.)

History: 1971 acts applied provisions equally with respect to either spouse where previously applicable only to wives receiving personal violence from husbands or to women charged with violation of specified sections; P.A. 77-360 prohibited comment upon neglect or refusal to testify "by the court or prosecuting official, except as provided in subsection (b) of this section" rather than comments "to the court or jury" and added Subsec. (b); P.A. 80-313 deleted provisions re spouse's competency as witness and option to testify or not except in cases involving violence against spouse or specified violations where testimony may be compelled.

Communication between husband and wife not privileged to extent of preventing one who overhears them from testifying thereto. 47 C. 540. Voluntary statements of accused before coroner or grand jury in no sense compulsory and are admissible in evidence. 56 C. 399. Attacking credit of accused where he does testify. 67 C. 290; 76 C. 94; 87 C. 22; 88 C. 150; 89 C. 417. Certain comments by state's attorney not objectionable. 73 C. 100; 96 C. 291. Commenting on refusal not always ground for new trial; accused must at once object. 79 C. 477. Effect of testimony by one of two jointly indicted. 82 C. 59. Remark by state's attorney in arguing question of evidence while putting in his own case, held not within rule. 83 C. 455. In absence of request, court need not charge as to rule. 90 C. 132. Proper course for accused to take to insure his rights under rule. 96 C. 291. Charge under rule. 108 C. 463, but see 127 C. 592. Does not prevent inference being drawn from failure to testify; but such failure must not be commented upon. 108 C. 463. Cited. 109 C. 134; Id., 497. For violence received from husband before marriage, wife may refuse to testify against him. 113 C. 291. Court may comment to jury on failure of accused to testify. 119 C. 35; 127 C. 591. Reference by state's attorney to fact defendant's attorney offered no testimony to refute state's witnesses, not a violation of section. 130 C. 549. Court may take into consideration failure of an accused to testify only if state has made out a prima facie case against him. 139 C. 124. Does not preclude cross-examination of the accused as to inconsistent statements made to spouse. 145 C. 60. It is violation of fifth and fourteenth amendments for court to comment on failure of defendant in a criminal trial to testify; interpretation before *Griffin v. California*, 380 U.S. 609. 154 C. 41. Cited. 171 C. 12; Id., 586. Section gives witness' spouse option of testifying against accused spouse. 172 C. 37. Cited. Id., 74; 179 C. 327; 197 C. 369; 201 C. 462; 206 C. 300; Id., 621; 213 C. 422; 222 C. 469; 223 C. 52; 233 C. 813. Prosecutorial comments on defendant's exercise of right not to testify discussed. 243 C. 324. State's attorney's comment in closing argument that "I gave you everything I had" not seen as comment on defendant's failure to testify. 244 C. 547.

Cited. 7 CA 292; 9 CA 169; judgment reversed, see 205 C. 370; 13 CA 386; 16 CA 264; 22 CA 321; 24 CA 642; 26 CA 674; 27 CA 601; Id., 643; 28 CA 369. Use of term "unfair" in lieu of term "unfavorable" inference discussed. 36 CA 41. Cited. 39 CA 96. Legislature could not have intended that instructions to venire panel would comply with dictates of section to give instructions to jury. 60 CA 301. Although the recorded out-of-court statement of defendant was not equivalent of in-court testimony where defendant puts his credibility in issue, prosecutor's admonition to jury to consider defendant's interest in the outcome of the case when evaluating defendant's statement was not a forbidden indirect comment on defendant's decision not to testify. 78 CA 535. Defendant's right to a no adverse inference instruction was violated by court's postcharge, supplemental instruction that materially and substantially misstated the nature of defendant's privilege not to testify. 83 CA 811. Prosecutor's statement that sexual assault cases are often decided on credibility of victim or defendant was not an improper comment on defendant's failure to testify. 86 CA 641. Prosecutor's comments made during rebuttal argument regarding defendant's failure to testify were a clear violation of section. 156 CA 138.

Where state's case rested entirely on defendant's testimony, held it was error not to inform defendant of his privilege against self-incrimination. 24 CS 353. Defendant does not have option to refuse to testify in civil proceeding for homicide by automobile on ground that he may be subject to criminal prosecution for some facts. 28 CS 59. Cited. 33 CS 505; Id., 700.

Defendant's failure to bring timely objection re comments on his refusal to testify results in waiver of right. 2 Conn. Cir. Ct. 68. Charge to jury that, if they concluded there was such a strong probability of defendant's guilt that denial or explanation by him was reasonably called for, then they would be entitled to consider his failure to testify, held in violation of due process and constituted reversible error. 3 Conn. Cir. Ct. 463, 464. Any comment by presiding judge or counsel forbidden; court's refusal to charge jury that no inference of guilt could be drawn or sinister meaning attached to defendant's failure to testify, proper. 4 Conn. Cir. Ct. 520, 522, 523. Cited. 5 Conn. Cir. Ct. 181. Defendants who took stand for limited purpose of testifying new counsel represented them entitled to assistance of counsel when questioning of them broadened out to other matters. Id., 242.

Subsec. (b):

Even though defense counsel did not object to the court's failure to give the "no unfavorable inference" instruction, the judgment was set. 182 C. 330. Cited. Id., 403. Failure to follow mandate of statute is reversible error despite failure to make a timely request or objection. Id., 580. Cited. 183 C. 444; 188 C. 681; 190 C. 1. Use of "unreasonable" instead of "unfavorable" in jury instruction constituted harmful error. 194 C. 594. Cited. 195 C. 421; Id., 444; 197 C. 574; Id., 588; 198 C. 77; 199 C. 322; 201 C. 659; 209 C. 636; 210 C. 751; 227 C. 910. Harmless error analysis applied to erroneous instruction under statute; judgment of Appellate Court in 31 CA 688 reversed. 229 C. 516. In context of entire jury charge re defendant's decision not to testify, reference to defendant's "failure to testify" was neither negative in substance nor improper; phrase "unless the defendant requests otherwise" does not obligate court to use defendant's requested language. 255 C. 581. When the jury charge contains no language that resembles the mandated instruction, it cannot be assumed that the jurors had sufficient knowledge of the law to be able to glean from the balance of instructions that they should draw no adverse inference from defendant's failure to testify. 322 C. 796.

Cited. 5 CA 79; 6 CA 124; 7 CA 477; 10 CA 302; 11 CA 425; 15 CA 342; Id., 749; 17 CA 490; 19 CA 48; Id., 618; 20 CA 721; 21 CA 162; 23 CA 28; Id., 151; 28 CA 290; 31 CA 688; judgment reversed, see 229 C. 516. Total omission of "no adverse interference" instruction is plain error that is not subject to harmless error analysis. 33 CA 126. Cited. 34 CA 153. Trial court's charge did not comply with requirements of statute because of improper reference to loss of defendant's presumption of innocence. Id., 250. Cited. 37 CA 672. Court will not infer a waiver of the mandatory instruction from defendant's silence.

59 CA 426. Where counsel had requested omission of instruction under section in the jury charge, it was not error for court to fail to inquire expressly of defendant if he also wanted the court to omit the instruction. 64 CA 340. Since trial court's instruction to jury not to draw any unfavorable inference from the fact that defendant did not testify given in the context of instructions concerning how jury was to find facts in general did not clearly inform jury that it could not use defendant's silence as a factor in its verdict and did not satisfy the statutory requirement that court convey a specific instruction to jury that no unfavorable inference could be drawn from the fact that defendant did not testify, and state failed to establish that the deficient instruction was clarified or remedied by the court and failed to demonstrate harmlessness of the constitutional violation beyond a reasonable doubt, judgment was reversed and the case remanded for new trial. 97 CA 266. Where lower court had inquired about specific instruction re failure to testify and court and defense counsel discussed instruction, such discussion constituted a request for a no unfavorable inference instruction; reiterated previous holding that provisions are not required to be waived personally by defendant but can be waived by defense counsel. 109 CA 679.

Cited. 36 CS 583.

(Return to Chapter Table of Contents)

(Return to List of Chapters)

(Return to List of Titles)

Sec. 54-84a. Testimony against spouse. (a) Except as provided in subsection (b) of this section, in any criminal proceeding, a person may elect or refuse to testify against his or her then lawful spouse.

(b) The testimony of a spouse may be compelled, in the same manner as for any other witness, in a criminal proceeding against the other spouse for (1) joint participation with the spouse in criminal conduct, (2) bodily injury, sexual assault or other violence attempted, committed or threatened upon the spouse, or (3) bodily injury, sexual assault, risk of injury pursuant to section 53-21, or other violence attempted, committed or threatened upon the minor child of either spouse, or any minor child in the care or custody of either spouse.

(P.A. 80-313, S. 45; P.A. 11-152, S. 14.)

History: (Revisor's note: In 1993, obsolete reference to repealed Sec. 53-25 was deleted editorially by the Revisors); P.A. 11-152 replaced former provisions with Subsec. (a) authorizing person to elect or refuse to testify against then lawful spouse in any criminal proceeding and Subsec. (b) re when testimony of spouse may be compelled.

Cited. 199 C. 631; 211 C. 555. Section codifies adverse spousal testimony privilege, as distinguished from marital communications privilege, and the privilege belongs to the witness spouse and is meant to protect against impact of the testimony on the marriage. 267 C. 710.

(Return to Chapter

Table of Contents)

(Return to

List of Chapters)

(Return to

List of Titles)

Sec. 54-84b. Testimony of spouse re confidential communications. (a) For the purposes of this section, "confidential communication" means any oral or written communication made between spouses during a marriage that is intended to be confidential and is induced by the affection, confidence, loyalty and integrity of the marital relationship.

(b) Except as provided in subsection (c) of this section, in any criminal proceeding, a spouse shall not be (1) required to testify to a confidential communication made by one spouse to the other during the marriage, or (2) allowed to testify to a confidential communication made by one spouse to the other during the marriage, over the objection of the other spouse.

(c) The testimony of a spouse regarding a confidential communication may be compelled, in the same manner as for any other witness, in a criminal proceeding against the other spouse for (1) joint participation with the spouse in what was, at the time the communication was made, criminal conduct or conspiracy to commit a crime, (2) bodily injury, sexual assault or other violence attempted, committed or threatened upon the spouse, or (3) bodily injury, sexual assault, risk of injury pursuant to section 53-21, or other violence attempted, committed or threatened upon the minor child of either spouse, or any minor child in the care or custody of either spouse.

(P.A. 11-152, S. 15.)

Language in Subsec. (a) re "induced by the affection, confidence, loyalty and integrity of the marital relationship" adds a separate element to, and effectively narrows the scope of, the common-law marital communications privilege; statements must be brought about or caused by the affection, confidence, loyalty and integrity of the marital relationship, and therefore, statements made by defendant for the purpose of furthering extramarital affair and attempting to murder her husband did not fall within language of Subsec. (a). 320 C. 123.

"Induced by affection" requirement limits privilege to subset of those confidential statements made between spouses in a valid marriage which are induced by the affection, confidence, loyalty and integrity of the marital relationship. 153 CA 419; judgment affirmed, see 320 C. 123.

(Return to Chapter

Table of Contents)

(Return to

List of Chapters)

(Return to

List of Titles)

Sec. 54-85. Witness to testify with regard to bribery at elections. A person summoned as a witness to testify regarding bribery at any election shall not be excused from testifying because his evidence may tend to disgrace or criminate him, nor shall he thereafter be prosecuted for anything connected with the transaction about which he so testifies, nor shall the evidence he may so give be used against him in any proceeding.

(1949 Rev., S. 8801; P.A. 80-313, S. 46.)

History: P.A. 80-313 restated provisions but made no substantive changes.

(Return to Chapter Table of Contents)

(Return to List of Chapters)

(Return to List of Titles)

Sec. 54-85a. Sequestering of witnesses in criminal prosecution. In any criminal prosecution, the court, upon motion of the state or the defendant, shall cause any witness to be sequestered during the hearing on any issue or motion or any part of the trial of such prosecution in which he is not testifying.

(1967, P.A. 498.)

Sequestration order merely prohibits sequestered witness from being present in courtroom when he is not testifying. 169 C. 322. Cited. Id., 428; 185 C. 211; 187 C. 6; 199 C. 62; 211 C. 672; 230 C. 591; 235 C. 711; 236 C. 112; 237 C. 284.

Cited. 11 CA 80; 13 CA 687; 16 CA 172; 20 CA 342; 21 CA 474; 32 CA 448; 33 CA 339; judgment reversed in part, see 232 C. 431; judgment reversed on issues of sufficiency of evidence and jury misconduct, see 235 C. 502; 34 CA 276; 38 CA 371. Scope of suppression order was not limited only to the suppression hearing and defendant did not establish that he had been prejudiced by police officers' discussion of their testimony with each other in the time between the hearing and the trial. 74 CA 802.

(Return to Chapter Table of Contents)

(Return to List of Chapters)

(Return to List of Titles)

Sec. 54-85b. Employment protection for witnesses and victims of crime. Penalty. Action for damages and reinstatement. (a) An employer shall not deprive an employee of employment, penalize or threaten or otherwise coerce an employee with respect to employment, because (1) the employee obeys a legal subpoena to appear before any court of this state as a witness in any criminal proceeding, (2) the employee attends a court proceeding or participates in a police investigation related to a criminal case in which the employee is a crime victim, or attends or participates in a court proceeding related to a civil case in which the employee is a victim of family violence, as defined in section 46b-38a, (3) a restraining order has been issued on the employee's behalf pursuant to section 46b-15, (4) a protective order has been issued on the employee's behalf by a court of this state or by a court of another state, provided if issued by a court of another state, the protective order shall be registered in this state pursuant to section 46b-15a, or (5) the employee is a victim of family violence, as defined in section 46b-38a. For the purposes of this section, "crime victim" means an employee who suffers direct or threatened physical, emotional or financial harm as a result of a crime or an employee who is an immediate family member or guardian of (A) a person who suffers such harm and is a minor, physically disabled, as defined in section 46a-51, or incompetent, or (B) a homicide victim.

(b) Any employer who violates subdivision (1) of subsection (a) of this section shall be guilty of criminal contempt and shall be fined not more than five hundred dollars or imprisoned not more than thirty days, or both.

(c) If an employer discharges, penalizes or threatens or otherwise coerces an employee in violation of subsection (a) of this section, the employee, not later than one hundred eighty days from the occurrence of such action, may bring a civil action for damages and for an order requiring the employee's reinstatement or otherwise rescinding such action. If the employee prevails, the employee shall be allowed a reasonable attorney's fee to be fixed by the court.

(P.A. 81-186; P.A. 02-136, S. 1; P.A. 10-144, S. 14.)

History: P.A. 02-136 amended Subsec. (a) by designating existing language as Subdiv. (1) and adding new Subdivs. (2) to (4) prohibiting employers from firing, penalizing or threatening employees who are crime victims because of their attendance at court proceedings, participation in police investigations or securement of a restraining or protective order, and made technical changes by adding reference to Subsec. (c) and made technical changes in Subsec. (c); P.A. 10-144 amended Subsec. (a) to make technical changes, including re attendance or participation in cases, re cases related to or illness and re employee is victim of family violence in Subdiv. (2) and to add Subdiv. (5) re employee who is victim of family violence and amended Subsec. (c) to substitute "one hundred eighty days" for "ninety days" re time limitation to bring action.

(Return to Chapter Table of Contents)

(Return to List of Chapters)

(Return to List of Titles)

Sec. 54-85c. Representative of homicide victim entitled to be present at trial of defendant. Exclusion. Hearing. (a) For the purposes of this section, "representative of a homicide victim" means the legal representative of a victim of a homicide or a member of such victim's immediate family selected by such family. In the event of a dispute, the court in its discretion may designate such representative.

(b) A representative of a homicide victim shall be entitled to be present at the trial or any proceeding concerning the prosecution of the defendant for the homicide, except that a judge may remove such representative from the trial or proceeding or any portion thereof for the same causes and in the same manner as the rules of court or provisions of the general statutes provide for the exclusion or removal of the defendant. No representative of a homicide victim may be excluded from the proceedings under this section without a hearing.

(c) The failure of a representative of a homicide victim to exercise any right granted by the provisions of this section shall not be cause or ground for an appeal of a conviction by a defendant or for any court to set aside, reverse or remand a criminal conviction.

(P.A. 88-278, S. 1.)

(Return to Chapter Table of Contents)

(Return to List of Chapters)

(Return to List of Titles)

Sec. 54-85d. Employer not to discharge employee who attends court as family member of or person designated by homicide victim. An employer shall not deprive an employee of employment, or threaten or otherwise coerce such employee with respect thereto, because the employee, as a parent, spouse, child or sibling of a victim of homicide, or as a person designated by the victim in accordance with section 1-56r, attends court proceedings with respect to the criminal case of the person or persons charged with committing the crime that resulted in the death of the victim.

(P.A. 99-247, S. 2; P.A. 02-105, S. 12.)

History: P.A. 02-105 added a person designated by a victim pursuant to Sec. 1-56r to employees protected in attending court proceedings.

(Return to Chapter Table of Contents)

(Return to List of Chapters)

(Return to List of Titles)

Sec. 54-85e. Photograph of deceased victim shown to jury during opening and closing arguments. A photograph not to exceed eight inches by ten inches solely of a deceased victim prior to the date of the offense for which the defendant is being tried, that is a fair and accurate representation of the victim and is not of itself inflammatory in nature, may be shown to the jury during the opening and closing arguments by the prosecutor.

(P.A. 00-200, S. 4.)

(Return to Chapter Table of Contents)

(Return to List of Chapters)

(Return to List of Titles)

Sec. 54-85f. Victim of violent crime or representative of deceased victim permitted to attend court proceedings. Any victim of a violent crime or the legal representative or member of the immediate family of a victim who is deceased shall be permitted to attend all court proceedings that are part of the court record.

(P.A. 00-200, S. 7.)

(Return to Chapter Table of Contents)

(Return to List of Chapters)

(Return to List of Titles)

Sec. 54-85g. Advisement to crime victims re constitutional rights by judge at arraignment. In order to ensure that any victim coming before the court has been advised of the victim's constitutional rights, any judge of the Superior Court shall, at the daily commencement of the regular criminal docket at which accused persons are arraigned, issue the following advisement: "If you are a victim of a crime with a case pending before this court, you are advised that you have the right: (1) To be treated fairly and with respect throughout the criminal justice process; (2) to timely disposition of the case; (3) to be protected from the accused; (4) to be notified of and attend court proceedings; (5) to speak with the prosecutor; (6) to object or support any plea agreement; (7) to make a statement to the court before the court accepts a plea agreement and at sentencing; (8) to restitution; and (9) to information about the arrest, conviction, sentence, imprisonment and release of the accused".

(P.A. 01-35.)

(Return to Chapter Table of Contents)

(Return to List of Chapters)

(Return to List of Titles)

Sec. 54-86. Depositions. (a) In any case involving an offense for which the punishment may be imprisonment for more than one year, the Superior Court or a judge thereof may, upon the application of the accused, order that the deposition of a witness shall be taken before a commissioner or magistrate, to be designated by the court or judge, if it appears that his testimony will be required at trial and that, by reason of bodily infirmity or residence out of this state, he will be unable to testify at trial.

(b) Reasonable notice of the time when and place where the examination will be had and of the interrogatories to be propounded shall be given to the state's attorney or assistant state's attorney for the judicial district in which the prosecution is pending; and such attorney may, within such time as the court or judge limits, file with the clerk of the court additional interrogatories to be propounded to the witness to be examined.

(c) Depositions so taken, opened by and filed with the clerk within such time as the court or judge directs, may be used at trial.

(1949 Rev., S. 8802; 1963, P.A. 642, S. 71; P.A. 73-116, S. 27; 73-667, S. 1, 2; P.A. 74-48; P.A. 75-567, S. 34, 80; P.A. 76-436, S. 476, 681; P.A. 78-280, S. 1, 127; P.A. 80-313, S. 34.)

History: 1963 act updated statute, deleting provisions for court of common pleas and prosecuting attorney; P.A. 73-116 added reference to judicial districts; P.A. 73-667 changed effective date of P.A. 73-667 from October 1, 1973, to December 31, 1973; P.A. 74-48 amended section to include depositions in circuit court cases involving Class D felonies, adding reference to prosecuting attorneys and circuits; P.A. 75-567 deleted changes enacted by P.A. 74-48, except for reference to prosecuting attorneys, reflecting reorganization of judicial system in P.A. 74-183; P.A. 76-436 applied provisions to cases where punishment may be imprisonment for more than one year and substituted assistant state's attorneys for prosecuting attorneys, effective July 1, 1978; P.A. 78-280 deleted reference to counties; P.A. 80-313 divided section into Subsecs. and restated provisions.

State cannot take deposition. 90 C. 381. Comment of state's attorney on accused's use of depositions held improper to extent of requiring new trial. 96 C. 165. Proper course of accused to protect his rights under statute. Id., 166, 168. Cited. 229 C. 716.

Cited. 19 CA 594; 29 CA 642; 36 CA 250; 42 CA 186; judgment reversed, see 241 C. 823.

(Return to Chapter Table of Contents)

(Return to List of Chapters)

(Return to List of Titles)

Sec. 54-86a. Certain evidence to be made available to defendant. (a) Upon motion of a defendant at any time after the filing of the indictment or information, and upon a showing that the items sought may be material to the preparation of his defense and that the request is reasonable, the court shall order the attorney for the state to permit the defendant to inspect and copy or photograph any relevant (1) written or recorded statements, admissions or confessions made by the defendant; (2) books, papers, documents or tangible objects obtained from or belonging to the defendant or obtained from others by seizure or process; (3) copies of records of any physical or mental examinations of the defendant; and (4) records of prior convictions of the defendant, or copies thereof, within the possession, custody or control of the state, the existence of which is known to the attorney for the state or to the defendant.

(b) An order of the court granting relief under subsection (a) of this section shall specify the time, place and manner of making the discovery and inspection permitted and may prescribe such terms and conditions as are just.

(c) A motion under subsection (a) of this section may be made only in a criminal case and shall include all relief sought under subsection (a) of this section. A subsequent motion may be made only upon a showing of cause why such motion would be in the interest of justice.

(d) Prior to the arraignment of any arrested person before the court to determine the existence of probable cause to believe such person committed the offense charged or to determine the conditions of such person's release pursuant to section 54-64a, the attorney for the state shall provide the arrested person or his counsel with a copy of any affidavit or report submitted to the court for the purpose of making such determination; except that the court may, upon motion of the attorney for the state and for good cause shown, limit the disclosure of any such affidavit or report, or portion thereof.

(1967, P.A. 706, S. 1, 2, 3; P.A. 78-289, S. 2; 78-290, S. 2; P.A. 91-242.)

History: P.A. 78-289 amended Subsec. (a) to delete provision allowing inspection, copying etc. of defendant's recorded testimony before a grand jury; P.A. 78-290 deleted provision in Subsec. (a) which had allowed inspection, copying etc. of exculpatory information or material; P.A. 91-242 added Subsec. (d) requiring the attorney for the state to provide the arrested person or his counsel with a copy of any affidavit or report submitted to the court for the purpose of determining probable cause or the conditions of release.

Cited. 158 C. 275; 159 C. 389. Examination in camera used to determine compliance. 166 C. 593. Cited. 187 C. 292; 190 C. 20; 200 C. 323; 229 C. 716.

Cited. 34 CA 58; judgment reversed, see 232 C. 537.

Section does not specifically require disclosure of name and address of the informant in trial of defendant charged with sale of marijuana. 28 CS 331. Cited. 33 CS 599; 42 CS 291.

Motion for further bill of particulars after plea of not guilty denied as untimely; preliminary motions in criminal case should be filed prior to plea unless grounds are not then known. 5 Conn. Cir. Ct. 269. Unless prosecutor is under some constitutional obligation, he need not allow defense complete and unqualified access to state's files. 6 Conn. Cir. Ct. 437.

Subsec. (a):

Subdiv. (1): Indiscriminate, wholesale, and blanket demands for "exculpatory" material under motion of discovery is not permissible; must be shown that evidence would have tendency to clear defendant. 29 CS 86.

(Return to Chapter

Table of Contents)

(Return to

List of Chapters)

(Return to

List of Titles)

Sec. 54-86b. Right of accused to examine statements. (a) In any criminal prosecution, after a witness called by the prosecution has testified on direct examination, the court shall on motion of the defendant order the prosecution to produce any statement oral or written of the witness in the possession of the prosecution which relates to the subject matter as to which the witness has testified, and the court shall order said statement to be delivered directly to the defendant for his examination and use.

(b) If the prosecution fails to comply with the order of the court, the court shall strike from the record the testimony of the witness and the trial shall proceed unless the court in its discretion shall determine that the interests of justice require that a mistrial be declared.

(1969, P.A. 680.)

Cited. 159 C. 264. Held unconstitutional, but assuming constitutional, procedure found to comply. 196 C. 519. Cited, 200 C. 323; 202 C. 259; 211 C. 555. Destruction of tapes discussed. 214 C. 161. Id., 215 C. 572; 221 C. 300; 223 C. 731; 224 C. 641; 229 C. 716; 231 C. 195.

Cited 10 CA 103. Destruction of tapes held to be harmless error in not striking defendant's testimony. 14 CA 189. Cited, 20 CA 536; 25 CA 255; Id., 503; 29 CA 68; judgment reversed, see 227 C. 566; Id., 304; Id., 755; Id., 803; 46 CA 118; Id., 545.

Cited. 42 CS 10; Id., 291.

(Return to Chapter

Table of Contents)

(Return to

List of Chapters)

(Return to

List of Titles)

Sec. 54-86c. Disclosure of exculpatory information or material. (a) Not later than thirty days after any defendant enters a plea of not guilty in a criminal case, the state's attorney, assistant state's attorney or deputy assistant state's attorney in charge of the case shall disclose any exculpatory information or material which he may have with respect to the defendant whether or not a request has been made therefor. If prior to or during the trial of the case, the prosecutorial official discovers additional information or material which is exculpatory, he shall promptly disclose the information or material to the defendant.

(b) Any state's attorney, assistant state's attorney or deputy assistant state's attorney may request an ex parte in camera hearing before a judge, who shall not be the same judge who presides at the hearing of the criminal case if the case is tried to the court, to determine whether any material or information is exculpatory.

(c) Each peace officer, as defined in subdivision (9) of section 53a-3, shall disclose in writing any exculpatory information or material which he may have with respect to any criminal investigation to the prosecutorial official in charge of such case.

(P.A. 78-290, S. 1; P.A. 80-313, S. 33.)

History: P.A. 80-313 replaced "such" with "the" where appearing.

Cited. 184 C. 258; 189 C. 183; 191 C. 12; 194 C. 258; 197 C. 17; Id., 298; 198 C. 285; 199 C. 207; Id., 399; 201 C. 517; 206 C. 512; 209 C. 143; 212 C. 387; 221 C. 264; 229 C. 716.

Cited. 14 CA 586; 17 CA 525; 22 CA 329; 24 CA 57; Id., 195; 34 CA 58; judgment reversed, see 232 C. 537; 36 CA 417; 38 CA 777.

Cited. 36 CS 89; 42 CS 291. Police officer lied in investigation of incident and therefore violated public policy; arbitration panel, in reinstating the police officer, violated this public policy. 50 CS 180.

(Return to Chapter Table of Contents)

(Return to List of Chapters)

(Return to List of Titles)

Sec. 54-86d. Nondisclosure of address and telephone number by victims of certain crimes. Any person who has been the victim of a sexual assault under section 53a-70, 53a-70a, 53a-71, 53a-72a, 53a-72b or 53a-73a, voyeurism under section 53a-189a, or injury or risk of injury, or impairing of morals under section 53-21, or of an attempt thereof, or family violence, as defined in section 46b-38a, shall not be required to divulge his or her address or telephone number during any trial or pretrial evidentiary hearing arising from the sexual assault, voyeurism or injury or risk of injury to, or impairing of morals of, a child, or family violence; provided the judge presiding over such legal proceeding finds: (1) Such information is not material to the proceeding, (2) the identity of the victim has been satisfactorily established, and (3) the current address of the victim will be made available to the defense in the same manner and time as such information is made available to the defense for other criminal offenses.

(P.A. 81-448, S. 1; P.A. 82-472, S. 145, 183; P.A. 93-340, S. 9, 19; P.A. 15-211, S. 23; 15-213, S. 6.)

History: P.A. 82-472 made technical corrections; P.A. 93-340 amended Subdiv. (3) to require the judge to find that the current address of the victim "will be made available to the defense in the same manner and time as such information is made available to the defense for other criminal offenses" rather than "is made available to the defense", effective July 1, 1993; P.A. 15-211 added references to family violence, effective July 1, 2015; P.A. 15-213 added references to voyeurism and made technical changes.

Cited. 8 CA 387; 20 CA 115.

Cited. 42 CS 291.

(Return to Chapter Table of Contents)

(Return to List of Chapters)

(Return to List of Titles)

Sec. 54-86e. Confidentiality of identifying information pertaining to victims of certain crimes. Availability of information to accused. Protective order information to be entered in registry. The name and address of the victim of a sexual assault under section 53a-70, 53a-70a, 53a-71, 53a-72a, 53a-72b or 53a-73a, voyeurism under section 53a-189a, or injury or risk of injury, or impairing of morals under section 53-21, or of an attempt thereof, or family violence, as defined in section 46b-38a and such other identifying information pertaining to such victim as determined by the court, shall be confidential and shall be disclosed only upon order of the Superior Court, except that (1) such information shall be available to the accused in the same manner and time as such information is available to persons accused of other criminal offenses, and (2) if a protective order is issued in a prosecution under any of said sections, the name and address of the victim, in addition to the information contained in and concerning the issuance of such order, shall be entered in the registry of protective orders pursuant to section 51-5c.

(P.A. 81-448, S. 3; P.A. 93-340, S. 10, 19; May 25 Sp. Sess. P.A. 94-1, S. 42, 130; P.A. 02-132, S. 59; P.A. 03-202, S. 15; P.A. 15-211, S. 24; 15-213, S. 7.)

History: P.A. 93-340 required name and address of victim to be available to the accused "in the same manner and time as such information is available to those accused of other criminal offenses", effective July 1, 1993; May 25 Sp. Sess. P.A. 94-1 made technical change, effective July 1, 1994; P.A. 02-132 designated exception re availability of information to accused as Subdiv. (1), added Subdiv. (2) re entry of information into registry of protective orders pursuant to Sec. 51-5c and made a technical change, effective January 1, 2003; P.A. 03-202 added provision re other identifying information pertaining to the victim as determined by the court; P.A. 15-211 added reference to family violence, effective July 1, 2015; P.A. 15-213 added reference to voyeurism.

Cited. 230 C. 43; 233 C. 403; 235 C. 145.

(Return to Chapter Table of Contents)

(Return to List of Chapters)

(Return to List of Titles)

Sec. 54-86f. Admissibility of evidence of sexual conduct. (a) In any prosecution for sexual assault under sections 53a-70, 53a-70a and 53a-71 to 53a-73a, inclusive, no evidence of the sexual conduct of the victim may be admissible unless such evidence is (1) offered by the defendant on the issue of whether the defendant was, with respect to the victim, the source of semen, disease, pregnancy or injury, or (2) offered by the defendant on the issue of credibility of the victim, provided the victim has testified on direct examination as to his or her sexual conduct, or (3) any evidence of sexual conduct with the defendant offered by the defendant on the issue of consent by the victim, when consent is raised as a defense by the defendant, or (4) otherwise so relevant and material to a critical issue in the case that excluding it would violate the defendant's constitutional rights. Such evidence shall be admissible only after an in camera hearing on a motion to offer such evidence containing an offer of proof. If the proceeding is a trial with a jury, such hearing shall be held in the absence of the jury. If, after a hearing, the court finds that the evidence meets the requirements of this section and that the probative value of the evidence outweighs its prejudicial effect on the victim, the court may grant the motion. The testimony of the defendant during a hearing on a motion to offer evidence under this section may not be used against the defendant during the trial if such motion is denied, except that such testimony may be admissible to impeach the credibility of the defendant if the defendant elects to testify as part of the defense.

(b) Any motion and supporting document filed pursuant to this section shall be filed under seal and may be unsealed only if the court rules the evidence is admissible and the case proceeds to trial. If the court determines that only part of the evidence contained in the motion is admissible, only that portion of the motion and any supporting document pertaining to the admissible portion may be unsealed. The court shall maintain any document remaining under seal for delivery to the Appellate Court in the event of an appeal.

(c) The court shall seal each court transcript, recording and record of a proceeding of a hearing held pursuant to this section. The court may unseal a transcript, recording or record only if the court rules the evidence in such transcript, recording or record is admissible and the case proceeds to trial. If the court determines that only part of such evidence is admissible, only the portion of such transcript, record or recording pertaining to the admissible evidence may be unsealed.

(d) Evidence described in subsection (a) of this section shall be subject to such other terms and conditions as the court may provide. No defendant, defense counsel or agent of the defendant or defense counsel shall further disclose such evidence disclosed by the state, except to persons employed by defense counsel in connection with the investigation or defense of the case or any successor counsel, without the prior approval of the prosecuting authority or the court.

(P.A. 82-230; P.A. 83-113; P.A. 85-347; P.A. 15-207, S. 2.)

History: P.A. 83-113 added requirement that motion to offer evidence of prior sexual conduct contain an offer of proof and provision re admissibility of testimony of defendant to impeach credibility if defendant elects to testify; P.A. 85-347 deleted "prior" before "sexual conduct" and added "any" before "evidence"; P.A. 15-207 designated existing provisions as Subsec. (a) and amended same to add provision re court to conduct an in camera hearing on a motion to offer evidence of prior sexual conduct and delete former provision re hearing held in camera subject to Sec. 51-164x, added Subsec. (b) re any motion and supporting document to be filed under seal, added Subsec. (c) re each court transcript, recording and record of a proceeding of a hearing to be filed under seal, and added Subsec. (d) re other terms and conditions the court may prescribe re evidence of prior sexual conduct.

Cited. 195 C. 253; 197 C. 280; 199 C. 193; Id., 481; 207 C. 403; 208 C. 365; 209 C. 143; 220 C. 345; 228 C. 456; 230 C. 43. Defendant failed to make an adequate preliminary showing of relevancy in order to justify cross examination of plaintiff's father about plaintiff's statement concerning a prior sexual assault investigation. 244 C. 640. Court sets forth standard applicable to child sexual abuse cases re determining whether prior sexual conduct should be admissible at trial for purposes of showing an alternative source for victim's sexual knowledge; standard also applicable for determining admissibility of evidence of prior sexual conduct for purposes of rebutting evidence offered by expert witness to show that a child exhibits behavior indicative of sexual abuse, by showing an alternative explanation for that behavior. 257 C. 156. Evidence of victim's prior history of prostitution admissible to establish consent to sexual relations or motive to provide false testimony but not to establish general unchaste character. 270 C. 826; overruled with respect to conclusion that "material" refers to the constitutional standard for materiality, see 320 C. 781. Court improperly excluded testimony proffered by defendant re victim's prior statements about past sexual conduct after victim testified to having no prior sexual experience at time of assault. 280 C. 36. Trial court properly exercised discretion by precluding inquiry into victim's prior sexual assaults, as they were not relevant to any critical issue in present case, and defendant never offered any specific evidence of falsity. 295 C. 758. Evidence of victim's prior sexual acts with a person other than defendant was not relevant to demonstrate alleged bias, motive or interest of victim and was properly excluded. 303 C. 589.

Cited. 3 CA 374; 8 CA 44; Id., 190; 11 CA 673; 14 CA 451; Id., 688; 20 CA 263; 21 CA 411; 23 CA 221; Id., 225; 29 CA 409; Id., 642; 30 CA 56; 34 CA 473; 35 CA 173; 38 CA 100; 42 CA 445; 43 CA 667; Id., 680; Id., 715; 45 CA 116. Defendant's rights under statute were impermissibly impaired when trial court excluded evidence of victim's consensual sexual relations with the lead detective investigating her claim of sexual assault; such evidence was relevant to the substantive issue of consent raised by defendant and was offered for sole purpose of determining victim's credibility and the inconsistency of her behavior following an alleged traumatic sexual assault. 57 CA 32. Court did not improperly exclude evidence of semen from third party on victim's clothing. 68 CA 470. Legislative intent of rape shield statute discussed; legislature also provided for exceptions in rare instances; defendant entitled to proffer direct testimony re physical evidence tending to show misidentification; Subdiv. (1) does not specify that such evidence offered by defendant may be rebuttal evidence only. 85 CA 96. Court did not improperly exclude evidence concerning victim's prior sexual conduct because court found that such evidence was not credible and therefore not relevant. 85 CA 575. Exclusion of evidence relating to victim's alleged sexual interactions with his brothers did not violate defendant's sixth amendment rights because such evidence was properly excluded as irrelevant. 99 CA 274. Trial court abused its discretion in refusing to grant evidentiary hearing to determine admissibility of evidence of plaintiff's prior sexual conduct; evidence from police reports of two prior allegations, which presented facts that tended to demonstrate the falsity of plaintiff's prior allegations, sufficient as offers of proof and relevant to the issue of whether defendant used force in committing the sexual assault. 106 CA 517; judgment reversed, see 295 C. 758. Defendant was properly prohibited from questioning victims about their sexual histories. 126 CA 437.

Subsec. (a):

Court improperly excluded DNA evidence re semen from individual other than defendant under Subdiv. (1) because evidence was offered by defendant to prove misidentification by victim, not to expose victim's past sexual conduct. 280 C. 285. Subdiv. (4): "Material" as used in section does not refer to the constitutional standard, but rather the evidentiary standard, that is, evidence is material when it has an influence, effect, or bearing on a fact in dispute at trial. 320 C. 781.

Psychological injury is not recognized as an injury for purposes of Subdiv. (1); Subdiv. (2) does not apply where the only sexual conduct to which victim testifies is alleged sexual conduct by defendant; evidence admitted under Subdiv. (4) must be both material and relevant in order to be so critical that its exclusion could lead to a violation of defendant's constitutional rights. 99 CA 274. Subdiv. (4): Trial court improperly precluded evidence of minor victim's sexual relationship with boyfriend because state conceded that defendant showed that victim may have had a motive to lie about defendant's sexual assault. 121 CA 534.

(Return to Chapter Table of Contents)   (Return to List of Chapters)   (Return to List of Titles)

Sec. 54-86g. Testimony of victim of child abuse. Court may order testimony taken outside courtroom. Procedure. (a) In any criminal prosecution of an offense involving assault, sexual assault or abuse of a child twelve years of age or younger, the court may, upon motion of the attorney for any party, order that the testimony of the child be taken in a room other than the courtroom in the presence and under the supervision of the trial judge hearing the matter and be televised by closed circuit equipment in the courtroom or recorded for later showing before the court. Only the judge, the defendant, the attorneys for the defendant and for the state, persons necessary to operate the equipment and any person who would contribute to the welfare and well-being of the child may be present in the room with the child during his testimony, except that the court may order the defendant excluded from the room or screened from the sight and hearing of the child only if the state proves, by clear and convincing evidence, that the child would be so intimidated, or otherwise inhibited, by the physical presence of the defendant that a compelling need exists to take the testimony of the child outside the physical presence of the defendant in order to insure the reliability of such testimony. If the defendant is excluded from the room or screened from the sight and hearing of the child, the court shall ensure that the defendant is able to observe and hear the testimony of the child, but that the child cannot see or hear the defendant. The defendant shall be able to consult privately with his attorney at all times during the taking of the testimony. The attorneys and the judge may question the child. If the court orders the testimony of a child to be taken under this subsection, the child shall not be required to testify in court at the proceeding for which the testimony was taken.

(b) In any criminal prosecution of an offense involving assault, sexual assault or abuse of a child twelve years of age or younger, the court may, upon motion of the attorney for any party, order that the following procedures be used when the testimony of the child is taken: (1) Persons shall be prohibited from entering and leaving the courtroom during the child's testimony; (2) an adult who is known to the child and with whom the child feels comfortable shall be permitted to sit in close proximity to the child during the child's testimony, provided such person shall not obscure the child from the view of the defendant or the trier of fact; (3) the use of anatomically correct dolls by the child shall be permitted; and (4) the attorneys for the defendant and for the state shall question the child while seated at a table positioned in front of the child, shall remain seated while posing objections and shall ask questions and pose objections in a manner which is not intimidating to the child.

(P.A. 85-587, S. 1; P.A. 89-177, S. 1; P.A. 90-230, S. 94, 101.)

History: P.A. 89-177 amended Subsec. (a) to permit the defendant to be present in the room during the child's testimony, to provide that the court may exclude the defendant from the room or screen him from the sight and hearing of the child only if the state proves by clear and convincing evidence that a compelling need exists to take the testimony of the child outside the physical presence of the defendant, to provide that the requirement that the defendant be able to observe and hear the child and that the child not be able to see or hear the defendant applies "if the defendant is excluded from the room or screened from the sight and hearing of the child", and to replace provision that the defendant "may consult with his attorney" with "shall be able to consult privately with his attorney at all times during the taking of the testimony", incorporated Subsec. (b) into Subsec. (a), and added a new Subsec. (b) authorizing the court to order that certain procedures be used when a child testifies in any criminal prosecution of an offense involving an assault, sexual assault or abuse of a child 12 years of age or younger and requiring the question of the competency of the child as a witness to be resolved prior to the time of the trial; P.A. 90-230 made technical change to Subsec. (b).

Not effective at time action initiated; videotaping procedure essentially followed by trial court discussed in connection with federal and state constitutional confrontation clauses. 204 C. 683. Cited. 210 C. 51; Id., 244; Id., 359; 211 C. 185. Judgment of Appellate Court in 36 CA 803 reversed and case remanded to Appellate Court for consideration of trial court's denial of state's motion to videotape pursuant to section. 235 C. 659. In 36 CA 803, 233 C. 902, 42 CA 186, 239 C. 934, judgment of Appellate Court reversed; trial court properly exercised its discretion to deny motion on videotaped testimony. 241 C. 823. It is insufficient, without further inquiry, to determine that because victim cried on the witness stand, victim is not reliable as a witness. 258 C. 42. Section does not specifically authorize the use of a dog, but trial court may exercise its discretion to permit a dog to provide comfort and support to a testifying witness. 321 C. 656.

Cited. 14 CA 333; 19 CA 445; 24 CA 146; 26 CA 674; 36 CA 803; judgment reversed, see 235 C. 659, see also 241 C. 823. Defendant not entitled to have a defense expert conduct a psychological or psychiatric examination of an alleged child victim as prerequisite to trial court's granting of motion filed pursuant to section. 42 CA 186; judgment reversed, see 241 C. 823. Cited. 39 CA 702. In this case, trial court properly permitted the state to videotape testimony of child victim outside the presence of defendant. 51 CA 753. Hearing re videotaping of remainder of the child's testimony outside the presence of defendant re her sexual assault pursuant to 204 C. 683 need not be conducted prior to trial or before testimony begins. 55 CA 717. Plain language of statute permits testimony via videotape of victim who is 12 years of age or younger at time of offense; victim's age at time of videotaping is not controlling under statute. 70 CA 171. Section does not give court specific authority to allow the presence of a dog while a child witness testifies. 150 CA 514; judgment reversed, see 321 C. 656.

Subsec. (a):

State's compelling interest in securing reliable testimony from a child victim may outweigh defendant's right of face-to-face confrontation. 284 C. 597.

Cited. 42 CA 186; judgment reversed, see 241 C. 823. Trial court's finding of compelling need for videotaped testimony upheld. 47 CA 199.

Sec. 54-86h. Competency of child as witness.

No witness shall be automatically adjudged incompetent to testify because of age and any child who is a victim of assault, sexual assault or abuse shall be competent to testify without prior qualification. The weight to be given the evidence and the credibility of the witness shall be for the determination of the trier of fact.

(P.A. 85-587, S. 2.)

Cited. 211 C. 555; 241 C. 823.

Cited. 12 CA 585; 13 CA 368; 19 CA 36; 20 CA 737; 23 CA 509; 24 CA 146; 25 CA 21; 42 CA 186; judgment reversed, see 241 C. 823.

Sec. 54-86i. Testimony of expert witness re mental state or condition of defendant.

No expert witness testifying with respect to the mental state or condition of a defendant in a criminal case may state an opinion or inference as to whether the defendant did or did not have the mental state or condition constituting an element of the crime charged or of a defense thereto, except that such expert witness may state his diagnosis of the mental state or condition of the defendant. The ultimate issue as to whether the defendant was criminally responsible for the crime charged is a matter for the trier of fact alone.

(P.A. 85-605.)

Cited. 207 C. 35; 209 C. 423; 210 C. 481; 216 C. 139; 224 C. 114; Id., 347; 225 C. 450; Id., 650.

Cited. 17 CA 257; 26 CA 94; 28 CA 425; 32 CA 170; 34 CA 629.

Sec. 54-86j. Polygraph examination of victims of sexual assault restricted.

(a) No member of any municipal police department, the state police or the Division of Criminal Justice may request or require any victim of a sexual assault under section 53a-70, 53a-70a, 53a-70b, 53a-71, 53a-72a, 53a-72b or 53a-73a to submit to or take a polygraph examination.

(b) For the purposes of this section, "polygraph" means any mechanical or electrical instrument or device of any type used or allegedly used to examine, test or question individuals for the purpose of determining truthfulness.

(P.A. 89-60.)

Sec. 54-86k. Admissibility of results of DNA analysis.

(a) In any criminal proceeding, DNA (deoxyribonucleic acid) testing shall be deemed to be a reliable scientific technique and the evidence of a DNA profile comparison may be admitted to prove or disprove the identity of any person. This section shall not otherwise limit the introduction of any relevant evidence bearing upon any question at issue before the court. The court shall, regardless of the results of the DNA analysis, if any, consider such other relevant evidence of the identity of the accused as shall be admissible in evidence.

(b) If the results of the DNA analysis tend to exculpate the accused, the prosecuting authority shall disclose such exculpatory information or material to the accused in accordance with section 54-86c.

(c) At least twenty-one days prior to commencement of the proceeding in which the results of a DNA analysis will be offered as evidence, the party intending to offer the evidence shall notify the opposing party, in writing, of the intent to offer the analysis and shall provide or make available copies of the profiles and the report or statement to be introduced. In the event that such notice is not given, and the person proffers such evidence, then the court may in its discretion either allow the opposing party a continuance or, under the appropriate circumstances, bar the person from presenting such evidence. The period of any such continuance shall not be counted for speedy trial purposes under section 54-82c. If the opposing party intends to object to the admissibility of such evidence he shall give written notice of that fact and the basis for his objections at least ten days prior to commencement of the proceedings.

(d) No blood sample submitted to the Division of Scientific Services within the Department of Emergency Services and Public Protection for analysis and use as provided in this section and no results of the analysis performed shall be included in the DNA data bank established by the division pursuant to section 54-102j or otherwise used in any way with identifying information on the person whose sample was submitted.

(P.A. 94-246, S. 7; P.A. 99-218, S. 9, 16; P.A. 11-51, S. 134.)

History: P.A. 99-218 amended Subsec. (d) by replacing the State Police Forensic Science Laboratory with the Division of Scientific Services within the Department of Public Safety, effective July 1, 1999; pursuant to P.A. 11-51, "Department of Public Safety" was changed editorially by the Revisors to "Department of Emergency Services and Public Protection" in Subsec. (d), effective July 1, 2011.

See Secs. 54-102g to 54-102l, inclusive, re DNA analysis procedures.

Trial court did not abuse its discretion when it denied defendant's motion to preclude DNA testing results produced by the state shortly before the trial was scheduled to begin where trial court ordered a continuance of the trial because of state's failure to comply with statute's timing requirements and defendant did not establish he was prejudiced by the late disclosure. 304 C. 383.

Sec. 54-86l. Admissibility in criminal or juvenile proceeding of statement by child twelve years of age or younger at time of statement relating to sexual offense or offense involving physical abuse against the child.

(a) Notwithstanding any other rule of evidence or provision of law, a statement by a child twelve years of age or younger at the time of the statement relating to a sexual offense committed against that child, or an offense involving physical abuse committed against that child by the child's parent or guardian or any other person exercising comparable authority over the child at the time of the offense, shall be admissible in a criminal or juvenile proceeding if: (1) The court finds, in a hearing conducted outside the presence of the jury, if any, that the circumstances of the statement, including its timing and content, provide particularized guarantees of its trustworthiness, (2) the statement was not made in preparation for a legal proceeding, (3) the proponent of the statement makes known to the adverse party an intention to offer the statement and the particulars of the statement including the content of the statement, the approximate time, date and location of the statement, the person to whom the statement was made and the circumstances surrounding the statement that indicate its trustworthiness, at such time as to provide the adverse party with a fair opportunity to prepare to meet it, and (4) either (A) the child testifies and is subject to cross-examination at the proceeding, or (B) the child is unavailable as a witness and (i) there is independent nontestimonial corroborative evidence of the alleged act, and (ii) the statement was made prior to the defendant's arrest or institution of juvenile proceedings in connection with the act described in the statement.

(b) Nothing in this section shall be construed to (1) prevent the admission of any statement under another hearsay exception, (2) allow broader definitions in other hearsay exceptions for statements made by children twelve years of age or younger at the time of the statement concerning any alleged act described in subsection (a) of this section than is done for other declarants, or (3) allow the admission pursuant to the residual hearsay exception of a statement described in subsection (a) of this section.

(P.A. 07-143, S. 11; June Sp. Sess. P.A. 07-5, S. 42; P.A. 09-63, S. 1.)

History: P.A. 07-143 effective July 1, 2007; June Sp. Sess. P.A. 07-5 deleted provision in Subsec. (a) re admissibility in civil proceedings, effective October 6, 2007; P.A. 09-63 amended Subsec. (a) to substitute "child twelve years of age or younger at the time of the statement" for "child under thirteen years of age" and replace provision re persons having authority or apparent authority over the child with provision re parent, guardian or other person exercising authority over the child at time of offense, and amended Subsec. (b) to substitute "children twelve years of age or younger" for "children under thirteen years of age".

See Sec. 54-86g re courtroom testimony of child abused or sexually assaulted.

Sec. 54-86m. Reproduction of property or material that constitutes child pornography prohibited.

Notwithstanding the provisions of section 54-86a, in any criminal proceeding, any property or material that constitutes child pornography shall remain in the care, custody and control of the state, and a court shall deny any request by the defendant to copy, photograph, duplicate or otherwise reproduce any property or material that constitutes child pornography provided the attorney for the state makes the property or material reasonably available to the defendant. Such property or material shall be deemed to be reasonably available to the defendant if the attorney for the state provides the defendant, the defendant's attorney or any individual the defendant may seek to qualify to furnish expert testimony at trial, ample opportunity for inspection, viewing and examination of the property or material at a state facility or at another facility agreed upon by the attorney for the state and the defendant. For the purposes of this section, "child pornography" has the same meaning as in section 53a-193.

(P.A. 07-246, S. 2; P.A. 10-36, S. 27.)

History: P.A. 10-36 made technical changes, effective July 1, 2010.

Sec. 54-86n. Appointment of advocate in proceeding re the welfare or custody of a cat or dog. Advocate's duties. Department of Agriculture to maintain list of eligible advocates.

(a) In any prosecution under section 53-247, or in any court proceeding pursuant to section 22-329a or in the criminal session of the Superior Court regarding the welfare or custody of a cat or dog, the court may order, upon its own initiative or upon request of a party or counsel for a party, that a separate advocate be appointed to represent the interests of justice. If a court orders that an advocate be appointed to represent the interests of justice, the court shall appoint such advocate from a list provided to the court by the Commissioner of Agriculture pursuant to subsection (c) of this section. A decision by the court denying a request to appoint a separate advocate to represent the interests of justice shall not be subject to appeal.

(b) The advocate may: (1) Monitor the case; (2) consult any individual with information that could aid the judge or fact finder and review records relating to the condition of the cat or dog and the defendant's actions, including, but not limited to, records from animal control officers, veterinarians and police officers; (3) attend hearings; and (4) present information or recommendations to the court pertinent to determinations that relate to the interests of justice, provided such information and recommendations shall be based solely upon the duties undertaken pursuant to this subsection.

(c) The Department of Agriculture shall maintain a list of attorneys with knowledge of animal issues and the legal system and a list of law schools that have students, or anticipate having students, with an interest in animal issues and the legal system. Such attorneys and law students shall be eligible to serve on a voluntary basis as advocates under this section. The provisions of sections 3-14 to 3-21, inclusive, of the Connecticut Practice Book shall govern a law student's participation as an advocate under this section.

(P.A. 16-30, S. 1.)

Sec. 54-87. Demurrer. Section 54-87 is repealed.

(1949 Rev., S. 8803; P.A. 80-313, S. 61.)

Sec. 54-88. State to open and close arguments.

In any criminal trial, the counsel for the state shall be entitled to open and close the argument.

(1949 Rev., S. 8804.)

There is no rigid requirement that prosecutor's final summation must be limited solely to rebuttal of matters raised in defendant's argument. 170 C. 417. Cited. 230 C. 351.

Sec. 54-89. Direction of court to jury. The court shall decide all issues of law and all questions of law arising in the trial of criminal cases. In committing the cause to the jury, if in the opinion of the court the evidence is not sufficient to justify the finding of guilt beyond a reasonable doubt, the court may direct the jury to find a verdict of not guilty; otherwise the court shall submit the facts to the jury without directing how to find their verdict.

(1949 Rev., S. 8806.)

How far jury judges of the law and of its constitutionality. 40 C. 248; 47 C. 551, 552; 69 C. 127. Cited. 46 C. 339. Jury as much bound by the law as the judge. 47 C. 551, 552. Comments on evidence permissible so long as they do not amount to directions as to verdict. 57 C. 529; 64 C. 329; 103 C. 486; 105

C. 764. Instance of charge in violation of spirit of statute. 63 C. 47. Proper for judge to state that the statute under which accused was prosecuted was valid, until repealed or pronounced otherwise by higher court. 65 C. 287; 69 C. 127. A judge has complied with provision of statute when he has given the jury instructions required to enable it to understand the nature of the offense and the questions it is to decide, to weigh the evidence applicable thereto and to intelligently decide thereon. 72 C. 43. Instruction permitting jury to determine law is error. 75 C. 218, 234. Court may state opinion on evidence; 64 C. 330; 67 C. 581; 72 C. 40; 78 C. 28; 81 C. 98; 83 C. 160; Id., 601; 87 C. 5; Id., 285; 98 C. 467; 109 C. 91; thus, may give opinion that newspaper is within statute as to obscene literature; 73 C. 18; may comment on testimony as to good character of accused; 83 C. 597; so as to testimony of an accomplice; 72 C. 321; 75 C. 326; 76 C. 342; 84 C. 152; Id., 411. Granting new trial. 65 C. 274; 69 C. 190. Rules same as in civil action. 72 C. 109; 74 C. 638; 79 C. 481. Capital case. 81 C. 22. Prior to 1921, court could not direct verdict of not guilty. 96 C. 639. But otherwise under present law. 99 C. 244; 100 C. 643. How far court may go in charge without violating rule against directing verdict of guilty. 99 C. 244; 103 C. 486; 105 C. 764. Direction of verdict of not guilty in case of one defendant held erroneous. 100 C. 643. Cited. 146 C. 327; 169 C. 377; 186 C. 696; 196 C. 519.

Cited. 8 CA 631; 10 CA 697; 15 CA 704; 19 CA 576.

Court may direct verdict of not guilty when reasoning mind could not reasonably reach conclusion other than that the evidence, under the law, is not sufficient to justify finding of guilty beyond reasonable doubt. 4 Conn. Cir. Ct. 192. Court may not direct jury to find verdict of guilty. 5 Conn. Cir. Ct. 222. Cited. 6 Conn. Cir. Ct. 650.

Sec. 54-89a. Court to inform jury on consequences of a finding of not guilty by reason of mental disease or defect.

If the court instructs the jury on a defense of mental disease or defect raised pursuant to section 53a-13, it shall, unless the defendant affirmatively objects, inform the jury of the consequences for the defendant if he is found not guilty by reason of mental disease or defect and of the confinement and release provisions of sections 17a-580 to 17a-602, inclusive, applicable to a person found not guilty by reason of mental disease or defect.

(P.A. 81-301, S. 3; P.A. 83-486, S. 6; P.A. 85-506, S. 30, 32.)

History: P.A. 83-486 replaced provision re court instructing jury "on the absence of criminal responsibility of a defendant on the grounds of mental disease or defect" with instruction "on a defense of mental disease or defect raised pursuant to section 53a-13", and replaced "a finding of guilty but not criminally responsible" with a finding of "not guilty by reason" of mental disease or defect; P.A. 85-506 replaced reference to repealed Sec. 53a-47 with sections 17-257a to 17-257w, inclusive.

Cited. 208 C. 125; 230 C. 183.

Cited. 10 CA 50. Section enacted in derogation of common law and is to be construed narrowly; court's instructions satisfied section where effect was to inform jury of consequences of a successful insanity defense and to allay jurors' fears that defendant could be released while a danger to society. 50 CA 312.

(Return to Chapter

Table of Contents)

(Return to

List of Chapters)

(Return to

List of Titles)

Secs. 54-90 and 54-90a. Transferred to Chapter 961a, Secs. 54-142a and 54-142b, respectively.

PART II SENTENCING AND APPEAL

Sec. 54-91. When sentence to be passed. Section 54-91 is repealed.

(1949 Rev., S. 8807; P.A. 76-336, S. 10.)

Sec. 54-91a. (Formerly Sec. 54-109). Presentence investigation of defendant. (a) No defendant convicted of a crime, other than a capital felony under the provisions of section 53a-54b in effect prior to April 25, 2012, or murder with special circumstances under the provisions of section 53a-54b in effect on or after April 25, 2012, the punishment for which may include imprisonment for more than one year, may be sentenced, or the defendant's case otherwise disposed of, until a written report of investigation by a probation officer has been presented to and considered by the court, if the defendant is so convicted for the first time in this state; but any court may, in its discretion, order a presentence investigation for a defendant convicted of any crime or offense other than a capital felony under the provisions of section 53a-54b in effect prior to April 25, 2012, or murder with special circumstances under the provisions of section 53a-54b in effect on or after April 25, 2012.

(b) A defendant who is convicted of a crime and is not eligible for sentence review pursuant to section 51-195 may, with the consent of the sentencing judge and the prosecuting official, waive the presentence investigation.

(c) Whenever an investigation is required, the probation officer shall promptly inquire into the circumstances of the offense, the attitude of the complainant or victim, or of the immediate family where possible in cases of homicide, and the criminal record, social history and present condition of the defendant. Such investigation shall include an inquiry into any damages suffered by the victim, including medical expenses, loss of earnings and property loss. All local and state police agencies shall furnish to the probation officer such criminal records as the probation officer may request. When in the opinion of the court or the investigating authority it is desirable, such investigation shall include a physical and mental examination of the defendant. If the defendant is committed to any institution, the investigating agency shall send the reports of such investigation to the institution at the time of commitment.

(d) Any information contained in the files or report of an investigation pursuant to this section shall be available to the Court Support Services Division for the purpose of performing the duties contained in section 54-63d and to the Department of Mental Health and Addiction Services for purposes of diagnosis and treatment.

(1955, S. 3337d; 1957, P.A. 639, S. 1; 1959, P.A. 615, S. 14; P.A. 76-336, S. 6; P.A. 78-188, S. 5, 8; P.A. 80-313, S. 48; P.A. 82-281; 82-298, S. 5; P.A. 85-98; P.A. 90-261, S. 12, 19; P.A. 95-225, S. 35; 95-261, S. 4; P.A. 00-64, S. 1; P.A. 02-132, S. 41; P.A. 03-48, S. 1; P.A. 12-5, S. 30.)

History: 1959 act required report of probation officer's investigation prior to sentencing if defendant's record discloses a conviction obtained prior to three years from present conviction; P.A. 76-336 substituted references to capital felony for references to first degree murder where appearing; P.A. 78-188 required that criminal records be furnished to restitution specialists upon their request; P.A. 80-313 divided section into Subsecs. and substituted "may" for "shall" in provision re required reports of probation officer in Subsec. (a); Sec. 54-109 transferred to Sec. 54-91a in 1981; P.A. 82-281 amended Subsec. (a)(2) to increase from three to five years the period of time between convictions, and inserted a new Subsec. (b) authorizing certain defendants to waive the investigation, relettering former Subsec. (b) accordingly; P.A. 82-298 deleted references to restitution specialists in newly relettered Subsec. (c); P.A. 85-98 amended Subsec. (c) by adding provision requiring the investigation to include an inquiry into any damages suffered by the victim; P.A. 90-261 amended Subsec. (c) by adding provision requiring the investigation to include an inquiry into whether the department of correction recommends that the defendant participate in a special alternative incarceration program; P.A. 95-225 and P.A. 95-261 both added substantially identical provisions as new Subsec. (d) authorizing the disclosure of information in the files or report of an investigation to the Office of the Bail Commission for the purpose of performing the duties in Sec. 54-63d (Revisor's note: P.A. 95-225 provided that "Any information contained in the files or report of an investigation made pursuant to this section may be disclosed to the Office of the Bail Commission ...", whereas P.A. 95-261 provided that "Any information contained in the files or report of an investigation pursuant to this section shall be available to the Office of the Bail Commission ..."); P.A. 00-64 amended Subsec. (a) by making technical changes and deleting provision that required investigation if record of defendant, as shown by prosecutor, discloses conviction obtained prior to five years from guilty finding in present prosecution, and amended Subsec. (d) by adding provision making information contained in files or report available to Department of Mental Health and Addiction Services for purposes of diagnosis and treatment; P.A. 02-132 amended Subsec. (d) by replacing "Office of the Bail Commission" with "Court Support Services Division"; P.A. 03-48 amended Subsec. (c) to delete provision requiring investigation to include an inquiry into whether the Department of Correction recommends that the defendant participate in a special alternative incarceration program in accordance with Sec. 53a-39b, reflecting repeal of said Sec. by the same public act; P.A. 12-5 amended Subsec. (a) to add references to provisions of Sec. 53a-54b in effect prior to April 25, 2012, re capital felony and add references to murder with special circumstances under Sec. 53a-54b, effective April 25, 2012.

Annotations to former section 54-109:

Refusal of court to allow defendant to question on the witness stand the probation officer who prepared report held not violation of right to be confronted by witnesses and to cross-examine them. 147 C. 125. Cited. 153 C. 673; 160 C. 151, 165. Request to withdraw nolo contendere plea after presentence report may validly be refused by court if it is deemed delaying action. 161 C. 20. Cited. 168 C. 623; 169 C. 263; 176 C. 270.

Sec. 54-91b. (Formerly Sec. 54-109a). Defendant may request copy of prior record and presentence investigation report.

In any case, without a showing of good cause, upon the request of the defendant or his attorney, prior to sentencing, the court shall provide the defendant or his attorney with a copy of his record of prior convictions and in any case wherein a presentence investigation is ordered, without a showing of good cause, the court shall provide the defendant or his attorney with a copy of the presentence investigation report at least twenty-four hours prior to the date set for sentencing and in both such cases shall hear motions addressed to the accuracy of any part of such record or report.

(1969, P.A. 129.)

History: Sec. 54-109a transferred to Sec. 54-91b in 1981.

Sec. 54-91c. Testimony of victim or representative of deceased victim prior to acceptance of plea agreement and at sentencing hearing. Terms of proposed plea agreement. Notification by state's attorney. (a) For the purposes of this section, "victim" means a person who is a victim of a crime, the legal representative of such person, a member of a deceased victim's immediate family or a person designated by a deceased victim in accordance with section 1-56r.

(b) Prior to the imposition of sentence upon any defendant who has been found guilty of any crime or has pleaded guilty or nolo contendere to any crime, and prior to the acceptance by the court of a plea of guilty or nolo contendere made pursuant to a plea agreement with the state wherein the defendant pleads to a lesser offense than the offense with which such defendant was originally charged, the court shall permit any victim of the crime to appear before the court for the purpose of making a statement for the record, which statement may include the victim's opinion of any plea agreement. In lieu of such appearance, the victim may submit a written statement or, if the victim of the crime is deceased, the legal representative or a member of the immediate family of such deceased victim may submit a statement of such deceased victim to the state's attorney, assistant state's attorney or deputy assistant state's attorney in charge of the case. Such state's attorney, assistant state's attorney or deputy assistant state's attorney shall file the statement with the sentencing court and the statement shall be made a part of the record at the sentencing hearing. Any such statement, whether oral or written, shall relate to the facts of the case, the appropriateness of any penalty and the extent of any injuries, financial losses and loss of earnings directly resulting from the crime for which the defendant is being sentenced. The court shall inquire on the record whether any victim is present for the purpose of making an oral statement or has submitted a written statement. If no victim is present and no such written statement has been submitted, the court shall inquire on the record whether an attempt has been made to notify any such victim as provided in subdivision (1) of subsection (c) of this section or, if the defendant was originally charged with a violation of section 53a-167c for assaulting a peace officer, whether the peace officer has been personally notified as provided in subdivision (2) of subsection (c) of this section. After consideration of any such statements, the court may refuse to accept, where appropriate, a negotiated plea or sentence, and the court shall give the defendant an opportunity to enter a new plea and to elect trial by jury or by the court.

(c) (1) Except as provided in subdivision (2) of this subsection, prior to the imposition of sentence upon such defendant and prior to the acceptance of a plea pursuant to a plea agreement, the state's attorney, assistant state's attorney or deputy assistant state's attorney in charge of the case shall notify the victim of such crime of the date, time and place of the original sentencing hearing or any judicial proceeding concerning the acceptance of a plea pursuant to a plea agreement, provided the victim has informed such state's attorney, assistant state's attorney or deputy assistant state's attorney that such victim wishes to make or submit a statement as provided in subsection (b) of this section and has complied with a request from such state's attorney, assistant state's attorney or deputy assistant state's attorney to submit a stamped, self-addressed postcard for the purpose of such notification.

(2) Prior to the imposition of sentence upon a defendant originally charged with a violation of section 53a-167c for assaulting a peace officer, and prior to the acceptance of a plea pursuant to a plea agreement, the state's attorney, assistant state's attorney or deputy assistant state's attorney in charge of the case shall personally notify the peace officer who was the victim of such crime of the date, time and place of the original sentencing hearing or any judicial proceeding concerning the acceptance of a plea pursuant to a plea agreement.

(3) If the state's attorney, assistant state's attorney or deputy assistant state's attorney is unable to notify the victim, such state's attorney, assistant state's attorney or deputy state's attorney shall sign a statement as to such notification.

(d) Upon the request of a victim, prior to the acceptance by the court of a plea of a defendant pursuant to a proposed plea agreement, the state's attorney, assistant state's attorney or deputy assistant state's attorney in charge of the case shall provide such victim with the terms of such proposed plea agreement in writing.

(e) The provisions of this section shall not apply to any proceedings held in accordance with section 46b-121 or section 54-76h.

(P.A. 81-324, S. 1–3, 5; P.A. 85-117; P.A. 86-401, S. 2, 7; P.A. 98-53; P.A. 99-247, S. 1; P.A. 00-200, S. 3; P.A. 01-211, S. 10; P.A. 02-105, S. 13; P.A. 03-179, S. 1; P.A. 10-42, S. 1.)

History: 85-117 amended Subsecs. (a) and (b) by adding "or a violation of section 53a-72a or 53a-72b"; P.A. 86-401 amended Subsecs. (b) and (c) permitting victim to make statement prior to acceptance plea of guilty or nolo contendere pursuant to plea agreement wherein defendant pleads to lesser offense and requiring state's attorney to notify victim of any such judicial proceeding; P.A. 98-53 amended Subsec. (b) by adding provision re statement by representative or family member of deceased victim and re inclusion of the appropriateness of penalty in any written or oral statement; P.A. 99-247 added new Subsec. (d) to require the prosecutorial official to provide a victim, upon such victim's request, with the terms of a proposed plea agreement in writing prior to the court's acceptance of the defendant's plea, relettering former Subsec. (d) as Subsec. (e), and made a technical change for purposes of gender neutrality; P.A. 00-200 amended Subsec. (b) by making a technical change and adding provision that statement of victim may include victim's opinion of plea agreement, and amended Subsec. (c) by providing that, if victim of crime is deceased, legal representative or family member shall inform prosecutor of wish to give statement and to be notified, and if prosecutor is unable to notify, such prosecutor shall sign statement as to notification; P.A. 01-211 amended Subsec. (a) to redefine "victim" as a person who is a victim of "a crime" rather than "a class A, B or C felony or a violation of section 53a-72a or 53a-72b", amended Subsec. (b) to make provisions applicable with respect to the sentencing of a defendant convicted of "any crime" rather than "any class A, B or C felony or a violation of section 53a-72a or 53a-72b" and amended Subsec. (c) to delete language re deceased crime victim; P.A. 02-105 amended Subsec. (a) by adding a person designated by a victim pursuant to Sec. 1-56r to definition of "victim"; P.A. 03-179 amended Subsec. (b) by replacing "permit the victim" with "permit any victim", adding provisions re inquiry of the court on the record and making technical changes; P.A. 10-42 amended Subsec. (b) to specify that notification of victim is as provided in Subsec. (c)(1) and add provision requiring court to inquire, if defendant was originally charged with violation of Sec. 53a-167c for assaulting a peace officer, whether peace officer has been personally notified as provided in Subsec. (c)(2) and amended Subsec. (c) to designate existing provisions re notification of victim as Subdiv. (1) and amend same by adding exception re Subdiv. (2) and replacing "advise" with "notify", add Subdiv. (2) re notification of peace officer assaulted in violation of Sec. 53a-167c and designate existing provision re statement of prosecutor if unable to notify victim as Subdiv. (3).

See Sec. 54-91e re notification of victim through automated system prior to acceptance of plea agreement.

Cited. 9 CA 686; 10 CA 591; 23 CA 431.

Cited. 41 CS 229.

Sec. 54-91d. Referral of persons to youth service bureaus. Section 54-91d is repealed.

(P.A. 93-432, S. 4, 6; P.A. 95-225, S. 51.)

Sec. 54-91e. Notification of victim through automated system prior to acceptance of plea agreement.

On and after the date on which the state-wide automated victim information and notification (SAVIN) system mandated by section 54-235 becomes operational, a victim of a crime who has requested notification through the Office of Victim Services within the Judicial Department, the Board of Pardons and Paroles or the Victim Services Unit within the Department of Correction shall receive notification through the SAVIN system prior to acceptance of a plea agreement by the court. Such notification shall be deemed to have occurred once the SAVIN system has been updated to reflect the offer of a plea agreement.

(Jan. Sp. Sess. P.A. 08-1, S. 32.)

History: Jan. Sp. Sess. P.A. 08-1 effective January 25, 2008.

Sec. 54-91f. Apology to victim by person convicted of motor vehicle offense that resulted in death or serious physical injury to another. Inadmissibility in civil or criminal proceeding.

Any person convicted of a motor vehicle offense that resulted in the death or serious physical injury of another person may, prior to sentencing for the offense, make a statement, affirmation, gesture or expression of apology, fault, sympathy, commiseration, condolence, compassion or a general sense of benevolence to the victim of such offense, a relative of the victim or a representative of the victim. Such statement, affirmation, gesture or expression shall be made before the court in a courtroom closed to the public at a time set by the court. Such statement, affirmation, gesture or expression shall be inadmissible as evidence of an admission of liability or as evidence of an admission against interest in any civil or criminal proceeding. For the purposes of this section, "serious physical injury" has the same meaning as provided in section 53a-3.

(P.A. 12-124, S. 1.)

Sec. 54-91g. Sentencing of a child for class A or B felony.

(a) If the case of a child, as defined in section 46b-120, is transferred to the regular criminal docket of the Superior Court pursuant to section 46b-127 and the child is convicted of a class A or B felony pursuant to such transfer, at the time of sentencing, the court shall:

(1) Consider, in addition to any other information relevant to sentencing, the defendant's age at the time of the offense, the hallmark features of adolescence, and any scientific and psychological evidence showing the differences between a child's brain development and an adult's brain development; and

(2) Consider, if the court proposes to sentence the child to a lengthy sentence under which it is likely that the child will die while incarcerated, how the scientific and psychological evidence described in subdivision (1) of this subsection counsels against such a sentence.

(b) Notwithstanding the provisions of section 54-91a, no presentence investigation or report may be waived with respect to a child convicted of a class A or B felony. Any presentence report prepared with respect to a child convicted of a class A or B felony shall address the factors set forth in subparagraphs (A) to (D), inclusive, of subdivision (1) of subsection (a) of this section.

(c) Whenever a child is sentenced pursuant to subsection (a) of this section, the court shall indicate the maximum period of incarceration that may apply to the child and whether the child may be eligible to apply for release on parole pursuant to subdivision (1) of subsection (f) of section 54-125a.

(d) The Court Support Services Division of the Judicial Branch shall compile reference materials relating to adolescent psychological and brain development to assist courts in sentencing children pursuant to this section.

(P.A. 15-84, S. 2.)

Sec. 54-92. Pronouncement of sentence.

Any sentence to imprisonment shall be pronounced by the judge in the presence and hearing of the convicted person.

(1949 Rev., S. 8809; P.A. 76-336, S. 13.)

History: P.A. 76-336 reworded section to omit reference to imprisonment specifically in Somers correctional facility.

Not error to impose sentence in capital case before passing on motion for new trial. 46 C. 339. Sentence for term of years, however long, not a life sentence. 60 C. 96. Sentence to be given before appeal is taken; suspending it; bail. 71 C. 457. Penalty of "fine and imprisonment" permits either. 75 C. 351. In capital case, if appeal decided before time set for execution, Supreme Court need not set day; 81 C. 22; in such case, not error to omit inquiry as to whether accused has anything to say. 47 C. 546. Appeal as supersedeas in capital case. 82 C. 68; 84 C. 566. Cited. 169 C. 13.

Cited. 31 CA 660. Legislature has designated court, rather than jury, to impose sentences on criminal defendants. 81 CA 824.

In absence of statute, sentences will be held to run concurrently where a person has received two or more separate sentences to imprisonment in the same penal institution and the judgments contain no provision that they shall run consecutively; where an accused is convicted on a number of counts, a general sentence is not invalid if the punishment does not exceed the maximum which could have been imposed for any single count. 23 CS 214. Habeas corpus brought on defendant's claim he had involuntarily agreed to lesser plea to obtain shorter sentence was denied where he had received sentence he anticipated and, on being sentenced, told court he had nothing he wanted to say. 28 CS 15.

Sec. 54-92a. (Formerly Sec. 54-120). Commitment to custody of Commissioner of Correction.

Commitment on findings of probable cause or on adjournments and punishment by imprisonment, including imprisonment for nonpayment of a fine, when not otherwise provided, shall be by commitment to the custody of the Commissioner of Correction in such institution or facility of the Department of Correction as he determines.

(1949 Rev., S. 8826; 1961, P.A. 580, S. 18; 1967, P.A. 152, S. 45.)

History: 1961 act deleted stipulation imprisonment be in jail of county where offense was committed and provided for commitment to jail administrator; 1967 act made commitment to correction commissioner in institution which he determines upon rather than in State Prison for sentences of at least one year with optional confinement in jail where sentence was for less than one year; Sec. 54-120 transferred to Sec. 54-92a in 1981.

Annotations to former section 54-120:

Cited. 99 C. 120; 115 C. 597. Where the maximum sentence for an offense is imprisonment for 1 year, it cannot be to the state prison. Id., 603. Before section was adopted, most criminal statutes specified whether imprisonment should be in jail or state prison. 127 C. 720. Cited. 152 C. 470; 153 C. 208.

Cited. 23 CS 296; 30 CS 71.

Sec. 54-92b. (Formerly Sec. 54-122). Discharge from community correctional center when held for nonpayment of fine.

Any person held in a community correctional center for the nonpayment of fine only may, upon application, be discharged from such imprisonment by the court by which he was committed or, when the court is not sitting, by any judge thereof, provided such notice of such application and the hearing thereon as the court or judge may direct shall be given to the prosecuting officer of the court.

(1949 Rev., S. 8822; 1967, P.A. 656, S. 63; 1969, P.A. 297.)

History: 1967 act substituted "when the court is not sitting" for "in vacation"; 1969 act substituted "community correctional center" for "jail"; Sec. 54-122 transferred to Sec. 54-92b in 1981.

Sec. 54-92c. (Formerly Sec. 17-381). Women attendants.

Whenever any female person is committed to the Commissioner of Correction or any reformatory institution for girls or women in this state, the court making such commitment shall, unless such person is to be accompanied by a member of her own family, direct that some responsible woman shall accompany her; provided, in emergency cases, where no such woman is available, the court may make such other order as security and respect for the person of the female may require. The necessary expenses and the compensation, if any is required, for such attendant shall be taxed and allowed by the court as costs in such action.

(1949 Rev., S. 2763; 1967, P.A. 152, S. 22.)

History: 1967 act substituted the commissioner of correction for correctional institutions, provided for court order in emergency cases and removed the exception of jails; Sec. 17-381 transferred to Sec. 54-92c in 1991.

Sec. 54-93. Clerks to notify warden of Connecticut Correctional Institution, Somers, of sentences.

Section 54-93 is repealed, effective October 1, 2002.

(1949 Rev., S. 8808; S.A. 02-12, S. 1.)

Sec. 54-93a. Court order to correct public record containing false information as a result of identity theft.

Whenever a person is convicted of a violation of section 53a-129a of the general statutes, revision of 1958, revised to January 1, 2003, section 53a-129b, 53a-129c, 53a-129d or 53a-129e, the court shall issue such orders as are necessary to correct a public record that contains false information as a result of such violation.

(P.A. 03-156, S. 6; P.A. 09-239, S. 8.)

History: P.A. 09-239 added reference to Sec. 53a-129e and replaced "may" with "shall" re court issuance of orders necessary to correct public record.

Sec. 54-94. Sentence of persons between sixteen and seventeen. Section 54-94 is repealed.

(1949 Rev., S. 8810; 1961, P.A. 580, S. 17.)

Sec. 54-94a. Conditional nolo contendere plea. Appeal of denial of motion to suppress or dismiss. When a defendant, prior to the commencement of trial, enters a plea of nolo contendere conditional on the right to take an appeal from the court's denial of the defendant's motion to suppress or motion to dismiss, the defendant after the imposition of sentence may file an appeal within the time prescribed by law provided a trial court has determined that a ruling on such motion to suppress or motion to dismiss would be dispositive of the case. The issue to be considered in such an appeal shall be limited to whether it was proper for the court to have denied the motion to suppress or the motion to dismiss. A plea of nolo contendere by a defendant under this section shall not constitute a waiver by the defendant of nonjurisdictional defects in the criminal prosecution.

(P.A. 82-17; P.A. 88-19; P.A. 01-13.)

History: P.A. 88-19 authorized the entry of a plea of nolo contendere conditional on the right to appeal the denial of a motion to suppress statements and evidence based on the involuntariness of a statement; P.A. 01-13 substituted "motion to suppress" for "motion to suppress evidence based on an unreasonable search or seizure, motion to suppress statements and evidence based on the involuntariness of a statement" and added proviso re determination by a trial court "that a ruling on such motion to suppress or motion to dismiss would be dispositive of the case".

Cited. 189 C. 42; 194 C. 331; 197 C. 17; Id., 620. Voluntariness of confession is not within purview of statute. 198 C. 92. Cited. 199 C. 591; 200 C. 412; 202 C. 39; Id., 369; Id., 443; 203 C. 97; 205 C. 560; 206 C. 90; Id., 323; Id., 346; 209 C. 1; 210 C. 435; 212 C. 485; 214 C. 476; 215 C. 667; 216 C. 402; 218 C. 714; 220 C. 38; 221 C. 635; 224 C. 593; Id., 627; 226 C. 265; 227 C. 207; Id., 363; 229 C. 824; 230 C. 372; 232 C. 345; 234 C. 78; 236 C. 18; Id., 216. Conditional plea could qualify for review of substantive claims under Practice Book Sec. 4003(b) rather than this section; judgment of Appellate Court in 37 CA 252 reversed. Id., 388. Cited. 240 C. 365; Id., 489; 242 C. 211; 243 C. 115; Id., 205. Defendant had no nonfrivolous grounds for appeal and defense counsel was not ineffective for failing to consult with defendant regarding appellate rights section would have preserved. 267 C. 414. Defendant's claim that trial court improperly denied his request for a continuance to change counsel does not fall within the narrow scope of section. 269 C. 454. Defendant's nolo contendre plea was not conditional even though trial court treated the plea as if it were conditional by conducting a sua sponte hearing; statute does not apply and Appellate Court has no good cause to review claim outside scope of statute. 276 C. 503.

Cited. 2 CA 219; 5 CA 207; Id., 441; 6 CA 394; 7 CA 265; Id., 354; 8 CA 330; Id., 361; Id., 542; 10 CA 7; Id., 561; Id., 667; 11 CA 11; Id., 140; Id., 540; judgment reversed, see 209 C. 1; 12 CA 427; 14 CA 134; Id., 205; Id., 356; 19 CA 296; Id., 626; 20 CA 168; judgment reversed, see 215 C. 667; Id., 336; 21 CA 210; 22 CA 10; 23 CA 50; Id., 215; Id., 495; 24 CA 115; Id., 438; 25 CA 3; Id., 99; 26 CA 103; Id., 481; judgment reversed, see 224 C. 494; 27 CA 128; Id., 248; Id., 370; Id., 461; Id., 741; 28 CA 508; 29 CA 207; 30 CA 712; Id., 917; 31 CA 669; 32 CA 656; judgment reversed in part, see 232 C. 345; Id., 849; 33 CA 107; Id., 409; Id., 590; 34 CA 492; Id., 557; 36 CA 106; judgment reversed, see 234 C. 78; Id., 710; 37 CA 205. Nothing in language of statute indicating that word "voluntariness" is meant to include claims of right to counsel. Id., 252; judgment reversed, see 236 C. 388. Cited. Id., 561; judgment reversed, see 236 C. 216; 38 CA 8; judgment reversed, see 236 C. 18; Id., 588; 39 CA 82; 40 CA 420; Id., 724; 41 CA 530; Id., 694; Id., 772; 42 CA 589; 43 CA 448; 44 CA 162; Id., 249; 45 CA 32; 46 CA 633. Trial court's exercise of discretion regarding youthful offender status not a claim encompassed by section. 51 CA 539. If defendant understood that, by entering a plea pursuant to statute, the only issue allowed on appeal was whether trial court improperly denied his motion to suppress, then defendant cannot raise other issues on appeal. 55 CA 217. Claim of insufficient evidence is not one of the particular claims that statute permits to be appealed. 67 CA 562. Although defendant's claim is cast as a challenge to court's denials of his motions to suppress and to dismiss, his claim is, in reality, a challenge to court's denial of his motion for disclosure; as such, his claim is not reviewable pursuant to section. 81 CA 492. Determination requirement of section is not a matter of convenience, but rather a matter of substance necessary to achieve the goals of statute, therefore, the requirement is mandatory. 83 CA 700. Statutory requirement that court make a determination that the ruling on a motion to suppress or dismiss would be dispositive of the case is a matter of substance necessary to achieve goals of statute and therefore is mandatory. 87 CA 122. In a matter where state stipulated before trial court that court's ruling on defendant's motion to suppress evidence of prior uncharged misconduct was dispositive of

Sec. 54-95. Appeal by defendant in criminal prosecution; stay of execution.

(a) Any defendant in a criminal prosecution, aggrieved by any decision of the Superior Court, upon the trial thereof, or by any error apparent upon the record of such prosecution, may be relieved by appeal, petition for a new trial or writ of error, in the same manner and with the same effect as in civil actions. No appeal may be taken from a judgment denying a petition for a new trial unless, within ten days after the judgment is rendered, the judge who heard the case or a judge of the Supreme Court or the Appellate Court, as the case may be, certifies that a question is involved in the decision which ought to be reviewed by the Supreme Court or by the Appellate Court. It shall be sufficient service of any such writ of error or petition for a new trial to serve it upon the state's attorney for the judicial district where it is brought.

(b) When such defendant is convicted and sentenced to a term of imprisonment and, within two weeks after final judgment, files with the clerk of the court wherein the conviction was had an appeal to the Supreme Court or gives oral or written notice of his intention to appeal to said court or to petition for a new trial, the appeal or the notice shall operate as a stay of execution pending the final determination of the case, provided the defendant is admitted to bail, except the appeal or the notice shall not operate as a stay of execution, if within five days after the filing of the appeal or notice thereof, the judge before whom the criminal prosecution was tried directs in writing that the appeal or the notice shall not operate as a stay of execution. Such order shall be accompanied by a written statement of the judge's reasons for denying the stay of execution. The order and the statement shall become a part of the files and record of the case. If any defendant has been admitted to bail following an oral or written notice of intent to appeal or petition for a new trial and such defendant has failed, within twenty days after the judgment from which the appeal is to be taken, or such further period as the court may grant, to perfect the appeal or petition, a mittimus for his arrest shall issue. If any defendant is imprisoned after sentencing and before he is admitted to bail, such period of imprisonment shall be counted toward satisfaction of his sentence. If any defendant is admitted to bail and subsequently surrendered and remitted to custody while his appeal is pending, the period of imprisonment following thereafter shall be counted toward satisfaction of his sentence.

(c) In any criminal prosecution in which the defendant has been sentenced to death and has taken an appeal to the Supreme Court of this state or the Supreme Court of the United States or brought a writ of error, writ of certiorari or petition for a new trial, the taking of the appeal, the making of the application for a writ of certiorari or the return into court of the writ of error or petition for a new trial shall, unless, upon application by the state's attorney and after hearing, the Supreme Court otherwise orders, stay the execution of the death penalty until the clerk of the court where the trial was had has received notification of the termination of any such proceeding by decision or otherwise, and for thirty days thereafter. No appellate procedure shall be deemed to have terminated until the end of the period allowed by law for the filing of a motion for reargument, or, if such motion is filed, until the proceedings consequent thereon are finally determined. When execution is stayed under the provisions of this section, the clerk of the court shall forthwith give notice thereof to the warden of the institution in which such defendant is in custody. If the original judgment of conviction has been affirmed or remains in full force at the time when the clerk has received the notification of the termination of any proceedings by appeal, writ of certiorari, writ of error or petition for a new trial, and the day designated for the infliction of the death penalty has then passed or will pass within thirty days thereafter, the defendant shall, within said period of thirty days, upon an order of the court in which the judgment was rendered at a regular or special criminal session thereof, be presented before said court by the warden of the institution in which the defendant is in custody or his deputy, and the court, with the judge assigned to hold the session presiding, shall thereupon designate a day for the infliction of the death penalty and the clerk of the court shall issue a warrant of execution, reciting therein the original judgment, the fact of the stay of execution and the final order of the court, which warrant shall be forthwith served upon the warden or his deputy.

(1949 Rev., S. 8811; 1953, S. 3328d; 1957, P.A. 483; 1959, P.A. 474; 1963, P.A. 416, S. 1; 642, S. 73; 1972, P.A. 66, S. 1; P.A. 76-336, S. 14; P.A. 78-280, S. 1, 127; 78-379, S. 22, 27; P.A. 80-313, S. 51; June Sp. Sess. P.A. 83-29, S. 51, 82.)

History: 1959 act amended Subsec. (b) to provide appeal operate as a stay "provided the defendant is admitted to bail or makes an election in writing not to commence service of the sentence" and added provisions re filing of election not to commence service and re factors determining when sentence is satisfied; 1963 acts amended Subsec. (a) to delete obsolete references to the court of common pleas and amended Subsec. (b) to provide for filing of appeal two weeks after final judgment rather than one week after conviction; 1972 act specified that notice of intention to appeal may be oral or written and provision re issuance of mittimus for arrest of person who fails to perfect appeal within 20 days from judgment in Subsec. (b); P.A. 76-336 replaced specific references to Somers correctional facility with general references to "institution in which such defendant is in custody"; P.A. 78-280 substituted "judicial district" for "county" where appearing; P.A. 78-379 restated provision in Subsec. (b) re judge's direction that appeal shall not stay execution and deleted provisions re defendant's power to elect not to commence service of sentence; P.A. 80-313 made minor changes in wording but made no substantive changes; June Sp. Sess. P.A. 83-29 included reference to appellate court in Subsec. (a).

See Sec. 52-582 re time limit for bringing petitions for new trial.

Plaintiff in error may not be heard on any cause of error not specially assigned, but court finding fatal defect may reverse the judgment. 10 C. 371. Petition for new trial not granted on merely formal grounds. 11 C. 418. True rule. Id.; 48 C. 93. New evidence must be such as was not discoverable at former trial. Id. Power to grant new trial may be exercised when verdict is without evidence or manifestly against weight of evidence. 12 C. 489. State cannot move for new trial. 16 C. 59. New trial for error in charge of court or for verdict against evidence can only be granted by Supreme Court. 43 C. 516. New trial not granted on ex parte affidavits alone. 45 C. 272. Policy of law. 69 C. 190. Accused may file motion for new trial for verdict against evidence. Id., 192. Law regulating new trials same in criminal as in civil cases. 72 C. 116. Accused is entitled to every doubt as regards materiality of error. 75 C. 334. But he cannot complain of ruling that several counts state but one offense. Id., 267. Costs not taxable to defendant who prevails. 82 C. 392. Supreme Court cannot support judgment by presumption or intendment. 84 C. 93. Full discussion of proper method of taking appeal in criminal case tried to court. 105 C. 327; 109 C. 28;

Id., 126, 139. Does not permit appeal from a city court in a criminal case. 128 C. 341. Time within which motions in arrest of judgment must be filed. 148 C. 57. Where appeal period had expired, convict could not by habeas corpus proceeding challenge validity of arrest warrant; by pleading to information against him, while represented by counsel, he waived defect in warrant and consented to jurisdiction of court. 155 C. 591, 627, 701, 703. Defendant's decision to waive his right to appeal must be voluntarily, knowingly and intelligently made. 175 C. 328. Denial of a motion for a new trial was not a final judgment and not appealable. 180 C. 141. Remedy of appeal afforded defendants in criminal prosecutions having been established by statute, state's delay in defending against appeal resulted in setting aside of the judgment and ordering of a new trial. 183 C. 586. Cited. 194 C. 510; 208 C. 420; 228 C. 552; 236 C. 388.

Cited. 1 CA 724; 12 CA 621; 19 CA 686; 37 CA 252; judgment reversed, see 236 C. 388; 41 CA 530. Statutory requirement that court make a determination that ruling on a motion to suppress or dismiss would be dispositive of the case is a matter of substance necessary to achieve goals of statute and therefore is mandatory. 87 CA 122. Denial of petition for certification made pursuant to section is not a bar to court's jurisdiction, but is a threshold issue on appeal. 88 CA 572.

Term "execution" means "to put into effect". 15 CS 273. Cited. 24 CS 60; 29 CS 339; 38 CS 552; 41 CS 454.

Cited. 2 Conn. Cir. Ct. 635; 5 Conn. Cir. Ct. 314.

Subsec. (a):

Cited. 183 C. 418; 229 C. 178; Id., 397. Since legislature did not expressly prohibit appellate review of the denial of certification to appeal, petitioner is entitled to appellate review of such denial; petitioner may establish an abuse of discretion in such denial if there are issues that are debatable among jurists of reason, if a court could resolve the issues in a different manner or if there are questions that are adequate to deserve encouragement to proceed further. 246 C. 514. Although petitioner's failure to seek certification to appeal pursuant to statute does not deprive appellate tribunal of jurisdiction over the appeal, appellate tribunal should nevertheless decline to entertain an appeal challenging denial of petition for a new trial until petitioner has satisfied the certification requirement of statute. 261 C. 533.

Cited. 23 CA 559.

Sec. 54-95a. (Formerly Sec. 54-17). Jurisdiction of Superior Court.

In any prosecution for the violation of any provision of any charter, ordinance or bylaw of a city or borough, the defendant shall have the right of appeal as in other cases.

(1949 Rev., S. 8743; 1959, P.A. 28, S. 142; 1963, P.A. 642, S. 62; P.A. 74-183, S. 133, 291; P.A. 76-436, S. 524, 681.)

History: 1959 act substituted circuit court for municipal court or trial justice, which were abolished; 1963 act updated statute, deleting provisions giving superior court jurisdiction of offenses not within jurisdiction of court of common pleas and concurrent jurisdiction of offense within its jurisdiction; P.A. 74-183 replaced circuit court with court of common pleas, reflecting reorganization of judicial system, effective December 31, 1974; P.A. 76-436 deleted provisions granting superior court sole jurisdiction of offenses not in common pleas court's jurisdiction and concurrent jurisdiction of offenses in common pleas court's jurisdiction, rendered obsolete by transfer of all trial jurisdiction to superior court, effective July 1, 1978; Sec. 54-17 transferred to Sec. 54-95a in 1981.

Annotations to former section 54-17:

Superior Court formerly had no power to try a criminal case without a jury, even on agreement of parties. 27 C. 281. General criminal jurisdiction of Superior Court. 97 C. 600; 106 C. 719. Cited. 145 C. 124; 153 C. 129. The general rule of jurisdiction is that nothing shall be intended to be out of the jurisdiction of the Superior Court but that which specially appears to be so; and, on the contrary, nothing shall be intended to be within the jurisdiction of an inferior court but that which is expressly so alleged. Id., 603, 612, 613. Cited. 154 C. 272, 278; 155 C. 595; 159 C. 150. Jurisdiction over the subject matter can neither be waived nor conferred by consent of the accused. 167 C. 228.

Cited. 9 CS 167. Held proper for police court to yield jurisdiction to Superior Court in certain gambling arrests in light of state's attorney's drive against gambling being carried on through Superior Court. 21 CS 246. Cited. 33 CS 708.

Cited. 5 Conn. Cir. Ct. 119.

Annotation to present section:

Cited. 14 CA 574.

Sec. 54-95b. Reopening judgment in certain motor vehicle and criminal cases.

Any judgment rendered in the Superior Court in any case involving prosecution for a motor vehicle violation or criminal offense adjudging the defendant to pay a fine only, may be reopened, provided a motion to reopen is filed within four months succeeding the date on which it was rendered.

(P.A. 82-153.)

Sec. 54-95c. Application to vacate prostitution conviction on basis of being a victim of trafficking in persons. Prosecutor's response. Court order. At any time after a judgment of conviction is entered pursuant to section 53a-82, the defendant may apply to the Superior Court to vacate any judgment of conviction on the basis that his or her participation in the offense was a result of having been a victim of conduct of another person that constitutes (1) trafficking in persons under section 53a-192a, or (2) a criminal violation of 18 USC Chapter 77, as amended from time to time. Prior to rendering a decision on a

271

defendant's application to vacate any judgment of conviction, the court shall afford the prosecutor a reasonable opportunity to investigate the defendant's claim and an opportunity to be heard to contest the defendant's application. If the defendant proves that he or she was a victim of trafficking in persons under said section or a victim of a criminal violation of said chapter at the time of the offense, the court shall vacate any judgment of conviction and dismiss any charges related to the offense. The vacating of a judgment of conviction and dismissal of charges pursuant to this section shall not constitute grounds for an award of compensation for wrongful arrest, prosecution, conviction or incarceration pursuant to section 54-102uu or any other provision of the general statutes.

(P.A. 13-166, S. 5; P.A. 16-71, S. 15.)

History: P.A. 16-71 replaced provision re at time of offense defendant was a victim of human trafficking with provision re defendant's participation in offense was a result of having been a victim of human trafficking and made technical changes.

Sec. 54-96. Appeals by the state from Superior Court in criminal cases. Appeals from the rulings and decisions of the Superior Court, upon all questions of law arising on the trial of criminal cases, may be taken by the state, with the permission of the presiding judge, to the Supreme Court or to the Appellate Court, in the same manner and to the same effect as if made by the accused.

(1949 Rev., S. 8812; 1963, P.A. 642, S. 74; P.A. 80-442, S. 23, 28; June Sp. Sess. P.A. 83-29, S. 52, 82.)

History: 1963 act deleted provisions re appeals from common pleas court; P.A. 80-442 allowed appeals to be taken to appellate session of superior court, effective July 1, 1981; June Sp. Sess. P.A. 83-29 deleted reference to appellate session of the superior court and added reference to appellate court.

Right of appeal not limited to errors during trial alone, but extends to errors in earlier part of proceedings. 58 C. 100. Section authorizes an appeal in the nature of a motion for a new trial after acquittal; bail. 65 C. 278; 106 C. 115. Proper method to pursue to secure rulings on evidence for appeal; asking prejudicial questions before jury to secure rulings on evidence held error. 100 C. 215. Proper method to be pursued by state in taking an appeal in a criminal case discussed. 106 C. 115. To review judgment of city court, state may bring writ of error. 118 C. 373. Statute held constitutional. 122 C. 542; 302 U.S. 319. Cited. 150 C. 246; 163 C. 230; 164 C. 637. Rulings and decisions appealable under section include any proceeding from which either criminal defendant or party to civil trial could appeal. 170 C. 337. State has right to appeal in criminal cases only from Superior Court on questions of law with permission of presiding judge. 171 C. 417. Cited. Id., 600; 174 C. 100; 176 C. 224. Double jeopardy does not attach as long as a retrial is not required in the event the state prevails in its appeal. 178 C. 450. Cited. 181 C. 284; 187 C. 109; 188 C. 183; Id., 626. State's motion for dismissal with prejudice in order to allow appeal from suppression order discussed. 189 C. 42. Cited. Id., 228; Id., 360; Id., 717; 191 C. 506; 192 C. 471; 194 C. 594; 197 C. 436. Jurisdictional predicate for appeal exists only if trial court abused discretion in denying motion for permission to appeal. 202 C. 300. Cited. 209 C. 23; 210 C. 110; 213 C. 66; Id., 708; 214 C. 657; Id., 692; 215 C. 189; 219 C. 752; 223 C. 411; 224 C. 656, see also 31 CA 452; 225 C. 355; 226 C. 514; 229 C. 178; 230 C. 427; Id., 608; 236 C. 659. Judgment of Appellate Court in 33 CA 550 reversed on appeal of state with respect to suppression of evidence pursuant to section.

238 C. 380. Cited. Id., 828; 240 C. 317; Id., 708; 241 C. 823. Trial court abuses its discretion in denying state permission to appeal under section if state demonstrates that the issues are debatable among jurists of reason, that a court could resolve the issues in a different manner, or that the questions are adequate to deserve encouragement to proceed further. 261 C. 395. In denying state permission to appeal, trial court misconstrued the law of unanimity in context of a capital felony penalty hearing and, by doing so, improperly concluded that jury reached a lawful verdict. 271 C. 338.

Cited. 1 CA 378; 2 CA 605; 3 CA 477; 4 CA 520; 7 CA 131; 10 CA 147; Id., 532; 15 CA 289; 17 CA 385; 18 CA 658; 19 CA 631; Id., 686; 20 CA 321. Appeal period runs from date permission to appeal is granted. 23 CA 559. Cited. 25 CA 235; 26 CA 667; 27 CA 427; 29 CA 512; 32 CA 1; 34 CA 1; 36 CA 803; judgment reversed, see 235 C. 659, see also 241 C. 823; 39 CA 550; judgment reversed with respect to suppression of evidence, see 238 C. 380; 40 CA 544; Id., 789; 42 CA 1; Id., 17; Id., 186; judgment reversed, see 241 C. 823; 43 CA 698; 45 CA 722; 46 CA 350. Probation revocation hearing is a criminal case that can be appealed under section. 50 CA 187. Trial court improperly denied state permission to appeal on the bases of inadequacy of record where state rectified record, lack of jurisdiction over defendant solely for prosecutor's failure to sign the information pursuant to Sec. 36-12, and state's failure to indicate its intention to appeal on date of dismissal of charges where state impliedly expressed its intent by seeking "one week" and planned to file motion to appeal within that period. 51 CA 676. In the absence of either permission to appeal or challenge to trial court's denial of permission to appeal, Appellate Court lacks subject matter jurisdiction to hear an appeal pursuant to section. 55 CA 250. Where there was sufficient basis in the evidence to support court's finding on a motion to suppress and there had been a full evidentiary hearing on such motion, the record was such that there was no clear, arbitrary and extreme abuse of discretion such that an injustice appears to have been done and, therefore, trial court's denial of state's request for permission to appeal was not an abuse of discretion. 64 CA 495. Despite the statutory language of section permitting the state to appeal "with the permission of the court", the state may directly appeal a question of law without the permission of the court after requesting permission to appeal if the request is expressly denied. 147 CA 465.

Cited. 38 CS 521.

Sec. 54-96a. (Formerly Sec. 54-13). Appeal vacated by payment of fine.

Any person appealing from the judgment of the Superior Court, adjudging him to pay a fine only, may pay the same at any time before the hearing in the Supreme Court or Appellate Court, without further cost, which payment shall vacate the appeal and restore the judgment.

(1949 Rev., S. 8734; 1959, P.A. 28, S. 139; P.A. 74-183, S. 131, 291; P.A. 76-436, S. 522, 681; June Sp. Sess. P.A. 83-29, S. 53, 82.)

History: 1959 act substituted circuit court for trial justice and municipal courts, which were abolished and changed technical operation of statute; P.A. 74-183 replaced circuit court with court of common pleas and specified appellate session as that of superior court, reflecting reorganization of judicial system, effective December 31, 1974; P.A. 76-436 replaced court of common pleas with superior court and appellate session of superior court with hearing in supreme court, effective July 1, 1978; Sec. 54-13 transferred to Sec. 54-96a in 1981; June Sp. Sess. P.A. 83-29 included reference to appellate court.

Sec. 54-96b. (Formerly Sec. 54-14). Withdrawal of appeal of person committed to community correctional center.

Any person appealing from any judgment of the superior court under which judgment such person may be committed to a community correctional center may, at any time before the hearing in the Supreme Court or Appellate Court, notify the Superior Court that such appeal is withdrawn, and, if such person is in a community correctional center in default of bail awaiting trial upon such appeal, the court shall forthwith forward a mittimus to the Community Correctional Center Administrator, and the term of such sentence shall run from the date of such notice, provided such term shall not run concurrently with any other sentence or term imposed upon such person unless so directed by such court. If any person taking such appeal is at large, such person shall forthwith surrender himself to the court from which such appeal was taken and such court shall issue a mittimus in the same manner as though no appeal had been taken. Upon the issuance of such mittimus, such appeal shall be vacated and the judgment shall be in force. In any case in which the judgment from which an appeal has been taken includes a community correctional center sentence and a fine, such appeal may be vacated upon compliance with the provisions of section 54-96a and of this section, and thereupon such judgment shall be in effect.

(1949 Rev., S. 8735; 1959, P.A. 28, S. 140; 1963, P.A. 642, S. 60; 1969, P.A. 297; P.A. 74-183, S. 132, 291; P.A. 76-436, S. 523, 681; June Sp. Sess. P.A. 83-29, S. 54, 82.)

History: 1959 act substituted circuit court for trial justice or municipal court and changed technical language of statute; 1963 act substituted jail administrator for keeper of the jail; 1969 act substituted community correctional centers and their administrators for jails and their administrators; P.A. 74-183 replaced circuit court with court of common pleas and specified appellate session as that of superior court, reflecting reorganization of judicial system, effective December 31, 1974; P.A. 76-436 replaced court of common pleas with superior court and appellate session of superior court with hearing in supreme court, effective July 1, 1978; Sec. 54-14 transferred to Sec. 54-96b in 1981; June Sp. Sess. P.A. 83-29 included reference to appellate court.

Sec. 54-97. Mittimus required for commitment to correctional facility.

No person may be committed to a correctional institution or a community correctional center without a mittimus signed by the judge or clerk of the court which committed such person or, with respect to a person sentenced to a period of special parole, signed by the chairperson of the Board of Pardons and Paroles, declaring the cause of commitment and requiring the warden or Community Correctional Center Administrator to receive and keep such person in the correctional institution or the community correctional center, as the case may be, for the period fixed by the judgment of said court or said board or until such person is legally discharged; and such mittimus shall be sufficient authority to the officer to commit such person, and to the warden or Community Correctional Center Administrator to receive and hold such person in custody, except that any community correctional center may receive any person as provided in section 7-135 without such mittimus.

(1949 Rev., S. 8813; 1959, P.A. 28, S. 194; 1961, P.A. 1, S. 3; 566, S. 3; 1963, P.A. 642, S. 75; 1969, P.A. 297; P.A. 80-313, S. 49; P.A. 04-234, S. 2, 7.)

History: 1959 act deleted obsolete reference to trial justice; 1961 acts added exception re Sec. 7-135; 1963 act deleted obsolete references to workhouses and substituted state jail administrator for warden or master; 1969 act replaced jails and their administrators with community correctional centers and their administrators; P.A. 80-313 substituted "may" for "shall" and added reference to incarceration in Somers facility for period fixed by court's judgment or until discharge effected; P.A. 04-234 replaced references to the Connecticut Correctional Institution, Somers with "correctional institution", authorized the commitment by a mittimus signed by the chairperson of the Board of Parole of a person sentenced to a period of special parole, authorized retention of the person for the period fixed by "said board" and made technical changes for purposes of gender neutrality, effective June 8, 2004, and replaced Board of Parole with Board of Pardons and Paroles, effective July 1, 2004.

Sec. 54-98. Execution of mittimus for commitment to Connecticut Correctional Institution, Somers.

The Chief Court Administrator or the administrator's designee shall execute each mittimus for the commitment of convicts to the Connecticut Correctional Institution, Somers, by delivering such convicts to the warden of said institution or such warden's agent at said institution.

(1949 Rev., S. 8814; 1959, P.A. 615, S. 11; 1969, P.A. 297; P.A. 00-99, S. 121, 154; P.A. 01-195, S. 71, 181.)

History: 1959 act substituted mittimus for warrant; 1969 act replaced "jail" with "community correctional center"; P.A. 00-99 replaced reference to sheriffs with the Chief Court Administrator or the administrator's designee and deleted provisions re fees payable to sheriffs for prisoner transportation, effective December 1, 2000; P.A. 01-195 made a technical change for the purpose of gender neutrality, effective July 11, 2001.

Cited. 185 C. 540.

Cited. 16 CS 79.

Sec. 54-99. Period within which death penalty inflicted.

Unless a reprieve or stay of execution is granted by competent authority, the penalty of death shall be inflicted within a period of not less than one month nor more than six months after conviction and sentence. All executions of the death penalty shall take place according to the provisions of this section and section 54-100 on the day, or within five days after the day, designated by the judge passing sentence.

(1949 Rev., S. 8815.)

Cited. 121 C. 197.

Sec. 54-100. Method of inflicting death penalty. Attendance at execution.

(a) The method of inflicting the punishment of death shall be by continuous intravenous injection of a substance or substances in a quantity sufficient to cause death, in accordance with procedures prescribed by the Commissioner of Correction in consultation with the Commissioner of Public Health. The Commissioner of Correction shall direct a warden of an appropriate correctional institution to appoint a suitable person or persons to perform the duty of executing sentences of the court requiring the infliction of the death penalty. Such person or persons shall receive, for such duty, such compensation as is determined by the Commissioner of Correction. When any person is sentenced to death by any court of this state having competent jurisdiction, he shall, within twenty days after final sentence, be conveyed to an appropriate correctional institution and such punishment shall be inflicted only within the walls of said institution, within an enclosure to be prepared for that purpose under direction of the warden of said institution. Such enclosure shall be so constructed as to exclude public view.

(b) Besides the warden or deputy warden and such number of correctional staff as he thinks necessary, the following persons may be present at the execution: The Commissioner of Correction, a physician, a clergyman in attendance upon the prisoner and such other adults, as the prisoner may designate, not exceeding three in number, news media representatives and such other persons as the commissioner deems appropriate. The total number of witnesses permitted at an execution shall be governed by space and security requirements and the Commissioner of Correction shall make the final determination of such number. News media representatives present at an execution shall include representatives of newspapers, broadcasters and news services, who shall report on behalf of all news media. The number of news media representatives present at an execution shall be nine, except that the commissioner, in his discretion, may authorize a greater number of such representatives or, for specified reasons of space or security, may reduce such number of representatives. The commissioner may exclude a witness for specified reasons of security.

(1949 Rev., S. 8816; 1963, P.A. 28, S. 6; P.A. 74-84; P.A. 95-16, S. 1, 5; 95-257, S. 12, 21, 58; P.A. 96-180, S. 130, 166; P.A. 97-184, S. 1.)

History: 1963 act provided electrocution be at prison in Somers rather than Wethersfield; P.A. 74-84 allowed attendance of "adults" designated by prisoner rather than attendance of "persons, adult males" designated by prisoner; P.A. 95-16 changed the method of inflicting the punishment of death from "electrocution" to "continuous intravenous injection of a substance or substances in a quantity sufficient to cause death, in accordance with procedures prescribed by the Commissioner of Correction in consultation with the Commissioner of Public Health and Addiction Services", replaced the requirement that the warden of the Connecticut Correctional Institution, Somers, appoint a suitable person to perform the execution and that such person's compensation be determined by the directors of said institution with the requirement that the Commissioner of Correction direct a warden of an appropriate correctional institution to appoint such a person and that such person's compensation be determined by said commissioner, required a person sentenced to death to be conveyed to an appropriate correctional institution rather than to "the Connecticut Correctional Institution, Somers" and that the enclosure be prepared under direction of the warden of said institution rather than the warden and board of directors of the Connecticut Correctional Institution, Somers, replaced "guards" with "correction officers", replaced as some of the persons authorized to be in attendance at the execution "the board of directors, the physician of the Connecticut Correctional Institution, Somers," with "the commissioner, a physician of a correctional institution", effective October 1, 1995, and applicable to executions carried out on or after said date; P.A. 95-257 replaced Commissioner and Department of Public Health and Addiction Services with Commissioner and Department of Public Health, effective July 1, 1995; P.A. 96-180 substituted "Commissioner of Correction" for "commissioner", effective June 3, 1996; P.A. 97-184 inserted Subsec. indicators, amended Subsec. (a) to authorize the appointment of more than one person to perform the execution and amended Subsec. (b) to revise the list of persons authorized to be present at the execution by replacing "correction officers" with "correctional staff", replacing "a physician of a correctional institution" with "a physician", deleting the "sheriff of the county in which the prisoner was tried and convicted", "representatives of not more than five newspapers in the county where the crime was committed" and "one reporter for each of the daily newspapers published in the city of Hartford" and adding "news media representatives" and "such other persons as the commissioner deems appropriate", provided that the total number of witnesses shall be governed by space and security requirements and be finally determined by the commissioner, provide that news media representatives shall include representatives of newspapers, broadcasters and news services reporting on behalf of all news media, provided that the number of news media representatives shall be nine subject to increase or reduction by the commissioner and authorize the commissioner to exclude a witness for security reasons.

Cited. 121 C. 197. Death penalty does not constitute cruel and unusual punishment and courts will not vitiate legislative determination of punishment for crimes. 158 C. 341. Cited. 238 C. 389.

Sec. 54-100a. Committee on news media access to executions. Selection of news media witnesses.

There shall be a committee on news media access to executions composed of news media representatives appointed by the Associated Press Managing Editors Association of Connecticut and the Connecticut Associated Press Broadcasters Association. The Commissioner of Correction or his designee shall be an ex-officio member of the committee. The committee shall receive applications from news media seeking to witness and report executions and select news media witnesses from such applicants. The committee shall consider applications from three categories of news media: (1) Newspapers, broadcasters and news services regularly reporting general news of the state; (2) newspapers and broadcasters nearest the locality where the crime was committed; and (3) newspapers and broadcasters that regularly cover the correctional institutions deemed appropriate by the commissioner as a location for the infliction of the death penalty. The committee shall select applicants from each category unless a category lacks a qualified applicant. The committee shall promptly inform the commissioner of its recommendations and inform the news media recommended to be witnesses. For any execution, the commissioner shall specify the number of news media witnesses that space and security requirements permit. The commissioner shall promptly inform the committee if any applicant it has recommended to be a witness is to be excluded for specified reasons of security.

(P.A. 97-184, S. 2.)

(Return to Chapter Table of Contents)

(Return to List of Chapters)

(Return to List of Titles)

Sec. 54-101. Disposition of person becoming insane after death sentence. When any person detained at the Connecticut Correctional Institution, Somers, awaiting execution of a sentence of death appears to the warden thereof to be insane, the warden may make application to the superior court for the judicial district of Tolland having either civil or criminal jurisdiction or, if said court is not in session, to any judge of the Superior Court, and, after hearing upon such application, notice thereof having been given to the state's attorney for the judicial district wherein such person was convicted, said court or such judge may, if it appears advisable, appoint three reputable physicians to examine as to the mental condition of the person so committed. Upon return to said court or such judge of a certificate by such physicians, or a majority of them, stating that such person is insane, said court or such judge shall order the sentence of execution to be stayed and such person to be transferred to any state hospital for mental illness for confinement, support and treatment until such person recovers sanity, and shall cause a mittimus to be issued to the Department of Correction for such commitment. If, at any time thereafter, the superintendent of the state hospital to which such person has been committed is of the opinion that such person has recovered sanity, the superintendent shall so report to the state's attorney for the judicial district wherein the conviction was had and such attorney shall thereupon make application to the superior court for such judicial district having criminal jurisdiction, for the issuance of a warrant of execution for such sentence, and, if said court finds that such person has recovered sanity, it shall cause a mittimus to be issued for such person's return to the Connecticut Correctional Institution, Somers, there to be received and kept until a day designated in the mittimus for the infliction of the death penalty, and thereupon said penalty shall be inflicted, in accordance with the provisions of the statutes.

(1949 Rev., S. 8817; 1963, P.A. 28, S. 7; P.A. 73-116, S. 28; 73-667, S. 1, 2; P.A. 78-280, S. 120, 127; P.A. 82-472, S. 146, 183; P.A. 00-99, S. 122, 154; P.A. 01-195, S. 72, 181.)

History: 1963 act substituted Tolland county for Hartford county; P.A. 73-116 added references to judicial districts and substituted "Connecticut Correctional Institution, Somers" for "State Prison"; P.A. 73-667 changed effective date of P.A. 73-116 from October 1, 1973, to April 25, 1973; P.A. 78-280 deleted references to counties; P.A. 82-472 deleted obsolete reference to counties; P.A. 00-99 replaced reference to sheriff of Tolland County or either deputy with the Department of Correction re to whom mittimus shall be issued, effective December 1, 2000; P.A. 01-195 made technical changes for purposes of gender neutrality, effective July 11, 2001.

Statute requires a determination of "sanity" only as a condition precedent to the carrying out of the death penalty, and mandates execution once such a determination is made. 169 C. 13.

Sec. 54-102. Burial or disposal of body of executed criminal.

The warden or his deputy shall cause the body of any executed criminal to be decently and quietly buried in any place in the United States that may be designated by the relatives or friends of the executed person, provided a request for such burial has been made to the warden or deputy on or before the day of execution. The amount of the expenses of the funeral and burial to be paid by the state shall not exceed one hundred and fifty dollars, which shall be paid out of any funds on hand appropriated for the maintenance and support of the Connecticut Correctional Institution, Somers. If the expenses of the funeral and burial at the place designated by such relatives or friends exceed one hundred and fifty dollars, such relatives or friends shall pay to the warden the amount required in excess of said sum before the warden causes the body of such criminal to be removed and buried at the place designated. If the body is not claimed by any relatives or friends on or before the day of execution, the warden or deputy shall dispose of it as provided by law for the unclaimed bodies of criminals who die in the Connecticut Correctional Institution, Somers. The warden shall endorse upon the death warrant a record of his execution thereof and shall return such warrant to the clerk of the superior court for the judicial district where the trial and conviction was had.

(1949 Rev., S. 8818; 1953, S. 3329d; P.A. 73-116, S. 29; 73-667, S. 1, 2; P.A. 82-472, S. 147, 183.)

History: P.A. 73-116 added reference to judicial districts; P.A. 73-667 changed effective date of P.A. 73-116 from October 1, 1973, to April 25, 1973; P.A. 82-472 deleted obsolete reference to counties.

See Sec. 19a-270 re municipal

PART IIa HIV AND DNA TESTING OF OFFENDERS

Sec. 54-102a. (Formerly Sec. 53a-90). Venereal examination and HIV testing of persons charged with certain sexual offenses.

(a) The court before which is pending any case involving a violation of any provision of sections 53a-65 to 53a-89, inclusive, may, before final disposition of such case, order the examination of the accused person or, in a delinquency proceeding, the accused child to determine whether or not the accused person or child is suffering from any venereal disease, unless the court from which such case has been transferred has ordered the examination of the accused person or child for such purpose, in which event the court to which such transfer is taken may determine that a further examination is unnecessary.

(b) Notwithstanding the provisions of section 19a-582, the court before which is pending any case involving a violation of section 53-21 or any provision of sections 53a-65 to 53a-89, inclusive, that involved a sexual act, as defined in section 54-102b, may, before final disposition of such case, order the testing of the accused person or, in a delinquency proceeding, the accused child for the presence of the etiologic agent for acquired immune deficiency syndrome or human immunodeficiency virus, unless the court from which such case has been transferred has ordered the testing of the accused person or child for such purpose, in which event the court to which such transfer is taken may determine that a further test is unnecessary. If the victim of the offense requests that the accused person or child be tested, the court may order the testing of the accused person or child in accordance with this subsection and the results of such test may be disclosed to the victim. The provisions of sections 19a-581 to 19a-585, inclusive, and section 19a-590, except any provision requiring the subject of an HIV-related test to provide informed consent prior to the performance of such test and any provision that would prohibit or limit the disclosure of the results of such test to the victim under this subsection, shall apply to a test ordered under this subsection and the disclosure of the results of such test.

(c) A report of the result of such examination or test shall be filed with the Department of Public Health on a form supplied by it. If such examination discloses the presence of venereal disease or if such test discloses the presence of the etiologic agent for acquired immune deficiency syndrome or human immunodeficiency virus, the court may make such order with reference to the continuance of the case or treatment or other disposition of such person as the public health and welfare require. Such examination or test shall be conducted at the expense of the Department of Public Health. Any person who fails to comply with any order of any court under the provisions of this section shall be guilty of a class C misdemeanor.

(1969, P.A. 828, S. 91; P.A. 77-614, S. 323, 610; P.A. 92-260, S. 34; P.A. 93-381, S. 9, 39; May Sp. Sess. P.A. 94-6, S. 27, 28; P.A. 95-257, S. 12, 21, 58; June Sp. Sess. P.A. 98-1, S. 40, 121; P.A. 10-43, S. 41.)

History: P.A. 77-614 replaced department of health with department of health services, effective January 1, 1979; P.A. 92-260 replaced "bound over" and "bindover" with "transferred" and "transfer", respectively; P.A. 93-381 replaced department of health services with department of public health and addiction services, effective July 1, 1993; May Sp. Sess. P.A. 94-6 added provisions designated as Subsec. (b) concerning acquired immune deficiency syndrome, relettered Subsec. (c) and made prior provisions Subsecs. (a) and (c), amending Subsec. (c) to apply to tests for acquired immune deficiency syndrome or human immunodeficiency virus, effective June 21, 1994; Sec. 53a-90 transferred to Sec. 54-102a in 1995; P.A. 95-257 replaced Commissioner and Department of Public Health and Addiction Services with Commissioner and Department of Public Health, effective July 1, 1995; June Sp. Sess. P.A. 98-1 made a technical change in Subsec. (a), effective June 24, 1998; P.A. 10-43 amended Subsecs. (a) and (b) to make provisions applicable to accused child in delinquency proceeding.

Sec. 54-102b. HIV testing of persons convicted of certain sexual offenses.

(a) Notwithstanding any provision of the general statutes, except as provided in subsection (b) of this section, a court entering a judgment of conviction or conviction of a child as delinquent for a violation of section 53a-70, 53a-70a, 53a-70b or 53a-71 or a violation of section 53-21, 53a-72a, 53a-72b or 53a-73a involving a sexual act, shall, at the request of the victim of such crime, order that the offender be tested for the presence of the etiologic agent for acquired immune deficiency syndrome or human immunodeficiency virus and that the results be disclosed to the victim and the offender. The test shall be performed by or at the direction of the Department of Correction or, in the case of a child convicted as delinquent, at the direction of the Court Support Services Division of the Judicial Department or the Department of Children and Families, in consultation with the Department of Public Health.

(b) The provisions of sections 19a-581 to 19a-585, inclusive, and section 19a-590, except the requirement that the subject of an HIV-related test provide informed consent prior to the performance of such test, shall apply to a test ordered under this section.

(c) For the purposes of this section and section 19a-112b, "sexual act" means contact between the penis and the vulva or the penis and the anus, where such contact involving the penis occurs upon penetration, however slight, or contact between the mouth and the penis, the mouth and the vulva or the mouth and the anus.

(May Sp. Sess. P.A. 94-6, S. 24, 28; P.A. 95-257, S. 12, 21, 58; P.A. 10-43, S. 42.)

History: May Sp. Sess. P.A. 94-6 effective June 21, 1994; P.A. 95-257 replaced Commissioner and Department of Public Health and Addiction Services with Commissioner and Department of Public Health, effective July 1, 1995; P.A. 10-43 amended Subsec. (a) to replace "an adjudication of delinquency" with "conviction of a child as delinquent" and require that, in case of child convicted as delinquent, test be performed at direction of Court Support Services Division or Department of Children and Families.

Sec. 54-102c. HIV information and test results provided to victim.

When a court orders a test pursuant to section 54-102a or 54-102b, the court shall provide the victim with (1) the educational materials about human immunodeficiency virus and acquired immune deficiency syndrome developed by the Department of Public Health pursuant to section 19a-112c, (2) information about and referral to HIV testing and counseling for victims of sexual acts provided through sites funded by such department pursuant to section 19a-112b, and (3) referrals and information regarding rape crisis centers. The court shall also inform the victim that the victim may designate a health care provider chosen by the victim or an HIV testing and counseling site funded by the department to receive the results of such test on behalf of the victim. The test results shall be disclosed to the victim by the designated health care provider or by a professional trained to provide counseling about HIV and acquired immune deficiency syndrome at the department-funded site designated by the victim.

(P.A. 04-165, S. 2.)

Secs. 54-102d to 54-102f. Reserved for future use.

Sec. 54-102g. Blood or other biological sample required from certain arrested or convicted persons for DNA analysis.

(a) Whenever any person is arrested on or after October 1, 2011, for the commission of a serious felony and, prior to such arrest, has been convicted of a felony but has not submitted to the taking of a blood or other biological sample for DNA (deoxyribonucleic acid) analysis pursuant to this section, the law enforcement agency that arrested such person shall, as available resources allow, require such person to submit to the taking of a blood or other biological sample for DNA (deoxyribonucleic acid) analysis to determine identification characteristics specific to the person. If the law enforcement agency requires such person to submit to the taking of such blood or other biological sample, such person shall submit to the taking of such sample prior to release from custody and at such time and place as the agency may specify. For purposes of this subsection, "serious felony" means a violation of section 53a-54a, 53a-54b, 53a-54c, 53a-54d, 53a-55, 53a-55a, 53a-56, 53a-56a, 53a-56b, 53a-57, 53a-59, 53a-59a, 53a-60, 53a-60a, 53a-60b, 53a-60c, 53a-70, 53a-70a, 53a-70b, 53a-72b, 53a-92, 53a-92a, 53a-94, 53a-94a, 53a-95, 53a-100aa, 53a-101, 53a-102, 53a-102a, 53a-103a, 53a-111, 53a-112, 53a-134, 53a-135, 53a-136, 53a-167c, 53a-179b, 53a-179c or 53a-181c.

(b) Any person who has been convicted of a criminal offense against a victim who is a minor, a nonviolent sexual offense or a sexually violent offense, as those terms are defined in section 54-250, or a felony, and has been sentenced on that conviction to the custody of the Commissioner of Correction, and who has not submitted to the taking of a blood or other biological sample pursuant to subsection (a) of this section with respect to such offense, shall, prior to release from custody and at such time as the commissioner may specify, submit to the taking of a blood or other biological sample of sufficient quality for DNA (deoxyribonucleic acid) analysis to determine identification characteristics specific to the person. If any person required to submit to the taking of a blood or other biological sample pursuant to this subsection refuses to do so, the Commissioner of Correction or the commissioner's designee shall notify the Department of Emergency Services and Public Protection within thirty days of such refusal for the initiation of criminal proceedings against such person.

(c) Any person who is convicted of a criminal offense against a victim who is a minor, a nonviolent sexual offense or a sexually violent offense, as those terms are defined in section 54-250, or a felony and is not sentenced to a term of confinement, and who has not submitted to the taking of a blood or other biological sample pursuant to subsection (a) of this section with respect to such offense, shall, as a condition of such sentence and at a time and place specified by the Court Support Services Division of the Judicial Department, submit to the taking of a blood or other biological sample of sufficient quality for DNA (deoxyribonucleic acid) analysis to determine identification characteristics specific to the person.

(d) Any person who has been found not guilty by reason of mental disease or defect pursuant to section 53a-13 of a criminal offense against a victim who is a minor, a nonviolent sexual offense or a sexually violent offense, as those terms are defined in section 54-250, or a felony, and is in the custody of the Commissioner of Mental Health and Addiction Services or the Commissioner of Developmental Services as a result of that finding, and who has not submitted to the taking of a blood or other biological sample pursuant to subsection (a) of this section with respect to such offense, shall, prior to a court hearing commenced in accordance with subsection (d) of section 17a-582, and at such time as the Commissioner of Mental Health and Addiction Services or the Commissioner of Developmental Services with whom such person has been placed may specify, submit to the taking of a blood or other biological sample of sufficient quality for DNA (deoxyribonucleic acid) analysis to determine identification characteristics specific to the person.

(e) Any person who has been convicted of a criminal offense against a victim who is a minor, a nonviolent sexual offense or a sexually violent offense, as those terms are defined in section 54-250, or a felony, and is serving a period of probation or parole, and who has not submitted to the taking of a blood or other biological sample pursuant to subsection (a), (b), (c) or (d) of this section, shall, prior to discharge from the custody of the Court Support Services Division or the Department of Correction and at such time as said division or department may specify, submit to the taking of a blood or other biological sample of sufficient quality for DNA (deoxyribonucleic acid) analysis to determine identification characteristics specific to the person.

(f) Any person who has been convicted or found not guilty by reason of mental disease or defect in any other state or jurisdiction of a felony or of any crime, the essential elements of which are substantially the same as a criminal offense against a victim who is a minor, a nonviolent sexual offense or a sexually violent offense, as those terms are defined in section 54-250, and is in the custody of the Commissioner of Correction, is under the supervision of the Judicial Department or the Board of Pardons and Paroles or is under the jurisdiction of the Psychiatric Security Review Board, shall, prior to discharge from such custody, supervision or jurisdiction submit to the taking of a blood or other biological sample of sufficient quality for DNA (deoxyribonucleic acid) analysis to determine identification characteristics specific to the person.

(g) If the blood or other biological sample taken from a person pursuant to this section is not of sufficient quality for DNA (deoxyribonucleic acid) analysis to determine identification characteristics specific to the person, the person shall submit to the taking of an additional sample or samples until a sample of sufficient quality is obtained.

(h) The analysis shall be performed by the Division of Scientific Services within the Department of Emergency Services and Public Protection, except that the division shall analyze samples taken pursuant to subsection (a) of this section only as available resources allow. The identification characteristics of the profile resulting from the DNA (deoxyribonucleic acid) analysis shall be stored and maintained by the division in a DNA data bank and shall be made available only as provided in section 54-102j.

(i) Any person who refuses to submit to the taking of a blood or other biological sample pursuant to this section or wilfully fails to appear at the time and place specified pursuant to subsection (b) of this section for the taking of a blood or other biological sample shall be guilty of a class D felony. Any person required to submit to the taking of a blood or other biological sample pursuant to subsection (c) of this section who wilfully fails to appear to submit to the taking of such sample within five business days of the time specified by the Court Support Services Division may be arrested pursuant to a warrant issued under section 54-2a.

(j) If any person required to submit to the taking of a blood or other biological sample pursuant to any provision of this section is in the custody of the Commissioner of Correction and refuses to submit to the taking of such sample, the commissioner or the commissioner's designee may use reasonable force to obtain a blood or other biological sample from such person.

(k) For the purposes of this section, a motor vehicle violation for which a sentence to a term of imprisonment of more than one year may be imposed shall be deemed an unclassified felony.

(P.A. 94-246, S. 1; P.A. 98-111, S. 10; P.A. 99-183, S. 11, 13; 99-218, S. 10, 16; P.A. 03-242, S. 1; P.A. 04-188, S. 1; 04-234, S. 2; 04-257, S. 121; P.A. 07-73, S. 2(b); P.A. 10-102, S. 2; P.A. 11-51, S. 134; 11-144, S. 1; 11-207, S. 1; P.A. 12-133, S. 20.)

History: P.A. 98-111 added new Subsec. (c) requiring any person found not guilty by reason of mental disease or defect of any violation specified in Subsec. (a) or (b) on or after October 1, 1994 to have a blood sample taken for DNA analysis prior to discharge from custody, redesignating former Subsec. (c) as Subsec. (d); P.A. 99-183 revised the crimes the conviction of which subjects a person to DNA testing by replacing "a violation of section 53a-70, 53a-70a, 53a-70b, 53a-71, 53a-72a or 53a-72b" in Subsecs. (a) and (b) and "any violation specified in subsection (a) or (b) of this section" in Subsec. (c) with "a criminal offense against a victim who is a minor, a nonviolent sexual offense or a sexually violent offense, as those terms are defined in section 54-250, or of a felony found by the sentencing court to have been committed for a sexual purpose, as provided in section 54-254", amended Subsec. (a) to make provisions applicable to a person convicted of any of the specified offenses who "is sentenced to the custody of the Commissioner of Correction" rather than a person who is convicted of any of the specified offenses "on or after October 1, 1994, and is sentenced to the custody of the Commissioner of Correction" or a person who has been convicted of any of the specified offenses "and on October 1, 1994, is in the custody of the Commissioner of Correction", amended Subsec. (b) to delete provision re applicability to persons convicted "on or after October 1, 1994", amended Subsec. (c) to delete provision re applicability to persons found not guilty by reason of mental disease or defect "on or after October 1, 1994" and include a discharge in accordance with Sec. 17a-588, and made technical changes for purposes of gender neutrality, effective July 1, 1999; P.A. 99-218 amended Subsec. (d) by replacing the State Police Forensic Science Laboratory with the Division of Scientific Services within the Department of Public Safety, effective July 1, 1999; P.A. 03-242 replaced in Subsecs. (a), (b) and (c) "a felony found by the sentencing court to have been committed for a sexual purpose as provided in section 54-254" with "a felony", amended Subsec. (a) to replace requirement that the person "at any time prior to release from custody, have a sample of such person's blood taken" with requirement that the person "prior to release from custody and at such time as the commissioner may specify, submit to the taking of a blood or other biological sample", amended Subsec. (b) to replace requirement that the person "have a sample of such person's blood taken" with requirement that the person "at such time as the sentencing court may specify, submit to the taking of a blood or other biological sample", amended Subsec. (c) to replace requirement that the person "at any time" prior to discharge from custody "have a sample of such person's blood taken" with requirement that the person prior to discharge from custody and "at such time as the superintendent of the hospital for psychiatric disabilities in which such person is confined or the Commissioner of Mental Retardation with whom such person has been placed may specify, submit to the taking of a blood or other biological sample", added new Subsec. (d) requiring any person who is convicted of a criminal offense against a victim who is a minor, nonviolent sexual offense, sexually violent offense or felony and is serving a period of probation or parole to submit to the taking of a blood or other biological sample prior to discharge from custody and redesignated existing Subsec. (d) as Subsec. (e); P.A. 04-188 amended Subsec. (a) to replace "is convicted" with "has been convicted", replace "is sentenced" with "has been sentenced on that conviction" and add provision re notification of Department of Public Safety when a person refuses to submit to the taking of a sample, amended Subsec. (c) to replace "is found not guilty" with "has been found not guilty", add condition that such person "is in custody as a result of that finding" and replace "superintendent of the hospital for psychiatric disabilities in which such person is confined" with "Commissioner of Mental Health and Addiction Services", added new Subsec. (e) re taking of samples from persons convicted or found not guilty by reason of mental disease or defect in another state or jurisdiction and who are in the custody or under the supervision or jurisdiction of certain agencies in this state, redesignated existing Subsec. (e) as Subsec. (f) and added Subsec. (g) to make it a class A misdemeanor to refuse to submit to the taking of a sample; P.A. 04-234 replaced Board of Parole with Board of Pardons and Paroles, effective July 1, 2004; P.A. 04-257 amended Subsec. (d) to replace references to "the Board of Parole" and "board" with "the Department of Correction" and "department", respectively, effective June 14, 2004; pursuant to P.A. 07-73 "Commissioner of Mental Retardation" was changed editorially by the Revisors to "Commissioner of Developmental Services", effective October 1, 2007; P.A. 10-102 amended Subsec. (b) to require submission to taking of sample "at a time and place specified by the Court Support Services Division of the Judicial Department" rather than "at such time as the sentencing court may specify" and amended Subsec. (g) to increase penalty from class A misdemeanor to class D felony and add provision re arrest by warrant of person who refuses to submit to taking of sample pursuant to Subsec. (b) within 5 days of time specified; pursuant to P.A. 11-51, "Department of Public Safety" was changed editorially by the Revisors to "Department of Emergency Services and Public Protection", effective July 1, 2011; P.A. 11-144 required sample taken be "of sufficient quality", amended Subsec. (c) to make applicable to person who is "in the custody of the Commissioner of Mental Health and Addiction Services or the Commissioner of Developmental Services", rather than "in custody", and require person to submit to taking of sample "prior to a court hearing commenced in accordance with subsection (d) of section 17a-582", rather than "prior to discharge from custody in accordance with subsection (e) of section 17a-582, section 17a-588 or subsection (g) of section 17a-593", added new Subsec. (f) to require person to submit to taking of additional sample or samples until sample of sufficient quality is obtained, redesignated existing Subsec. (f) as Subsec. (g), redesignated existing Subsec. (g) as Subsec. (h) and amended same to make penalty applicable to person who "wilfully fails to appear at the time and place specified pursuant to subsection (b) of this section for the taking of a blood or other biological sample" and replace "refuses" with "wilfully fails to appear" and added Subsec. (i) to authorize use of reasonable force to obtain sample from person in custody of Commissioner of Correction who refuses to submit to taking of sample; P.A. 11-207 added new Subsec. (a) re taking of blood or other biological sample for DNA analysis of person arrested on or after October 1, 2011, for commission of serious felony who prior to such arrest has been convicted of a felony but has not submitted to the taking of such a sample, redesignated existing Subsecs. (a) to (g) as Subsecs. (b) to (h), amended Subsecs. (b) to (d) to add condition that such person "has not submitted to the taking of a blood or other biological sample pursuant to subsection (a) of this section with respect to such offense", amended Subsec. (e) to make a technical change, amended Subsec. (g) to add exception that division shall analyze samples taken pursuant to Subsec. (a) only as available resources allow and make a technical change, and amended Subsec. (h) to make a technical change; P.A. 12-133 added Subsec. (k) re motor vehicle violation for which sentence to a term of imprisonment of more than 1 year may be imposed deemed an unclassified felony.

Purpose of section is to further the regulatory, nonpunitive goal of maintaining a DNA data bank to assist in criminal investigations, not to punish those convicted of crimes by requiring them to submit a DNA sample; penalty provision of section does not render the entire statutory scheme punitive in fact; prior to the legislature's amendment of the section in 2011, section was ambiguous as to whether it was permissible for the trial court to authorize the state to use reasonable physical force to obtain a sample of a defendant's DNA, but the use of reasonable force to obtain a DNA sample from an unwilling individual was inherent in section; section is regulatory in nature, rather than punitive, and does not violate the federal constitution's bar on ex post facto laws under article one, section 10. 321 C. 821.

Section is regulatory in nature and does not violate the ex post facto clause, and the state may use reasonable force to obtain a DNA sample. 143 CA 485; judgment affirmed, see 321 C. 821. Defendant's double jeopardy claim fails because refusal to provide DNA sample is new, postconviction conduct and constitutes a separate crime. Id., 510.

Sec. 54-102h. Procedure for collection of blood or other biological sample for DNA analysis.

(a)(1) The collection of a blood or other biological sample from persons required to submit to the taking of such sample pursuant to subsection (a) of section 54-102g shall be the responsibility of the law enforcement agency that arrested such person and shall be taken at a time and place specified by that agency prior to such person's release from custody.

(2) The collection of a blood or other biological sample from persons required to submit to the taking of such sample pursuant to subsection (b) of section 54-102g shall be the responsibility of the Department of Correction and shall be taken at a time and place specified by the Department of Correction.

(3) The collection of a blood or other biological sample from persons required to submit to the taking of such sample pursuant to subsection (c) of section 54-102g shall be the responsibility of the Judicial Department and shall be taken at a time and place specified by the Court Support Services Division.

(4) The collection of a blood or other biological sample from persons required to submit to the taking of such sample pursuant to subsection (d) of section 54-102g shall be the responsibility of the Commissioner of Mental Health and Addiction Services or the Commissioner of Developmental Services, as the case may be, and shall be taken at a time and place specified by said commissioner.

(5) The collection of a blood or other biological sample from persons required to submit to the taking of such sample pursuant to subsection (e) of section 54-102g shall be the responsibility of the Judicial Department if such person is serving a period of probation and of the Department of Correction if such person is serving a period of parole and shall be taken at a time and place specified by the Court Support Services Division or the Department of Correction, as the case may be.

(6) The collection of a blood or other biological sample from persons required to submit to the taking of such sample pursuant to subsection (f) of section 54-102g shall be the responsibility of the agency in whose custody or under whose supervision such person has been placed, and shall be taken at a time and place specified by such agency.

(b) Only a person licensed to practice medicine and surgery in this state, a qualified laboratory technician, a registered nurse or a phlebotomist shall take any blood sample to be submitted to analysis.

(c) No civil liability shall attach to any person authorized to take a blood or other biological sample as provided in this section as a result of the act of taking such sample from any person submitting thereto, if the blood or other biological sample was taken according to recognized medical procedures, provided no person shall be relieved from liability for negligence in the taking of any such sample.

(d) (1) Chemically clean sterile disposable needles and vacuum draw tubes shall be used for all blood samples. The tube or container for a blood or other biological sample shall be sealed and labeled with the subject's name, Social Security number, date of birth, race and gender, the name of the person collecting the sample, and the date and place of collection. The tube or container shall be secured to prevent tampering with the contents.

(2) Only collection kits approved by the Division of Scientific Services within the Department of Emergency Services and Public Protection may be used for the collection of biological samples by buccal swabs.

(e) The steps set forth in this section relating to the taking, handling, identification and disposition of blood or other biological samples are procedural and not substantive. Substantial compliance therewith shall be deemed to be sufficient. The samples shall be transported to the Division of Scientific Services within the Department of Emergency Services and Public Protection not more than fifteen days following their collection and shall be analyzed and stored in the DNA data bank in accordance with sections 54-102i and 54-102j.

(P.A. 94-246, S. 2; P.A. 99-218, S. 11, 16; P.A. 03-242, S. 2; P.A. 04-188, S. 2; 04-234, S. 2; P.A. 07-73, S. 2(b); 07-158, S. 5; P.A. 10-102, S. 3; P.A. 11-51, S. 134; 11-207, S. 2.)

History: P.A. 99-218 amended Subsec. (b) by replacing the State Police Forensic Science Laboratory with the Division of Scientific Services within the Department of Public Safety, effective July 1, 1999; P.A. 03-242 amended Subsec. (a) to make provisions applicable to "other biological" samples in addition to blood samples, provide that samples be "taken" rather than "withdrawn" and rephrase provisions re withdrawal of samples accordingly, add provision requiring samples from persons who are found not guilty by reason of mental disease or defect and are confined in a hospital for psychiatric disabilities or placed with the Commissioner of Mental Retardation be taken at a time and place specified by the superintendent or the commissioner, add provision requiring samples from persons serving probation or parole be taken at a time and place specified by the Court Support Services Division or the Board of Parole and make provision that requires certain medical personnel to withdraw any sample applicable only to the taking of "blood" samples, amended Subsec. (b) to make provision requiring the use of needles and vacuum draw tubes applicable to "blood" samples and include references to the "container" for the sample, designated existing provisions re procedure and substantial compliance therewith and requirements re transportation, analysis and storage as Subsec. (c) and amended said Subsec. to make provisions applicable to "other biological" samples and replace "withdrawal" with "their collection"; P.A. 04-188 amended Subsec. (a) to insert Subdiv. designators, amended Subsec. (a)(1) to provide that collection of the sample shall be the responsibility of Department of Correction, that samples collected are "from persons required to submit to the taking of such sample pursuant to subsection (a) of section 54-102g" rather than "pursuant to section 54-102g from persons who are to be incarcerated" and that samples be taken at "a time and place specified" by department rather than "at the receiving unit or at such other place as is designated" by department, amended Subsec. (a)(2) to provide that collection of the sample shall be the responsibility of Department of Public Safety and that samples collected are from "persons required to submit to the taking of such sample pursuant to subsection (b) of section 54-102g" rather than from "persons who are not sentenced to a term of confinement", amended Subsec. (a)(3) to provide that collection of the sample shall be responsibility of the Commissioner of Mental Health and Addiction Services or Commissioner of Mental Retardation, as the case may be, that samples collected are from "persons required to submit to the taking of such sample pursuant to subsection (c) of section 54-102g" rather than "persons who are found not guilty by reason of mental disease or defect pursuant to section 53a-13 and are confined in a hospital for psychiatric disabilities or placed with the Commissioner of Mental Retardation" and that sample be taken at a time and place specified by "said commissioner" rather than by "the superintendent of such hospital or said commissioner, as the case may be", amended Subsec. (a)(4) to provide that collection of the sample shall be the responsibility of Judicial Department if the person is serving a period of probation and of Board of Parole if the person is serving a period of parole and that samples collected are from "persons required to submit to the taking of such sample pursuant to subsection (d) of section 54-102g" rather than from "persons who are serving periods of probation or parole", added new Subdiv. (5) re agency responsible for collection of a sample from persons required to submit to the taking of a sample pursuant to Sec. 54-102g(e), designated existing provision of Subsec. (a) re persons authorized to take a blood sample as new Subsec. (b), designated existing provision of Subsec. (a) re liability of persons taking a sample as new Subsec. (c), redesignated existing Subsec. (b) re needles, tubes and containers as Subsec. (d), and redesignated existing Subsec. (c) re procedure and substantial compliance therewith and requirements re transportation, analysis and storage as Subsec. (e); P.A. 04-234 replaced Board of Parole with Board of Pardons and Paroles, effective July 1, 2004; pursuant to P.A. 07-73 "Commissioner of Mental Retardation" was changed editorially by the Revisors to "Commissioner of Developmental Services", effective October 1, 2007; P.A. 07-158 amended Subsec. (a)(4) to substitute "Department of Correction" for "Board of Pardons and Paroles" re collection from certain parolees; P.A. 10-102 amended Subsec. (a)(2) to provide that collection of a sample shall be responsibility of Judicial Department, rather than Department of Public Safety, and shall be taken at time and place specified by Court Support Services Division, rather than sentencing court, and amended Subsec. (d) to designate existing provisions as Subdiv. (1) and add Subdiv. (2) re collection kits approved for collection of biological samples by buccal swabs; pursuant to P.A. 11-51, "Department of Public Safety" was changed editorially by the Revisors to "Department of Emergency Services and Public Protection", effective July 1, 2011; P.A. 11-207 amended Subsec. (a) to add new Subdiv. (1) re responsibility of arresting law enforcement agency to collect sample from persons required to submit to taking of sample pursuant to Sec. 54-102g(a) and requirement that sample be taken at time and place specified by agency prior to person's release from custody, and to redesignate existing Subdivs. (1) to (5) as Subdivs. (2) to (6) and amend same by making technical changes to statutory references.

Sec. 54-102i. Procedure for conducting DNA analysis of blood or other biological sample.

(a) Whether or not the results of an analysis are to be included in the data bank, the Division of Scientific Services within the Department of Emergency Services and Public Protection shall conduct the DNA analysis in accordance with procedures adopted by the division to determine identification characteristics specific to the individual whose blood or other biological sample is being analyzed. Such procedures shall conform to nationally recognized and accepted standards for DNA analysis. The Commissioner of Emergency Services and Public Protection or the commissioner's designee shall complete and maintain on file a form indicating the name of the person whose sample is to be analyzed, the date and by whom the sample was received and examined, and a statement that the seal on the tube or container had not been broken or otherwise tampered with. The remainder of a sample submitted for analysis and inclusion in the data bank pursuant to section 54-102g may be divided, labeled as provided for the original sample, and securely stored by the division in accordance with specific procedures set forth in regulations adopted by the Department of Emergency Services and Public Protection in accordance with the provisions of chapter 54 to ensure the integrity and confidentiality of the samples. All or part of the remainder of that sample may be used only (1) to create a statistical data base provided no identifying information on the individual whose sample is being analyzed is included, or (2) for retesting by the division to validate or update the original analysis.

(b) A report of the results of a DNA analysis conducted by the division as authorized, including the profile and identifying information, shall be made and maintained at the division. A certificate and the results of the analysis shall be admissible in any court as evidence of the facts therein stated. Except as specifically provided in this section and section 54-102j, the results of the analysis shall be securely stored and shall remain confidential.

(P.A. 94-246, S. 3; P.A. 96-2; P.A. 99-218, S. 12, 16; P.A. 03-242, S. 3; P.A. 11-51, S. 134.)

History: P.A. 96-2 amended Subsec. (b) to provide for the initiation of a DNA testing process rather than conducting a DNA analysis; P.A. 99-218 replaced the State Police Forensic Science Laboratory with the Division of Scientific Services within the Department of Public Safety, and made conforming changes, effective July 1, 1999; P.A. 03-242 amended Subsec. (a) to make provisions applicable to "other biological" samples in addition to blood samples, add reference to a "container" and make conforming and technical changes, and amended Subsec. (b) to delete provision that required the division to initiate a

DNA testing process not later than 45 days after receipt of a blood sample; pursuant to P.A. 11-51, "Commissioner of Public Safety" and "Department of Public Safety" were changed editorially by the Revisors to "Commissioner of Emergency Services and Public Protection" and "Department of Emergency Services and Public Protection", respectively, in Subsec. (a), effective July 1, 2011.

Sec. 54-102j. Dissemination of information in DNA data bank.

(a) It shall be the duty of the Division of Scientific Services within the Department of Emergency Services and Public Protection to receive blood or other biological samples and to analyze, classify and file the results of DNA identification characteristics profiles of blood or other biological samples submitted pursuant to section 54-102g and to make such information available as provided in this section, except that the division shall analyze samples taken pursuant to subsection (a) of section 54-102g only as available resources allow. The results of an analysis and comparison of the identification characteristics from two or more blood or other biological samples shall be made available directly to federal, state and local law enforcement officers upon request made in furtherance of an official investigation of any criminal offense. Only when a sample or DNA profile supplied by the person making the request satisfactorily matches a profile in the data bank shall the existence of data in the data bank be confirmed or identifying information from the data bank be disseminated, except that if the results of an analysis and comparison do not reveal a match between the sample or samples supplied and a DNA profile contained in the data bank, the division may, upon request of the law enforcement officer, indicate whether the DNA profile of a named individual is contained in the data bank provided the law enforcement officer has a reasonable and articulable suspicion that such individual has committed the criminal offense being investigated. A request pursuant to this subsection may be made by personal contact, mail or electronic means. The name of the person making the request and the purpose for which the information is requested shall be maintained on file with the division.

(b) Upon the request of a person from whom a blood or other biological sample has been taken pursuant to sections 54-102g and 54-102h, a copy of such person's DNA profile shall be furnished to such person.

(c) Upon the request of any person identified and charged with an offense as the result of a search of information in the data bank, a copy of the request for a search shall be furnished to such person so identified and charged.

(d) The Department of Emergency Services and Public Protection shall adopt regulations, in accordance with the provisions of chapter 54, governing (1) the methods of obtaining information from the data bank in accordance with this section, and (2) procedures for verification of the identity and authority of the person making the request. The department shall specify the positions in that agency which require regular access to the data bank and samples submitted as a necessary function of the job.

(e) The Division of Scientific Services shall create a separate statistical data base comprised of DNA profiles of blood or other biological samples of persons whose identity is unknown. Nothing in this section or section 54-102k shall prohibit the Division of Scientific Services from sharing or otherwise disseminating the information in the statistical data base with law enforcement or criminal justice agencies within or without the state.

(f) The Division of Scientific Services may charge a reasonable fee to search and provide a comparative analysis of DNA profiles in the data bank to any authorized law enforcement agency outside of the state.

(P.A. 94-246, S. 4; P.A. 98-2; P.A. 99-218, S. 13, 16; P.A. 03-242, S. 4; P.A. 11-51, S. 134; 11-144, S. 2; 11-207, S. 4.)

History: P.A. 98-2 added "or other biological samples" to Subsec. (a); P.A. 99-218 replaced the State Police Forensic Science Laboratory with the Division of Scientific Services within the Department of Public Safety and made conforming changes, and reworded part of Subsec. (b) for gender neutrality, effective July 1, 1999; P.A. 03-242 amended Subsec. (a) to include "other biological" samples, added new Subsec. (b) to provide that upon request of a person from whom a blood or other biological sample has been taken, a copy of such person's DNA profile shall be furnished to such person, redesignated existing Subsecs. (b), (c), (d) and (e) as new Subsecs. (c), (d), (e) and (f), respectively, made technical changes in Subsec. (d) and amended Subsec. (e) to include "other biological" samples; pursuant to P.A. 11-51, "Department of Public Safety" was changed editorially by the Revisors to "Department of Emergency Services and Public Protection", effective July 1, 2011; P.A. 11-144 amended Subsec. (a) to add provision re confirmation or dissemination of information in data bank only when there is a satisfactory match, said provision formerly being part of Subsec. (c), and add exception re authority of division to indicate whether profile of a named individual is contained in data bank when there is no match but officer has reasonable and articulable suspicion that such individual committed offense being investigated, and amended Subsec. (c) to delete provision re confirmation or dissemination of information in data bank only when there is a satisfactory match; P.A. 11-207 amended Subsec. (a) to add exception re division to analyze samples taken pursuant to Sec. 54-102g(a) only as available resources allow.

Sec. 54-102k. Unauthorized dissemination or use of DNA data bank information. Obtaining blood sample without authority. Penalties.

Any person who, without authority, disseminates information contained in the data bank shall be guilty of a class C misdemeanor. Any person who disseminates, receives or otherwise uses or attempts to so use information in the data bank, knowing that such dissemination, receipt or use is for a purpose other than as authorized by law, shall be guilty of a class A misdemeanor. Except as authorized by law, any person who, for purposes of having a DNA analysis performed, obtains or attempts to obtain any sample submitted to the Division of Scientific Services for analysis shall be guilty of a class D felony.

(P.A. 94-246, S. 5; P.A. 99-218, S. 14, 16.)

History: P.A. 99-218 replaced the forensic science laboratory with the Division of Scientific Services, effective July 1, 1999.

Sec. 54-102*l*. Expungement of DNA data bank records and destruction of samples.

(a) A DNA profile that has been included in the data bank pursuant to sections 54-102g to 54-102k, inclusive, shall be expunged in the event that (1) the criminal conviction or the finding of not guilty by reason of mental disease or defect on which the authority for including the person's DNA profile was based has been reversed and the case dismissed, or (2) if the DNA profile of a person has been included in the data bank on account of the person being arrested as provided in subsection (a) of section 54-102g, the charge has been dismissed or nolled or the person has been acquitted of the charge.

(b) The Division of Scientific Services within the Department of Emergency Services and Public Protection shall purge all records and identifiable information in the data bank pertaining to the person and destroy all samples from the person upon receipt of a certified copy of (1) the court order reversing and dismissing the conviction or the finding of not guilty by reason of mental disease or defect, or (2) the court order dismissing or nolling the charge or acquitting the person of the charge.

(P.A. 94-246, S. 6; P.A. 10-36, S. 28; P.A. 11-91, S. 2; 11-207, S. 3.)

History: P.A. 10-36 made provisions applicable upon reversal of finding of not guilty by reason of mental disease or defect and made technical changes, effective July 1, 2010; P.A. 11-91 substituted "State Police Forensic Science Laboratory" with "Division of Scientific Services within the Department of Public Safety", effective July 8, 2011 (Revisor's note: "Department of Public Safety" was changed editorially by the Revisors to "Department of Emergency Services and Public Protection" to conform with changes made by P.A. 11-51); P.A. 11-207 inserted Subsec. (a) and (b) designators, amended Subsec. (a) to replace provision re person "may request expungement" of DNA profile upon reversal of conviction or finding of not guilty by reason of mental disease or defect and dismissal of case with provision re profile "shall be expunged" upon such reversal and dismissal, designate existing provision re reversal and dismissal as Subdiv. (1) and add new Subdiv. (2) re dismissal, nolle or acquittal of charge when profile included on account of person being arrested as provided in Sec. 54-102g(a), and amended Subsec. (b) to delete former Subdiv. (1) re written request for expungement, redesignate existing Subdiv. (2) re court order reversing and dismissing conviction or finding of not guilty by reason of mental disease or defect as Subdiv. (1) and add new Subdiv. (2) re court order dismissing or nolling the charge or acquitting the person of the charge.

Sec. 54-102m. DNA Data Bank Oversight Panel.

(a) There is established a DNA Data Bank Oversight Panel composed of the Chief State's Attorney, the Attorney General, the Commissioner of Emergency Services and Public Protection, the Commissioner of Correction, the executive director of the Court Support Services Division of the Judicial Department and the Chief Public Defender, or their designees. The Chief State's Attorney shall serve as chairperson of the panel and shall coordinate the agencies responsible for the implementation and maintenance of the DNA data bank established pursuant to section 54-102j.

(b) The panel shall take such action as necessary to assure the integrity of the data bank including the destruction of inappropriately obtained samples and the purging of all records and identifiable information pertaining to the persons from whom such inappropriately obtained samples were collected.

(c) The panel shall meet on a quarterly basis and shall maintain records of its meetings. Such records shall be retained by the chairperson. The meetings and records of the panel shall be subject to the provisions of the Freedom of Information Act, as defined in section 1-200, except that discussions and records of personally identifiable DNA information contained in the data bank shall be confidential and not subject to disclosure pursuant to the Freedom of Information Act. The Chief Public Defender, or the Chief Public Defender's designee, shall not participate in discussions concerning, or have access to records of, personally identifiable DNA information contained in the data bank.

(P.A. 03-242, S. 5; P.A. 04-188, S. 3; P.A. 10-102, S. 4; P.A. 11-9, S. 1; 11-51, S. 134.)

History: P.A. 04-188 amended Subsec. (c) to add provision that the meetings and records of the panel shall be subject to the Freedom of Information Act, except that discussions and records of personally identifiable DNA information contained in the data bank shall be confidential and not subject to disclosure pursuant to that act; P.A. 10-102 amended Subsec. (a) to add executive director of Court Support Services Division as member of panel; P.A. 11-9 amended Subsec. (a) to add Chief Public Defender as member of panel and amended Subsec. (c) to prohibit Chief Public Defender or designee from participating in discussions concerning, or having access to records of, personally identifiable DNA information contained in data bank, effective May 24, 2011; pursuant to P.A. 11-51, "Commissioner of Public Safety" was changed editorially by the Revisors to "Commissioner of Emergency Services and Public Protection" in Subsec. (a), effective July 1, 2011.

Secs. 54-102n to 54-102q. Reserved for future use.

Sec. 54-102r. Registration of persons convicted of sexual assault upon release from correctional facility or completion or termination of probation. Section 54-102r is repealed, effective October 1, 1998.

(P.A. 94-246, S. 8–12; P.A. 95-142, S. 10; 95-175, S. 12; P.A. 97-183, S. 1, 2; P.A. 98-111, S. 12.)

Sec. 54-102s. Transferred to Chapter 969, Sec. 54-260.

Secs. 54-102t to 54-102z. Reserved for future use.

PART IIb TESTING FOR TUBERCULOSIS INFECTION

Sec. 54-102aa. Tuberculosis testing: Definitions. Requirements.

(a) As used in this part:

(1) "Active tuberculosis" has the same meaning as provided in subdivision (1) of subsection (a) of section 19a-265;

(2) "Infectious tuberculosis" has the same meaning as provided in subdivision (2) of subsection (a) of section 19a-265; and

(3) "Latent tuberculosis" means having a positive tuberculin skin test with no clinical, bacteriologic or radiologic evidence of active tuberculosis.

(b) Any person who has been committed to the custody of the Commissioner of Correction and remains in custody for a period of at least five consecutive days shall be tested to determine if such person has active tuberculosis or latent tuberculosis infection. Any person testing positive for active tuberculosis or infectious tuberculosis shall be subject to the provisions of sections 19a-255 and 19a-262 to 19a-265, inclusive. Any person testing positive for latent tuberculosis infection shall be first medically evaluated for infectious tuberculosis and then offered treatment for latent tuberculosis infection as recommended at the time by the National Centers for Disease Control and Prevention, provided the scheduled period of custody of such person is such that the treatment may be completed prior to the release of such person from custody.

(P.A. 02-63, S. 1; P.A. 03-278, S. 108; Sept. Sp. Sess. P.A. 09-3, S. 52; P.A. 14-122, S. 195.)

History: P.A. 03-278 made technical changes in Subsecs. (a) and (b), effective July 9, 2003; Sept. Sp. Sess. P.A. 09-3 amended Subsec. (b) by deleting reference to Sec. 19a-256, effective October 6, 2009; P.A. 14-122 made technical changes in Subsec. (a).

Sec. 54-102bb. Procedures for evaluation of tuberculosis infection.

In facilities operated by the Department of Correction, the medical director, contractor and chief administrator of the facility shall ensure that: (1) Each incarcerated inmate, upon incarceration, has a tuberculin skin test, unless already known to be positive, a symptom evaluation and if indicated according to the most recent recommendations from the National Centers for Disease Control and Prevention, a chest radiograph for tuberculosis, provided each inmate who is asymptomatic and who has had a chest radiograph in a correctional facility within six months of incarceration need not have an additional chest radiograph; (2) each incarcerated inmate has an evaluation for active tuberculosis or infectious tuberculosis whenever the inmate develops a cough lasting more than two weeks; (3) each incarcerated inmate has at least an annual tuberculin skin test, unless already known to be positive; and (4) information on the results of testing for infectious tuberculosis and latent tuberculosis infection as described in subdivisions (1) to (3), inclusive, of this section and all efforts to treat each inmate for active tuberculosis or latent tuberculosis infection and discharges of inmates who have not completed therapy for tuberculosis or latent tuberculosis infection are reported promptly to the central Department of Correction tuberculosis registry.

(P.A. 02-63, S. 2; P.A. 03-278, S. 109.)

History: P.A. 03-278 made technical changes, effective July 9, 2003.

Sec. 54-102cc. Tuberculosis infection control committee.

(a) The Department of Correction shall establish a tuberculosis infection control committee. Said committee shall include, but not be limited to, the following members: (1) The Commissioner of Correction or said commissioner's designee; (2) the medical director for the Department of Correction; and (3) a medical contractor or consultant currently executing any tuberculosis control contract with the Department of Correction. Said committee may consult with the Commissioner of Public Health or said commissioner's designee.

(b) The committee established pursuant to subsection (a) of this section shall develop guidelines and protocols for the purpose of implementing section 54-102bb. Said guidelines shall include, but not be limited to, the following tuberculosis infection control activities: (1) Screening of inmates; (2) containment; and (3) assessment of guidelines implementation. Any guidelines established shall be consistent with the most recent recommendations from the National Centers for Disease Control and Prevention.

(P.A. 02-63, S. 3; P.A. 03-278, S. 110.)

History: P.A. 03-278 made a technical change in Subsec. (a), effective July 9, 2003.

Sec. 54-102dd. Inmates with infectious tuberculosis required to be isolated. Persons exposed encouraged to be tested.

(a) Any inmate found to have evidence of infectious tuberculosis shall be isolated from any public contact until such time as the inmate has received treatment and has been evaluated and found to be free of infection.

(b) If an inmate found to have infectious tuberculosis is believed, based on subsequent investigation, to have exposed visitors or employees to tuberculosis, efforts shall be made to inform such persons and encourage such persons to have an evaluation for tuberculosis infection.

(P.A. 02-63, S. 4.)

Sec. 54-102ee. Department contract option for testing of tuberculosis.

The Department of Correction may enter into a contract agreement with an appropriate health care provider to manage the responsibilities as it relates to testing, screening or treatment of inmates for tuberculosis.

(P.A. 02-63, S. 5.)

Secs. 54-102ff to 54-102ii. Reserved for future use.

PART IIc POST-CONVICTION REMEDIES

Sec. 54-102jj. Preservation of biological evidence.

(a) For the purposes of this section and section 54-102kk:

(1) "DNA testing" means forensic deoxyribonucleic acid testing; and

(2) "Agent" means a person, firm or corporation to whom the state police or a local police department entrusts or delivers evidence to undergo DNA testing.

(b) Upon the conviction of a person of a capital felony under the provisions of section 53a-54b in effect prior to April 25, 2012, or murder with special circumstances under the provisions of section 53a-54b in effect on or after April 25, 2012, or the conviction of a person of a crime after trial, or upon order of the court for good cause shown, the state police, all local police departments, any agent of the state police or a local police department and any other person to whom biological evidence has been transferred shall preserve all biological evidence acquired during the course of the investigation of such crime for the term of such person's incarceration.

(c) The state police, a local police department, an agent or any person to whom biological evidence has been transferred may be relieved of the obligation to preserve biological evidence as provided in subsection (b) of this section by applying to the court in which the defendant's case was prosecuted for permission to destroy such biological evidence. Upon receipt of the application, the court shall give notice to all defendants charged in connection with the prosecution and shall hold a hearing. After such hearing, the court shall grant the application if it finds that the Connecticut Supreme Court has decided the defendant's appeal and the defendant does not seek further preservation of the biological evidence, or for good cause shown.

(P.A. 03-242, S. 6; P.A. 12-5, S. 31.)

History: P.A. 12-5 amended Subsec. (b) to add reference to provisions of Sec. 53a-54b in effect prior to April 25, 2012, re capital felony and add reference to murder with special circumstances under Sec. 53a-54b, effective April 25, 2012.

Sec. 54-102kk. DNA testing of biological evidence.

(a) Notwithstanding any other provision of law governing postconviction relief, any person who was convicted of a crime and sentenced to incarceration may, at any time during the term of such incarceration, file a petition with the sentencing court requesting the DNA testing of any evidence that is in the possession or control of the Division of Criminal Justice, any law enforcement agency, any laboratory or the Superior Court. The petitioner shall state under penalties of perjury that the requested testing is related to the investigation or prosecution that resulted in the petitioner's conviction and that the evidence sought to be tested contains biological evidence.

(b) After notice to the prosecutorial official and a hearing, the court shall order DNA testing if it finds that:

(1) A reasonable probability exists that the petitioner would not have been prosecuted or convicted if exculpatory results had been obtained through DNA testing;

(2) The evidence is still in existence and is capable of being subjected to DNA testing;

(3) The evidence, or a specific portion of the evidence identified by the petitioner, was never previously subjected to DNA testing, or the testing requested by the petitioner may resolve an issue that was never previously resolved by previous testing; and

(4) The petition before the Superior Court was filed in order to demonstrate the petitioner's innocence and not to delay the administration of justice.

(c) After notice to the prosecutorial official and a hearing, the court may order DNA testing if it finds that:

(1) A reasonable probability exists that the requested testing will produce DNA results which would have altered the verdict or reduced the petitioner's sentence if the results had been available at the prior proceedings leading to the judgment of conviction;

(2) The evidence is still in existence and is capable of being subjected to DNA testing;

(3) The evidence, or a specific portion of the evidence identified by the petitioner, was never previously subjected to DNA testing, or the testing requested by the petitioner may resolve an issue that was never previously resolved by previous testing; and

(4) The petition before the Superior Court was filed in order to demonstrate the petitioner's innocence and not to delay the administration of justice.

(d) The costs of DNA testing ordered pursuant to this section shall be borne by the state or the petitioner, as the court may order in the interests of justice, except that DNA testing shall not be denied because of the inability of the petitioner to pay the costs of such testing.

(e) In a proceeding under this section, the petitioner shall have the right to be represented by counsel and, if the petitioner is indigent, the court shall appoint counsel for the petitioner in accordance with section 51-296.

(P.A. 03-242, S. 7.)

Reasonable probability under Subsec. (b)(1) means a probability sufficient to undermine confidence in the outcome; a petitioner may succeed by demonstrating a reasonable probability that he or she would not have been prosecuted or convicted if exculpatory DNA evidence had been available. 295 C. 50. In light of determination that defendant did not establish "reasonable probability" under Subsec. (b), trial court properly denied petition under Subsec. (c). Id., 74. Under Subsec. (b)(1), petitioner was not entitled to DNA testing as there was no reasonable probability that petitioner would not have been prosecuted or convicted if exculpatory DNA test results had been obtained prior to trial because even if the court assumed the most favorable result from DNA testing, it would not have undermined the confidence in the verdict given the strength of the state's case against petitioner. 309 C. 567.

Subsec. (b)(1) requires court to consider the effect of the most favorable result possible from DNA testing of evidence, and in this case, petitioner did not establish a reasonable probability under Subsec. (b)(1) because evidence amply supported conclusion that petitioner, in fact, committed the crimes. 129

Secs. 54-102ll to 54-102oo. Reserved for future use.

Sec. 54-102pp. Review of wrongful convictions. Section 54-102pp is repealed, effective October 1, 2014.

(P.A. 03-242, S. 8; P.A. 11-51, S. 134; P.A. 14-207, S. 17.)

Secs. 54-102qq to 54-102tt. Reserved for future use.

Sec. 54-102uu. Compensation for wrongful incarceration.

(a) A person is eligible to receive compensation for wrongful incarceration if:

(1) Such person has been convicted by this state of one or more crimes and has been sentenced to a term of imprisonment for such crime or crimes and has served all or part of such sentence; and

(2) Such person's conviction was vacated or reversed and (A) the complaint or information dismissed on grounds of innocence, or (B) the complaint or information dismissed on a ground citing an act or omission that constitutes malfeasance or other serious misconduct by any officer, agent, employee or official of the state that contributed to such person's arrest, prosecution, conviction or incarceration.

(b) A person who meets the eligibility requirements of subsection (a) of this section may present a claim against the state for such compensation with the Claims Commissioner in accordance with the provisions of chapter 53. The provisions of said chapter shall be applicable to the presentment, hearing and determination of such claim except as otherwise provided in this section.

(c) At the hearing on such claim, such person shall have the burden of establishing by a preponderance of the evidence that such person meets the eligibility requirements of subsection (a) of this section. In addition, such person shall present evidence as to (1) the person's age, income, vocational training and level of education at the time of conviction, (2) loss of familial relationships, (3) damage to reputation, (4) the severity of the crime for which such person was convicted and whether such person was under a sentence of death pursuant to section 53a-46a for any period of time, (5) whether such person was required to register pursuant to section 54-251 or 54-252, and for what length of time such person complied with the registration requirements of chapter 969, and (6) any other damages such person may have suffered arising from or related to such person's arrest, prosecution, conviction and incarceration.

(d) (1) If the Claims Commissioner determines that such person has established such person's eligibility under subsection (a) of this section by a preponderance of the evidence, the Claims Commissioner shall order the immediate payment to such person of compensation for such wrongful incarceration in an amount determined pursuant to subdivision (2) of this subsection, unless (A) such compensation award is in an amount exceeding twenty thousand dollars, or (B) such person requests, in accordance with section 4-158, that the General Assembly review such compensation award, in which cases the Claims Commissioner shall submit any such claim to the General Assembly in the same manner as provided under section 4-159, not later than five business days after such award determination is made or such review is requested. The General Assembly shall review any such compensation award and the claim from which it arose not later than forty-five days after such claim is submitted to the General Assembly and may deny such claim or confirm or modify such compensation award. If the General Assembly modifies the amount of the compensation award, the General Assembly may award any amount of compensation the General Assembly deems just and reasonable. If the General Assembly takes no action on such compensation award or the claim from which it arose, the determination made by the Claims Commissioner shall be deemed confirmed.

(2) In determining the amount of such compensation, the Claims Commissioner shall award an amount that is at a minimum, but may be up to two hundred per cent of the median household income for the state for each year such person was incarcerated, as determined by the United States Department of Housing and Urban Development, adjusted for inflation using the consumer price index for urban consumers, provided the amount for any partial year shall be prorated in order to compensate only for the portion of such year in which such person was incarcerated. The Claims Commissioner may decrease or further the award amount by twenty-five per cent based on an assessment of relevant factors including, but not limited to, the evidence presented by the person under subdivisions (1) to (6), inclusive, of subsection (c) of this section.

(e) In addition to the compensation paid under subsection (d) of this section, the Claims Commissioner may order payment for the expenses of employment training and counseling, tuition and fees at any constituent unit of the state system of higher education and any other services such person may need to facilitate such person's reintegration into the community.

(f) Any person claiming compensation under this section based on a pardon that was granted or the dismissal of a complaint or information that occurred before October 1, 2008, shall file such claim not later than two years after October 1, 2008. Any person claiming compensation under this section based on a pardon that was granted or the dismissal of a complaint that occurred on or after October 1, 2008, shall file such claim not later than two years after the date of such pardon or dismissal.

(g) Any person who is compensated pursuant to this section shall sign a release providing that such person voluntarily relinquishes any right to pursue any other action or remedy at law or in equity that such person may have arising out of such wrongful conviction and incarceration.

(P.A. 08-143, S. 1; P.A. 16-127, S. 29.)

History: P.A. 16-127 amended Subsec. (a)(1) by deleting ", of which the person was innocent,", amended Subsec. (a)(2) by designating existing provision re complaint or information dismissed on grounds of innocence as Subpara. (A) and amending same to delete provision re complaint or information dismissed on ground consistent with innocence and by adding Subpara. (B) re complaint or information dismissed on ground citing act or omission that constitutes malfeasance or other serious misconduct by officer, agent, employee or official of the state, amended Subsec. (c) by replacing former provision re person to present evidence of damages suffered with Subdivs. (1) to (6) re same, amended Subsec. (d) by designating existing provisions re payment of compensation as Subdiv. (1), designating existing provisions re amount of compensation as Subdiv. (2) and substantially amending Subdivs. (1) and (2) including adding provisions re award amount and General Assembly to review compensation award, amended Subsec. (g) by deleting provisions re person's pursuit of action or remedy at law or in equity against the state and any political subdivision of the state and officer, agent, employee or official thereof and adding provision re person who is compensated to sign release, and made technical and conforming changes, effective June 9, 2016.

PART III PROBATION, PAROLE AND PARDON

Sec. 54-103. Commission on Adult Probation. Section 54-103 is repealed.

(1955, S. 3331d; 1971, P.A. 259, S. 1; P.A. 74-183, S. 154, 291; P.A. 76-436, S. 553, 681; P.A. 78-303, S. 119, 136.)

Sec. 54-103a. Office of Adult Probation. Section 54-103a is repealed, effective October 1, 2002.

(P.A. 77-614, S. 278, 610; P.A. 02-132, S. 82.)

Sec. 54-103b. Services for probation referrals. Duties of Court Support Services Division. Contractual services and alternative incarceration program.

The Court Support Services Division shall implement liaison with local community service providers throughout the state for the purpose of improving services delivery for probation referrals. Contractual services purchased shall be predominantly for the purpose of, but not limited to, employment, psychiatric and psychological evaluation and counseling, drug and alcohol dependency treatment, and other services towards more effective control and rehabilitation of probation referrals. The Chief Court Administrator, as part of a publicly bid contract for an alternative incarceration program, may include a requirement that the contractor provide such space as is necessary for staff of the Court Support Services Division to meet with probationers and to conduct any business that may be necessary to oversee and monitor such program. Other outside professional service fees consonant with the primary purpose of improved direct services shall be within the scope of the authority granted by this section.

(P.A. 79-585, S. 14, 15; P.A. 02-132, S. 42; P.A. 06-152, S. 6.)

History: P.A. 02-132 replaced "Office of Adult Probation" with "Court Support Services Division"; P.A. 06-152 authorized Chief Court Administrator to include space requirement in publicly bid contract for alternative incarceration program, effective June 6, 2006.

Sec. 54-104. Appointment of Director of Probation and probation officers. Qualifying examinations. Section 54-104 is repealed, effective October 1, 2002.

(1949 Rev., S. 8839; 1955, S. 3332d; P.A. 76-436, S. 554, 681; P.A. 77-614, S. 67, 279, 610; P.A. 79-585, S. 11, 15; P.A. 02-132, S. 43, 82.)

Sec. 54-105. Duties of executive director of Court Support Services Division re probation. Intensive probation program. Community service program. Caseload limitation.

(a) The executive director of the Court Support Services Division shall be responsible for the supervision of the probation officers and other employees and may require reports from them. The executive director shall (1) formulate methods of investigation, supervision, record-keeping and reports, (2) compile statistics on the work of all probation officers, (3) maintain a record of all probationers, (4) perform such other duties as may be necessary to establish and maintain an efficient probation service in the Superior Court, and (5) prepare and publish such reports as may be required by the Chief Court Administrator. In the pursuance of such duties, the executive director shall have access to the records of probation officers.

(b) The Judicial Department shall establish within the Court Support Services Division an intensive probation program. The purpose of intensive probation is to place persons in the community under close supervision and restriction to ensure public safety, reduce prison overcrowding and contribute to the rehabilitation of persons in the program. There shall be periodic testing for drug or alcohol use for those probationers on intensive probation who have been identified as having histories of drug or alcohol abuse. Any defendant placed on intensive probation who fails to comply with the conditions of his intensive probation shall be presented to the court as provided in subsection (a) of section 53a-32 for a hearing to be conducted in accordance with said subsection. If such defendant is found by the court to have violated any condition of his intensive probation, the sentencing court or judge may continue such defendant on intensive probation, modify or enlarge the conditions of intensive probation or revoke the intensive probation and either require the defendant to serve the balance of the sentence imposed or impose any lesser sentence. The executive director of the Court Support Services Division shall have the same powers and duties with respect to the intensive probation program as the executive director has with respect to regular probation under subsection (a) of this section. Persons may be placed on intensive probation pursuant to an order of a court or judge under section 53a-30 or 53a-39a or as required by the Court Support Services Division.

(c) Subject to the approval of the Chief Court Administrator, the executive director of the Court Support Services Division may establish within the Court Support Services Division a community service program, including a community service labor program, which will assign, supervise and report compliance of persons sentenced to perform community service as a condition of probation or conditional discharge.

(d) The executive director of the Court Support Services Division shall establish within the Court Support Services Division a program wherein eighty-four probation officers shall have a caseload of not more than thirty-five probationers per officer for the purpose of providing high level supervision. This program shall be implemented with funds appropriated pursuant to section 48 of public act 90-213*, provided such caseload may be increased at the discretion of the executive director if funding for the current service level for the Court Support Services Division is reduced.

(1955, S. 3333d; P.A. 76-436, S. 555, 681; P.A. 77-614, S. 280, 610; P.A. 78-379, S. 23, 27; P.A. 79-585, S. 12, 15; P.A. 80-483, S. 137, 186; P.A. 84-505, S. 4, 6; P.A. 85-354, S. 2, 3; P.A. 87-538, S. 3, 5; P.A. 89-383, S. 5, 16; P.A. 90-213, S. 5, 14, 56; 90-261, S. 8, 19; P.A. 02-132, S. 44.)

*Note: Section 48 of public act 90-213 is special in nature and therefore has not been codified but remains in full force and effect according to its terms.

History: P.A. 76-436 revised section to reflect transfer of all trial jurisdiction to superior court, eliminating references to other courts, effective July 1, 1978; P.A. 77-614 replaced commission on adult probation with office of adult probation, eliminating limitations of director's powers requiring commission approval for various actions, specified that salaries are subject to compensation plan under Sec. 51-12, deleted director's duties to prescribe districts and assign probation officers to them and to conduct training courses for staff, and required publication of reports determined by chief court administrator rather than by commission or court, effective January 1, 1979; P.A. 78-379 added temporary provision re director's power to enter into contracts, effective July 1, 1978, through December 31, 1978; P.A. 79-585 authorized judges to take action re salaries through committee; P.A. 80-483 made technical grammatical correction; P.A. 84-505 added Subsec. (b) requiring the director of probation to establish an intensive probation program and specifying the purpose and nature of such program, effective June 13, 1984, to July 1, 1987; P.A. 85-354 amended Subsec. (b) to replace the requirement of "weekly" testing for drug and alcohol use with "periodic" testing and replace the requirement that the director of probation immediately inform the court of the failure of a probationer to comply with the rules, regulations and orders of the intensive probation program with provisions requiring any defendant who fails to comply with the conditions of his intensive probation to be presented to the court for a hearing and provisions specifying the options of the sentencing court or judge upon finding the defendant has violated any condition of his intensive probation; P.A. 87-538 reenacted and continued in effect on and after July 1, 1987, the provisions of this section previously effective from June 13, 1984, until July 1, 1987; P.A. 89-383 amended Subsec. (b) to delete from the stated purposes of intensive probation the removal of convicted persons from incarceration and added Subsec. (c) authorizing the director to establish a community service program, specifying the nature of the program and specifying the director's duties if he establishes such a program; P.A. 90-213 amended Subsec. (c) to authorize the establishment of a community service labor program and to require the director prior to the establishment of such program to certify that all anticipated costs can be paid for within available appropriations and added Subsec. (d) requiring the director to establish a program for the high level supervision of probationers by probation offices, providing for the funding of such program and authorizing an increase in the caseload if funding is reduced; P.A. 90-261 amended Subsec. (b) to delete the intensive probation caseload limit of twenty probationers per probation officer and the requirement that each week the officer have at least three contacts with each probationer and one or more collateral contacts, to delete the requirement that the director inform a court which ordered a sentenced defendant discharged on intensive probation of the progress of such probationer, to make the requirement of periodic drug or alcohol testing applicable to those probationers "on intensive probation", to provide that a defendant is "placed" rather than "discharged" on intensive probation, and to replace the provision that "Persons may only be placed in the intensive probation program pursuant to an order of a court or judge under section 53a-39" with "Persons may be placed on intensive probation pursuant to an order of a court or judge under section 53a-30 or 53a-39a, or as required by the office of adult probation"; P.A. 02-132 amended Subsec. (a) by deleting provisions re Director of Probation and re appointment and salaries of probation officers and other employees, adding provisions re responsibilities of the executive director of the Court Support Services Division and making technical changes, amended Subsec. (b) by replacing "Director of Probation shall establish within the Office of Adult Probation" with "Judicial Department shall establish within the Court Support Services Division", deleting provisions re separate operation of program and re sharing of facilities and administrative services, replacing "director" with "executive director of the Court Support Services Division" and replacing "Office of Adult Probation" with "Court Support Services Division", amended Subsec. (c) by replacing "Director of Probation" with "executive director of the Court Support Services Division", replacing "Office of Adult Probation" with "Court Support Services Division" and deleting provisions re duties of Director of Probation and amended Subsec. (d) by replacing "Director of Probation" with "executive director of the Court Support Services Division" and replacing "Office of Adult Probation" with "Court Support Services Division".

Sec. 54-105a. Funds for the probation transition program and technical violation units.

For the fiscal year ending June 30, 2008, and each fiscal year thereafter, any revenue derived by the Department of Administrative Services from the contract for the provision of pay telephone service to inmates of correctional facilities that is remaining after any required transfer to the Department of Correction pursuant to section 18-81x, or that is remaining after any of such revenue is made available to the Department of Administrative Services to administer the criminal justice information system, shall be transferred to the Judicial Department for staffing and services necessary for the state-wide expansion of the probation transition program and the technical violation units.

(June Sp. Sess. P.A. 07-4, S. 36; P.A. 11-51, S. 76.)

History: June Sp. Sess. P.A. 07-4 effective July 1, 2007; pursuant to P.A. 11-51, "Department of Information Technology" was changed editorially by the Revisors to "Department of Administrative Services", effective July 1, 2011.

Secs. 54-106 and 54-107. General Assembly to provide for expenses; central office; quarters. Appointment of probation officers. Sections 54-106 and 54-107 are repealed, effective October 1, 2002.

(1949 Rev., S. 8833; 1955, S. 3334d; 1955, June, 1955, S. 3335d; November, 1955, S. N231; P.A. 76-436, S. 556, 681; P.A. 77-562, S. 1, 2; 77-614, S. 281, 282, 610; P.A. 79-585, S. 13, 15; 79-631, S. 35, 111, P.A. 80-483, S. 138, 186, P.A. 87-496, S. 107, 110, P.A. 02-132, S. 45, 82.)

Sec. 54-108. Duties of probation officers.

(a) Probation officers shall investigate all cases referred to them for investigation by the executive director or by the court. They shall furnish to each person released under their supervision a written statement of the conditions of probation and shall instruct him regarding the same. They shall keep informed of his conduct and condition and use all suitable methods to aid and encourage him and to bring about improvement in his conduct and condition.

(b) Probation officers shall supervise and enforce all conditions of probation ordered pursuant to section 53a-30.

(c) Any interference with any probation officer or with any person placed in his charge shall render the person so interfering liable to the provisions of section 53a-167a.

(1949 Rev., S. 8834, 8835; 1955, S. 3336d; 1959, P.A. 28, S. 155; 1963, P.A. 642, S. 76; 1969, P.A. 297; P.A. 74-183, S. 155, 291; 74-338, S. 37, 94; P.A. 76-436, S. 557, 681; P.A. 11-155, S. 2.)

History: 1959 act substituted circuit court for municipal court or trial justice; 1963 act updated statute, excluding court of common pleas and reference to appeal by minor and substituting state jail administrator for jailer; 1969 act substituted community correctional centers and their administrators for jails and their administrators; P.A. 74-183 replaced circuit court with court of common pleas, reflecting reorganization of judicial system, and substituted "section 53a-167a" for "section 53-165", effective December 31, 1974; P.A. 74-338 repeated change in section reference enacted by P.A. 74-183; P.A. 76-436 reworded section to reflect transfer of all trial jurisdiction to superior court, deleting references implying other courts' jurisdiction, effective July 1, 1978; P.A. 11-155 inserted Subsec. (a) and (c) designators, amended Subsec. (a) to delete provisions re duty of probation officers to collect and disburse moneys and account therefor and to send record of all probations to director, re duty of police to notify probation officer whenever any minor has been arrested and re authority of court to commit minor to custody of probation officer while case is being investigated or when minor is in default of bail and is committed to a community correctional center and to make a technical change, and added Subsec. (b) requiring probation officers to supervise and enforce all conditions of probation ordered pursuant to Sec. 53a-30, effective July 1, 2011.

Cited. 207 C. 152. Where, pursuant to a plea bargain, defendant pleads guilty to sexual assault in fourth degree in violation of Sec. 53a-73a and public indecency in violation of Sec. 53a-186, trial court acted within its discretion in permitting Office of Adult Probation to notify members of defendant's community. 250 C. 280.

Cited. 31 CA 660. Section does not provide remedy for failure of probation officer to comply with statute and does not require that defendant's signature be on conditions of probation; section is directory and not mandatory and violation of statute by probation officer does not excuse defendant from requirement that he not violate a condition of probation as long as probation officer advised defendant of conditions of his probation and consequences of violating those conditions. 55 CA 622. Section is directory and not mandatory and violation of section by probation officer does not excuse defendant from requirement that he not violate a condition of probation. 58 CA 153.

Sec. 54-108a. Supervision of probationers. Section 54-108a is repealed, effective October 1, 2002.

(P.A. 98-38; P.A. 02-132, S. 82.)

Sec. 54-108b. Risk assessment and monitoring standards developed by Chief Court Administrator.

The Chief Court Administrator shall develop a system to accurately assess the risk that an individual under the supervision of an adult probation officer has to the community and shall develop classification categories and standards of monitoring for such individuals based upon the assessment. The purpose of the classification system shall be to ensure close supervision and restriction, public safety, effective alternatives to incarceration and maximum rehabilitation of persons placed in the community under the supervision of an adult probation officer.

(June Sp. Sess. P.A. 00-1, S. 33, 46.)

History: June Sp. Sess. P.A. 00-1 effective July 1, 2000.

Sec. 54-108c. Availability of information on outstanding arrest warrants for probation violations.

The Court Support Services Division of the Judicial Branch shall make available on the Internet (1) information concerning all outstanding arrest warrants for violation of probation including the name, address and photographic image of the probationer named in such warrant, except that information concerning such an outstanding warrant shall not be made available on the Internet if (A) there is reason to believe that making such information available might endanger the safety of the probationer or any other person, or (B) the probationer is a person adjudicated as a youthful offender, and (2) a quarterly report listing by court of issuance all arrest warrants for violation of probation made available under subdivision (1) of this section, including the name and address of the probationer named in each such warrant and the date of issuance of such warrant.

(Jan. Sp. Sess. P.A. 08-1, S. 21; P.A. 10-43, S. 27.)

History: Jan. Sp. Sess. P.A. 08-1 effective January 25, 2008; P.A. 10-43 amended Subdiv. (1) to add exception re unavailability of information if safety of probationer or other person might be endangered or probationer is youthful offender and amended Subdiv. (2) to make provisions applicable to all arrest warrants made available under Subdiv. (1), rather than all outstanding arrest warrants, effective July 1, 2010.

Sec. 54-108d. Authority of probation officers to detain certain persons, seize contraband and act as member of fugitive task force.

(a) A probation officer may, in the performance of his or her official duties, detain for a reasonable period of time and until a police officer arrives to make an arrest (1) any person who has one or more unexecuted state or federal arrest warrants lodged against him or her, and (2) any person who such officer has probable cause to believe has violated a condition of probation and is the subject of a probation officer's authorization to arrest pursuant to subsection (a) of section 53a-32. If a police officer is unable to come to the location where the person is being detained within a reasonable period of time, a probation officer may transport the person to the nearest location where a police officer is able to make an arrest.

(b) A probation officer may seize and take into custody any contraband, as defined in subsection (a) of section 54-36a, that such officer discovers in the performance of his or her official duties. Such probation officer shall promptly process such contraband in accordance with the provisions of section 54-36a.

(c) A probation officer may, in the performance of his or her official duties, act as a member of a state or federal ad hoc fugitive task force that seeks out and arrests persons who have unexecuted state or federal arrest warrants lodged against such persons and such officer shall be deemed to be acting as an employee of the state while carrying out the duties of the task force.

(P.A. 10-43, S. 29; P.A. 11-155, S. 3.)

History: P.A. 11-155 amended Subsec. (a) to add provision re authority of probation officer to transport detained person to nearest location where police officer is able to make an arrest, effective July 1, 2011.

Sec. 54-108e. Duties of probation officers. Availability of information contained in alternative sentencing plan or community release plan.

(a) Probation officers shall provide intensive pretrial supervision services, in accordance with guidelines developed by the Court Support Services Division, whenever ordered to do so by the court.

(b) Probation officers shall complete alternative sentencing plans, in accordance with guidelines developed by the Court Support Services Division, for persons who have entered into a stated plea agreement that includes a term of imprisonment of two years or less, whenever ordered to do so by the court.

(c) Probation officers may evaluate persons sentenced to a term of imprisonment of two years or less who have been confined under such sentence for at least ninety days and have complied with institutional rules and necessary treatment programs of the Department of Correction, and may develop a community release plan for such persons in accordance with guidelines developed by the Court Support Services Division. If a probation officer develops a community release plan, the probation officer shall apply for a sentence modification hearing under section 53a-39.

(d) Information contained in an alternative sentencing plan or a community release plan shall be available only to: (1) Employees of the Judicial Branch who in the performance of their duties require access to the information contained in such plan; (2) employees and authorized agents of state or federal agencies involved in the design and delivery of treatment services to the person who is the subject of such plan; (3) employees of state or community-based agencies providing services directly to the person who is the subject of such plan; (4) an attorney representing the person who is the subject of such plan in any proceeding in which such plan is relevant; (5) employees of the Division of Criminal Justice who are assigned to the court location where the court ordered completion of an alternative sentencing plan pursuant to subsection (b) of this section, or where a sentence modification hearing will be heard pursuant to subsection (c) of this section; and (6) employees of the Department of Correction.

(P.A. 11-51, S. 21; P.A. 12-133, S. 33; P.A. 14-173, S. 3.)

History: P.A. 11-51 effective June 30, 2011; P.A. 12-133 added Subsec. (d) re availability of information contained in alternative sentencing plan or community release plan; P.A. 14-173 amended Subsec. (d) to add Subdiv. (5) re employees of Division of Criminal Justice assigned to court location and Subdiv. (6) re employees of Department of Correction.

Sec. 54-108f. Issuance of certificate of rehabilitation by Court Support Services Division. Modification or revocation.

(a) The Court Support Services Division of the Judicial Branch may issue a certificate of rehabilitation to an eligible offender who is under the supervision of the division while on probation or other supervised release, or may issue a new certificate of rehabilitation to enlarge the relief previously granted under such certificate of rehabilitation or revoke any such certificate of rehabilitation in accordance with the provisions of section 54-130e that are applicable to certificates of rehabilitation. If the division issues, enlarges the relief previously granted under a certificate of rehabilitation or revokes a certificate of rehabilitation under this section, the division shall immediately file written notice of such action with the Board of Pardons and Paroles.

(b) Not later than October 1, 2015, and annually thereafter, the Court Support Services Division shall submit to the Office of Policy and Management and the Connecticut Sentencing Commission, in such form as the office may prescribe, data regarding the administration of certificates of rehabilitation, which shall include data on the number of certificates issued by the division and the number of certificates revoked by the division.

(P.A. 14-27, S. 3.)

Sec. 54-108g. Prohibition against disclosure of personal information of probation officers to certain individuals under the Freedom of Information Act.

Any personal information of a current or former probation officer employed by the Judicial Branch that is not related to the performance of such officer's duties or employment, including, but not limited to, such officer's (1) date of birth, (2) Social Security number, (3) current or former electronic mail address, telephone number or residential address, (4) photograph, and (5) driver's license information, shall not be subject to disclosure under the Freedom of Information Act, as defined in section 1-200, to any individual under the supervision of the Court Support Services Division or any individual committed to the custody or supervision of the Commissioner of Correction pursuant to section 53a-32 for a violation of probation.

(P.A. 14-34, S. 1.)

History: P.A. 14-34 effective July 1, 2014.

Secs. 54-109 and 54-109a. Transferred to Secs. 54-91a and 54-91b, respectively.

Secs. 54-110 to 54-119. Report on person with prior conviction. Restitution investigation and report. Information to be included in report. Appointment of restitution specialists and other personnel. Optional treatment of person found guilty of crime. Probation or suspension of sentence, generally. Penalty for common law high crimes and misdemeanors. Punishment upon second and third conviction. Second and subsequent convictions of crimes while armed with firearm. Additional penalties for conviction of crimes while armed with firearm. Court may impose additional sentence. Sections 54-110 to 54-119, inclusive, are repealed.

(1949 Rev., S. 8819—8821, 8836, 8837; 1955, S. 3338d—3341d; 1957, P.A. 287, S. 1, 2; 580, S. 1; 639, S. 2; 1959, P.A. 28, S. 204; 615, S. 15; 1963, P.A. 170; 368; 1969, P.A. 605, S. 1, 2; 828, S. 214; 1971, P.A. 871, S. 129; P.A. 78-188, S. 1—3, 8; P.A. 80-313, S. 61; P.A. 82-298, S. 9.)

Sec. 54-120. Transferred to Sec. 54-92a.

Sec. 54-121. Indeterminate sentence. Section 54-121 is repealed.

(1949 Rev., S. 8825; 1969, P.A. 828, S. 214.)

Sec. 54-122. Transferred to Sec. 54-92b.

Sec. 54-123. Transportation of prisoner discharged from jail. Section 54-123 is repealed.

(1949 Rev., S. 8824; 1959, P.A. 152, S. 82; 1961, P.A. 580, S. 19; 1967, P.A. 152, S. 46.)

Sec. 54-123a. Judicial Department duties re alternative sanctions and incarceration programs. The Judicial Department shall:

(1) Oversee and coordinate the implementation of alternative sanctions for both the regular criminal docket and the docket for juvenile matters of the Superior Court;

(2) Evaluate the effectiveness of alternative sanctions and their impact on juvenile and adult offenders, prison and jail overcrowding, court backlogs and community safety;

(3) Plan and establish new alternative sanctions;

(4) Develop criteria for determining the types of offenders appropriate to receive alternative sanctions and for determining the effectiveness of those sanctions for specific offender populations;

(5) Contract with nonprofit organizations providing alternative incarceration programs, halfway houses and other similar services;

(6) Contract for independent evaluations with respect to the use of alternative sanctions;

(7) Apply for, receive, allocate, disburse and account for grants of funds made available by the United States, the state, foundations, corporations and other businesses, agencies or individuals;

(8) Enter into agreements with the United States which may be required to obtain federal funds, and do all things necessary to apply or qualify for, accept and distribute any state and federal funds allotted under any federal or state law for alternative incarceration programs;

(9) Enter into contracts and cooperate with local government units and any combination of such units to carry out the duties imposed by this section;

(10) Enter into agreements necessary, convenient or desirable for carrying out the purposes of this section with foundations, agencies, corporations and other businesses or individuals; and

(11) Accept gifts or donations of funds, services, materials or property from any source and use such gifts or donations as is appropriate to implement the provisions of this section.

(P.A. 90-213, S. 1, 56; P.A. 95-225, S. 36; P.A. 02-132, S. 46.)

History: P.A. 95-225 amended Subsec. (b)(1) to require that the office oversee and coordinate the implementation of alternative sanctions "for both the regular criminal docket and the docket for juvenile matters of the Superior Court" and Subsec. (b)(2) to require that the office evaluate the impact of alternative sanctions on "juvenile and adult" offenders; P.A. 02-132 deleted Subsec. (a) re Office of Alternative Sanctions, deleted Subsec. (b) designator, replaced "The duties and responsibilities of the office shall be to" with "The Judicial Department shall", deleted former Subdiv. (5) re annual report to the General Assembly, renumbered existing Subdivs. (6) to (12) as Subdivs. (5) to (11) and made a technical change.

Secs. 54-123b and 54-123c. Advisory committee concerning adult offenders. Advisory committee concerning juvenile offenders. Sections 54-123b and 54-123c are repealed, effective October 1, 2003.

(P.A. 90-213, S. 2, 56; P.A. 95-225, S. 37, 38; P.A. 02-132, S. 47, 48; P.A. 03-202, S. 25.)

Sec. 54-123d. Establishment of alternative incarceration center providing mental health services.

(a) The Judicial Branch may establish, within available appropriations, in the judicial district of New Haven, an alternative incarceration center that, in addition to the programs and services offered by an alternative incarceration center, provides a residential and day reporting program for accused and convicted persons with mental health needs.

309

(b) A full range of mental health services shall, within available appropriations, be provided to the program participants. A clinical coordinator shall work with the director of the alternative incarceration center in facilitating timely access to appropriate services and shall develop a network of community, social and vocational rehabilitation supports that will enhance successful program participation and long-term community integration.

(June Sp. Sess. P.A. 01-9, S. 77, 131.)

History: June Sp. Sess. P.A. 01-9 effective July 1, 2001.

Sec. 54-124. Board of Parole. Appointment and duties of executive secretary. Section 54-124 is repealed.

(1957, P.A. 461, S. 1, 2; 1959, P.A. 276; 1967 P.A. 152, S. 49; 453, S. 1.)

Sec. 54-124a. Board of Pardons and Paroles.

(a)(1) There shall be a Board of Pardons and Paroles within the Department of Correction, for administrative purposes only. On and after July 1, 2015, the board shall consist of ten full-time and up to five part-time members appointed by the Governor with the advice and consent of both houses of the General Assembly. The term of any part-time member serving on the board on June 30, 2015, shall expire on said date. On or after July 1, 2015, the Governor may appoint up to five persons to serve as part-time members. In the appointment of the members, the Governor shall specify if the member is being appointed as full-time or part-time. In the appointment of the members, the Governor shall comply with the provisions of section 4-9b. The Governor shall appoint a chairperson from among the membership. The members of the board shall be qualified by education, experience or training in the administration of community corrections, parole or pardons, criminal justice, criminology, the evaluation or supervision of offenders or the provision of mental health services to offenders. Each appointment of a member of the board submitted by the Governor to the General Assembly, except as provided in subdivision (2) of this subsection, shall be referred, without debate, to the joint standing committee of the General Assembly having cognizance of matters relating to the judiciary which shall report on each appointment not later than thirty legislative days after the date of reference.

(2) If, not later than September 1, 2015, the Governor appoints a part-time member and such member was previously a member whose term expired June 30, 2015, such appointment shall take effect immediately without confirmation by the General Assembly.

(b) The term of each member of the board shall be coterminous with the term of the Governor or until a successor is chosen, whichever is later. Any vacancy in the membership of the board shall be filled for the unexpired portion of the term by the Governor.

(c) Ten of the members of the board shall devote full time to the performance of their duties under this section and shall be compensated therefor in such amount as the Commissioner of Administrative Services determines, subject to the provisions of section 4-40. The other members of the board shall receive one hundred ten dollars for each day spent in the performance of their duties and shall be reimbursed for necessary expenses incurred in the performance of such duties. The chairperson or, in the chairperson's absence or inability to act, a member designated by the chairperson to serve temporarily as chairperson, shall be present at all meetings of the board and participate in all decisions.

(d) The chairperson shall be the executive and administrative head of said board and shall have the authority and responsibility for (1) overseeing all administrative affairs of the board, (2) assigning members to panels, (3) establishing procedural rules for members to follow when conducting hearings, reviewing recommendations made by employees of the board and making decisions, (4) adopting policies in all areas of pardons and paroles including, but not limited to, granting pardons, commutations of punishments or releases, conditioned or absolute, in the case of any person convicted of any offense against the state and commutations from the penalty of death, risk-based structured decision making and release criteria, (5) consulting with the Department of Correction on shared issues including, but not limited to, prison overcrowding, (6) consulting with the Judicial Branch on shared issues of community supervision, and (7) signing and issuing subpoenas to compel the attendance and testimony of witnesses at parole proceedings. Any such subpoena shall be enforceable to the same extent as subpoenas issued pursuant to section 52-143.

(e) Each parole release panel shall be composed of two members and the chairperson or a full-time member designated by the chairperson to serve temporarily as chairperson. On and after January 1, 2016, not less than three members shall be present at each parole hearing. Each pardons panel shall be composed of three members, one of whom may be the chairperson, except that for hearings on commutations from the penalty of death, one member of the panel shall be the chairperson.

(f) The Board of Pardons and Paroles shall have independent decision-making authority to (1) grant or deny parole in accordance with sections 54-125, 54-125a, 54-125e and 54-125g, (2) establish conditions of parole or special parole supervision in accordance with section 54-126, (3) rescind or revoke parole or special parole in accordance with sections 54-127 and 54-128, (4) grant commutations of punishment or releases, conditioned or absolute, in the case of any person convicted of any offense against the state and commutations from the penalty of death in accordance with section 54-130a.

(g) The Department of Correction shall be responsible for the supervision of any person transferred to the jurisdiction of the Board of Pardons and Paroles during such person's period of parole or special parole.

(h) The chairperson, or the chairperson's designee, and two members of the board shall conduct all parole release hearings, and shall approve or deny all (1) parole revocations and parole rescissions recommended by an employee of the board pursuant to section 54-127a, and (2) recommendations for parole pursuant to section 54-125i. No panel of the Board of Pardons and Paroles shall hold a hearing to determine the suitability for parole release of any person unless the chairperson of the board has made reasonable efforts to determine the existence of and obtain all information deemed pertinent to the panel's decision and has certified that all such pertinent information determined to exist has been obtained or is unavailable.

(i) The chairperson of the board shall appoint an executive director. The executive director shall oversee the administration of the agency and, at the discretion of the chairperson, shall: (1) Direct and supervise all administrative affairs of the board, (2) prepare the budget and annual operation plan, (3) assign staff to administrative reviews, (4) organize pardons and parole release hearing calendars, (5) implement a uniform case filing and processing system, and (6) create programs for staff and board member development, training and education.

(j) The chairperson, in consultation with the executive director, shall adopt regulations, in accordance with chapter 54, concerning:

(1) Parole revocation and rescission hearings that include implementing due process requirements;

(2) An expedited pardons review that allows an applicant convicted of a crime to be granted a pardon with respect to such crime without a hearing, unless a victim of such crime requests such a hearing, if such applicant was convicted of a nonviolent crime;

(3) Requiring board members to issue written statements containing the reasons for rejecting any application for a pardon.

(k) The Board of Pardons and Paroles shall hold a pardons hearing at least once every three months and shall hold such hearings in various geographical areas of the state. The board shall not hold a pardons hearing within or on the grounds of a correctional facility except when solely for the benefit of applicants who are incarcerated at the time of such hearing.

(l) The chairperson and executive director shall establish:

(1) In consultation with the Department of Correction, a parole orientation program for all parole-eligible inmates upon their transfer to the custody of the Commissioner of Correction that will provide general information on the laws and policies regarding parole release, calculation of time-served standards, general conditions of release, supervision practices, revocation and rescission policies, and procedures for administrative review and panel hearings, and any other information that the board deems relevant for preparing inmates for parole;

(2) An incremental sanctions system for parole violations including, but not limited to, reincarceration based on the type, severity and frequency of the violation and specific periods of incarceration for certain types of violations; and

(3) A formal training program for members of the board and parole officers that shall include, but not be limited to, an overview of the criminal justice system, the parole system including factors to be considered in granting parole, victim rights and services, reentry strategies, risk assessment, case management and mental health issues. Each member shall complete such training annually.

(m) The board shall employ at least one psychologist with expertise in risk assessment and recidivism of criminal offenders who shall be under the supervision of the chairperson and assist the board in its parole release decisions.

(n) In the event of the temporary inability of any member other than the chairperson to perform his or her duties, the Governor, at the request of the board, may appoint a qualified person to serve as a temporary member during such period of inability.

(o) The chairperson of the Board of Pardons and Paroles shall: (1) Adopt an annual budget and plan of operation, (2) adopt such rules as deemed necessary for the internal affairs of the board, and (3) submit an annual report to the Governor and General Assembly.

(p) Any decision of the board or a panel of the board shall be made by a majority of those members present.

(1967, P.A. 152, S. 48; 1969, P.A. 537, S. 1; 1971, P.A. 230; 1972, P.A. 23, S. 1; P.A. 74-338, S. 57, 94; P.A. 77-614, S. 134, 610; P.A. 79-560, S. 32, 39; June Sp. Sess. P.A. 83-18; P.A. 93-219, S. 3, 14; P.A. 94-183, S. 1, 3; May 25 Sp. Sess. P.A. 94-1, S. 64, 130; P.A. 95-189, S. 1, 2; P.A. 98-234, S. 1, 5; June 30 Sp. Sess. P.A. 03-6, S. 161; P.A. 04-234, S. 1; P.A. 05-84, S. 1, 2; 05-288, S. 187; Jan. Sp. Sess. P.A. 08-1, S. 12; Sept. Sp. Sess. P.A. 09-7, S. 36; P.A. 10-14, S. 1; 10-36, S. 29; P.A. 14-27, S. 8; June Sp. Sess. P.A. 15-2, S. 9.)

History: 1969 act specified that board of parole is autonomous body within department of correction solely for fiscal and budgetary purposes, increased membership from 7 to 9 and provided for their appointment, updated previous appointment provisions to provide ongoing applicability, deleted provision requiring 3 members for quorum and added provisions re assignment of members to panels and duties of panels; 1971 act deleted obsolete provision re appointment of additional members enacted in 1969 and added provision re appointment of temporary members; 1972 act increased membership to 11 and provided for their appointment; P.A. 74-338 deleted obsolete provision re initial appointment of additional members provided for in 1972 act; P.A. 77-614 provided for compensation of chairman as determined by commissioner of administrative services rather than by personnel policy board; P.A. 79-560 specified that board is within department of correction for "administrative" rather than for "fiscal and budgetary" purposes; June Sp. Sess. P.A. 83-18 increased the per diem compensation of members from $75 to $110; P.A. 93-219 inserted Subsec. indicators, amended Subsec. (a) to increase the number of members on and after July 1, 1994, from 11 to 13, require the chairman to be qualified by training, experience or education in law, criminal justice, parole matters or other related fields and require the governor to endeavor to reflect the racial diversity of the state when making appointments, added a new Subsec. (b) to require the term of the chairman to be coterminous with that of the governor, provide that the terms of all other members expire on July 1, 1994, that on and after said date 6 members shall be appointed for 2 years and 6 members appointed for 4 years and that thereafter all members shall serve for terms of 4 years and require the governor to fill any vacancy, amended Subsec. (d) to set forth the powers and duties of the chairman and added a new Subsec. (g) to set forth the duties of the board, effective July 1, 1994; P.A. 94-183 and May 25 Sp. Sess. P.A. 94-1 both amended Subsec. (a) to delete provision that the board of parole "shall be an autonomous body and within the department of correction for administrative purposes only", effective July 1, 1994; P.A. 95-189 added new Subsec. (d)(10) re noninstitutional, community-based service programs, renumbering former Subdiv. (10) as Subdiv. (11), effective July 1, 1995; P.A. 98-234 amended Subsec. (a) to increase the number of members on and after July 1, 1998 from 13 to 15, provide for the appointment of 2 vice-chairmen and make the provision re qualifications of the chairman also applicable to the vice-chairmen, amended Subsec. (b) to provide that the term of each vice-chairman shall be the same as that of the chairman, amended Subsec. (c) to make provision re performance of duties by and compensation of the chairman also applicable to the vice-chairmen, and added Subsec. (d)(12) authorizing the signing and issuing of subpoenas and add provision that any such subpoena shall be enforceable to the same extent as subpoenas issued under Sec. 52-143, effective July 1, 1998; June 30 Sp. Sess. P.A. 03-6 amended Subsec. (a) to place board "within the Department of Correction" and delete an obsolete date, amended Subsec. (c) to delete requirement that the vice-chairmen devote their entire time to the performance of their duties and replace "entire time" with "full time" and amended Subsec. (d) to delete provision that designated the chairman as the executive and administrative head of the board, designate the Commissioner of Correction rather than the chairman as the person having the authority and responsibility for the duties set forth in said Subsec., delete former Subdiv. (11) re consulting with the Department of Correction on shared issues including, but not limited to, prison overcrowding, and redesignate existing Subdiv. (12) as new Subdiv. (11), effective August 20, 2003; P.A. 04-234 amended Subsec. (a) to rename "Board of Parole" as "Board of Pardons and Paroles", provide that board is within Department of Correction "for administrative purposes only", provide that on and after October 1, 2004, board shall consist of 13 rather than 15 members, require that all 13 members, rather than only chairman and 2 vice-chairmen, be appointed by the Governor with advice and consent of either house of the General Assembly, provide that chairperson shall be qualified by education, experience and training "in the administration of community corrections, parole or pardons" rather than "in law, criminal justice, parole matters or other related fields", delete provision re qualifications of vice-chairmen and other members and add provision requiring the Governor to appoint chairperson from among membership, amended Subsec. (b) to add provision that term of each appointed member of board serving on September 30, 2004, shall expire on that date, provide that term of each member of board beginning on or after October 1, 2004, rather than only term of chairman and each vice-chairman, shall be coterminous with term of the Governor, and delete provision re appointment on or after July 1, 1994, of members other than chairman for staggered terms, amended Subsec. (c) to make technical changes, amended Subsec. (d) to designate chairperson rather than Commissioner of Correction as person having authority and responsibility for duties set forth in said Subsec., provide that chairperson shall be executive and administrative head of the board, replace in Subdiv. (1) "directing and supervising" with "overseeing", delete former Subdivs. (2) to (5), inclusive, to reflect transfer of duties to executive director under new Subsec. (i)(2) to (5), redesignate existing Subdiv. (6) as new Subdiv. (2) and amend said Subdiv. to replace "establishing policy in all areas of parole including, but not limited to, decision making, release criteria and supervision standards" with "adopting policies in all areas of pardons and paroles including, but not limited to, granting pardons, commutations of punishments or releases, conditioned or absolute, in the case of any person convicted of any offense against the state and commutations from the penalty of death, risk-based structured decision-making and release criteria", delete former Subdiv. (7) re establishing specialized parole units, delete former Subdiv. (8) re entering into contracts with service providers, community programs and consultants, delete former Subdiv. (9) to reflect transfer of duty to executive director under new Subsec. (i)(6), delete former Subdiv. (10) re establishing, developing and maintaining noninstitutional, community-based service programs, add new Subdiv. (3) re consulting with Department of Correction on shared issues including, but not limited to, prison overcrowding, add new Subdiv. (4) re consulting with Judicial Department on shared issues of community supervision, and redesignate existing Subdiv. (11) re subpoenas as new Subdiv. (5), amended Subsec. (e) to authorize chairperson to serve on both pardons panels and parole release panels, require chairperson to assign 7 members exclusively to parole release hearings and 5 members exclusively to pardons hearings, prohibit member assigned to one type of hearing to be subsequently assigned to other type of hearing, add provision re composition of each pardons panel and make technical changes, added new Subsec. (f) re independent decision-making authority of the board, added new Subsec. (g) re responsibility of Department of Correction for supervision of persons on parole or special parole, added new Subsec. (h) re conduct of parole release hearings and approval or denial of all parole releases, revocations and rescissions recommended by employee of board, added new Subsec. (i) re appointment and powers of executive director, added new Subsec. (j) re adoption of regulations re parole revocation and rescission hearings, an administrative pardons process and requiring written statement re reasons for rejecting pardons application, added new Subsec. (k) re frequency and location of pardons hearings, added new Subsec. (l) re establishment of parole orientation program and incremental sanctions system for parole violations, redesignated existing Subsec. (f) as Subsec. (m) and amended said Subsec. to make a technical change, and redesignated existing Subsec. (g) as Subsec. (n) and amended said Subsec. to replace "The Board of Parole" with "The chairperson of the Board of Pardons and Paroles" and replace in Subdiv. (3) "develop policy for and administer the operation" of the Interstate Parole Compact with "adopt regulations, in accordance with chapter 54, for the administration" of said compact, effective July 1, 2004; P.A. 05-84 amended Subsec. (j)(2)(A)(ii) to reduce from 10 years to 5 years the period of time prior to the granting of the pardon during which the applicant must not have been convicted of a crime, amended Subsec. (j)(2)(B) to increase from 5 years to 10 years the period of time after the date of conviction or the applicant's release from incarceration, whichever is later, that must elapse prior to the granting of the pardon and deleted former Subsec. (n)(3) re the adoption of regulations for the administration of the Interstate Parole Compact, redesignating existing Subdiv. (4) as Subdiv. (3); P.A. 05-288 made a technical change in Subsec. (f)(4), effective July 13, 2005; Jan. Sp. Sess. P.A. 08-1 amended Subsec. (a) to provide that from February 1, 2008, to July 1, 2008, board shall consist of not more than 25 members, rather than 13 members, that on and after July 1, 2008, board shall consist of 18 members, that on and after February 1, 2008, the Governor shall appoint all members of board with advice and consent of "both houses" of the General Assembly, rather than "either house", that on and after July 1, 2008, 12 members shall serve exclusively on parole release panels, 5 members shall serve exclusively on pardons panels and chairperson may serve on both such panels, and that on and after February 1, 2008, the Governor shall specify the member being appointed chairperson, the full-time and part-time members being appointed to serve on parole release panels and the members being appointed to serve on pardons panels, replace requirement that in appointment of members the Governor "shall endeavor to reflect the racial diversity of the state" with "shall comply with the provisions of section 4-9b", require that all members of the board appointed on or after February 1, 2008, rather than only chairperson, be qualified by education, experience or training in administration of community corrections, parole or pardons and add "criminal justice, criminology, the evaluation or supervision of offenders or the provision of mental health services to offenders", and add provision requiring each appointment submitted by the Governor to the General Assembly on or after February 1, 2008, be referred to the judiciary committee which shall report thereon not later than 30 legislative days thereafter, amended Subsec. (b) to provide that term of each member serving on June 30, 2008, who had been assigned exclusively to parole hearings shall expire on said date, provide that term of each member serving on June 30, 2008, who had been appointed chairperson, had been assigned by chairperson exclusively to pardons hearings or has been appointed on or after February 1, 2008, shall be coterminous with the Governor or until a successor is chosen, whichever is later, and delete provisions re expiration of term of members serving on September 30, 2004, and duration of term of members beginning on or after October 1, 2004, amended Subsec. (c) to make the provision re devotion of full time to duties and manner of compensation applicable to five members appointed on or after February 1, 2008, to serve on parole release panels, amended Subsec. (d) to add new Subdiv. (2) re assigning members to panels, add new Subdiv. (3) re establishing procedural rules and redesignate existing Subdivs. (2), (3), (4) and (5) as Subdivs. (4), (5), (6) and (7), amended Subsec. (e) to delete provision authorizing chairperson to serve on both panels and granting chairperson responsibility for assigning members to panels, make provision requiring chairperson to assign 7 members to parole release hearings and 5 members to pardons hearings applicable with respect to "members appointed prior to February 1, 2008", replace provision

315

re each parole release panel shall be composed of two members and chairperson or designee with provision re "prior to July 1, 2008", each parole release panel shall be composed of two members "from among the members assigned by the chairperson exclusively to parole release hearings or the members appointed by the Governor on or after February 1, 2008, to serve exclusively on parole release panels" and chairperson or designee, provide that "On and after July 1, 2008, each parole release panel shall be composed of two members appointed by the Governor on or after February 1, 2008, to serve on parole release panels, at least one of whom is a full-time member, and the chairperson or a full-time member designated to serve temporarily as chairperson, for each correctional institution" and replace "Each pardons panel shall be composed of three members, one of whom may be the chairperson" with "Each pardons panel shall be composed of three members from among the members assigned by the chairperson exclusively to pardons hearings or the members appointed by the Governor on or after February 1, 2008, to serve on pardons panels, one of whom may be the chairperson", amended Subsec. (h) to replace "The chairperson, or the chairperson's designee, and two members of the board shall conduct all parole release hearings" with "The chairperson, or the chairperson's designee, and two members of the board from among the members assigned by the chairperson to serve exclusively on parole release panels or the members appointed by the Governor on or after February 1, 2008, to serve on parole release panels, shall conduct all parole release hearings", make existing requirement that panel approve or deny all parole releases recommended by employee of the board pursuant to Sec. 54-125b applicable to period "prior to July 1, 2008" and add provision prohibiting panel holding hearing or meeting re parole release unless chairperson has made reasonable efforts to determine existence of and obtain all information deemed pertinent to panel's decision and certified that all such pertinent information determined to exist has been obtained or is unavailable, amended Subsec. (l) to add Subdiv. (3) re establishment of formal training program for board members and parole officers, added new Subsec. (m) re employment of psychologist, and redesignated existing Subsecs. (m) and (n) as Subsecs. (n) and (o), effective January 25, 2008; Sept. Sp. Sess. P.A. 09-7 amended Subsec. (e) to make existing provision requiring parole release panel to have at least 1 full-time member in addition to chairperson or a full-time member designated as chairperson applicable to panels "prior to October 5, 2009," and to add "On and after October 5, 2009, each parole release panel shall be composed of two members appointed by the Governor to serve on parole release panels and the chairperson or a full-time member designated to serve temporarily as chairperson, for each correctional institution", effective October 5, 2009; P.A. 10-14 amended Subsec. (a) to provide that on and after July 1, 2010, the board shall consist of 20 members and that 7 members shall serve exclusively on pardons panels and to delete obsolete language, effective May 5, 2010; P.A. 10-36 amended Subsec. (h) to delete obsolete provisions re panel action on parole releases recommended by employee of board pursuant to Sec. 54-125b, effective July 1, 2010; P.A. 14-27 made a technical change in Subsec. (d)(6); June Sp. Sess. P.A. 15-2 amended Subsec. (a) to designate existing provisions as Subdiv. (1) and amend same to replace provision re make-up of board from July 1, 2008, to July 1, 2010, and on and after July 1, 2010, with provision re make-up of board on and after July 1, 2015, add provision re expiration of part-time members' terms on June 30, 2015, and appointment of 5 part-time members on or after July 1, 2015, add reference to Subdiv. (2) and make technical changes, and to add Subdiv. (2) re appointments of part-time members not later than September 1, 2015, amended Subsec. (b) to delete references to dates in 2008 and provisions re members assigned exclusively to pardons hearings, amended Subsec. (c) to replace provision re 5 members appointed to serve on parole release panels with provision re 10 members devoting full time and make a technical change, amended Subsec. (e) to delete provisions re assignments of members exclusively to parole release and pardons hearings for members appointed prior to February 1, 2008, composition of each panel

316

prior to July 1, 2008, and on and after July 1, 2008, and prior to October 5, 2009, each panel's temporary chairperson to be designated by the chairperson, delete provision re panel for each correctional institution, add provisions re on and after January 1, 2016, 3 members to be present at each hearing and delete provision re exclusive assignment to pardons panels, amended Subsec. (h) to delete provision re exclusive assignment or appointment to parole release panels, designate existing provision re parole revocations or rescissions as Subdiv. (1) and add Subdiv. (2) re recommendations pursuant to Sec. 54-125i, amended Subsec. (j)(2) to replace "administrative pardons process" with "expedited pardons review", add provision re process for applicant convicted of nonviolent crime and delete former Subparas. (A) and (B) re misdemeanor conviction or conviction for a violation of Sec. 21a-277, 21a-278 or 21a-279, deleted reference to assignment to pardons hearings in Subsec. (j)(3), added provision re training to be completed annually in Subsec. (l)(3) and added Subsec. (p) re decisions to be made by a majority of members present, effective June 30, 2015.

See Sec. 4-38f for definition of "administrative purposes only".

See Sec. 18-101f re nondisclosure of member or employee files to inmates.

Cited. 170 C. 124; 171 C. 691.

Sec. 54-124b. Caseload of parole officers.

The chairman of the Board of Pardons and Paroles, in consultation with the members of the board and representatives of parole officers, shall annually review and establish goals for parole officer to parolee caseload ratio.

(1967, P.A. 152, S. 50; 1972, P.A. 112, S. 1; P.A. 90-261, S. 6, 19; P.A. 93-219, S. 7, 14; P.A. 94-183, S. 2, 3; May 25 Sp. Sess. P.A. 94-1, S. 65, 130; P.A. 04-234, S. 2.)

History: 1972 act deleted proviso which had made superintendent of Niantic correctional facility responsible for direction and control of parole of women; P.A. 90-261 designated existing provisions as Subsec. (a) and added Subsec. (b) establishing a maximum caseload of twenty-five parolees per supervisor on and after July 1, 1995; P.A. 93-219 amended Subsec. (a) to delete responsibility of commissioner to "carry out field services, parolee supervision and other duties requisite to the proper administration of the parole process" and amended Subsec. (b) to replace provision establishing a maximum caseload of twenty-five parolees per supervisor as of July 1, 1995, with requirement that the chairman of the board of parole, in consultation with board members and representatives of parole officers, annually review and establish goals for parole officer to parolee caseload ratio, effective July 1, 1994; P.A. 94-183 and May 25 Sp. Sess. P.A. 94-1 both deleted Subsec. (a) that had required the commissioner of correction to furnish all necessary clerical, administrative and fiscal services to the board of parole, effective July 1, 1994; P.A. 04-234 replaced Board of Parole with Board of Pardons and Paroles, effective July 1, 2004.

Cited. 170 C. 129.

Sec. 54-124c. Responsibility of the Department of Correction for supervision of persons released from confinement.

Notwithstanding any provision of the general statutes, the Department of Correction shall be responsible for the supervision of all persons released from confinement in a correctional institution or facility into the community, until their sentence to the custody of the Commissioner of Correction is completed.

(P.A. 93-219, S. 6, 14; P.A. 04-234, S. 32.)

History: P.A. 93-219 effective July 1, 1993; P.A. 04-234 replaced "Board of Parole" with "Department of Correction", deleted obsolete date and deleted exception for "persons released pursuant to section 18-100c", effective June 8, 2004.

Sec. 54-124d. Criminal history records check of Board of Parole personnel. Section 54-124d is repealed, effective June 14, 2004.

(P.A. 01-175, S. 29, 32; P.A. 04-257, S. 135.)

Sec. 54-124e. Board of Pardons and Paroles as successor department to Board of Pardons and Board of Parole.

(a) The Board of Pardons and Paroles shall be a successor department to the Board of Pardons and the Board of Parole in accordance with the provisions of sections 4-38d and 4-39.

(b) Wherever the words "Board of Pardons" or "Board of Parole" are used in the general statutes or the public acts of 2003 and 2004, the words "Board of Pardons and Paroles" shall be substituted in lieu thereof.

(c) The Legislative Commissioners' Office shall, in codifying the provisions of this section, make such technical, grammatical and punctuation changes as are necessary to carry out the purposes of this section.

(P.A. 04-234, S. 2.)

History: P.A. 04-234 effective July 1, 2004.

Sec. 54-125. Parole of prisoner serving indeterminate sentence.

Any person confined for an indeterminate sentence, after having been in confinement under such sentence for not less than the minimum term, or, if sentenced for life, after having been in confinement under such sentence for not less than the minimum term imposed by the court, less such time as may have been earned under the provisions of section 18-7, may be allowed to go at large on parole in the discretion of the panel of the Board of Pardons and Paroles for the institution in which the person is confined, if (1) it appears from all available information, including such reports from the Commissioner of Correction as such panel may require, that there is reasonable probability that such inmate will live and remain at liberty without violating the law and (2) such release is not incompatible with the welfare of society. Such parolee shall be allowed in the discretion of such panel to return to his home or to reside in a residential community center, or to go elsewhere, upon such terms and conditions, including personal reports from such paroled person, as such panel prescribes, and to remain, while on parole, in the legal custody and control of the board until the expiration of the maximum term or terms for which he was sentenced. Any parolee released on condition that he reside in a residential community center may be required to contribute to the cost incidental to such residence. Each order of parole shall fix the limits of the parolee's residence, which may be changed in the discretion of such panel. Within one week after the commitment of each person sentenced for more than one year during any criminal term of the Superior Court, the state's attorney of each county and judicial district shall send to the Board of Pardons and Paroles the record, if any, of such person. In the case of an inmate serving a sentence at the John R. Manson Youth Institution, Cheshire, or at the York Correctional Institution, the Board of Pardons and Paroles shall establish, by rule, the date upon which said board shall notify the inmate that his eligibility for parole will be considered. At any time prior thereto the Commissioner of Correction may recommend that parole be granted and, under special and unusual circumstances, the commissioner may recommend that an inmate be discharged from the institution.

(1949 Rev., S. 8827; 1957, P.A. 461, S. 4; 1967, P.A. 152, S. 51; 1969, P.A. 575; 1971, P.A. 781, S. 2; 825; 1972, P.A. 25, S. 1; P.A. 73-116, S. 30; 73-667, S. 1, 2; P.A. 76-336, S. 7; P.A. 80-442, S. 26, 28; P.A. 86-186, S. 19; P.A. 04-234, S. 2; P.A. 15-14, S. 37.)

History: 1967 act, effective July 1, 1968, included State Prison for Women, required quorum rather than majority of board to parole prisoner, deleted provisions for notice to State Prison inmate of parole eligibility and for notice to and action by state's attorney relative to paroles and added provisions re determination of date on which inmate will be notified of parole eligibility in cases involving indeterminate sentences at Connecticut Reformatory or Connecticut State Farm for Women and re superintendent's power to recommend early parole or discharge; 1969 act substituted references to Connecticut Correctional Institutions at Somers, Niantic and Cheshire for references to State Prison, State Prison or State Farm for Women and Connecticut Reformatory; 1971 acts added references to parole to residence in residential community center and replaced superintendent with commissioner of correction; 1972 act amended section to reflect parole powers vested in panels of parole board where previously parole powers were vested in the entire board acting if quorum was present; P.A. 73-116 referred to judicial districts generally, deleting specific reference to actions of state's attorney in judicial district of Waterbury; P.A. 73-667 changed effective date of P.A. 73-116 from October 1, 1973, to April 25, 1973; P.A. 76-336 deleted specific references to the various correctional institutions, allowed parole of person sentenced for life after serving minimum term imposed by court rather than after serving 25 years and specified that records of persons sentenced for more than 1 year be sent to parole board where previously such records were required to be sent in all cases; P.A. 80-442 deleted provision which allowed reduction of minimum sentence by not more than 5 years; P.A. 86-186 changed the name of the Connecticut Correctional Institution, Cheshire, to the John R. Manson Youth Institution, Cheshire; P.A. 04-234 replaced Board of Parole with Board of Pardons and Paroles, effective July 1, 2004; P.A. 15-14 made a technical change.

Cited. 126 C. 220; 145 C. 60; 152 C. 601; 168 C. 389; 169 C. 263; 170 C. 129; 171 C. 691; 172 C. 126; 196 C. 655; 210 C. 519; 213 C. 38, 48. To establish a cognizable claim under the ex post facto clause, habeas petitioner need only make a colorable showing that new law creates a genuine risk that petitioner will be incarcerated longer under the new law than under the old. 258 C. 804. Cited. Id., 830.

Sec. 54-125a. Parole of inmate serving sentence of more than two years. Eligibility. Hearing to determine suitability for parole release of certain inmates.

(a) A person convicted of one or more crimes who is incarcerated on or after October 1, 1990, who received a definite sentence or total effective sentence of more than two years, and who has been confined under such sentence or sentences for not less than one-half of the total effective sentence less any risk reduction credit earned under the provisions of section 18-98e or one-half of the most recent sentence imposed by the court less any risk reduction credit earned under the provisions of section 18-98e, whichever is greater, may be allowed to go at large on parole (1) in accordance with the provisions of section 54-125i, or (2) in the discretion of a panel of the Board of Pardons and Paroles, if (A) it appears from all available information, including any reports from the Commissioner of Correction that the panel may require, that there is a reasonable probability that such inmate will live and remain at liberty without violating the law, and (B) such release is not incompatible with the welfare of society. At the discretion of the panel, and under the terms and conditions as may be prescribed by the panel including requiring the parolee to submit personal reports, the parolee shall be allowed to return to the parolee's home or to reside in a residential community center, or to go elsewhere. The parolee shall, while on parole, remain under the jurisdiction of the board until the expiration of the maximum term or terms for which the parolee was sentenced less any risk reduction credit earned under the provisions of section 18-98e. Any parolee released on the condition that the parolee reside in a residential community center may be required to contribute to the cost incidental to such residence. Each order of parole shall fix the limits of the parolee's residence, which may be changed in the discretion of the board and the Commissioner of Correction. Within three weeks after the commitment of each person sentenced to more than two years, the state's attorney for the judicial district shall send to the Board of Pardons and Paroles the record, if any, of such person.

(b) (1) No person convicted of any of the following offenses, which was committed on or after July 1, 1981, shall be eligible for parole under subsection (a) of this section: (A) Capital felony, as provided under the provisions of section 53a-54b in effect prior to April 25, 2012, (B) murder with special circumstances, as provided under the provisions of section 53a-54b in effect on or after April 25, 2012, (C) felony murder, as provided in section 53a-54c, (D) arson murder, as provided in section 53a-54d, (E) murder, as provided in section 53a-54a, or (F) aggravated sexual assault in the first degree, as provided in section 53a-70a. (2) A person convicted of (A) a violation of section 53a-100aa or 53a-102, or (B) an offense, other than an offense specified in subdivision (1) of this subsection, where the underlying facts and circumstances of the offense involve the use, attempted use or threatened use of physical force against another person shall be ineligible for parole under subsection (a) of this section until such person has served not less than eighty-five per cent of the definite sentence imposed.

(c) The Board of Pardons and Paroles shall, not later than July 1, 1996, adopt regulations in accordance with chapter 54 to ensure that a person convicted of an offense described in subdivision (2) of subsection (b) of this section is not released on parole until such person has served eighty-five per cent of the definite sentence imposed by the court. Such regulations shall include guidelines and procedures for classifying a person as a violent offender that are not limited to a consideration of the elements of the offense or offenses for which such person was convicted.

(d) The Board of Pardons and Paroles may hold a hearing to determine the suitability for parole release of any person whose eligibility for parole release is not subject to the provisions of subsection (b) of this section upon completion by such person of seventy-five per cent of such person's definite or total effective sentence less any risk reduction credit earned under the provisions of section 18-98e. An employee of the board or, if deemed necessary by the chairperson, a panel of the board shall assess the suitability for parole release of such person based on the following standards: (1) Whether there is reasonable probability that such person will live and remain at liberty without violating the law, and (2) whether the benefits to such person and society that would result from such person's release to community supervision substantially outweigh the benefits to such person and society that would result from such person's continued incarceration. If a hearing is held, and if the board determines that continued confinement is necessary, the board shall articulate for the record the specific reasons why such person and the public would not benefit from such person serving a period of parole supervision while transitioning from incarceration to the community. If a hearing is not held, the board shall document the specific reasons for not holding a hearing and provide such reasons to such person. No person shall be released on parole without receiving a hearing. The decision of the board under this subsection shall not be subject to appeal.

(e) The Board of Pardons and Paroles may hold a hearing to determine the suitability for parole release of any person whose eligibility for parole release is subject to the provisions of subdivision (2) of subsection (b) of this section upon completion by such person of eighty-five per cent of such person's definite or total effective sentence. An employee of the board or, if deemed necessary by the chairperson, a panel of the board shall assess the suitability for parole release of such person based on the following standards: (1) Whether there is a reasonable probability that such person will live and remain at liberty without violating the law, and (2) whether the benefits to such person and society that would result from such person's release to community supervision substantially outweigh the benefits to such person and society that would result from such person's continued incarceration. If a hearing is held, and if the board determines that continued confinement is necessary, the board shall articulate for the record the specific reasons why such person and the public would not benefit from such person serving a period of parole supervision while transitioning from incarceration to the community. No hearing pursuant to the provisions of this subsection may proceed unless the parole release panel is in possession of the complete file for such applicant, including any documentation from the Department of Correction, the trial transcript, the sentencing record and any file of any previous parole hearing. Each member of the panel shall certify that all such documentation has been reviewed in preparation for such hearing. If a hearing is not held, the board shall document the specific reasons for not holding a hearing and provide such reasons to such person. No person shall be released on parole without receiving a hearing. The decision of the board under this subsection shall not be subject to appeal.

(f) (1) Notwithstanding the provisions of subsections (a) to (e), inclusive, of this section, a person convicted of one or more crimes committed while such person was under eighteen years of age, who is incarcerated on or after October 1, 2015, and who received a definite sentence or total effective sentence of more than ten years for such crime or crimes prior to, on or after October 1, 2015, may be allowed to go at large on parole in the discretion of the panel of the Board of Pardons and Paroles for the institution in which such person is confined, provided (A) if such person is serving a sentence of fifty years or less, such person shall be eligible for parole after serving sixty per cent of the sentence or twelve years, whichever is greater, or (B) if such person is serving a sentence of more than fifty years, such person shall be eligible for parole after serving thirty years. Nothing in this subsection shall limit a person's eligibility for parole release under the provisions of subsections (a) to (e), inclusive, of this section if such person would be eligible for parole release at an earlier date under any of such provisions.

(2) The board shall apply the parole eligibility rules of this subsection only with respect to the sentence for a crime or crimes committed while a person was under eighteen years of age. Any portion of a sentence that is based on a crime or crimes committed while a person was eighteen years of age or older shall be subject to the applicable parole eligibility, suitability and release rules set forth in subsections (a) to (e), inclusive, of this section.

(3) Whenever a person becomes eligible for parole release pursuant to this subsection, the board shall hold a hearing to determine such person's suitability for parole release. At least twelve months prior to such hearing, the board shall notify the office of Chief Public Defender, the appropriate state's attorney, the Victim Services Unit within the Department of Correction, the Office of the Victim Advocate and the Office of Victim Services within the Judicial Department of such person's eligibility for parole release pursuant to this subsection. The office of Chief Public Defender shall assign counsel for such person pursuant to section 51-296 if such person is indigent. At any hearing to determine such person's suitability for parole release pursuant to this subsection, the board shall permit (A) such person to make a statement on such person's behalf, (B) counsel for such person and the state's attorney to submit reports and other documents, and (C) any victim of the crime or crimes to make a statement pursuant to section 54-126a. The board may request testimony from mental health professionals or other relevant witnesses, and reports from the Commissioner of Correction or other persons, as the board may require. The board shall use validated risk assessment and needs assessment tools and its risk based structured decision making and release criteria established pursuant to subsection (d) of section 54-124a in making a determination pursuant to this subsection.

(4) After such hearing, the board may allow such person to go at large on parole with respect to any portion of a sentence that was based on a crime or crimes committed while such person was under eighteen years of age if the board finds that such parole release would be consistent with the factors set forth in subdivisions (1) to (4), inclusive, of subsection (c) of section 54-300 and if it appears, from all available information, including, but not limited to, any reports from the Commissioner of Correction, that (A) there is a reasonable probability that such person will live and remain at liberty without violating the law, (B) the benefits to such person and society that would result from such person's release to community supervision substantially outweigh the benefits

322

to such person and society that would result from such person's continued incarceration, and (C) such person has demonstrated substantial rehabilitation since the date such crime or crimes were committed considering such person's character, background and history, as demonstrated by factors, including, but not limited to, such person's correctional record, the age and circumstances of such person as of the date of the commission of the crime or crimes, whether such person has demonstrated remorse and increased maturity since the date of the commission of the crime or crimes, such person's contributions to the welfare of other persons through service, such person's efforts to overcome substance abuse, addiction, trauma, lack of education or obstacles that such person may have faced as a child or youth in the adult correctional system, the opportunities for rehabilitation in the adult correctional system and the overall degree of such person's rehabilitation considering the nature and circumstances of the crime or crimes.

(5) After such hearing, the board shall articulate for the record its decision and the reasons for its decision. If the board determines that continued confinement is necessary, the board may reassess such person's suitability for a new parole hearing at a later date to be determined at the discretion of the board, but not earlier than two years after the date of its decision.

(6) The decision of the board under this subsection shall not be subject to appeal.

(g) Any person released on parole under this section shall remain in the custody of the Commissioner of Correction and be subject to supervision by personnel of the Department of Correction during such person's period of parole.

(P.A. 90-261, S. 5; P.A. 92-114; P.A. 93-219, S. 2, 14; P.A. 94-37, S. 2; P.A. 95-255, S. 1–3; P.A. 99-196, S. 2; June Sp. Sess. P.A. 01-9, S. 74, 131; P.A. 04-234, S. 2, 3; Jan. Sp. Sess. P.A. 08-1, S. 5; P.A. 10-36, S. 30; P.A. 11-51, S. 25; P.A. 12-5, S. 32; P.A. 13-3, S. 59; 13-247, S. 376; P.A. 15-84, S. 1; June Sp. Sess. P.A. 15-2, S. 12–15.)

History: P.A. 92-114 amended Subsec. (a) to make eligible for parole a person convicted of "one or more crimes" who received "a definite sentence or aggregate sentence of more than one year and has been confined under such sentence or sentences for not less than one-half of the aggregate sentence or one-half of the most recent sentence imposed by the court, whichever is greater", rather than only a person convicted of "a felony" who received "a definite sentence of more than one year who has been confined under such sentence for not less than one-half of the sentence imposed by the court"; P.A. 93-219 amended Subsec. (a) to limit parole eligibility to persons who received a sentence of more than two years, rather than more than one year, effective July 1, 1993; P.A. 94-37 amended Subsec. (b) to make ineligible for parole a person convicted of an offense committed with a firearm in or on, or within 1,500 feet of, the real property comprising a public or private elementary or secondary school; P.A. 95-255 amended Subsec. (b) to add Subdiv. (2) re parole eligibility of persons convicted of offenses involving the use, attempted use or threatened use of physical force, designating existing provision re parole ineligibility of certain offenders as Subdiv. (1) and existing provision re parole eligibility of persons convicted of offenses carrying a mandatory minimum sentence as Subdiv. (3), effective July 1, 1996, and added Subsec. (c) requiring the Board of Parole to adopt regulations re the classification and release of violent offenders, effective July 1, 1995; P.A. 99-196 amended Subsec. (b) to delete Subdiv. (3) re parole eligibility date of a person convicted of an offense carrying a mandatory minimum sentence; June Sp. Sess. P.A. 01-9 added Subsec. (d) requiring the Board of Parole to submit reports re the number of persons whose eligibility for parole release is subject to Subsec. (a) and who have completed 75% of their definite sentence but have not been approved for parole release and made technical changes for purposes of gender neutrality in Subsec. (a), effective July 1, 2001; P.A. 04-234 amended Subsec. (a) to provide that parolee shall, while on parole, remain "under the jurisdiction" of board rather than "in the legal custody" of board and provide that limits of parolee's residence may be changed in discretion of "the board and the Commissioner of Correction" rather than in discretion of "such panel", amended Subsec. (b) to delete provision making ineligible for parole a person convicted of offense committed with a firearm in or on, or within 1,500 feet of an elementary or secondary school, add provision making ineligible for parole a person convicted of aggravated assault in the first degree, as provided in Sec. 53a-70a and make technical changes, deleted former Subsec. (d) requiring Board of Parole to submit reports re the number of persons whose eligibility for parole release is subject to Subsec. (a) and who have completed 75% of their definite sentence but have not been approved for parole release, added new Subsec. (d) to require board to hold hearing to determine suitability for parole release of any person whose eligibility for parole release is not subject to Subsec. (b) upon completion of 75% of such person's sentence, require employee or panel to reassess suitability for parole release of such a person, specify standards for reassessment, require board to articulate for the record its reasons if it determines that continued confinement is necessary and provide that decision of board is not appealable, added new Subsec. (e) to require board to hold hearing to determine suitability for parole release of any person whose eligibility for parole release is not subject to Subsec. (b)(2) upon completion of 85% of such person's sentence, require employee or panel to assess suitability for parole release of such a person, specify standards for reassessment, require board to articulate for the record its reasons if it determines that continued confinement is necessary and provide that decision of board is not appealable and added new Subsec. (f) to provide that a person remains in custody of Commissioner of Correction and is subject to supervision by personnel of Department of Correction while on parole, effective June 8, 2004, and replaced Board of Parole with Board of Pardons and Paroles, effective July 1, 2004; Jan. Sp. Sess. P.A. 08-1 amended Subsec. (b)(2) to add Subpara. (A) re person convicted of a violation of Sec. 53a-100aa or 53a-102 and designate existing provision as Subpara. (B), effective March 1, 2008; P.A. 10-36 amended Subsec. (a) to require state's attorney to send board the record, if any, of each person sentenced to more than 2 years, rather than more than 1 year, effective July 1, 2010; P.A. 11-51 provided for deduction from person's sentence of any risk reduction credit earned under Sec. 18-98e when calculating parole eligibility date under Subsecs. (a) to (c), length of time under jurisdiction of board under Subsec. (a) and date for parole suitability hearing under Subsecs. (d) and (e), effective July 1, 2011; P.A. 12-5 amended Subsec. (b)(1) to insert Subpara. designators (A) and (C) to (F), add reference to provisions of Sec. 53a-54b in effect prior to April 25, 2012, re capital felony in Subpara. (A) and add Subpara. (B) re murder with special circumstances under Sec. 53a-54b, effective April 25, 2012; P.A. 13-3 amended Subsecs. (b)(2), (c) and (e) to delete provisions re deduction for risk reduction credit earned under Sec. 18-98e, effective July 1, 2013; P.A. 13-247 amended Subsecs. (d) and (e) by changing "shall" to "may" re hearing by board to determine suitability for parole release, adding provisions re board to document specific reasons for not holding a hearing and re no person to be released on parole without receiving a hearing, and making technical changes, effective July 1, 2013; P.A. 15-84 amended Subsecs. (a), (d) and (e) by replacing "aggregate sentence" with "total effective sentence", adding new Subsec. (f) re person convicted of one or more crimes committed while the person was under 18 years of age, redesignating existing Subsec. (f) as Subsec. (g), and making a technical change; June Sp. Sess. P.A. 15-2 amended Subsec. (a) by adding new Subdiv. (1) re parole in accordance with Sec. 54-125i and by designating existing provision re discretion of panel of the board as Subdiv. (2) and amending same to delete provision re panel for the institution in which person is confined, redesignate existing Subdivs. (1) and (2) as Subparas. (A) and (B) and make a technical change, and amended Subsec. (e) by adding provisions re possession of complete file for applicant and certification by each member that all documentation has been reviewed, effective July 1, 2015.

See Sec. 18-100c re release of inmates with sentences of two years or less.

Broad discretionary nature of statute does not grant inmate the right to parole eligibility after serving one half of sentence and there is no liberty interest in parole release. 281 C. 241. Holding in *Miller v. Alabama*, 132 S. Ct. 2455, applies retroactively to cases on collateral review; life sentence for a juvenile includes a sentence of 50 years or more. 317 C. 52.

Board of Parole did not abuse discretion where there was misinterpretation of statute concerning parole eligibility unless petitioner served more time as a result of misinterpretation. 96 CA 26.

Cited. 44 CS 417.

Subsec. (b):

Requirement under Subdiv. (2) that a person shall remain ineligible for parole until completing not less than 85 per cent of the definite sentence imposed not applicable to persons who committed offenses prior to July 1, 1996. 258 C. 804. Cited. Id., 830.

Defendant's guilty plea for murder charge remains effective, even when trial court, in accepting guilty plea, failed to advise defendant that murder conviction would make him ineligible for parole pursuant to Subdiv. (1), as long as record indicates that defendant understood actual sentencing possibilities. 53 CA 90. Petitioner alleged sufficient facts to make a colorable showing that he would serve more prison time as result of Board of Pardons and Paroles application of revised section, as amended by Jan. Sp. Sess. P.A. 08-1, that specified he would not be eligible for parole until he served 85 per cent, rather than 50 per cent, of his sentence. 121 CA 1.

Subsec. (f):

Parole hearing under section offers a constitutionally adequate remedy to juvenile offenders who are facing life without parole or its functional equivalent and who were entitled to be, but were not, sentenced with consideration of the mitigating factors of youth as required by *Miller v. Alabama*, 132 S. Ct. 2455. 167 CA 744.

Sec. 54-125b. Parole of prisoner after administrative review without a hearing.

Section 54-125b is repealed, effective July 1, 2008.

(P.A. 93-219, S. 5, 14; P.A. 00-86; P.A. 04-234, S. 2, 4; Jan. Sp. Sess. P.A. 08-1, S. 44.)

(Return to Chapter

Table of Contents)

(Return to

List of Chapters)

(Return to

List of Titles)

Sec. 54-125c. Sexual offender treatment as precondition for parole hearing.

The Board of Pardons and Paroles, within available appropriations, may require an inmate to undergo specialized sexual offender treatment for at least one year before the board will schedule a date for a hearing to consider such inmate's eligibility for parole.

(P.A. 95-142, S. 8; P.A. 04-234, S. 2.)

History: P.A. 04-234 replaced Board of Parole with Board of Pardons and Paroles, effective July 1, 2004.

Sec. 54-125d. Deportation parole of aliens.

(a) The Board of Pardons and Paroles shall enter into an agreement with the United States Immigration and Naturalization Service for the deportation of parolees who are aliens as described in 8 USC 1252a(b)(2) and for whom an order of deportation has been issued pursuant to 8 USC 1252(b) or 8 USC 1252a(b).

(b) The Department of Correction shall determine those inmates who shall be referred to the Board of Pardons and Paroles based on intake interviews by the department and standards set forth by the United States Immigration and Naturalization Service for establishing immigrant status.

(c) Notwithstanding the provisions of subdivision (2) of subsection (b) of section 54-125a, any person whose eligibility for parole is restricted under said subdivision shall be eligible for deportation parole under this section after having served fifty per cent of the definite sentence imposed by the court.

(d) Notwithstanding any provision of the general statutes, a sentencing court may refer any person convicted of an offense other than a capital felony under the provisions of section 53a-54b in effect prior to April 25, 2012, or a class A felony who is an alien to the Board of Pardons and Paroles for deportation under this section.

(e) Any person who is approved for deportation under this section shall have his sentence placed in a hold status for a period of ten years. If the parolee reenters the United States within such ten-year period, he shall be in violation of his parole agreement, the remainder of his sentence shall be reinstated and he shall be ineligible for parole consideration.

(f) Any person approved for deportation parole shall not be eligible for any form of bond whether by the state or the federal government. Any person approved for deportation parole shall be transferred to the United States Immigration and Naturalization Service for deportation in accordance with the agreement entered into pursuant to subsection (a) of this section. Any person approved for deportation parole shall waive all rights to appeal his conviction, extradition and deportation.

(P.A. 97-256, S. 1; P.A. 04-234, S. 2; P.A. 12-5, S. 33.)

History: P.A. 04-234 replaced Board of Parole with Board of Pardons and Paroles, effective July 1, 2004; P.A. 12-5 amended Subsec. (d) to add reference to provisions of Sec. 53a-54b in effect prior to April 25, 2012, re conviction of a capital felony, effective April 25, 2012.

Sec. 54-125e. Special parole. Conditions. Duration. Violation. Hearing. Disposition.

(a) Any person convicted of a crime committed on or after October 1, 1998, who received a definite sentence of more than two years followed by a period of special parole shall, at the expiration of the maximum term or terms of imprisonment imposed by the court, be automatically transferred to the jurisdiction of the chairperson of the Board of Pardons and Paroles or, if such person has previously been released on parole pursuant to subsection (a) of section 54-125a or section 54-131a, remain under the jurisdiction of said chairperson until the expiration of the period of special parole imposed by the court. The Department of Correction shall be responsible for the supervision of any person transferred to the jurisdiction of the chairperson of the Board of Pardons and Paroles under this section during such person's period of special parole.

(b) When sentencing a person to a period of special parole, the court may recommend that such person comply with any or all of the requirements of subsection (a) of section 53a-30. The court shall cause a copy of any such recommendation to be delivered to such person and to the Department of Correction. The Board of Pardons and Paroles may require that such person comply with the requirements of subsection (a) of section 53a-30 which the court recommended. Any person sentenced to a period of special parole shall also be subject to such rules and conditions as may be established by the Board of Pardons and Paroles or its chairperson pursuant to section 54-126.

(c) The period of special parole shall be not less than one year or more than ten years, except that such period may be for more than ten years for a person convicted of a violation of subdivision (2) of section 53-21 of the general statutes in effect prior to October 1, 2000, subdivision (2) of subsection (a) of section 53-21 or section 53a-70, 53a-70a, 53a-70b, 53a-71, 53a-72a or 53a-72b or sentenced as a persistent dangerous felony offender pursuant to subsection (i) of section 53a-40 or as a persistent serious felony offender pursuant to subsection (k) of section 53a-40.

(d) Whenever a parolee has, in the judgment of such parolee's parole officer, violated the conditions of his or her special parole, the board shall cause the parolee to be brought before it without unnecessary delay for a hearing on the violation charges. At such hearing, the parolee shall be informed of the manner in which such parolee is alleged to have violated the conditions of such parolee's special parole and shall be advised by the employee of the board conducting the hearing of such parolee's due process rights.

(e) If such violation is established, the board may: (1) Continue the period of special parole; (2) modify or enlarge the conditions of special parole; or (3) revoke the sentence of special parole.

(f) If the board revokes special parole for a parolee, the chairperson may issue a mittimus for the commitment of such parolee to a correctional institution for any period not to exceed the unexpired portion of the period of special parole.

(g) Whenever special parole has been revoked for a parolee, the board may, at any time during the unexpired portion of the period of special parole, allow the parolee to be released again on special parole without court order.

(P.A. 98-234, S. 3; June Sp. Sess. P.A. 99-2, S. 52; P.A. 01-84, S. 21, 26; P.A. 04-234, S. 2, 5; P.A. 05-84, S. 3; 05-288, S. 188; P.A. 07-143, S. 14; 07-217, S. 196; June Sp. Sess. P.A. 15-2, S. 20.)

History: June Sp. Sess. P.A. 99-2 amended Subsec. (c) to provide that the period of special parole for the specified offenses "may be for more than ten years" rather than "shall be not less than ten years nor more than thirty-five years" and to make technical changes in statutory references; P.A. 01-84 amended Subsec. (c) to replace reference to "a violation of subdivision (2) of section 53-21" with "a violation of subdivision (2) of section 53-21 of the general statutes in effect prior to October 1, 2000," and include a violation of "subdivision (2) of subsection (a) of section 53-21", effective July 1, 2001; P.A. 04-234 replaced "chairman" with "chairperson" where appearing, amended Subsec. (a) to require the person be "automatically" transferred to the jurisdiction of the chairperson, delete provision that the person is transferred "from the custody of the Commissioner of Correction" and add provision requiring that Department of Correction be responsible for supervision of any person transferred to the jurisdiction of the chairperson during such person's period of special parole, added Subsec. (d) re a hearing on an alleged violation of the conditions of a parolee's special parole, added Subsec. (e) re authorized dispositions by the board upon establishing a violation, added Subsec. (f) re authority of the chairperson to issue a mittimus upon revocation of special parole and added Subsec. (g) re authority of the board to release again on special parole a parolee whose special parole has been revoked, effective June 8, 2004, and replaced Board of Parole with Board of Pardons and Paroles, effective July 1, 2004; P.A. 05-84 amended Subsec. (e)(1) to replace "sentence of special parole" with "period of special parole"; P.A. 05-288 made technical changes in Subsec. (c), effective July 13, 2005; P.A. 07-143 amended Subsec. (b) to add provisions authorizing court to order compliance with any or all of the requirements of Sec. 53a-30(a), requiring court to cause a copy of the order to be delivered to the person and Department of Correction and authorizing Board of Pardons and Paroles to require compliance with any or all of the requirements of Sec. 53a-30(a) which court could have imposed and are not inconsistent with any condition actually imposed by court; P.A. 07-217 amended Subsec. (b) to replace provision that court may "as a condition of the sentence, order such person to comply" with any or all of requirements of Sec. 53a-30(a) with provision re court may "recommend that such person comply" with such requirements, require delivery of copy of "recommendation", rather than copy of "order", and authorize board to require compliance with "the requirements of subsection (a) of section 53a-30 which the court recommended", rather than "any or all of the requirements of subsection (a) of section 53a-30 which the court could have imposed and which are not inconsistent with any condition actually imposed by the court"; June Sp. Sess. P.A. 15-2 made technical changes in Subsec. (c).

Subsec. (a):

Regardless of whether a person has been convicted of one offense or multiple offenses, legislature has used the phrase "period of special parole" to refer to that duration of time in which a person is transferred to the jurisdiction of the chairperson of the Board of Pardons and Paroles for supervision. 133 CA 140.

Subsec. (c):

With respect to 1999 revision, when sentencing provisions of Sec. 54-128(c) and Subsec. conflict, legislature intended the maximum statutory limit in Sec. 54-128(c) to control; defendant's sentence of 10 years of imprisonment followed by 10 years of special parole violated Sec. 54-128(c) and was an illegal sentence because total length of terms of imprisonment and special parole combined exceeded maximum term of imprisonment authorized for sexual assault in the second degree by Sec. 53a-35a(6) and Sec. 53a-71(b). 279 C. 527. Subsec. can be given effect only to the extent that it does not conflict with Sec. 54-128(c). 292 C. 417. Legislature intended to provide trial court with authority to impose a sentence of up to 10 years of special parole for each offense for which defendant is convicted and has not expressed intention to prevent a trial court from imposing such sentences of special parole consecutively if it deems appropriate, regardless of whether such consecutive sentences impose a total effective sentence of more than 10 years of special parole. 310 C. 693.

Court exceeded its authority by sentencing defendant to 16 years of special parole, beyond the 10-year maximum, where defendant had not been convicted of one of the enumerated exceptions for which a longer period of special parole may be imposed. 133 CA 140; judgment reversed, see 310 C. 693.

Sec. 54-125f. Pilot zero-tolerance drug supervision program.

(a) Not later than October 1, 1998, the chairman of the Board of Pardons and Paroles shall establish a pilot zero-tolerance drug supervision program. Eligibility for participation in the program shall be limited to individuals who are eligible for release on parole and shall be based upon criteria, including a limit on the maximum number of eligible participants, established by the chairman of the Board of Pardons and Paroles.

(b) Any person entering such program shall, as a condition of participating in such program, agree to: (1) Submit to periodic urinalysis drug tests, (2) detention in a halfway house facility for a period of two days each time such test produces a positive result, and (3) comply with all rules established by the halfway house if detained in such facility.

(c) Participants in the zero-tolerance drug supervision program shall submit to periodic urinalysis drug tests. If the test produces a positive result, the participant may be detained in a halfway house facility for a period of two days.

(d) Any person who has submitted to a urinalysis drug test pursuant to subsection (c) of this section that produced a positive result may request that a second urinalysis drug test be administered, at such person's expense, to confirm the results of the first test, except that if the participant is determined to be indigent, based upon financial affidavits, the Board of Pardons and Paroles shall pay the cost of the test. The second drug test shall be a urinalysis drug test, separate and independent of the initial test. The participant may be detained in a halfway house pending the results of the second test. If such second test does not produce a positive result, the participant, if detained in a halfway house, shall be released and the fee, if paid by the participant, shall be refunded to the participant.

(e) If at any time during participation in the zero-tolerance drug supervision program, the chairman of the Board of Pardons and Paroles determines that the public safety will be served by the incarceration of a participant, such participant may be returned to a correctional facility.

(P.A. 98-145, S. 1, 4; P.A. 99-34, S. 1, 2; P.A. 02-89, S. 84; P.A. 03-278, S. 111; P.A. 04-234, S. 2.)

History: P.A. 99-34 amended Subsec. (a) to delete provision that limited the program to individuals eligible for release on parole "in accordance with section 54-125b", effective May 27, 1999; P.A. 02-89 deleted as obsolete Subsec. (f) requiring the chairman of the Board of Parole, the Commissioner of Correction and the Chief Court Administrator to submit a report on the program to the committee of the General Assembly having cognizance of matters relating to criminal justice not later than January 1, 2000; P.A. 03-278 made a technical change in Subsec. (a), effective July 9, 2003; P.A. 04-234 replaced Board of Parole with Board of Pardons and Paroles, effective July 1, 2004.

See Sec. 18-100e re pilot zero-tolerance drug supervision program established by Commissioner of Correction.

Sec. 54-125g. Parole of prisoner nearing end of maximum sentence.

Notwithstanding the provisions of sections 18-100d, 54-124c and 54-125a, any person who has six months or less to the expiration of the maximum term or terms for which such person was sentenced, may be allowed to go at large on parole pursuant to section 54-125i or following a hearing pursuant to section 54-125a, provided such person agrees (1) to be subject to supervision by personnel of the Department of Correction for a period of one year, and (2) to be retained in the institution from which such person was paroled for a period equal to the unexpired portion of the term of his or her sentence if such person is found to have violated the terms or conditions of his or her parole. Any person subject to the provisions of subdivision (1) or (2) of subsection (b) of section 54-125a shall only be eligible to go at large on parole under this section after having served ninety-five per cent of the definite sentence imposed.

(P.A. 99-196, S. 1; P.A. 04-257, S. 122; June Sp. Sess. P.A. 15-2, S. 16.)

History: P.A. 04-257 replaced "Board of Parole" with "Department of Correction", effective June 14, 2004; June Sp. Sess. P.A. 15-2 added references to Secs. 54-125a and 54-125i, effective July 1, 2015.

Sec. 54-125h. Transfer of prisoner granted parole and nearing parole release date.

Notwithstanding the provisions of section 54-125a, the chairperson of the Board of Pardons and Paroles may transfer to any public or private nonprofit halfway house, group home or mental health facility or to an approved community or private residence any person confined in a correctional institution or facility who has been granted parole release and is within eighteen months of the parole release date established by the board. Any person released from confinement pursuant to this section shall be transferred to the jurisdiction of the chairperson of the Board of Pardons and Paroles. Such person shall remain in the custody of the Commissioner of Correction during the period of such release and employees of the Department of Correction shall be responsible for the supervision of such person while such person is residing at such halfway house, group home, mental health facility or community or private residence. Such person may, at any time, be returned to confinement in a correctional facility.

(P.A. 04-234, S. 2, 9.)

History: P.A. 04-234 effective June 8, 2004 (Revisor's note: Effective July 1, 2004, references to "Board of Parole" or "Board of Pardons" in the general statutes and in the public and special acts of the 2003 and 2004 regular and special sessions of the General Assembly were replaced with "Board of Pardons and Paroles" pursuant to Sec. 2 of P.A. 04-234).

Sec. 54-125i. Parole of prisoner without a hearing.

(a) An inmate (1) not convicted of a crime for which there is a victim, as defined in section 54-201 or section 54-226, who is known by the Board of Pardons and Paroles, (2) whose eligibility for parole release is not subject to the provisions of subsection (b) of section 54-125a, (3) who was not convicted of a violation of section 53a-55, 53a-55a, 53a-56, 53a-56a, 53a-56b, 53a-57, 53a-58, 53a-59, 53a-59a, 53a-60, 53a-60a, 53a-60c, 53a-64aa, 53a-64bb, 53a-70, 53a-70b, 53a-72b, 53a-92, 53a-92a, 53a-94a, 53a-95, 53a-100aa, 53a-101, 53a-102, 53a-102a, 53a-103a, 53a-111, 53a-112, 53a-134, 53a-135, 53a-136, 53a-167c, 53a-179b, 53a-179c or 53a-181c, and (4) who is not otherwise prohibited from being granted parole for any reason, may be allowed to go at large on parole in accordance with the provisions of section 54-125a or section 54-125g, pursuant to the provisions of subsections (b) and (c) of this section.

(b) A member of the board, or an employee of the board qualified by education, experience or training in the administration of community corrections, parole, pardons, criminal justice, criminology, the evaluation or supervision of offenders or the provision of mental health services to offenders, may evaluate whether parole should be granted to an inmate pursuant to this section. The board member or employee shall (1) use risk-based structured decision making and release criteria developed under policies adopted by the board pursuant to subsection (d) of section 54-124a, and (2) review the inmate's offender accountability plan, including, but not limited to, the environment to which the inmate plans to return upon release, to determine whether parole should be recommended for such inmate.

(c) If the board member or qualified employee recommends parole for an inmate, the chairperson of the board shall present such recommendation and all pertinent information to a parole release panel for approval. No parole release panel may review such recommendation and determine the suitability for parole release of an inmate unless the chairperson has made reasonable efforts to determine the existence of and obtain all information deemed pertinent to the panel's decision and has certified that all such pertinent information determined to exist has been obtained or is unavailable. No applicant may be granted parole pursuant to this section unless each board member or parole officer who reviewed such inmate's file certifies that he or she reviewed such recommendation and all such pertinent information.

(June Sp. Sess. P.A. 15-2, S. 11.)

History: June Sp. Sess. P.A. 15-2 effective July 1, 2015.

Sec. 54-126. Rules and regulations concerning parole. Enforcement.

Said Board of Pardons and Paroles may establish such rules and regulations as it deems necessary, upon which such convict may go upon parole, and the panel for the particular case may establish special provisions for the parole of a convict. The chairman of the board shall enforce such rules, regulations and provisions and retake and reimprison any convict upon parole, for any reason that such panel, or the chairman with the approval of the panel, deems sufficient; and the chairman may detain any convict or inmate pending approval by the panel of such retaking or reimprisonment.

(1949 Rev., S. 8828; 1967, P.A. 152, S. 52; 1972, P.A. 25, S. 2; P.A. 93-219, S. 8, 14; P.A. 04-234, S. 2.)

History: 1967 act, effective July 1, 1968, provided for enforcement by correction commissioner and added provision for detention by commissioner at end of section; 1972 act amended section to reflect transfer of parole power for entire board or quorum to panels and authorized panels to set special conditions for parole; P.A. 93-219 replaced the commissioner of correction with the chairman of the board as the official responsible for enforcement, recapture and detention, effective July 1, 1994; P.A. 04-234 replaced Board of Parole with Board of Pardons and Paroles, effective July 1, 2004.

Cited. 132 C. 306; 162 C. 434; 170 C. 118; 171 C. 691; Id., 691; 172 C. 126.

Cited. 4 CS 365. Rule of board which conflicted with Sec. 54-128(a) declared void. 27 CS 439.

Sec. 54-126a. Testimony of crime victim at parole hearing. Notification to victim.

(a) For the purposes of this section, "victim" means a person who is a victim of a crime, the legal representative of such person, a member of a deceased victim's immediate family or a person designated by a deceased victim in accordance with section 1-56r.

(b) (1) When a hearing is scheduled by the Board of Pardons and Paroles for the purpose of determining the eligibility for parole of an inmate incarcerated for the commission of any crime, the Office of Victim Services shall notify any victim of such crime who is registered with the board of the time, date and location of the hearing and include information that such victim may make a statement or submit a written statement pursuant to this section.

(2) A panel of said board shall permit any victim of the crime for which the inmate is incarcerated to appear before the panel for the purpose of making a statement for the record concerning whether the inmate should be released on parole or the nature of any terms or conditions to be imposed upon any such release. In lieu of such appearance, the victim may submit a written statement to the panel and the panel shall make such statement a part of the record at the parole hearing. At any such hearing, the record shall reflect that all reasonable efforts to notify registered victims were undertaken.

(c) If an inmate is scheduled to appear before the Board of Pardons and Paroles who (1) is serving an indeterminate sentence or a sentence for felony murder, and (2) was sentenced prior to July 1, 1981, the Office of Victim Services shall work with the Board of Pardons and Paroles to locate victims and victims' families and to notify them of the date, time and location of any parole hearing that is scheduled. If the victim of a crime committed by an inmate described in this subsection is a peace officer, and that peace officer is deceased, the Office of Victim Services shall notify the chief law enforcement officer of the town in which such crime occurred of the time, date and location of such hearing.

(d) Nothing in this section shall be construed to prohibit the board from exercising its discretion to permit a member or members of a victim's immediate family to appear before the panel and make a statement in accordance with subsection (b) of this section.

(P.A. 83-416; P.A. 85-566, S. 2; P.A. 91-389, S. 7, 12; P.A. 01-211, S. 9; P.A. 02-105, S. 14; P.A. 04-234, S. 2; Jan. Sp. Sess. P.A. 08-1, S. 13; June Sp. Sess. P.A. 15-2, S. 17; P.A. 16-193, S. 30.)

History: P.A. 85-566 amended Subsec. (c) to replace provision that nothing in the section shall be construed to require the state to give notice to a victim of a scheduled parole hearing with provision that the board shall notify a victim of the date, time and place of the hearing if the victim requests notice and provides a current address; P.A. 91-389 amended Subsec. (a) to revise the definition of "victim" and deleted Subsec. (c) re the requirement that the board notify a victim who has requested notice of the date, time and place of the hearing, effective April 1, 1992; P.A. 01-211 amended Subsec. (a) to redefine "victim" and amended Subsec. (b) to make provisions applicable at a hearing for an inmate incarcerated for the commission of "any crime" rather than "a class A, B or C felony or a violation of section 53a-60a, 53a-80c, 53a-72b, 53a-103a or 53a-216", P.A. 02-105 amended Subsec. (a) by adding a person designated by a victim pursuant to Sec. 1-56r to definition of "victim"; P.A. 04-234 replaced Board of Parole with Board of Pardons and Paroles, effective July 1, 2004; Jan. Sp. Sess. P.A. 08-1 added Subsec. (c) re board's discretion to permit a member or members of victim's immediate family to appear before panel and make a statement, effective January 25, 2008; June Sp. Sess. P.A. 15-2 amended Subsec. (b) by designating existing provisions re hearing for determining eligibility for parole as Subdiv. (1) and amending same to replace "At a hearing held by a panel of" with "When a hearing is scheduled by" and add provision re Office of Victim Services to notify any registered victim of the crime, and by designating existing provisions re appearance of victim as Subdiv. (2) and amending same to add provision re record to reflect all reasonable efforts to notify registered victims, added new Subsec. (c) re notification of victims and victims' families, and redesignated existing Subsec. (c) as Subsec. (d), effective July 1, 2015; P.A. 16-193 made a technical change in Subsec. (b)(2).

See Sec. 54-220a re assignment of victim advocates to assist victims at hearings.

Cited. 32 CA 438.

(Return to Chapter Table of Contents)

(Return to List of Chapters)

(Return to List of Titles)

Sec. 54-127. Rearrest.

The request of the Commissioner of Correction or any officer of the Department of Correction so designated by the commissioner, or of the Board of Pardons and Paroles or its chairman shall be sufficient warrant to authorize any officer of the Department of Correction or any officer authorized by law to serve criminal process within this state, to return any convict or inmate on parole into actual custody; and any such officer, police officer, constable or state marshal shall arrest and hold any parolee or inmate when so requested, without any written warrant.

(1949 Rev., S. 8829; March, 1958, P.A. 27, S. 38; 1967, P.A. 152, S. 53; 1969, P.A. 271; 1971, P.A. 62; May Sp. Sess. P.A. 94-6, S. 22, 28; P.A. 00-99, S. 123, 154; P.A. 04-234, S. 2; 04-257, S. 123.)

History: 1967 act, effective July 1, 1968, added correction commissioner to those authorized to request rearrest, deleted provision for parole board to authorize persons to so request and substituted officers of the correction department for officers of the board or the State Prison; 1969 act applied provisions to correction department officers designated by commissioner; 1971 act authorized chairman of board of parole to request custody; May Sp. Sess. P.A. 94-6 added "any officer of the board of parole designated by the chairman", made technical changes and deleted provision pertaining to compensation, effective July 1, 1994; P.A. 00-99 replaced reference to sheriff with state marshal, effective December 1, 2000; P.A. 04-234 replaced Board of Parole with Board of Pardons and Paroles, effective July 1, 2004; P.A. 04-257 deleted "any officer of the Board of Parole designated by the chairman" from individuals authorized to request the return to custody of a convict or inmate and deleted an officer "of the Board of Parole" from officers authorized to return a convict or inmate to custody, effective June 14, 2004.

Sec. 54-127a. Parole revocation and rescission hearings.

All parole revocation and rescission hearings shall be conducted by an employee of the Board of Pardons and Paroles. The parole of a person who has been allowed to go on parole in accordance with subsection (a) of section 54-125a or section 54-125g, or who has been sentenced to a period of special parole in accordance with subdivision (9) of subsection (b) of section 53a-28, shall be revoked or rescinded if, after such hearing, the employee recommends such revocation or rescission and such recommendation is approved by at least two members of a panel of the board.

(P.A. 04-234, S. 2, 6.)

History: P.A. 04-234 effective June 8, 2004 (Revisor's note: Effective July 1, 2004, references to "Board of Parole" or "Board of Pardons" in the general statutes and in the public and special acts of 2003 and 2004 regular and special sessions of the General Assembly were replaced with "Board of Pardons and Paroles" pursuant to Sec. 2 of P.A. 04-234).

Sec. 54-128. Period of confinement in correctional institution after parole violation.

 (a) Any paroled inmate who has been returned to any institution of the Department of Correction for violation of such inmate's parole may be retained in a correctional institution for a period equal to the unexpired portion of the term of such inmate's sentence at the date of the request or order for such inmate's return less any commutation or diminution of such inmate's sentence earned, except that the Board of Pardons and Paroles may, in its discretion, determine that such inmate shall forfeit any or all of such earned time, or may be again paroled by said board.

(b) Each parolee or inmate, subject to the provisions of section 18-7, shall be subject to loss of all or any portion of time earned.

(c) Any person who, during the service of a period of special parole imposed in accordance with subdivision (9) of subsection (b) of section 53a-28, has been returned to any institution of the Department of Correction for violation of such person's parole, may be retained in a correctional institution for a period equal to the unexpired portion of the period of special parole. The total length of the term of incarceration and term of special parole combined shall not exceed the maximum sentence of incarceration authorized for the offense for which the person was convicted.

(1949 Rev., S. 8830; 1957, P.A. 461, S. 5; 1967, P.A. 152, S. 54; P.A. 98-234, S. 4; P.A. 04-234, S. 2, 8; 04-257, S. 84, 124.)

History: 1967 act, effective July 1, 1968, extended section to all correctional institutions rather than State Prison alone, added reference to correction commissioner and deleted restriction of subsection (b) to serious acts of insubordination and refusal to conform to prison or parole regulations; P.A. 98-234 added new Subsec. (c) re the period of time that a person who has violated his special parole may be retained in the institution from which he was paroled; P.A. 04-234 replaced where appearing "the institution from which he was paroled" with "a correctional institution" as the place where a returned inmate may be retained, amended Subsec. (a) to delete reference to a paroled "convict", amended Subsec. (c) to delete provision re returning an inmate to "the custody of the Commissioner of Correction", and made technical changes, effective June 8, 2004, and replaced Board of Parole with Board of Pardons and Paroles, effective July 1, 2004; P.A. 04-257 amended Subsec. (a) to delete reference to a paroled "convict", delete provision re returning an inmate to "the custody of the Commissioner of Correction", replace "the institution from which he was paroled" with "a correctional institution" as the place where a returned inmate may be retained and make technical changes for purposes of gender neutrality, and made a technical change in Subsec. (c), effective June 14, 2004.

For purposes of determining amount of diminution for good time earned or its forfeiture, sentences imposed under several counts are to be regarded as one continuous term. 129 C. 164. It is for court, not Board of Parole, to determine whether second sentence given parolee shall run concurrently or consecutively with unexpired portion of first. 132 C. 307. Cited. 162 C. 434; 170 C. 129; 172 C. 126; 184 C. 222; 213 C. 38.

Cited. 12 CA 1.

Cited. 4 CS 365; 11 CS 284; 13 CS 309. Sentence runs for parolee until date of order for return. 16 CS 22. Cited. Id., 80. When prisoner was returned for violation of parole, term he was to serve should have been computed by subtracting, from time he was to serve, period he had served up to date of order for his return as parole violator. 27 CS 439. When a man is returned to prison for parole violation, he may be held only for the balance of time after the date of the issuance of the order for his return. 32 CS 190.

Subsec. (c):

When sentencing provisions of Sec. 54-125e(c) and Subsec. conflict, legislature intended the maximum statutory limit in Subsec. to control; defendant's sentence of 10 years of imprisonment followed by 10 years of special parole violated Subsec. and was an illegal sentence because total length of terms of imprisonment and special parole combined exceeded maximum term of imprisonment authorized for sexual assault in the second degree by Sec. 53a-35a(6) and Sec. 53a-71(b). 279 C. 527. Sec. 54-125e(c) can be given effect only to the extent that it does not conflict with Subsec. 292 C. 417.

Sec. 54-129. Discharge of paroled prisoner

. If it appears to the appropriate panel of the Board of Pardons and Paroles that any convict or inmate on parole or eligible for parole will lead an orderly life, said panel, by a unanimous vote of all the members present at any regular meeting thereof, may declare such convict or inmate discharged from the custody of the Commissioner of Correction and shall thereupon deliver to him a written certificate to that effect under the seal of the Board of Pardons and Paroles and signed by its chairman and the commissioner.

(1949 Rev., S. 8831; 1957, P.A. 461, S. 6; 1967, P.A. 152, S. 55; 1972, P.A. 25, S. 3; P.A. 04-234, S. 2.)

History: 1967 act, effective July 1, 1968, substituted custody of correction commissioner for "said prison" and provided certificate be signed by chairman of board of parole and commissioner rather than executive secretary of board and warden; 1972 act applied provisions to persons eligible for parole and transferred duties formerly held by entire parole board or quorum to panels of board; P.A. 04-234 replaced Board of Parole with Board of Pardons and Paroles, effective July 1, 2004.

Cited. 170 C. 129; 213 C. 38.

Cited. 8 CA 656.

Cited. 4 CS 365; 16 CS 80.

Sec. 54-130. State Prison for Women not covered. Section 54-130 is repealed.

(1957, P.A. 461, S. 7; 1967, P.A. 152, S. 56.)

Sec. 54-130a. (Formerly Sec. 18-26). Jurisdiction and authority of board to grant commutations of punishment, releases, pardons and certificates of rehabilitation.

(a) Jurisdiction over the granting of, and the authority to grant, commutations of punishment or releases, conditioned or absolute, in the case of any person convicted of any offense against the state and commutations from the penalty of death shall be vested in the Board of Pardons and Paroles.

(b) The board shall have authority to grant pardons, conditioned, provisional or absolute, or certificates of rehabilitation for any offense against the state at any time after the imposition and before or after the service of any sentence.

(c) The board may accept an application for a pardon three years after an applicant's conviction of a misdemeanor or violation and five years after an applicant's conviction of a felony, except that the board, upon a finding of extraordinary circumstances, may accept an application for a pardon prior to such dates.

(d) Whenever the board grants an absolute pardon to any person, the board shall cause notification of such pardon to be made in writing to the clerk of the court in which such person was convicted, or the Office of the Chief Court Administrator if such person was convicted in the Court of Common Pleas, the Circuit Court, a municipal court, or a trial justice court.

(e) Whenever the board grants a provisional pardon or a certificate of rehabilitation to any person, the board shall cause notification of such provisional pardon or certificate of rehabilitation to be made in writing to the clerk of the court in which such person was convicted. The granting of a provisional pardon or a certificate of rehabilitation does not entitle such person to erasure of the record of the conviction of the offense or relieve such person from disclosing the existence of such conviction as may be required.

(f) In the case of any person convicted of a violation for which a sentence to a term of imprisonment may be imposed, the board shall have authority to grant a pardon, conditioned, provisional or absolute, or a certificate of rehabilitation in the same manner as in the case of any person convicted of an offense against the state.

(1949 Rev., S. 3020; 1959, P.A. 410, S. 4; P.A. 74-163, S. 5; P.A. 76-388, S. 5, 6; 76-436, S. 10a, 595, 681; P.A. 04-234, S. 2; P.A. 06-187, S. 86; P.A. 07-57, S. 1; P.A. 14-27, S. 1.)

History: 1959 act extended jurisdiction in Subsec. (a) from cases of persons confined in State Prison to persons convicted of any offense against the state; P.A. 74-163 added Subsec. (c) re notice of absolute pardon; P.A. 76-388 included circuit court and replaced "chief clerk" of court of common pleas with "chief judge" in Subsec. (c); P.A. 76-436 replaced "chief judge of common pleas court" with "office of the chief court administrator", effective July 1, 1978; P.A. 04-234 replaced Board of Pardons with Board of Pardons and Paroles, effective July 1, 2004; Sec. 18-26 transferred to Sec. 54-130a in 2005; P.A. 06-187 amended Subsec. (b) to authorize board to grant "provisional" pardons, amended Subsec. (c) to provide that the "board", rather than the "secretary of said board", shall cause notification to be made and added Subsec. (d) to require that board cause written notification of the granting of provisional pardon to be made to clerk of the court in which the person granted such pardon was convicted and provide that granting of provisional pardon does not entitle the person to erasure of conviction record or relieve person from disclosing existence of conviction as may be required; P.A. 07-57 made a technical change in Subsec. (b), added new Subsec. (c) authorizing board to accept a pardon application 3 years after a misdemeanor or violation conviction and 5 years after a felony conviction or prior to such dates if extraordinary circumstances are found, redesignated existing Subsecs. (c) and (d) as Subsecs. (d) and (e) and added new Subsec. (f) authorizing board to grant a pardon to a person convicted of a violation for which a sentence to a term of imprisonment may be imposed in the same manner as a person convicted of an offense against the state; P.A. 14-27 amended Subsecs. (b), (e) and (f) to add references to certificates of rehabilitation.

Annotations to former section 18-26:

Cited. 124 C. 123; 145 C. 60; 152 C. 601. Board may revoke an absolute commutation prior to actual release of prisoner if factual basis for commutation proves to be erroneous and justification for granting commutation thereby abrogated. 206 C. 267. Cited. 208 C. 420.

Cited. 15 CA 161; 26 CA 132.

Sec. 54-130b. (Formerly Sec. 18-26a). Commutation of punishment and deportation of inmates who are aliens.

(a) The Board of Pardons and Paroles shall enter into an agreement with the United States Immigration and Naturalization Service for the deportation of persons incarcerated in correctional facilities in the state who are aliens upon the conditioned commutation of their punishment by said board.

(b) The Board of Pardons and Paroles may grant a commutation of punishment in the case of any person incarcerated in a correctional facility in the state who is an alien and transfer such person to the United States Immigration and Naturalization Service for deportation in accordance with the agreement entered into pursuant to subsection (a) of this section provided such person agrees not to contest his criminal conviction and deportation.

(P.A. 95-162; P.A. 04-234, S. 2.)

History: P.A. 04-234 replaced Board of Pardons with Board of Pardons and Paroles, effective July 1, 2004; Sec. 18-26a transferred to Sec. 54-130b in 2005.

Sec. 54-130c. (Formerly Sec. 18-30). Information about prisoner.

Said board may institute inquiries by correspondence or otherwise as to the previous history or character of any prisoner, and each prosecuting officer, judge, police officer or other person shall give said board, upon request, such information as he may possess with reference to the habits, disposition, career and associates of any prisoner.

(1949 Rev., S. 3024.)

History: Sec. 18-30 transferred to Sec. 54-130c in 2005.

Sec. 54-130d. (Formerly Sec. 18-27a). Testimony of crime victim at session of board. Notification of Office of Victim Services of board's action.

(a) For the purposes of this section, "victim" means a person who is a victim of a crime, the legal representative of such person or a member of a deceased victim's immediate family.

(b) At a session held by the Board of Pardons and Paroles to consider whether to grant a commutation of punishment or release, conditioned or absolute, a commutation from the penalty of death or a pardon, conditioned or absolute, to any person convicted of any crime, the board shall permit any victim of the crime for which the person was convicted to appear before the board for the purpose of making a statement for the record concerning whether the convicted person should be granted such commutation, release or pardon. In lieu of such appearance, the victim may submit a written statement to the board and the board shall make such statement a part of the record at the session.

(c) If the Board of Pardons and Paroles is prepared to grant a commutation of punishment or release, conditioned or absolute, a commutation from the penalty of death or a pardon, conditioned or absolute, to a person convicted of an offense involving the use, attempted use or threatened use of physical force against another person or resulting in the physical injury, serious physical injury or death of another person, it shall make reasonable efforts to locate and notify any victim of the crime for which such person was convicted prior to granting such commutation, release or pardon and shall permit such victim to appear before the board and make a statement or submit a statement as provided in subsection (b) of this section.

(d) Upon the granting to any person of a commutation of punishment or release, conditioned or absolute, a commutation from the penalty of death or a pardon, conditioned or absolute, the Board of Pardons and Paroles shall forthwith notify the Office of Victim Services of its action.

(P.A. 91-389, S. 8, 12; P.A. 99-247, S. 3; P.A. 01-211, S. 8; P.A. 04-234, S. 2.)

History: P.A. 91-389, S. 8 effective April 1, 1992; (Revisor's note: In 1995 the reference to "Commission on Victim Services" in Subsec. (c) was changed editorially by the Revisors to "Office of Victim Services" to carry out the provisions of Public Act 93-310); P.A. 99-247 added new Subsec. (c) to require the board to make reasonable efforts to locate and notify any victim of a crime of violence prior to granting the person convicted of such crime a commutation, release or pardon and to permit such victim to appear before the board and make or submit a statement, relettering former Subsec. (c) as Subsec. (d); P.A. 01-211 amended Subsec. (a) to redefine "victim" as "a person who is a victim of a crime, the legal representative of such person or a member of a deceased victim's immediate family" rather than "the victim, the legal representative of the victim or a member of a deceased victim's immediate family", amended Subsec. (b) to make provisions applicable at a session for a person convicted of "any crime" rather than "a class A, B or C felony or a violation of section 53a-60a, 53a-60c, 53a-72b, 53a-103a or 53a-216" and amended Subsec. (c) to make provisions applicable with respect to a person convicted of an offense "resulting in the physical injury, serious physical injury or death of another person"; P.A. 04-234 replaced Board of Pardons with Board of Pardons and Paroles, effective July 1, 2004; Sec. 18-27a transferred to Sec. 54-130d in 2005.

Sec. 54-130e. Provisional pardons. Certificates of rehabilitation.

(a) For the purposes of this section and sections 31-51i, 46a-80, 54-108f, 54-130a and 54-301:

(1) "Barrier" means a denial of employment or a license based on an eligible offender's conviction of a crime without due consideration of whether the nature of the crime bears a direct relationship to such employment or license;

(2) "Direct relationship" means that the nature of criminal conduct for which a person was convicted has a direct bearing on the person's fitness or ability to perform one or more of the duties or responsibilities necessarily related to the applicable employment or license;

(3) "Certificate of rehabilitation" means a form of relief from barriers or forfeitures to employment or the issuance of licenses, other than a provisional pardon, that is granted to an eligible offender by (A) the Board of Pardons and Paroles pursuant to this section, or (B) the Court Support Services Division of the Judicial Branch pursuant to section 54-108f;

(4) "Eligible offender" means a person who has been convicted of a crime or crimes in this state or another jurisdiction and who is a resident of this state and (A) is applying for a provisional pardon or is under the jurisdiction of the Board of Pardons and Paroles, or (B) with respect to a certificate of rehabilitation under section 54-108f, is under the supervision of the Court Support Services Division of the Judicial Branch;

(5) "Employment" means any remunerative work, occupation or vocation or any form of vocational training, but does not include employment with a law enforcement agency;

(6) "Forfeiture" means a disqualification or ineligibility for employment or a license by reason of law based on an eligible offender's conviction of a crime;

(7) "License" means any license, permit, certificate or registration that is required to be issued by the state or any of its agencies to pursue, practice or engage in an occupation, trade, vocation, profession or business; and

(8) "Provisional pardon" means a form of relief from barriers or forfeitures to employment or the issuance of licenses granted to an eligible offender by the Board of Pardons and Paroles pursuant to subsections (b) to (i), inclusive, of this section.

(b) The Board of Pardons and Paroles may issue a provisional pardon or a certificate of rehabilitation to relieve an eligible offender of barriers or forfeitures by reason of such person's conviction of the crime or crimes specified in such provisional pardon or certificate of rehabilitation. Such provisional pardon or certificate of rehabilitation may be limited to one or more enumerated barriers or forfeitures or may relieve the eligible offender of all barriers and forfeitures. Such certificate of rehabilitation shall be labeled by the board as a "Certificate of Employability" or a "Certificate of Suitability for Licensure", or both, as deemed appropriate by the board. No provisional pardon or certificate of rehabilitation shall apply or be construed to apply to the right of such person to retain or be eligible for public office.

(c) The Board of Pardons and Paroles may, in its discretion, issue a provisional pardon or a certificate of rehabilitation to an eligible offender upon verified application of such eligible offender. The board may issue a provisional pardon or a certificate of rehabilitation at any time after the sentencing of an eligible offender, including, but not limited to, any time prior to the eligible offender's date of release from the custody of the Commissioner of Correction, probation or parole. Such provisional pardon or certificate of rehabilitation may be issued by a pardon panel of the board or a parole release panel of the board.

(d) The board shall not issue a provisional pardon or a certificate of rehabilitation unless the board is satisfied that:

(1) The person to whom the provisional pardon or the certificate of rehabilitation is to be issued is an eligible offender;

(2) The relief to be granted by the provisional pardon or the certificate of rehabilitation may promote the public policy of rehabilitation of ex-offenders through employment; and

(3) The relief to be granted by the provisional pardon or the certificate of rehabilitation is consistent with the public interest in public safety, the safety of any victim of the offense and the protection of property.

(e) In accordance with the provisions of subsection (d) of this section, the board may limit the applicability of the provisional pardon or the certificate of rehabilitation to specified types of employment or licensure for which the eligible offender is otherwise qualified.

(f) The board may, for the purpose of determining whether such provisional pardon or certificate of rehabilitation should be issued, request its staff to conduct an investigation of the applicant and submit to the board a report of the investigation. Any written report submitted to the board pursuant to this subsection shall be confidential and shall not be disclosed except to the applicant and where required or permitted by any provision of the general statutes or upon specific authorization of the board.

(g) If a provisional pardon or a certificate of rehabilitation is issued by the board pursuant to this section before an eligible offender has completed service of the offender's term of incarceration, probation or parole, or any combination thereof, the provisional pardon or the certificate of rehabilitation shall be deemed to be temporary until the eligible offender completes such eligible offender's term of incarceration, probation or parole. During the period that such provisional pardon or certificate of rehabilitation is temporary, the board may revoke such provisional pardon or certificate of rehabilitation for a violation of the conditions of such eligible offender's probation or parole. After the eligible offender completes such eligible offender's term of incarceration, probation or parole, the temporary provisional pardon or certificate of rehabilitation shall become permanent.

(h) The board may at any time issue a new provisional pardon or certificate of rehabilitation to enlarge the relief previously granted, and the provisions of subsections (b) to (f), inclusive, of this section shall apply to the issuance of any new provisional pardon or certificate of rehabilitation.

(i) The application for a provisional pardon or a certificate of rehabilitation, the report of an investigation conducted pursuant to subsection (f) of this section, the provisional pardon or the certificate of rehabilitation and the revocation of a provisional pardon or a certificate of rehabilitation shall be in such form and contain such information as the Board of Pardons and Paroles shall prescribe.

(j) If a temporary certificate of rehabilitation issued under this section or section 54-108f is revoked, barriers and forfeitures thereby relieved shall be reinstated as of the date the person to whom the temporary certificate of rehabilitation was issued receives written notice of the revocation. Any such person shall surrender the temporary certificate of rehabilitation to the issuing board or division upon receipt of the notice.

(k) The board shall revoke a provisional pardon or certificate of rehabilitation if the person to whom it was issued is convicted of a crime, as defined in section 53a-24, after the issuance of the provisional pardon or certificate of rehabilitation.

(l) Not later than October 1, 2015, and annually thereafter, the board shall submit to the Office of Policy and Management and the Connecticut Sentencing Commission, in such form as the office may prescribe, data on the number of applications received for provisional pardons and certificates of rehabilitation, the number of applications denied, the number of applications granted and the number of provisional pardons and certificates of rehabilitation revoked.

(P.A. 06-187, S. 84, 85; P.A. 14-27, S. 2.)

History: P.A. 14-27 added provisions re certificate of rehabilitation throughout, amended Subsec. (a) to add references to Secs. 54-108f and 54-301, add new Subdiv. (2) defining "direct relationship", add new Subdiv. (3) defining "certificate of rehabilitation", redesignate existing Subdivs. (2) to (6) as Subdivs. (4) to (8) and redefine "eligible offender" in redesignated Subdiv. (4), amended Subsec. (c) to add provisions re issuance at any time prior to eligible offender's date of release and re issuance by panel, amended Subsec. (d)(3) to add provision re safety of any victim of offense, amended Subsec. (g) to add provisions re issuance before eligible offender has completed service of term and re when temporary provisional pardon or certificate of rehabilitation becomes permanent, added Subsec. (j) re revocation of temporary certificate of rehabilitation, added Subsec. (k) re revocation of provisional pardon or certificate of rehabilitation, added Subsec. (l) re submission of data to Office of Policy and Management and Connecticut Sentencing Commission, and made technical and conforming changes.

Sec. 54-130f. Pardon eligibility notice.

Not later than January 1, 2016, the Board of Pardons and Paroles shall develop a pardon eligibility notice containing written explanatory text of the pardons process set forth in this chapter. The board, in conjunction with the Judicial Department and Department of Correction, shall ensure that such notice is provided to a person at the time such person (1) is sentenced, (2) is released by the Department of Correction, including any pretrial release pursuant to section 18-100f, (3) has completed or been discharged from a period of parole, and (4) has completed a period of probation or conditional discharge pursuant to section 53a-29 or 53a-33. The board shall update such notice as deemed necessary by the board.

(June Sp. Sess. P.A. 15-2, S. 10.)

History: June Sp. Sess. P.A. 15-2 effective July 1, 2015.

Sec. 54-130g. Pardon for violation of certain provisions of section 53a-61aa or 53a-62. Criteria.

The Board of Pardons and Paroles shall grant an absolute pardon to any person who applies for such pardon with respect to a conviction of a violation of subdivision (4) of subsection (a) of section 53a-61aa or subdivision (3) of subsection (a) of section 53a-62, if (1) such person committed such offense

343

prior to attaining the age of eighteen years, (2) at least three years have elapsed from the date of such conviction or such person's discharge from the supervision of the court or the care of any institution or agency to which such person has been committed by the court, whichever is later, (3) such person has no subsequent juvenile proceeding or adult criminal proceeding that is pending, (4) such person has attained the age of eighteen years, and (5) such person has not been convicted as an adult of a felony or misdemeanor during the three-year period specified in subdivision (2) of this section.

(P.A. 16-67, S. 8.)

Sec. 54-131. Employment of paroled or discharged prisoners. Interviews.

Community Partners in Action and the Commissioner of Correction shall make all reasonable efforts to secure employment and provide directly or by contract other necessary services for any convict or inmate paroled or discharged from the custody of the commissioner and any institution of the Department of Correction, and the agents of said association are authorized, in carrying out this duty, to interview inmates of said correctional institutions prior to discharge.

(1949 Rev., S. 8832; 1949, S. 3330d; 1963 P.A. 642, S. 77; 1967, P.A. 152, S. 57; P.A. 15-14, S. 39.)

History: 1963 act substituted state jails for county jails; 1967 act, effective July 1, 1968, substituted correction commissioner for parole board and substituted department institutions for State Prison, reformatory and jails; P.A. 15-14 replaced "The Connecticut Prison Association" with "Community Partners in Action".

See Sec. 18-81c re Community Partners in Action.

Cited. 170 C. 129.

Cited. 4 CS 365; 27 CS 327.

Sec. 54-131a. Release of inmate on medical parole.

The Board of Pardons and Paroles may determine, in accordance with sections 54-131a to 54-131g, inclusive, when and under what conditions an inmate serving any sentence of imprisonment may be released on medical parole.

(P.A. 89-383, S. 6, 16; P.A. 04-234, S. 2.)

History: P.A. 04-234 replaced Board of Parole with Board of Pardons and Paroles, effective July 1, 2004.

Sec. 54-131b. Eligibility for medical parole.

The Board of Pardons and Paroles may release on medical parole any inmate serving any sentence of imprisonment, except an inmate convicted of a capital felony under the provisions of section 53a-54b in effect prior to April 25, 2012, or murder with special circumstances under the provisions of section 53a-54b in effect on or after April 25, 2012, who has been diagnosed pursuant to section 54-131c as suffering from a terminal condition, disease or syndrome, and is so debilitated or incapacitated by such condition, disease or syndrome as to be physically incapable of presenting a danger to society. Notwithstanding any provision of the general statutes to the contrary, the Board of Pardons and Paroles may release such inmate at any time during the term of such inmate's sentence.

(P.A. 89-383, S. 7, 16; P.A. 04-234, S. 2; P.A. 12-5, S. 34.)

History: P.A. 04-234 replaced Board of Parole with Board of Pardons and Paroles, effective July 1, 2004; P.A. 12-5 added reference to provisions of Sec. 53a-54b in effect prior to April 25, 2012, re capital felony, added reference to murder with special circumstances under Sec. 53a-54b and made technical changes, effective April 25, 2012.

Sec. 54-131c. Medical diagnosis.

A diagnosis that an inmate is suffering from a terminal condition, disease or syndrome shall be made by a physician licensed under chapter 370 and shall include but need not be limited to (1) a description of such terminal condition, disease or syndrome, (2) a prognosis concerning the likelihood of recovery from such condition, disease or syndrome and (3) a description of the inmate's physical incapacity. A diagnosis made by a physician other than one employed by the Department of Correction or a hospital or medical facility used by the Department of Correction for medical treatment of inmates may be reviewed by a physician appointed by the Commissioner of Correction or reviewed by the medical director of the Department of Correction. For purposes of this section "terminal condition, disease or syndrome" includes, but is not limited to, any prognosis by a licensed physician that the inmate has six months or less to live.

(P.A. 89-383, S. 8, 16.)

Sec. 54-131d. Conditions of release on medical parole.

(a) The Board of Pardons and Paroles shall require as a condition of release on medical parole that the parolee agree to placement and that he is able to be placed for a definite or indefinite period of time in a hospital or hospice or other housing accommodation suitable to his medical condition, including his family's home, as specified by the board.

(b) The Board of Pardons and Paroles may require as a condition of release on medical parole periodic diagnoses as described in section 54-131c. If after review of such diagnoses the board finds that a parolee released pursuant to sections 54-131a to 54-131g, inclusive, is no longer so debilitated or incapacitated as to be physically incapable of presenting a danger to society, such parolee shall be returned to any institution of the Department of Correction.

(P.A. 89-383, S. 9, 16; P.A. 04-234, S. 2; 04-257, S. 125.)

History: P.A. 04-234 replaced Board of Parole with Board of Pardons and Paroles, effective July 1, 2004; P.A. 04-257 amended Subsec. (b) to provide that a parolee shall be returned to "any institution" of the Department of Correction rather than to "the custody" of said department, effective June 14, 2004.

Sec. 54-131e. Requests for medical diagnosis.

A request for a medical diagnosis in order to determine eligibility for medical parole under sections 54-131a to 54-131g, inclusive, may be made by the Board of Pardons and Paroles, the Commissioner of Correction, or a correctional institution warden or superintendent, or by request made to the board, commissioner, warden or superintendent by an inmate, an inmate's spouse, parent, guardian, grandparent, aunt or uncle, sibling, child over the age of eighteen years, or attorney.

(P.A. 89-383, S. 10, 16; P.A. 04-234, S. 2.)

History: P.A. 04-234 replaced Board of Parole with Board of Pardons and Paroles, effective July 1, 2004.

Sec. 54-131f. Special panel. Emergency review.

The Board of Pardons and Paroles may appoint a special panel to implement the provisions of sections 54-131a to 54-131g, inclusive. The board or special panel shall review and decide requests for medical parole under said sections on an emergency basis, and in all cases shall act in as expeditious a manner as possible.

(P.A. 89-383, S. 11, 16; P.A. 04-234, S. 2.)

History: P.A. 04-234 replaced Board of Parole with Board of Pardons and Paroles, effective July 1, 2004.

Sec. 54-131g. Effect on parole or other release.

The provisions of sections 54-131a to 54-131f, inclusive, shall not affect an inmate's eligibility for any other form of parole or release provided by law.

(P.A. 89-383, S. 12, 16.)

Secs. 54-131h to 54-131j. Reserved for future use.

Sec. 54-131k. Compassionate parole release.

(a) The Board of Pardons and Paroles may grant a compassionate parole release to any inmate serving any sentence of imprisonment, except an inmate convicted of a capital felony under the provisions of section 53a-54b in effect prior to April 25, 2012, or murder with special circumstances under the provisions of section 53a-54b in effect on or after April 25, 2012, if it finds that such inmate (1) is so physically or mentally debilitated, incapacitated or infirm as a result of advanced age or as a result of a condition, disease or syndrome that is not terminal as to be physically incapable of presenting a danger to society, and (2) (A) has served not less than one-half of such inmate's definite or aggregate sentence, or (B) has served not less than one-half of such inmate's remaining definite or aggregate sentence after commutation of the original sentence by the Board of Pardons and Paroles.

(b) Any person granted a compassionate parole release pursuant to this section shall be released subject to such terms and conditions as may be established by the Board of Pardons and Paroles and shall be supervised by the Department of Correction.

(P.A. 04-234, S. 2, 28; P.A. 12-5, S. 35.)

History: P.A. 04-234 effective June 8, 2004 (Revisor's note: Effective July 1, 2004, references to "Board of Parole" or "Board of Pardons" in the general statutes and in the public and special acts of the 2003 and 2004 regular and special sessions of the General Assembly were replaced with "Board of Pardons and Paroles" pursuant to Sec. 2 of P.A. 04-234); P.A. 12-5 amended Subsec. (a) to add reference to provisions of Sec. 53a-54b in effect prior to April 25, 2012, re capital felony, add reference to murder with special circumstances under Sec. 53a-54b and make a technical change, effective April 25, 2012.

Sec. 54-132. Definitions. Section 54-132 is repealed, effective June 19, 2002.*

(1951, S. 3346d; 1957, P.A. 340; 1963, P.A. 642, S. 78; P.A. 00-185, S. 4, 5.)

*Note: P.A. 00-185 repealed this section effective "July 1, 2001, or upon enactment of the Interstate Compact for Adult Offender Supervision by thirty-five jurisdictions, whichever is later"; Pennsylvania became the thirty-fifth enacting jurisdiction on June 19, 2002.

Sec. 54-133. Interstate Compact for Adult Offender Supervision.

The Interstate Compact for Adult Offender Supervision is hereby enacted into law and entered into by this state with all jurisdictions legally joining therein, in the form substantially as follows:

ARTICLE I

PURPOSE

The compacting states to this Interstate Compact recognize that each state is responsible for the supervision of adult offenders in the community who are authorized pursuant to the bylaws and rules of this compact to travel across state lines both to and from each compacting state in such a manner as to:

Track the location of offenders, transfer supervision authority in an orderly and efficient manner, and when necessary return offenders to the originating jurisdictions.

The compacting states also recognize that Congress, by enacting the Crime Control Act, 4 USC Section 112 (1965), has authorized and encouraged compacts for cooperative efforts and mutual assistance in the prevention of crime.

It is the purpose of this compact and the Interstate Commission created hereunder, through means of joint and cooperative action among the compacting states: To provide the framework for the promotion of public safety and protect the rights of victims through the control and regulation of the interstate movement of offenders in the community; to provide for the effective tracking, supervision and rehabilitation of these offenders by the sending and receiving states; and to equitably distribute the costs, benefits and obligations of the compact among the compacting states.

In addition, this compact will: Create an Interstate Commission which will establish uniform procedures to manage the movement between states of adults placed under community supervision and released to the community under the jurisdiction of courts, paroling authorities, corrections or other criminal justice agencies which will promulgate rules to achieve the purpose of this compact; ensure an opportunity for input and timely notice to victims and to jurisdictions where defined offenders are authorized to travel or to relocate across state lines; establish a system of uniform data collection, access to information on active cases by authorized criminal justice officials and regular reporting of compact activities to heads of state councils, state executive, judicial and legislative branches and criminal justice administrators; monitor compliance with rules governing interstate movement of offenders and initiate interventions to address and correct noncompliance; and coordinate training and education regarding regulation of interstate movement of offenders for officials involved in such activity.

The compacting states recognize that there is no right of any offender to live in another state and that duly accredited officers of a sending state may at all times enter a receiving state and there apprehend and retake any offender under supervision subject to the provisions of this compact and bylaws and rules promulgated hereunder.

It is the policy of the compacting states that the activities conducted by the Interstate Commission created herein are the formation of public policies and are therefore public business.

ARTICLE II

DEFINITIONS

As used in this compact, unless the context clearly requires a different construction:

A. "Adult" means both individuals legally classified as adults and juveniles treated as adults by court order, statute or operation of law.

B. "Bylaws" means those bylaws established by the Interstate Commission for its governance or for directing or controlling the Interstate Commission's actions or conduct.

C. "Compact administrator" means the individual in each compacting state appointed pursuant to the terms of this compact responsible for the administration and management of the state's supervision and transfer of offenders subject to the terms of this compact, the rules adopted by the Interstate Commission and policies adopted by the state council under this compact.

D. "Compacting state" means any state which has enacted the enabling legislation for this compact.

E. "Commissioner" means the voting representative of each compacting state appointed pursuant to Article III of this compact.

F. "Interstate Commission" means the Interstate Commission for Adult Offender Supervision established by this compact.

G. "Member" means the commissioner of a compacting state or designee, who shall be a person officially connected with the commissioner.

H. "Noncompacting state" means any state which has not enacted the enabling legislation for this compact.

I. "Offender" means an adult placed under, or subject to, supervision as the result of the commission of a criminal offense and released to the community under the jurisdiction of courts, paroling authorities, corrections or other criminal justice agencies.

J. "Person" means any individual, corporation, business enterprise, or other legal entity, either public or private.

K. "Rules" means acts of the Interstate Commission, duly promulgated pursuant to Article VII of this compact, substantially affecting interested parties in addition to the Interstate Commission, which shall have the force and effect of law in the compacting states.

L. "State" means a state of the United States, the District of Columbia and any other territorial possession of the United States.

M. "State Council" means the resident members of the State Council for Interstate Adult Offender Supervision created by each state under Article III of this compact.

ARTICLE III

THE COMPACT COMMISSION

A. The compacting states hereby create the "Interstate Commission for Adult Offender Supervision". The Interstate Commission shall be a body corporate and joint agency of the compacting states. The Interstate Commission shall have all the responsibilities, powers and duties set forth herein, including the power to sue and be sued, and such additional powers as may be conferred upon it by subsequent action of the respective legislatures of the compacting states in accordance with the terms of this compact.

B. The Interstate Commission shall consist of commissioners selected and appointed by resident members of a State Council for Interstate Adult Offender Supervision for each state. While each member state may determine the membership of its own State Council, its membership must include at least one representative from the legislative, judicial and executive branches of government, victims groups and compact administrators. Each State Council shall appoint as its commissioner the compact administrator from that state to serve on the Interstate Commission in such capacity under or pursuant to applicable law of the member state. Each compacting state retains the right to determine the qualifications of the compact administrator who shall be appointed by the State Council or by the Governor in consultation with the legislature and the judiciary.

In addition to appointment of its commissioner to the Interstate Commission, each State Council shall exercise oversight and advocacy concerning its participation in Interstate Commission activities and other duties as may be determined by each member state, including, but not limited to, development of policy concerning operations and procedures of the compact within that state.

C. In addition to the commissioners who are the voting representatives of each state, the Interstate Commission shall include individuals who are not commissioners but who are members of interested organizations; such noncommissioner members must include a member of the national organizations of governors, legislators, state chief justices, attorneys general and crime victims. All noncommissioner members of the Interstate Commission shall be ex officio, nonvoting, members. The Interstate Commission may provide in its bylaws for such additional, ex officio, nonvoting members as it deems necessary.

D. Each compacting state represented at any meeting of the Interstate Commission is entitled to one vote. A majority of the compacting states shall constitute a quorum for the transaction of business, unless a larger quorum is required by the bylaws of the Interstate Commission.

E. The Interstate Commission shall meet at least once each calendar year. The chairperson may call additional meetings and, upon the request of twenty-seven or more compacting states, shall call additional meetings. Public notice shall be given of all meetings and meetings shall be open to the public.

F. The Interstate Commission shall establish an executive committee which shall include commission officers, members and others as shall be determined by the bylaws. The executive committee shall have the power to act on behalf of the Interstate Commission during periods when the Interstate Commission is not in session, with the exception of rulemaking and/or amendment to the compact. The executive committee oversees the day-to-day activities managed by the executive director and Interstate Commission staff; administers enforcement and compliance with the provisions of the compact, its bylaws and as directed by the Interstate Commission and performs other duties as directed by the Interstate Commission or set forth in the bylaws.

ARTICLE IV

POWERS AND DUTIES OF THE INTERSTATE COMMISSION

The Interstate Commission shall have the following powers:

1. To adopt a seal and suitable bylaws governing the management and operation of the Interstate Commission.

2. To promulgate rules which shall have the force and effect of statutory law and shall be binding in the compacting states to the extent and in the manner provided in this compact.

3. To oversee, supervise and coordinate the interstate movement of offenders subject to the terms of this compact and any bylaws adopted and rules promulgated by the compact commission.

4. To enforce compliance with compact provisions, Interstate Commission rules, and bylaws, using all necessary and proper means including, but not limited to, the use of judicial process.

5. To establish and maintain offices.

6. To purchase and maintain insurance and bonds.

7. To borrow, accept or contract for services of personnel, including, but not limited to, members and their staffs.

8. To establish and appoint committees and hire staff which it deems necessary for the carrying out of its functions including, but not limited to, an executive committee as required by Article III which shall have the power to act on behalf of the Interstate Commission in carrying out its powers and duties hereunder.

9. To elect or appoint such officers, attorneys, employees, agents or consultants, and to fix their compensation, define their duties and determine their qualifications; and to establish the Interstate Commission's personnel policies and programs relating to, among other things, conflicts of interest, rates of compensation and qualifications of personnel.

10. To accept any and all donations and grants of money, equipment, supplies, materials and services, and to receive, utilize and dispose of same.

11. To lease, purchase, accept contributions or donations of, or otherwise to own, hold, improve or use any property, real, personal or mixed.

12. To sell, convey, mortgage, pledge, lease, exchange, abandon or otherwise dispose of any property, real, personal or mixed.

13. To establish a budget and make expenditures and levy dues as provided in Article IX of this compact.

14. To sue and be sued.

15. To provide for dispute resolution among compacting states.

16. To perform such functions as may be necessary or appropriate to achieve the purposes of this compact.

17. To report annually to the legislatures, governors, judiciary and state councils of the compacting states concerning the activities of the Interstate Commission during the preceding year. Such reports shall also include any recommendations that may have been adopted by the Interstate Commission.

18. To coordinate education, training and public awareness regarding the interstate movement of offenders for officials involved in such activity.

19. To establish uniform standards for the reporting, collecting and exchanging of data.

ARTICLE V

ORGANIZATION AND OPERATION OF THE INTERSTATE COMMISSION

Section A. Bylaws

1. The Interstate Commission shall, by a majority of the members, within twelve months of the first Interstate Commission meeting, adopt bylaws to govern its conduct as may be necessary or appropriate to carry out the purposes of the compact, including, but not limited to:

a. Establishing the fiscal year of the Interstate Commission;

b. Establishing an executive committee and such other committees as may be necessary;

c. Providing reasonable standards and procedures: (i) For the establishment of committees, and (ii) governing any general or specific delegation of any authority or function of the Interstate Commission;

d. Providing reasonable procedures for calling and conducting meetings of the Interstate Commission, and ensuring reasonable notice of each such meeting;

e. Establishing the titles and responsibilities of the officers of the Interstate Commission;

f. Providing reasonable standards and procedures for the establishment of the personnel policies and programs of the Interstate Commission. Notwithstanding any civil service or other similar laws of any compacting state, the bylaws shall exclusively govern the personnel policies and programs of the Interstate Commission;

g. Providing a mechanism for winding up the operations of the Interstate Commission and the equitable return of any surplus funds that may exist upon the termination of the compact after the payment and/or reserving of all of its debts and obligations;

h. Providing transition rules for "start up" administration of the compact; and

i. Establishing standards and procedures for compliance and technical assistance in carrying out the compact.

Section B. Officers and staff

1. The Interstate Commission shall, by a majority of the members, elect from among its members a chairperson and a vice chairperson, each of whom shall have such authority and duties as may be specified in the bylaws. The chairperson or, in his or her absence or disability, the vice chairperson, shall preside at all meetings of the Interstate Commission. The officers so elected shall serve without compensation or remuneration from the Interstate Commission; provided that, subject to the availability of budgeted funds, the officers shall be reimbursed for any actual and necessary costs and expenses incurred by them in the performance of their duties and responsibilities as officers of the Interstate Commission.

2. The Interstate Commission shall, through its executive committee, appoint or retain an executive director for such period, upon such terms and conditions and for such compensation as the Interstate Commission may deem appropriate. The executive director shall serve as secretary to the Interstate Commission, and hire and supervise such other staff as may be authorized by the Interstate Commission, but shall not be a member.

Section C. Corporate records of the Interstate Commission

The Interstate Commission shall maintain its corporate books and records in accordance with the bylaws.

Section D. Qualified immunity, defense and indemnification

1. The members, officers, executive director and employees of the Interstate Commission shall be immune from suit and liability, either personally or in their official capacity, for any claim for damage to or loss of property or personal injury or other civil liability caused or arising out of any actual or alleged act, error or omission that occurred within the scope of Interstate Commission employment, duties or responsibilities; provided, that nothing in this paragraph shall be construed to protect any such person from suit and/or liability for any damage, loss, injury or liability caused by the intentional or wilful and wanton misconduct of any such person.

2. The Interstate Commission shall defend the commissioner of a compacting state, or his or her representatives or employees, or the Interstate Commission's representatives or employees, in any civil action seeking to impose liability, arising out of any actual or alleged act, error or omission that occurred within the scope of Interstate Commission employment, duties or responsibilities, or that the defendant had a reasonable basis for believing occurred

within the scope of Interstate Commission employment, duties or responsibilities; provided, that the actual or alleged act, error or omission did not result from intentional wrongdoing on the part of such person.

3. The Interstate Commission shall indemnify and hold the commissioner of a compacting state, the appointed designee or employees, or the Interstate Commission's representatives or employees, harmless in the amount of any settlement or judgment obtained against such persons arising out of any actual or alleged act, error or omission that occurred within the scope of Interstate Commission employment, duties or responsibilities, or that such persons had a reasonable basis for believing occurred within the scope of Interstate Commission employment, duties or responsibilities, provided, that the actual or alleged act, error or omission did not result from gross negligence or intentional wrongdoing on the part of such person.

ARTICLE VI

ACTIVITIES OF THE INTERSTATE COMMISSION

1. The Interstate Commission shall meet and take such actions as are consistent with the provisions of this compact.

2. Except as otherwise provided in this compact and unless a greater percentage is required by the bylaws, in order to constitute an act of the Interstate Commission, such act shall have been taken at a meeting of the Interstate Commission and shall have received an affirmative vote of a majority of the members present.

3. Each member of the Interstate Commission shall have the right and power to cast a vote to which that compacting state is entitled and to participate in the business and affairs of the Interstate Commission. A member shall vote in person on behalf of the state and shall not delegate a vote to another member state. However, a State Council shall appoint another authorized representative, in the absence of the commissioner from that state, to cast a vote on behalf of the member state at a specified meeting. The bylaws may provide for members' participation in meetings by telephone or other means of telecommunication or electronic communication. Any voting conducted by telephone or other means of telecommunication or electronic communication shall be subject to the same quorum requirements of meetings where members are present in person.

4. The Interstate Commission shall meet at least once during each calendar year. The chairperson of the Interstate Commission may call additional meetings at any time and, upon the request of a majority of the members, shall call additional meetings.

5. The Interstate Commission's bylaws shall establish conditions and procedures under which the Interstate Commission shall make its information and official records available to the public for inspection or copying. The Interstate Commission may exempt from disclosure any information or official records to the extent they would adversely affect personal privacy rights or proprietary interests. In promulgating such rules, the Interstate Commission may make available to law enforcement agencies records and information otherwise exempt from disclosure, and may enter into agreements with law enforcement agencies to receive or exchange information or records subject to nondisclosure and confidentiality provisions.

6. Public notice shall be given of all meetings and all meetings shall be open to the public, except as set forth in the rules or as otherwise provided in the compact. The Interstate Commission shall promulgate rules consistent with the principles contained in the "Government in Sunshine Act", 5 USC Section 552(b), as may be amended. The Interstate Commission and any of its committees may close a meeting to the public where it determines by two-thirds vote that an open meeting would be likely to: a. Relate solely to the Interstate Commission's internal personnel practices and procedures; b. disclose matters specifically exempted from disclosure by statute; c. disclose trade secrets or commercial or financial information which is privileged or confidential; d. involve accusing any person of a crime, or formally censuring any person; e. disclose information of a personal nature where disclosure would constitute a clearly unwarranted invasion of personal privacy; f. disclose investigatory records compiled for law enforcement purposes; g. disclose information contained in or related to examination, operating or condition reports prepared by, or on behalf of or for the use of, the Interstate Commission with respect to a regulated entity for the purpose of regulation or supervision of such entity; h. disclose information, the premature disclosure of which would significantly endanger the life of a person or the stability of a regulated entity; i. specifically relate to the Interstate Commission's issuance of a subpoena, or its participation in a civil action or proceeding.

7. For every meeting closed pursuant to this provision, the Interstate Commission's chief legal officer shall publicly certify that, in his or her opinion, the meeting may be closed to the public, and shall reference each relevant exemptive provision. The Interstate Commission shall keep minutes which shall fully and clearly describe all matters discussed in any meeting and shall provide a full and accurate summary of any actions taken, and the reasons therefor, including a description of each of the views expressed on any item and the record of any roll call vote (reflected in the vote of each member on the question). All documents considered in connection with any action shall be identified in such minutes.

8. The Interstate Commission shall collect standardized data concerning the interstate movement of offenders as directed through its bylaws and rules which shall specify the data to be collected, the means of collection and data exchange and reporting requirements.

ARTICLE VII

RULEMAKING FUNCTIONS OF THE INTERSTATE COMMISSION

1. The Interstate Commission shall promulgate rules in order to effectively and efficiently achieve the purposes of the compact including transition rules governing administration of the compact during the period in which it is being considered and enacted by the states.

2. Rulemaking shall occur pursuant to the criteria set forth in this article and the bylaws and rules adopted pursuant thereto. Such rulemaking shall substantially conform to the principles of the federal Administrative Procedure Act, 5 USC Section 551 et seq., and the Federal Advisory Committee Act, 5 USC App. 2, Section 1 et seq., as may be amended (hereinafter "APA").

3. All rules and amendments shall become binding as of the date specified in each rule or amendment.

4. If a majority of the legislatures of the compacting states rejects a rule, by enactment of a statute or resolution in the same manner used to adopt the compact, then such rule shall have no further force and effect in any compacting state.

5. When promulgating a rule, the Interstate Commission shall: a. Publish the proposed rule stating with particularity the text of the rule which is proposed and the reason for the proposed rule; b. allow persons to submit written data, facts, opinions and arguments, which information shall be publicly available; c. provide an opportunity for an informal hearing; and d. promulgate a final rule and its effective date, if appropriate, based on the rulemaking record.

6. Not later than sixty days after a rule is promulgated, any interested person may file a petition in the United States District Court for the District of Columbia or in the federal district court where the Interstate Commission's principal office is located for judicial review of such rule. If the court finds that the Interstate Commission's action is not supported by substantial evidence, as defined in the APA, in the rulemaking record, the court shall hold the rule unlawful and set it aside.

7. Subjects to be addressed within twelve months after the first meeting must at a minimum include: a. Notice to victims and opportunity to be heard; b. offender registration and compliance; c. violations/returns; d. transfer procedures and forms; e. eligibility for transfer; f. collection of restitution and fees from offenders; g. data collection and reporting; h. the level of supervision to be provided by the receiving state; i. transition rules governing the operation of the compact and the Interstate Commission during all or part of the period between the effective date of the compact and the date on which the last eligible state adopts the compact; j. mediation, arbitration and dispute resolution.

The existing rules governing the operation of the previous compact superseded by this compact shall be null and void twelve months after the first meeting of the Interstate Commission created hereunder.

8. Upon determination by the Interstate Commission that an emergency exists, it may promulgate an emergency rule which shall become effective immediately upon adoption, provided that the usual rulemaking procedures provided hereunder shall be retroactively applied to said rule as soon as reasonably possible, in no event later than ninety days after the effective date of the rule.

ARTICLE VIII

OVERSIGHT, ENFORCEMENT AND DISPUTE RESOLUTION
BY THE INTERSTATE COMMISSION

Section A. Oversight

1. The Interstate Commission shall oversee the interstate movement of adult offenders in the compacting states and shall monitor such activities being administered in noncompacting states which may significantly affect compacting states.

2. The courts and executive agencies in each compacting state shall enforce this compact and shall take all actions necessary and appropriate to effectuate the compact's purposes and intent. In any judicial or administrative proceeding in a compacting state pertaining to the subject matter of this compact which may affect the powers, responsibilities or actions of the Interstate Commission, the Interstate Commission shall be entitled to receive all service of process in any such proceeding, and shall have standing to intervene in the proceeding for all purposes.

Section B. Dispute resolution

1. The compacting states shall report to the Interstate Commission on issues or activities of concern to them, and cooperate with and support the Interstate Commission in the discharge of its duties and responsibilities.

2. The Interstate Commission shall attempt to resolve any disputes or other issues which are subject to the compact and which may arise among compacting states and noncompacting states.

3. The Interstate Commission shall enact a bylaw or promulgate a rule providing for both mediation and binding dispute resolution for disputes among the compacting states.

Section C. Enforcement

The Interstate Commission, in the reasonable exercise of its discretion, shall enforce the provisions of this compact using any or all means set forth in Article XI, Section B, of this compact.

ARTICLE IX

FINANCE

1. The Interstate Commission shall pay or provide for the payment of the reasonable expenses of its establishment, organization and ongoing activities.

2. The Interstate Commission shall levy on and collect an annual assessment from each compacting state to cover the cost of the internal operations and activities of the Interstate Commission and its staff which must be in a total amount sufficient to cover the Interstate Commission's annual budget as approved each year. The aggregate annual assessment amount shall be allocated based upon a formula to be determined by the Interstate Commission, taking into consideration the population of the state and the volume of interstate movement of offenders in each compacting state and shall promulgate a rule binding upon all compacting states which governs said assessment.

3. The Interstate Commission shall not incur any obligations of any kind prior to securing the funds adequate to meet the same; nor shall the Interstate Commission pledge the credit of any of the compacting states, except by and with the authority of the compacting state.

4. The Interstate Commission shall keep accurate accounts of all receipts and disbursements. The receipts and disbursements of the Interstate Commission shall be subject to the audit and accounting procedures established under its bylaws. However, all receipts and disbursements of funds handled by the Interstate Commission shall be audited yearly by a certified or licensed public accountant and the report of the audit shall be included in and become part of the annual report of the Interstate Commission.

ARTICLE X

COMPACTING STATES, EFFECTIVE DATE AND AMENDMENT

1. Any state, as defined in Article II of this compact, is eligible to become a compacting state.

2. The compact shall become effective and binding upon legislative enactment of the compact into law by no less than thirty-five of the states. The initial effective date shall be the later of July 1, 2001, or upon enactment into law by the thirty-fifth jurisdiction. Thereafter it shall become effective and binding, as to any other compacting state, upon enactment of the compact into law by that state. The governors of nonmember states or their designees will be invited to participate in Interstate Commission activities on a nonvoting basis prior to adoption of the compact by all states and territories of the United States.

3. Amendments to the compact may be proposed by the Interstate Commission for enactment by the compacting states. No amendment shall become effective and binding upon the Interstate Commission and the compacting states unless and until it is enacted into law by unanimous consent of the compacting states.

ARTICLE XI

WITHDRAWAL, DEFAULT, TERMINATION AND JUDICIAL
ENFORCEMENT

Section A. Withdrawal

1. Once effective, the compact shall continue in force and remain binding upon each and every compacting state; provided, that a compacting state may withdraw from the compact ("withdrawing state") by enacting a statute specifically repealing the statute which enacted the compact into law.

2. The effective date of withdrawal is the effective date of the repeal.

3. The withdrawing state shall immediately notify the chairperson of the Interstate Commission in writing upon the introduction of legislation repealing this compact in the withdrawing state.

4. The Interstate Commission shall notify the other compacting states of the withdrawing state's intent to withdraw within sixty days of its receipt thereof.

5. The withdrawing state is responsible for all assessments, obligations and liabilities incurred through the effective date of withdrawal, including any obligations, the performance of which extend beyond the effective date of withdrawal.

6. Reinstatement following withdrawal of any compacting state shall occur upon the withdrawing state reenacting the compact or upon such later date as determined by the Interstate Commission.

Section B. Default

1. If the Interstate Commission determines that any compacting state has at any time defaulted ("defaulting state") in the performance of any of its obligations or responsibilities under this compact, the bylaws or any duly promulgated rules, the Interstate Commission may impose any or all of the following penalties:

a. Fines, fees and costs in such amounts as are deemed to be reasonable as fixed by the Interstate Commission;

b. Remedial training and technical assistance as directed by the Interstate Commission;

c. Suspension and termination of membership in the compact. Suspension shall be imposed only after all other reasonable means of securing compliance under the bylaws and rules have been exhausted. Immediate notice of suspension shall be given by the Interstate Commission to the Governor, the Chief Justice or chief judicial officer of the state; the majority and minority leaders of the defaulting state's legislature, and the State Council. The grounds for default include, but are not limited to, failure of a compacting state to perform such obligations or responsibilities imposed upon it by this compact, Interstate Commission bylaws, or duly promulgated rules. The Interstate Commission shall immediately notify the defaulting state in writing of the penalty imposed by the Interstate Commission on the defaulting state pending a cure of the default. The Interstate Commission shall stipulate the conditions and the time period within which the defaulting state must cure its default. If the defaulting state fails to cure the default within the time period specified by the Interstate Commission, in addition to any other penalties imposed herein, the defaulting state may be terminated from the compact upon an affirmative vote of a majority of the compacting states and all rights, privileges and benefits conferred by this compact shall be terminated from the effective date of suspension.

2. Within sixty days of the effective date of termination of a defaulting state, the Interstate Commission shall notify the Governor, the Chief Justice or chief judicial officer and the majority and minority leaders of the defaulting state's legislature and the State Council of such termination.

3. The defaulting state is responsible for all assessments, obligations and liabilities incurred through the effective date of termination including any obligations, the performance of which extends beyond the effective date of termination.

4. The Interstate Commission shall not bear any costs relating to the defaulting state unless otherwise mutually agreed upon between the Interstate Commission and the defaulting state.

5. Reinstatement following termination of any compacting state requires both a reenactment of the compact by the defaulting state and the approval of the Interstate Commission pursuant to the rules.

Section C. Judicial enforcement

The Interstate Commission may, by majority vote of the members, initiate legal action in the United States District Court for the District of Columbia or, at the discretion of the Interstate Commission, in the federal district where the Interstate Commission has its offices to enforce compliance with the provisions of the compact, its duly promulgated rules and bylaws, against any compacting state in default. In the event judicial enforcement is necessary the prevailing party shall be awarded all costs of such litigation including reasonable attorneys' fees.

Section D. Dissolution of compact

1. The compact dissolves effective upon the date of the withdrawal or default of the compacting state which reduces membership in the compact to one compacting state.

2. Upon the dissolution of this compact, the compact becomes null and void and shall be of no further force or effect, and the business and affairs of the Interstate Commission shall be wound up and any surplus funds shall be distributed in accordance with the bylaws.

ARTICLE XII

SEVERABILITY AND CONSTRUCTION

1. The provisions of this compact shall be severable, and if any phrase, clause, sentence or provision is deemed unenforceable, the remaining provisions of the compact shall be enforceable.

2. The provisions of this compact shall be liberally construed to effectuate its purposes.

ARTICLE XIII

BINDING EFFECT OF COMPACT AND OTHER LAWS

Section A. Other laws

1. Nothing herein prevents the enforcement of any other law of a compacting state that is not inconsistent with this compact.

2. All compacting states' laws conflicting with this compact are superseded to the extent of the conflict.

Section B. Binding effect of the compact

1. All lawful actions of the Interstate Commission, including all rules and bylaws promulgated by the Interstate Commission, are binding upon the compacting states.

2. All agreements between the Interstate Commission and the compacting states are binding in accordance with their terms.

3. Upon the request of a party to a conflict over meaning or interpretation of Interstate Commission actions, and upon a majority vote of the compacting states, the Interstate Commission may issue advisory opinions regarding such meaning or interpretation.

4. In the event any provision of this compact exceeds the constitutional limits imposed on the legislature of any compacting state, the obligations, duties, powers or jurisdiction sought to be conferred by such provision upon the Interstate Commission shall be ineffective and such obligations, duties, powers or jurisdiction shall remain in the compacting state and shall be exercised by the agency thereof to which such obligations, duties, powers or jurisdiction are delegated by law in effect at the time this compact becomes effective.

(1949 Rev., S. 8841; 1951, S. 3345d; P.A. 00-185, S. 3, 5.)

History: (Revisor's note: In 1995 the indicators (a) and (b) in Subsec. (a)(1) were changed editorially by the Revisors to (A) and (B) respectively for consistency with statutory usage); P.A. 00-185 replaced former provisions re the "Uniform Act for Out-of-State Parolee Supervision" with the "Interstate Compact for Adult Offender Supervision", effective July 1, 2001, or upon enactment of the Interstate Compact for Adult Offender Supervision by thirty-five jurisdictions, whichever is later; Pennsylvania became the thirty-fifth enacting jurisdiction on June 19, 2002.

See Sec. 54-76b re youthful offenders.

Receiving state terminates its supervision when parolee moves to another state after notice given to pending state of request of parolee to transfer; Connecticut could retake parolee who had moved from the receiving state of Maine to Massachusetts without reporting to Connecticut authorities and was convicted of drug possession in Massachusetts. 167 C. 639. Cited. 215 C. 418.

Constitutionality of statute upheld; waiver of extradition as a condition of parole not repugnant to fourteenth amendment of U.S. Constitution. 17 CS 101.

Sec. 54-133a. Motor vehicle violation deemed a criminal offense for purposes of Interstate Compact for Adult Offender Supervision.

For the purposes of section 54-133, a motor vehicle violation for which a sentence to a term of imprisonment of more than one year may be imposed shall be deemed a criminal offense.

(P.A. 12-133, S. 21.)

Secs. 54-134 to 54-138b. Designation of "Compact Institutions". Transfers to other correctional institutions. Incarceration in receiving state not to affect rights in sending state. Reimbursement for expenses. Ratification; regulations. Retaking of parolee. Unauthorized residency by parolee from another state; penalty. Sections 54-134 to 54-138b, inclusive, are repealed, effective June 19, 2002.*

(1951, S. 3347d–3351d; 1963, P.A. 128; 1969, P.A. 297; P.A. 87-282, S. 21; P.A. 98-97; P.A. 00-185, S. 4, 5.)

*Note: P.A. 00-185 repealed these sections effective "July 1, 2001, or upon enactment of the Interstate Compact for Adult Offender Supervision by thirty-five jurisdictions, whichever is later"; Pennsylvania became the thirty-fifth enacting jurisdiction on June 19, 2002.

Secs. 54-139 to 54-141. Transferred to Chapter 961, Secs. 54-82c to 54-82e, inclusive.

Sec. 54-142. Destruction of notes received for unpaid fines. Section 54-142 is repealed.

(1949 Rev., S. 8823; 1963, P.A. 642, S. 80; P.A. 76-336, S. 10.)

CHAPTER 962 COSTS, FEES AND EXPENSES IN CRIMINAL PROCEEDINGS OR PROSECUTIONS

Table of Contents

Sec. 54-143. Costs imposed in prosecutions.

Sec. 54-143a. Cost imposed for infractions and certain motor vehicle violations.

Sec. 54-143b. Forfeited bonds for motor vehicle violations.

Sec. 54-143c. Additional fine for sexual assault offenses.

Sec. 54-144. Payment of expenses.

Secs. 54-145 and 54-146. Refunds to clerk of municipal court or to town treasurer. Report to clerk or town treasurer.

Sec. 54-147. Rules for payment of expenses. Waiver of fee or cost.

Sec. 54-148. Support of prisoners after sentence.

Sec. 54-149. Payment for board of prisoners.

Sec. 54-150. Compensation of physicians.

Sec. 54-151. Cost of transcript and printing on appeal.

Sec. 54-152. Allowance to witnesses from another state in criminal prosecutions.

Sec. 54-153. Where witnesses for accused paid by state.

Sec. 54-154. Taxing expenses in search and seizure cases.

Sec. 54-155. Expenses of requisitions of fugitives.

Sec. 54-143. Costs imposed in prosecutions.

(a) A cost of twenty dollars shall be imposed against any person convicted of a felony, and a cost of fifteen dollars shall be imposed against any person convicted of a misdemeanor or convicted under section 14-219, 14-222, 14-224, 14-225, 14-227a or 14-227m or subdivision (1) or (2) of subsection (a) of section 14-227n, or who pleads nolo contendere to a violation of section 14-219 and pays the fine by mail, and the taxation of costs or the collection of fees and expenses as provided by law may be imposed on appeal to the Supreme Court or Appellate Court.

(b) A cost of fifteen dollars shall be imposed against any person not a resident of this state who is summoned for allegedly having committed an infraction or a violation under section 14-219 and forfeits a cash bond or guaranteed bail bond certificate posted under section 14-140a or under reciprocal agreements made with other states. Such cost shall be included in the amount of such bond.

(c) Under no condition shall a political subdivision be held liable for the payment of any cost imposed under this section. The words "felony" and "misdemeanor" as used in this section do not include infractions or violations of any state or local housing code or violation of the regulations of the Department of Energy and Environmental Protection.

(1949 Rev., S. 8842; P.A. 76-336, S. 9; P.A. 78-261, S. 15, 17; P.A. 79-505, S. 4, 7; P.A. 80-276, S. 3, 6; 80-390, S. 4, 5; 80-483, S. 181, 186; P.A. 81-23, S. 2; June Sp. Sess. P.A. 83-29, S. 55, 82; P.A. 84-313, S. 3; P.A. 11-80, S. 1; P.A. 16-126, S. 36.)

History: P.A. 76-336 deleted provision which had specified that section does not act to prevent dismissal of complaint or information or entry of nolle prosequi upon payment of sum fixed by court and rephrased provision re taxation of costs and collection of fees and expenses upon appeal to supreme court; P.A. 78-261 imposed $10 cost imposed against persons convicted of crime or convicted under specified sections in title 14, replacing provision which prohibited imposition of prosecution costs except on appeals to supreme court, and added Subsec. (b) protecting political subdivisions from liability for costs and specifying that crime does not include infractions or violations of housing codes or violation of environmental protection department regulations; P.A. 79-505 added reference to Sec. 14-219 in Subsec. (a); P.A. 80-276 applied Subsec. (a) to persons who plead nolo contendere to violation of Sec. 14-219 and pays fine by mail, inserted new Subsec. (b) re $10 cost imposed against nonresidents and relettered Subsec. (c) accordingly; P.A. 80-390 replaced $10 cost in Subsec. (a) with $20 cost for felony conviction and $15 cost for other convictions and applied provision to persons convicted of misdemeanors; P.A. 80-483 raised cost imposed in Subsec. (b) from $10 to $15 and amended Subsec. (c) to refer to "felony" and "misdemeanor" rather than to crime; P.A. 81-23 amended Subsec. (b) to include violations under Sec. 14-219 and forfeitures of bond required under reciprocal agreements with other states; June Sp. Sess. P.A. 83-29 included reference to appellate court in Subsec. (a); P.A. 84-313 amended Subsec. (b) to replace "required to be posted under section 51-164o" with "posted under section 14-140a"; pursuant to P.A. 11-80, "Department of Environmental Protection" was changed editorially by the Revisors to "Department of Energy and Environmental Protection" in Subsec. (c), effective July 1, 2011; P.A. 16-126 amended Subsec. (a) by adding references to Secs. 14-227m and 14-227n(a)(1) and (2) and by making technical changes.

Annotations to former statute:

Town not liable for support of prisoner legally committed to jail. 5 C. 185; 7 C. 529. Payment of costs part of punishment. 16 C. 50. Assumpsit will not lie for recovery of officer's fees. 46 C. 498. Costs not taxable in favor of accused who prevails on appeal to Supreme Court. 82 C. 392. Cited. 127 C. 58.

Annotation to present section:

Cited. 34 CS 275.

Sec. 54-143a. Cost imposed for infractions and certain motor vehicle violations.

A cost of twenty dollars shall be imposed against any person convicted of a violation, as defined in section 53a-27, under any provision of section 12-487 or sections 13b-410a to 13b-410c, inclusive; any regulation adopted in accordance with the provisions of section 12-484, 12-487 or 13b-410; or a violation of section 14-147, 14-219, 14-266, 14-267a, 14-269 or 14-270, chapter 268 or subsection (a) of section 22a-250, or any section of the general statutes the violation of which is deemed an infraction, or who forfeits a cash bond or guaranteed bail bond certificate posted under section 14-140a or under reciprocal agreements made with other states for the alleged violation of any of said sections, or who pleads nolo contendere to a violation of any of said sections and pays the fine by mail; except that such cost shall be thirty-five dollars for a violation of any section of the general statutes the violation of which is deemed an infraction and carries a fine of thirty-five dollars or more. The costs imposed by this section shall be deposited in the General Fund and shall be in addition to any costs imposed by section 54-143.

(P.A. 81-63, S. 1, 2; P.A. 84-313, S. 4; 84-429, S. 77; P.A. 90-213, S. 6; May Sp. Sess. P.A. 92-6, S. 83, 117; P.A. 93-307, S. 28, 34; June 30 Sp. Sess. P.A. 03-1, S. 104; June 30 Sp. Sess. P.A. 03-6, S. 165.)

History: P.A. 84-313 added provision to impose the cost against a person who forfeits a cash bond or guaranteed bail bond certificate or under reciprocal agreements with other states; P.A. 84-429 made technical changes for statutory consistency; P.A. 90-213 increased the cost from $10 to $20 and expanded applicability of section by imposing cost against any person convicted under Sec. 14-219 and replacing provision imposing cost against any person convicted under Sec. 14-36, 14-80, 14-80b, 14-80h or 14-80i, Secs. 14-96a to 14-96cc, inclusive, or Sec. 14-99f, 14-217, 14-218a, 14-230, 14-251 or 14-299 with provision imposing cost against any person convicted of "any section of the general statutes the violation of which is deemed an infraction"; May Sp. Sess. P.A. 92-6 added violations under Secs. 12-487, 13b-404, 13b-404a, 13b-405, 14-147, 14-219, 14-266, 14-267a, 14-269 or 14-270, chapter 268 or Sec. 22a-250(a) or under regulations adopted pursuant to Secs. 12-484, 12-487 and 13b-410; P.A. 93-307 amended the section by deleting references to Secs. 13b-404, 13b-404a and 13b-405 which were repealed by the same act, substituting references to Secs. 13b-410a to 13b-410c, inclusive, effective June 29, 1993; June 30 Sp. Sess. P.A. 03-1 added provision re cost of $35 for infraction if fine is $35 as provided by statute or if fine is established by Superior Court judges pursuant to Sec. 51-164m; June 30 Sp. Sess. P.A. 03-6 replaced provision re cost of $35 for infraction if fine is $35 as provided by statute or if fine is established by Superior Court judges pursuant to Sec. 51-164m with provision re cost of $35 for violation of statute which is deemed an infraction and carries a fine of $35 or more.

Sec. 54-143b. Forfeited bonds for motor vehicle violations.

The total amount of any forfeited bond for a motor vehicle violation, when such bond is composed in part of an additional fee established under subsection (c) or (d) of section 51-56a, any cost established under subsection (b) of section 54-143 or any cost established under section 54-143a, shall be deposited in the General Fund as one undifferentiated lump sum amount or deposited in the Special Transportation Fund as one undifferentiated lump sum amount as may be required by statute.

(P.A. 88-103, S. 3, 4; P.A. 12-133, S. 24.)

History: P.A. 12-133 substituted "subsection (c) or (d) of section 51-56a" for "subsection (c) of section 51-56a".

Sec. 54-143c. Additional fine for sexual assault offenses.

In addition to any fine, fee or cost that may be imposed pursuant to any provision of the general statutes, the court shall impose a fine of one hundred fifty-one dollars on any person who, on or after July 1, 2004, is convicted of or pleads guilty or nolo contendere to a violation of subdivision (2) of subsection (a) of section 53-21 or section 53a-70, 53a-70a, 53a-70b, 53a-71, 53a-72a, 53a-72b or 53a-73a. Fines collected under this section shall be deposited in the sexual assault victims account established under section 19a-112d.

(P.A. 04-121, S. 2.)

History: P.A. 04-121 effective July 1, 2004.

Sec. 54-144. Payment of expenses.

Any expenses necessarily incurred in any criminal proceeding or prosecution, except such expenses as are incurred by the Division of Criminal Justice, when approved by the court in which the proceeding or prosecution is had, shall be paid in the same manner as are other expenses of maintenance of the court. The court may allow the payment of any fees charged by such court by means of a credit card, charge card or debit card and may charge the person making such payment a service fee for any such payment made by any such card. The fee shall not exceed any charge by the card issuer, including any discount rate.

(1949 Rev., S. 8843; P.A. 73-122, S. 15, 27; P.A. 13-247, S. 64.)

History: P.A. 73-122 added exception re expenses incurred by criminal justice division and deleted reference to payments "from the same treasury" as other expenses of maintaining court; P.A. 13-247 added provisions re payment of fees by credit card, charge card or debit card and charging service fee therefor, effective July 1, 2013.

Secs. 54-145 and 54-146. Refunds to clerk of municipal court or to town treasurer. Report to clerk or town treasurer.   Sections 54-145 and 54-146 are repealed.

(1949 Rev., S. 8844, 8845; 1959, P.A. 28, S. 204.)

Sec. 54-147. Rules for payment of expenses. Waiver of fee or cost.

(a) The judges of the Superior Court may establish rules, in addition to those established by statute, for the payment of the expenses of all criminal proceedings or prosecutions, except such expenses as are incurred by the Division of Criminal Justice.

(b) No fee or cost imposed pursuant to any provision of the general statutes on a person who is a defendant or has been convicted in a criminal proceeding or prosecution shall be waived by the court, except as authorized by such provision or for good cause shown.

(1949 Rev., S. 8846; P.A. 73-122, S. 16, 27; P.A. 03-97, S. 1.)

History: P.A. 73-122 added exception re expenses incurred by criminal justice division; P.A. 03-97 designated existing provisions as Subsec. (a), making a technical change therein, and added Subsec. (b) re waiver of fee or cost.

Sec. 54-148. Support of prisoners after sentence.

The support of prisoners in community correctional centers, sentenced to a correctional institution, or sentenced to death, shall be paid by the state.

(1949 Rev., S. 8848; 1969, P.A. 297; P.A. 95-16, S. 2.)

History: 1969 act substituted "community correctional centers" for "jails"; P.A. 95-16 replaced "sentenced to the Connecticut Correctional Institution, Somers, or to be electrocuted" with "sentenced to a correctional institution, or sentenced to death".

Sec. 54-149. Payment for board of prisoners.

Section 54-149 is repealed.

(1949 Rev., S. 8849; 1959, P.A. 152, S. 99.)

Sec. 54-150. Compensation of physicians.

Physicians shall receive a reasonable compensation for services rendered in criminal cases.

(1949 Rev., S. 3612.)

Sec. 54-151. Cost of transcript and printing on appeal.

In any appeal in a criminal action, where it appears to the trial court that the accused is without funds with which to defray the costs of securing a transcript of the evidence, or printing the briefs and the appendices to the briefs, such costs shall be defrayed by the state.

(1949 Rev., S. 8850; 1957, P.A. 17; 1967, P.A. 421, S. 1.)

History: 1967 act deleted language restricting section to appeals to the supreme court.

Cited. 139 C. 401; 154 C. 631, 636; 155 C. 719.

Finding of fact after comprehensive examination of facts and circumstances is required where indigency is controverted. 5 Conn. Cir. Ct. 313.

Sec. 54-152. Allowance to witnesses from another state in criminal prosecutions.

When, in any criminal prosecution, it is necessary to obtain the testimony of any witnesses residing without this state, the Chief State's Attorney may allow them a reasonable sum for their time and expenses in going to, attending upon and returning from the court and may allow a reasonable sum for the expense of procuring their attendance or procuring any document from without this state necessary to be used as evidence on the trial of such prosecution, to be from the appropriation for the Division of Criminal Justice.

(1949 Rev., S. 8851; 1963, P.A. 642, S. 81; 1967, P.A. 844; P.A. 73-122, S. 17, 27.)

History: 1963 act deleted obsolete reference to criminal prosecution before common pleas court; 1967 act removed limitation of section to prosecutions in superior court; P.A. 73-122 made chief state's attorney rather than the court responsible for determining witnesses' expenses and specified that payments are to be made from criminal justice division appropriations, replacing provision whereby they were "taxed and paid as in other criminal cases".

See Sec. 51-275 for applicable definitions.

Sec. 54-153. Where witnesses for accused paid by state.

The court before which any criminal prosecution is pending may order such number of witnesses as the court approves to be summoned on behalf of the accused at the expense of the state.

(1949 Rev., S. 8852.)

Cited. 17 CA 359.

Sec. 54-154. Taxing expenses in search and seizure cases.

In any case in which the statutes provide for a search warrant and seizure, the court, judge or judge trial referee issuing such warrant may tax for the officer's services thereon the same fees for service, travel, copies and endorsements as are taxed in civil cases, and such sum for securing, care and destruction of property as such court, judge or judge trial referee, under the circumstances, deems reasonable, such fees and sum to be paid from the appropriation for the Division of Criminal Justice.

(1949 Rev., S. 8853; 1959, P.A. 28, S. 195; P.A. 73-122, S. 18, 27; P.A. 01-72, S. 7.)

History: 1959 act deleted references to trial justice; P.A. 73-122 specified that payments are to be made from criminal justice division appropriation; P.A. 01-72 added references to judge trial referee.

Sec. 54-155. Expenses of requisitions of fugitives.

When a requisition is made by the governor upon the executive authority of another state for the delivery of any fugitive from justice, the necessary expenses of such requisition and of the removal of such fugitive shall be ascertained and allowed by the superior court for the judicial district within which the crime charged is alleged to have been committed, and shall be paid from the appropriation for the Division of Criminal Justice, if application therefor is made within one year after such expenses have been incurred.

(1949 Rev., S. 8854; P.A. 73-122, S. 19, 27; P.A. 80-313, S. 52.)

History: P.A. 73-122 added reference to judicial districts and specified that expenses incurred under section are to be paid from criminal justice division appropriations rather than "by the state"; P.A. 80-313 deleted references to counties in accordance with provisions of P.A. 76-436 and P.A. 78-28.

CHAPTER 963* FRESH PURSUIT

*Statutory provisions governing arrest of fugitives from justice to be strictly complied with; arrest of fugitive without warrant unlawful. 115 C. 649.

Table of Contents

Sec. 54-156. Pursuit of suspected criminals.

Sec. 54-156. Pursuit of suspected criminals.

(a) Any member of a duly organized state, county or municipal peace unit of another state of the United States who enters this state in fresh pursuit, and continues within this state in such fresh pursuit, of a person, in order to arrest him on the ground that he is believed to have committed a felony in such other state, shall have the same authority to arrest and hold such person in custody as has any member of any duly organized state, county or municipal peace unit of this state to arrest and hold in custody a person on the ground that he is believed to have committed a felony in this state.

(b) If an arrest is made in this state by an officer of another state in accordance with the provisions of subsection (a) of this section, he shall, without unnecessary delay, take the person arrested before a judge of the superior court for the judicial district in which the arrest was made, who shall conduct a hearing for the purpose of determining the lawfulness of the arrest. If such judge determines that the arrest was lawful, he shall commit the person arrested to await for a reasonable time the issuance of an extradition warrant by the Governor of this state or admit him to bail for such purpose. If such judge determines that the arrest was unlawful, he shall discharge the person arrested.

(c) Subsection (a) of this section shall not be construed so as to make unlawful any arrest in this state which would otherwise be lawful.

(d) For the purpose of this section the word "state" shall include the District of Columbia.

(e) The term "fresh pursuit" as used in this section shall include fresh pursuit as defined by the common law, and also the pursuit of a person who has committed a felony or who is reasonably suspected of having committed a felony. It shall also include the pursuit of a person suspected of having committed a supposed felony, though no felony has actually been committed, if there is reasonable ground for believing that a felony has been committed. Fresh pursuit, as used herein, shall not necessarily imply instant pursuit, but pursuit without unreasonable delay.

(f) The provisions of this section shall apply only to those states which by their laws grant similar rights to the duly constituted officers of this state.

(1949 Rev., S. 8870; P.A. 73-116, S. 31; 73-667, S. 1, 2; P.A. 82-472, S. 148, 183; P.A. 05-288, S. 189.)

History: P.A. 73-116 added reference to judicial districts in Subsec. (b); P.A. 73-667 changed effective date of P.A. 73-116 from October 1, 1973, to April 25, 1973; P.A. 82-472 deleted obsolete reference to counties; P.A. 05-288 made a technical change in Subsecs. (b) and (c), effective July 13, 2005.

Charges of several offenses, if they are of the same character, shall be tried together unless the court shall order otherwise. 139 C. 234.

CHAPTER 964* UNIFORM CRIMINAL EXTRADITION ACT

*Cited. 149 C. 70; 157 C. 407; 171 C. 366; 180 C. 153; 182 C. 470; 185 C. 562; 186 C. 404; 188 C. 364. Burden of proof for contesting fugitive states discussed. 190 C. 631. Violation of rights under Ch. 965 and its effect on requested extradition discussed. 193 C. 116. Cited. Id., 270; 194 C. 702. Remanding state, rather than custodial state, must determine if arrest is constitutionally defective for lack of probable cause. 195 C. 465. Cited. 196 C. 309. Under Uniform Criminal Extradition Act, a person who leaves the demanding state involuntarily under government compulsion is a fugitive from justice subject to mandatory extradition provisions of the act. 281 C. 380.

Cited. 26 CA 254; 33 CA 41.

Cited. 26 CS 470. Discussed. 34 CS 78. Cited. 41 CS 320; 42 CS 569.

Table of Contents

Sec. 54-157. Definitions.

Sec. 54-158. Governor's duty to arrest and deliver up fugitive.

Sec. 54-159. Requirements for recognition of extradition demand.

Sec. 54-160. State's attorney and prosecuting attorney to assist Governor.

Sec. 54-161. Return to this state of person imprisoned or held in another state.

Sec. 54-162. Return to another state of person whose act in this state caused crime.

Sec. 54-163. Arrest warrant signed by Governor.

Sec. 54-164. Authorization under warrant.

Sec. 54-165. Power of arresting officer.

Sec. 54-166. Appearance of accused in court. Habeas corpus.

Sec. 54-167. Penalty for failure of officer to present accused in court.

Sec. 54-168. Confinement, when.

Sec. 54-169. Arrest warrant of judge.

Sec. 54-170. Arrest without warrant.

Sec. 54-171. Commitment pending Governor's warrant.

Sec. 54-172. Allowance and conditions of bail bond.

Sec. 54-173. Discharge or recommitment after expiration of period specified in warrant or bond.

Sec. 54-174. Forfeiture of bond.

Sec. 54-175. Surrender of person against whom criminal prosecution pending in this state.

Sec. 54-176. Governor not to inquire into guilt or innocence of accused.

Sec. 54-177. Recall or new issuance of Governor's warrant.

Sec. 54-178. Governor seeking extradition to issue warrant to agent to receive accused.

Sec. 54-179. Application by state's attorney, Board of Pardons and Paroles or Correction Commissioner for return of accused.

Sec. 54-180. Immunity of accused to process in civil action arising from same facts.

Sec. 54-181. Waiver by accused.

Sec. 54-182. State's rights not waived.

Sec. 54-183. Trial for crimes other than those specified in extradition requisition.

Sec. 54-184. Interpretation of chapter.

Sec. 54-185. Short title: Uniform Criminal Extradition Act.

Sec. 54-157. Definitions.

Where appearing in this chapter, the term "Governor" includes any person performing the functions of Governor by authority of the law of this state. The term "executive authority" includes the Governor and any person performing the functions of Governor in a state other than this state. The term "state", referring to a state other than this state, includes any other state or territory, organized or unorganized, of the United States of America.

(1957, P.A. 362, S. 1.)

Annotations to former statute:

One who escapes from imprisonment considered still to be "charged with crime" within meaning of statute. 68 C. 441; 105 C. 374. What crimes included. 84 C. 370; 92 C. 542; 100 C. 292; 105 C. 374; 109 C. 404. One residing in Connecticut as a paroled prisoner of California is not immune from liability to extradition by Michigan for a crime committed there. 105 C. 374.

Annotations to present section:

Cited. 186 C. 404; 190 C. 631.

Cited. 26 CA 254.

Sec. 54-158. Governor's duty to arrest and deliver up fugitive.

Subject to the provisions of this chapter, the provisions of the Constitution of the United States controlling, and any and all acts of Congress enacted in pursuance thereof, it is the duty of the Governor of this state to have arrested and delivered up to the executive authority of any other state of the United States any person charged in that state with treason, felony or other crime, who has fled from justice and is found in this state.

(1957, P.A. 362, S. 2.)

Cited. 163 C. 394; 186 C. 404; 190 C. 631; 193 C. 116.

Cited. 3 CA 512.

Words "or other crime" necessarily include misdemeanors. 25 CS 179.

Sec. 54-159. Requirements for recognition of extradition demand.

No demand for the extradition of a person charged with crime in another state shall be recognized by the Governor unless in writing alleging, except in cases arising under section 54-162, that the accused was present in the demanding state at the time of the commission of the alleged crime, and that thereafter he fled from the state, and accompanied by a copy of an indictment found or by information supported by affidavit in the state having jurisdiction of the crime, or by a copy of an affidavit made before a magistrate there, together with a copy of any warrant which was issued thereupon; or by a copy of a judgment of conviction or of a sentence imposed in execution thereof, together with a statement by the executive authority of the demanding state that the person claimed has escaped from confinement or has broken the terms of his bail, probation or parole. The indictment, information or affidavit made before the magistrate must substantially charge the person demanded with having committed a crime under the law of that state; and the copy of indictment, information, affidavit, judgment of conviction or sentence must be authenticated by the executive authority making the demand.

(1957, P.A. 362, S. 3.)

As long as copy of judgment recited plaintiff's conviction and sentence as second offender, copy of information upon which he was presented as second offender not essential to validity of extradition request. 149 C. 73. Cited. 157 C. 407; 161 C. 329; 186 C. 404; 188 C. 364; 190 C. 631; 193 C. 270; 194 C. 702. Provisions of Sec. 1-36 not applicable to extradition documentation. 195 C. 465. Cited. 196 C. 557; 201 C. 162.

Recognition of extradition requests under federal law and this statute discussed. 3 CA 512. Cited. 26 CA 254; 33 CA 41; 36 CA 678.

Affiant's statement that she "believes" plaintiff to be the perpetrator of the crimes charged in Florida is not a substantial charge hereunder and writ of habeas corpus releasing plaintiff was granted. 31 CS 412. Implements Art. IV, Sec. 2 of U.S. Constitution; person demanded may resist extradition by proving, in habeas corpus proceeding, that he was not present in demanding state at time of alleged offense and is, therefore, not a fugitive from its justice. 34 CS 78. Judicial finding of probable cause should be explicitly made. 40 CS 179. Cited. 42 CS 569.

Sec. 54-160. State's attorney and prosecuting attorney to assist Governor.

When a demand is made upon the Governor of this state by the executive authority of another state for the surrender of a person so charged with crime, the Governor may call upon any state's attorney or prosecuting attorney in this state to investigate or assist in investigating the demand, and to report to him the situation and circumstances of the person so demanded, and whether he ought to be surrendered.

(1957, P.A. 362, S. 4; P.A. 75-221.)

History: P.A. 75-221 added reference to prosecuting attorneys.

Cited. 186 C. 404; 190 C. 631; 234 C. 539.

Sec. 54-161. Return to this state of person imprisoned or held in another state.

When it is desired to have returned to this state a person charged in this state with a crime, and such person is imprisoned or is held under criminal proceedings then pending against him in another state, the Governor of this state may agree with the executive authority of such other state for the extradition of such person before the conclusion of such proceedings or his term of sentence in such other state, upon condition that such person be returned to such other state at the expense of this state as soon as the prosecution in this state is terminated. The Governor of this state may also surrender on demand of the executive authority of any other state any person in this state who is charged in the manner provided in section 54-179 with having violated the laws of the state whose executive authority is making the demand, even though such person left the demanding state involuntarily.

(1957, P.A. 362, S. 5.)

Cited. 186 C. 404; 190 C. 631.

Plain language of section makes it clear that Connecticut's extradition law does not make it mandatory to extradite a nonfugitive; section governs extradition of persons who have been removed involuntarily from the demanding state by government compulsion and such persons properly are treated as nonfugitives. 88 CA 178.

Sec. 54-162. Return to another state of person whose act in this state caused crime.

The Governor of this state may also surrender, on demand of the executive authority of any other state, any person in this state charged in such other state in the manner provided in section 54-159 with committing an act in this state, or in a third state, intentionally resulting in a crime in the state whose executive authority is making the demand, and the provisions of this chapter not otherwise inconsistent shall apply to such cases, even though the accused was not in that state at the time of the commission of the crime and has not fled therefrom.

(1957, P.A. 362, S. 6.)

Cited. 157 C. 414; 186 C. 404; 190 C. 631; 201 C. 162.

Governor of rendering state exercises informed legal discretion, as extradition is not required by Art. IV, Sec. 2 of the U.S. Constitution; where both governors falsely believed person was a fugitive, extradition will not be granted under section and person must be released, as discretion was not exercised. 34 CS 78.

Sec. 54-163. Arrest warrant signed by Governor.

If the Governor decides that the demand should be complied with, he shall sign a warrant of arrest, which shall be sealed with the state seal, and be directed to any peace officer or other person whom he may think fit to entrust with the execution thereof. The warrant shall substantially recite the facts necessary to the validity of its issuance.

(1957, P.A. 362, S. 7.)

Procedure before Governor and effect of issuance of warrant by him. 78 C. 150; 84 C. 370; 160 U.S. 231. Warrant necessary for arrest under Uniform Criminal Extradition Act. 146 C. 509. Cited. 157 C. 38. In habeas corpus challenging detention under warrant, indigent plaintiff entitled to assistance to assert his legal rights. Id., 403. Cited. 161 C. 329; 163 C. 394; 168 C. 274; 180 C. 153; 182 C. 470; 186 C. 404; 190 C. 631; 201 C. 162.

Cited. 26 CS 469.

ꞁ

Sec. 54-164. Authorization under warrant.

Such warrant shall authorize the peace officer or other person to whom directed to arrest the accused at any time and any place where he is found within the state and to command the aid of all peace officers or other persons in the execution of the warrant, and to deliver the accused, subject to the provisions of this chapter, to the duly authorized agent of the demanding state.

(1957, P.A. 362, S. 8.)

Cited. 186 C. 404; 190 C. 631.

Sec. 54-165. Power of arresting officer.

Every such officer or other person empowered to make the arrest shall have the same authority, in arresting the accused, to command assistance therein as peace officers have by law in the execution of any criminal process directed to them, with like penalties against those who refuse their assistance.

(1957, P.A. 362, S. 9.)

Cited. 186 C. 404; 190 C. 631.

Sec. 54-166. Appearance of accused in court. Habeas corpus.

No person arrested upon such warrant shall be delivered over to the agent whom the executive authority demanding him has appointed to receive him unless he is first taken forthwith before a judge of any court having criminal jurisdiction in this state, who shall inform him of the demand made for his surrender and of the crime with which he is charged, and that he has the right to demand and procure legal counsel; and if the prisoner or his counsel states that he or they desire to test the legality of his arrest, the judge of such court shall fix a reasonable time to be allowed him within which to apply for a writ of habeas corpus. When such writ is applied for, notice thereof, and of the time and place of hearing thereon, shall be given to the state's attorney of the county in which the arrest is made and in which the accused is in custody, and to the agent of the demanding state.

(1957, P.A. 362, S. 10; 1959, P.A. 28, S. 156.)

History: 1959 act deleted reference to trial justice.

Prior to 1960: Court of Common Pleas may, in its discretion, admit prisoner to bail pending appeal from its decision dismissing writ of habeas corpus. 100 C. 291. Demanding state is forum in which issue of violation of due process must be raised; argument re arrest must be confined to legalities. 151 C. 155. Indigent must be afforded means to assert his rights on such hearings. 157 C. 403. Cited. 159 C. 150. United States court will not ordinarily issue writ pending final determination of case in state courts. 160 U.S. 231. Cited. 171 C. 366; 186 C. 404; 188 C. 364; 190 C. 631; 193 C. 270; 196 C. 309; 218 C. 791.

Scope and limits of the hearing on habeas corpus discussed; in habeas corpus proceeding, plaintiff argued that his return to North Carolina would be in violation of his constitutional rights, particularly those relating to cruel and unusual punishment, excessive fines and right to counsel; held that, if his constitutional rights were violated, his remedy lies in an appeal from the decision of the North Carolina court. 21 CS 12.

Sec. 54-167. Penalty for failure of officer to present accused in court.

Any officer who delivers to the agent for extradition of the demanding state a person in his custody under the Governor's warrant, in wilful disobedience to section 54-166, shall be fined not more than one thousand dollars or be imprisoned not more than six months or both.

(1957, P.A. 362, S. 11.)

Cited. 186 C. 404; 190 C. 631.

Sec. 54-168. Confinement, when.

The officer or person executing the Governor's warrant of arrest, or the agent of the demanding state to whom the prisoner has been delivered, may, when necessary, confine the prisoner in any community correctional center or in the jail of any city through which he passes; and the Community Correctional Center Administrator or the keeper of such jail shall receive and safely keep the prisoner until the officer or person having charge of him is ready to proceed on his route, such officer or person being chargeable with the expense of keeping. The officer or agent of a demanding state to whom a prisoner has been delivered following extradition proceedings in another state, or to whom a prisoner has been delivered after waiving extradition in such other state, and who is passing through this state with such a prisoner for the purpose of immediately returning such prisoner to the demanding state may, when necessary, confine the prisoner in any community correctional center or in the jail of any city through which he passes; and the Community Correctional Center

Administrator or keeper of such jail shall receive and safely keep the prisoner until the officer or agent having charge of him is ready to proceed on his route, such officer or agent being chargeable with the expense of keeping; provided such officer or agent shall produce and show to the Community Correctional Center Administrator or the keeper of such jail satisfactory written evidence of the fact that he is actually transporting such prisoner to the demanding state after a requisition by the executive authority of such demanding state. Such prisoner shall not be entitled to demand a new requisition while in this state.

(1957, P.A. 362, S. 12; 1963, P.A. 642, S. 82; 1969, P.A. 297.)

History: 1963 act substituted state jail for county jail and included jail administrator; 1969 act replaced jails and jail administrators with community correctional centers and their administrators.

Cited. 186 C. 404; 190 C. 631.

Sec. 54-169. Arrest warrant of judge.

Whenever any person within this state is charged on the oath of any credible person before any judge of any court of this state having criminal jurisdiction with the commission of any crime in any other state and, except in cases arising under section 54-162, with having fled from justice, or having been convicted of a crime in that state and having escaped from confinement, or having broken the terms of his bail, probation or parole, or whenever complaint has been made before such judge in this state setting forth on the affidavit of any credible person in another state that a crime has been committed in such other state and that the accused has been charged in such state with the commission of the crime and, except in cases arising under section 54-162, has fled from justice, or with having been convicted of a crime in that state and having escaped from confinement, or having broken the terms of his bail, probation or parole, and is believed to be in this state, the judge shall issue a warrant directed to any peace officer commanding him to apprehend the person named therein, wherever he may be found in this state, and to bring him before the same or any other judge or court who or which may be available in or convenient of access to the place where the arrest may be made, to answer the charge or complaint and affidavit, and a certified copy of the sworn charge or complaint and affidavit upon which the warrant is issued shall be attached to the warrant.

(1957, P.A. 362, S. 13; 1959, P.A. 28, S. 157.)

History: 1959 act deleted references to trial justice.

Warrant necessary for arrest under Uniform Criminal Extradition Act. 146 C. 509. Cited. 157 C. 38; 186 C. 404; 190 C. 631; 193 C. 116; Id., 270.

Cited. 26 CS 469.

Sec. 54-170. Arrest without warrant.

The arrest of a person may be lawfully made also by any peace officer or a private person, without a warrant, upon reasonable information that the accused stands charged in the courts of a state with a crime punishable by death or imprisonment for a term exceeding one year, but when so arrested the accused shall be taken before such a judge with all practicable speed and complaint shall be made against him under oath setting forth the ground for the arrest as in section 54-169; and thereafter his answer shall be heard as if he had been arrested on a warrant.

(1957, P.A. 362, S. 14; 1959, P.A. 28, S. 196.)

History: 1959 act deleted reference to trial justice.

Cited. 186 C. 404; 190 C. 631; 193 C. 270.

Sec. 54-171. Commitment pending Governor's warrant.

If from the examination before the judge it appears that the person held is the person charged with having committed the crime alleged and, except in cases arising under section 54-162, that he has fled from justice, the judge shall, by a warrant reciting the accusation, commit him to a community correctional center for such a time, not exceeding thirty days and specified in the warrant, as will enable the arrest of the accused to be made under a warrant of the Governor on a requisition of the executive authority of the state having jurisdiction of the offense, unless the accused gives bail as provided in section 54-172, or until he is legally discharged.

(1957, P.A. 362, S. 15; 1959, P.A. 28, S. 158; 1969, P.A. 297.)

History: 1959 act deleted reference to trial justice; 1969 act substituted "community correctional center" for "jail".

Cited. 180 C. 153; 186 C. 404; 190 C. 631.

Sec. 54-172. Allowance and conditions of bail bond.

Unless the offense with which the prisoner is charged is shown to be an offense punishable by death or life imprisonment under the laws of the state in which it was committed, such a judge in this state may admit the person arrested to bail by bond, with sufficient sureties, and in such sum as he deems proper, conditioned for his appearance before him at a time specified in such bond, and for his surrender, to be arrested upon the warrant of the Governor of this state.

(1957, P.A. 362, S. 16; 1959, P.A. 28, S. 159.)

History: 1959 act deleted reference to trial justices.

Sec. 54-173. Discharge or recommitment after expiration of period specified in warrant or bond.

If the accused is not arrested under warrant of the Governor by the expiration of the time specified in the warrant or bond, such judge may discharge him or may recommit him for a further period not to exceed sixty days, or a judge may again take bail for his appearance and surrender as provided in section 54-172, but within a period not to exceed sixty days after the date of such new bond.

(1957, P.A. 362, S. 17; 1959, P.A. 28, S. 160.)

History: 1959 act deleted references to trial justice.

Cited. 163 C. 394; 186 C. 404; 190 C. 631.

Sec. 54-174. Forfeiture of bond.

If the prisoner is admitted to bail, and fails to appear and surrender himself according to the conditions of his bond, the judge, by proper order, shall declare the bond forfeited and order his immediate arrest without warrant if he is within the state. Recovery may be had on such bond in the name of the state as in the case of other bonds given by the accused in criminal proceedings within this state.

(1957, P.A. 362, S. 18; 1959, P.A. 28, S. 161.)

History: 1959 act deleted reference to trial justice.

Cited. 186 C. 404; 190 C. 631.

Sec. 54-175. Surrender of person against whom criminal prosecution pending in this state.

If a criminal prosecution has been instituted against such person under the laws of this state and is still pending, the Governor, in his discretion, may either surrender him on demand of the executive authority of another state or hold him until he has been tried and discharged or convicted and punished in this state.

(1957, P.A. 362, S. 19.)

Sec. 54-176. Governor not to inquire into guilt or innocence of accused.

The guilt or innocence of the accused as to the crime of which he is charged may not be inquired into by the Governor or in any proceeding after the demand for extradition accompanied by a charge of crime in legal form as above provided has been presented to the Governor, except as it may be involved in identifying the person held as the person charged with the crime.

(1957, P.A. 362, S. 20.)

Sec. 54-177. Recall or new issuance of Governor's warrant.

The Governor may recall his warrant of arrest or may issue another warrant whenever he deems proper.

(1957, P.A. 362, S. 21.)

Sec. 54-178. Governor seeking extradition to issue warrant to agent to receive accused.

Whenever the Governor of this state demands a person charged with crime or with escaping from confinement or breaking the terms of his bail, probation or parole in this state, from the executive authority of any other state, or from the Chief Justice or an associate justice of the Supreme Court of the District of Columbia authorized to receive such demand under the laws of the United States, he shall issue a warrant, under the seal of this state, to some agent, commanding him to receive the person so charged if delivered to him and convey him to the proper officer of the county in this state in which the offense was committed.

(1957, P.A. 362, S. 22.)

Sec. 54-179. Application by state's attorney, Board of Pardons and Paroles or Correction Commissioner for return of accused.

(a) When the return to this state of a person charged with crime in this state is required, the state's attorney shall present to the Governor his written application for a requisition for the return of the person charged, in which application shall be stated the name of the person so charged, the crime charged against him, the approximate time, place and circumstances of its commission, the state in which he is believed to be, including the location of the accused therein, at the time the application is made and certifying that, in the opinion of the state's attorney, the ends of justice require the arrest and return of the accused to this state for trial and that the proceeding is not instituted to enforce a private claim.

(b) When the return to this state is required of a person who has been convicted of a crime in this state and has escaped from confinement or broken the terms of his bail, probation or parole, the state's attorney of the county in which the offense was committed, the Board of Pardons and Paroles, or the Commissioner of Correction, shall present to the Governor a written application for a requisition for the return of such person, in which application shall be stated the name of the person, the crime of which he was convicted, the circumstances of his escape from confinement or of the breach of the terms of his bail, probation or parole and the state in which he is believed to be, including the location of the person therein at the time application is made.

(c) The application shall be verified by affidavit, shall be executed in duplicate and shall be accompanied by two certified copies of the indictment returned, or information and affidavit filed, or of the complaint made to the judge, stating the offense with which the accused is charged, or of the judgment of conviction or of the sentence. The state's attorney, Board of Pardons and Paroles or Commissioner of Correction may also attach such further affidavits and other documents in duplicate as he deems proper to be submitted with such application. One copy of the application, with the action of the Governor indicated by endorsement thereon, and one of the certified copies of the indictment, complaint, information and affidavits or of the judgment of conviction or of the sentence, shall be filed in the office of the Secretary of the State, to remain of record in that office. The other copies of all papers shall be forwarded with the Governor's requisition.

(1957, P.A. 362, S. 23; 1961, P.A. 517, S. 52; 1967, P.A. 656, S. 64, 64a; June Sp. Sess. P.A. 98-1, S. 76, 121; P.A. 04-234, S. 2.)

History: 1961 act amended subsection (c) by deleting obsolete reference to trial justice; 1967 act, effective July 1, 1968, amended subsections (b) and (c) to substitute correction commissioner for warden or sheriff; June Sp. Sess. P.A. 98-1 made technical changes in Subsecs. (b) and (c), effective June 24, 1998; P.A. 04-234 replaced Board of Parole with Board of Pardons and Paroles, effective July 1, 2004.

Cited. 186 C. 404; 190 C. 631; 196 C. 557.

Cited. 34 CS 219.

Sec. 54-180. Immunity of accused to process in civil action arising from same facts.

A person brought into this state by, or after waiver of, extradition based on a criminal charge shall not be subject to service of personal process in civil actions arising out of the same facts as the criminal proceedings to answer which he is being or has been returned, until he has been convicted in the criminal proceeding or, if acquitted, until he has had reasonable opportunity to return to the state from which he was extradited.

(1957, P.A. 362, S. 24.)

Sec. 54-181. Waiver by accused.

Any person arrested in this state charged with having committed any crime in another state or alleged to have escaped from confinement, or broken the terms of his bail, probation or parole may waive the issuance and service of the warrant provided for in sections 54-163 and 54-164 and all other procedure incidental to extradition proceedings, by executing or subscribing in the presence of a judge of any court having criminal jurisdiction within this state a writing which states that he consents to return to the demanding state; provided, before such waiver is executed or subscribed by such person, such judge shall inform such person of his rights to the issuance or service of a warrant of extradition and to obtain a writ of habeas corpus as provided in section 54-166. If and when such consent has been executed, it shall forthwith be forwarded to the office of the Governor of this state and filed therein. The judge shall direct the officer having such person in custody to deliver forthwith such person to the duly accredited agent or agents of the demanding state, and shall deliver or cause to be delivered to such agent or agents a copy of such consent; provided nothing in this section shall be deemed to limit the rights of the accused person to return voluntarily and without formality to the demanding state, nor shall this waiver procedure be deemed to be an exclusive procedure or to limit the powers, rights or duties of the officers of the demanding state or of this state.

(1957, P.A. 362, S. 25; 1961, P.A. 517, S. 53.)

History: 1961 act deleted obsolete references to trial justices.

Sec. 54-182. State's rights not waived.

Nothing contained in this chapter shall be deemed to constitute a waiver by the state of its right, power or privilege to try such demanded person for crime committed within this state, or of its right, power or privilege to regain custody of such person by extradition proceedings or otherwise for the purpose of trial, sentence or punishment for any crime committed within this state, nor shall any proceedings had under this chapter which result in, or fail to result in, extradition be deemed a waiver by this state of any of its rights, privileges or jurisdiction.

(1957, P.A. 362, S. 26.)

Sec. 54-183. Trial for crimes other than those specified in extradition requisition.

After a person has been brought back to this state by, or after waiver of, extradition proceedings, he may be tried in this state for other crimes which he is charged with having committed here as well as that specified in the requisition for his extradition.

(1957, P.A. 362, S. 27.)

Cited. 186 C. 404; 190 C. 631.

Sec. 54-184. Interpretation of chapter.

The provisions of this chapter shall be so interpreted and construed as to effectuate the general purpose to make uniform the law of those states which enact it.

(1957, P.A. 362, S. 28.)

Cited. 186 C. 404; 190 C. 631.

Cited. 36 CS 327.

Sec. 54-185. Short title: Uniform Criminal Extradition Act.

This chapter may be cited as the "Uniform Criminal Extradition Act".

(1957, P.A. 362, S. 30.)

Cited. 186 C. 404; 190 C. 631.

Since chapter is a uniform law, precedents from other states are particularly valuable in construing it. 34 CS 78.

CHAPTER 965* DETAINERS

*Cited. 185 C. 562. Violation of rights under chapter and its effects on requested extradition under Ch. 964 discussed. 193 C. 116. Cited. 196 C. 309. Interstate Agreement on Detainers cited. 210 C. 78; 215 C. 418; 219 C. 629.

Interstate Agreement on Detainers cited. 20 CA 205; 36 CA 691.

Table of Contents

Sec. 54-186. Agreement on Detainers.

Sec. 54-187. Agreement on Detainers: Appropriate court defined.

Sec. 54-188. Agreement on Detainers: Enforcement of agreement.

Sec. 54-189. Agreement on Detainers: Second or subsequent offense penalty not applicable.

Sec. 54-190. Agreement on Detainers: Penalty for escape while in another state.

Sec. 54-191. Agreement on Detainers: Warden to surrender inmate.

Sec. 54-192. Agreement on Detainers: Commissioner of Correction to make rules and regulations.

Secs. 54-192a to 54-192g. **Reserved**

Sec. 54-192h. Civil immigration detainers.

Sec. 54-186. Agreement on Detainers.

The Agreement on Detainers is hereby entered into by this state with all jurisdictions legally joining therein in form substantially as follows: The contracting states solemnly agree that:

Article I

The party states find that charges outstanding against a prisoner, detainers based on untried indictments, informations or complaints, and difficulties in securing speedy trial of persons already incarcerated in other jurisdictions, produce uncertainties which obstruct programs of prisoner treatment and rehabilitation. Accordingly, it is the policy of the party states and the purpose of this agreement to encourage the expeditious and orderly disposition of such charges and determination of the proper status of any and all detainers based on untried indictments, informations or complaints. The party states also find that proceedings with reference to such charges and detainers, when emanating from another jurisdiction, cannot properly be had in the absence of cooperative procedures. It is the further purpose of this agreement to provide such cooperative procedures.

Article II

As used in this agreement: (a) "State" shall mean a state of the United States; the United States of America; a territory or possession of the United States; the District of Columbia; the Commonwealth of Puerto Rico. (b) "Sending state" shall mean a state in which a prisoner is incarcerated at the time that he initiates a request for final disposition pursuant to article III hereof or at the time that a request for custody or availability is initiated pursuant to article IV hereof. (c) "Receiving state" shall mean the state in which trial is to be had on an indictment, information or complaint pursuant to article III or article IV hereof.

Article III

(a) Whenever a person has entered upon a term of imprisonment in a penal or correctional institution of a party state, and whenever during the continuance of the term of the imprisonment there is pending in any other party state any untried indictment, information or complaint on the basis of which a detainer has been lodged against the prisoner, he shall be brought to trial within one hundred eighty days after he shall have caused to be delivered to the prosecuting officer and the appropriate court of the prosecuting officer's jurisdiction written notice of the place of his imprisonment and his request for a final disposition to be made of the indictment, information or complaint; provided that for good cause shown in open court, the prisoner or his counsel being present, the court having jurisdiction of the matter may grant any necessary or reasonable continuance. The request of the prisoner shall be accompanied by a certificate of the appropriate official having custody of the prisoner, stating the term of commitment under which the prisoner is being held, the time already served, the time remaining to be served on the sentence, the amount of good time earned, the time of parole eligibility of the prisoner, and any decisions of the state parole agency relating to the prisoner.

(b) The written notice and request for final disposition referred to in paragraph (a) hereof shall be given or sent by the prisoner to the warden, commissioner of correction or other official having custody of him, who shall promptly forward it together with the certificate to the appropriate prosecuting official and court by registered or certified mail, return receipt requested.

(c) The warden, commissioner of correction or other official having custody of the prisoner shall promptly inform him of the source and contents of any detainer lodged against him and shall also inform him of his right to make a request for final disposition of the indictment, information or complaint on which the detainer is based.

(d) Any request for final disposition made by a prisoner pursuant to paragraph (a) hereof shall operate as a request for final disposition of all untried indictments, informations or complaints on the basis of which detainers have been lodged against the prisoner from the state to whose prosecuting official the request for final disposition is specifically directed. The warden, commissioner of correction or other official having custody of the prisoner shall forthwith notify all appropriate prosecuting officers and courts in the several jurisdictions within the state to which the prisoner's request for final disposition is being sent of the proceeding being initiated by the prisoner. Any notification sent pursuant to this paragraph shall be accompanied by copies of the prisoner's written notice, request, and the certificate. If trial is not had on any indictment, information or complaint contemplated hereby prior to the return of the prisoner to the original place of imprisonment, such indictment, information or complaint shall not be of any further force or effect, and the court shall enter an order dismissing the same with prejudice.

(e) Any request for final disposition made by a prisoner pursuant to paragraph (a) hereof shall also be deemed to be a waiver of extradition with respect to any charge or proceeding contemplated thereby or included therein by reason of paragraph (d) hereof, and a waiver of extradition to the receiving state to serve any sentence there imposed upon him, after completion of his term of imprisonment in the sending state. The request for final disposition shall also constitute a consent by the prisoner to the production of his body in any court where his presence may be required in order to effectuate the purposes of this agreement and a further consent voluntarily to be returned to the original place of imprisonment in accordance with the provisions of this agreement. Nothing in this paragraph shall prevent the imposition of a concurrent sentence if otherwise permitted by law.

(f) Escape from custody by the prisoner subsequent to his execution of the request for final disposition referred to in paragraph (a) hereof shall void the request.

Article IV

(a) The appropriate officer of the jurisdiction in which an untried indictment, information or complaint is pending shall be entitled to have a prisoner against whom he has lodged a detainer and who is serving a term of imprisonment in any party state made available in accordance with article V(a) hereof upon presentation of a written request for temporary custody or availability to the appropriate authorities of the state in which the prisoner is incarcerated; provided that the court having jurisdiction of such indictment, information or complaint shall have duly approved, recorded and transmitted the request; and provided further that there shall be a period of thirty days after receipt by the appropriate authorities before the request be honored, within which period the governor of the sending state may disapprove the request for temporary custody or availability, either upon his own motion or upon motion of the prisoner.

(b) Upon receipt of the officer's written request as provided in paragraph (a) hereof, the appropriate authorities having the prisoner in custody shall furnish the officer with a certificate stating the term of commitment under which the prisoner is being held, the time already served, the time remaining to be served on the sentence, the amount of good time earned, the time of parole eligibility of the prisoner, and any decisions of the state parole agency relating to the prisoner. Said authorities simultaneously shall furnish all other officers and appropriate courts in the receiving state who have lodged detainers against the prisoner with similar certificates and with notices informing them of the request for custody or availability and of the reasons therefor.

(c) In respect of any proceeding made possible by this article, trial shall be commenced within one hundred twenty days of the arrival of the prisoner in the receiving state, but for good cause shown in open court, the prisoner or his counsel being present, the court having jurisdiction of the matter may grant any necessary or reasonable continuance.

(d) Nothing contained in this article shall be construed to deprive any prisoner of any right which he may have to contest the legality of his delivery as provided in paragraph (a) hereof, but such delivery may not be opposed or denied on the ground that the executive authority of the sending state has not affirmatively consented to or ordered such delivery.

(e) If trial is not had on any indictment, information or complaint contemplated hereby prior to the prisoner's being returned to the original place of imprisonment pursuant to article V(e) hereof, such indictment, information or complaint shall not be of any further force or effect, and the court shall enter an order dismissing the same with prejudice.

Article V

(a) In response to a request made under article III or article IV hereof, the appropriate authority in a sending state shall offer to deliver temporary custody of such prisoner to the appropriate authority in the state where such indictment, information or complaint is pending against such person in order that speedy and efficient prosecution may be had. If the request for final disposition is made by the prisoner, the offer of temporary custody shall accompany the written notice provided for in article III of this agreement. In the case of a federal prisoner, the appropriate authority in the receiving state shall be entitled to temporary custody as provided by this agreement or to the prisoner's presence in federal custody at the place for trial, whichever custodial arrangement may be approved by the custodian.

(b) The officer or other representative of a state accepting an offer of temporary custody shall present the following upon demand: (1) Proper identification and evidence of his authority to act for the state into whose temporary custody the prisoner is to be given. (2) A duly certified copy of the indictment, information or complaint on the basis of which the detainer has been lodged and on the basis of which the request for temporary custody of the prisoner has been made.

(c) If the appropriate authority shall refuse or fail to accept temporary custody of said person, or in the event that an action on the indictment, information or complaint on the basis of which the detainer has been lodged is not brought to trial within the period provided in article III or article IV hereof, the appropriate court of the jurisdiction where the indictment, information or complaint has been pending shall enter an order dismissing the same with prejudice, and any detainer based thereon shall cease to be of any force or effect.

(d) The temporary custody referred to in this agreement shall be only for the purpose of permitting prosecution on the charge or charges contained in one or more untried indictments, informations or complaints which form the basis of the detainer or detainers or for prosecution on any other charge or charges arising out of the same transaction. Except for his attendance at court and while being transported to or from any place at which his presence may be required, the prisoner shall be held in a suitable jail or other facility regularly used for persons awaiting prosecution.

(e) At the earliest practicable time consonant with the purposes of this agreement, the prisoner shall be returned to the sending state.

(f) During the continuance of temporary custody or while the prisoner is otherwise being made available for trial as required by this agreement, time being served on the sentence shall continue to run but good time shall be earned by the prisoner only if, and to the extent that, the law and practice of the jurisdiction which imposed the sentence may allow.

(g) For all purposes other than that for which temporary custody as provided in this agreement is exercised, the prisoner shall be deemed to remain in the custody of and subject to the jurisdiction of the sending state and any escape from temporary custody may be dealt with in the same manner as an escape from the original place of imprisonment or in any other manner permitted by law.

(h) From the time that a party state receives custody of a prisoner pursuant to this agreement until such prisoner is returned to the territory and custody of the sending state, the state in which the one or more untried indictments, informations or complaints are pending or in which trial is being had shall be responsible for the prisoner and shall also pay all costs of transporting, caring for, keeping and returning the prisoner. The provisions of this paragraph shall govern unless the states concerned shall have entered into a supplementary agreement providing for a different allocation of costs and responsibilities as between or among themselves. Nothing herein contained shall be construed to alter or affect any internal relationship among the departments, agencies and officers of and in the government of a party state, or between a party state and its subdivisions, as to the payment of costs, or responsibilities therefor.

Article VI

(a) In determining the duration and expiration dates of the time periods provided in articles III and IV of this agreement, the running of said time periods shall be tolled whenever and for as long as the prisoner is unable to stand trial, as determined by the court having jurisdiction of the matter.

(b) No provision of this agreement, and no remedy made available by this agreement, shall apply to any person who is adjudged to be mentally ill.

Article VII

Each state party to this agreement shall designate an officer who, acting jointly with like officers of other party states, shall promulgate rules and regulations to carry out more effectively the terms and provisions of this agreement, and who shall provide, within and without the state, information necessary to the effective operation of this agreement.

Article VIII

This agreement shall enter into full force and effect as to a party state when such state has enacted the same into law. A state party to this agreement may withdraw herefrom by enacting a statute repealing the same. However, the withdrawal of any state shall not affect the status of any proceedings already initiated by inmates or by state officers at the time such withdrawal takes effect, nor shall it affect their rights in respect thereof.

Article IX

This agreement shall be liberally construed so as to effectuate its purposes. The provisions of this agreement shall be severable and if any phrase, clause, sentence or provision of this agreement is declared to be contrary to the constitution of any party state or of the United States or the applicability thereof to any government, agency, person or circumstance is held invalid, the validity of the remainder of this agreement and the applicability thereof to any government, agency, person or circumstance shall not be affected thereby. If this agreement shall be held contrary to the constitution of any state party hereto, the agreement shall remain in full force and effect as to the state affected as to all severable matters.

(1957, P.A. 404, S. 1.)

Cited. 180 C. 153. Remedial relief must be sought in charging state. 185 C. 562. Cited. 193 C. 116; Id., 270. Phrase "shall have caused to be delivered" in Article III(a) discussed. 194 C. 297. Cited. 202 C. 93; 203 C. 494; 210 C. 78; 215 C. 418; 218 C. 791; 219 C. 629; 224 C. 163.

Cited. 12 CA 1; 14 CA 244; 20 CA 205; 21 CA 298; 23 CA 642; judgment reversed, see 219 C. 629; 26 CA 254; Id., 698; 36 CA 691. Defendant's right to speedy trial under Article III not violated when delay due to administrative error in transporting defendant. 49 CA 121. Purpose of section discussed. 57 CA 478. Petitioner who made oral request for disposition and repeatedly disregarded Connecticut's Interstate Agreement on Detainers procedures was precluded from complaining that he was denied his right to a speedy trial. 62 CA 24. Provisions apply only to trial on charges that form the basis of the detainer. 63 CA 386. Article IV(c): Time limit within which a trial must commence may be tolled by virtue of delays attributable to defendant; and thus continuances granted at the request of defendant's attorney tolled the statutory time period. 78 CA 610.

The 180-day period during which plaintiff was required under Article III to be brought to trial in the other party state having elapsed, plaintiff's habeas corpus petition granted and he is ordered discharged. 26 CS 469. Agreement on Detainers may serve as a statute of limitations on right of a state to extradite prisoner in another state. 34 CS 128. Motions for discovery filed by defendant do not toll the 180-day speedy trial period under Article III. 36 CS 327. Cited. 40 CS 354; 41 CS 320.

Sec. 54-187. Agreement on Detainers: Appropriate court defined.

The phrase "appropriate court" as used in the Agreement on Detainers, as provided in section 54-186, shall, with reference to the courts of this state, mean the Superior Court.

(1957, P.A. 404, S. 2.)

Sec. 54-188. Agreement on Detainers: Enforcement of agreement.

All courts, departments, agencies, officers and employees of the state and its political subdivisions shall enforce said agreement and cooperate with one another and with other party states in enforcing said agreement and effectuating its purpose.

(1957, P.A. 404, S. 3.)

Sec. 54-189. Agreement on Detainers: Second or subsequent offense penalty not applicable.

Nothing in this chapter or in the Agreement on Detainers shall be construed to require the application of any penalty for second or subsequent offenses under any provision of the general statutes to any person on account of any conviction had in a proceeding brought to final disposition by reason of the use of said agreement.

(1957, P.A. 404, S. 4.)

54-190. Agreement on Detainers: Penalty for escape while in another state.

Any person who escapes or attempts to escape from custody while in another state pursuant to said agreement shall be subject to the penalties provided in section 53a-169.

(1957, P.A. 404, S. 5; 1971, P.A. 871, S. 123.)

History: 1971 act substituted reference to Sec. 53a-169 for reference to Sec. 53-155.

Sec. 54-191. Agreement on Detainers: Warden to surrender inmate.

The warden or other official in charge of any correctional institution in this state shall give over the person of any inmate thereof whenever so required by the operation of the Agreement on Detainers.

(1957, P.A. 404, S. 6.)

Sec. 54-192. Agreement on Detainers: Commissioner of Correction to make rules and regulations.

The Commissioner of Correction is designated as the officer provided for in article VII of said agreement.

(1957, P.A. 404, S. 7; 1971, P.A. 116.)

History: 1971 act replaced director of probation with commissioner of correction.

Secs. 54-192a to 54-192g. Reserved for future use.

Sec. 54-192h. Civil immigration detainers.

(a) For the purposes of this section:

(1) "Civil immigration detainer" means a detainer request issued pursuant to 8 CFR 287.7;

(2) "Convicted of a felony" means that a person has been convicted of a felony, as defined in section 53a-25, pursuant to a final judgment of guilt entered by a court in this state or in a court of competent jurisdiction within the United States upon a plea of guilty, a plea of nolo contendere or a finding of guilty by a jury or the court notwithstanding any pending appeal or habeas corpus proceeding arising from such judgment;

(3) "Federal immigration authority" means any officer, employee or other person otherwise paid by or acting as an agent of United States Immigration and Customs Enforcement or any division thereof or any officer, employee or other person otherwise paid by or acting as an agent of the United States Department of Homeland Security who is charged with enforcement of the civil provisions of the Immigration and Nationality Act; and

(4) "Law enforcement officer" means:

(A) Each officer, employee or other person otherwise paid by or acting as an agent of the Department of Correction;

(B) Each officer, employee or other person otherwise paid by or acting as an agent of a municipal police department;

(C) Each officer, employee or other person otherwise paid by or acting as an agent of the Division of State Police within the Department of Emergency Services and Public Protection; and

(D) Each judicial marshal and state marshal.

(b) No law enforcement officer who receives a civil immigration detainer with respect to an individual who is in the custody of the law enforcement officer shall detain such individual pursuant to such civil immigration detainer unless the law enforcement official determines that the individual:

(1) Has been convicted of a felony;

(2) Is subject to pending criminal charges in this state where bond has not been posted;

(3) Has an outstanding arrest warrant in this state;

(4) Is identified as a known gang member in the database of the National Crime Information Center or any similar database or is designated as a Security Risk Group member or a Security Risk Group Safety Threat member by the Department of Correction;

(5) Is identified as a possible match in the federal Terrorist Screening Database or similar database;

(6) Is subject to a final order of deportation or removal issued by a federal immigration authority; or

(7) Presents an unacceptable risk to public safety, as determined by the law enforcement officer.

(c) Upon determination by the law enforcement officer that such individual is to be detained or released, the law enforcement officer shall immediately notify United States Immigration and Customs Enforcement. If the individual is to be detained, the law enforcement officer shall inform United States Immigration and Customs Enforcement that the individual will be held for a maximum of forty-eight hours, excluding Saturdays, Sundays and federal holidays. If United States Immigration and Customs Enforcement fails to take custody of the individual within such forty-eight-hour period, the law enforcement officer shall release the individual. In no event shall an individual be detained for longer than such forty-eight-hour period solely on the basis of a civil immigration detainer.

(P.A. 13-155, S. 1.)

History: P.A. 13-155 effective January 1, 2014.

CHAPTER 966 LIMITATION OF PROSECUTIONS

Table of Contents

Sec. 54-193. Limitation of prosecution for certain violations or offenses.

Sec. 54-193a. Limitation of prosecution for offenses involving sexual abuse of minor.

Sec. 54-193b. Limitation of prosecution for sexual assault offenses when DNA evidence available.

Sec. 54-193. Limitation of prosecution for certain violations or offenses.

(a) There shall be no limitation of time within which a person may be prosecuted for (1) a capital felony under the provisions of section 53a-54b in effect prior to April 25, 2012, a class A felony or a violation of section 53a-54d or 53a-169, (2) a violation of section 53a-165aa or 53a-166 in which such person renders criminal assistance to another person who has committed an offense set forth in subdivision (1) of this subsection, (3) a violation of section 53a-156 committed during a proceeding that results in the conviction of another person subsequently determined to be actually innocent of the offense or offenses of which such other person was convicted, or (4) a motor vehicle violation or offense that resulted in the death of another person and involved a violation of subsection (a) of section 14-224.

(b) No person may be prosecuted for any offense, other than an offense set forth in subsection (a) of this section, for which the punishment is or may be imprisonment in excess of one year, except within five years next after the offense has been committed.

(c) No person may be prosecuted for any offense, other than an offense set forth in subsection (a) or (b) of this section, except within one year next after the offense has been committed.

(d) If the person against whom an indictment, information or complaint for any of said offenses is brought has fled from and resided out of this state during the period so limited, it may be brought against such person at any time within such period, during which such person resides in this state, after the commission of the offense.

(e) When any suit, indictment, information or complaint for any crime may be brought within any other time than is limited by this section, it shall be brought within such time.

(1949 Rev., S. 8871; P.A. 76-35, S. 1, 2; P.A. 77-604, S. 40, 84; P.A. 80-313, S. 53; P.A. 86-197; P.A. 00-87, S. 1, 2; P.A. 10-180, S. 6; P.A. 12-5, S. 36; P.A. 14-185, S. 1.)

History: P.A. 76-35 replaced reference to crimes and misdemeanors, treason, etc. with general reference to offenses, adding exceptions re capital felonies and class A felonies, deleted specific reference to imprisonment in Somers facility, substituting applicability based on imprisonment for more than one year, and specified that there is no limitation for prosecution of capital and class A felonies; P.A. 77-604 made no change; P.A. 80-313 reordered and rephrased provisions, dividing section into Subsecs.; P.A. 86-197 provided that there shall be no time limitation on the prosecution of a person for a violation of Sec. 53a-54d; P.A. 00-87 amended Subsecs. (a) and (b) to provide that there shall be no time limitation on the prosecution of a person for a violation of Sec. 53a-169 and made technical changes for purposes of gender neutrality in Subsec. (c), effective May 26, 2000, and applicable to any offense committed prior to, on or after said date; P.A. 10-180 amended Subsec. (a) to designate existing offenses for which there is no time limitation as Subdiv. (1), add Subdiv. (2) re violation of Sec. 53a-165aa or 53a-166 and add Subdiv. (3) re violation of Sec. 53a-156, amended Subsec. (b) to replace "except a capital felony, a class A felony or a violation of section 53a-54d or 53a-169" with "other than an offense set forth in subsection (a) of this section", designated existing provision re offenses subject to one-year time limitation as Subsec. (c) and amended same to replace "any other offense, except a capital felony, a class A felony or a violation of section 53a-54d or 53a-169" with "any offense, other than an offense set forth in subsection (a) or (b) of this section" and redesignated existing Subsecs. (c) and (d) as Subsecs. (d) and (e), effective June 8, 2010, and applicable to any offense committed on or after that date and to any offense committed prior to that date for which the statute of limitations in effect at the time of the commission of the offense had not yet expired as of that date; P.A. 12-5 amended Subsec. (a)(1) to add reference to provisions of Sec. 53a-54b in effect prior to April 25, 2012, re capital felony, effective April 25, 2012; P.A. 14-185 amended Subsec. (a) to add Subdiv. (4) re motor vehicle violation or offense that resulted in death of another and involved a violation of Sec. 14-224(a).

Qui tam information amendable, notwithstanding no new information for same cause could be brought. 10 C. 472. Grand juror's complaint and information of state's attorney part of same proceeding and prevents running of statute. 49 C. 437. Statute does not run as to conspiracy until last overt act is committed. 126 C. 85. Cited. 150 C. 229; 163 C. 230. Prosecution within 1 year for first offender. Id., 234. P.A. 76-35, which amended statute to remove the 5-year limitation on prosecutions for capital or class A felonies, was not applied retroactively to crimes committed while 5-year limitation was in effect in absence of language clearly necessitating such construction. 189 C. 346. Cited. 197 C. 436; Id., 507. Protection afforded by statute may be waived; treated as an affirmative defense, not as jurisdictional. 199 C. 631. Prosecution for violation of Sec. 53a-54(a)(1) not barred by this section. 201 C. 435. Cited. 204 C. 98; 213 C. 388; 233 C. 403; 235 C. 145; 242 C. 409. Amendment to statute of limitations applies retroactively to crimes committed before its effective date but for which the preamendment limitation period had not yet expired. 276 C. 633. Plainly and unambiguously provides that statute of limitations runs from the date of the offense. 301 C. 630.

Cited. 28 CA 91; 34 CA 473; 35 CA 754; 41 CA 476.

It is not necessary in criminal prosecution to prove the precise day the acts were committed. 4 CS 259. Cited. 6 CS 349; 24 CS 312. After a nolle prosequi has been entered, statute of limitations continues to run and a prosecution may be resumed only on a new information and a new arrest. 32 CS 504. Cited. 35 CS 565. Issuance of arrest warrant starts prosecution and tolls statute of limitations. 38 CS 377. The prosecution of defendant began with his arrest; once prosecution has commenced within time period allowed by appropriate statute of limitations, the prosecutor has broad discretion as to what crimes to charge in any particular situation. 39 CS 347.

Subsec. (b):

Cited. 202 C. 86; Id., 93. Issuance of arrest warrant is sufficient initiation of a prosecution to toll statute of limitations if warrant served with due diligence. Id., 443. Cited. 209 C. 52; 211 C. 441; 228 C. 393. Although the case against defendant under Sec. 20-427 was initially dismissed based on statute of limitations, state's successful appeal on statute of limitations calculation and subsequent trial did not constitute unlawful double jeopardy. 250 C. 1. When the state files an amended or substitute information after the limitations period has passed, a timely information will toll statute of limitations only if the amended or substitute information does not broaden or substantially amend the charges made in the timely information. 305 C. 330.

Cited. 15 CA 222; 21 CA 449; 26 CA 674; 42 CA 790. Pursuant to Subsec., charged violations of Sec. 14-227a were subject to a 1-year limitations period because they were not punishable by a term of imprisonment of more than 1 year; trial court did not improperly deny defendant's motion to dismiss counts of information on grounds that statute of limitations precluded prosecution of counts where court found no evidence that defendant raised statute of limitations as an affirmative defense at trial. 61 CA 90. Prosecution was time barred where the police department did not make sufficient effort to ensure that warrant was timely served and therefore the state could not demonstrate that delay of nearly 3 years on service of arrest warrant was reasonable to toll statute of limitations. 130 CA 734.

Subsec. (d):

Re meaning of "fled" in former Subsec. (c), plain language does not require defendant to leave the state with intent to avoid prosecution, and Subsec. may toll statute of limitations when defendant absents himself from the jurisdiction with reason to believe that an investigation may ensue as a result of his actions. 306 C. 698.

Sec. 54-193a. Limitation of prosecution for offenses involving sexual abuse of minor.

Notwithstanding the provisions of section 54-193, no person may be prosecuted for any offense, except a class A felony, involving sexual abuse, sexual exploitation or sexual assault of a minor except within thirty years from the date the victim attains the age of majority or within five years from the date the victim notifies any police officer or state's attorney acting in such police officer's or state's attorney's official capacity of the commission of the offense, whichever is earlier, provided if the prosecution is for a violation of subdivision (1) of subsection (a) of section 53a-71, the victim notified such police officer or state's attorney not later than five years after the commission of the offense.

(P.A. 90-279, S. 2; P.A. 91-406, S. 14, 29; P.A. 93-340, S. 11, 19; P.A. 02-138, S. 1.)

History: P.A. 91-406 inserted "after the commission of the offense" after "seven years"; P.A. 93-340 replaced "or seven years after the commission of the offense, whichever is less" with "or within five years from the date the victim notifies any police officer or state's attorney acting in his official capacity of the commission of the offense, whichever is earlier", effective July 1, 1993; P.A. 02-138 added exception re class A felony, extended time limitation on possible prosecution from within 2 to within 30 years from the date the victim attains the age of majority, deleted proviso that required the time period to be in no event less than 5 years after the commission of the offense, added proviso that required the victim to have notified the police officer or state's attorney not later than 5 years after the commission of the offense if the prosecution is for a violation of Sec. 53a-71(a)(1) and made a technical change for purposes of gender neutrality, effective May 23, 2002, and applicable to any offense committed on or after said date.

See Sec. 52-577d re statute of limitations in civil action.

Sec. 54-193b. Limitation of prosecution for sexual assault offenses when DNA evidence available.

Notwithstanding the provisions of sections 54-193 and 54-193a, there shall be no limitation of time within which a person may be prosecuted for a violation of section 53a-70, 53a-70a, 53a-70b, 53a-71, 53a-72a or 53a-72b, provided (1) the victim notified any police officer or state's attorney acting in such police officer's or state's attorney's official capacity of the commission of the offense not later than five years after the commission of the offense, and (2) the identity of the person who allegedly committed the offense has been established through a DNA (deoxyribonucleic acid) profile comparison using evidence collected at the time of the commission of the offense.

(P.A. 00-80, S. 1, 3; June Sp. Sess. P.A. 07-4, S. 89.)

History: P.A. 00-80 effective May 16, 2000, and applicable to any offense committed prior to, on or after said date; June Sp. Sess. P.A. 07-4 deleted former limitation of time within which a person may be prosecuted for specified offenses of "not later than twenty years from the date of the commission of the offense" and provided that "there shall be no limitation of time" within which a person may be so prosecuted, effective July 1, 2007.

CHAPTER 967 GENERAL PROVISIONS

Table of Contents

Sec. 54-194. Effect of the repeal of a criminal statute.

Sec. 54-195. Penalty when no penalty provided.

Secs. 54-196 to 54-198. Accessories. Conspiracy. Attempt to commit statutory crime.

Sec. 54-199. Parent or guardian to accompany minor in court. Representatives of commissioner.

Sec. 54-200. When acquittal or conviction not a bar to further complaint.

Sec. 54-194. Effect of the repeal of a criminal statute.

The repeal of any statute defining or prescribing the punishment for any crime shall not affect any pending prosecution or any existing liability to prosecution and punishment therefor, unless expressly provided in the repealing statute that such repeal shall have that effect.

(1949 Rev., S. 8872.)

See Sec. 1-1 re words and phrases in general use throughout statutes.

Cited. 121 C. 200; 142 C. 29; 152 C. 81; 171 C. 524, 528. Repeal of any statute defining a crime shall not affect pending prosecutions thereunder unless expressly provided in repealing statute. 172 C. 242. Cited. 198 C. 158.

Cited. 22 CA 601. There is no express language in P.A. 11-71 or any indication in the legislative history that the legislature clearly and unequivocally intended P.A. 11-71 to apply retroactively and thus the savings statutes apply and the law in effect at the time of defendant's offense for possession of marijuana and use of drug paraphernalia controls. 147 CA 232.

Cited. 29 CS 132; Id., 333.

Sec. 54-195. Penalty when no penalty provided.

Any person who is convicted of a violation of any provision of the general statutes for which violation no penalty is expressly provided shall be fined not more than one hundred dollars.

(1949 Rev., S. 8874.)

Secs. 54-196 to 54-198. Accessories. Conspiracy. Attempt to commit statutory crime. Sections 54-196 to 54-198, inclusive, are repealed.

(1949 Rev., S. 8875-8877; 1955, S. 3352d; 1969, P.A. 828, S. 214.)

Sec. 54-199. Parent or guardian to accompany minor in court. Representatives of commissioner.

Whenever any minor charged with the commission of an offense is to appear in any court, he shall be accompanied by one of his parents, if such parent is physically capable of appearing and is within the jurisdiction of such court, or by his legally appointed guardian, if any. In the case of any child committed to the guardianship of the Commissioner of Social Services or the Commissioner of Children and Families, said commissioner may designate any member of his department to act as his representative. If any such parent, guardian or representative fails to appear in court as required by this section, the court may continue the case until he so appears and may issue a subpoena to compel his attendance. Failure to appear in response to such subpoena shall be punishable as contempt of court. The judge of such court may, in his discretion and for good cause, waive the requirement that a minor be accompanied by his parent, guardian or a Department of Social Services representative.

(1955, S. 3353d; 1957, P.A. 598; 1969, P.A. 297; 395; P.A. 74-251, S. 14; P.A. 75-420, S. 4, 6; P.A. 77-614, S. 521, 610; P.A. 93-91, S. 1, 2; 93-262, S. 1, 87.)

History: 1969 act added provision allowing judge to waive requirement that minor be accompanied by parent, guardian or welfare department representative; P.A. 74-251 included cases involving children committed to commissioner of children and youth services; P.A. 75-420 replaced welfare commissioner and department with commissioner and department of social services; P.A. 77-614 replaced commissioner and department of social services with commissioner and department of human resources, effective January 1, 1979; P.A. 93-91 substituted commissioner and department of children and families for commissioner and department of children and youth services, effective July 1, 1993; P.A. 93-262 authorized substitution of commissioner and department of social services for commissioner and department of human resources, effective July 1, 1993.

Since a grand jury is essentially an investigatory body and not a court, the provisions of section are not applicable when minor is to appear before a grand jury; a juvenile defendant shall be accompanied by guardian ad litem if he has one, but appointment of guardian ad litem is not required. 171 C. 644.

Cited. 8 CA 607.

Cited. 4 Conn. Cir. Ct. 413.

Sec. 54-200. When acquittal or conviction not a bar to further complaint.

No acquittal or conviction for any criminal offense, had upon any complaint issued by the procurement or at the solicitation of the person committing it, shall be a bar to another complaint or information for the same offense.

(1949 Rev., S. 8878.)

Fraudulent procurement of conviction by authorities a bar, as defendant must be personally concerned in such fraud. 26 C. 207. Nature and limitations of doctrine as to former conviction. 65 C. 271. If crimes are distinct, though evidence much the same, it does not apply. 77 C. 201. Acquittal for receiving stolen goods bars prosecution for theft; but discharge on hearing as to probable cause not an acquittal. 83 C. 286.

CHAPTER 968 VICTIM SERVICES

Table of Contents

Sec. 54-201. Definitions.

Sec. 54-202. Compensation commissioners; appointment; Chief Victim Compensation Commissioner; temporary victim compensation commissioners; compensation.

Sec. 54-202a. Executive director. Appointment; term; salary; duties. Deputy director of compensation. Deputy director of victim services.

Sec. 54-203. Office of Victim Services established. Powers and duties.

Sec. 54-204. Application for compensation or restitution services. Report and examination. Confidential information.

Sec. 54-205. Evaluation of application. Determination. Request for review by compensation commissioner.

Sec. 54-206. Payment of attorneys as part of order.

Sec. 54-207. Regulations to prescribe procedures.

Sec. 54-207a. Chief Court Administrator to prescribe policies and procedures.

Sec. 54-208. Order of payment of compensation. Criminal intent. Circumstances considered. Prosecution not necessary. Amount and manner of payments. Unclaimed award.

Sec. 54-209. When compensation may be ordered. Order inadmissible in civil or criminal proceeding.

Sec. 54-210. Compensation ordered for expenses, loss of earnings, pecuniary loss and other losses.

Sec. 54-211. Time limitation on filing application for compensation. Restrictions on award of compensation. Amount of compensation.

Sec. 54-211a. Appeal.

Sec. 54-212. Office of Victim Services to have subrogated cause of action against person responsible for crime.

Sec. 54-213. Award not subject to execution or attachment.

Sec. 54-214. Annual report to legislature and to appropriations committee.

Sec. 54-215. Criminal Injuries Compensation Fund.

Sec. 54-216. Restitution services.

Sec. 54-217. Emergency award pending final determination on claim.

Sec. 54-218. Profits derived as result of crime of violence. Recovery of money judgment by victim. Payment to Criminal Injuries Compensation Fund.

Sec. 54-219. Victim Services Technical Assistance Fund.

Sec. 54-220. Victim advocates. Responsibilities and duties.

Sec. 54-220a. Assignment of victim advocates to assist victims before Board of Pardons and Paroles.

Sec. 54-221. Appointment of advocates for victims of crime by court.

Sec. 54-222. Brochure re rights of victims and victim services. Notice concerning services for victims of human trafficking.

Sec. 54-222a. Duty of peace officer regarding crime victim. Regulations.

Sec. 54-223. Failure to afford rights to victim shall not constitute grounds for vacating conviction or voiding sentence or parole determination.

Sec. 54-224. Liability of state re failure to afford rights to victim.

Sec. 54-225. Voluntary program for lawyers for protection of persons injured in person or property by civil wrong.

Sec. 54-226. Definitions.

Sec. 54-227. Notification of Office of Victim Services and Victim Services Unit within Department of Correction by inmate or sexual offender seeking release or other relief.

Sec. 54-227a. Transferred

Sec. 54-228. Request by victim or family member of inmate for notification.

Sec. 54-229. Request by prosecuting authority for notification.

Sec. 54-230. Notification of victims and other persons by Office of Victim Services when inmate or sexual offender seeks release or other relief or is released from a correctional institution.

Sec. 54-230a. Notification of victims and other persons by Department of Correction when inmate or sexual offender seeks release or other relief.

Sec. 54-231. Notification of Office of Victim Services by Department of Correction upon release of inmate. Access to criminal history record information.

Sec. 54-232. Disposition of requests for notification received prior to April 1, 1992.

Sec. 54-233. Compensation of victim of tort occurring prior to July 1, 1993.

Sec. 54-234. Development of response system for victims of offense of trafficking in persons. Contracts.

Sec. 54-234a. Display of notice re services for victims of human trafficking at highway service plazas, hotels, adults-only businesses and liquor permittee premises.

Sec. 54-235. State-wide automated victim information and notification system.

Secs. 54-236 to 54-239. Reserved

Sec. 54-201. Definitions.

As used in sections 54-201 to 54-233, inclusive:

(1) "Victim" means a person who is injured or killed as provided in section 54-209;

(2) "Personal injury" means (A) actual bodily harm and mental anguish which is the direct result of bodily injury and includes pregnancy and any condition thereof, or (B) injury to a guide dog or assistance dog owned or kept by a blind or disabled person;

(3) "Dependent" means any relative of a deceased victim or a person designated by a deceased victim in accordance with section 1-56r who was wholly or partially dependent upon his income at the time of his death or the child of a deceased victim and shall include the child of such victim born after his death;

(4) "Relative" means a person's spouse, parent, grandparent, stepparent, child, including a natural born child, stepchild and adopted child, grandchild, brother, sister, half brother or half sister or a parent of a person's spouse;

(5) "Crime" means any act which is a felony, as defined in section 53a-25, or misdemeanor, as defined in section 53a-26, and includes any crime committed by a juvenile.

(P.A. 78-261, S. 1, 17; P.A. 87-554, S. 17; P.A. 95-175, S. 4; P.A. 02-105, S. 15; P.A. 03-129, S. 1; P.A. 10-36, S. 31.)

History: P.A. 87-554 redefined "dependents" to include children of deceased victims and added definition of "crime"; P.A. 95-175 redefined crime to include crimes committed by juveniles; P.A. 02-105 amended Subdiv. (3) by making technical changes and adding a person designated by a victim pursuant to Sec. 1-56r to definition of "dependent"; P.A. 03-129 redefined "personal injury" in Subdiv. (2) by inserting Subpara. (A) designator and adding Subpara. (B) to include injury to a guide dog or assistance dog owned or kept by a blind or disabled person; P.A. 10-36 amended Subdiv. (4) to make technical changes, effective July 1, 2010.

Sec. 54-202. Compensation commissioners; appointment; Chief Victim Compensation Commissioner; temporary victim compensation commissioners; compensation.

(a) On or before July 1, 1993, the Governor shall appoint five victim compensation commissioners for a term of four years to conduct hearings and make determinations as provided in sections 54-201 to 54-233, inclusive. To be eligible for appointment, a victim compensation commissioner shall have been admitted to the practice of law in this state for at least five years prior to the appointment.

(b) Each victim compensation commissioner shall be eligible for reappointment and may be removed by the Governor for inefficiency, neglect of duty or malfeasance in office after due notice and hearing.

(c) A Chief Victim Compensation Commissioner shall be designated by the Chief Court Administrator from among the five victim compensation commissioners appointed by the Governor. The Chief Court Administrator may appoint qualified attorneys to serve as temporary victim compensation commissioners when victim compensation commissioners are not available or when additional victim compensation commissioners are necessary for the expeditious processing of claims. Temporary victim compensation commissioners shall have the same qualifications for appointment and the same powers as victim compensation commissioners.

(d) Each victim compensation commissioner and temporary victim compensation commissioner shall receive one hundred twenty-five dollars for each day of service.

(P.A. 78-261, S. 2, 17; P.A. 80-390, S. 1, 5; P.A. 83-311; P.A. 87-554, S. 1; P.A. 89-35; P.A. 91-389, S. 9; P.A. 92-153, S. 1; May Sp. Sess. P.A. 92-11, S. 49, 70; P.A. 93-310, S. 1, 32.)

History: P.A. 80-390 replaced previous provision in Subsec. (c) which had allowed members no compensation but had allowed reimbursement for expenses incurred in performing duties with provision authorizing $50 per diem; P.A. 83-311 amended Subsec. (c) by increasing compensation from $50 to $100 per day; P.A. 87-554 changed "criminal injuries compensation board" to "commission on victim services" and amended Subsec. (c) to specify that expenses are in addition to $100 per diem; P.A. 89-35 amended Subsec. (d) by adding provision permitting administrator to make preliminary evaluation and order of compensation not to exceed $2,000; P.A. 91-389 amended Subsec. (d) to replace provision permitting administrator to make preliminary evaluation and order of compensation not to exceed $2,000 with provision permitting administrator to make a preliminary evaluation of an application; P.A. 92-153 increased members from three to five, required that one member have at least five years' experience in delivery of victim services and one member have at least five years' experience in insurance handling personal injury claims, deleted restriction specifying that members must never have been victims themselves or be related to a victim, added provisions re expiration of terms of members on September 30, 1992, appointment of members as of October 1, 1992, and re term length, revised provision re compensation of members and appeals panel, and changed "administrator" to "executive director"; May Sp. Sess. P.A. 92-11 made a technical change in Subsec. (a); P.A. 93-310 extensively revised section, changing "members of the commission" to "victim compensation commissioners", providing for chief victim compensation commissioner, authorizing appointment of temporary victim compensation commissioners, replacing provision authorizing reimbursement for expenses and payment of $100 per day with set compensation of $125 per day and deleting prior provisions re hearing officers, effective July 1, 1993.

Sec. 54-202a. Executive director. Appointment; term; salary; duties. Deputy director of compensation. Deputy director of victim services. Section 54-202a is repealed, effective July 1, 1993.

(P.A. 92-153, S. 2; P.A. 93-310, S. 31, 32.)

Sec. 54-203. Office of Victim Services established. Powers and duties.

(a) There is established an Office of Victim Services within the Judicial Department.

(b) The Office of Victim Services shall have the following powers and duties:

(1) To direct each hospital, whether public or private, to display prominently in its emergency room posters giving notice of the availability of compensation and assistance to victims of crime or their dependents pursuant to sections 54-201 to 54-233, inclusive, and to direct every law enforcement agency of the state to inform victims of crime or their dependents of their rights pursuant to sections 54-201 to 54-233, inclusive;

(2) To request from the office of the state's attorney, state police, local police departments or any law enforcement agency such investigation and data as will enable the Office of Victim Services to determine if in fact the applicant was a victim of a crime or attempted crime and the extent, if any, to which the victim or claimant was responsible for his own injury;

(3) To request from the Department of Correction, other units of the Judicial Department and the Board of Pardons and Paroles such information as will enable the Office of Victim Services to determine if in fact a person who has requested notification pursuant to section 54-228 was a victim of a crime;

(4) To direct medical examination of victims as a requirement for payment under sections 54-201 to 54-233, inclusive;

(5) To take or cause to be taken affidavits or depositions within or without the state;

(6) To apply for, receive, allocate, disburse and account for grants of funds made available by the United States, by the state, foundations, corporations and other businesses, agencies or individuals to implement a program for victim services which shall assist witnesses and victims of crimes as the Office of Victim Services deems appropriate within the resources available and to coordinate services to victims by state and community-based agencies, with priority given to victims of violent crimes, by (A) assigning, in consultation with the Division of Criminal Justice, such victim advocates as are necessary to provide assistance; (B) administering victim service programs; and (C) awarding grants or purchase of service contracts to private nonprofit organizations or local units of government for the direct delivery of services, except that the provision of training and technical assistance of victim service providers and the development and implementation of public education campaigns may be provided by private nonprofit or for-profit organizations or local units of government. Such grants and contracts shall be the predominant method by which the Office of Victim Services shall develop, implement and operate direct service programs and provide training and technical assistance to victim service providers;

(7) To provide each person who applies for compensation pursuant to section 54-204, within ten days of the date of receipt of such application, with a written list of rights of victims of crime involving personal injury and the programs available in this state to assist such victims. The Office of Victim Services, the state or any agent, employee or officer thereof shall not be liable for the failure to supply such list or any alleged inadequacies of such list. Such list shall include, but not be limited to:

(A) Subject to the provisions of sections 18-81e and 51-286e, the victim shall have the right to be informed concerning the status of his or her case and to be informed of the release from custody of the defendant;

(B) Subject to the provisions of section 54-91c, the victim shall have the right to present a statement of his or her losses, injuries and wishes to the prosecutor and the court prior to the acceptance by the court of a plea of guilty or nolo contendere made pursuant to a plea agreement with the state wherein the defendant pleads to a lesser offense than the offense with which the defendant was originally charged;

(C) Subject to the provisions of section 54-91c, prior to the imposition of sentence upon the defendant, the victim shall have the right to submit a statement to the prosecutor as to the extent of any injuries, financial losses and loss of earnings directly resulting from the crime;

(D) Subject to the provisions of section 54-126a, the victim shall have the right to appear before a panel of the Board of Pardons and Paroles and make a statement as to whether the defendant should be released on parole and any terms or conditions to be imposed upon any such release;

(E) Subject to the provisions of section 54-36a, the victim shall have the right to have any property the victim owns which was seized by police in connection with an arrest to be returned;

(F) Subject to the provisions of sections 54-56e and 54-142c, the victim shall have the right to be notified of the application by the defendant for the pretrial program for accelerated rehabilitation and to obtain from the court information as to whether the criminal prosecution in the case has been dismissed;

(G) Subject to the provisions of section 54-85b, the victim cannot be fired, harassed or otherwise retaliated against by an employer for appearing under a subpoena as a witness in any criminal prosecution;

(H) Subject to the provisions of section 54-86g, the parent or legal guardian of a child twelve years of age or younger who is a victim of child abuse or sexual assault may request special procedural considerations to be taken during the testimony of the child;

(I) Subject to the provisions of section 46b-15, the victim of assault by a spouse or former spouse, family or household member has the right to request the arrest of the offender, request a protective order and apply for a restraining order;

(J) Subject to the provisions of sections 52-146k, 54-86e and 54-86f, the victim of sexual assault or domestic violence can expect certain records to remain confidential; and

(K) Subject to the provisions of section 53a-32, the victim and any victim advocate assigned to assist the victim may receive notification from a probation officer whenever the officer has notified a police officer that the probation officer has probable cause to believe that the offender has violated a condition of such offender's probation;

(8) Within available appropriations, to establish a victim's assistance center which shall provide a victims' rights information clearinghouse which shall be a central repository of information regarding rights of victims of crime and services available to such victims and shall collect and disseminate such information to assist victims;

(9) To provide a victims' notification clearinghouse which shall be a central repository for requests for notification filed pursuant to sections 54-228 and 54-229, and to notify persons who have filed such a request whenever an inmate has applied for release from a correctional institution or reduction of sentence or review of sentence pursuant to section 54-227 or whenever an inmate is scheduled to be released from a correctional institution and to provide victims of family violence crimes, upon request, information concerning any modification or termination of criminal orders of protection;

(10) To provide a telephone helpline that shall provide information on referrals for various services for victims of crime and their families;

(11) To provide staff services to a state advisory council. The council shall consist of not more than fifteen members to be appointed by the Chief Justice and shall include the Chief Victim Compensation Commissioner and members who represent victim populations, including but not limited to, homicide survivors, family violence victims, sexual assault victims, victims of drunk drivers, and assault and robbery victims, and members who represent the judicial branch and executive branch agencies involved with victims of crime. The members shall serve for terms of four years. Any vacancy in the membership shall be filled by the appointing authority for the balance of the unexpired term. The members shall receive no compensation for their services. The council shall meet at least six times a year. The council shall recommend to the Office of Victim Services program, legislative or other matters which would improve services to victims of crime and develop and coordinate needs assessments for both court-based and community-based victim services. The Chief Justice shall appoint two members to serve as cochairmen. Not later than December fifteenth of each year, the council shall report the results of its findings and activities to the Chief Court Administrator;

(12) To utilize such voluntary and uncompensated services of private individuals, agencies and organizations as may from time to time be offered and needed;

(13) To recommend policies and make recommendations to agencies and officers of the state and local subdivisions of government relative to victims of crime;

(14) To provide support and assistance to state-wide victim services coalitions and groups;

(15) Within available appropriations to establish a crime victims' information clearinghouse which shall be a central repository for information collected pursuant to subdivision (9) of this subsection and information made available through the criminal justice information system, to provide a toll-free telephone number for access to such information and to develop a plan, in consultation with all agencies required to provide notification to victims, outlining any needed statutory changes, resources and working agreements necessary to make the Office of Victim Services the lead agency for notification of victims, which plan shall be submitted to the General Assembly not later than February 15, 2000;

(16) To provide a training program for judges, prosecutors, police, probation and parole personnel, bail commissioners, intake, assessment and referral specialists, officers from the Department of Correction and judicial marshals to inform them of victims' rights and available services;

(17) To establish a sexual assault forensic examiners program that will train and make available sexual assault forensic examiners to adolescent and adult victims of sexual assault who are patients at participating acute care hospitals. In order to establish and implement such program, the Office of Victim Services may apply for, receive, allocate, disburse and account for grants of funds made available by the United States, the state, foundations, corporations and other businesses, agencies or individuals;

(18) To provide victims of crime and the general public with information detailing the process by which a victim may register to receive notices of hearings of the Board of Pardons and Paroles; and

(19) To submit to the joint standing committee of the General Assembly having cognizance of matters relating to victim services, in accordance with the provisions of section 11-4a, on or before January 15, 2000, and biennially thereafter a report of its activities under sections 54-201 to 54-233, inclusive, including, but not limited to, implementation of training activities and mandates. Such report shall include the types of training provided, entities providing training and recipients of training.

(P.A. 78-261, S. 3, 17; P.A. 80-390, S. 2, 5; P.A. 83-341; P.A. 85-609, S. 1; P.A. 86-401, S. 1; P.A. 87-514, S. 1, 4; 87-554, S. 2; P.A. 91-389, S. 10; P.A. 92-153, S. 3; P.A. 93-91, S. 1, 2; 93-262, S. 1, 87; 93-310, S. 2, 32; 93-381, S. 9, 39; P.A. 95-257, S. 12, 21, 58; P.A. 96-97, S. 1; P.A. 97-257, S. 3, 13; P.A. 99-184, S. 1 -3; P.A. 00-99, S. 125, 154; 00-196, S. 44; P.A. 04-234, S. 2; P.A. 05-288, S. 190; Sept. Sp. Sess. P.A. 09-3, S. 49; P.A. 12-114, S. 17; 12-133, S. 25; P.A. 13-214, S. 2; June Sp. Sess. P.A. 15-2, S. 18.)

History: P.A. 80-390 added Subdiv. (e) re implementation of programs to assist witnesses and crime victims; P.A. 83-341 amended Subsec. (e) to permit board to apply for and receive grants of funds for victim services program; P.A. 85-609 added Subsec. (f) re provision of comprehensive state-wide victim assistance program and appointment and assignment of victim advocates; P.A. 86-401 amended Subsec. (f) to permit transfer of any person employed in classified service as a victim advocate on October 1, 1986, to the criminal injuries compensation board as classified employee as victim advocate without reduction in salary or grade and added Subsec. (g) re written list of rights provided to victim; P.A. 87-514 added Subsecs. (h) to (k), inclusive, adding duty to provide victims' rights information and telephone hotline for referrals; to continue study by task force on civil liability, assist in implementing recommendations thereof and report findings; to utilize voluntary services and recommend policies to state and local government re rights of victims of crime and victims of torts; P.A. 87-554 changed name of "criminal injuries compensation board" to "commission on victim services"; P.A. 91-389 amended Subsec. (a) to include notice of the availability of "assistance" to crime victims, inserted a new Subsec. (c) to authorize the commission to request information to verify that a person who has requested notification pursuant to Sec. 54-228 was a victim of crime and relettering the remaining Subsecs. accordingly, amended Subsec. (g) to delete provision re transfer to the commission as a classified employee any person employed in the unclassified service as a victim advocate on October 1, 1986, added Subsec. (h)(6) to (10), inclusive, re additional rights of victims to be included in the list, inserted a new Subsec. (j) re the establishment of a victims' notification clearinghouse and the notification of persons who have requested notification, relettering the remaining Subsecs. accordingly, deleted former Subsec. (j) re the study by the task force on civil liability, and added Subsec. (l) re the establishment, composition and duties of a victim services coordinating council, relettering the remaining Subsec. accordingly; P.A. 92-153 established division of crime victims' compensation and division of victim services under supervision of executive director and deputy directors, revised provisions re coordination of victim services, added provision re notification of victims of family violence crimes and modification or termination of criminal orders of protection not later than April 1, 1993, deleted provision re victim services coordinating council and added provision re state advisory council and added responsibility of development of comprehensive plan for administration of crime victims' compensation and coordination of delivery of services in coordination with department of human resources, department of health services, office of policy and management, judicial branch, department of children and youth services and division of criminal justice; P.A. 93-91 substituted commissioner and department of children and families for commissioner and department of children and youth services, effective July 1, 1993; P.A. 93-262 authorized substitution of commissioner and department of social services for commissioner and department of human resources, effective July 1, 1993; P.A. 93-310 revised section by deleting references to victim compensation commission, establishing office of victim compensation within the judicial department, deleting references to victims of torts, adding deadline of January 1, 1994, for establishment of victims' notification clearinghouse, requiring chief justice to appoint members of council, including the chief victim compensation commissioner, and two members to serve as cochairmen, effective July 1, 1993; P.A. 93-381 replaced department of health services with department of public health and addiction services, effective July 1, 1993; P.A. 95-257 replaced Commissioner and Department of Public Health and Addiction Services with Commissioner and Department of Public Health, effective July 1, 1995; P.A. 96-97 amended Subsec. (b)(9) by adding "scheduled to be" before "released"; P.A. 97-257 amended Subsec. (b)(8) by adding "Within available appropriations, to establish a victim's assistance center which shall" and added Subdivs. (16) re establishment of victim's information clearinghouse and provision of toll-free number for access to information and (17) re training program for judges, prosecutors, police, probation and parole personnel, bail commissioners, correctional officers and special deputy sheriffs, effective July 1, 1997; P.A. 99-184 amended Subsec. (b)(6) by adding provision that training and technical assistance for providers and development and implementation of public education campaigns may be provided by nonprofit or for-profit organizations or local units of government, amended Subsec. (b)(16) by adding provision requiring the Office of Victim Services to develop a plan in consultation with other agencies for notification of victims, making Office of Victim Services the lead agency for notification of victims and requiring plan to be submitted to General Assembly not later than February 15, 2000, and added Subdiv. (18) requiring Office of Victim Services to submit report of its activities, including training activities and mandates, to the General Assembly on or before January 15, 2000, and biennially thereafter; P.A. 00-99 replaced reference to special deputy sheriffs with judicial marshals in Subsec. (b)(17), effective December 1, 2000; P.A. 00-196 made a technical change in Subsec. (b)(18); P.A. 04-234 replaced Board of Pardons and Board of Parole with Board of Pardons and Paroles, effective July 1, 2004; P.A. 05-288 made a technical change in Subsec. (b)(16), effective July 13, 2005; Sept. Sp. Sess. P.A. 09-3 amended Subsec. (b) to add new Subdiv. (18) re establishment of sexual assault forensic examiners program and redesignate existing Subdiv. (18) as Subdiv. (19), effective October 6, 2009; P.A. 12-114 amended Subsec. (b)(7) to add Subpara. (K) re notice to victim that probation officer has notified police officer of probable cause re probation violation by offender; P.A. 12-133 amended Subsec. (b) to substitute "helpline" for "hotline" in Subdiv. (10), delete former Subdiv. (15) re development of comprehensive plan to administer crime victims' compensation, redesignate existing Subdivs. (16) to (19) as Subdivs. (15) to (18), add "intake, assessment and referral specialists" in redesignated Subdiv. (16), and make technical changes; P.A. 13-214 amended Subsec. (b)(7)(K) to add provision re notice to any victim advocate assigned to assist the

Sec. 54-204. Application for compensation or restitution services. Report and examination. Confidential information.

(a) Any person who may be eligible for compensation or restitution services, or both, pursuant to sections 54-201 to 54-233, inclusive, may make application therefor to the Office of Victim Services. If the person entitled to make application is a minor or incompetent person, the application may be made on such person's behalf by a parent, guardian or other legal representative of the minor or incompetent person.

(b) In order to be eligible for compensation or restitution services under sections 54-201 to 54-233, inclusive, the applicant shall prior to a determination on any application made pursuant to sections 54-201 to 54-233, inclusive, submit reports if reasonably available from all physicians or surgeons or advanced practice registered nurses who have treated or examined the victim in relation to the injury for which compensation is claimed at the time of or subsequent to the victim's injury or death. If in the opinion of the Office of Victim Services or, on review, a victim compensation commissioner, reports on the previous medical history of the victim, examination of the injured victim and a report thereon or a report on the cause of death of the victim by an impartial medical expert would be of material aid to its just determination, said office or commissioner shall order such reports and examinations. Any information received which is confidential in accordance with any provision of the general statutes shall remain confidential while in the custody of the Office of Victim Services or a victim compensation commissioner.

(P.A. 78-261, S. 4, 17; P.A. 79-505, S. 1, 7; P.A. 87-554, S. 3; P.A. 91-39; P.A. 93-310, S. 3, 32; P.A. 16-39, S. 72.)

History: P.A. 79-505 added references to restitution services; P.A. 87-554 substituted "commission" for "board"; P.A. 91-39 amended Subsec. (b) by adding provision that confidential information received by the commission shall remain confidential while in the custody of the commission; P.A. 93-310 changed "commission" to "office of victims services", added "of the minor or incompetent person" after "representative", changed "hearing" to "determination", changed "commission or hearing examiner" to "office of victim services or, on review, a victim compensation commissioner" and "office of victim services or a victim compensation commissioner", effective July 1, 1993; P.A. 16-39 amended Subsec. (b) by adding reference to advanced practice registered nurses.

Sec. 54-205. Evaluation of application. Determination. Request for review by compensation commissioner.

(a) Upon application made under the provisions of sections 54-201 to 54-233, inclusive, the Office of Victim Services shall evaluate such application, make an appropriate determination in writing, and provide notice to the applicant of such determination. In order to make a determination on an application, the Office of Victim Services may administer oaths or affirmations, may subpoena any witness to appear or may issue a subpoena duces tecum, provided no subpoena shall be issued except under the signature of a victim compensation commissioner. Any application to any court for aid in enforcing such subpoena may be made in the name of the Office of Victim Services only by a victim compensation commissioner. Subpoenas shall be served by any person designated by a victim compensation commissioner.

(b) An applicant may request that a determination made pursuant to subsection (a) of this section be reviewed by a victim compensation commissioner by filing a request for review with the Office of Victim Services, on a form prescribed by the Office of the Chief Court Administrator, within thirty days from mailing of the notice of such determination.

(c) For the purposes of carrying out the provisions of sections 54-201 to 54-233, inclusive, a victim compensation commissioner shall hear any request for review filed by an applicant pursuant to sections 54-201 to 54-233, inclusive, to which such commissioner is assigned and shall make a written determination on such application for compensation. A victim compensation commissioner shall hold such hearings and take such testimony as such commissioner may deem advisable. A commissioner may administer oaths or affirmations to witnesses and shall have full power to subpoena any witness to appear and give testimony or to issue a subpoena duces tecum. Subpoenas shall be served by any person designated by a victim compensation commissioner.

(d) No witness under subpoena authorized to be issued by the provisions of this section shall be excused from testifying or from producing records, papers or documents. If any person disobeys such process or, having appeared in obedience thereto, refuses to answer any pertinent question put to him by the victim compensation commissioner or to produce any records, papers or documents and appears pursuant thereto, said commissioner may apply to the superior court for the judicial district of Hartford, setting forth such disobedience to process or refusal to answer. The court shall cite such person to appear before said court to answer such question or to produce such records, papers or documents or to show cause why a question put to him should not be answered or why such records, papers or documents should not be produced. Upon such person's refusal to answer or produce records, papers or documents or to show cause, the court may commit such person to a community correctional center until such person complies, but not for a longer period than sixty days. Notwithstanding any such commitment of such person, the victim compensation commissioner may proceed with the hearing as if such witness had testified adversely regarding his interest in the proceeding.

(e) The applicant and any other person having a substantial interest in a proceeding may appear before the victim compensation commissioner and be heard, produce evidence and cross-examine witnesses in person or by his attorney. The victim compensation commissioner also may hear such other persons as in the commissioner's judgment may have relevant evidence to submit.

(f) Any statement, document, information or matter may be considered by the Office of Victim Services or, on review, by a victim compensation commissioner, if in the opinion of said office or commissioner, it contributes to a determination of the claim, whether or not the same would be admissible in a court of law.

(g) If any person has been convicted of any offense with respect to an act on which a claim under sections 54-201 to 54-233, inclusive, is based, proof of that conviction shall be taken as conclusive evidence that the offense has been committed by such person, unless an appeal or any proceeding with regard thereto is pending.

(P.A. 78-261, S. 5, 17; P.A. 87-554, S. 4; P.A. 93-142, S. 4, 7, 8; 93-310, S. 4, 32; P.A. 95-220, S. 4-6; P.A. 96-97, S. 2; P.A. 03-189, S. 1.)

History: P.A. 87-554 changed "board" to "commission"; P.A. 93-310 revised section, changing "commission" to "office of victim services", changing "hearing" to "determination", providing revised procedure for determination of claims by office of victim services and upon request of applicant, review by a victim compensation commissioner and adding provision re witness under subpoena, effective July 1, 1993 (Revisor's note: P.A. 88-230, P.A. 90-98 and P.A. 93-142 authorized substitution of "judicial district of Hartford" for "judicial district of Hartford-New Britain" in public acts of the 1993 session of the general assembly, effective September 1, 1996); P.A. 95-220 changed the effective date of P.A. 88-230 from September 1, 1996, to September 1, 1998, effective July 1, 1995; P.A. 96-97 amended Subsec. (b) by increasing time for filing a request for review from 14 to 30 days from mailing notice of determination; P.A. 03-189 amended Subsec. (a) by replacing "review such application" with "evaluate such application".

Sec. 54-206. Payment of attorneys as part of order.

The Office of Victim Services or, on review, a victim compensation commissioner may, as part of any order entered under sections 54-201 to 54-233, inclusive, determine and allow reasonable attorney's fees, which shall not exceed fifteen per cent of the amount awarded as compensation under section 54-208, to be paid out of but not in addition to the amount of such compensation. No such attorney shall ask for, contract for or receive any larger sum than the amount so allowed.

(P.A. 78-261, S. 6, 17; P.A. 87-554, S. 5; P.A. 93-310, S. 5, 32; P.A. 01-211, S. 19; P.A. 03-189, S. 2.)

History: P.A. 87-554 substituted "commission" for "board"; P.A. 93-310 changed "The commission" to "A victim compensation commissioner", effective July 1, 1993; P.A. 01-211 designated existing provisions as Subsec. (a) and added new Subsec. (b) re direct payment to health care providers for health care services rendered to the victim; P.A. 03-189 deleted Subsec. (a) designator, added reference to the Office of Victim Services and provision re review by victim compensation commissioner and deleted former Subsec. (b) re payment to health care providers.

Sec. 54-207. Regulations to prescribe procedures. Section 54-207 is repealed, effective July 1, 1993.

(P.A. 78-261, S. 7, 17; P.A. 87-554, S. 6; P.A. 92-153, S. 7; P.A. 93-310, S. 31, 32.)

Sec. 54-207a. Chief Court Administrator to prescribe policies and procedures.

The Office of the Chief Court Administrator shall prescribe such policies and procedures, as deemed necessary, to implement the provisions of sections 54-201 to 54-233, inclusive, and may formulate standards for the uniform application of the payment of compensation of claims.

(P.A. 93-310, S. 6, 32.)

History: P.A. 93-310 effective July 1, 1993.

Sec. 54-208. Order of payment of compensation. Criminal intent. Circumstances considered. Prosecution not necessary. Amount and manner of payments. Unclaimed award.

(a) If a person is injured or killed as provided in section 54-209, the Office of Victim Services or, on review, a victim compensation commissioner may order the payment of compensation in accordance with the provisions of sections 54-201 to 54-233, inclusive: (1) To or for the benefit of the injured person; (2) in the case of personal injury of the victim, to any person responsible for the maintenance of the victim who has suffered pecuniary loss as a result of such injury; or (3) in the case of death of the victim, to or for the benefit of any one or more of the dependents of the victim including any dependent child of a homicide victim who was killed by the other parent or to any person who has suffered pecuniary loss, including but not limited to funeral expenses, as a result of such death.

(b) For the purposes of sections 54-201 to 54-233, inclusive, a person shall be deemed to have intended an act notwithstanding that, by reason of age, insanity, drunkenness or otherwise, he was legally incapable of forming a criminal intent.

(c) In determining whether to make an order under this section, the Office of Victim Services or, on review, a victim compensation commissioner shall consider all circumstances determined to be relevant, including but not limited to provocation, consent or any other behavior of the victim which directly or indirectly contributed to such victim's injury or death, the extent of the victim's cooperation in investigating the application and the extent of the victim's cooperation with law enforcement agencies in their efforts to apprehend and prosecute the offender, and any other relevant matters.

(d) An order may be made under this section whether or not any person is prosecuted or convicted of any offense arising out of such act. Upon application made by an appropriate prosecuting authority, the Office of Victim Services or a victim compensation commissioner may suspend making any determination or any proceedings, as the case may be, under sections 54-201 to 54-233, inclusive, for such period as it deems appropriate on the ground that a prosecution for an offense arising out of such act or omission has been commenced or is imminent.

(e) In determining the amount of compensation to be allowed, the Office of Victim Services or, on review, a victim compensation commissioner shall take into consideration amounts that the applicant has received or is eligible to receive from any other source or sources, including, but not limited to, payments from state and municipal agencies, health insurance benefits, and workers' compensation awards, as a result of the incident or offense giving rise to the application. For purposes of this section, life insurance benefits received by the applicant shall not be taken into consideration by the Office of Victim Services or a victim compensation commissioner.

(f) Payments shall be made in a manner to be determined by the Office of Victim Services, including, but not limited to, lump sum or periodic payments. If an award is not claimed by the applicant within forty-five days after notice of the award, the Office of Victim Services may vacate such award or may order payments from such award to health care providers or victim service providers and vacate any remaining amount of such award.

(P.A. 78-261, S. 8, 17; P.A. 80-90; P.A. 82-397, S. 1, 7; P.A. 87-554, S. 7; P.A. 93-310, S. 7, 32; P.A. 95-175, S. 5; P.A. 02-132, S. 79; P.A. 15-85, S. 22.)

History: P.A. 80-90 amended Subsec. (a)(3) to include payments to victim's estate; P.A. 82-397 deleted references to "incurred expenses" associated with injury or death in Subsec. (a), referring instead to "pecuniary loss" in both instances, added provision re extent of victim's cooperation with board and law enforcement agencies in Subsec. (c), restated Subsec. (e) and added specific reference to payments from state and municipal agencies, insurance benefits and workers' compensation awards and added Subsec. (f) re method of payment; P.A. 87-554 changed "board" to "commission" and amended Subsec. (a) by adding "including any child of a homicide victim who was killed by the other parent, provided the proceeds of any payment of compensation shall be placed in a trust fund for the benefit of any such child until such child or children reach the age of eighteen"; P.A. 93-310 changed "commission" to "office of victim services, or on review a victim compensation commissioner", made technical changes, and in Subsec. (f) changed "commission" to "office of victim services", eliminated annuities or deposits in accounts held in trust for applicant and added provision permitting vacation of award if not claimed within 45 days, effective July 1, 1993; P.A. 95-175 amended Subsec. (c) to delete "need for financial aid" as factor to be considered; P.A. 02-132 amended Subsec. (f) by adding provisions re order of payments to health care providers or victim service providers from unclaimed award and making technical changes; P.A. 15-85 amended Subsec. (e) by substituting "health insurance benefits" for "insurance benefits", adding provision re Office of Victim Services or victim compensation commissioner not to consider life insurance benefits received by applicant, and making technical changes.

Sec. 54-209. When compensation may be ordered. Order inadmissible in civil or criminal proceeding.

(a) The Office of Victim Services or, on review, a victim compensation commissioner may order the payment of compensation in accordance with the provisions of sections 54-201 to 54-233, inclusive, for personal injury or death which resulted from: (1) An attempt to prevent the commission of crime or to apprehend a suspected criminal or in aiding or attempting to aid a police officer so to do, (2) the commission or attempt to commit by another of any crime as provided in section 53a-24, (3) any crime involving international terrorism as defined in Section 2331 of Title 18 of the United States Code.

(b) The Office of Victim Services or, on review, a victim compensation commissioner may also order the payment of compensation in accordance with the provisions of sections 54-201 to 54-233, inclusive, for personal injury or death that resulted from the operation of a motor vehicle by another person who was subsequently convicted with respect to such operation for a violation of subsection (a) or subdivision (1) of subsection (b) of section 14-224, section

14-227a or 14-227m, subdivision (1) or (2) of subsection (a) of section 14-227n or section 53a-56b or 53a-60d. In the absence of a conviction, the Office of Victim Services or, on review, a victim compensation commissioner may order payment of compensation under this section if, upon consideration of all circumstances determined to be relevant, the office or commissioner, as the case may be, reasonably concludes that another person has operated a motor vehicle in violation of subsection (a) or subdivision (1) of subsection (b) of section 14-224, section 14-227a or 14-227m, subdivision (1) or (2) of subsection (a) of section 14-227n or section 53a-56b or 53a-60d.

(c) Except as provided in subsection (b) of this section, no act involving the operation of a motor vehicle which results in injury shall constitute a crime for the purposes of sections 54-201 to 54-233, inclusive, unless the injuries were intentionally inflicted through the use of the vehicle.

(d) In instances where a violation of section 53-21, 53a-70, 53a-70a, 53a-70b, 53a-70c, 53a-71, 53a-72a, 53a-72b or 53a-73a has been alleged, the Office of Victim Services or, on review, a victim compensation commissioner may order compensation be paid if (1) the personal injury has been disclosed to: (A) A physician or surgeon licensed under chapter 370; (B) a resident physician or intern in any hospital in this state, whether or not licensed; (C) a physician assistant licensed under chapter 370; (D) an advanced practice registered nurse, registered nurse or practical nurse licensed under chapter 378; (E) a psychologist licensed under chapter 383; (F) a police officer; (G) a mental health professional; (H) an emergency medical services provider licensed or certified under chapter 368d; (I) an alcohol and drug counselor licensed or certified under chapter 376b; (J) a marital and family therapist licensed under chapter 383a; (K) a domestic violence counselor or a sexual assault counselor, as defined in section 52-146k; (L) a professional counselor licensed under chapter 383c; (M) a clinical social worker licensed under chapter 383b; or (N) an employee of the Department of Children and Families; and (2) the office or commissioner, as the case may be, reasonably concludes that a violation of any of said sections has occurred.

(e) Evidence of an order for the payment of compensation by the Office of Victim Services or a victim compensation commissioner in accordance with the provisions of sections 54-201 to 54-233, inclusive, shall not be admissible in any civil proceeding to prove the liability of any person for such personal injury or death or in any criminal proceeding to prove the guilt or innocence of any person for any crime.

(P.A. 78-261, S. 9, 17; P.A. 85-529, S. 2, 4; P.A. 87-554, S. 8; P.A. 89-49; P.A. 93-310, S. 8, 32; P.A. 95-175, S. 6; P.A. 97-59, S. 1, 4; P.A. 12-133, S. 26; P.A. 13-214, S. 14; P.A. 14-130, S. 39; P.A. 16-126, S. 37.)

History: P.A. 85-529 inserted Subsec. indicators and added Subsec. (a)(3) and an exception to Subsec. (b) to authorize the board to pay compensation for injury or death resulting from the operation of a motor vehicle by another person subsequently convicted of a violation of Sec. 14-227a, 53a-56b or 53a-60d; P.A. 87-554 changed "board" to "commission"; P.A. 89-49 inserted new Subsec. (b) permitting payment of compensation in absence of conviction if commission reasonably concludes person operated motor vehicle in violation of Sec. 14-227a, 53a-56b or 53a-60d, relettering former Subsec. (b) accordingly, and added Subsec. (d) re inadmissibility of order of compensation in civil or criminal proceeding to prove liability or guilt or innocence of any person; P.A. 93-310 changed "commission" to "office of victim services or, on review, a victim compensation commissioner", effective July 1, 1993; P.A. 95-175 amended Subsecs. (a) and (b) by adding references to Sec. 14-224(a); P.A. 97-59 added Subsec. (a)(4) re crime involving international terrorism,

413

effective May 8, 1997; P.A. 12-133 amended Subsec. (a) by deleting former Subdiv. (3) re operation of motor vehicle by another person who was subsequently convicted of violation and redesignating existing Subdiv. (4) as Subdiv. (3), replaced former Subsec. (b) with new Subsec. (b) re compensation in cases involving motor vehicle violations, made a conforming change in Subsec. (c), added new Subsec. (d) re order to pay compensation if personal injury is disclosed to and conclusion re violation is made by certain professionals, and redesignated existing Subsec. (d) as Subsec. (e); P.A. 13-214 amended Subsec. (d)(1)(K) to substitute "domestic violence counselor" for "battered women's counselor"; P.A. 14-130 amended Subsec. (b) by adding references to Sec. 14-224(b)(1); P.A. 16-126 amended Subsec. (b) by adding references to Secs. 14-227m and 14-227n(a)(1) and (2).

Sec. 54-210. Compensation ordered for expenses, loss of earnings, pecuniary loss and other losses.

(a) The Office of Victim Services or a victim compensation commissioner may order the payment of compensation under sections 54-201 to 54-233, inclusive, for: (1) Expenses actually and reasonably incurred as a result of the personal injury or death of the victim, provided coverage for the cost of medical care and treatment of a crime victim who does not have medical insurance or who has exhausted coverage under applicable health insurance policies or Medicaid shall be ordered; (2) loss of earning power as a result of total or partial incapacity of such victim; (3) pecuniary loss to the spouse or dependents of the deceased victim, provided the family qualifies for compensation as a result of murder or manslaughter of the victim; (4) pecuniary loss to the relatives or dependents of a deceased victim for attendance at court proceedings with respect to the criminal case of the person or persons charged with committing the crime that resulted in the death of the victim; and (5) any other loss, except as set forth in section 54-211, resulting from the personal injury or death of the victim which the Office of Victim Services or a victim compensation commissioner, as the case may be, determines to be reasonable.

(b) Payment of compensation under sections 54-201 to 54-233, inclusive, may be made to a person who is a recipient of public assistance or state-administered general assistance for necessary and reasonable expenses related to injuries resulting from a crime and not provided for by the income assistance program in which such person is a participant. Unless required by federal law, no such payment shall be considered an asset for purposes of eligibility for such assistance.

(P.A. 78-261, S. 10, 17; P.A. 87-217; 87-554, S. 9; P.A. 92-153, S. 6; P.A. 93-310, S. 9, 32; P.A. 97-257, S. 5, 13; June 18 Sp. Sess. P.A. 97-2, S. 111, 165; P.A. 99-128, S. 1; 99-184, S. 4; P.A. 00-200, S. 1; P.A. 04-76, S. 41; P.A. 10-43, S. 36; P.A. 12-133, S. 27.)

History: P.A. 87-217 added Subsec. (b) permitting board to order compensation to recipient of income assistance for expenses related to injuries resulting from crime and not provided for by income assistance program and providing that no such payment shall be considered asset for purposes of eligibility for assistance unless required by federal law; P.A. 87-554 changed "board" to "commission"; P.A. 92-153 made no change; P.A. 93-310 changed "commission" to "office of victim services" or "office of victim services or a victim compensation commissioner, as the case may be", effective July 1, 1993; P.A. 97-257 amended Subsec. (a) by requiring order of coverage for cost of medical care of victim who does not have medical insurance or who has exhausted coverage, effective July 1, 1998; June 18 Sp. Sess. P.A. 97-2 amended Subsec. (b) to make technical and conforming changes re references to assistance programs, effective July 1, 1997; P.A. 99-128 amended Subsec. (a) by adding provision re compensation for pecuniary loss to relatives or

Sec. 54-211. Time limitation on filing application for compensation. Restrictions on award of compensation. Amount of compensation.

(a)(1) No order for the payment of compensation shall be made under section 54-210 unless (A) the application has been made within two years after the date of the personal injury or death, (B) the personal injury or death was the result of an incident or offense listed in section 54-209, and (C) such incident or offense has been reported to the police within five days of its occurrence or, if the incident or offense could not reasonably have been reported within such period, within five days of the time when a report could reasonably have been made, except that a victim of a sexual assault shall not be ineligible for the payment of compensation by reason of failing to make a report pursuant to this subparagraph if such victim presented himself or herself to a health care facility within seventy-two hours of such sexual assault for examination and collection of evidence of such sexual assault in accordance with the provisions of section 19a-112a. (2) Notwithstanding the provisions of subdivision (1) of this subsection, any person who, before, on or after October 1, 2005, fails to make application for compensation within two years after the date of the personal injury or death as a result of physical, emotional or psychological injuries caused by such personal injury or death may apply for a waiver of such time limitation. The Office of Victim Services, upon a finding of such physical, emotional or psychological injury, may grant such waiver. (3) Notwithstanding the provisions of subdivision (1) of this subsection, any minor, including, but not limited to, a minor who is a victim of conduct by another person that constitutes a violation of section 53a-192a or a criminal violation of 18 USC Chapter 77, who, before, on or after October 1, 2005, fails to make application for compensation within two years after the date of the personal injury or death through no fault of the minor, may apply for a waiver of such time limitation. The Office of Victim Services, upon a finding that such minor is not at fault, may grant such waiver. (4) Notwithstanding the provisions of subdivision (1) of this subsection, a person who is a dependent of a victim may make application for payment of compensation not later than two years from the date that such person discovers or in the exercise of reasonable care should have discovered that the person upon whom the applicant was dependent was a victim or ninety days after May 26, 2000, whichever is later. Such person shall file with such application a statement signed under penalty of false statement setting forth the date when such person discovered that the person upon whom the applicant was dependent was a victim and the circumstances that prevented such person discovering that the person upon whom the applicant was dependent was a victim until more than two years after the date of the incident or offense. There shall be a rebuttable presumption that a person who files such a statement and is otherwise eligible for compensation pursuant to sections 54-201 to 54-233, inclusive, is entitled to compensation. (5) Any waiver denied by the Office of Victim Services under this subsection may be reviewed by a victim compensation commissioner, provided such request for review is made by the applicant within thirty days from the mailing of the notice of denial by the Office of Victim Services. If a victim compensation commissioner grants such waiver, the commissioner shall refer the application for compensation to the Office of Victim Services for a determination pursuant to section 54-205. (6) Notwithstanding the provisions of subdivision (1), (2) or (3) of this subsection, the Office of Victim Services may, for good cause shown and upon a finding of compelling equitable circumstances, waive the time limitations of subdivision (1) of this subsection.

(b) No compensation shall be awarded if: (1) The offender is unjustly enriched by the award, provided compensation awarded to a victim which would benefit the offender in a minimal or inconsequential manner shall not be considered unjust enrichment; (2) the victim violated a penal law of this state, which violation caused or contributed to his injuries or death.

(c) No compensation shall be awarded for losses sustained for crimes against property or for noneconomic detriment such as pain and suffering.

(d) (1) No compensation shall be in an amount in excess of fifteen thousand dollars except that compensation to or for the benefit of the dependents of a homicide victim shall be in an amount not to exceed twenty-five thousand dollars. The claims of the dependents of a deceased victim, as provided in section 54-208, shall be considered derivative of the claim of such victim and the total compensation paid for all claims arising from the death of such victim shall not exceed a maximum of twenty-five thousand dollars.

(2) Notwithstanding the provisions of subdivision (1) of this subsection, the Office of Victim Services or a victim compensation commissioner may, for good cause shown and upon a finding of compelling equitable circumstances, award compensation in an amount in excess of the maximum amounts set forth in said subdivision.

(e) Orders for payment of compensation pursuant to sections 54-201 to 54-233, inclusive, may be made only as to injuries or death resulting from incidents or offenses arising on and after January 1, 1979, except that orders for payment of compensation pursuant to subsection (b) of section 54-209 may be made only as to injuries or death resulting from incidents or offenses arising on and after July 1, 1985.

(f) Compensation shall be awarded pursuant to sections 54-201 to 54-233, inclusive, for bodily injury or death resulting from a crime which occurs (1) within this state, regardless of the residency of the applicant; (2) outside this state but within the territorial boundaries of the United States, provided the victim, at the time of injury or death, was a resident of this state and the state in which such crime occurred does not have a program for compensation of victims for which such victim is eligible; and (3) outside the territorial boundaries of the United States, provided the applicant is a victim of international terrorism, as defined in Section 2331 of Title 18 of the United States Code, and was a resident of this state at the time of injury or death.

(P.A. 78-261, S. 11, 17; P.A. 81-23, S. 1; P.A. 82-397, S. 4, 7; P.A. 85-529, S. 3, 4; 85-538, S. 3; P.A. 87-554, S. 10; P.A. 90-22, S. 1; 90-279, S. 1; P.A. 93-310, S. 10, 32; P.A. 95-175, S. 7; P.A. 97-59, S. 2, 4; P.A. 00-110, S. 1, 2; P.A. 05-249, S. 7; P.A. 06-100, S. 2, 3; P.A. 12-133, S. 28; P.A. 15-195, S. 6.)

History: P.A. 81-23 added Subsec. (e) prohibiting compensation to nonresident victims unless a reciprocal victim compensation provision has been enacted in the state in which the victim is a resident; P.A. 82-397 amended Subsec. (a) by deleting provision prohibiting compensation award if victim is relative of offender or living with offender as member of family or household or maintaining a sexual relationship with offender or member of family of offender and added prohibition of compensation to victim if offender benefits or if victim was living with offender by mutual consent in relationship of cohabitation, regardless of legal status, and amended Subsec. (c) by deleting requirement that all payments be made in a lump sum; P.A. 85-529 amended Subsec. (d) by providing that compensation pursuant to Sec. 54-209(a)(3) is limited to incidents or offenses arising on and after July 1, 1985; P.A. 85-538 amended Subsec. (b) adding "unless the parties have separated, are no longer in a relationship of cohabitation and there is no expectation that the parties will resume a relationship of cohabitation in the future, and deleted Subsec. (e) which required reciprocity for nonresident victim; P.A. 87-554 amended Subsec. (c) by increasing maximum compensation to $15,000, except that the maximum compensation for dependents of homicide victim shall be $25,000 and providing that claims of dependents of deceased victim shall be considered derivative of claim of victim and total of all claims shall not exceed $25,000, and amended Subsec. (e) re compensation for bodily injury or death from crime occurring in this state, regardless of residency of the applicant; P.A. 90-22 amended Subsec. (b) by adding provisions prohibiting compensation if offender may be unjustly enriched and amended Subsec. (e) by authorizing award of compensation to resident victim of a crime committed outside the state; P.A. 90-279 amended Subsec. (a) by permitting application for and granting of waiver of time limitation for benefits if failure to file within two-year period was a result of physical, emotional or psychological injuries or the negligence of the parent, guardian or custodian of a minor who failed to file within the two-year period; P.A. 93-310 changed "commission" to "office of victim services", added provision re review of denial of waiver, deleted provision in Subsec. (b) re investigation where unjust enrichment, added provision prohibiting compensation for crimes against property or for noneconomic detriment such as pain and suffering and made technical changes, effective July 1, 1993; P.A. 95-175 amended Subsec. (a) by replacing failure to make application through "negligence of the parent, guardian or custodian" of a minor with failure to apply "through no fault of" the minor; P.A. 97-59 amended Subsec. (a) by changing "fourteen" days from the mailing of the notice of denial to "thirty" days from such mailing, amended Subsec. (f)(2) by adding "but within the territorial boundaries of the United States" and added Subdiv. (3) re crime outside territorial boundaries provided applicant is victim of international terrorism and resident of state at time of injury or death, effective May 8, 1997; P.A. 00-110 added new Subsec. (a)(4) re time limitation and procedure for a person to make application for compensation upon discovering that the person upon whom the applicant was dependent was a victim, redesignating former Subdiv. (4) as Subdiv. (5), effective May 26, 2000; P.A. 05-249 amended Subsec. (a)(2) to make provisions applicable to any person who "before, on or after October 1, 2005," fails to make a timely application for compensation and delete the condition that an application for a waiver be filed not later than six years after the date of the personal injury or death, amended Subsec. (a)(3) to make provisions applicable to any minor who "before, on or after October 1, 2005," fails to make a timely application for compensation and delete the condition that an application for a waiver be filed not later than two years after the minor attains the age of majority or seven years after the date of the personal injury or death, whichever is sooner, and made technical changes in Subsec. (a); P.A. 06-100 amended Subsec. (a) to insert Subpara. designators and make technical changes in Subdiv. (1), add exception in Subdiv. (1)(C) re sexual assault victim who presents himself or herself to health care facility within 72 hours for examination and collection of evidence of such sexual assault, and add Subdiv. (6) authorizing office to waive time limitations of Subdiv. (1) for good cause shown and upon a finding of compelling equitable circumstances and amended Subsec. (d) to designate existing provisions as Subdiv. (1) and add Subdiv. (2) authorizing office to award compensation in excess of maximum amounts set forth in Subdiv. (1) for good cause shown and upon finding of compelling equitable circumstances; P.A. 12-133 amended Subsec. (d)(1) by deleting provision re no compensation awarded for first $100 of injury sustained and making a technical change and amended Subsec. (e) by substituting "subsection (b) of section 54-209" for "subdivision (3) of subsection (a) of section 54-209"; P.A. 15-195 amended Subsec. (a)(3) to add provision re waiver of time limits of Subsec. (a)(1) for minor who is a victim of conduct that constitutes a violation of Sec. 53a-192a or a criminal violation of 18 USC Chapter 77.

Sec. 54-211a. Appeal.

Any applicant aggrieved by an order or decision of a victim compensation commissioner may appeal by way of a demand for a trial de novo to the superior court for the judicial district of Hartford. The appeal shall be taken within thirty days after mailing of the order or decision, or if there is no mailing, within thirty days after personal delivery of such order or decision.

(P.A. 82-397, S. 3, 7; P.A. 87-554, S. 11; P.A. 88-230, S. 1, 12; 88-364, S. 72, 123; P.A. 90-98, S. 1, 2; P.A. 93-142, S. 4, 7, 8; 93-310, S. 11, 32; P.A. 95-220, S. 4 6.)

History: P.A. 87-554 changed "board" to "commission"; P.A. 88-230 replaced "judicial district of Hartford-New Britain" with "judicial district of Hartford", effective September 1, 1991; P.A. 88-364 made technical changes; P.A. 90-98 changed the effective date of P.A. 88-230 from September 1, 1991, to September 1, 1993; P.A. 93-142 changed the effective date of P.A. 88-230 from September 1, 1993, to September 1, 1996, effective June 14, 1993; P.A. 93-310 changed "commission" to "victim compensation commissioner" and added provision re appeal by way of trial de novo and requirement that appeal be taken within 30 days, effective July 1, 1993; P.A. 95-220 changed the effective date of P.A. 88-230 from September 1, 1996, to September 1, 1998, effective July 1, 1995.

Appeal from decision of commissioner pursuant to section constitutes a civil action; plaintiff's service of process on defendant within 30 days of mailing of notice of commissioner's decision satisfies requirements of section. 319 C. 697.

Court lacked subject matter jurisdiction to hear administrative appeal and lacked authority to enter order to pay plaintiff's medical expenses where plaintiff failed to comply strictly with provisions of section and did not take appeal until approximately 210 days after receiving notice of commissioner's decision. 61 CA 151.

Sec. 54-212. Office of Victim Services to have subrogated cause of action against person responsible for crime.

(a) Whenever an order for the payment of compensation for personal injury or death or for the provision of restitution services is or has been made under sections 54-201 to 54-233, inclusive, the Office of Victim Services shall, upon payment of the amount of the order or the provision of such services,

418

be subrogated to the cause of action of the applicant against the person or persons responsible for such injury or death. The Attorney General, on behalf of the Office of Victim Services, shall be entitled to bring an action and, if the Attorney General declines to do so, the office may hire a private attorney to bring an action against such person or persons and to recover, whether by judgment, settlement or compromise settlement before or after judgment, the amount of damages sustained by the applicant and shall furnish the applicant with a copy of the action taken within thirty days of the filing of such action. If an amount greater than two-thirds of that paid pursuant to any such order is recovered and collected in any such action, whether by judgment, settlement or compromise settlement before or after judgment, the state shall pay the balance exceeding two-thirds of the amount paid pursuant to such order to the applicant less any costs and expenses incurred therefor.

(b) If the applicant brings an action against the person or persons responsible for such injury or death to recover damages arising out of the crime for which an award has been granted, or, if the applicant recovers money from any other source or sources including, but not limited to, payments from state or municipal agencies, insurance benefits or workers' compensation awards as a result of the incident or offense giving rise to the application, the Office of Victim Services shall have a lien on the applicant's recovery for the amount to which the office is entitled to reimbursement. If an action is brought by the applicant against the person or persons responsible for the injury or death, the applicant shall notify the Office of Victim Services of the filing of such complaint within thirty days of the filing of the complaint in court. Whenever an applicant recovers damages, whether by judgment, settlement or compromise settlement before or after judgment, from the person or persons responsible for such injury, and whenever an applicant recovers money from any other source or sources including, but not limited to, payments from state or municipal agencies, insurance benefits or workers' compensation awards as a result of the incident or offense giving rise to the application, the Office of Victim Services is entitled to reimbursement from the applicant for two-thirds of the amount paid pursuant to any order for the payment of compensation for personal injury or death or for the provision of restitution services.

(c) Notwithstanding the provisions of subsection (a) of this section, if the Office of Victim Services finds that enforcement of its subrogation rights would cause undue harm to the applicant, the office may abrogate such rights. Notwithstanding the provisions of subsection (b) of this section, if the Office of Victim Services finds that enforcement of its lien rights would cause undue harm to the applicant, the office may abrogate such rights. "Undue harm" includes, but is not limited to, considerations of victim safety and recovery by the applicant of an amount that is less than the applicant's compensable economic losses.

(P.A. 78-261, S. 12, 17; P.A. 79-505, S. 6, 7; P.A. 81-149; P.A. 82-397, S. 5, 7; P.A. 85-538, S. 4; P.A. 87-554, S. 12; P.A. 93-310, S. 12, 32; P.A. 95-175, S. 8; P.A. 12-133, S. 29.)

History: P.A. 79-505 added references to orders for provision of restitution services; P.A. 81-149 provided that if an amount greater than two-thirds of restitution payment is recovered by judgment or settlement, the state shall pay the excess to the applicant, less any costs and expenses, where previously the excess was paid to applicant when any amount greater than that paid was recovered; P.A. 82-397 enabled board to recover, whether by judgment settlement or compromise settlement before or after judgment the amount of damages sustained by applicant and to contract with private attorneys to undertake subrogation actions on its behalf and deleted provision re payment by state of balance exceeding two-thirds of amount paid pursuant to order;

P.A. 85-538 added provision that if an amount greater than two-thirds of order is recovered, the state shall pay balance exceeding two-thirds to the applicant less costs and expenses, and added Subsec. (b) stating whenever applicant recovers damages, the board is entitled to two-thirds of amount paid pursuant to order; P.A. 87-554 changed "board" to "commission" and amended Subsec. (a) by adding provision requiring commission to furnish applicant with copy of action to recover damages within 30 days of filing such action and requiring applicant who brings any such action to provide similar notice to commission; P.A. 93-310 changed "commission" to "office of victim services" and "the attorney general, on behalf of the office of victim services", added provision that if attorney general declines to bring an action, the office of victim services may hire private attorney to bring action, and made technical changes, effective July 1, 1993; P.A. 95-175 amended Subsec. (b) by adding provision re lien by Office of Victim Services on applicants recovery and added Subsec. (c) re abrogation of subrogation and lien rights if it would cause undue harm to the applicant; P.A. 12-133 amended Subsec. (b) by adding provision re Office of Victim Services to have a lien on any money received by applicant from any other source, adding provision re applicant to notify office when applicant recovers money from any other source as a result of incident or offense giving rise to the application and making a conforming change.

Sec. 54-213. Award not subject to execution or attachment.

No award made pursuant to sections 54-201 to 54-233, inclusive, shall be subject to execution or attachment other than for expenses resulting from the injury which is the basis for the claim.

(P.A. 78-261, S. 13, 17.)

Sec. 54-214. Annual report to legislature and to appropriations committee. Section 54-214 is repealed, effective July 1, 1993.

(P.A. 78-261, S. 14, 17; P.A. 82-397, S. 2, 7; P.A. 84-179; P.A. 85-609, S. 5; P.A. 87-554, S. 13; P.A. 92-153, S. 4; P.A. 93-310, S. 31, 32.)

Sec. 54-215. Criminal Injuries Compensation Fund.

(a) The Office of Victim Services shall establish a Criminal Injuries Compensation Fund for the purpose of funding the compensation and restitution services provided for by sections 54-201 to 54-233, inclusive. The fund may contain any moneys required by law to be deposited in the fund and shall be held by the Treasurer separate and apart from all other moneys, funds and accounts. The interest derived from the investment of the fund shall be credited to the fund. Amounts in the fund may be expended only pursuant to appropriation by the General Assembly, except that any recovery from the person or persons responsible for the injury or death or any reimbursement from the applicant received by the Office of Victim Services pursuant to section 54-212 and deposited in the fund may be expended in the subsequent fiscal year. Any balance remaining in the fund at the end of any fiscal year shall be carried forward in the fund for the fiscal year next succeeding.

(b) The cost paid into court under section 54-143 shall be deposited in the General Fund and shall be credited to and become a part of the Criminal Injuries Compensation Fund. Any restitution collected by the Court Support Services Division pursuant to section 46b-140, 53a-30 or 54-56e which is not disbursed within five years after the date such restitution is collected, because the victim could not be located, shall be deposited in the Criminal Injuries Compensation Fund. Any restitution collected pursuant to section 46b-140 or 54-56e on or before May 8, 1997, that has not been disbursed as of October 1, 2003, shall be deposited in the fund. If payment is awarded under section 54-210 and thereafter the court orders the defendant in the criminal case from which such injury or death resulted to make restitution, any money collected as restitution shall be paid to the fund unless the court directs otherwise. The Office of Victim Services may apply for and receive moneys for the fund from any federal, state or private source.

(c) Any administrative costs related to the operation of the Criminal Injuries Compensation Fund, including credits to and payments of compensation therefrom, shall be paid from the fund. Administrative costs of providing direct services, the proportionate share of any fixed costs associated with such services, the costs of providing direct services to victims and witnesses of crimes in accordance with subdivision (6) of subsection (b) of section 54-203, and any services offered by the Office of Victim Services to witnesses and victims of crime may be budgeted for payment from the fund.

(P.A. 78-261, S. 16, 17; P.A. 79-505, S. 2, 7; P.A. 80-390, S. 3, 5; P.A. 82-397, S. 6, 7; P.A. 86-312, S. 13, 21; P.A. 87-554, S. 14; P.A. 92-153, S. 5; May Sp. Sess. P.A. 92-14, S. 6, 11; P.A. 93-310, S. 13, 32; P.A. 97-59, S. 3, 4; P.A. 02-132, S. 50; P.A. 03-189, S. 3; 03-278, S. 112; P.A. 10-43, S. 35.)

History: P.A. 79-505 added reference to restitution services and deleted provision requiring termination of fund on June 30, 1979, and transfer of remaining moneys to general fund; P.A. 80-390 deleted specific reference to ten-dollar cost under Sec. 54-143, that amount having been increased and specified that costs of services to witnesses and crime victims are to be paid from fund; P.A. 82-397 included cost of encouraging volunteer activities on board's behalf as administrative cost and required board to invest balance of fund in short term investment fund, with any interest earned deposited in criminal injuries compensation fund, effective July 1, 1983; P.A. 86-312 changed criminal injuries compensation "fund" to a separate nonlapsing "account" within the general fund; P.A. 87-554 changed "board" to "commission" and authorized commission to apply for and receive state funds; P.A. 92-153 changed "account" to "fund" and provided that amounts in fund may be expended only pursuant to appropriation by the general assembly, and deleted costs of volunteer activities and costs of services to witnesses and victims of crime from payments to be made from the fund; May Sp. Sess. P.A. 92-14 added provision that administrative costs of direct services and proportionate share of fixed costs for such services to witnesses and victims of crime may be paid from the fund; P.A. 93-310 changed "commission on victim services" to "office of victim services", effective July 1, 1993; (Revisor's note: In 1995, a reference to "said account" was changed editorially by the Revisors to "said fund" to reflect the changes enacted by P.A. 92-153); P.A. 97-59 added provision re deposit into fund of restitution collected by Office of Adult Probation and not disbursed to victim and added provision re payment of costs of providing direct services to victims and witnesses of crime from fund, effective May 8, 1997; P.A. 02-132 replaced "Office of Adult Probation" with "Court Support Services Division" and made technical changes; P.A. 03-189 divided existing provisions into Subsecs. (a) to (c), added provisions re restitution collected pursuant to Secs. 46b-140 and 54-56e, re deposit of such restitution into the fund and re disbursement within five years after the date restitution is collected in Subsec. (b) and made technical changes; P.A. 03-278 made technical changes, effective July 9, 2003; P.A. 10-43 amended Subsec. (a) to add exception authorizing expenditure in subsequent fiscal year of any recovery or reimbursement received pursuant to Sec. 54-212 and deposited in fund.

Sec. 54-216. Restitution services.

(a) The Office of Victim Services or, on review, a victim compensation commissioner may order that services be provided for the restitution of any person eligible for such services in accordance with the provisions of sections 54-201 to 54-233, inclusive. Such services may include but shall not be limited to medical, psychiatric, psychological and social services and social rehabilitation services.

(b) The Office of Victim Services or, on review, a victim compensation commissioner may order that such restitution services be provided to victims of child abuse and members of their families, victims of sexual assault and members of their families, victims of domestic violence and members of their families, members of the family of any victim of homicide, and children who witness domestic violence, including, but not limited to, children who are not related to the victim. For the purposes of this subsection, "members of their families" or "member of the family" does not include the person responsible for such child abuse, sexual assault, domestic violence or homicide.

(c) The Office of Victim Services may contract with any public or private agency for any services ordered under this section.

(P.A. 79-505, S. 3, 7; P.A. 85-538, S. 1; P.A. 87-554, S. 15; P.A. 93-310, S. 14, 32; P.A. 95-175, S. 9; P.A. 11-152, S. 6; P.A. 12-114, S. 18.)

History: P.A. 85-538 inserted new Subsec. (b) re restitution services to victims of child abuse and their families and members of the family of any victim of homicide, relettering former Subsec. (b) accordingly; P.A. 87-554 replaced "board" with "commission"; P.A. 93-310 changed "commission" to "office of victim services or, on review, a victim compensation commissioner", effective July 1, 1993; P.A. 95-175 amended Subsec. (b) by including victims of sexual assault and members of their families; P.A. 11-152 amended Subsec. (b) to add restitution services for victims of domestic violence and members of their families, and provide that "members of their families" or "member of the family" does not include the person responsible for child abuse, sexual assault, domestic violence or homicide; P.A. 12-114 amended Subsec. (b) to add provision re restitution services for children who witness domestic violence, including children who are not related to the victim.

Sec. 54-217. Emergency award pending final determination on claim.

Notwithstanding the provisions of sections 54-204 and 54-205, if it appears to the Office of Victim Services, prior to taking action upon a claim and based upon a review of all information then available to the Office of Victim Services, that such claim is one with respect to which an award probably will be made and undue hardship will result to the claimant if payment is not expedited, the Office of Victim Services may make an emergency award to the claimant pending a final determination on the claimant's application, provided (1) the amount of such emergency award shall not exceed two thousand dollars, (2) the amount of such emergency award shall be deducted from any final award made to the claimant, and (3) the excess of the amount of such emergency award over the final award, or the full amount of the emergency award if no final award is made, shall be repaid by the claimant to the Office of Victim Services.

(P.A. 79-505, S. 5, 7; P.A. 87-554, S. 16; P.A. 90-22, S. 2; P.A. 93-310, S. 15, 32; P.A. 03-189, S. 4; P.A. 10-43, S. 37.)

History: P.A. 87-554 changed "board" to "commission"; P.A. 90-22 increased maximum amount of emergency award from $500 to $1,000; P.A. 93-310 changed "commission on victim services" to "office of victim services", effective July 1, 1993; P.A. 03-189 increased maximum amount of emergency award from $1,000 to $2,000 and made technical changes; P.A. 10-43 added provision re decision to make emergency award based upon review of all information then available to Office of Victim Services and conditioned finding that undue hardship will result if payment is not expedited, rather than if immediate payment is not made.

Sec. 54-218. Profits derived as result of crime of violence. Recovery of money judgment by victim. Payment to Criminal Injuries Compensation Fund.

(a) Any person, firm, corporation, partnership, association or other legal entity contracting with any person or the representative or assignee of any person accused of a crime of violence in this state, with respect to the reenactment of such crime, by way of a movie, book, magazine article, radio or television presentation, live entertainment of any kind, or from the expression of such person's thoughts, feelings, opinions or emotions regarding such crime, shall pay over to the Office of Victim Services any moneys which would otherwise, by terms of such contract, be owing to the persons so accused or the accused's representatives. The Office of Victim Services shall deposit such moneys in an interest-bearing escrow account for the benefit of and payable to such accused person for the expenses of his or her defense and any victim of a crime of violence committed by such person, provided such person is finally convicted of a crime of violence for which compensation may be paid and, provided further such victim brings a civil action in a court of competent jurisdiction within five years of the date of the crime and recovers a money judgment against such person or his or her representatives. Any covenant, promise, agreement or understanding entered into or in connection with or collateral to a contract or agreement relative to the payment of any person accused or convicted of a crime of violence which attempts to circumvent the provisions of this section is prohibited.

(b) If no victim brings a civil action within five years of the date of the crime and recovers a money judgment, the moneys in any such escrow account shall be paid to the Criminal Injuries Compensation Fund established under section 54-215. If there is an affirmative finding that the person accused of the crime is not guilty within such five-year period, the money in any such escrow account shall be returned to such person.

(P.A. 82-328; P.A. 93-310, S. 16, 32; P.A. 95-175, S. 11.)

History: P.A. 93-310 deleted "clerk of the court of the judicial district in which the crime is alleged to have been committed" to the "office of victim services" and made technical changes, effective July 1, 1993; P.A. 95-175 amended Subsec. (b) by adding provision re return of money if affirmative finding that person accused of crime is not guilty.

Sec. 54-219. Victim Services Technical Assistance Fund.

Section 54-219 is repealed.

(P.A. 85-609, S. 3; P.A. 88-185, S. 1, 2; P.A. 92-153, S. 13.)

Sec. 54-220. Victim advocates. Responsibilities and duties.

(a) Victim advocates shall have the following responsibilities and duties: (1) To provide initial screening of each personal injury case; (2) to assist victims in the preparation of victim impact statements to be placed in court files; (3) to notify victims of their rights and request that each victim so notified attest to the fact of such notification of rights on a form developed by the Office of the Chief Court Administrator, which form shall be signed by the victim advocate and the victim and be placed in court files and a copy of which form shall be provided to the victim; (4) to provide information and advice to victims in order to assist such victims in exercising their rights throughout the criminal justice process; (5) to direct victims to public and private agencies for service; (6) to coordinate victim applications to the Office of Victim Services; and (7) to assist victims in the processing of claims for restitution.

(b) Within available appropriations, the Office of Victim Services may contract with any public or private agency for victim advocate services in geographical area courts.

(P.A. 85-609, S. 2; P.A. 87-554, S. 1; P.A. 93-310, S. 17, 32; P.A. 95-175, S. 10; P.A. 03-179, S. 3; P.A. 05-152, S. 11.)

History: (Revisor's note: In 1991 the term "commission on victim services" was substituted editorially for "criminal injuries compensation board" pursuant to public act 87-554); P.A. 93-310 amended Subdiv. (3) by deleting "prosecutors by gathering victim or witness" and inserting "victims by providing", amended Subdiv. (4) by deleting requirement of counsel, and amended Subdiv. (6) by changing "commission" to "office of victim services", effective July 1, 1993; P.A. 95-175 amended Subsec. (a) by adding Subdiv. (7) re assistance of victims in processing claims for restitution and added Subsec. (b) re contracting with public or private agency for victim advocates in geographical area courts; P.A. 03-179 amended Subsec. (a) by replacing "prepare" with "assist victims in the preparation of" in Subdiv. (2), replacing provision re providing information needed for processing of cases with provisions re notification of rights and attestation on form in Subdiv. (3), and deleting reference to "individual" and adding provision re assisting victims in exercising their rights throughout the criminal justice process in Subdiv. (4); P.A. 05-152 amended Subsec. (a)(3) by inserting "so notified".

Sec. 54-220a. Assignment of victim advocates to assist victims before Board of Pardons and Paroles.

The Office of Victim Services shall assign two victim advocates to provide full-time assistance to victims who appear before a panel of the Board of Pardons and Paroles or submit a written statement to such panel, as authorized by section 54-126a.

(Jan. Sp. Sess. P.A. 08-1, S. 14.)

History: Jan. Sp. Sess. P.A. 08-1 effective January 25, 2008.

Sec. 54-221. Appointment of advocates for victims of crime by court.

Section 54-221 is repealed, effective October 1, 2010.

(P.A. 85-538, S. 2; P.A. 10-43, S. 43.)

Sec. 54-222. Brochure re rights of victims and victim services. Notice concerning services for victims of human trafficking.

(a) The Office of the Chief Court Administrator shall develop a concise card or brochure concerning information to victims of crime concerning their rights as victims and any services available to them. The Office of Victim Services shall distribute such cards or brochures to municipalities and the state police who shall distribute such cards or brochures to crime victims.

(b) The Office of the Chief Court Administrator shall develop a concise notice concerning services available to victims of human trafficking. Such notice shall indicate that any person who is forced to engage in any activity and who cannot leave may contact a state or federal anti-trafficking hotline, and shall indicate the toll-free telephone numbers for such hotlines. The office shall make copies of such notice available to persons who are required to post such notice pursuant to section 54-234a.

(P.A. 85-609, S. 4; P.A. 87-554, S. 1; P.A. 93-310, S. 18, 32; P.A. 13-166, S. 6.)

History: (Revisor's note: In 1991 the term "commission on victim services" was substituted editorially for "criminal injuries compensation board" and "commission" for "board" pursuant to public act 87-554); P.A. 93-310 changed reference to "commission on victim services" to "office of the chief court administrator", changed "commission" to "office of victim services" and added "and the state police" after "municipalities", effective July 1, 1993; P.A. 13-166 designated existing provisions as Subsec. (a) and amended same to delete "bilingual" re card or brochure, and added Subsec. (b) re notice concerning services for victims of human trafficking.

Sec. 54-222a. Duty of peace officer regarding crime victim. Regulations.

(a) Whenever a peace officer determines that a crime has been committed, such officer shall: (1) Render immediate assistance to any crime victim, including obtaining medical assistance for any such crime victim if such assistance is required; (2) present a card prepared by the Office of the Chief Court Administrator to the crime victim informing the crime victim of services available and the rights of crime victims in this state; and (3) refer the crime victim to the Office of Victim Services for additional information on rights and services. A peace officer shall not be liable for failing to present an informational card to any crime victim as provided in subdivision (2) of this subsection or for failing to refer any crime victim to the Office of Victim Services as provided in subdivision (3) of this subsection. For the purposes of this subsection, "crime victim" has the same meaning as provided in section 1-1k.

(b) The Commissioner of Emergency Services and Public Protection shall adopt regulations in accordance with chapter 54 to implement the provisions of subsection (a) of this section.

(P.A. 88-260; P.A. 93-310, S. 19, 32; P.A. 05-169, S. 4; P.A. 11-51, S. 134; P.A. 14-122, S. 196.)

History: P.A. 93-310 changed "commission on victims services" to "office of chief court administrator" and changed "said commission" to "the office of victim services", effective July 1, 1993; P.A. 05-169 amended Subsec. (a) by replacing references to victim with references to crime victim, deleting provision re victim who has suffered physical injury, adding provision re peace officer not liable for failure to present informational card or refer crime victim to Office of Victim Services, defining "crime victim" and making technical changes; pursuant to P.A. 11-51, "Commissioner of Public Safety" was changed editorially by the Revisors to "Commissioner of Emergency Services and Public Protection" in Subsec. (b), effective July 1, 2011; P.A. 14-122 made a technical change in Subsec. (a).

Sec. 54-223. Failure to afford rights to victim shall not constitute grounds for vacating conviction or voiding sentence or parole determination.

Failure to afford the victim of a crime any of the rights provided pursuant to any provision of the general statutes shall not constitute grounds for vacating an otherwise lawful conviction or voiding an otherwise lawful sentence or parole determination.

(P.A. 86-401, S. 3, 7.)

Sec. 54-224. Liability of state re failure to afford rights to victim.

Except as provided in subsection (d) of section 46b-38b, the state or any agent, employee or officer thereof shall not be liable for (1) the failure to afford the victim of a crime any of the rights provided pursuant to any provision of the general statutes or (2) the failure to provide the victim of a crime with any notice pursuant to any provision of the general statutes.

(P.A. 86-401, S. 4, 7; P.A. 93-310, S. 20, 32.)

History: P.A. 93-310 inserted "Except as provided in subsection (d) of section 46b-38b, the", added Subdiv. indicators, designating as Subdiv. (2) new provision re failure to provide notice to victim, effective July 1, 1993.

Sec. 54-225. Voluntary program for lawyers for protection of persons injured in person or property by civil wrong.

There shall be a program for the protection of persons injured in person or property by a civil wrong. Lawyers may voluntarily participate in such program. Under the program, a lawyer shall inform any person injured in person or property by a civil wrong of his right to (1) bring an action to recover damages for such injury within the time limited by law, (2) the competent assistance of counsel, (3) notification of all court proceedings concerning his action, (4) full compensation for his injury, and (5) a written list of the rights of civil victims and the agencies or programs available to assist such victims. No lawyer who participates in such program or any law firm with which he is associated may solicit, accept or agree to accept any compensation from any such victim.

(P.A. 87-514, S. 2, 4.)

Sec. 54-226. Definitions.

For the purposes of sections 54-226 to 54-231, inclusive, "furlough" means the temporary custodial transfer of an inmate from incarcerative custody to community custody for an authorized purpose under the supervision of a verified community sponsor, and "victim" means the victim, the legal representative of the victim or a member of the deceased victim's immediate family.

(P.A. 91-389, S. 1, 12; P.A. 92-153, S. 8.)

History: P.A. 91-389, S. 1 effective April 1, 1992; P.A. 92-153 added definition of "furlough".

Sec. 54-227. Notification of Office of Victim Services and Victim Services Unit within Department of Correction by inmate or sexual offender seeking release or other relief.

(a) Any inmate who makes an application to the Board of Pardons and Paroles or the Department of Correction for release other than a furlough from a correctional institution, who applies to the sentencing court or judge for a reduction in sentence pursuant to section 53a-39 or who applies to the review division for a review of sentence pursuant to section 51-195, shall notify the Office of Victim Services and the Victim Services Unit within the Department of Correction of such application on a form prescribed by the Office of the Chief Court Administrator. Notwithstanding any provision of the general statutes, no such application shall be accepted unless the applicant has notified the Office of Victim Services and the Victim Services Unit within the Department of Correction pursuant to this subsection and provides proof of such notice as part of the application.

(b) Any person who files an application with the court to be exempted from the registration requirements of section 54-251 pursuant to subsection (b) or (c) of said section and any person who files a petition with the court pursuant to section 54-255 for an order restricting the dissemination of the registration information or removing such restriction shall notify the Office of Victim Services and the Victim Services Unit within the Department of Correction of the filing of such application or petition on a form prescribed by the Office of the Chief Court Administrator. Notwithstanding any provision of the general statutes, no such application or petition shall be considered unless such person has notified the Office of Victim Services and the Victim Services Unit within the Department of Correction pursuant to this subsection and provides proof of such notice as part of the application or petition.

(c) Notwithstanding any provision of the general statutes to the contrary, the Board of Pardons and Paroles, sentencing court and sentence review division may make available to the Office of Victim Services and the Victim Services Unit within the Department of Correction direct access to records in their custody, including computerized criminal history record information, for the purpose of performing said office's and department's duties regarding victim notification.

(P.A. 91-389, S. 2, 12; P.A. 92-153, S. 9; P.A. 93-310, S. 21, 32; P.A. 96-97, S. 3; P.A. 01-211, S. 3; P.A. 04-234, S. 2; P.A. 05-146, S. 2; Jan. Sp. Sess. P.A. 08-1, S. 26.)

History: P.A. 91-389, S. 2 effective April 1, 1992; P.A. 92-153 added phrase "other than a furlough"; P.A. 93-310 changed "commission on victim services" to "office of victim services", effective July 1, 1993; P.A. 96-97 added Subsec. (b) permitting Board of Pardons, Board of Parole, sentencing court and sentence review division to allow Office of Victim Services direct access to records; P.A. 01-211 amended Subsec. (a) to require the inmate to also notify the Department of Correction of such application, added new Subsec. (b) to require any person who files an application to be exempted from the registration requirements of Sec. 54-251 or who files a petition pursuant to Sec. 54-255 for order restricting dissemination of registration information or removing such restriction to notify the Office of Victim Services and the Department of Correction of the filing of such application or petition and to prohibit the consideration of such application or petition unless such notice has been given and redesignated existing Subsec. (b) as Subsec. (c) and amended to allow the Department of Correction direct access to records in the custody of the specified agencies; P.A. 04-234 replaced Board of Pardons and Board of Parole with Board of Pardons and Paroles, effective July 1, 2004; P.A. 05-146 specified that the notice under Subsecs. (a) and (b) should be given to, and the records under Subsec. (c) made available to, the "Victim Services Unit" within the Department of Correction; Jan. Sp. Sess. P.A. 08-1 amended Subsec. (a) to make technical changes, effective January 25, 2008.

Sec. 54-227a. Transferred to Chapter 886, Sec. 51-286g.

Sec. 54-228. Request by victim or family member of inmate for notification.

(a) Any victim of a crime or any member of an inmate's immediate family who desires to be notified whenever an inmate makes an application to the Board of Pardons and Paroles, Department of Correction, sentencing court or judge or review division as provided in section 54-227, or whenever an inmate is scheduled to be released from a correctional institution other than on a furlough, may complete and file a request for notification with the Office of Victim Services or the Victim Services Unit within the Department of Correction.

(b) Any victim of a criminal offense against a victim who is a minor, a nonviolent sexual offense or a sexually violent offense, as those terms are defined in section 54-250, or a felony found by the sentencing court to have been committed for a sexual purpose, as provided in section 54-254, who desires to be notified whenever the person who was convicted or found not guilty by reason of mental disease or defect of such offense files an application with the court to be exempted from the registration requirements of section 54-251 pursuant to subsection (b) or (c) of said section or files a petition with the court pursuant to section 54-255 for an order restricting the dissemination of the registration information, or removing such restriction, may complete and file a request for notification with the Office of Victim Services or the Victim Services Unit within the Department of Correction.

(c) A request for notification filed pursuant to this section shall be in such form and content as the Office of the Chief Court Administrator may prescribe. Such request for notification shall be confidential and shall remain confidential while in the custody of the Office of Victim Services and the Department of Correction and shall not be disclosed. It shall be the responsibility of the victim to notify the Office of Victim Services and the Victim Services Unit within the Department of Correction of his or her current mailing address and telephone number, which shall be kept confidential and shall not be disclosed by the Office of Victim Services and the Department of Correction. Nothing in this section shall be construed to prohibit the Office of Victim Services, the Board of

428

Pardons and Paroles and the Victim Services Unit within the Department of Correction from communicating with each other for the purpose of facilitating notification to a victim and disclosing to each other the name, mailing address and telephone number of the victim, provided such information shall not be further disclosed.

(P.A. 91-389, S. 3, 12; P.A. 92-153, S. 10; P.A. 93-219, S. 13, 14; 93-310, S. 22, 32; P.A. 96-97, S. 4; P.A. 01-211, S. 4; P.A. 04-234, S. 2; P.A. 05-146, S. 3; 05-152, S. 12; Jan. Sp. Sess. P.A. 08-1, S. 27, 28.)

History: P.A. 91-389, S. 3 effective April 1, 1992; P.A. 92-153 deleted reference to confidentiality "as provided in section 54-204" and inserted provision specifying that requests for notification "shall not be disclosed"; P.A. 93-219 authorized any member of an inmate's immediate family to complete and file a request for notification, effective July 1, 1993; P.A. 93-310 changed "commission" to "office of victim services", changed "commission on victim services" to "office of the chief court administrator", and added provision re responsibility of victim to notify office of current mailing address, which shall be kept confidential, effective July 1, 1993; P.A. 96-97 added phrase "scheduled to be" before "released"; P.A. 01-211 designated existing provisions authorizing a victim to file a request for notification as Subsec. (a) and amended same. to authorize the victim to file request with the Department of Correction, added a new Subsec. (b) to authorize the victim of certain sexual offenses to file a request for notification whenever the perpetrator seeks to be exempted from the sexual offender registration requirements or to restrict the dissemination of the registration information or remove such restriction and designated existing provisions re the form and confidentiality of the victim's request for notification as Subsec. (c) and amended same to make the confidentiality and nondisclosure provisions applicable to the Department of Correction and require the victim to also notify the Department of Correction of his or her current mailing address; P.A. 04-234 replaced Board of Pardons and Board of Parole with Board of Pardons and Paroles, effective July 1, 2004; P.A. 05-146 specified that the request for notification under Subsecs. (a) and (b) should be filed with, and the notice of the victim's current mailing address under Subsec. (c) should be given to, the "Victim Services Unit" within the Department of Correction; P.A. 05-152 amended Subsec. (a) by adding exception re furlough granted for the purpose of reintegrating an inmate into the community and amended Subsec. (c) by providing that nothing in section shall be construed to prohibit communication between Office of Victim Services and Department of Correction re current mailing address of victim and disclosure of such address to each other; Jan. Sp. Sess. P.A. 08-1 amended Subsec. (a) to delete provision re victim notification whenever inmate is to be released on furlough granted for the purpose of reintegrating the inmate into the community and amended Subsec. (c) to require victim to provide his or her current telephone number, replace provision allowing Office of Victim Services and Department of Correction to communicate with each other to determine if either has current mailing address of victim and, if so, to disclose that address to each other for purpose of facilitating notice to victim with provision allowing Office of Victim Services, Board of Pardons and Paroles and Victim Services Unit within Department of Correction to communicate with each other for purpose of facilitating notice to victim and disclosing to each other the name, mailing address and telephone number of victim, prohibit further disclosure of "such information", rather than "such mailing address", and make technical changes, effective January 25, 2008.

Sec. 54-229. Request by prosecuting authority for notification.

Any state's attorney, assistant state's attorney or deputy assistant state's attorney who desires to be notified whenever an inmate makes an application to the Board of Pardons and Paroles, Department of Correction, sentencing court or judge or review division as provided in section 54-227 may complete and file a request for notification with the Office of Victim Services or the Victim Services Unit within the Department of Correction. Such request for notification shall be in such form and content as the Office of the Chief Court Administrator may prescribe.

(P.A. 91-389, S. 4, 12; P.A. 93-310, S. 23, 32; P.A. 04-234, S. 2; P.A. 05-146, S. 1.)

History: P.A. 91-389, S. 4 effective April 1, 1992; P.A. 93-310 deleted "commission on" and inserted "office of" and deleted "commission on victim services" and inserted "office of chief court administrator" effective July 1, 1993; P.A. 04-234 replaced Board of Pardons and Board of Parole with Board of Pardons and Paroles, effective July 1, 2004; P.A. 05-146 authorized the filing of a request for notification with the Victim Services Unit within the Department of Correction.

Sec. 54-230. Notification of victims and other persons by Office of Victim Services when inmate or sexual offender seeks release or other relief or is released from a correctional institution.

(a) Upon receipt of notice from an inmate pursuant to section 54-227, the Office of Victim Services shall notify by certified mail all persons who have requested to be notified pursuant to subsection (a) of section 54-228 and section 54-229 whenever such inmate makes application for release or sentence reduction or review. Such notice shall be in writing and notify each person of the nature of the release or sentence reduction or review being applied for, the address and telephone number of the board or agency to which the application by the inmate was made, and the date and place of the hearing or session, if any, scheduled on the application.

(b) Upon receipt of notice from a person pursuant to subsection (b) of section 54-227, the Office of Victim Services shall notify by certified mail all persons who have requested to be notified pursuant to subsection (b) of section 54-228 whenever such person files an application with the court to be exempted from the registration requirements of section 54-251 pursuant to subsections (b) or (c) of said section or files a petition with the court pursuant to section 54-255 for an order restricting the dissemination of the registration information, or removing such restriction. Such notice shall be in writing and notify each person of the nature of the exemption or of the restriction or removal of the restriction being applied for, the address and telephone number of the court to which the application or petition by the person was made, and the date and place of the hearing or session, if any, scheduled on the application or petition.

(c) Upon compliance with the notification requirements of this section, the Office of Victim Services shall notify, on a form prescribed by the Office of the Chief Court Administrator, the board, agency or court to which the application or petition was made of such compliance.

(d) Upon receipt of notice from the Department of Correction pursuant to section 54-231, the Office of Victim Services shall notify by certified mail all victims who have requested to be notified pursuant to section 54-228 whenever such inmate is scheduled to be released from a correctional institution. Such notice shall be in writing and notify each victim of the date of such inmate's release. The victim shall notify the Office of Victim Services of his or her current mailing address and telephone number, which shall be kept confidential and shall not be disclosed by the Office of Victim Services. Nothing in this section shall be construed to prohibit the Office of Victim Services, the Board of Pardons and Paroles and the Victim Services Unit within the Department of Correction from communicating with each other for the purpose of facilitating notification to a victim and disclosing to each other the name, mailing address and telephone number of the victim, provided such information shall not be further disclosed.

(P.A. 91-389, S. 5, 12; P.A. 92-153, S. 11; P.A. 93-310, S. 24, 32; P.A. 96-97, S. 5; P.A. 01-211, S. 5; P.A. 05-152, S. 13; Jan. Sp. Sess. P.A. 08-1, S. 29.)

History: P.A. 91-389, S. 5 effective April 1, 1992; P.A. 92-153 deleted requirement that victim be notified of "place" where inmate is released; P.A. 93-310 changed "commission on" to "office of" and added provision in Subsec. (b) re responsibility of victim to notify office of current mailing address which shall be kept confidential, effective July 1, 1993; P.A. 96-97 amended Subsec. (b) by adding phrase "scheduled to be" before "released"; P.A. 01-211 amended Subsec. (a) to require notice to be sent by "certified" mail and replace reference to "section 54-228" with "subsection (a) of section 54-228", added new Subsec. (b) re notification by the Office of Victim Services of victims who have requested notification whenever a sexual offender seeks to be exempted from sexual offender registration requirements or to restrict the dissemination of registration information or remove such restriction, added new Subsec. (c) requiring the Office of Victim Services to notify the board, agency or court to which the application or petition was made of said office's compliance with the notification requirements of section and redesignated existing Subsec. (b) as Subsec. (d) and amended same to require notice to be sent by "certified" mail; P.A. 05-152 amended Subsec. (d) by providing that nothing in section shall be construed to prohibit communication between Office of Victim Services and Department of Correction re current mailing address of victim and disclosure of such address to each other; Jan. Sp. Sess. P.A. 08-1 amended Subsec. (d) to require victim to provide his or her current telephone number, replace provision allowing Office of Victim Services and Department of Correction to communicate with each other to determine if either has current mailing address of victim and, if so, to disclose that address to each other for purpose of facilitating notice to victim with provision allowing Office of Victim Services, Board of Pardons and Paroles and Victim Services Unit within Department of Correction to communicate with each other for purpose of facilitating notice to victim and disclosing to each other the name, mailing address and telephone number of victim and prohibit further disclosure of "such information", rather than "such mailing address", effective January 25, 2008.

Sec. 54-230a. Notification of victims and other persons by Department of Correction when inmate or sexual offender seeks release or other relief.

(a) Upon receipt of notice from an inmate pursuant to section 54-227, the Victim Services Unit within the Department of Correction shall notify by certified mail all persons who have requested to be notified pursuant to subsection (a) of section 54-228 and section 54-229 whenever such inmate makes application for release or sentence reduction or review. Such notice shall be in writing and notify each person of the nature of the release or sentence reduction or review being applied for, the address and telephone number of the board or agency to which the application by the inmate was made, and the date and place of the hearing or session, if any, scheduled on the application.

(b) Upon receipt of notice from a person pursuant to subsection (b) of section 54-227, the Victim Services Unit within the Department of Correction shall notify by certified mail all persons who have requested to be notified pursuant to subsection (b) of section 54-228 whenever such person files an application with the court to be exempted from the registration requirements of section 54-251 pursuant to subsections (b) or (c) of said section or files a petition with the court pursuant to section 54-255 for an order restricting the dissemination of the registration information, or removing such restriction. Such notice shall be in writing and notify each person of the nature of the exemption or of the restriction or the removal of the restriction being applied for, the address and telephone number of the court to which the application or petition by the person was made, and the date and place of the hearing or session, if any, scheduled on the application or petition.

(c) Upon compliance with the notification requirements of this section, the Victim Services Unit within the Department of Correction shall notify, on a form prescribed by the Office of the Chief Court Administrator, the board, agency or court to which the application or petition was made of such compliance.

(P.A. 01-211, S. 6; P.A. 05-146, S. 4.)

History: P.A. 05-146 specified that the required notice be given by the "Victim Services Unit" within the Department of Correction.

Sec. 54-231. Notification of Office of Victim Services by Department of Correction upon release of inmate. Access to criminal history record information.

The Department of Correction shall notify the Office of Victim Services whenever the department schedules the release of an inmate from a correctional institution other than on a furlough. Notwithstanding any provision of the general statutes to the contrary, the Department of Correction may make available to the Office of Victim Services direct access to any records in its custody, including computerized criminal history record information, for the purpose of assisting said office to perform its duties regarding victim notification.

(P.A. 91-389, S. 6, 12; P.A. 92-153, S. 12; P.A. 93-310, S. 25, 32; P.A. 96-97, S. 6; P.A. 05-68, S. 1; Jan. Sp. Sess. P.A. 08-1, S. 30.)

History: P.A. 91-389, S. 6 effective April 1, 1992; P.A. 92-153 specified that correction department need not notify commission of inmate's release on furlough; P.A. 93-310 changed "commission on victim services" to "office of victim services", effective July 1, 1993; P.A. 96-97 changed "releases" to "schedules the release of" and added provision permitting Department of Correction to allow Office of Victim Services direct access to records; P.A. 05-68 required notification when an inmate is scheduled to be released on a furlough that is granted for the purpose of reintegrating the inmate into the community and allows the inmate to serve the period immediately preceding the inmate's parole release or discharge date in the community; Jan. Sp. Sess. P.A. 08-1 deleted provision requiring notification whenever inmate is to be released on furlough granted for the purpose of reintegrating the inmate into the community and made a technical change, effective January 25, 2008.

Sec. 54-232. Disposition of requests for notification received prior to April 1, 1992. Section 54-232 is repealed, effective July 1, 1993.

(P.A. 91-389, S. 11; P.A. 93-310, S. 31, 32.)

Sec. 54-233. Compensation of victim of tort occurring prior to July 1, 1993.

Nothing in sections 4-141, 18-85, 18-101, 54-202 to 54-206, inclusive, 54-207a to 54-212, inclusive, 54-215 to 54-218, inclusive, 54-220, 54-222, 54-222a, 54-224 and 54-227 to 54-231, inclusive, shall preclude any victim of a tort occurring prior to July 1, 1993, from seeking compensation pursuant to the provisions of this chapter, revision of 1958, revised to January 1, 1993.

(P.A. 93-310, S. 29, 32.)

History: P.A. 93-310 effective July 1, 1993.

Sec. 54-234. Development of response system for victims of offense of trafficking in persons. Contracts.

(a) The Office of Victim Services within the Judicial Department shall, within available appropriations, contract with nongovernmental organizations to develop a coordinated response system to assist victims of the offense of trafficking in persons.

(b) Such contracts shall be entered into for the following purposes, including, but not limited to:

(1) Developing a uniform curriculum to address rights and services for such victims;

(2) Developing information and materials on available resources and services for such victims;

(3) Actively seeking out quality training and other educational opportunities regarding the identification and assistance of such victims that take into consideration such victims' cultural context and needs; and

(4) Promoting and disseminating information on training and other educational opportunities concerning the assistance of such victims to emergency medical services, faith-based communities, sexual assault service providers, domestic violence service providers and state and local governmental agencies.

(June Sp. Sess. P.A. 07-4, S. 29.)

Sec. 54-234a. Display of notice re services for victims of human trafficking at highway service plazas, hotels, adults-only businesses and liquor permittee premises.

(a) The operator of any publicly or privately operated highway service plaza, any hotel, motel, inn or similar lodging or any business that sells or offers for sale materials or promotes performances intended for an adult-only audience and each person who holds an on-premises consumption permit for the retail sale of alcoholic liquor pursuant to title 30 shall post the notice developed pursuant to subsection (b) of section 54-222 in plain view in a conspicuous location where sales are to be carried on.

(b) The provisions of subsection (a) of this section shall not apply to any person who holds an on-premises consumption permit for the retail sale of alcoholic liquor pursuant to title 30 that consists of only one or more of the following: (1) A caterer, railroad, boat, airline, military, charitable organization, special club, temporary liquor or temporary beer permit, or (2) a manufacturer permit for a farm winery, a manufacturer permit for beer, manufacturer permits for beer and brew pubs, or any other manufacturer permit issued under title 30.

(P.A. 13-166, S. 7; P.A. 16-71, S. 10.)

History: P.A. 16-71 amended Subsec. (a) by replacing provisions re truck stop with provisions re highway service plaza, hotel, motel, inn or similar lodging and business that sells materials or promotes performances intended for adult-only audiences, amended Subsec. (b) by deleting former Subdiv. (2) re restaurant permits and by redesignating existing Subdiv. (3) as Subdiv. (2), and made technical and conforming changes.

Sec. 54-235. State-wide automated victim information and notification system.

The Judicial Branch shall contract for the establishment and implementation of a state-wide automated victim information and notification system to provide automatic notice of relevant offender information and status reports to registered crime victims. Such system shall be used to provide victim notification by the Office of Victim Services within the Judicial Department, the Victim Services Unit within the Department of Correction, the Board of Pardons and Paroles and the Division of Criminal Justice. Such system shall be operational on July 1, 2009, or not later than thirty days after receipt of notice of the award of federal funds for the establishment and implementation of such system, whichever is earlier.

(Jan. Sp. Sess. P.A. 08-1, S. 31.)

History: Jan. Sp. Sess. P.A. 08-1 effective January 25, 2008.

Secs. 54-236 to 54-239. Reserved for future use.

CHAPTER 968a ADDRESS CONFIDENTIALITYPROGRAM

Table of Contents

Sec. 54-240. Definitions.

Sec. 54-240a. Program purpose. Regulations.

Sec. 54-240b. Application for program participation. Application assistants.

Sec. 54-240c. Certification as program participant. Application requirements.

Sec. 54-240d. Certification card.

Sec. 54-240e. Program address. Forwarding of mail.

Sec. 54-240f. Confidentiality of marriage records.

Sec. 54-240g. Listing on voter registry list.

Sec. 54-240h. Agency use of program address.

Sec. 54-240i. Exemption from use of program address by agency.

Sec. 54-240j. Renewal of program certification.

Sec. 54-240k. Cancellation of program certification. Notice. Reapplication to program. Withdrawal from program.

Sec. 54-240l. Secretary of the State as agent for program participant. Service on program participant.

Sec. 54-240m. Confidentiality of records re program participant. Exceptions. Notice of disclosure.

Sec. 54-240n. Nondisclosure of confidential address in criminal or civil proceeding.

Sec. 54-240o. Custody or visitation order in effect prior to or during participation in program.

Secs. 54-241 to 54-249. **Reserved**

Sec. 54-240. Definitions.

As used in this chapter:

(1) "Address confidentiality program" or "program" means the program established pursuant to this chapter;

(2) "Agency" has the same meaning as "public agency" or "agency", as provided in section 1-200;

(3) "Application assistant" means a person authorized by the Secretary of the State to assist applicants in the completion of applications for program participation;

(4) "Authorized personnel" means an employee in the office of the Secretary of the State who has been designated by the Secretary of the State, or an employee of an agency who has been designated by the chief executive officer of such agency, to process and have access to records pertaining to a program participant, including, but not limited to, voter registration applications, voting records and marriage records;

(5) "Certification card" means a card issued by the Secretary of the State pursuant to section 54-240d;

(6) "Confidential address" means a program participant's address or addresses as listed on such participant's application for program participation that are not to be disclosed, including such participant's residential address in this state and work and school addresses in this state, if any;

(7) "Family violence" has the same meaning as provided in section 46b-38a;

(8) "Injury or risk of injury to a child" means any act or conduct that constitutes a violation of section 53-21;

(9) "Law enforcement agency" means the office of the Attorney General, the office of the Chief State's Attorney, the Division of State Police within the Department of Emergency Services and Public Protection or any municipal police department;

(10) "Marriage records" means an application for a marriage license, an issued marriage license, a license certificate or other documents related thereto;

(11) "Program address" means the post office box number and fictitious street address assigned to a program participant by the Secretary of the State;

(12) "Program participant" or "participant" means any person certified by the Secretary of the State to participate in the address confidentiality program;

(13) "Record" has the same meaning as "public records or files" as provided in section 1-200;

(14) "Sexual assault" means any act that constitutes a violation of section 53a-70, 53a-70a, 53a-70b, 53a-71, 53a-72a, 53a-72b or 53a-73a; and

(15) "Stalking" means any act that constitutes a violation of section 53a-181c, 53a-181d or 53a-181e.

(P.A. 03-200, S. 1; P.A. 11-51, S. 134; P.A. 14-122, S. 197 199.)

History: P.A. 03-200 effective January 1, 2004; pursuant to P.A. 11-51, "Department of Public Safety" was changed editorially by the Revisors to "Department of Emergency Services and Public Protection" in Subdiv. (9), effective July 1, 2011; P.A. 14-122 made technical changes in Subdivs. (2), (7) and (13).

Sec. 54-240a. Program purpose. Regulations.

(a) There shall be an address confidentiality program established in the office of the Secretary of the State to provide a substitute mailing address for any person who has been a victim of family violence, injury or risk of injury to a child, sexual assault or stalking, and who wishes to keep such person's residential address confidential because of safety concerns.

(b) The Secretary of the State shall adopt regulations, in accordance with the provisions of chapter 54, to carry out the provisions of this chapter. Such regulations may include, but need not be limited to, provisions for applications for participation in the address confidentiality program, certification of program participants, certification cancellation, agency use of program addresses, forwarding of program participants' mail, voting by program participants and recording of vital statistics for program participants.

(P.A. 03-200, S. 2.)

History: P.A. 03-200 effective January 1, 2004.

Sec. 54-240b. Application for program participation. Application assistants.

(a) An adult person, a guardian or conservator of the person acting on behalf of an adult person, or a parent or guardian acting on behalf of a minor may apply to the Secretary of the State for participation in the address confidentiality program and to have the Secretary of the State designate a program address to serve as the address of the adult person or of the minor. Each application for program participation shall be completed with the assistance of an application assistant.

(b) The Secretary of the State shall make available a list of entities that employ application assistants to assist applicants in applying for participation in the address confidentiality program, provided no entity shall be included on such list unless the entity has received sufficient funds from federal or state sources as reimbursement for the reasonable costs of implementing the provisions of this chapter.

(P.A. 03-200, S. 3.)

History: P.A. 03-200 effective January 1, 2004.

Sec. 54-240c. Certification as program participant. Application requirements.

The Secretary of the State shall certify an applicant or the person on whose behalf an application is made as a program participant if the application is filed in the manner and on the application form prescribed by the Secretary of the State and includes:

(1) A statement made under penalty of false statement, as provided in section 53a-157b, that (A) the applicant or the person on whose behalf the application is made is a victim of family violence, injury or risk of injury to a minor, sexual assault or stalking, and (B) the applicant fears for the applicant's safety, for the safety of the applicant's children, for the safety of the person on whose behalf the application is made, or for the safety of the children of the person on whose behalf the application is made;

(2) Documentation supporting the statement made pursuant to subdivision (1) of this section;

(3) A designation of the Secretary of the State as the agent of the applicant or the person on whose behalf the application is made for service of process and for receipt of first class mail;

(4) The residential address in this state, the work and school addresses in this state, if any, and the phone number or numbers, if available, that are to remain confidential, but which may be used by the Secretary of the State or authorized personnel to contact the applicant or the person on whose behalf the application is made; and

(5) The application preparation date, the applicant's signature and the signature of the application assistant who assisted the applicant in completing the application.

(P.A. 03-200, S. 4.)

History: P.A. 03-200 effective January 1, 2004.

Sec. 54-240d. Certification card.

Upon certification of an applicant or a person on whose behalf an application is made as a program participant pursuant to section 54-240c, the Secretary of the State shall issue a certification card to such applicant or person, as appropriate. The certification card shall include the program participant's name and signature, a certification code, the program address and the certification expiration date. Such certification expiration date shall be four years from the date of issuance of the certification card.

(P.A. 03-200, S. 5.)

History: P.A. 03-200 effective January 1, 2004.

Sec. 54-240e. Program address. Forwarding of mail.

(a) The Secretary of the State shall maintain a post office box for the exclusive use of the program. The post office box number and a fictitious street address shall be the program address for program participants.

(b) The Secretary of the State shall open the post office box each day, other than Saturdays, Sundays and state holidays, and retrieve the contents. All first class mail addressed to a program participant shall be placed, unopened, into envelopes addressed to the participant and deposited at a United States post office the same day for delivery by first class mail to the participant at the confidential address indicated on the application by the participant or by the person applying on behalf of the participant.

(P.A. 03-200, S. 6.)

History: P.A. 03-200 effective January 1, 2004.

Sec. 54-240f. Confidentiality of marriage records.

A program participant may request that the participant's marriage records be kept confidential by appearing in person with the participant's spouse or intended spouse before the authorized personnel for the office of the registrar of vital statistics in the municipality where the marriage was or is to be celebrated and presenting the participant's certification card to such personnel. Upon such request, such registrar shall keep the participant's marriage records confidential and shall not make available for inspection or copying the name and address of a program participant or of the participant's spouse or intended spouse contained in the participant's marriage records, except (1) if requested by a law enforcement agency, to the law enforcement agency, (2) if directed by a court order, to a person identified in such order, or (3) if notified by the Secretary of the State that the program participant's certification has been cancelled.

(P.A. 03-200, S. 7.)

History: P.A. 03-200 effective January 1, 2004.

Sec. 54-240g. Listing on voter registry list.

A program participant may request to be listed on a voter registry list without the participant's street and house number by presenting the participant's certification card to the authorized personnel for the office of the registrar of voters for the municipality in which the participant is eligible to vote, or has applied for such eligibility. Upon such request, the registrar of voters shall list the participant by name only in accordance with subsection (d) of section 9-35. Such registrar shall keep the participant's confidential address confidential and shall not make such address available for inspection or copying, except (1) if requested by a law enforcement agency, to the law enforcement agency, (2) if directed by a court order, to a person identified in such order, or (3) if notified by the Secretary of the State that the program participant's certification has been cancelled.

(P.A. 03-200, S. 8.)

History: P.A. 03-200 effective January 1, 2004.

Sec. 54-240h. Agency use of program address.

(a) A program participant may request that an agency use the program address as the participant's residential, work or school address for all purposes for which the agency requires or requests such residential, work or school address. A program participant shall present the participant's certification card to any agency official creating a new record pertaining to the participant and request the use in such record of the program address appearing on the certification card. The agency official may make a photocopy of the certification card for the records of the agency and thereafter shall immediately return the certification card to the program participant.

(b) If a program participant requests that an agency use the program address pursuant to subsection (a) of this section, the agency shall accept and use the program address as the program participant's residential, work or school address, in lieu of the participant's confidential address, unless the agency receives an exemption from such use granted by the Secretary of the State pursuant to section 54-240i.

(P.A. 03-200, S. 9.)

History: P.A. 03-200 effective January 1, 2004.

Sec. 54-240i. Exemption from use of program address by agency.

(a) An agency may request an exemption from the use of a program participant's program address pursuant to section 54-240h by providing, in writing, to the Secretary of the State: (1) Identification of the statute or regulation that specifies the agency's statutory or regulatory requirement for the use of the program participant's confidential address; (2) a statement that the confidential address will be used only for such statutory or regulatory purposes; (3) identification of the specific program participant with respect to whom the exemption is requested; (4) identification of the persons who will have access to the confidential address; and (5) an explanation of how the agency's acceptance of the program address would prevent the agency from meeting its obligations under the law and why it cannot meet its statutory or regulatory obligation by a change in its internal procedures.

(b) During the review and evaluation by the Secretary of the State, and any appeal, if applicable, of an agency's exemption request, the agency shall use the program participant's program address.

(c) The Secretary of the State's determination to grant or deny an exemption request shall be based on, but need not be limited to, an evaluation of the information provided by the agency pursuant to subsection (a) of this section.

(d) If the Secretary of the State determines that there is a statutory or regulatory requirement that the agency use the program participant's confidential address and that the confidential address will be used only to comply with such requirement, the Secretary of the State shall issue a written exemption for the agency. The Secretary of the State may include in the exemption (1) the agency's obligation to maintain the confidentiality of the program participant's confidential address, (2) limitations on the use of or access to the confidential address, (3) the term for which the exemption is granted, (4) a designation of the record format in which the confidential address may be maintained, (5) a designation of a disposition date after which the agency may no longer maintain a record of the participant's confidential address, and (6) any other provisions and qualifications deemed appropriate by the Secretary of the State. Any agency that is granted an exemption may not make the program participant's confidential address available for inspection or copying by persons other than those identified in the exemption request as having access to the confidential address, except (A) if directed by a court order, to a person identified in such order, or (B) if notified by the Secretary of the State that the program participant's certification has been cancelled.

(e) Prior to granting an exemption, the Secretary of the State shall notify the program participant of the exemption, including the name of the agency and the reason or reasons for the exemption.

(f) If the Secretary of the State determines that there is no statutory or regulatory requirement that the agency use the program participant's confidential address, the Secretary of the State shall issue a written denial of the exemption request. Such written denial shall include a statement of the reason or reasons for the denial.

(g) The granting or denial of the agency's exemption request pursuant to this section constitutes a final decision. The program participant or any other party aggrieved by such decision may appeal therefrom in accordance with the provisions of section 4-183.

(P.A. 03-200, S. 10.)

History: P.A. 03-200 effective January 1, 2004.

Sec. 54-240j. Renewal of program certification.

(a) A program participant, a guardian or conservator of the person acting on behalf of an adult program participant, or a parent or guardian acting on behalf of a minor program participant may apply to renew the participant's program certification by filing with the Secretary of the State (1) the participant's current certification card, (2) a properly completed certification renewal form, and (3) a new certification card form. The program participant or the person acting on behalf of the program participant shall provide all the information required on the certification renewal form and the program participant shall sign and date the certification card form.

(b) The Secretary of the State shall (1) certify a program participant who has satisfied the filing requirements of subsection (a) of this section to participate in the program for an additional four-year term, and (2) issue to such program participant a new certification card with a new certification expiration date.

(P.A. 03-200, S. 11.)

History: P.A. 03-200 effective January 1, 2004.

Sec. 54-240k. Cancellation of program certification. Notice. Reapplication to program. Withdrawal from program.

(a) The Secretary of the State may cancel a program participant's certification and invalidate the participant's certification card if:

(1) The program participant changes the participant's name from the name listed on the program application and fails to notify the Secretary of the State in writing of the name change not later than thirty days after the change;

(2) The program participant changes the participant's confidential address from the address listed on the program application and fails to notify the Secretary of the State in writing of the change not later than thirty days after the change;

(3) Mail forwarded to the program participant is returned as nondeliverable;

(4) The term of the program participant's certification has expired and the participant has not applied for renewal; or

(5) The application for program participation or renewal filed by or on behalf of the program participant contains false information.

(b) The Secretary of the State shall send written notice of cancellation to the program participant at the confidential address shown in the Secretary of the State's records regarding the participant. The notice shall specify the reason or reasons for cancellation. The program participant shall have thirty days from the date the notice was mailed by the Secretary of the State to appeal the cancellation in accordance with regulations adopted pursuant to section 54-240a.

(c) A person may reapply to the address confidentiality program at any time after such person's certification has been cancelled for any reason.

(d) (1) The Secretary of the State shall notify in writing the authorized personnel of the appropriate agency when a participant's certification in the program has been cancelled. After receipt of such notice, the agency shall not be responsible for maintaining the confidentiality of the record or address of a program participant whose certification has been cancelled.

(2) If the marriage records of a program participant whose certification has been cancelled were kept confidential pursuant to section 54-240f, the Secretary of the State shall notify in writing the authorized personnel of the appropriate office of the registrar of vital statistics of the cancellation.

(3) If the participant whose certification has been cancelled was listed on a voter registry list without the participant's street and house number pursuant to section 54-240g, the Secretary of the State shall notify in writing the authorized personnel of the appropriate office of the registrar of voters of the cancellation.

(e) A program participant may withdraw from the program by submitting to the Secretary of the State written notice of the participant's withdrawal and the participant's current certification card. The Secretary of the State shall cancel the participant's certification effective on the date of receipt of such notice by the Secretary of the State.

(P.A. 03-200, S. 12.)

History: P.A. 03-200 effective January 1, 2004.

Sec. 54-240*l*. Secretary of the State as agent for program participant. Service on program participant.

(a) The Secretary of the State shall be a program participant's agent upon whom any summons, writ, notice, demand or process in any action, proceeding or other matter involving the program participant shall be served.

(b) The Secretary of the State shall notify the chairperson of the State Marshal Commission of the names of program participants and the commission shall create a list to be used by state marshals to determine if a person upon whom process is to be served is a program participant. If a person is identified on the list as a program participant, a state marshal shall make service upon the Secretary of the State in accordance with subsection (c) of this section. Prior to making service, a state marshal shall verify the participation of a specific program participant as provided in subdivision (3) of subsection (a) of section 54-240m.

(c) A program participant may be served by any proper officer or other person lawfully empowered to make service by leaving two true and attested copies of such summons, writ, notice, demand or process, together with the required fee, at the office of the Secretary of the State or depositing the same in the United States mail, by registered or certified mail, postage prepaid, addressed to the Secretary of the State's office and marked "Address Confidentiality Program". The Secretary of the State shall file one copy of the summons, writ, notice, demand or process and keep a record of the date and hour of receipt. The Secretary of the State shall, not later than two business days after such service, forward by registered or certified mail the copy of such summons, writ, notice, demand or process to the program participant at the confidential address shown on the records of the Secretary of the State.

(d) Service is effective pursuant to this section as of the date and hour received by the Secretary of the State as shown on the records of the Secretary of the State.

(P.A. 03-200, S. 13; P.A. 06-100, S. 5.)

History: P.A. 03-200 effective January 1, 2004; P.A. 06-100 added new Subsec. (b) re notification of chairperson of State Marshal Commission of names of program participants, creation by said commission of list of program participants to be used by state marshals and responsibilities of state marshals when a person is identified as a program participant and redesignated existing Subsecs. (b) and (c) as Subsecs. (c) and (d), respectively, effective June 2, 2006.

Sec. 54-240m. Confidentiality of records re program participant. Exceptions. Notice of disclosure.

(a) The Secretary of the State may not make any records in a program participant's file, other than the program address, available for inspection or copying, except:

(1) If requested by a law enforcement agency or by the State Elections Enforcement Commission, to such law enforcement agency or said commission, provided the request is in writing, on agency or commission letterhead stationery signed by the agency's chief law enforcement officer, a commanding officer in the Division of State Police within the Department of Emergency Services and Public Protection or the executive director of the State Elections Enforcement Commission, as the case may be, and contains the request date and the name of the program participant;

(2) If directed by a court order, to a person identified in such order;

(3) To verify the participation of a specific program participant, in which case the Secretary of the State may only confirm information supplied by the requestor; or

(4) If the program participant's certification has been cancelled.

(b) If the Secretary of the State discloses records pursuant to subdivision (2) or (3) of subsection (a) of this section, the Secretary of the State shall forthwith notify the program participant of such disclosure.

(P.A. 03-200, S. 14; P.A. 11-51, S. 134.)

History: P.A. 03-200 effective January 1, 2004; pursuant to P.A. 11-51, "Department of Public Safety" was changed editorially by the Revisors to "Department of Emergency Services and Public Protection" in Subsec. (a)(1), effective July 1, 2011.

Sec. 54-240n. Nondisclosure of confidential address in criminal or civil proceeding.

No employee of any law enforcement agency or any state or municipal social service agency, and no other witness, shall be compelled to disclose a program participant's confidential address during the discovery phase of, or during testimony in, any criminal or civil proceeding unless the court finds that nondisclosure may prejudice a party to the proceeding.

(P.A. 03-200, S. 15.)

History: P.A. 03-200 effective January 1, 2004.

Sec. 54-240o. Custody or visitation order in effect prior to or during participation in program.

No custody or visitation order in effect prior to or during a person's participation in the address confidentiality program shall be affected by such participation or by any provision of this chapter.

(P.A. 03-200, S. 16.)

History: P.A. 03-200 effective January 1, 2004.

Secs. 54-241 to 54-249. Reserved for future use.

CHAPTER 969* REGISTRATION OF SEXUAL OFFENDERS

*Megan's Law does not apply retroactively to employee's prior convictions or establish public policy in favor of registration or monitoring of employee who had been acquitted of an enumerated offense. 51 CS 467.

Table of Contents

Sec. 54-250. Definitions.

Sec. 54-251. Registration of person who has committed a criminal offense against a victim who is a minor or a nonviolent sexual offense.

Sec. 54-252. Registration of person who has committed a sexually violent offense.

Sec. 54-253. Registration of person who has committed a sexual offense in another jurisdiction.

Sec. 54-254. Registration of person who has committed a felony for a sexual purpose.

Sec. 54-255. Restriction on dissemination of registration information for certain offenders.

Sec. 54-256. Responsibilities of courts and agencies in registration process.

Sec. 54-257. Registry. Suspension of registration. Verification of address. Retake of photographic image. Change of name.

Sec. 54-258. Availability of registration information. Immunity.

Sec. 54-258a. Warning against wrongful use of registry information.

Sec. 54-259. Sexual Offender Registration Committee.

Sec. 54-259a. Risk Assessment Board. Development and use of risk assessment scale. Report.

Sec. 54-260. (Formerly Sec. 54-102s). Notification of change of name or address of sexual offenders on parole or probation.

Sec. 54-260a. Report on number of registrants being electronically monitored and need for additional resources.

Sec. 54-260b. Criminal investigation of registrants using the Internet. Ex parte court order to compel disclosure of basic subscriber information of registrants.

Sec. 54-261. Community response education program.

Secs. 54-262 to 54-279. **Reserved**

Sec. 54-250. Definitions.

For the purposes of sections 54-102g and 54-250 to 54-258a, inclusive:

(1) "Conviction" means a judgment entered by a court upon a plea of guilty, a plea of nolo contendere or a finding of guilty by a jury or the court notwithstanding any pending appeal or habeas corpus proceeding arising from such judgment.

(2) "Criminal offense against a victim who is a minor" means (A) a violation of subdivision (2) of section 53-21 of the general statutes in effect prior to October 1, 2000, subdivision (2) of subsection (a) of section 53-21, subdivision (2) of subsection (a) of section 53a-70, subdivision (1), (4), (8) or (10) or subparagraph (B) of subdivision (9) of subsection (a) of section 53a-71, subdivision (2) of subsection (a) of section 53a-72a, subdivision (2) of subsection (a) of section 53a-86, subdivision (2) of subsection (a) of section 53a-87, section 53a-90a, 53a-196a, 53a-196b, 53a-196c, 53a-196d, 53a-196e or 53a-196f, (B) a violation of subparagraph (A) of subdivision (9) of subsection (a) of section 53a-71 or section 53a-92, 53a-92a, 53a-94, 53a-94a, 53a-95, 53a-96 or 53a-186, provided the court makes a finding that, at the time of the offense, the victim was under eighteen years of age, (C) a violation of any of the offenses specified in subparagraph (A) or (B) of this subdivision for which a person is criminally liable under section 53a-8, 53a-48 or 53a-49, or (D) a violation of any predecessor statute to any offense specified in subparagraph (A), (B) or (C) of this subdivision the essential elements of which are substantially the same as said offense.

(3) "Identifying factors" means fingerprints, a photographic image, and a description of any other identifying characteristics as may be required by the Commissioner of Emergency Services and Public Protection. The commissioner shall also require a sample of the registrant's blood or other biological sample be taken for DNA (deoxyribonucleic acid) analysis, unless such sample has been previously obtained in accordance with section 54-102g.

(4) "Mental abnormality" means a congenital or acquired condition of a person that affects the emotional or volitional capacity of the person in a manner that predisposes that person to the commission of criminal sexual acts to a degree that makes the person a menace to the health and safety of other persons.

(5) "Nonviolent sexual offense" means (A) a violation of section 53a-73a or subdivision (2), (3) or (4) of subsection (a) of section 53a-189a, or (B) a violation of any of the offenses specified in subparagraph (A) of this subdivision for which a person is criminally liable under section 53a-8, 53a-48 or 53a-49.

(6) "Not guilty by reason of mental disease or defect" means a finding by a court or jury of not guilty by reason of mental disease or defect pursuant to section 53a-13 notwithstanding any pending appeal or habeas corpus proceeding arising from such finding.

(7) "Personality disorder" means a condition as defined in the most recent edition of the Diagnostic and Statistical Manual of Mental Disorders, published by the American Psychiatric Association.

(8) "Registrant" means a person required to register under section 54-251, 54-252, 54-253 or 54-254.

(9) "Registry" means a central record system in this state, any other state or the federal government that receives, maintains and disseminates information on persons convicted or found not guilty by reason of mental disease or defect of criminal offenses against victims who are minors, nonviolent sexual offenses, sexually violent offenses and felonies found by the sentencing court to have been committed for a sexual purpose.

(10) "Release into the community" means, with respect to a conviction or a finding of not guilty by reason of mental disease or defect of a criminal offense against a victim who is a minor, a nonviolent sexual offense, a sexually violent offense or a felony found by the sentencing court to have been committed for a sexual purpose, (A) any release by a court after such conviction or finding of not guilty by reason of mental disease or defect, a sentence of probation or any other sentence under section 53a-28 that does not result in the offender's immediate placement in the custody of the Commissioner of Correction; (B) release from a correctional facility at the discretion of the Board of Pardons and Paroles, by the Department of Correction to a program authorized by section 18-100c or upon completion of the maximum term or terms of the offender's sentence or sentences, or to the supervision of the Court Support Services Division in accordance with the terms of the offender's sentence; or (C) temporary leave to an approved residence by the Psychiatric Security Review Board pursuant to section 17a-587, conditional release from a hospital for mental illness or a facility for persons with intellectual disability by the Psychiatric Security Review Board pursuant to section 17a-588, or release upon termination of commitment to the Psychiatric Security Review Board.

(11) "Sexually violent offense" means (A) a violation of section 53a-70, except subdivision (2) of subsection (a) of said section, 53a-70a, 53a-70b, 53a-71, except subdivision (1), (4), (8) or (10) or subparagraph (B) of subdivision (9) of subsection (a) of said section or subparagraph (A) of subdivision (9) of subsection (a) of said section if the court makes a finding that, at the time of the offense, the victim was under eighteen years of age, 53a-72a, except subdivision (2) of subsection (a) of said section, or 53a-72b, or of section 53a-92 or 53a-92a, provided the court makes a finding that the offense was committed with intent to sexually violate or abuse the victim, (B) a violation of any of the offenses specified in subparagraph (A) of this subdivision for which a person is criminally liable under section 53a-8, 53a-48 or 53a-49, or (C) a violation of any predecessor statute to any of the offenses specified in subparagraph (A) or (B) of this subdivision the essential elements of which are substantially the same as said offense.

(12) "Sexual purpose" means that a purpose of the defendant in committing the felony was to engage in sexual contact or sexual intercourse with another person without that person's consent. A sexual purpose need not be the sole purpose of the commission of the felony. The sexual purpose may arise at any time in the course of the commission of the felony.

(13) "Employed" or "carries on a vocation" means employment that is full-time or part-time for more than fourteen days, or for a total period of time of more than thirty days during any calendar year, whether financially compensated, volunteered or for the purpose of government or educational benefit.

(14) "Student" means a person who is enrolled on a full-time or part-time basis, in any public or private educational institution, including any secondary school, trade or professional institution or institution of higher learning.

(P.A. 98-111, S. 1; P.A. 99-183, S. 1, 13; P.A. 01-84, S. 22, 26; P.A. 02-89, S. 85; 02-132, S. 51; May 9 Sp. Sess. P.A. 02-7, S. 78; P.A. 04-139, S. 10; 04-188, S. 4; 04-234, S. 2; P.A. 06-187, S. 31–33; 06-196, S. 292; P.A. 11-51, S. 134; 11-129, S. 20; P.A. 13-73, S. 1; P.A. 15-213, S. 3.)

History: P.A. 99-183 made definitions applicable to new Sec. 54-258a but specific reference not added since said Sec. already included in existing reference to Secs. 54-250 to 54-259, inclusive, amended the definition of "conviction" to add "notwithstanding any pending appeal or habeas corpus proceeding arising from such judgment", amended definition of "criminal offense against a victim who is a minor" to revise Subpara. (A) by deleting a violation of "subparagraph (A) or (D) of subdivision (1) of subsection (a) or subdivision (6) of subsection (a) of section 53a-73a" and including a violation of section "53a-196c or 53a-196d" and to add Subpara. (D) re a violation of any predecessor statute with substantially the same essential elements, amended the definition of "identifying factors" to replace "photographs" with "a photographic image", added definition of "nonviolent sexual offense" as new Subdiv. (5), renumbering the remaining definitions accordingly, amended definition of "not guilty by reason of mental disease or defect" to add "notwithstanding any pending appeal or habeas corpus proceeding arising from such finding", amended definition of "registry" to include a central record system in "the federal government", include information on persons convicted or found not guilty by reason of mental disease or defect of "nonviolent sexual offenses" and replace "sexual purposes" with "a sexual purpose", amended the definition of "release into the community" to add reference to "a nonviolent sexual offense", replace "sexual purposes" with "a sexual purpose", and revise Subpara. (A) by including "any release by a court after such conviction or finding of not guilty by reason of mental disease or defect" and replacing "offender's placement" with "offender's immediate placement", amended definition of "sexually violent offense" to delete from Subpara. (A) reference to a violation of section "53a-73a, except subparagraph (A) or (D) of subdivision (1) of subsection (a) of said section or subdivision (6) of subsection (a) of said section" and to add Subpara. (C) re a violation of any predecessor statute with substantially the same essential elements, and added definition of "sexual purpose" as Subdiv. (12), effective July 1, 1999; P.A. 01-84 amended Subdiv. (2)(A) to replace reference to "a violation of subdivision (2) of section 53-21" with "a violation of subdivision (2) of section 53-21 of the general statutes in effect prior to October 1, 2000," and include a violation of "subdivision (2) of subsection (a) of section 53-21", effective July 1, 2001; P.A. 02-89 replaced reference in the introductory language to Sec. 54-259 with Sec. 54-258a, reflecting repeal of Sec. 54-259 by the same public act; P.A. 02-132 amended Subdiv. (10)(B) by replacing "Office of Adult Probation" with "Court Support Services Division"; May 9 Sp. Sess. P.A. 02-7 added Subdiv. (13) defining "employed" or "carries on a vocation" and Subdiv. (14) defining "student", effective August 15, 2002; P.A. 04-139 amended Subdiv. (2)(A) to include a violation of Sec. 53a-90a, 53a-196e or 53a-196f; P.A. 04-188 amended Subdiv. (3) to authorize the commissioner to require the taking of a biological sample other than a blood sample; P.A. 04-234 replaced Board of Parole with Board of Pardons and Paroles, effective July 1, 2004; P.A. 06-187 amended Subdiv. (2)(A) to include a violation of Sec. 53a-71(a)(9)(B) or Sec. 53a-71(a)(10), amended Subdiv. (2)(B) to include a violation of Sec. 53a-71(a)(9)(A), amended Subdiv. (5) to designate the specified violation of Sec. 53a-73a as Subpara. (A) and include therein a violation of Sec. 53a-189a(a)(2) and add Subpara. (B) to include a violation of any of the offenses specified in Subpara. (A) for which a person is criminally liable under Sec. 53a-8, 53a-48 or 53a-49, and amended Subdiv. (11)(A) to exclude a violation of Sec. 53a-71(a)(9)(B) or Sec. 53a-71(a)(10) and exclude a violation of Sec. 53a-71(a)(9)(A) if court finds that, at the time of the offense, the victim was under 18 years of age, effective July 1, 2006; P.A. 06-196 changed effective date of P.A. 06-187, S. 31–33 from July 1, 2006, to October 1, 2006, effective June 7, 2006; pursuant to P.A. 11-51, "Commissioner of Public Safety" was changed editorially by the Revisors to "Commissioner of Emergency Services and Public Protection" in Subdiv. (3), effective July 1, 2011; pursuant to P.A. 11-129, "mental retardation" was changed editorially by the Revisors to "intellectual disability" in Subdiv. (10); P.A. 13-73 redefined "release into the community" in Subdiv. (10) by adding provision re temporary leave to an approved residence by the Psychiatric Security Review Board pursuant to Sec. 17a-587 and making technical changes in Subpara. (C), effective July 1, 2013; P.A. 15-213 redefined "nonviolent sexual offense" in Subdiv. (5) by adding reference to Sec. 53a-189a(a)(3) or (4).

Pursuant to Subdiv. (2)(B), trial court retains jurisdiction with respect to the finding of a trigger for registration, even after the rendering of judgment. 264 C. 484.

Sec. 54-251. Registration of person who has committed a criminal offense against a victim who is a minor or a nonviolent sexual offense.

(a) Any person who has been convicted or found not guilty by reason of mental disease or defect of a criminal offense against a victim who is a minor or a nonviolent sexual offense, and is released into the community on or after October 1, 1998, shall, within three days following such release or, if such person is in the custody of the Commissioner of Correction, at such time prior to release as the commissioner shall direct, and whether or not such person's place of residence is in this state, register such person's name, identifying factors, criminal history record, residence address and electronic mail address, instant message address or other similar Internet communication identifier, if any, with the Commissioner of Emergency Services and Public Protection, on such forms and in such locations as the commissioner shall direct, and shall maintain such registration for ten years from the date of such person's release into the community, except that any person who has one or more prior convictions of any such offense or who is convicted of a violation of subdivision (2) of subsection (a) of section 53a-70 shall maintain such registration for life. Prior to accepting a plea of guilty or nolo contendere from a person with respect to a criminal offense against a victim who is a minor or a nonviolent sexual offense, the court shall (1) inform the person that the entry of a finding of guilty after acceptance of the plea will subject the person to the registration requirements of this section, and (2) determine that the person fully understands the consequences of the plea. If any person who is subject to registration under this section changes such person's name, such person shall, without undue delay, notify the Commissioner of Emergency Services and Public Protection in writing of the new name. If any person who is subject to registration under this section changes such person's address, such person shall, without undue delay, notify the Commissioner of Emergency Services and Public Protection in writing of the new address and, if the new address is in another state, such person shall also register with an appropriate agency in that state, provided that state has a registration requirement for such offenders. If any person who is subject to registration under this section establishes or changes an electronic mail address, instant message address or other similar Internet communication identifier, such person shall, without undue delay, notify the Commissioner of Emergency Services and Public Protection in writing of such identifier. If any person who is subject to registration under this section is employed at, carries on a vocation at or is a student at a trade or professional institution or institution of higher learning in this state, such person shall, without undue delay, notify the Commissioner of Emergency Services and Public Protection of such status and of any change in such status. If any person who is subject to registration under this section is employed in another state, carries on a vocation in another state or is a student in another state, such person shall, without undue delay, notify the Commissioner of Emergency Services and Public Protection and shall also register with an appropriate agency in that state, provided that state has a registration requirement for such offenders. During such period of registration, each registrant shall complete and return forms mailed to such registrant to verify such registrant's residence address and shall submit to the retaking of a photographic image upon request of the Commissioner of Emergency Services and Public Protection.

(b) Notwithstanding the provisions of subsection (a) of this section, the court may exempt any person who has been convicted or found not guilty by reason of mental disease or defect of a violation of subdivision (1) of subsection (a) of section 53a-71 from the registration requirements of this section if the court finds that such person was under nineteen years of age at the time of the offense and that registration is not required for public safety.

(c) Notwithstanding the provisions of subsection (a) of this section, the court may exempt any person who has been convicted or found not guilty by reason of mental disease or defect of a violation of subdivision (2) of subsection (a) of section 53a-73a or subdivision (2), (3) or (4) of subsection (a) of section 53a-189a, from the registration requirements of this section if the court finds that registration is not required for public safety.

(d) Any person who files an application with the court to be exempted from the registration requirements of this section pursuant to subsection (b) or (c) of this section shall, pursuant to subsection (b) of section 54-227, notify the Office of Victim Services and the Victim Services Unit within the Department of Correction of the filing of such application. The Office of Victim Services or the Victim Services Unit within the Department of Correction, or both, shall, pursuant to section 54-230 or 54-230a, notify any victim who has requested notification of the filing of such application. Prior to granting or denying such application, the court shall consider any information or statement provided by the victim.

(e) Any person who violates the provisions of subsection (a) of this section shall be guilty of a class D felony, except that, if such person violates the provisions of this section by failing to notify the Commissioner of Emergency Services and Public Protection without undue delay of a change of name, address or status or another reportable event, such person shall be subject to such penalty if such failure continues for five business days.

(P.A. 98-111, S. 2; P.A. 99-183, S. 2, 13; P.A. 01-211, S. 1; May 9 Sp. Sess. P.A. 02-7, S. 79; P.A. 05-146, S. 5; P.A. 06-187, S. 34–36; 06-196, S. 292; June Sp. Sess. P.A. 07-4, S. 90; P.A. 11-51, S. 134; P.A. 15-211, S. 5; 15-213, S. 4.)

History: P.A. 99-183 amended Subsec. (a) to make provisions applicable to any person convicted or found not guilty by reason of mental disease or defect of "a nonviolent sexual offense", require a person to register "whether or not such person's place of residence is in this state", add exception requiring any person who has one or more prior convictions of any such offense or who is convicted of a violation of Sec. 53a-70(a)(2) to maintain registration for life, revise provision re changing address to and registering in another state, add provision requiring a person who regularly travels into or within another state or temporarily resides in another state to notify the Commissioner of Public Safety and register with an appropriate agency in that state if that state has a registration requirement, add provision requiring registrants to submit to the retaking of a photographic image upon request and make technical changes for purposes of gender neutrality, added new Subsec. (b) to authorize the court to exempt any person convicted or found not guilty by reason of mental disease or defect of violation of Sec. 53a-71(a)(1) from the registration requirement under certain circumstances, added new Subsec. (c) to authorize the court to exempt any person convicted or found not guilty by reason of mental disease or defect of violation of Sec. 53a-73(a)(2) from the registration requirement under certain circumstances, and redesignated former Subsec. (b) as Subsec. (d), effective July 1, 1999; P.A. 01-211 added new Subsec. (d) requiring any person who files an application to be exempted to notify the Office of Victim Services and the Department of Correction of the filing of such application, requiring said office or department, or both, to notify any victim who has requested notification of the filing of such application and requiring the court to consider any information or statement provided by the victim prior to granting or denying such application and redesignated existing Subsec. (d) as Subsec. (e) and amended same to specify that penalty is for a violation of "subsection (a)" of this section; May 9 Sp. Sess. P.A. 02-7 amended Subsec. (a) to make requirement that a person subject to registration under this section notify the commissioner and register with an appropriate agency in another state applicable if such person "is employed in another state, carries on a vocation in another state or is a student in another state" rather than if such person "regularly travels into or within another state or temporarily resides in another state for purposes including, but not limited to employment or schooling" and to add provision requiring any person subject to registration under this section who is employed at, carries on a vocation at or is a student at a trade or professional institution or institution of higher learning in this state to notify the commissioner of such status and any change in such status, effective August 15, 2002; P.A. 05-146 amended Subsec. (d) to specify that it is the "Victim Services Unit" within the Department of Correction to which a person gives notice of the filing of an application and which notifies any victim who requested notification of the filing of the application; P.A. 06-187 amended Subsec. (a) to require person in custody of Commissioner of Correction to register at such time prior to release as commissioner directs, require person who changes such person's name to notify commissioner in writing of new name without undue delay, replace requirement that person who changes such person's address register new address in writing with commissioner within five days with requirement that such person notify commissioner in writing of new address without undue delay, reposition provision re notification of employment, vocational or student status at trade or professional institution or institution of higher learning in this state and of any change in such status, require that such notification be made "without undue delay", and require that notification person must give re employment, vocational or student status in another state be given "without undue delay", amended Subsec. (c) to include a violation of Sec. 53a-189a(a)(2) and amended Subsec. (e) to add exception that person who fails to notify commissioner without undue delay of change of name, address or status or another reportable event is subject to penalty if such failure continues for five business days, effective July 1, 2006; P.A. 06-196 changed effective date of P.A. 06-187, S. 34–36 from July 1, 2006, to October 1, 2006, effective June 7, 2006; June Sp. Sess. P.A. 07-4 amended Subsec. (a) to require registration of person's "electronic mail address, instant message address or other similar Internet communication identifier, if any," and require registrant who establishes or changes such an identifier to notify Commissioner of Public Safety in writing of such identifier without undue delay; pursuant to P.A. 11-51, "Commissioner of Public Safety" was changed editorially by the Revisors to "Commissioner of Emergency Services and Public Protection", effective July

1, 2011; P.A. 15-211 amended Subsec. (a) to add provision re 10-year registration period to start from date of person's release into the community; P.A. 15-213 amended Subsec. (c) to add reference to Sec. 53a-189a(a)(3) or (4).

Because statute imposes strict liability, actual notice to defendant and mens rea are not elements of the offense and therefore trial court's instructions were not constitutionally deficient. 286 C. 191. "Residence" means the act or fact of living in a given place for some time, but does not include temporary stays; "undue delay" means unwarranted or excessive postponement; legislature did not intend to adopt a bright-line definition for undue delay applicable to every situation but, rather, intended to make allowance for vagaries of individual conditions; "without undue delay" does not always mean within 5 business days. 306 C. 149.

Trial court erred when concluding that a finding of homelessness always constitutes a change of address. 148 CA 760.

Subsec. (a):

Court's failure to advise defendant of registration requirement prior to defendant's *Alford* plea does not render defendant exempt from registration requirement. 296 C. 305.

Absent clear expression of legislative intent, provisions do not apply to violations before effective date of section. 99 CA 358. Residence means any place of abode or dwelling place, however temporary it may be; court rejected defendant's claim that, due to the fact he was homeless, it was impossible for him to comply with the statutory requirement that he provide a residence address for registration purposes. 112 CA 458. Manifest injustice found where court not only failed to inform defendant that he would be required to register as a sex offender, but also failed to correct defendant's mistaken belief that by entering guilty plea pursuant to Sec. 53-21(a)(2), he would avoid such registration requirement. 127 CA 760. Because there was sufficient evidence supporting defendant's conviction of kidnapping in the second degree and because victim was under 18 at time offense was committed, Subsec. mandates defendant, upon release, register as a sex offender for a period of 10 years. 147 CA 598.

Subsec. (b):

Under the "may exempt" language in Subsec., even when the two enumerated factors are satisfied in a given case, the court still may decline to grant the registry exemption. 281 C. 5. Phrase "may exempt" means that a court may exercise its discretion to grant an exemption from registration once an individual has been convicted of violation of Sec. 53a-71(a)(1), regardless of whether the individual's obligation to register has commenced, as long as the two criteria set forth in Subsec. are satisfied, and therefore defendant retained statutory right to file application for exemption after having been placed on registry for approximately 7 years; plain language of Subsec. indicates that individual's right to seek exemption arises upon entry of judgment of conviction and continues throughout his or her obligation to register; Subsec. contains no provision imposing a temporal limitation on individual's statutory right to file application for exemption from registration. 320 C. 426.

Sec. 54-252. Registration of person who has committed a sexually violent offense.

(a) Any person who has been convicted or found not guilty by reason of mental disease or defect of a sexually violent offense, and (1) is released into the community on or after October 1, 1988, and prior to October 1, 1998, and resides in this state, shall, on October 1, 1998, or within three days of residing in this state, whichever is later, or (2) is released into the community on or after October 1, 1998, shall, within three days following such release or, if such person is in the custody of the Commissioner of Correction, at such time prior to release as the commissioner shall direct, register such person's name, identifying factors and criminal history record, documentation of any treatment received by such person for mental abnormality or personality disorder, and such person's residence address and electronic mail address, instant message address or other similar Internet communication identifier, if any, with the Commissioner of Emergency Services and Public Protection on such forms and in such locations as said commissioner shall direct, and shall maintain such registration for life. Prior to accepting a plea of guilty or nolo contendere from a person with respect to a sexually violent offense, the court shall (A) inform the person that the entry of a finding of guilty after acceptance of the plea will subject the person to the registration requirements of this section, and (B) determine that the person fully understands the consequences of the plea. If any person who is subject to registration under this section changes such person's name, such person shall, without undue delay, notify the Commissioner of Emergency Services and Public Protection in writing of the new name. If any person who is subject to registration under this section changes such person's address, such person shall, without undue delay, notify the Commissioner of Emergency Services and Public Protection in writing of the new address and, if the new address is in another state, such person shall also register with an appropriate agency in that state, provided that state has a registration requirement for such offenders. If any person who is subject to registration under this section establishes or changes an electronic mail address, instant message address or other similar Internet communication identifier, such person shall, without undue delay, notify the Commissioner of Emergency Services and Public Protection in writing of such identifier. If any person who is subject to registration under this section is employed at, carries on a vocation at or is a student at a trade or professional institution or institution of higher learning in this state, such person shall, without undue delay, notify the Commissioner of Emergency Services and Public Protection of such status and of any change in such status. If any person who is subject to registration under this section is employed in another state, carries on a vocation in another state or is a student in another state, such person shall, without undue delay, notify the Commissioner of Emergency Services and Public Protection and shall also register with an appropriate agency in that state, provided that state has a registration requirement for such offenders. During such period of registration, each registrant shall complete and return forms mailed to such registrant to verify such registrant's residence address and shall submit to the retaking of a photographic image upon request of the Commissioner of Emergency Services and Public Protection.

(b) Any person who has been subject to the registration requirements of section 54-102r of the general statutes, revised to January 1, 1997, as amended by section 1 of public act 97-183, shall, not later than three working days after October 1, 1998, register under this section and thereafter comply with the provisions of sections 54-102g and 54-250 to 54-258a, inclusive, except that any person who was convicted or found not guilty by reason of mental disease or defect of an offense that is classified as a criminal offense against a victim who is a minor under subdivision (2) of section 54-250 and that is subject to a ten-year period of registration under section 54-251 shall maintain such registration for ten years from the date of such person's release into the community.

(c) Notwithstanding the provisions of subsections (a) and (b) of this section, during the initial registration period following October 1, 1998, the Commissioner of Emergency Services and Public Protection may phase in completion of the registration procedure for persons released into the community prior to said date over the first three months following said date, and no such person shall be prosecuted for failure to register under this section during those three months provided such person complies with the directives of said commissioner regarding registration procedures.

(d) Any person who violates the provisions of this section shall be guilty of a class D felony, except that, if such person violates the provisions of this section by failing to notify the Commissioner of Emergency Services and Public Protection without undue delay of a change of name, address or status or another reportable event, such person shall be subject to such penalty if such failure continues for five business days.

(P.A. 98-111, S. 3; P.A. 99-183, S. 3, 13; P.A. 02-89, S. 86; May 9 Sp. Sess. P.A. 02-7, S. 80; P.A. 06-187, S. 37; 06-196, S. 292; June Sp. Sess. P.A. 07-4, S. 91; P.A. 11-51, S. 134; P.A. 15-211, S. 6.)

History: P.A. 99-183 amended Subsec. (a) to replace provision requiring a person who "is released into the community on or after October 1, 1988," to register "within three days following such release or October 1, 1998, whichever is later" with provisions requiring a person who "is released into the community on or after October 1, 1988, and prior to October 1, 1998, and resides in this state" to register "on October 1, 1998, or within three days of residing in this state, whichever is later" and requiring a person who "is released into the community on or after October 1, 1998," to register "within three days of such release", to require that a person maintain registration "for life" rather than "until released from this obligation in accordance with section 54-255", to revise provision re changing address to and registering in another state, to add provision requiring a person who regularly travels into or within another state or temporarily resides in another state to notify the Commissioner of Public Safety and register with an appropriate agency in that state if that state has a registration requirement, and to add provision requiring registrants to submit to the retaking of a photographic image upon request and made technical changes, effective July 1, 1999; P.A. 02-89 amended Subsec. (b) to replace reference to Sec. 54-259 with Sec. 54-258a, reflecting repeal of Sec. 54-259 by the same public act; May 9 Sp. Sess. P.A. 02-7 amended Subsec. (a) to make requirement that a person subject to registration under this section notify the commissioner and register with an appropriate agency in another state applicable if such person "is employed in another state, carries on a vocation in another state or is a student in another state" rather than if such person "regularly travels into or within another state or temporarily resides in another state for purposes including, but not limited to employment or schooling" and to add provision requiring any person subject to registration under this section who is employed at, carries on a vocation at or is a student at a trade or professional institution or institution of higher learning in this state to notify the commissioner of said status and any change in such status, effective April 4, 2016; P.A. 06-187 amended Subsec. (a) to require person in custody of Commissioner of Correction to register at such time prior to release as commissioner directs, require person who changes such person's name to notify commissioner in writing of new name without undue delay, replace requirement that person who changes address register new address in writing with commissioner within five days with requirement that such person notify commissioner in writing of new address without undue delay, reposition provision re notification of employment, vocational or student status at trade or professional institution or institution of higher learning in this state and of any change in such status, require that such notification be made "without undue delay", and require that notification person must give re employment, vocational or student status in another state be given "without undue delay", amended Subsec. (b) to add exception re maintenance of registration for 10 years for offense classified as a criminal offense against victim who is a minor and that is subject to 10-year period of registration and amended Subsec. (d) to add exception that person who fails to notify commissioner without undue delay of change of name, address or status or another reportable event is subject to penalty if such failure continues for 5 business days, effective July 1, 2006; P.A. 06-196 changed effective date of P.A. 06-187, S. 37 from July 1, 2006, to October 1, 2006, effective June 7, 2006; June Sp. Sess. P.A. 07-4 amended Subsec. (a) to require registration of person's "electronic mail address, instant message address or other similar Internet communication identifier, if any," require registrant who establishes or changes such an identifier to notify Commissioner of Public Safety in writing of such identifier without undue delay and make technical changes; pursuant to P.A. 11-51, "Commissioner of Public Safety" was changed editorially by the Revisors to "Commissioner of Emergency Services and Public Protection", effective July 1, 2011; P.A. 15-211 amended Subsec. (b) to add provision re 10-year registration period to start from date of person's release into the community.

Violation of section is a threat to the public in general, thus the state has an important interest at stake, and involuntary administration of medication to render the accused competent for trial is justified. 122 CA 664. Defendant's federal and state equal protection challenges properly denied because defendant failed to demonstrate lack of a rational basis for the lifetime registration requirement for those convicted of violent second degree sexual assaults as compared to the 10-year registration requirement for those convicted of nonviolent second degree sexual assaults; requiring lifetime sexual offender registration for those convicted of violent second degree sexual assaults is rationally related to the government's legitimate interest in protecting the public from sexual offenders whose actions demonstrate a willingness to use force or the threat of force. 151 CA 658.

Subsec. (b):

Registration of nonviolent offenders under another statute does not negate requirement that sexual offenders register under repealed Sec. 52-102n. 99 CA 358.

Sec. 54-253. Registration of person who has committed a sexual offense in another jurisdiction.

(a) Any person who has been convicted or found not guilty by reason of mental disease or defect in any other state, in a federal or military court or in any foreign jurisdiction of any crime (1) the essential elements of which are substantially the same as any of the crimes specified in subdivisions (2), (5) and (11) of section 54-250, or (2) which requires registration as a sexual offender in such other state or in the federal or military system, and who resides in

455

this state on and after October 1, 1998, shall, without undue delay upon residing in this state, register with the Commissioner of Emergency Services and Public Protection in the same manner as if such person had been convicted or found not guilty by reason of mental disease or defect of such crime in this state, except that the commissioner shall maintain such registration until such person is released from the registration requirement in such other state, federal or military system or foreign jurisdiction.

(b) If any person who is subject to registration under this section changes such person's name, such person shall, without undue delay, notify the Commissioner of Emergency Services and Public Protection in writing of the new name. If any person who is subject to registration under this section changes such person's address, such person shall, without undue delay, notify the Commissioner of Emergency Services and Public Protection in writing of the new address and, if the new address is in another state, such person shall also register with an appropriate agency in that state, provided that state has a registration requirement for such offenders. If any person who is subject to registration under this section establishes or changes an electronic mail address, instant message address or other similar Internet communication identifier, such person shall, without undue delay, notify the Commissioner of Emergency Services and Public Protection in writing of such identifier. If any person who is subject to registration under this section is employed at, carries on a vocation at or is a student at a trade or professional institution or institution of higher learning in this state, such person shall, without undue delay, notify the Commissioner of Emergency Services and Public Protection of such status and of any change in such status. If any person who is subject to registration under this section is employed in another state, carries on a vocation in another state or is a student in another state, such person shall, without undue delay, notify the Commissioner of Emergency Services and Public Protection and shall also register with an appropriate agency in that state, provided that state has a registration requirement for such offenders. During such period of registration, each registrant shall complete and return forms mailed to such registrant to verify such registrant's residence address and shall submit to the retaking of a photographic image upon request of the Commissioner of Emergency Services and Public Protection.

(c) Any person not a resident of this state who is registered as a sexual offender under the laws of any other state and who is employed in this state, carries on a vocation in this state or is a student in this state, shall, without undue delay after the commencement of such employment, vocation or education in this state, register such person's name, identifying factors and criminal history record, locations visited on a recurring basis, and such person's residence address, if any, in this state, residence address in such person's home state and electronic mail address, instant message address or other similar Internet communication identifier, if any, with the Commissioner of Emergency Services and Public Protection on such forms and in such locations as said commissioner shall direct and shall maintain such registration until such employment, vocation or education terminates or until such person is released from registration as a sexual offender in such other state. If such person terminates such person's employment, vocation or education in this state, changes such person's address in this state or establishes or changes an electronic mail address, instant message address or other similar Internet communication identifier such person shall, without undue delay, notify the Commissioner of Emergency Services and Public Protection in writing of such termination, new address or identifier.

(d) Any person not a resident of this state who is registered as a sexual offender under the laws of any other state and who travels in this state on a recurring basis for periods of less than five days shall notify the Commissioner of Emergency Services and Public Protection of such person's temporary residence in this state and of a telephone number at which such person may be contacted.

(e) Any person who violates the provisions of this section shall be guilty of a class D felony, except that, if such person violates the provisions of this section by failing to register with the Commissioner of Emergency Services and Public Protection without undue delay or notify the Commissioner of Emergency Services and Public Protection without undue delay of a change of name, address or status or another reportable event, such person shall be subject to such penalty if such failure continues for five business days.

(P.A. 98-111, S. 4; P.A. 99-183, S. 4, 13; May 9 Sp. Sess. P.A. 02-7, S. 81; P.A. 06-187, S. 38; 06-196, S. 292; June Sp. Sess. P.A. 07-4, S. 92, 93; P.A. 11-51, S. 134.)

History: P.A. 99-183 amended Subsec. (a) to include crimes specified in Subdiv. "(5)" of Sec. 54-250, replace reference to Subdiv. "(10)" with Subdiv. "(11)" of Sec. 54-250, make the registration requirement applicable to a person who "resides" rather than "establishes residence" in this state, require registration within ten days of "residing in this state" rather than within ten days of "establishing such residence", delete reference to the ten-year period of registration under Sec. 54-255, and make technical changes, added new Subsec. (b) re registration and notice requirements of a nonresident who is registered as a sexual offender in another state and regularly travels into or within this state or temporarily resides in this state, and redesignated former Subsec. (b) as Subsec. (c), effective July 1, 1999; May 9 Sp. Sess. P.A. 02-7 amended Subsec. (b) to make requirement that a nonresident registered sexual offender register with the commissioner applicable if such person "is employed in this state, carries on a vocation in this state or is a student in this state" rather than if such person "regularly travels into or within this state or temporarily resides in this state for purposes including, but not limited to employment or schooling", require such person to register "within five days after the commencement of such employment, vocation or education in this state" rather than "within three days after the commencement of such travel or residence in this state", and replace references to "travel or residence" with "employment, vocation or education" where appearing, added new Subsec. (c) requiring any person subject to registration under this section who is employed at, carries on a vocation at or is a student at a trade or professional institution or institution of higher learning in this state to notify the commissioner of such status and any change in such status, added new Subsec. (d) requiring any nonresident registered sexual offender who travels in this state on a recurring basis for periods of less than five days to notify the commissioner of such person's temporary residence and telephone number and redesignated existing Subsec. (c) as Subsec. (e), effective August 15, 2002; P.A. 06-187 amended Subsec. (a) to designate existing provision re crime the essential elements of which are substantially the same as Sec. 54-250(2), (3) or (11) as Subdiv. (1) and add Subdiv. (2) re crime which requires registration as a sexual offender in other state or in federal or military system, require person to register "without undue delay" upon residing in this state, rather than "within ten days" of residing in this state, and replace former exception re determining ten-year period of registration with exception re commissioner to maintain registration until person is released from registration requirement in other state, federal or military system or foreign jurisdiction, added Subsec. (b) requiring person subject to registration to notify commissioner if person changes such person's name or address, is employed at, carries on a vocation at or is a student at trade or professional institution or institution of higher learning in this state or is employed in another state, carries on a vocation in another state or is a student in another state and requiring registrant to verify address and submit to retaking of photographic image upon request, redesignated existing Subsec. (b) as Subsec. (c) and amended same to require person to register with commissioner "without undue delay", rather than "within five days", after commencement of employment, vocation or education in this state and require person to notify commissioner of termination of employment, vocation or education in this state or change of address "without undue delay", rather than "within five days", deleted former Subsec. (c) re notification of employment, vocational or student status at trade or professional institution or institution of higher learning in this state and of any change in such status, and amended Subsec. (e) to add exception that person who fails to register with commissioner without undue delay or notify commissioner without undue delay of change of name, address or status or another reportable event is subject to penalty if such failure continues for five business days, effective July 1, 2006; P.A. 06-196 changed effective date of P.A. 06-187, S. 38 from July 1, 2006, to October 1, 2006, effective June 7, 2006; June Sp. Sess. P.A. 07-4 amended Subsecs. (b) and (c) re notification and registration requirements regarding registrants' electronic mail addresses, instant message addresses or other similar Internet communication identifiers and made technical changes in Subsec. (c); pursuant to P.A. 11-51, "Commissioner of Public Safety" was changed editorially by the Revisors to "Commissioner of Emergency Services and Public Protection", effective July 1, 2011.

Sec. 54-254. Registration of person who has committed a felony for a sexual purpose.

(a) Any person who has been convicted or found not guilty by reason of mental disease or defect in this state on or after October 1, 1998, of any felony that the court finds was committed for a sexual purpose, may be required by the court upon release into the community or, if such person is in the custody of the Commissioner of Correction, at such time prior to release as the commissioner shall direct to register such person's name, identifying factors, criminal history record, residence address and electronic mail address, instant message address or other similar Internet communication identifier, if any, with the Commissioner of Emergency Services and Public Protection, on such forms and in such locations as the commissioner shall direct, and to maintain such registration for ten years from the date of such person's release into the community. If the court finds that a person has committed a felony for a sexual purpose and intends to require such person to register under this section, prior to accepting a plea of guilty or nolo contendere from such person with respect to such felony, the court shall (1) inform the person that the entry of a finding of guilty after acceptance of the plea will subject the person to the registration requirements of this section, and (2) determine that the person fully understands the consequences of the plea. If any person who is subject to registration under this section changes such person's name, such person shall, without undue delay, notify the Commissioner of Emergency Services and Public Protection in writing of the new name. If any person who is subject to registration under this section changes such person's address, such person shall, without undue delay, notify the Commissioner of Emergency Services and Public Protection in writing of the new address and, if the new address is in another state, such person shall also register with an appropriate agency in that state, provided that state has a registration requirement for such offenders. If any person who is subject to registration under this section establishes or changes an electronic mail address, instant message address or other similar Internet communication identifier, such person shall, without undue delay, notify the Commissioner of Emergency Services and Public Protection in writing of such identifier. If any person who is subject to registration under this section is employed at, carries on a vocation at or is a student at a trade or professional

458

institution or institution of higher learning in this state, such person shall, without undue delay, notify the Commissioner of Emergency Services and Public Protection of such status and of any change in such status. If any person who is subject to registration under this section is employed in another state, carries on a vocation in another state or is a student in another state, such person shall, without undue delay, notify the Commissioner of Emergency Services and Public Protection and shall also register with an appropriate agency in that state, provided that state has a registration requirement for such offenders. During such period of registration, each registrant shall complete and return forms mailed to such registrant to verify such registrant's residence address and shall submit to the retaking of a photographic image upon request of the Commissioner of Emergency Services and Public Protection.

(b) Any person who violates the provisions of this section shall be guilty of a class D felony, except that, if such person violates the provisions of this section by failing to notify the Commissioner of Emergency Services and Public Protection without undue delay of a change of name, address or status or another reportable event, such person shall be subject to such penalty if such failure continues for five business days.

(P.A. 98-111, S. 5; P.A. 99-183, S. 5, 13; May 9 Sp. Sess. P.A. 02-7, S. 82; P.A. 06-187, S. 39; 06-196, S. 292; June Sp. Sess. P.A. 07-4, S. 94; P.A. 11-51, S. 134; P.A. 15-211, S. 7.)

History: P.A. 99-183 amended Subsec. (a) to replace "sexual purposes" with "a sexual purpose" where appearing, revise provision re changing address to and registering in another state, add provision requiring a person who regularly travels into or within another state or temporarily resides in another state to notify the Commissioner of Public Safety and register with an appropriate agency in that state if that state has a registration requirement, add provision requiring registrants to submit to the retaking of a photographic image upon request and make technical changes for purposes of gender neutrality, effective July 1, 1999; May 9 Sp. Sess. P.A. 02-07 amended Subsec. (a) to add provision requiring any person subject to registration under this section who is employed at, carries on a vocation at or is a student at a trade or professional institution or institution of higher learning in this state to notify the commissioner of such status and any change in such status and to make requirement that a person subject to registration under this section notify the commissioner and register with an appropriate agency in another state applicable if such person "is employed in another state, carries on a vocation in another state or is a student in another state" rather than if such person "regularly travels into or within another state or temporarily resides in another state for purposes including, but not limited to employment or schooling", effective August 15, 2002; P.A. 06-187 amended Subsec. (a) to require person in custody of Commissioner of Correction to register at such time prior to release as commissioner directs, require person who changes such person's name to notify commissioner in writing of new name without undue delay, replace requirement that person who changes address register new address in writing with commissioner within five days with requirement that such person notify commissioner in writing of new address without undue delay and require that notification person must give re employment, vocational or student status at trade or professional institution or institution of higher learning in this state and any change in such status and re employment, vocational or student status in another state be given "without undue delay" and amended Subsec. (b) to add exception that person who fails to notify commissioner without undue delay of change of name, address or status or another reportable event is subject to penalty if such failure continues for five business days, effective July 1, 2006; P.A. 06-196 changed effective date of P.A. 06-187, S. 39 from July 1, 2006, to October 1, 2006, effective June 7, 2006; June Sp. Sess. P.A. 07-4 amended Subsec. (a) to require registration of person's "electronic mail address, instant message address or other similar Internet communication identifier, if any," and require registrant who establishes or changes such an identifier to notify Commissioner of Public Safety in writing of such identifier without undue delay; pursuant to P.A. 11-51, "Commissioner of Public Safety" was changed editorially by the Revisors to "Commissioner of Emergency Services and Public Protection", effective July 1, 2011; P.A. 15-211 amended Subsec. (a) to add provision re 10-year registration period to start from date of person's release into the community.

Court concluded that section is not a sentence enhancement statute; court found that evidentiary hearing is required on issue of whether the crime was committed for a sexual purpose and stated that the fact is to be found by a fair preponderance of the evidence. 69 CA 516.

Subsec. (a):

Order to register as sex offender not required to be based on finding that defendant posed risk of reoffense or danger to public safety but can be based on finding that crime was committed for sexual purpose. 288 C. 582.

Sec. 54-255. Restriction on dissemination of registration information for certain offenders.

(a) Upon the conviction or finding of not guilty by reason of mental disease or defect of any person for a violation of section 53a-70b, the court may order the Department of Emergency Services and Public Protection to restrict the dissemination of the registration information to law enforcement purposes only and to not make such information available for public access, provided the court finds that dissemination of the registration information is not required for public safety and that publication of the registration information would be likely to reveal the identity of the victim within the community where the victim resides. The court shall remove the restriction on the dissemination of such registration information if, at any time, the court finds that public safety requires that such person's registration information be made available to the public or that a change of circumstances makes publication of such registration information no longer likely to reveal the identity of the victim within the community where the victim resides. Prior to ordering or removing the restriction on the dissemination of such person's registration information, the court shall consider any information or statements provided by the victim.

(b) Upon the conviction or finding of not guilty by reason of mental disease or defect of any person of a criminal offense against a victim who is a minor, a nonviolent sexual offense or a sexually violent offense, where the victim of such offense was, at the time of the offense, under eighteen years of age and related to such person within any of the degrees of kindred specified in section 46b-21, the court may order the Department of Emergency Services and Public Protection to restrict the dissemination of the registration information to law enforcement purposes only and to not make such information available for public access, provided the court finds that dissemination of the registration information is not required for public safety and that publication of the registration information would be likely to reveal the identity of the victim within the community where the victim resides. The court shall remove the restriction on the dissemination of such registration information if, at any time, it finds that public safety requires that such person's registration information be made available to the public or that a change in circumstances makes publication of the registration information no longer likely to reveal the identity of the victim within the community where the victim resides.

(c) Any person who: (1) Has been convicted or found not guilty by reason of mental disease or defect of a violation of subdivision (1) of subsection (a) of section 53a-71 between October 1, 1988, and June 30, 1999, and was under nineteen years of age at the time of the offense; (2) has been convicted or found not guilty by reason of mental disease or defect of a violation of subdivision (2) of subsection (a) of section 53a-73a between October 1, 1988, and June 30, 1999; (3) has been convicted or found not guilty by reason of mental disease or defect of a criminal offense against a victim who is a minor, a nonviolent sexual offense or a sexually violent offense, between October 1, 1988, and June 30, 1999, where the victim of such offense was, at the time of the offense, under eighteen years of age and related to such person within any of the degrees of kindred specified in section 46b-21; (4) has been convicted or found not guilty by reason of mental disease or defect of a violation of section 53a-70b between October 1, 1988, and June 30, 1999; or (5) has been convicted or found not guilty by reason of mental disease or defect of any crime between October 1, 1988, and September 30, 1998, which requires registration under sections 54-250 to 54-258a, inclusive, and (A) served no jail or prison time as a result of such conviction or finding of not guilty by reason of mental disease or defect, (B) has not been subsequently convicted or found not guilty by reason of mental disease or defect of any crime which would require registration under sections 54-250 to 54-258a, inclusive, and (C) has registered with the Department of Emergency Services and Public Protection in accordance with sections 54-250 to 54-258a, inclusive; may petition the court to order the Department of Emergency Services and Public Protection to restrict the dissemination of the registration information to law enforcement purposes only and to not make such information available for public access. Any person who files such a petition shall, pursuant to subsection (b) of section 54-227, notify the Office of Victim Services and the Victim Services Unit within the Department of Correction of the filing of such petition. The Office of Victim Services or the Victim Services Unit within the Department of Correction, or both, shall, pursuant to section 54-230 or 54-230a, notify any victim who has requested notification pursuant to subsection (b) of section 54-228 of the filing of such petition. Prior to granting or denying such petition, the court shall consider any information or statements provided by the victim. The court may order the Department of Emergency Services and Public Protection to restrict the dissemination of the registration information to law enforcement purposes only and to not make such information available for public access, provided the court finds that dissemination of the registration information is not required for public safety.

(P.A. 98-111, S. 6; P.A. 99-183, S. 6, 13; P.A. 01-211, S. 2; P.A. 02-89, S. 87; P.A. 05-146, S. 6; P.A. 11-51, S. 134.)

History: P.A. 99-183 entirely replaced existing provisions that had authorized a person registered under Sec. 54-252 to apply to the court after 10 years for release from the obligation to register, that had required the court to grant such application if the person proved by clear and convincing evidence that he does not suffer from a mental abnormality or personality disorder that makes him likely to engage in sexually violent offenses and that had specified the procedure for the court to follow in acting on such application with new provisions authorizing the court under certain circumstances to order the Department of Public Safety to restrict the dissemination of registration information with respect to certain offenders to law enforcement purposes only and not make such information available for public access, effective July 1, 1999; P.A. 01-211 amended Subsec. (c) to add provisions requiring any person who files a petition to notify the Office of Victim Services and the Department of Correction of the filing of such petition, requiring said office or department, or both, to notify any victim who has requested notification of the filing of such petition and requiring the court to consider any information or statements provided by the victim prior to granting or denial of such petition; P.A. 02-89 amended Subsec. (a) by replacing references to Sec. 54-259 with Sec. 54-258a, reflecting repeal of Sec. 54-259 by the same public act; P.A. 05-146 amended Subsec. (c) to specify that it is the "Victim Services Unit" within the Department of Correction to which a person gives notice of the filing of a petition and which notifies any victim who requested notification of the filing of the petition; pursuant to P.A. 11-51, "Department of Public Safety" was changed editorially by the Revisors to "Department of Emergency Services and Public Protection", effective July 1, 2011.

"Registration information" means any information that is received, maintained and disseminated by the registry, and restricted registration information should not be disclosed except as provided in Sec. 54-258(a)(4). 298 C. 703.

Sec. 54-256. Responsibilities of courts and agencies in registration process.

(a) Any court, the Commissioner of Correction or the Psychiatric Security Review Board, prior to releasing into the community any person convicted or found not guilty by reason of mental disease or defect of a criminal offense against a victim who is a minor, a nonviolent sexual offense, a sexually violent offense or a felony found by the sentencing court to have been committed for a sexual purpose, except a person being released unconditionally at the conclusion of such person's sentence or commitment, shall require as a condition of such release that such person complete the registration procedure established by the Commissioner of Emergency Services and Public Protection under sections 54-251, 54-252 and 54-254. The court, the Commissioner of Correction or the Psychiatric Security Review Board, as the case may be, shall provide the person with a written summary of the person's obligations under sections 54-102g and 54-250 to 54-258a, inclusive, and transmit the completed registration package to the Commissioner of Emergency Services and Public Protection who shall enter the information into the registry established under section 54-257. If a court transmits the completed registration package to the Commissioner of Emergency Services and Public Protection with respect to a person released by the court, such package need not include identifying factors for such person. In the case of a person being released unconditionally who declines to complete the registration package through the court or the releasing agency, the court or agency shall: (1) Except with respect to information that is not available to the public pursuant to court order, rule of court or any provision of the general statutes, provide to the Commissioner of Emergency Services and Public Protection the person's name, date of release into the community, anticipated residence address, if known, and criminal history record, any known treatment history of such person, any electronic mail address, instant message address or other similar Internet communication identifier for such person, if known, and any other relevant information; (2) inform the person that such person has an obligation to register within three days with the Commissioner of Emergency Services and Public Protection for a period of ten years following the date of such person's release or for life, as the case may be, that if such person changes such person's address such person shall within five days register the new address in writing with the Commissioner of Emergency Services and Public Protection and, if the new address is in another state or if such person is employed in another state, carries on a vocation in another state or is a student in another state, such person shall also register with an appropriate agency in that state, provided that state has a registration requirement for such offenders, and that if such person establishes or changes an electronic mail address, instant message address or other similar Internet communication identifier such person shall, within five days, register such identifier with the Commissioner of Emergency Services and Public Protection; (3) provide the person with a written summary of the person's obligations

462

under sections 54-102g and 54-250 to 54-258a, inclusive, as explained to the person under subdivision (2) of this subsection; and (4) make a specific notation on the record maintained by that agency with respect to such person that the registration requirements were explained to such person and that such person was provided with a written summary of such person's obligations under sections 54-102g and 54-250 to 54-258a, inclusive.

(b) Whenever a person is convicted or found not guilty by reason of mental disease or defect of an offense that will require such person to register under section 54-251, 54-252 or 54-254, the court shall provide to the Department of Emergency Services and Public Protection a written summary of the offense that includes the age and sex of any victim of the offense and a specific description of the offense. Such summary shall be added to the registry information made available to the public through the Internet.

(P.A. 98-111, S. 7; P.A. 99-183, S. 7, 13; P.A. 02-89, S. 88; May 9 Sp. Sess. P.A. 02-7, S. 83; P.A. 06-187, S. 28; 06-196, S. 291; June Sp. Sess. P.A. 07-4, S. 95; P.A. 11-51, S. 134.)

History: P.A. 99-183 deleted the Board of Parole from requirements of section, made provisions applicable to a person "found not guilty by reason of mental disease or defect" of the specified offenses, added "a nonviolent sexual offense" to specified offenses, replaced "sexual purposes" with "a sexual purpose", required the court or specified agencies to "provide the person with a written summary of the person's obligations under sections 54-102g and 54-250 to 54-259, inclusive,", added provision that if a court transmits the completed registration package to the Commissioner of Public Safety with respect to a person released by the court, the package need not include identifying factors for the person, required the court or agency to inform the person that the obligation to register is for 10 years "or for life" rather than "or until released from such obligation in accordance with section 54-255", revised provision re changing address to and registering in another state, added provision requiring the court or agency to inform a person that if such person regularly travels into or within another state or temporarily resides in another state such person shall register with an appropriate agency in that other state if that state has a registration requirement and made technical changes for purposes of gender neutrality, effective July 1, 1999; P.A. 02-89 replaced references to Sec. 54-259 with Sec. 54-258a, reflecting repeal of Sec. 54-259 by the same public act; May 9 Sp. Sess. P.A. 02-7 amended Subdiv. (2) to require the court or agency to inform the person of requirement to register with an appropriate agency in another state if such person "is employed in another state, carries on a vocation in another state or is a student in another state" rather than if such person "regularly travels into or within another state or temporarily resides in another state for purposes including, but not limited to employment or schooling", effective August 15, 2002; P.A. 06-187 designated existing provisions as Subsec. (a) and added Subsec. (b) requiring that court provide Department of Public Safety with written summary of offense and that summary be added to registry information available to the public through the Internet, effective July 1, 2006; P.A. 06-196 changed effective date of P.A. 06-187, S. 28 from July 1, 2006, to July 1, 2007, effective June 7, 2006; June Sp. Sess. P.A. 07-4 amended Subsec. (a)(1) to require court or agency to provide commissioner with "any electronic mail address, instant message address or other similar Internet communication identifier for such person, if known," and make technical changes and amended Subsec. (a)(2) to require court or agency to inform person that if such person establishes or changes such an identifier such person shall, within 5 days, register such identifier with commissioner; pursuant to P.A. 11-51, "Commissioner of Public Safety" and "Department of Public Safety"

Sec. 54-257. Registry. Suspension of registration. Verification of address. Retake of photographic image. Change of name.

(a) The Department of Emergency Services and Public Protection shall, not later than January 1, 1999, establish and maintain a registry of all persons required to register under sections 54-251, 54-252, 54-253 and 54-254. The department shall, in cooperation with the Office of the Chief Court Administrator, the Department of Correction and the Psychiatric Security Review Board, develop appropriate forms for use by agencies and individuals to report registration information, including changes of address. Upon receipt of registration information, the department shall enter the information into the registry and notify the local police department or state police troop having jurisdiction where the registrant resides or plans to reside. If a registrant notifies the Department of Emergency Services and Public Protection that such registrant is employed at, carries on a vocation at or is a student at a trade or professional institution or institution of higher learning in this state, the department shall notify the law enforcement agency with jurisdiction over such institution. If a registrant reports a residence in another state, the department shall notify the state police agency of that state or such other agency in that state that maintains registry information, if known. The department shall also transmit all registration information, conviction data, photographic images and fingerprints to the Federal Bureau of Investigation in such form as said bureau shall require for inclusion in a national registry.

(b) The Department of Emergency Services and Public Protection may suspend the registration of any person registered under section 54-251, 54-252, 54-253 or 54-254 while such person is incarcerated, under civil commitment or residing outside this state. During the period that such registration is under suspension, the department is not required to verify the address of the registrant pursuant to subsection (c) of this section and may withdraw the registration information from public access. Upon the release of the registrant from incarceration or civil commitment or resumption of residency in this state by the registrant, the department shall reinstate the registration, redistribute the registration information in accordance with subsection (a) of this section and resume verifying the address of the registrant in accordance with subsection (c) of this section. Suspension of registration shall not affect the date of expiration of the registration obligation of the registrant under section 54-251, 54-252 or 54-253.

(c) Except as provided in subsection (b) of this section, the Department of Emergency Services and Public Protection shall verify the address of each registrant by mailing a nonforwardable verification form to the registrant at the registrant's last reported address. Such form shall require the registrant to sign a statement that the registrant continues to reside at the registrant's last reported address and return the form by mail by a date which is ten days after the date such form was mailed to the registrant. The form shall contain a statement that failure to return the form or providing false information is a violation of section 54-251, 54-252, 54-253 or 54-254, as the case may be. Each person required to register under section 54-251, 54-252, 54-253 or 54-254 shall have such person's address verified in such manner every ninety days after such person's initial registration date. In the event that a registrant fails to return the address verification form, the Department of Emergency Services and Public Protection shall notify the local police department or the state police troop having jurisdiction over the registrant's last reported address, and that agency shall apply for a warrant to be issued for the registrant's arrest under section 54-251, 54-252, 54-253 or 54-254, as the case may be. The Department of Emergency Services and Public Protection shall not verify the address of registrants whose last reported address was outside this state.

(d) The Department of Emergency Services and Public Protection shall include in the registry the most recent photographic image of each registrant taken by the department, the Department of Correction, a law enforcement agency or the Court Support Services Division of the Judicial Department and shall retake the photographic image of each registrant at least once every five years.

(e) Whenever the Commissioner of Emergency Services and Public Protection receives notice from a superior court pursuant to section 52-11 or a probate court pursuant to section 45a-99 that such court has ordered the change of name of a person, and the department determines that such person is listed in the registry, the department shall revise such person's registration information accordingly.

(f) The Commissioner of Emergency Services and Public Protection shall develop a protocol for the notification of other state agencies, the Judicial Department and local police departments whenever a person listed in the registry changes such person's name and notifies the commissioner of the new name pursuant to section 54-251, 54-252, 54-253 or 54-254 or whenever the commissioner determines pursuant to subsection (e) of this section that a person listed in the registry has changed such person's name.

(P.A. 98-111, S. 8; P.A. 99-183, S. 8, 13; May 9 Sp. Sess. P.A. 02-7, S. 84; P.A. 03-202, S. 19; P.A. 06-187, S. 40; 06-196, S. 292; P.A. 11-51, S. 134.)

History: P.A. 99-183 amended Subsec. (a) to delete the Board of Parole from list of agencies cooperating with the department in the development of forms to report registration information, added new Subsec. (b) re suspension of registration while a person is incarcerated, under civil commitment or residing out of state, redesignated former Subsec. (b) as Subsec. (c) and amended said Subsec. to add exception to address verification requirement when registration is suspended under Subsec. (b), to add reference to Sec. 54-253 in provision requiring the form to contain a statement that failure to return the form or providing false information is a violation of the specified statutes, to delete provision establishing an affirmative defense in a prosecution for failure to return the address verification form and to make technical changes for purposes of gender neutrality, and added Subsec. (d) to require the retaking of the photographic image of each registrant at least once every five years, effective July 1, 1999; May 9 Sp. Sess. P.A. 02-7 amended Subsec. (a) to add provision that if a registrant notifies the department that such registrant is employed at, carries on a vocation at or is a student at a trade or professional institution or institution of higher learning in this state, the department shall notify the law enforcement agency with jurisdiction over such institution and amended Subsec. (c) to require verification of address of a person required to register under Sec. 54-251 or 54-254 "every ninety days after such person's initial registration date" rather than "annually on the anniversary of such person's initial registration date" and to require verification of address of a person required to register under Sec. 54-253 "every ninety days after such person's initial registration date" rather than "either annually on the anniversary of such person's initial registration date or every ninety days after such person's initial registration date depending upon whether, after such initial registration, such person is subject to the requirements of section 54-251 or section 54-252, respectively", effective August 15, 2002; P.A. 03-202 added Subsec. (e) re revision of registration information upon notice of court ordered change of name; P.A. 06-187 amended Subsec. (d) to require department to include in registry most recent photographic image of each registrant taken by department, Department of Correction, law enforcement agency or Court Support Services Division and added Subsec. (f) re development of protocol for notification of other state agencies, Judicial Department and local police departments whenever commissioner is notified or determines that person listed in the registry has changed such person's name, effective July 1, 2006; P.A. 06-196 changed effective date of P.A. 06-187, S. 40 from July 1, 2006, to October 1, 2006, effective June 7, 2006; pursuant to P.A. 11-51, "Commissioner of Public Safety" and "Department of Public Safety" were changed editorially by the Revisors to "Commissioner of Emergency Services and Public Protection" and "Department of Emergency Services and Public Protection", respectively, effective July 1, 2011.

Because statute imposes strict liability, actual notice to defendant and mens rea are not elements of the offense, and therefore trial court's instructions were not constitutionally deficient. 286 C. 191.

Sec. 54-258. Availability of registration information. Immunity.

(a)(1) Notwithstanding any other provision of the general statutes, except subdivisions (3), (4) and (5) of this subsection, the registry maintained by the Department of Emergency Services and Public Protection shall be a public record and shall be accessible to the public during normal business hours. The Department of Emergency Services and Public Protection shall make registry information available to the public through the Internet. Not less than once per calendar quarter, the Department of Emergency Services and Public Protection shall issue notices to all print and electronic media in the state regarding the availability and means of accessing the registry. Each local police department and each state police troop shall keep a record of all registration information transmitted to it by the Department of Emergency Services and Public Protection, and shall make such information accessible to the public during normal business hours.

(2) (A) Any state agency, the Judicial Department, any state police troop or any local police department may, at its discretion, notify any government agency, private organization or individual of registration information when such agency, said department, such troop or such local police department, as the case may be, believes such notification is necessary to protect the public or any individual in any jurisdiction from any person who is subject to registration under section 54-251, 54-252, 54-253 or 54-254.

(B) (i) Whenever a registrant is released into the community, or whenever a registrant changes such registrant's address and notifies the Department of Emergency Services and Public Protection of such change pursuant to section 54-251, 54-252, 54-253 or 54-254, the Department of Emergency Services and Public Protection shall, by electronic mail, notify the superintendent of schools for the school district in which the registrant resides, or plans to reside, of such release or new address, and provide such superintendent with the same registry information for such registrant that the department makes available to the public through the Internet under subdivision (1) of this subsection.

(ii) Whenever a registrant is released into the community, or whenever a registrant changes such registrant's address and notifies the Department of Emergency Services and Public Protection of such change pursuant to section 54-251, 54-252, 54-253 or 54-254, the Department of Emergency Services and Public Protection shall, by electronic mail, notify the chief executive officer of the municipality in which the registrant resides, or plans to reside, of such release or new address, and provide such chief executive officer with the same registry information for such registrant that the department makes available to the public through the Internet under subdivision (1) of this subsection.

(3) Notwithstanding the provisions of subdivisions (1) and (2) of this subsection, state agencies, the Judicial Department, state police troops and local police departments shall not disclose the identity of any victim of a crime committed by a registrant or treatment information provided to the registry pursuant to sections 54-102g and 54-250 to 54-258a, inclusive, except to government agencies for bona fide law enforcement or security purposes.

(4) Notwithstanding the provisions of subdivisions (1) and (2) of this subsection, registration information the dissemination of which has been restricted by court order pursuant to section 54-255 and which is not otherwise subject to disclosure, shall not be a public record and shall be released only for law enforcement purposes until such restriction is removed by the court pursuant to said section.

(5) Notwithstanding the provisions of subdivisions (1) and (2) of this subsection, a registrant's electronic mail address, instant message address or other similar Internet communication identifier shall not be a public record, except that the Department of Emergency Services and Public Protection may release such identifier for law enforcement or security purposes in accordance with regulations adopted by the department. The department shall adopt regulations in accordance with chapter 54 to specify the circumstances under which and the persons to whom such identifiers may be released including, but not limited to, providers of electronic communication service or remote computing service, as those terms are defined in section 54-260b, and operators of Internet web sites, and the procedure therefor.

(6) When any registrant completes the registrant's term of registration or is otherwise released from the obligation to register under section 54-251, 54-252, 54-253 or 54-254, the Department of Emergency Services and Public Protection shall notify any state police troop or local police department having jurisdiction over the registrant's last reported residence address that the person is no longer a registrant, and the Department of Emergency Services and Public Protection, state police troop and local police department shall remove the registrant's name and information from the registry.

(b) Neither the state nor any political subdivision of the state nor any officer or employee thereof, shall be held civilly liable to any registrant by reason of disclosure of any information regarding the registrant that is released or disclosed in accordance with subsection (a) of this section. The state and any political subdivision of the state and, except in cases of wanton, reckless or malicious conduct, any officer or employee thereof, shall be immune from liability for good faith conduct in carrying out the provisions of subdivision (2) of subsection (a) of this section.

(P.A. 98-111, S. 9; P.A. 99-183, S. 9, 13; P.A. 02-89, S. 89; June Sp. Sess. P.A. 07-4, S. 96; P.A. 09-199, S. 1; P.A. 11-51, S. 134; P.A. 14-192, S. 6; 14-213, S. 1; P.A. 15-14, S. 18.)

History: P.A. 99-183 amended Subsec. (a) to add exception for Subdivs. (3) and (4) of said Subsec., designate provisions re notification as new Subdiv. (2) and amend said Subdiv. to replace "The Department of Public Safety" with "Any state agency, the Judicial Department" and make technical changes, redesignate former Subdiv. (2) as Subdiv. (3) and amend said Subdiv. to replace "Notwithstanding the provisions of subdivision (1) of this subsection, the Department of Public Safety," with "Notwithstanding the provisions of subdivisions (1) and (2) of this subsection, state agencies, the Judicial Department,", add Subdiv. (4) providing that registration information the dissemination of which has been restricted by court order pursuant to Sec. 54-255 and is not otherwise subject to disclosure shall not be a public record and shall be released only for law enforcement purposes, redesignate former Subdiv. (3) as Subdiv. (5) and amend said Subdiv. to make provisions applicable when a registrant "completes the registrant's term of registration or is otherwise released from the obligation to register" rather than when a registrant "is released from the obligation to register" and to replace provision that when notified a person is no longer a registrant the Department of Public Safety, state police troop and local police department "shall remove and destroy all registration information pertaining to the person and shall make no further disclosure of such information to any government agency, private organization or individual" with provision that said department, troop and local police department "shall remove the registrant's name and information from the registry", amended Subsec. (b) to replace "Neither the state nor any municipality, nor any branch, agency or employee thereof, shall be liable" with "Neither the state nor any political subdivision of the state nor any officer or employee thereof, shall be held civilly liable" and to add provision that the state and any political subdivision of the state and, except in cases of wanton, reckless or malicious conduct, any officer or employee thereof, shall be immune from liability for good faith conduct in carrying out Subsec. (a)(2), effective July 1, 1999; P.A. 02-89 amended Subsec. (a)(3) to replace reference to Sec. 54-259 with Sec. 54-258a, reflecting repeal of Sec. 54-259 by the same public act; June Sp. Sess. P.A. 07-4 amended Subsec. (a) to except in Subdiv. (1) the provisions of Subdiv. (5), add new Subdiv. (5) re confidentiality and authorized release of registrant's electronic mail address, instant message address or other similar Internet communication identifier and adoption of regulations specifying when and to whom such identifiers may be released and the procedure therefor and redesignate existing Subdiv. (5) as Subdiv. (6); P.A. 09-199 amended Subsec. (a)(2) to designate existing provisions as Subpara. (A) and add Subpara. (B) re notification by electronic mail of, and provision of registry information to, the appropriate superintendent of schools whenever a registrant is released into the community, effective September 1, 2009; pursuant to P.A. 11-51, "Department of Public Safety" was changed editorially by the Revisors to "Department of Emergency Services and Public Protection" in Subsec. (a), effective July 1, 2011; P.A. 14-192 amended Subsec. (a)(2)(B) to designate existing provisions as Subdiv. (1) and add Subdiv. (2) re notice to chief executive officer of municipality in which registrant resides or plans to reside, effective July 1, 2014; P.A. 14-213 amended Subsec. (a)(2)(B) to designate existing provisions as Subdiv. (1) and amend same to add provision re notification when registrant changes address and notifies Department of Emergency Services and Public Protection of such change, and to add Subdiv. (2) re notification to chief executive officer of municipality upon release or change of address of registrant, effective July 1, 2014; P.A. 15-14 made technical changes in Subsec. (a)(2).

"Registration information" in Subsec. (a)(4) means any information that is received, maintained and disseminated by the registry. 298 C. 703.

Sec. 54-258a. Warning against wrongful use of registry information.

Any agency of the state or any political subdivision thereof that provides public access to information contained in the registry shall post a warning that states: "Any person who uses information in this registry to injure, harass or commit a criminal act against any person included in the registry or any other person is subject to criminal prosecution." Such warning shall be in a suitable size and location to ensure that it will be seen by any person accessing registry information.

(P.A. 99-183, S. 10, 13.)

History: P.A. 99-183 effective July 1, 1999.

Sec. 54-259. Sexual Offender Registration Committee. Section 54-259 is repealed, effective October 1, 2002.

(P.A. 98-111, S. 11; P.A. 02-89, S. 90.)

Sec. 54-259a. Risk Assessment Board. Development and use of risk assessment scale. Report.

Section 54-259a is repealed, effective July 1, 2013.

(P.A. 06-187, S. 30; 06-196, S. 295; June Sp. Sess. P.A. 07-4, S. 99; P.A. 11-51, S. 134; P.A. 13-299, S. 95.)

Sec. 54-260. (Formerly Sec. 54-102s). Notification of change of name or address of sexual offenders on parole or probation.

(a) For the purposes of this section, "sexual offender" means any person convicted of a violation of subdivision (2) of section 53-21 of the general statutes in effect prior to October 1, 2000, subdivision (2) of subsection (a) of section 53-21, section 53a-70, 53a-70a, 53a-70b, 53a-71, 53a-72a or 53a-72b committed on or after October 1, 1995.

(b) Any sexual offender who is released from a correctional institution on parole or who is sentenced to a period of probation shall, during the period of such parole or probation and as a condition of such parole or probation, immediately notify such person's parole officer or probation officer, as the case may be, whenever such person changes such person's name or residence address. Each parole officer or probation officer who is notified of such change of address shall notify the chief of police of the police department or resident state trooper for the municipality of the new address of the parolee or probationer and any other law enforcement official such parole officer or probation officer deems appropriate.

(c) Nothing in this section shall be construed to prohibit a parole officer or probation officer acting in the performance of his duties and within the scope of his employment from disclosing any information concerning the parolee or probationer to any person whenever he deems such disclosure to be appropriate.

(P.A. 95-142, S. 6; P.A. 01-84, S. 23, 26; P.A. 03-202, S. 20.)

History: Sec. 54-102s transferred to Sec. 54-260 in 1999 (Revisor's note: In Subsec. (c) the words "or section 54-102r" were deleted editorially by the Revisors to reflect the repeal of Sec. 54-102r by P.A. 98-111); P.A. 01-84 amended Subsec. (a) to replace reference to "a violation of subdivision (2) of section 53-21" with "a violation of subdivision (2) of section 53-21 of the general statutes in effect prior to October 1, 2000," and include a violation of "subdivision (2) of subsection (a) of section 53-21", effective July 1, 2001; P.A. 03-202 amended Subsec. (b) by adding provision re change of name and making technical changes.

Annotation to former section 54-102s:

Legislature, in enacting statute, did not intend to restrict discretionary power of Office of Adult Probation to notify public in cases in which probationer has been convicted under a provision not enumerated in Subsec. (a). 250 C. 280.

Annotation to present section:

Section does not give probation and parole officers unrestrained discretionary power to disseminate sex offender registration information to the public and is not punitive for ex post facto purposes. 256 C. 23.

Sec. 54-260a. Report on number of registrants being electronically monitored and need for additional resources.

Not later than January fifteenth of each year, the Department of Correction, the Board of Pardons and Paroles and the Court Support Services Division of the Judicial Department shall each submit a report setting forth the number of persons subject to registration under this chapter who are being electronically monitored while being supervised in the community by such agency, including monitoring by global positioning system devices, and what, if any, additional resources are needed by such agency to ensure that persons subject to registration under this chapter are being supervised while in the community.

(P.A. 06-187, S. 41.)

History: P.A. 06-187 effective July 1, 2006.

Sec. 54-260b. Criminal investigation of registrants using the Internet. Ex parte court order to compel disclosure of basic subscriber information of registrants.

(a) For the purposes of this section:

(1) "Basic subscriber information" means: (A) Name, (B) address, (C) age or date of birth, (D) electronic mail address, instant message address or other similar Internet communication identifier, and (E) subscriber number or identity, including any assigned Internet protocol address;

(2) "Electronic communication" means "electronic communication" as defined in 18 USC 2510, as amended from time to time;

(3) "Electronic communication service" means "electronic communication service" as defined in 18 USC 2510, as amended from time to time;

(4) "Registrant" means a person required to register under section 54-251, 54-252, 54-253 or 54-254; and

(5) "Remote computing service" means "remote computing service" as defined in section 18 USC 2711, as amended from time to time.

(b) The Commissioner of Emergency Services and Public Protection shall designate a sworn law enforcement officer to serve as liaison between the Department of Emergency Services and Public Protection and providers of electronic communication services or remote computing services to facilitate the exchange of non-personally-identifiable information concerning registrants.

(c) Whenever such designated law enforcement officer ascertains from such exchange of non-personally-identifiable information that there are subscribers, customers or users of such providers who are registrants, such officer shall initiate a criminal investigation to determine if such registrants are in violation of the registration requirements of section 54-251, 54-252, 54-253 or 54-254 or of the terms and conditions of their parole or probation by virtue of being subscribers, customers or users of such providers.

(d) Such designated law enforcement officer may request an ex parte order from a judge of the Superior Court to compel a provider of electronic communication service or remote computing service to disclose basic subscriber information pertaining to subscribers, customers or users who have been identified by such provider to be registrants. The judge shall grant such order if the law enforcement officer offers specific and articulable facts showing that there are reasonable grounds to believe that the basic subscriber information sought is relevant and material to the ongoing criminal investigation. The order shall state upon its face the case number assigned to such investigation, the date and time of issuance and the name of the judge authorizing the order. The law enforcement officer shall have any ex parte order issued pursuant to this subsection signed by the authorizing judge within forty-eight hours or not later than the next business day, whichever is earlier.

(e) A provider of electronic communication service or remote computing service shall disclose basic subscriber information to such designated law enforcement officer when an order is issued pursuant to subsection (d) of this section.

(f) A provider of electronic communication service or remote computing service that provides information in good faith pursuant to an order issued pursuant to subsection (d) of this section shall be afforded the legal protections provided under 18 USC 3124, as amended from time to time, with regard to such actions.

(June Sp. Sess. P.A. 07-4, S. 98; P.A. 10-36, S. 32; P.A. 11-51, S. 134.)

History: P.A. 10-36 amended Subsec. (a) to delete former Subdiv. (6) defining "wire communication", effective July 1, 2010; pursuant to P.A. 11-51, "Commissioner of Public Safety" and "Department of Public Safety" were changed editorially by the Revisors to "Commissioner of Emergency Services and Public Protection" and "Department of Emergency Services and Public Protection", respectively, in Subsec. (b), effective July 1, 2011.

Sec. 54-261. Community response education program.

(a) The Court Support Services Division, in conjunction with state-wide experts in law enforcement, the treatment of sexual offenders and sexual assault victim services, shall, within available appropriations, develop a community response education program to be offered to neighborhoods and municipalities that have been notified pursuant to section 54-258 that a person who has registered under said section is or will be residing in that community.

(b) The purpose of such program shall be to assist neighborhoods, parents and children to learn how to better protect themselves from sexual abuse and sexual assault. The program shall develop educational materials and community information resources on prevention and risk reduction concerning sexual abuse and sexual assault and the enforcement of requirements concerning the registration and supervision of sexual offenders and the notification of communities where such offenders reside.

(c) The program may include the following:

(1) An initial community meeting following a community notification, sponsored by the Court Support Services Division and held in conjunction with the chief of police, chief elected officials, the superintendent of schools and other municipal officials of the community, to discuss the implementation of the statutory requirements concerning the registration of a sexual offender and the notification of the community where such offender resides, to provide information on the crime or crimes involved and to provide information on how the offender will be monitored by the Court Support Services Division and the specific conditions of probation applicable to the offender;

(2) Information on how and where concerned residents may report observed violations by an offender of the conditions of such offender's probation;

(3) Resources to educate families and children in the prevention and avoidance of sexual abuse and sexual assault and for parents seeking supportive methods for discussing relevant issues with their children;

(4) Resources on when and how a community may wish to establish a network of "Safe Houses" for neighborhood children to use when they seek safe shelter or the creation of a neighborhood block watch or crime watch;

(5) Resources for police departments and boards of education to use in consulting with parents on appropriate school-based classroom programs stressing safety, prevention and risk reduction and to use in developing educational programs for parents to discuss relevant issues with their children; and

472

(6) Compilation and distribution of a list of child protective agencies, child guidance clinics and rape crisis centers for families seeking more in-depth counseling after a community notification has occurred.

(d) The Court Support Services Division may apply for and receive grants from the federal government or any agency thereof or from any foundation, corporation, association or individual for purposes of the development of the community response education program under this section.

(P.A. 98-135, S. 1, 2; June Sp. Sess. P.A. 98-1, S. 111; P.A. 02-132, S. 52.)

History: P.A. 98-135 effective May 27, 1998; June Sp. Sess. P.A. 98-1 made a technical change in Subsec. (a); P.A. 02-132 replaced "Office of Adult Probation" with "Court Support Services Division" throughout and made a technical change in Subsec. (c).

Secs. 54-262 to 54-279. Reserved for future use.

CHAPTER 969a REGISTRATION OF CERTAIN OFFENDERS

Table of Contents

Sec. 54-280. Definitions. Registry of offenders convicted of offense committed with a deadly weapon. Suspension of registration. Registration information. Notification protocol. Confidentiality.

Sec. 54-280a. Registration of person convicted of offense committed with a deadly weapon. Personal appearance requirement. Penalty.

Sec. 54-280b. Registration information.

Secs. 54-281 to 54-299. **Reserved**

Sec. 54-280. Definitions. Registry of offenders convicted of offense committed with a deadly weapon. Suspension of registration. Registration information. Notification protocol. Confidentiality.

(a) For the purposes of this section and sections 45a-99, 52-11, 54-280a and 54-280b:

(1) "Commissioner" means the Commissioner of Emergency Services and Public Protection;

(2) "Convicted" means that a person has a judgment entered in this state against such person by a court upon a plea of guilty, a plea of nolo contendere or a finding of guilty by a jury or the court notwithstanding any pending appeal or habeas corpus proceeding arising from such judgment;

(3) "Deadly weapon" means a deadly weapon, as defined in section 53a-3;

(4) "Department" means the Department of Emergency Services and Public Protection;

(5) "Identifying factors" means fingerprints, a photographic image, and a description of any other identifying characteristics as may be required by the Commissioner of Emergency Services and Public Protection;

(6) "Not guilty by reason of mental disease or defect" means a finding by a court or jury of not guilty by reason of mental disease or defect pursuant to section 53a-13 notwithstanding any pending appeal or habeas corpus proceeding arising from such finding;

(7) "Offender convicted of committing a crime with a deadly weapon" or "offender" means a person who has been convicted of an offense committed with a deadly weapon;

(8) "Offense committed with a deadly weapon" or "offense" means: (A) A violation of subsection (c) of section 2-1e, subsection (e) of section 29-28, subsections (a) to (e), inclusive, or (i) of section 29-33, section 29-34, subsection (a) of section 29-35, section 29-36, 29-36k, 29-37a or 29-37e, subsection (c) of section 29-37g, section 29-37j, subsection (b), (c) or (g) of section 53-202, section 53-202b, 53-202c, 53-202j, 53-202k, 53-202*l*, 53-202aa or 53-206b, subsection (b) of section 53a-8, section 53a-55a, 53a-56a, 53a-60a, 53a-60c, 53a-72b, 53a-92a, 53a-94a, 53a-102a, 53a-103a, 53a-211, 53a-212, 53a-216, 53a-217, 53a-217a, 53a-217b or 53a-217c, or a second or subsequent violation of section 53-202g; or (B) a violation of any section of the general statutes which constitutes a felony, as defined in section 53a-25, provided the court makes a finding that, at the time of the offense, the offender used a deadly weapon, or was armed with and threatened the use of or displayed or represented by words or conduct that the offender possessed a deadly weapon;

(9) "Registrant" means a person required to register under section 54-280a;

(10) "Registry" means a central record system in this state that is established pursuant to this section and receives, maintains and disseminates to law enforcement agencies information on persons convicted or found not guilty by reason of mental disease or defect of an offense committed with a deadly weapon; and

(11) "Release into the community" means, with respect to a conviction or a finding of not guilty by reason of mental disease or defect of an offense committed with a deadly weapon, (A) any release by a court after such conviction or finding of not guilty by reason of mental disease or defect, a sentence of probation or any other sentence under section 53a-28 that does not result in the offender's immediate placement in the custody of the Commissioner of

Correction; (B) release from a correctional facility at the discretion of the Board of Pardons and Paroles, by the Department of Correction to a program authorized by section 18-100c or upon completion of the maximum term or terms of the offender's sentence or sentences, or to the supervision of the Court Support Services Division in accordance with the terms of the offender's sentence; or (C) temporary leave to an approved residence by the Psychiatric Security Review Board pursuant to section 17a-587, conditional release from a hospital for mental illness or a facility for persons with intellectual disability by the Psychiatric Security Review Board pursuant to section 17a-588 or release upon termination of commitment to the Psychiatric Security Review Board.

(b) The Department of Emergency Services and Public Protection shall, not later than January 1, 2014, establish and maintain a registry of all persons required to register under section 54-280a as offenders convicted of an offense committed with a deadly weapon. The department shall, in cooperation with the Office of the Chief Court Administrator, the Department of Correction and the Psychiatric Security Review Board, develop appropriate forms for use by agencies and individuals to report registration information, including changes of address. Upon receipt of registration information, the department shall enter the information into the registry and notify the local police department or state police troop having jurisdiction where the registrant resides or plans to reside. Upon receiving notification pursuant to section 54-280a that a registrant has changed his or her address, the department shall enter the information into the registry and notify the local police departments or state police troops having jurisdiction where the registrant previously resided and the jurisdiction where the registrant has relocated. The Commissioner of Emergency Services and Public Protection shall also ensure that the name and residence address of each registrant is available through the Connecticut on-line law enforcement communication teleprocessing system maintained by the department. If a registrant reports a residence in another state, the department may notify the state police agency of that state or such other agency in that state that maintains registry information, if known.

(c) The Department of Emergency Services and Public Protection may suspend the registration of any person registered under section 54-280a while such person is incarcerated, under civil commitment or residing outside this state. During the period that such registration is under suspension, the department may withdraw the registration information from access to law enforcement agencies. Upon the release of the registrant from incarceration or civil commitment or resumption of residency in this state by the registrant, the department shall reinstate the registration and redistribute the registration information in accordance with subsection (b) of this section. Suspension of registration shall not affect the date of expiration of the registration obligation of the registrant under section 54-280a.

(d) The Department of Emergency Services and Public Protection shall include in the registry the most recent photographic image of each registrant taken by the department, the Department of Correction, a law enforcement agency or the Court Support Services Division of the Judicial Department.

(e) Whenever the Commissioner of Emergency Services and Public Protection receives notice from a superior court pursuant to section 52-11 or a probate court pursuant to section 45a-99 that such court has ordered the change of name of a person, and the department determines that such person is listed in the registry, the department shall revise such person's registration information accordingly.

(f) The Commissioner of Emergency Services and Public Protection shall develop a protocol for the notification of other state agencies, the Judicial Department and local police departments whenever a person listed in the registry changes such person's name and notifies the commissioner of the new name pursuant to section 54-280a or whenever the commissioner determines pursuant to subsection (e) of this section that a person listed in the registry has changed such person's name.

(g) The information in the registry shall not be a public record or file for the purposes of section 1-200. Any information disclosed pursuant to this section or section 54-280a or 54-280b, shall not be further disclosed unless such disclosure is permitted under this section or section 54-280a or 54-280b.

(P.A. 13-3, S. 18.)

History: P.A. 13-3 effective January 1, 2014.

Sec. 54-280a. Registration of person convicted of offense committed with a deadly weapon. Personal appearance requirement. Penalty.

(a)(1) Any person who has been convicted or found not guilty by reason of mental disease or defect of an offense committed with a deadly weapon and is released into the community on or after January 1, 2014, shall, within fourteen calendar days following such release or, if such person is in the custody of the Commissioner of Correction, at such time prior to release as the Commissioner of Correction shall direct, and whether or not such person's place of residence is in this state, register such person's name, identifying factors, criminal history record, residence address and electronic mail address with the Commissioner of Emergency Services and Public Protection, on such forms and in such locations as the Commissioner of Emergency Services and Public Protection shall direct, and shall maintain such registration for five years.

(2) Prior to accepting a plea of guilty or nolo contendere from a person with respect to an offense committed with a deadly weapon, the court shall (A) inform the person that the entry of a finding of guilty after acceptance of the plea will subject the person to the registration requirements of this section, and (B) determine that the person fully understands the consequences of the plea.

(3) If any person who is subject to registration under this section changes such person's name, such person shall, without undue delay, notify the Commissioner of Emergency Services and Public Protection in writing of the new name. If any person who is subject to registration under this section changes such person's address, such person shall, without undue delay, notify the Commissioner of Emergency Services and Public Protection in writing of the new address. During such period of registration, each registrant shall complete and return any forms mailed to such registrant to verify such registrant's residence address and shall submit to the retaking of a photographic image upon request of the Commissioner of Emergency Services and Public Protection.

(b) Any offender convicted of committing a crime with a deadly weapon who is required to register under this section shall, not later than twenty calendar days after each anniversary date of such initial registration, until the date such registration requirement expires under subdivision (1) of subsection (a) of this section, personally appear at the local police department or state police troop having jurisdiction where the registrant resides to verify and update, as appropriate, the contents of his or her registration. The local police department or state police troop, as the case may be, may defer such requirement to personally appear to a later date for good cause shown. Not later than thirty calendar days prior to such anniversary date, the Department of Emergency Services and Public Protection shall mail written notice of the personal appearance requirement of this subsection to the registrant and the local police department or state police troop having jurisdiction where the registrant resides. Not later than thirty calendar days after the anniversary date of each registrant, the local police department or state police troop having jurisdiction where the registrant resides shall notify the Commissioner of Emergency Services and Public Protection, on such form as the commissioner may prescribe, (1) whether the registrant complied with the personal appearance requirement of this subsection or whether such personal appearance requirement was deferred to a later date for good cause shown, and (2) if the personal appearance requirement was deferred to a later date for good cause shown, the local police department or state police troop shall indicate the later date established for such personal appearance and describe the good cause shown.

(c) Any person who is subject to registration under this section who violates any provisions of subsection (a) or (b) of this section, except a violation consisting of failure to notify the Commissioner of Emergency Services and Public Protection of a change of name or address, shall be guilty of a class D felony. Any person who is subject to registration under this section who fails to notify the Commissioner of Emergency Services and Public Protection of a change of name or address not later than five business days after such change of name or address shall be guilty of a class D felony.

(P.A. 13-3, S. 19.)

History: P.A. 13-3 effective January 1, 2014.

Sec. 54-280b. Registration information.

(a) The registration information for each registrant shall include:

(1) The offender's name, including any other name by which the offender has been legally known, and any aliases used by the offender;

(2) Identifying information, including a physical description of the offender;

(3) The current residence address of the offender;

(4) The date of conviction of the offense;

(5) A description of the offense; and

(6) If the offender was sentenced to a term of incarceration for such offense, a portion of which was not suspended, the date the offender was released from such incarceration.

(b) The offender shall sign and date the registration.

(c) At the time that the offender appears for the purpose of registering, the Department of Emergency Services and Public Protection shall photograph the offender and arrange for the fingerprinting of the offender and include such photograph and a complete set of fingerprints in the registry. If the offender is required to submit to the taking of a blood or other biological sample of sufficient quality for DNA (deoxyribonucleic acid) analysis pursuant to section 54-102g, and has not submitted to the taking of such sample, the commissioner shall also require such sample to be taken for analysis pursuant to section 54-102g.

(d) The Department of Emergency Services and Public Protection may require the offender to provide documentation to verify the contents of his or her registration.

(P.A. 13-3, S. 20.)

History: P.A. 13-3 effective January 1, 2014.

Secs. 54-281 to 54-299. Reserved for future use.

CHAPTER 970 CONNECTICUT SENTENCING COMMISSION

Table of Contents

Sec. 54-300. Sentencing Commission.

Sec. 54-301. Posting of data and evaluation re provisional pardons and certificates of rehabilitation. Reports.

Sec. 54-300. Sentencing Commission.

(a) There is established, within existing budgetary resources, a Connecticut Sentencing Commission which shall be within the Office of Policy and Management for administrative purposes only.

(b) The mission of the commission shall be to review the existing criminal sentencing structure in the state and any proposed changes thereto, including existing statutes, proposed criminal justice legislation and existing and proposed sentencing policies and practices and make recommendations to the Governor, the General Assembly and appropriate criminal justice agencies.

(c) In fulfilling its mission, the commission shall recognize that: (1) The primary purpose of sentencing in the state is to enhance public safety while holding the offender accountable to the community, (2) sentencing should reflect the seriousness of the offense and be proportional to the harm to victims and the community, using the most appropriate sanctions available, including incarceration, community punishment and supervision, (3) sentencing should have as an overriding goal the reduction of criminal activity, the imposition of just punishment and the provision of meaningful and effective rehabilitation and reintegration of the offender, and (4) sentences should be fair, just and equitable while promoting respect for the law.

(d) The commission shall be composed of the following members:

(1) Eight persons appointed one each by: (A) The Governor, (B) the Chief Justice of the Supreme Court, (C) the president pro tempore of the Senate, (D) the speaker of the House of Representatives, (E) the majority leader of the Senate, (F) the majority leader of the House of Representatives, (G) the minority leader of the Senate, and (H) the minority leader of the House of Representatives, all of whom shall serve for a term of four years;

(2) Two judges appointed by the Chief Justice of the Supreme Court, one of whom shall serve for a term of one year and one of whom shall serve for a term of three years;

(3) One representative of the Court Support Services Division of the Judicial Branch appointed by the Chief Justice of the Supreme Court, who shall serve for a term of two years;

(4) The Commissioner of Correction, who shall serve for a term coterminous with his or her term of office;

(5) The Chief State's Attorney, who shall serve for a term coterminous with his or her term of office;

(6) The Chief Public Defender, who shall serve for a term coterminous with his or her term of office;

(7) One state's attorney appointed by the Chief State's Attorney, who shall serve for a term of three years;

(8) One member of the criminal defense bar appointed by the president of the Connecticut Criminal Defense Lawyers Association, who shall serve for a term of three years;

(9) The Victim Advocate, who shall serve for a term coterminous with his or her term of office;

(10) The chairperson of the Board of Pardons and Paroles, who shall serve for a term coterminous with his or her term of office;

(11) The Commissioner of Emergency Services and Public Protection, who shall serve for a term coterminous with his or her term of office;

(12) A municipal police chief appointed by the president of the Connecticut Police Chiefs Association, who shall serve for a term of two years;

(13) The Commissioner of Mental Health and Addiction Services, who shall serve for a term coterminous with his or her term of office;

(14) The undersecretary of the Criminal Justice Policy and Planning Division within the Office of Policy and Management, who shall serve for a term coterminous with his or her term of office; and

(15) An active or retired judge appointed by the Chief Justice of the Supreme Court, who shall serve as chairperson of the commission and serve for a term of four years.

(e) The commission shall elect a vice-chairperson from among the membership. Appointed members of the commission shall serve for the term specified in subsection (d) of this section and may be reappointed. Any vacancy in the appointed membership of the commission shall be filled by the appointing authority for the unexpired portion of the term.

(f) The commission shall:

(1) Facilitate the development and maintenance of a state-wide sentencing database in collaboration with state and local agencies, using existing state databases or resources where appropriate;

(2) Evaluate existing sentencing statutes, policies and practices including conducting a cost-benefit analysis;

(3) Conduct sentencing trends analyses and studies and prepare offender profiles;

(4) Provide training regarding sentencing and related issues, policies and practices;

(5) Act as a sentencing policy resource for the state;

(6) Preserve judicial discretion and provide for individualized sentencing;

(7) Evaluate the impact of pretrial, sentencing diversion, incarceration and post-release supervision programs;

(8) Perform fiscal impact analyses on selected proposed criminal justice legislation; and

(9) Identify potential areas of sentencing disparity related to racial, ethnic, gender and socioeconomic status.

(g) Upon completing the development of the state-wide sentencing database pursuant to subdivision (1) of subsection (f) of this section, the commission shall review criminal justice legislation as requested and as resources allow.

(h) The commission shall make recommendations concerning criminal justice legislation, including proposed modifications thereto, to the joint standing committee of the General Assembly having cognizance of matters relating to the judiciary which shall hold a hearing thereon.

(i) The commission shall have access to confidential information received by sentencing courts and the Board of Pardons and Paroles including, but not limited to, arrest data, criminal history records, medical records and other nonconviction information.

(j) The commission shall obtain full and complete information with respect to programs and other activities and operations of the state that relate to the criminal sentencing structure in the state.

(k) The commission may request any office, department, board, commission or other agency of the state or any political subdivision of the state to supply such records, information and assistance as may be necessary or appropriate in order for the commission to carry out its duties. Each officer or employee of such office, department, board, commission or other agency of the state or any political subdivision of the state is authorized and directed to cooperate with the commission and to furnish such records, information and assistance.

(l) The commission may accept, on behalf of the state, any grants of federal or private funds made available for any purposes consistent with the provisions of this section.

(m) Any records or information supplied to the commission that is confidential in accordance with any provision of the general statutes shall remain confidential while in the custody of the commission and shall not be disclosed. Any penalty for the disclosure of such records or information applicable to the officials, employees and authorized representatives of the office, department, board, commission or other agency of the state or any political subdivision of the state that supplied such records or information shall apply in the same manner and to the same extent to the members, staff and authorized representatives of the commission.

(n) The commission shall be deemed to be a criminal justice agency as defined in subsection (b) of section 54-142g.

(o) The commission shall meet at least once during each calendar quarter and at such other times as the chairperson deems necessary.

(p) Not later than January 15, 2012, and annually thereafter, the commission shall submit a report, in accordance with the provisions of section 11-4a, to the Governor, the General Assembly and the Chief Justice of the Supreme Court.

(P.A. 10-129, S. 1; P.A. 11-51, S. 134.)

History: P.A. 10-129 effective February 1, 2011; pursuant to P.A. 11-51, "Commissioner of Public Safety" was changed editorially by the Revisors to "Commissioner of Emergency Services and Public Protection" in Subsec. (d)(11), effective July 1, 2011.

See Sec. 4-38f for definition of "administrative purposes only".

Sec. 54-301. Posting of data and evaluation re provisional pardons and certificates of rehabilitation. Reports.

(a) Not later than January 1, 2016, the Connecticut Sentencing Commission shall post data on its Internet web site that the commission received from the Board of Pardons and Paroles pursuant to subsection (l) of section 54-130e and the Court Support Services Division of the Judicial Branch pursuant to section 54-108f, and shall update such data on its Internet web site annually thereafter.

(b) The Connecticut Sentencing Commission, or its designee, shall evaluate the effectiveness of provisional pardons and certificates of rehabilitation issued pursuant to section 54-130e and certificates of rehabilitation issued pursuant to section 54-108f, at promoting the public policy of rehabilitating ex-offenders consistent with the public interest in public safety, the safety of crime victims and the protection of property. Such evaluation shall continue for a period of three years from October 1, 2015. The commission shall submit a report to the joint standing committee of the General Assembly having cognizance of matters relating to the judiciary not later than January 15, 2016, January 15, 2017, and January 15, 2018, on the effectiveness of such provisional pardons and certificates of rehabilitation at promoting such public policy and public interest. Such report shall include recommendations, if any, for amendments to the general statutes governing such provisional pardons and certificates of rehabilitation in order to promote such public policy and public interest.

(P.A. 14-27, S. 4.)

Made in the USA
Middletown, DE
30 June 2020